THE ETHOS OF THE COSMOS

The Ethos of the Cosmos

The Genesis of Moral Imagination
in the Bible

William P. Brown

WILLIAM B. EERDMANS PUBLISHING COMPANY
GRAND RAPIDS, MICHIGAN / CAMBRIDGE, U.K.

© 1999 Wm. B. Eerdmans Publishing Co.
255 Jefferson Ave. S.E., Grand Rapids, Michigan 49503 /
P.O. Box 163, Cambridge CB3 9PU U.K.

Printed in the United States of America

04 03 02 01 00 99   7 6 5 4 3 2 1

Library of Congress Cataloging-in-Publication Data

Brown, William P., 1958
The ethos of the cosmos: the genesis of moral imagination
in the Bible / William P. Brown.
      p.   cm.
Includes bibliographical references (p.   ).
ISBN 0-8028-4539-8 (pbk.: alk. paper)
1. Creation — Biblical teaching.   2. Ethics in the Bible.
3. Bible — Socio-rhetorical criticism.   I. Title.
      BS652.B76   1999
231.7'65 — dc21   98-50871
                                        CIP

Unless otherwise noted, Scripture quotations represent the author's direct translation from the Hebrew or Greek.

Contents

v

Preface

In this study I have tried to convey a measure of the formative power of creation for the contemporary church by capturing something of the communicative intent behind the various models of creation found in the Bible, primarily the Old Testament. The approach employed diverges significantly from most theological treatments of creation, which typically seek to discern a uniform doctrine of creation, as well as from many historical studies that seek to uncover primarily the mythological precursors to the various traditions. Despite the plethora of studies, from historical to ecological, I am convinced that there is a richness to the biblical notions of creation that is yet to be tapped, partly because biblical scholars have too often fancied themselves as objective scientists observing the biblical cosmos with telescopes, narrow in focus and far removed from the claims and concerns of the text. But to the believer, the world of the Bible cannot be grasped by such tunnel vision. Moreover, the encompassing reality conveyed by Scripture invariably beckons the reader to enter and participate in its fullness or multidimensionality.

To be sure, the cultural and historical gap between an ancient preindustrial society and a so-called postmodern, market-driven one is, like the incomprehensible distance between earth and the distant galaxies, a real one. Nevertheless, like the gifted and informed artists who paint Saturn's rings from the perspective of its moons, communities of faith have no option except to imagine themselves, informed by faith and understanding, living within the formative and normative contours of the biblical world. Such imagination is no flight of fancy. To the contrary, Christians are, in the words of Luke Timothy Johnson, called to a life of "imagining the world Scripture imagines," a life guided by faithful and moral imagination. Contrary to what the subtitle might suggest, I do not investigate the *historical* roots of Israel's moral imagination, but the role of such imagination in the depiction of creation in the Bible.

To press the analogy, I have tried in this study to imagine myself more as a planetary explorer than as an astronomer, who observes only from a distance. What has prompted me to make this leap of perspective, from observation to contact, is a conviction that the moral character of ancient Israel and the early church has much to say to the contemporary church as it moves into the twenty-first century and reexamines its mission to the world. My investigation, consequently, moves from broaching the issue of culture and worldview, where most biblical studies begin and end, to that of ethics, with creation serving as the overarching context or ethos. I have found the results to be nothing short of surprising. Indeed, I attempt, no doubt presumptuously, to bridge two often disparate fields of theological study with the intent of breaking ground in both: on the one hand, the field of biblical scholarship, with its traditional emphasis on the history and religion of ancient Israel and the early church, and on the other, the intentionally relevant study of theological ethics or moral theology. The liability of such interdisciplinary research is, of course, that neither the biblical scholar (which I would classify myself as) nor the ethicist (which I am not) will feel satisfied that sufficient attention has been directed to his or her respective field. But that is a perennial risk I gladly accept. My fondest hope is that such a study will help to facilitate some measure of mutual dialogue, which is just beginning in fits and starts.

My interest and work in creation began with a dissertation that focused on certain variants within the Hebrew and Greek textual traditions of Genesis 1. In my research I realized that more was at stake in these variants than simply textual tinkering. Conflicting ideologies and theological visions were behind these seemingly innocuous differences. After some years, my interest in creation was rekindled in the classroom of Union-PSCE, an academic institution that seeks to integrate various fields of theological study in a way that effectively equips women and men of diverse backgrounds to ministry in the church and to the world. As Bill Moyers was studying the book of Genesis with a stellar group of artists, authors, and religious scholars on PBS, a group of similarly diverse, but admittedly less well-known, participants was calling

---

1. The phrase is borrowed from the title of Johnson's essay, "Imagining the World Scripture Imagines," *Modern Theology* 14/2 (1998) 165.

itself the "Genesis Seminar" in room 203 of Watts Hall in the fall of 1996. Therein, creationists and scientists, conservative and liberal budding theologians conducted open discussions about what creation could have meant to an ancient faith community and what it means today. I am grateful for the ways in which these students modeled a discussion that was consistently respectful, critically engaged, and thoroughly edifying for all participants, including the instructor. Such was the impetus for this study.

I enjoyed another, no less edifying conversation at the Center of Theological Inquiry in Princeton during my sabbatical leave. There, a group of diverse theologians, ethicists, historians, and biblical scholars shared research and conversation. At the center, the direction of my own research was sharpened in new and startling ways. I am particularly thankful for the comments and reflections of theologians David Fergusson, Niels Gregersen, George Hunsinger, and Eric Springsted, who brought a fledgling biblical scholar up to speed on the contemporary theological scene. Special thanks also go to ethicist Nancy Duff, who reacquainted me with the profound work of her mentor, Paul Lehmann. On the biblical scene, I am particularly grateful for the constant conversation and fellowship I enjoyed with János Bolyki, a Hungarian New Testament scholar new to American culture who was also working on the topic of creation. Special thanks also go to Michael Welker, whose work on creation and culture has profoundly influenced my own, and to William Schweiker, whose research interests overlapped mine considerably.

Others who have read parts of my project and have given me invaluable comments include particular members of the biblical department at Princeton Theological Seminary: Choon-Leong Seow, J. J. M. Roberts, Patrick D. Miller Jr., Dennis T. Olson, A. K. M. Adam, and Beverly R. Gaventa. I must also express my gratitude to Don Browning, the senior director of research at the center, whose wide range of knowledge and encouragement were indispensable to the development of my own work. Finally, a special word of thanks goes to Wallace M. Alston Jr., the center's director, for his hospitality and his incisive theological insights, which accompanied all our conversations at the center. Whatever is found to be helpful in this study came from them. Whatever errors or evidence of unclear thinking is to be found came only from me.

My work at the center, however, could not have been possible without the support of Union-PSCE, which granted me an academic leave for 1997 after five and a half years of teaching. My two treasured colleagues in Old Testament, W. Sibley Towner and S. Dean McBride Jr., have been a constant source of encouragement and insight throughout the shaping of this project. Thanks also go to John T. Carroll, coeditor of *Interpretation,* for taking on the lion's share of editorial responsibility during my sabbatical leave. On the topic of undeserved burden, I must also convey my appreciation to the first person to read the entire draft of the manuscript before its submission to Wm. B. Eerdmans Publishing Company, Kathy Davis, whose own insights I have very much appreciated during the editing of two previous books. Once again, Ms. Davis took on the arduous task of reading and correcting page after page while also serving the dean as secretary, a monumental feat! In addition, thanks go to Cheryl Hubbard for carefully checking my bibliography and developing the index of Scripture references, as well as to the graduate students in biblical studies at Union for hearing me out as I continued to develop my study. I am most grateful to editors Allen C. Myers and Gary Lee, as well as the staff of Eerdmans Publishing Company, for once again accepting and preparing a work for publication that seeks to be groundbreaking in scholarship yet is accessible and relevant to a larger audience.

Finally, and most importantly, words cannot express my love and appreciation for my partner in the dance of life, Gail King Brown, who has not only given me the space to complete a project that turned out to be more ambitious and time consuming than originally planned, but has also been a source of inspiration and a graciously willing participant in the agony and ecstasy of academic life. To her and to our children, Ella Rebekah and Hannah Grace, who constantly kindle within us the wonder of God's creation, I dedicate this work.

> *Rorate coeli desuper!*
> Heavens, distil your balmy showers;
> For now is risen the bright Day-star,
> From the rose Mary, flower of flowers;
> The clear sun, whom no cloud devours,
> Surmounting Phoebes in the east,
> Is comen of his heavn'ly towers,
> *Et nobis puer natus est.*
>
> William Dunbar (1460-1521?)

Christmas, 1997

Abbreviations

AARSR	American Academy of Religion Studies in Religion
AB	Anchor Bible
ABC	A. K. Grayson, ed., *Assyrian and Babylonian Chronicles*
ABD	D. N. Freedman, ed., *Anchor Bible Dictionary,* 6 vols.
AES	*Archives européenes de sociologie*
AHw	W. von Soden, *Akkadisches Handwörterbuch,* 3 vols.
AnBib	Analecta Biblica
ANE	Ancient Near East(ern)
ANET	J. B. Pritchard, ed., *Ancient Near Eastern Texts,* 3rd ed. with supplement
ANETS	Ancient Near Eastern Texts and Studies
AnSt	*Anatolian Studies*
AOAT	Alter Orient und Altes Testament
AR 1	A. K. Grayson, ed., *Assyrian Rulers of the Third and Second Millennia* BC *(to 1115* BC*)*
AR 2	A. K. Grayson, ed., *Assyrian Rulers of the Early First Millennium* BC *I (1114-859* BC*)*
AR 3	A. K. Grayson, ed., *Assyrian Rulers of the Early First Millennium* BC *II (858-745* BC*)*
ARAB	D. D. Luckenbill, ed., *Ancient Records of Assyria and Babylonia,* 2 vols.
ARE	J. H. Breasted, ed., *Ancient Records of Egypt,* 4 vols.
ATANT	Abhandlungen zur Theologie des Alten und Neuen Testaments
AzT	Arbeiten zur Theologie

BA	*Biblical Archaeology*
BAR	*The Biblical Archaeologist Reader*
BASOR	*Bulletin of the American Schools of Oriental Research*
BBB	Bonner biblische Beiträge
BDB	F. Brown, S. R. Driver, and C. A. Briggs, *Hebrew and English Lexicon of the Old Testament*
BES	Biblical Encounter Series
BHS	*Biblia hebraica stuttgartensia*
BHT	Beiträge zur historischen Theologie
BI	*Biblical Interpretation*
Bib	*Biblica*
BJRL	*Bulletin of the John Rylands University Library of Manchester*
BJS	Brown Judaic Studies
BLS	Bible and Literature Series
BN	*Biblische Notizen*
BR	*Bible Review*
BWANT	Beiträge zur Wissenschaft vom Alten und Neuen Testament
BZ	*Biblische Zeitschrift*
BZAW	Beihefte zur *ZAW*
CBQ	*Catholic Biblical Quarterly*
CBQMS	*Catholic Biblical Quarterly* Monograph Series
ConBOT	Coniectanea biblica, Old Testament Series
CThM	Calwer theologische Monographien
Ebib	Etudes bibliques
EvT	*Evangelische Theologie*
FCB	Feminist Companion to the Bible
FRC	Family, Religion, and Culture
FRLANT	Forschungen zur Religion und Literatur des Alten und Neuen Testaments
GKC	E. Kautzsch, ed., and A. E. Cowley, trans., *Gesenius' Hebrew Grammar*
HALAT	W. Baumgartner et al., ed., *Hebräisches und aramäisches Lexikon zum Alten Testament*
HAR	*Hebrew Annual Review*
HAT	Handkommentar zum Alten Testament
HBT	*Horizons in Biblical Theology*
HSM	Harvard Semitic Monographs
HTR	*Harvard Theological Review*
HUCA	*Hebrew Union College Annual*
IBT	Interpreting Biblical Texts

IDBSup	K. Crim, ed., *The Interpreter's Dictionary of the Bible: Supplementary Volume*
Int	*Interpretation*
ITC	International Theological Commentary
IRT	Issues in Religion and Theology
JAAR	*Journal of the American Academy of Religion*
JAARS	*Journal of the American Academy of Religion Studies*
JANES	*Journal of the Ancient Near Eastern Society of Columbia University*
JAOS	*Journal of the American Oriental Society*
JBL	*Journal of Biblical Literature*
JBS	Jerusalem Biblical Studies
JBT	Jahrbuch für biblische Theologie
JETS	*Journal of the Evangelical Theological Society*
JNES	*Journal of Near Eastern Studies*
JQR	*Jewish Quarterly Review*
JR	*Journal of Religion*
JRE	*Journal of Religious Ethics*
JSOT	*Journal for the Study of the Old Testament*
JSOTSup	*Journal for the Study of the Old Testament* Supplement Series
KAI	H. Donner and W. Röllig, eds., *Kanaanäische und aramäische Inschriften*
KJV	King James Version
KTU	*Die keilalphabetischen Texte aus Ugarit*
LCL	Loeb Classical Library
LEC	Library of Early Christianity
LSJ	H. G. Liddell, R. Scott, and H. S. Jones, eds., *Greek-English Lexicon*, 9th ed.
LUÅ	Lunds universitets årsskrifft
LXX	Septuagint
MT	Masoretic text
NCBC	New Century Bible Commentary
NICOT	New International Commentary on the Old Testament
NIV	New International Version
NJPSV	New Jewish Publication Society Version
NRSV	New Revised Standard Version
OBO	Orbis biblicus et orientalis
OBT	Overtures to Biblical Theology
OTL	Old Testament Library
OTS	Oudtestamentische Studiën

OTStudies	Old Testament Studies
PSB	*Princeton Seminary Bulletin*
QD	Questiones disputatae
RB	*Revue biblique*
RIMA	The Royal Inscriptions of Mesopotamia — Assyrian Periods
RIMB	The Royal Inscriptions of Mesopotamia — Babylonian Periods
ROB	G. Frame, ed., *Rulers of Babylonia: From the Second Dynasty of Isin to the End of Assyrian Domination*, vol. 2
SBLDS	Society of Biblical Literature Dissertation Series
SBLMS	Society of Biblical Literature Monograph Series
SBLSCS	Society of Biblical Literature Septuagint and Cognate Studies
SBS	Stuttgarter Bibelstudien
SBT	Studies in Biblical Theology
SBTS	Sources for Biblical and Theological Study
SEPR	Studies in Ethics and the Philosophy of Religion
SJLA	Studies in Judaism in Late Antiquity
SJOT	*Scandinavian Journal of the Old Testament*
SJT	*Scottish Journal of Theology*
SPSH	Scholars Press Studies in the Humanities
ST	*Studia theologica*
TBü	Theologische Bücherei
TS	*Theological Studies*
TToday	*Theology Today*
TUMSR	Texas University Monograph Series
TW	Theologische Wissenschaft
TZ	*Theologische Zeitshrift*
VT	*Vetus Testamentum*
VTSup	*Vetus Testamentum*, Supplements
WBC	Word Biblical Commentary
WMANT	Wissenschaftliche Monographien zum Alten und Neuen Testament
ZAH	*Zeitschrift für Althebräistik*
ZAW	*Zeitschrift für die alttestamentliche Wissenschaft*
ZKT	*Zeitschrift für katholische Theologie*
ZTK	*Zeitschrift für Theologie und Kirche*

CHAPTER 1

Introduction: The Ethos of Creation

To believe in God the Creator means to believe that he created me along with all other created beings. Few have progressed so far as to believe this in the fullest sense.

Martin Luther[1]

To find the essence of virtue, not in the day-to-day give-and-take of domestic life, but embedded somewhere in the impersonal structure of things: that would be to discover a true Talisman.

Stephen Toulmin[2]

O f the various scientific models that account for the genesis of the cosmos, none addresses the central issue with which the cosmologists of antiquity wrestled: the creation of culture.[3] Unlike their modern counter-

1. Quoted from D. J. A. Clines, *Job 1–20* (WBC 17; Waco: Word, 1989) 248.
2. S. Toulmin, *The Return of Cosmology: Postmodern Science and the Theology of Nature* (Berkeley: University of California Press, 1982) 70.
3. So R. J. Clifford, "The Hebrew Scriptures and the Theology of Creation," *TS* 46 (1985) 508-12. Such a claim, however, requires some nuance. One should note that modern cosmology and physics employ clear examples of valuative language. Whereas the ancient cosmogonies deliberately forged a connection between cosmos and community, modern cosmologies and other scientific models of physical and biological nature are

parts, ancient Near Eastern cosmologies presumed a seamless connection between cosmos and society. Without categorical distinction, nature and civilization, cosmos and community, were the inseparable products of divinely instituted creation. Human culture, including its organization and moral character, was of utmost concern for the ancient cosmologists, whether they comprised the ruling class of Babylonian society responsible for the *Enuma elish* or Israel's priestly hierarchy behind Gen 1:1–2:3(4a). For every tradition in which creation is its context, the moral life of the community is a significant subtext. Succinctly put, every model of the cosmos conveys an ethos as well as a mythos.[4]

Despite the recent spate of studies on biblical creation, much remains to be done in identifying the cultural, particularly moral, concerns and values conveyed by the creation texts. Far from being unnecessary baggage or accidental features, the social and moral values of a particular community were instrumental in determining the various ways in which creation was portrayed in Israel's literature. For example, neglect in modern studies of the moral values that undergird the creation texts has resulted in woefully one-sided discussions of creation theology and environmental concerns. As Heidi Hadsell notes, such impoverishment of theological discourse runs counter to the richness of the Judeo-Christian tradition, in which strong precedence for discerning an inherent relationship between ecology and social justice can be found.[5] Despite such catchphrases as "eco-justice" and the "integrity of creation," issues of the environment and social justice, of ecology and community, are all too often polarized in contemporary discussions.[6]

---

more subtle and inadvertent — yet in some cases intentional — in preserving the connection (see below).

4. For the standard explication of ethos as law and mythos as story in the context of biblical narrative, see J. A. Sanders, *From Sacred Story to Sacred Text* (Philadelphia: Fortress, 1987) 15-18. I take the latter term to refer more broadly to the moral context established by a given cosmology that informs a community's identity and conduct (see below). In my investigation of particular creation texts, I do not discern any monolithic conception of universal law or doctrine of natural rights, both of which come under the domain of "natural law." What I do find are various imaginative and formative contexts — rather than a single epistemological criterion — for Israel's moral living.

5. H. Hadsell, "Creation and Theology and the Doing of Ethics," *HBT* 14 (1992) 97.

6. Since her article, a growing awareness of the interconnectedness of environmental and social justice issues is being articulated in various disciplines. In biblical theology, see, e.g., W. Wink, "Biblical Theology and Social Ethics," in *Biblical Theology: Problems and Perspectives* (ed. S. J. Kraftchick et al.; Nashville: Abingdon, 1995) 260-75. From the sociological field, P. Lichterman offers a penetrating analysis of community formation among minority groups doing environmental justice in the face of the disproportionate siting of toxic wastes in poor neighborhoods (*The Search for Political Community: American Activ-*

Sustaining this polarization is the still prevailing assumption that creation consists of exclusively natural elements while the realm of social relations is of a different category altogether.[7] The proliferation of recent biblical studies of creation is in part impelled by a concern to "heal creation," but lacking, by and large, is a concomitant concern for healing the community.[8] This study aims to address this lack. How the fundamentally moral values and perspectives of ancient Israel that make up its multifaceted ethos are profiled in the very contours of creation to shape the theological landscape and memory of a people is the focus. Instead of determining how the biblical views of creation reflect ancient mythology, can solve the environmental crisis, or complement modern science (all worthy objectives on which this study depends),[9] my aim is to examine biblical creation's distinctly *moral* significance for both ancient and contemporary communities of faith. Even the common category "worldview," which has gained widespread currency in sociological research of the Bible, albeit indispensable, comes up short, for it remains morally neutral in its implications. Ethos is its ethical counterpart, a distinctly moral *Weltanschauung*.

---

ists Reinventing Commitment [Cambridge: Cambridge University Press, 1996], esp. 105-45). On a different front, Croatian theologian M. Volf probes the Genesis creation traditions in order to construct a viable political theology (*Exclusion and Embrace: A Theological Exploration of Identity, Otherness, and Reconciliation* [Nashville: Abingdon, 1996], esp. 64-85). Hadsell herself constructively employs the Reformed concept of "work" as an ethical category that highlights the interrelationships between community and nature ("Creation," 98-103). Indeed, her conclusions find much support in the Yahwistic view of creation (see chapter 2 below).

7. See E. Elnes's assessment in an article inspired in part by Hadsell's analysis ("Creation and Tabernacle: The Priestly Writer's 'Environmentalism,'" *HBT* 16 [1994] 144). See also W. P. Brown, *Structure, Role, and Ideology in the Hebrew and Greek Texts of Genesis 1:1–2:3* (SBLDS 132; Atlanta: Scholars Press 1993) 207-34.

8. This is clear from the fact that almost every recent exploration of biblical creation responds in some fashion to Lynn White's charge that the Judeo-Christian heritage is directly responsible for the demise of the natural environment ("The Historical Roots of Our Ecological Crisis," *Science* 144 [March 10, 1967] 1203-7). See below.

9. Regarding the latter, two recent yet strikingly different works are of note: C. Hyers, *The Meaning of Creation: Genesis and Modern Science* (Atlanta: John Knox, 1984), who employs the fruits of documentary-historical research; and L. R. Bailey, *Genesis, Creation, and Creationism* (New York: Paulist, 1993), who deliberately eschews this staple of pentateuchal research.

Culture and Ecology in Recent Biblical Scholarship

Ever since Gerhard von Rad's influential study on creation and redemption, biblical scholars have labored intensely over identifying the theological value (or lack thereof) of creation in the Bible.[10] Most recently, the trend has shifted slightly to highlighting the cultural roots from which the creation traditions sprang forth. The works of Richard Clifford, Ronald Simkins, and Theodore Hiebert are the most noteworthy examples.[11] Each in his own way focuses on the significance of creation in relation to Israel's worldview and culture. There is, however, no unanimity of approach among their studies. Moreover, each treats the phenomenon of culture in different ways.

From a theoretical perspective, Clifford ably points out the link between creation and certain *institutional* forms of culture in the ancient Near Eastern

10. G. von Rad, "The Theological Problem of the Old Testament Doctrine of Creation," in *The Problem of the Hexateuch and Other Essays* (tr. E. W. Trueman Dicken; London: SCM, 1966 [German originally published in 1936]) 131-43. Some of the more recent contributors include C. Westermann, "Creation and History in the Old Testament" (tr. D. Dutton), in *The Gospel and Human Destiny* (ed. V. Vajta; Minneapolis: Augsburg, 1971) 11-38; idem, *Creation* (tr. J. J. Scullion; Philadelphia: Fortress, 1974); idem, *Genesis 1–11* (tr. J. J. Scullion; Continental Commentary; Minneapolis: Augsburg, 1984) 1-73; J. D. Levenson, *Creation and the Persistence of Evil: The Jewish Drama of Divine Omnipotence* (San Francisco: Harper & Row, 1988 [2d ed.; Princeton: Princeton University Press, 1994]); H. H. Schmid, *Gerechtigkeit als Weltordnung: Hintergrund und Geschichte des alttestamentlichen Gerechtigkeitsbegriffes* (BHT 40; Tübingen: Mohr [Siebeck], 1968); idem, "Creation, Righteousness, and Salvation: 'Creation Theology' as the Broad Horizon of Biblical Theology" (tr. B. W. Anderson and D. G. Johnson), in *Creation in the Old Testament* (ed. B. W. Anderson; IRT 6; Philadelphia: Fortress, 1984) 102-17; B. W. Anderson, *Creation Versus Chaos* (New York: Association, 1967; repr. Philadelphia: Fortress, 1987); idem, *From Creation to New Creation: Old Testament Perspectives* (OBT; Minneapolis: Fortress, 1994); W. Harrelson, *From Fertility Cult to Worship* (Garden City, N.Y.: Doubleday, 1969); R. P. Knierim, "Cosmos and History in Israel's Theology," *HBT* 3 (1981) 59-124; T. E. Fretheim, "The Plagues as Ecological Signs of Historical Disaster," *JBL* 110 (1991) 385-96; idem, *Exodus* (Interpretation; Louisville: John Knox, 1991); J. Barr, *Biblical Faith and Natural Theology* (Oxford: Clarendon, 1993); J. R. Middleton, "Is Creation Theology Inherently Conservative? A Dialogue with Walter Brueggemann," *HTR* 87 (1994) 257-77. From a distinctly theological framework, a number of these scholars have helped to establish pride of place for creation theology over and against the once prevailing "history of salvation" paradigm that so dominated biblical scholarship until the 1970s. See W. Brueggemann's survey in "The Loss and Recovery of Creation in Old Testament Theology," *TToday* 53 (1996) 177-90.

11. For example, R. J. Clifford, *Creation Accounts in the Ancient Near East and in the Bible* (CBQMS 26; Washington, D.C.: Catholic Biblical Association of America, 1994); R. A. Simkins, *Creator and Creation: Nature in the Worldview of Ancient Israel* (Peabody, Mass.: Hendrickson, 1994); T. Hiebert, *The Yahwist's Landscape: Nature and Religion in Early Israel* (New York: Oxford University Press, 1996).

4

cosmogonies, including Israel's, but his discussions remain by and large on the level of generality.[12] By contrast, Ronald Simkins's approach addresses explicitly the issue of cultural valuation in his examination of the creation traditions. Drawing from the "value orientation preference model" developed by Kluckhohn and Strodtbeck, Simkins aims at systematizing those values held by ancient Israel that concern the relationship between culture and nature.[13] He places the various creation traditions under three categories: subjugation-to-nature, harmony-with-nature, and mastery-over-nature. His analysis is helpful as far as it goes, but it is unclear to me whether his classifications represent distinct worldviews or a single worldview shared throughout the ancient Near East (even though he claims the latter).[14] Given his ostensible preference for the latter, the question then naturally arises whether such a unified worldview can possibly account for all the various cosmologies found in biblical literature.

It would be hard to imagine, for example, a single worldview that could include the evolutionary drama of the Priestly creation account in Gen 1:1–2:3(4a) and Qohelet's musings on the wearisome repetitions of the cosmos in Eccl 1:3-8. Even if one were to develop a theoretical system that could subsume these two opposing models, of what significant heuristic use would it be? Israel's diverse perspectives on creation need not be described solely in terms of bloodless abstractions or subsumed under a "plain vanilla" worldview.[15] To his credit, Simkins admits that his unified worldview "does not reflect the many complexities of the *real world* in which [the Israelites] lived" and encourages more work to be done in this area.[16] Nevertheless, Simkins's attempt to formulate a unified worldview on which all the traditions are to be predicated is well-nigh impossible. Perhaps the time is ripe to enter into the cosmological fray of Israel's "real world."

12. See his discussion in "Hebrew Scriptures," 507-12; and in *Creation Accounts,* 7-10. My only criticism is that Clifford's work does not sufficiently probe the various valuative contexts that the biblical cosmogonies evince in their particular socioliterary contexts. His explications of the creation accounts remain frequently on the level of retelling the story without drawing any particular cultural or moral implications (e.g., his treatment of *Atrahasis* on pp. 74-82). When he does refer explicitly to culture, he invariably profiles it in its *institutional* forms, such as kingship in *Enuma elish* (pp. 91-93). He does not say much about the complex array of values imparted by the traditions for the general life of the ancient community. In addition, Clifford's monograph seems to be decidedly weighted toward the extrabiblical creation traditions at the expense of giving the biblical cosmologies their cultural and theological due.

13. Simkins, *Creator and Creation,* 31-33.

14. See, e.g., ibid., 23, 26, 75, 117-20, 252-55.

15. Ibid., 120.

16. Ibid. (italics added).

More useful is the eclectic approach followed by Ted Hiebert in his recent monograph *The Yahwist's Landscape,* in which he appropriately distinguishes the Priestly and Yahwistic worldviews.[17] Drawing from the results of archaeology, anthropology, and historical analysis, as well as those of source and literary analysis, Hiebert offers a finely nuanced view of the Yahwist's perspective on nature. As he makes clear repeatedly, the driving force behind the study is his ecological concern for humanity's place in the physical environment. Consequently his primary focus is on the agricultural practice presupposed by the Yahwist. More so than Clifford, Hiebert is able to derive certain moral conclusions from the Yahwist's epic, but they are exclusively environmental or "agricultural" in scope. In conclusion, Hiebert passionately calls for "the inevitable rehabilitation of a more traditional kind of agriculture" to redress the damage done by modern industrial practice on the environment.[18] In short, he reduces culture to agriculture.[19] Given his environmental focus, he does not move significantly beyond the material realm of agriculture in his discussion of Israelite culture, nor does he need to.[20]

Hiebert is not alone in his use of the biblical materials to address the mounting environmental crisis. Others such as Simkins and Bernhard W. Anderson have identified the environmental crisis as the raison d'être of much their work.[21] Typical surveys of biblical interpretation on the topic of nature and the Bible invariably place Lynn White Jr. (an environmentalist misinterpreting biblical traditions) and Gerhard von Rad (a biblical scholar allegedly misinterpreting creation traditions) practically side by side as foils for current research.[22] For White, the invention of the fixed plow, harnessed to the biblical mandate to subdue the earth (Gen 1:26), gave birth to Western culture's tendency to view nature as no more than a machine to be used and ultimately abused.[23] This "knife," as it were, lacerated the land, turning the farmer into a warrior, "an exploiter of nature." As many scholars suggest, von Rad also wielded a knife of sorts, namely, Hegel's philosophy of history, which severed

17. Hiebert, *Yahwist's Landscape,* 155-62.

18. Ibid., 148-49.

19. Hiebert casts the issue in reverse form, as indicated in his subtitle, "Agriculture as Culture: The Human as a Farmer" (*Yahwist's Landscape,* 141).

20. See ibid., 68-72, 141-49.

21. See the brief survey in Simkins, *Creator and Creation,* 3; B. W. Anderson, "Human Dominion over Nature," in idem, *From Creation to New Creation,* 112, 116 (repr. from *Biblical Studies in Contemporary Thought* [ed. M. Ward; Somerville, Mass.: Greeno, Hadden, 1975] 27-28, 32).

22. For example, Simkins, *Creator and Creation,* 4-9; T. Hiebert, "Re-Imaging Nature," *Int* 50 (1996) 38-39; idem, *Yahwist's Landscape,* 4-5, 13-18, esp. 18.

23. White, "Historical Roots," 1203-7.

all connection between history and nature.[24] Consequently the Hebrew tradents were viewed primarily as historians who by and large drowned out the music of the spheres with the drumbeat of salvation history.

An often-used citation from von Rad's influential essay maintains that the doctrine of creation is "but a magnificent foil for the message of salvation."[25] Critics charge that the subordination of cosmology to soteriology represents another example of Western civilization's tendency to set human culture and history over and against the natural realm. But for all the criticism leveled against his seminal essay, von Rad's argument is more nuanced than his detractors suggest. His expressed intent was not to sever, once and for all, the doctrines of creation and redemption but rather to determine their interrelationships. Second Isaiah marked for von Rad the exemplar of their integration.[26]

Granted, von Rad argues that the doctrine of creation in Second Isaiah performs "only an ancillary function."[27] Elsewhere, however, he refers to creation and redemption as synonymous dimensions of the "same divine dispensation."[28] In short, the web connecting creation and redemption could not be drawn more taut. Admittedly, von Rad's assumption that the respective doctrines were heretofore at loggerheads is problematic, for nature and history never really formed such a polarity in the biblical literature, as many have recently demonstrated.[29] Nevertheless, such criticism simply proves von Rad's main point: creation rarely serves itself in biblical literature — a thesis that he was able to demonstrate on behalf of the Priestly creation account but could not for certain psalms and much of the wisdom literature. Consequently, these anomalous traditions were relegated to foreign status from the purview of Yahwistic faith.[30] At his best, von Rad attempted to mend the cleavage of history and creation rather than drive the wedge deeper.[31] At his

24. R. A. Simkins, *Yahweh's Activity in History and Nature in the Book of Joel* (ANETS 10; Lewiston, N.Y.: Edwin Mellen, 1991) 3-10; Hiebert, "Re-Imaging Nature," 39; idem, *Yahwist's Landscape*, 5, 15-16.

25. Von Rad, "Doctrine of Creation," 134; cf. 142.

26. Ibid., 135.

27. Ibid., 134.

28. Ibid., 135.

29. For example, B. W. Anderson, *Creation Versus Chaos*, 51-52; T. E. Fretheim, "The Reclamation of Creation: Redemption and Law in Exodus," *Int* 45 (1991) 354-65; Schmid, "Creation," 102-17; Hiebert, *Yahwist's Landscape*, 3-29.

30. Von Rad, "Doctrine of Creation," 139-42.

31. Even in this early essay, von Rad sowed the seeds that were to produce 28 years later the following conclusion: "The Old Testament draws no such distinction between nature and history, regarding them as one single area of reality under the control of God." Nature and history are "merely vast ciphers, so many images projected" onto reality

worst, he accomplished the mending by trivializing nature, a theological move that was by and large contextually driven,[32] yet often interpreted as epitomizing the West's proclivity to deprecate the natural realm.

As for Western civilization's allegedly intractable antinature bias, British historian and cultural critic Simon Schama has done much to loosen that wedge.[33] Contrary to popular opinion, there is much in Western tradition, Schama claims, that embodies a sincere reverence of nature.

> The cultural habits of humanity have always made room for the sacredness of nature. All our landscapes, from the city park to the mountain hike, *are imprinted with our tenacious, inescapable obsessions.* So that to take the many and several ills of the environment seriously does not, I think, require that we trade in our cultural legacy or its posterity. It asks instead that we simply see it for what it has truly been: not the repudiation, but the veneration of nature.[34]

Schama is not suggesting that Western culture has consistently venerated nature. Such a claim would be naively romantic. Fully acknowledging the legacy of the West's abuse of nature, Schama nevertheless finds resources within Western culture that transcend the dichotomy between culture and nature. Indeed, nature is inexorably stamped with the contours of culture. By "culture" Schama does not mean the material remains of picnics and campsites. We perceive, engage, even construct nature from the perspective of culture. From the landscape lyrics of "America the Beautiful" to Shakespeare's eulogy of the "sceptred isle" pronounced by the dying John of Gaunt, "landscapes *can* be self-consciously designed to express *the virtues of a particular political or social community.*"[35]

Culture's indelible imprint on nature thus need not conjure up fears of

---

("Some Aspects of the Old Testament World-View," in *Problem of the Hexateuch, 154-55 [German originally published in 1964]*).

32. R. Albertz and others have noted that von Rad's subordination of the doctrine of nature in his 1936 essay was, like the Barmen Declaration (1934), in part polemically inspired to discredit the National Socialist use of creation ("Blood and Soil Religion") for ideological purposes (*Weltschöpfung und Menschenschöpfung untersucht bei Deuterojesaja, Hiob und in den Psalmen* [CThM 3; Stuttgart: Calwer, 1974] 174). See also Brueggemann, "Loss and Recovery," 177-78.

33. S. Schama, *Landscape and Memory* (New York: Knopf, 1995).

34. Ibid., 18 (italics added).

35. Ibid., 15 (italics added). Cast modally, Schama's statement cannot be taken as a bid for social reductionistic or constructionistic views of nature. His point is simply that the way in which the world is perceived and interpreted *can* reflect a particular society's values.

environmental rape and exploitation. The cultural legacy of nature need not be disparaged but can be celebrated as a constructive way toward rediscovering nature's value and, in turn, toward rediscovering ourselves.[36] As moral philosopher Mary Midgley contends, the issue of culture is analogous to that of sense perception.[37] We can think of our senses as a "screen or barrier set up between us and the real world," a veritable barricade or prison. Or we can think of them as our window to the world. To aspire to be free of culture for nature's sake is tantamount to being skinless, Midgley argues, since culture, whether we like it or not, is essential to human nature. From an epistemological standpoint, nature is invariably cultured. Through the filter of culture, our perceptions of the environment in some measure reflect back on ourselves, imbuing our "virtues" and "obsessions" with cosmic significance. A forest, a mountain, or a river can serve as a symbol that evokes social meaning, even self-recognition and reorientation. Such is the moral sense of nature through the eyes of the moral agent.

In sum, biblical scholars who attempt to draw distinctly cultural implications from the creation traditions invariably treat the phenomenon of culture as a black box, something exogenous to the larger realm of discourse that shapes and preserves a particular community's identity. As Simkins ably demonstrates, culture has everything to do with a valuative worldview; it is difficult, if not impossible, however, to construct a generalized, monolithic *Weltanschauung* apart from the changing mores and historical vicissitudes a community faces throughout any given period of time. As sociologist of religion Stephen Hart points out, cultural processes include the active creation, communication, transformation, and application of articulated values or "codes."[38] Culture is no doubt evinced in some established institutional forms, as Clifford occasionally highlights, but it certainly cannot be limited to them alone. Studies that are environmentally driven, such as Hiebert's and Simkins's, tend to construe culture only in ecological terms. Yet culture is more expansive and concrete. As noted above, the way in which nature is perceived can say much about the matrix of a particular culture's root values and convictions, its ethos, which is in

36. See C. J. Glacken's classic treatment of the relationship between self-perception and nature in *Traces on the Rhodian Shore: Nature and Culture in Western Thought from Ancient Times to the End of the Eighteenth Century* (Berkeley: University of California Press, 1967).

37. M. Midgley, *Beast and Man: The Roots of Human Nature* (2d ed.; New York: Routledge, 1995) 290-91.

38. S. Hart, "The Cultural Dimension of Social Movements: A Theoretical Reassessment and Literature Review," *Sociology of Religion* 57 (1996) 90-91.

THE ETHOS OF THE COSMOS

continual formation as much as the culture is in constant development historically.

By "culture" I mean to include the moral life of a particular community as conveyed in its theological and symbolic discourse, although nothing static is implied. Most studies that deal with ancient Israel's culture rely on Clifford Geertz's seminal definition of culture as "an historically transmitted pattern of meanings embodied in symbols."[39] But rare is any accounting of what Geertz refers to as "the autonomous process of symbolic formation" that is often "passed over in virtual silence."[40] Culture is the result of a complex *process*, an interaction between a community's preexisting traditions and codes and its current social contexts and practices by which certain values are interpreted, appropriated, transformed, and applied. Culture is "craftwork"[41] aimed at conveying an ethos or, more accurately, "ethoses" (Greek *ethē*), various compatible ways of perceiving the world and acting in it in appropriate ways. The world, even as nature, is not an external, monolithic object to be handled, whether reverently or abusively, by detached subjects; it is at its core a community.

Cosmos and Ethos

If what Y. Lotman and B. Uspensky say is true, that "culture is the generator of structuredness" that "creates a social sphere around [humankind] which, like the biosphere, makes life possible,"[42] then the way in which the cosmos is structured says something significant about the way in which the cultural, including moral, contours of the community have been and should be shaped, that is, something of the community's ethos. As ethicist Paul Lehmann has

39. C. Geertz, *The Interpretation of Cultures: Selected Essays* (New York: Basic Books, 1973) 90. See, e.g., the most recent work on Israelite culture in J. A. Dearman, *Religion and Culture in Ancient Israel* (Peabody, Mass.: Hendrickson, 1992) 2.

40. Geertz, *Interpretation of Culture*, 207. See Hart's similar critique of recent sociological studies of culture movements (Hart, "Cultural Dimension," 98).

41. Hart, "Cultural Dimension," 98.

42. Y. Lotman and B. Uspensky, "On the Semiotic Mechanism of Culture," *New Literary History* 9 (1978) 213.

43. P. Lehmann, *Ethics in a Christian Context* (New York: Harper & Row, 1963) 23-24. See also M. Heidegger, "Letter on Humanism," in *Basic Writings from* Being and Time *(1927) to* The Task of Thinking *(1964)* (ed. D. F. Krell; New York: Harper & Row, 1977) 23; E. O. Springsted, "'Thou Hast Given Me Room': Simone Weil's Retheologization of the Political," *Cahiers Simone Weil* 20/2 (1997) 87-98. As Lehmann points out, the term originally applied to animals rather than to human beings. The definition of ἦθος in classical

pointed out, *ethos*, from Greek ἦθος, originally meant "stall" or "dwelling."[43] At base, it designates a sense of *place* or habitation.[44] The term signifies an environment that makes possible and sustains moral living, establishing the direction and parameters of human conduct. Ethos defines the setting that is conducive for the formation of a community's character. Thus "ethics," also derived from Greek *ethos,* is "concerned with that which holds human society together. It is, so to say, the 'cement' of human society."[45] As the sphere of moral existence, ethos suggests a "moral ontology, that is, an account of the meaning of our being in the world and how to orient ourselves in the world."[46]

The position and orientation of the moral subject vis-à-vis the environment are thus central to the issue of moral ethos. To illustrate biblically, the first question addressed to the disobedient man in the garden is "Where are you?" (Gen 3:9), after which God broaches the nature of the disobedience: "What is this that you have done?" (v. 13). The primal man's posture and relationship to the garden have all to do with the crime he has committed. Similarly, in God's encounter with Cain the first question posed is "Where is your brother Abel?" (4:9), followed by "What have you done?" (v. 10). The question of place, of location and relation (locus), is primary, and it cuts to the very heart of ethos. In both cases the moral subject has ventured out of bounds. The nature of those bounds and the quality of existence within them are the foci of any investigation of ethos. Although the nature of the relationship between ethos and ethic is organically complex, ethos confirms the primacy of place in moral discourse. In the two biblical examples, the question of location opens an inquiry and an exchange of dialogue before the violation itself, be it illicit eating or malicious slaughter, is addressed. Perhaps one lesson to be learned is that the ethos or moral context presupposed by a certain prescribed mode of conduct is just as important as the particular ethic or moral principles at work. In any case, ethos provides the sustaining environment or context for an ethic to function and for a moral subject to perform. The normative claim of a particular ethic and the integrity of the moral self are determined in part by the place they assume in the larger ethos.

Greek ranges from "accustomed place" (e.g., *Iliad* 6.511; Herodotus 7.125) to "custom" (e.g., Hesiod *Theogony* 66; Herodotus 1.15, 157) and "moral character" (e.g., Aristotle *Nicomachean Ethics* 1139a1). See LSJ, 766.

44. See E. S. Casey, *The Fate of Place: A Philosophical History* (Berkeley: University of California Press, 1997) xiv.

45. Lehmann, *Ethics,* 25.

46. W. Schweiker, *Responsibility and Christian Ethics* (Cambridge: Cambridge University Press, 1995) 38.

As the cosmic habitation of moral agency, creation, biblically speaking, divulges an ethos of the cosmos. Whether viewed by ancient or by modern faith communities, the created order is perceived to exhibit the most fundamental relationships and values, building blocks in the formation of a community's identity. The way in which creation is configured has as much to do with how the moral community structures itself as with the way the natural world is ordered. Such a recognition is nothing new.

From Antiquity to Modern Science: A Cosmopolitical Sampling

From antiquity to the most recent developments in modern science (e.g., quantum physics and social biology), valuative discourse about the nature of the universe has in various ways forged links of correspondence. A clear example of the link between ethos and cosmos drawn from classical antiquity is found in Philo:

> We must now give the reason why he [Moses] began his law book with the history, and put the commands and prohibitions in the second place. He did not, like any historian, make it his business to leave behind for posterity records of ancient deeds for the pleasant but unimproving entertainment which they give; but, in relating the history of early times, and going for its beginning right to the creation of the universe, he wished to shew two most essential things: first that the Father and Maker of the world was in the truest sense also its Lawgiver, secondly that he who would observe the laws will accept gladly the duty of following nature and live in accordance with the ordering of the universe, so that his deeds are attuned to harmony with his words and his words with his deeds.[47]

Not only do history and law interpret one another in reciprocal fashion, but the cosmos, as the beginning point of history, offers for Philo a paradigm of ethical conduct. As in Psalms 19 and 119, the order of the cosmos reflects in some discernible sense Torah, and vice versa.[48] In his own words, the laws of Moses are "stamped (sesēmasmena), as it were, with the seals of nature herself."[49] The model of harmonious integrity imparted by law is reflected in the

47. *Moses* 2.48, translated by F. H. Colson in *Philo* (LCL; Cambridge: Harvard University Press, 1935) 6:471-73.

48. See J. D. Levenson's discussion of the cosmological basis of Torah evinced in these two psalms and elsewhere ("The Theologies of Commandment in Biblical Israel," *HTR* 73 [1980] 28-33).

49. *Moses* 2.14 (Colson, *Philo*, 457).

very "ordering of the universe." Philo gives both a theological and a moral warrant. First, law and creation find their nexus in God. Second, observing the law involves living in accordance with the cosmic order, an order that is also embodied in the correspondence ("harmony") between the individual's discourse and conduct. Cosmic order, consequently, is reflected in the microcosmic harmony of the individual. Like the law, the cosmos mandates such integrity. As lawgiver and creator, God is the ultimate cause that brings about the moral coherence of nature. As moral agents, human beings must act in accordance with creation to effect their integrity, one that mirrors the coherence of the natural order. To borrow from the scientific view of causation, one could say that Philo has both a "bottom-up" and a "top-down" view of moral reality.[50] In his mediation of Hellenism and Judaism, Philo has fashioned an ethos of harmony, a moral coherence between human virtue and cosmic order.

Philo is but one example of the cosmic coherence that typified a moral worldview from antiquity up through at least the seventeenth century in the West. Stephen Toulmin aptly describes this kind of worldview as a "cosmopolis": a harmony between the order of the cosmos and that of human affairs.[51] John Donne's lament over the decay of nature and the loss of all social coherence in early seventeenth-century Europe is but one prime example.[52] Toulmin does not see, however, the notion of cosmopolis altogether jettisoned in the modern period but rather resurfacing in radically altered forms, whether in the rise of nation-states in the eighteenth century, in which hierarchy and stability were the hallmarks of society and nature (à la Newton), or in the twentieth century, with the focus on adaptation (à la Darwin).[53] Yet Toulmin observes that the Cartesian split between mind and matter has had an irreparable effect on the cosmopolitical vision since the seventeenth century, for it drove a deep wedge between nature and humanity to the point of separating them out as "self-contained" realms.[54] In short, beginning with

50. See the explanation of these two frameworks of causation in Nancey Murphy and George F. R. Ellis, *On the Moral Nature of the Universe: Theology, Cosmology, and Ethics* (Minneapolis: Fortress, 1996) 16, 24-27.

51. S. Toulmin, *Cosmopolis: The Hidden Agenda of Modernity* (New York: Free Press, 1990) 67-69.

52. Ibid., 65-67. Donne's poetic elegies over the natural and social realms, cited by Toulmin, remind me of the despairing tone of the Egyptian "Admonitions of Ipuwer," frequently associated, albeit erroneously, with the First Intermediate Period. See M. Lichtheim, *Ancient Egyptian Literature*, vol. 1: *The Old and Middle Kingdoms* (Berkeley: University of California Press, 1975) 149-63.

53. Toulmin, *Cosmopolis*, 133, 191.

54. Ibid., 105-16, 133.

the Enlightenment and particularly with the rise of Cartesian philosophy and Newtonian physics, the *organic unity* of the cosmopolis was effectively wrenched. Although the natural and social orders could mirror each other, they could do so only as discrete, independent realms.

In a similar fashion, theologian Nancey Murphy and mathematician George F. R. Ellis point out that the modern period has seen a virtual chasm yawn open between the cosmos and the polis.[55] Most recently, however, scientific and theological circles are beginning to rebridge the gulf and recapture in various ways the cosmopolitical unity of reality. It can no longer be claimed, as biblical theologian Bernhard Anderson once did in his urgent call for dialogue, that the language of science is essentially neutral in meaning and that theology and science, consequently, speak two absolutely different languages.[56] That the cosmos exhibits a kind of ethos is increasingly recognized in modern science. To put it another way, the language of modern science is no longer finding it necessary to eschew the language of ethos and prescription altogether, particularly in its most comprehensive claims about physical reality on both the macro- and microscopic levels.[57] As is often noted, science exhibits a much wider role than the presumed neutral one of purveying information about a world conceived as utterly "objective."[58] Indeed, if the findings of "pure" science were utterly bereft of social or moral import, how could any dialogue between theology and science be entertained at all?

Historians of science Ian G. Barbour and Frederic B. Burnham, for example, have had much to say about the social and theological implications of scientific views of the cosmos. Although Barbour appropriately offers a word of caution about identifying the religious idea of creation too closely with scientific cosmology, he finds some intriguing, if not necessary, connections.[59] For

55. Murphy and Ellis, *Moral Nature*, 2.

56. B. W. Anderson, "Theology and Science: Cosmic Dimensions of the Creation Account in Genesis," in idem, *From Creation to New Creation*, 97-110 (repr. from the *Drew Gateway* 56 [1986] 1-13). See Murphy's and Ellis's critique of the "fact-value distinction" and of the notion of value-free, "pure" social sciences (*Moral Nature*, 5-6, 91-100). See also H. Rolston III's discussion of the relatedness of biology and theology in "Does Nature Need to Be Redeemed?" *HBT* 14 (1992) 145-46. That both the Bible and biology offer a "concept of nature, a worldview," allows for congenial lines of heuristic connection.

57. The claim is not made that the scientific method is itself an inherently moral enterprise, only that the results can be morally significant. For a critical examination of the mythic underpinnings as well as pretensions of modern science, see M. Midgley, *Science as Salvation: A Modern Myth and its Meaning* (London: Routledge, 1992) esp. 84-108.

58. Ibid., 92.

59. I. G. Barbour, "Creation and Cosmology," in *Cosmos as Creation* (ed. T. Peters; Nashville: Abingdon, 1989) 120.

instance, scientific models of the cosmos and the biosphere highlight the interdependence of all things within a hierarchy of existence that is distinctively holistic.[60] Barbour has characterized the universe as a complex "community of
beings."[61] Recognizing an ethos of interdependence on a cosmic level naturally
invites an ethic that values the integrity of all creation.

Frederic Burnham casts the issue more sharply when he draws certain
"anthropological implications" from the realm of quantum physics.[62]
Burnham quotes physicist Henry Stapp: "An elementary particle is not an in-
dependently-existing, isolated entity. It is, in essence, a set of relationships
reaching out to other things." Burnham then argues vigorously for the co-
gency of replacing the words "elementary particle" with "human being." The
result of such a hermeneutical move coheres well, according to Burnham,
with biblical anthropology. By such a move, Bernham imaginatively identifies
the moral agent with the subatomic particle, splitting the Adam, as it were,
and placing the human agent within a cosmic ethos of interdependence.

Most recently, Murphy and Ellis have collaborated to produce a programmatic vision for the integration of science and ethics. Their claim is that
a particular moral vision is in fact supported by the sciences.[63] In combination with scientific evidence of the "fine-tuning" of the cosmos and the
"anthropic principle," as well as biological evidence of natural cycles, Murphy
and Ellis discern a "kenotic" ethos, an ethic of noncoercive renunciation, operative in the natural world.[64] They find, consequently, a "natural-scientific
context for morality" that is conducive to theology.[65]

As investigated by the various fields of scientific inquiry, from biology to
cosmology and elementary physics, the world so described at its most fundamental level or cosmic scope is open for the language of ethos. For instance, Paul
Davies speaks of the laws of physics as "precluding cosmic anarchy" and evincing
a "link between mind and cosmos."[66] The view of cosmos as lawful has always

---

60. Ibid., 146-47.

61. Barbour, "Science, God, and Nature," lecture given at the Carl Howie Center for
Science, Art, and Theology at Union Theological Seminary in Virginia, Nov. 30, 1995.

62. F. B. Burnham, "Maker of Heaven and Earth: A Perspective of Contemporary
Science," *HBT* 12/2 (1990) 13.

63. Murphy and Ellis, *Moral Nature,* 1.

64. Ibid., 208-13. They admit that cosmology in and of itself is not sufficient for for-
mulating a moral worldview, but by forging a route through the "pure" social sciences,
their conclusions, they claim, receive cosmological confirmation (p. 63).

65. Ibid., 219.

66. P. C. W. Davies, "The Intelligibility of Nature," in *Quantum Cosmology and the
Laws of Nature* (ed. R. J. Russell et al.; Berkeley: Center for Theology and Natural Sciences,
1993) 148, 160.

been a staple of mathematics and physics, from Newton to Einstein, but recent discussions have begun to move significantly beyond mechanistic views of the universe. John Polkinghorne eschews the language of determinism in describing the "wonderful order of the cosmos," a fact that "we know as surely as we know anything that we are not automata."[67] The way Polkinghorne casts the epistemological issue is telling: knowledge of the world and knowledge of the self are bound up together. The universe's "reliability and openness" lead naturally from "matter to mind," forming a link between the physical and the noetic.[68]

Such discourse allows for ascribing moral valuation to scientific descriptions of reality, as in Philip Hefner's striking statement that the evolution of the biosphere is a "value-driven process," rife with "oughtness."[69] As Niels Gregersen ably demonstrates, it does not take much of a leap from Darwinian evolutionism to apprehend the universe as a "cosmology of freedom."[70] Similarly from the side of physics, "We can certainly say . . . that physics makes free will possible, and so has built into it the foundations of the possibility of moral choice."[71] Finally, gravitational theorist Lee Smolin has recently likened the universe to a "city," a place of "endless negotiation, an endless construction of the new out of the old, . . . where novelty may emerge without violence, where we might imagine a continual process of improvement without revolution, . . . continually confronted with each other as the makers of our shared world."[72] The language of Smolin's cosmic vision is implicitly rife with prescription, evoking the ideal of nonviolent, even democratic, evolution. Through the work of a physicist, the cosmopolitical vision has come full circle.

Such cursory examples by no means do justice to the wealth of recent studies, projects, and consultations currently underway that aim at building solid bridges between science and theology. My point is simply to show that they do more than suggest that theology or ethics and science are simply compatible yet separate areas of study. Science and theology are no longer talking past each other or staying out of each other's hair. Science is recognizing its own limitations in its

---

67. J. Polkinghorne, "The Laws of Nature and the Laws of Physics," in *Quantum Cosmology and the Laws of Nature,* ed. R. J. Russell et al. (Vatican City State: Vatican Observatory; Berkeley: Center for Theology and Natural Sciences, 1993), 448.

68. Ibid., 444.

69. P. Hefner, *The Human Factor: Evolution, Culture, and Religion* (Minneapolis: Fortress, 1993) 31.

70. N. H. Gregersen, "Theology in a Neo-Darwinian World," *ST* 48 (1994) 137. See more recently the application of Darwinianism to cosmogony by the gravitational theorist L. Smolin in *The Life of the Cosmos* (New York: Oxford University Press, 1997).

71. Murphy and Ellis, *Moral Nature,* 223.

72. Quoted from D. Overbye, "The Cosmos According to Darwin," *The New York Times Magazine,* July 13, 1997, 26.

cosmological investigations, and theology is acknowledging its need for scientific input, even vision, in its accounting of the cosmos as creation.[73] The examples surveyed above have a discernible blending of moral and scientific discourse. Terms like "interdependence," "hierarchy," "community," "freedom," and "negotiation without revolution" can characterize the cosmos from a distinctly scientific perspective as much as they can describe a human community from a distinctly moral (or immoral) perspective. Even physical "law" bears some correspondence to a moral ethos. Isolationism, coercion, and anarchy are not only moral failings; according to physicists, they are ultimately unnatural, as much as the unintegrated self is, according to Philo, morally deficient.

Rejoining What Has Been Rent Asunder

The works of Murphy and Ellis, as well as those of other scientists and theologians, represent concerted efforts in overcoming the artificial separation of ethics from science and theology, in regaining a cosmopolis that is theologically significant as well as scientifically credible. A comparable division is strongly evident in two significant areas of inquiry that have remained by and large separate in biblical studies until recently: creation theology and ethics.[74] Most stu-

73. Murphy and Ellis, *Moral Nature*, 60-63.
74. Among general treatments four important works are to be noted: B. C. Birch, *Let Justice Roll Down: The Old Testament, Ethics, and the Christian Life* (Louisville: Westminster John Knox, 1991) 71-104; E. Otto, *Theologische Ethik des Alten Testaments* (TW 3/2; Stuttgart: Kohlhammer, 1994); C. J. H. Wright, *Walking in the Ways of the Lord: The Ethical Authority of the Old Testament* (Downers Grove, Ill.: InterVarsity Press, 1995); and J. Barton, *Ethics and the Old Testament* (Harrisburg, Pa.: Trinity Press International, 1998). Following a canonical order, Birch begins his survey with a chapter on creation, which touches on some of the theological highlights of the creation traditions — most notably Gen 1:1–2:3(4a); 2:4b–3:24; and Second Isaiah — but overlooks many of their distinctly moral implications. Otto injects the theme of creation into his discussion of Old Testament ethics by referring to creation's "legitimization" of an ethos of divine solidarity in certain psalms (pp. 94-99), to the created order presupposed in the wisdom literature (pp. 117-74), and to creational background of the gendered relationship in Gen 2:4b–3:24 (pp. 61-64). Genesis 1, however, receives scant attention (cf. p. 231). Wright focuses on creation in terms of its general moral and ecological ramifications in relation to the dominant theme of land (pp. 118-27, 181-87). Barton's discussion of natural law as an important background to Old Testament ethics is limited only to certain prophetic passages, Proverbs, and the dietary laws in Leviticus and Deuteronomy (pp. 58-76). In all four works, Job 38–41 remains either unaddressed or a veritable afterthought (see Birch, *Let Justice Roll Down*, 344-45). In addition to the above works, the theme of creation is virtually absent in W. Janzen's recent survey in *Old Testament Ethics: A Paradigmatic Approach* (Louisville: Westminster John Knox, 1994). See n. 115.

dents of creation theology have explored the biblical traditions in terms of their mythological roots, their connection to the history of salvation, or their compatibility with modern science.[75] Only recently, however, have a number of biblical studies taken on a tone of moral urgency, particularly of ecological sensitivity in light of the mounting environmental crisis, as noted above. Nonetheless, one must admit at the outset that the biblical tradents themselves were no environmentalists, although their care for the land no doubt exceeded ours in many respects. To the contrary, the movers and shakers of biblical tradition were primarily concerned with shaping and preserving Israel's faith and practice, in short, the community's character.

Apart from the growing interest in creation theology from various fields of inquiry, biblical scholarship is enjoying a resurgence of interest in moral issues pertaining to ancient Israel and the early church.[76] The focus of these studies has moved significantly beyond the study of legal formulations and moral principles in recent years. There is an emerging interest in how ancient faith communities imparted certain fundamental values through various forms of discourse, from narrative to admonition. Biblical scholars are increasingly recognizing that each genre plays an integral role in the development of "communities of character."[77] Although not a genre in itself, the creation account plays an indisputable role in moral formation, since it defines how the community is appropriately to discern its environment and thereby act within it. Among ethicists, the role of perception is widely acknowledged as an indispensable factor in the formation of moral character.[78] One's perception of the world has ev-

75. The representative works listed in n. 10 address these issues in varying degree without explicitly or, at best, only peripherally exploring the distinctly moral implications of creation for the ancient community.

76. For example, W. P. Brown, *Character in Crisis: A Fresh Approach to the Wisdom Literature of the Old Testament* (Grand Rapids: Eerdmans, 1996); Janzen, *Old Testament Ethics*; Wright, *Walking in the Ways*; Birch, *Let Justice Roll Down*; idem and L. Rasmussen, *Bible and Ethics in the Christian Life* (rev. ed.; Minneapolis: Augsburg, 1989); G. H. Matties, *Ezekiel 18 and the Rhetoric of Moral Discourse* (SBLDS 126; Atlanta: Scholars Press, 1990); W. A. Meeks, *The Origins of Christian Morality: The First Two Centuries* (New Haven: Yale University Press, 1993); idem, *The Moral World of the First Christians* (LEC 6; Philadelphia: Westminster, 1986).

77. To borrow from S. Hauerwas, *A Community of Character: Toward a Constructive Christian Social Ethic* (Notre Dame: University of Notre Dame Press, 1981). His work has been influential in many of the works cited above. For biblical scholarship, Hauerwas's work has opened up new fields of ethical inquiry, particularly the area of narrative, as they relate to the moral life of the community. See Hauerwas and D. Burrell, "From System to Story: An Alternative Pattern for Rationality in Ethics," in *Why Narrative?* (ed. S. Hauerwas and L. G. Jones; Grand Rapids: Eerdmans, 1989) 158-90.

78. See Birch and Rasmussen, *Bible and Ethics*, 77; S. Hauerwas, *Character and the*

erything to do with how one engages the world and acts in it. Perception involves the way one selects, interprets, and evaluates the environment. The role of perception cannot be overemphasized in the development of character. As the foundation to any moral worldview or ethos, perception constitutes the nexus between the human subject and the environment.

This study proposes to facilitate a convergence of such divergent fields of inquiry, the study of creation on the one hand, and that of Israel's moral ethos on the other. To date, no one has explored Israel's own "cosmopolis" by examining the various creation traditions of the Hebrew Bible. The aim of this study is to show that the created world reflects certain discernible moral ethoses, or prescriptively sustaining contexts, in which the ancient community was to live its faith. Any given account of creation consequently reflects something of the moral perceptions of the community that produced and treasured it. Conversely, a model of creation imparts those perceptions and values to future generations of listeners and readers in the ongoing transmission of tradition. In short, creation and community *interact*.[79]

The Role of Moral Imagination in Creation

As the early church's doctrine of creation helped to define the ethos of the Christian community over against that of rival philosophies,[80] Israel's various views of creation contributed to its own self-definition vis-à-vis the imposing cultural terrain of the ancient Near East. The cultivation of cosmologies drew deeply from the well of Israel's theological and intellectual imagination. Indeed, such imagination was necessarily a *moral* imagination, one that powerfully informed the community of its identity and conduct, invariably sharpening and broadening its character and praxis.

The role of imagination in moral discourse and conduct has been a lively topic of recent discussion in theology and hermeneutics.[81] Yet some might find

---

Christian Life: A Study in Theological Ethics (TUMSR 3; San Antonio: Trinity University Press, 1975) 203; Brown, *Character in Crisis*, 7-8.

79. The question of whether creation morally defines community or community defines creation is an unnecessary and unanswerable chicken-or-the-egg question. My approach is more integrative; I simply assume that the biblical creation traditions are the result of Israel's interaction with its environment, with a world and community affirmed to be created and sustained by God.

80. For example, Hellenistic dualism and Gnostic teachings. See Barbour, "Creation and Cosmology," 124.

81. For recent discussions of the role of theological imagination in the development

19

the concept of "moral imagination" an oxymoron at best. What can be distinctly imaginative about the business of normative thinking and moral formation? Nevertheless, imagination remains at the core of moral reflection. Moral imagination generates the world of what ought to be, thereby making moral living possible.[82] Drawing from the work of Kathleen Fischer, Benedict Guevin describes the kind of imagination that is indispensable for moral, specifically Christian, living by identifying three of its characteristic elements:[83]

1. "Imagination is the tool by which we perceive reality concretely." Far from being abstract, the reality grasped by the imagination is relationally defined.
2. The language of imagination is essentially metaphorical. Paul Ricoeur defines the metaphorical process as the operation of "seeing as,"[84] an exercise of the imagination and a matter of perception.[85] Similarly, Iris Murdoch defines "moral imagination" as an act of willful attention, of discernment.[86]

---

and interpretation of biblical texts and traditions, see, e.g., W. Brueggemann, "Imagination as a Mode of Fidelity," in *Understanding the Word: Essays in Honour of Bernhard W. Anderson* (ed. J. T. Butler et al.; JSOTSup 37; Sheffield: JSOT Press, 1985) 13-36; L. Perdue, *Wisdom and Creation: The Theology of Wisdom Literature* (Nashville: Abingdon, 1994) 49-62; idem, *The Collapse of History* (OBT; Minneapolis: Fortress, 1994) 229-62; R. B. Hays, *The Moral Vision of the New Testament: A Contemporary Introduction to New Testament Ethics* (New York: HarperCollins, 1996) 298-304. For the term "moral imagination," see I. Murdoch, *The Sovereignty of Good* (New York: Schocken, 1971) 37; P. J. Rossi, "Moral Imagination and the Narrative Modes of Moral Discourse," *Renascence* 31 (1979) 131-41; idem, "Moral Interest and Moral Imagination in Kant," *The Modern Schoolman* 57 (1980) 149-58; idem, *Together Toward Hope: A Journey to Moral Theology* (Notre Dame: University of Notre Dame Press, 1983) 45-50; Hauerwas, *Character and the Christian Life*, 213; B. M. Guevin, "The Moral Imagination and the Shaping Power of the Parables," *JRE* 17 (1989) 63-79; M. Antonaccio, "Imagining the Good: Iris Murdoch's Godless Theology," in *The Annual of the Society of Christian Ethics, 1996* (Washington, D.C.: Georgetown University Press, 1996) 223-42, esp. 233-40. Frequently overlooked, however, is the indispensable role of moral imagination in the ethics of R. Niebuhr (e.g., *Moral Man and Immoral Society: A Study in Ethics and Politics* [New York: Charles Scribner's Sons, 1953] 53, 60-61).

82. Rossi, *Together Toward Hope*, 45.

83. Guevin, "The Moral Imagination," 64.

84. P. Ricoeur, *The Rule of Metaphor* (tr. R. Czerny et al.; Toronto: University of Toronto Press, 1981) 212-13.

85. P. S. Keane, S.S., *Christian Ethics and Imagination: A Theological Inquiry* (New York: Paulist, 1984) 100-101.

86. Murdoch, *The Sovereignty of the Good*, 37. See also Lehmann's related concept of "apperception" or discernment explicated by N. Duff, "Introduction," in P. L. Lehmann, *The Decalogue and a Human Future* (Grand Rapids: Eerdmans, 1995) 8-9.

3. Imagination is the vehicle that drives the moral subject out of his or her own world and into the world of others, the world of Thou. Through imagination, the moral subject enters into community and thereby expands the moral horizons of the self.

Harnessed to conceptual thought, imagination multiplies our moral options by forming "all manner of incompatible schemes and allowing us to know what we are missing."[87] In short, imagination drives the self outward into an awareness and knowledge of others and, in turn, to self-knowledge. Yet it can also lead to self-deception, if not used properly.[88] Moral reflection provides the direction, indeed the criterion, for the constructive use of imagination; otherwise, the exercise of imagination can lead to irrelevant flights of fancy or, more worrisome, to self-serving nightmarish scenarios that promote violence and destruction. For example, Iris Murdoch carefully distinguishes between fantasy and imagination. The former by definition is egoistic in orientation, "mechanically generating narrowly banal false pictures," whereas "liberated truth-seeking creative imagination" freely explores "the world, moving toward the expression and elucidation (and in art, celebration) of what is true and deep."[89] For Murdoch, the imagination is rooted in the free exercise of the will that enables contact with a moral absolute, the Good.

Essential to the formation of moral character, the exercise of imagination is abundantly evident in the various depictions of creation. The ancients ordered their world of wonder and warning, making sense of it for faith and practice before the Creator. In contemporary terms, Murdoch perhaps puts it best in her Gifford Lectures:

> The world is not given to us "on a plate," it is given to us as a creative task. It is impossible to banish morality from this picture. We *work,* using or failing to use our honesty, our courage, our truthful imagination, at the interpretation of what is present to us, as we of necessity shape it and "make some-

87. Midgley, *Beast and Man,* 283.
88. See D. Burrell and S. Hauerwas, "Self-Deception and Autobiography: Theological and Ethical Reflections on Speer's *Inside the Third Reich,*" *JRE* 2 (1974) 99-117. Burrell and Hauerwas examine Albert Speer's story as a paradigmatic example of self-deception that "covers up what is destructive."
89. I. Murdoch, *Metaphysics as a Guide to Morals* (New York: Viking, Penguin, 1992) 321. See Antonaccio's discussion of Murdoch's distinction between moral vision and imagination, which in my opinion is not as clear-cut as she presents it ("Imagining the Good," 234-35).

thing of it." We help it to be. We work at the meeting point where we deal with a world which is other than ourselves.[90]

For Murdoch, imagination is more than a matter of immediate perception of a moral world; the imagination constructs the moral world. "Our deepest imaginings . . . structure the world in which 'moral judgments' occur."[91] Similarly, Erazim Kohák avers that "the way we perceive the world is a function of the way we conceive of it — and if the practice that follows from it is flawed, then the solution is to be sought in a more adequate conception."[92]

To perceive the world in its cosmically expansive proportions, in all of its glory and chaos, requires the exercise of imagination's moral faculty. Through imagination, the created order becomes fraught with moral significance, as it most certainly was for the ancient tradents of Scripture. Throughout the biblical cosmologies, as in ancient Near Eastern lore, creation was both the locus of transcendence and the habitation of chaos.[93] Ever in tension, order and chaos made their presence felt at the most basic levels of moral living, from community to individual. Whether in defeat or in full command, chaos has its role and place in the created order. For the ancients, the created order was no fanciful daydream devoid of moral significance — it was the product of discerning and faithful imagination.

The biblical tradents remind us that the moral world, the ethos of the cosmos, is quite real. Yet it is not purely a matter of empirical observation, for "there is no implacable barrier between fact statements and value statements, between what 'is' and what 'ought to be.'"[94] The biblical cosmologists drew both from the imaginative world of myth and from the immediate world of sensory perception for articulating their various accounts. Yet myth and the visible world were not discrete realms of knowledge for the ancients. The sky, readily apprehensible by sight, was also the dwelling of transcendence.[95] The barren Wadi er-Rababeh, otherwise known as the Valley of Hinnom or Gehenna, also bore cosmic significance.[96] In the ancient

90. Murdoch, *Metaphysics,* 215.

91. Ibid., 314.

92. Quoted from Schweiker, *Responsibility and Christian Ethics,* 110.

93. For a systematic and historical accounting of the various levels of opposition chaos poses against Yahweh and Israel's social order, see Levenson, *Creation and the Persistence of Evil.*

94. W. C. Booth, *Critical Understanding: The Powers and Limits of Pluralism* (Chicago: University of Chicago Press, 1979) 363n.18.

95. See H. Gese, "The Question of a World View," in *Essays on Biblical Theology* (tr. K. Crim; Minneapolis: Augsburg, 1981) 232-33.

96. See L. Bailey, "Gehenna: The Topography of Hell," *BA* 49 (1986) 187-91.

cosmologies, moral imagination constituted a generative nexus between mythos and ethos, between sense perception and faith. What ought to be and what is, what could be and what has been, find their sublime convergence in creation and, as modern ethicists point out, in the exercise of moral conduct.

A Theological Advance: Breaking an Impasse

Treating the creation texts of Scripture as the outgrowth of the ancients' moral imagination, harnessed and directed for the purpose of shaping Israel's character, is significant theologically. The current debate over the theological significance of biblical creation has become mired in exclusively either/or categories, specifically in treating the traditions as texts of either liberation or oppression.[97] Lamentably, the latter has been more typical in Old Testament research. Through his penetrating sociological analysis, Walter Brueggemann has vigorously argued for viewing many creation texts as serving simply the status quo of Israel's royal establishment.[98] For example, in contrast to the psalms of "disorientation," the creation psalms are by and large deemed as psalms of "orientation" that legitimate structure and thereby suppress the abrasive pain of the marginalized.[99]

By generalizing his conclusions, Brueggemann has developed a one-sided view of the creation traditions that ironically fails to integrate his own reading of Genesis 1 as an empowering text for the exilic community under Babylonian domination.[100] Citing the examples of biblical scholar Terence

---

97. A similar impasse can be found in recent discussions of the nature and sociotraditional roots of apocalyptic literature. See the contrasting views of P. Hanson, *The Dawn of Apocalyptic* (Philadelphia: Fortress, 1978) 1-31; idem, *Old Testament Apocalyptic* (IBT; Nashville: Abingdon, 1987); and S. L. Cook, *Prophecy and Apocalypticism: The Postexilic Social Setting* (Minneapolis: Fortress, 1995).

98. For example, W. Brueggemann, *The Prophetic Imagination* (Philadelphia: Fortress, 1978) 16-19; idem, *Israel's Praise: Doxology against Idolatry and Ideology* (Philadelphia: Fortress, 1988) 101, 106, 108. See my critique of Brueggemann's position in *Structure, Role,* 226-27, 245n.87. For a more thorough critique, see Middleton, "Is Creation Theology Inherently Conservative?" 257-77.

99. W. Brueggemann, *The Message of the Psalms: A Theological Commentary* (Minneapolis: Augsburg Fortress, 1984) 25-49; idem, *Israel's Praise,* 89-121.

100. W. Brueggemann, "The Kerygma of the Priestly Writers," in Brueggemann and H. W. Wolff, *The Vitality of Old Testament Traditions* (2d ed.; Atlanta: John Knox, 1982) 101-14 (repr. from *ZAW* 84 [1972] 397-413); idem, *Genesis* (Interpretation; Atlanta: John Knox, 1982) 31-39.

Fretheim and liberation theologian Pedro Trigo, J. R. Middleton points out that Brueggemann has ignored much recent work by biblical scholars and liberation theologians who view the creation texts as inherently liberating.[101] In contrast to Brueggemann, Middleton finds "creation to be an explosive category, profoundly liberating from otherworldly pietism and empowering for redemptive activity in a world that belongs to God."[102]

The debate over the social and theological status of the creation traditions has unfortunately come down to such seemingly irreconcilable extremes. Both Brueggemann and Middleton reveal the contextual bases of their interpretations, the former admitting that his work throughout the years has been "invariably ad hoc" in his struggle against potentially oppressive theologies,[103] and the latter having struggled with the issues of postcolonialism as a student in Jamaica during the mid-1970s.[104] Recognizing that the social context of the interpreter is inescapably formative, it is laudable, if not mandatory, for interpreters to make such revelations in their debates. Questions remain, however, regarding whether such contextually based interpretations of the creation traditions leave liberation and ideology as the *exclusive* hermeneutical options. Taken to the extreme, such debates tend to focus almost exclusively on issues of power: who has it, who is empowered by it, who is subjected to it, and who suffers from it. The resulting danger is that such discussions can easily overlook issues of moral valuation, which reach beyond without excluding questions of ideology.[105] The shape and scope of moral values, mediated through cosmological discourse, as well as their impact on the life of the community, are left largely unaddressed.

On the one hand, the prominent concern for social order and structure among the creation traditions suggests that more is at stake than simply liberation for its own sake. On the other hand, the cosmic/social order profiled in these traditions is invariably cast as the result of change and transformation, whether from arduous struggle or from artistic activity. As a potential corrective to both extremes of the debate, H. H. Schmid en-

101. Middleton, "Is Creation Theology Inherently Conservative?" 265-66, 272-74.
102. Ibid., 277. In his response, Brueggemann all but concedes Middleton's critique without granting that liberation is "self-evident in the creation texts that focus upon order" (W. Brueggemann, "Response to J. Richard Middleton," *HTR* 87 [1994] 288).
103. Brueggemann, "Response," 280.
104. Middleton, "Is Creation Theology Inherently Conservative?" 277.
105. I am not accusing either Brueggemann or Middleton of neglecting issues of value and moral worth, but simply flag the concern as a danger that can naturally grow out of debates that focus exclusively on the ideological status of certain creation traditions.

tertains the following hermeneutical question: "What might be the specific contribution of a [creation] theology in our time? . . . Theology would have to point out and consider the obvious discrepancy between the evident demands of a universal righteousness and the actual possibilities and performances of human beings."[106] Schmid finds a distinctly moral relevance to creation theology. Given creation theology's stress on divine righteousness, the discrepancy to which he refers is charged with convictional force, potent with the power to inform and embolden the moral "performances of human beings." Each in its own way, the creation traditions of Scripture were and potentially remain instrumental in forming the moral identity of communities of faith. The modern tendency to sunder and keep separate at arm's length what the ancient cosmologists, in varying degrees, presented as seamlessly connected — transformation and order, mythos and ethos — only diminishes the formative power of creation for faith communities.

The Crisis of Culture

Taking my cue from Brueggemann and Middleton in their debate, let me enter the fray by sharing something of my own contextual basis and concerns. As the environmental crisis has prompted renewed appreciation of the creation traditions in the biblical corpus among many scholars, I see another crisis looming on the horizon that prompts me to take a fresh look at the creation texts — the crisis of culture. Many perceive that American society is on the verge of violent fragmentation, owing to the breakdown of community at all levels, from nation to church and family. Such emerging conflict reflects tectonic shifts in cultural values. Divisive confrontation, complaint, and blame have come to characterize much of our public discourse. The level of constructive participation in understanding and solving common problems is on the wane, fueled in part by the dramatic rise of electronic mass media, which by their selectivity and superficiality generate only illusions of participation that are both empty and divisive, reducing the level of discourse to mere sound bites. Ever more graphic depictions of violence and sex are the means by which the network media, the market-driven networks in particular, retain their lock on the public's attention and imagination. Sports and entertainment seem to constitute the only sense of common ground left in the public arena, offering only a "second-hand

106. Schmid, "Creation," 113.

life,"[107] all the while neighborhoods are turning into gated enclaves and persons or groups are routinely demonized or turned into stepping-stones for self-serving ends.

In addition to mass media, the market is relentlessly shaping our existence by finding new ways to demonstrate how incomplete we are without certain possessions, including the latest technologies. Yet in the mad rush toward material self-fulfillment, ever elusive, most of the planet goes hungry and remains destitute. In the United States, moreover, medical care is turning into an aggressive marketplace as hospitals adopt profit-enhancing strategies at the expense of community health. In short, human beings have been reduced to either material commodities or insatiable consumers, in either case given only instrumental worth.

In the commercialization of the world, education, even knowledge itself, has become redefined. Memory and hope, tradition and knowledge, are the commodities that advanced, market-driven societies seem to have in increasingly short supply. As Michael Welker puts it, "The educational ideal is shifting from the acquisition and cultivation of ordered knowledge to a skillful selectivity that is adequate to the situation and function in question."[108] Education is becoming increasingly functionalized, indeed, commercialized; and knowledge, as a whole, is measured primarily for its instrumental value, pressed into the utilitarian service of dominating or subsuming others and, in turn, aggrandizing the self.

With the global market economy reaching new heights of influence, any sense of abiding place, particularly among less-developed countries, is quickly crumbling. This crisis of existence is heightened in the face of perennial and seemingly irresolvable regional conflicts, forced migrations of peoples, enslavement, ethnic cleansing, and the ever persistent threat of nuclear annihilation, all suggesting that "the world is nothing but a scene of endless displacement."[109] The global village is turning out to be a "placeless place."[110] Also suffering from the withering effects of the so-called culture wars, the church is fast losing any sense of place in an increasingly pluralistic and conflictive world. As communities of faith face challenging ethical issues and ways in which to communicate the gospel, caustic divisiveness has come to replace edifying discourse. Some call the church back to a controlling and insulated, even sectarian, center, while others push the church toward new fron-

---

107. M. Welker (with W. Schweiker) *Integrity — Dignity — Truth: Beyond the Crisis of Christianity in the West* (forthcoming).
108. Ibid.
109. Casey, *Fate of Place*, xiii.
110. Ibid.

tiers of engagement with an increasingly pluralistic society to the point of either wholesale assimilation or fragmentation. In either case, the church is losing its distinctive voice for the world.

Given such a bleak picture, I need to be reminded that conflict and change, assimilation and fragmentation, placelessness and despair, were nothing new to ancient Israel. Such dynamics were both mediated and mitigated in the various formulations of narrative, law, prophecy, and sapiential instruction. The creation accounts formulated by ancient Israel are especially fertile fields for examination in relation to the crisis of culture, since they deal with order and structure as well as with conflict and change — in short, transformation and preservation on the grandest of scales. Conveying a vision of how the complex web of social relationships and roles are best (re)woven, any model of creation renders in some measure a moral performance in its larger literary and existential context. It conveys, in essence, an ethos. To recognize a certain cosmology's power to shape the character of a community by no means diminishes its theological import. Indeed, as Schmid suggests, it may very well constitute creation theology's "specific contribution." I hope that an investigation of how these creation traditions performed for ancient Israel, of their moral implications for the life of the community, will contribute constructive models of understanding and conduct within a conflicted church and world such as ours.

Modus Operandi

"When we ask how our world takes shape, we are at the same time asking how the self takes shape."[111] Such is the thrust of this investigation. More specifically, by examining particular creation texts, I want to discern something of Israel's view of itself as a community, of its moral topography, formed and fashioned by God. As will become clear, it is not possible to formulate a comprehensive model that can systematize and thereby homogenize Israel's view of nature and itself. Recognizing that culture is a social process, I hope to demonstrate that the various views Israel held about its environment reflect a dynamic and multidimensional moral ecology, one that imaginatively reflected as well as imparted distinctive values that contributed to shaping Israel's identity and conduct, an *ecology of community*. As the study of the mutual relations between organisms and their environment or "home" (Greek

---

111. L. S. Mudge, "Paul Ricoeur on Biblical Interpretation," in P. Ricoeur, *Essays on Biblical Interpretation* (ed. L. S. Mudge; Philadelphia: Fortress, 1980) 10.

oikos),[112] ecology need not be limited simply to examining the material impact of human beings on the physical environment. I am more interested in the reverse relationship, in the environment's impact, as conveyed by certain codified traditions, on Israel's cultural identity, particularly on its moral character. Moreover, the study of cultural process and change — "the autonomous process of symbolic formation," to borrow from Geertz — in relation to the physical environment constitutes an essential component.

The creation accounts and traditions of the Old Testament, which are quite diverse yet in their received form not entirely discrete, are stamped with Israel's complex and multidimensional character. Like the various legislative texts present in the Pentateuch and in Ezekiel, the creation texts in their final form were dialogically related, distinguishing themselves from as well as adapting and contextualizing one another. On the one hand, many worthy studies on creation have mined the ancient traditions for their mythological roots, environmental sensitivity, and relevance for our scientific age. But such studies rarely enter into the fray of Israel's culture making. On the other hand, the most recent general treatment of Israelite culture by and large ignores the creation traditions in their particular forms.[113] The same can be said of many general works on biblical ethics.[114] Given this significant gap, the goal of this study is to introduce a commonly overlooked feature into the current mix of studies on biblical creation and ethics: creation's moral ethos.

Creation discourse is, in theme and content, processual by nature: biblical cosmogonies recount God's craftwork on nature and culture. Similarly, the biblical tradents exercised their imaginative craftwork in developing and transmitting the ancient traditions. In order to assess the creation traditions according to their moral import, one must take account of the cultural land-

112. See H. Rolston III's definition of ecology as "a logic of the whole that is a home (*eco-logos*) a logic of the self in relation to the whole" ("The Bible and Ecology," *Int* 50 [1996] 22).

113. Dearman treats creation only briefly within his chapter on wisdom (*Religion and Culture*, 224).

114. For example, Janzen, *Old Testament Ethics;* Birch and Rasmussen, *Bible and Ethics;* W. C. Kaiser Jr., *Toward Old Testament Ethics* (Grand Rapids: Zondervan, 1983); B. Gerhardsson, *The Ethos of the Bible* (tr. S. Westerholm; Philadelphia: Fortress, 1979) 21; S. C. Mott, *Biblical Ethics and Social Change* (New York: Oxford University Press, 1982); R. E. O. White, *Biblical Ethics* (Atlanta: John Knox, 1979); H. G. Mitchell, *The Ethics of the Old Testament* (Chicago: University of Chicago Press, 1912). But cf. Hays, *Moral Vision,* 198, 292; 307-8, in which "new creation" constitutes one of three "focal images" in synthesis of the various textual witnesses to ethics in the New Testament. For other exceptions among general Old Testament treatments, see n. 74.

scape in which ancient Israel lived, the ancient Near Eastern context. Therein lies a constellation of preexisting codes and traditions. Though the focus here will be on *Israel's* creation traditions, the larger realm of ancient Near Eastern traditions (e.g., Mesopotamian, Egyptian, and Canaanite) must serve as an indispensable backdrop for comparison, particularly in sifting out common as well as distinctive nuances in each tradition. Such a comparative approach hopes to avoid resorting to reductive parallelomania, on the one hand, and introducing artificial distinctions, on the other. Though extensive work has been done in this area of comparative research, more work needs to be done in comparing the various biblical traditions themselves. A particular creation text is neither a free innovation composed in a vacuum nor a slavish imitation of previous traditions. Any given text is part of a larger conversation that addresses how the world — and the faith community embedded therein — is and should be configured. Indeed, the creation accounts themselves invite examination in terms of what they say in relationship to each other in their historical, dialogical, and ultimately canonical contexts.[115]

The realm of nature provides an unlimited stock of concrete images, relationships, and structures — a vast amount of raw material with which to construct a particular cosmology. Yet the stuff of nature is never perceived unfiltered. Similarly, any creation text or tradition draws from and transforms preexisting traditions available from within the community or from the community's larger cultural context. Such is the craftwork of culture on its textual legacies. However one relates the plethora of creation models within Scripture, a central lens is required in order to afford focused comparisons. That lens is provided by the texts themselves. Every creation text posits a network of relationships among a selective host of cosmic elements and characters, including divine and human, within a particular cultural, including moral, context or setting, an ethos. The moral significance of these ele-

---

115. A comparative study of the *biblical* creation traditions themselves has never been conducted, although a move in this direction is found in M. Weinfeld, "God the Creator in Gen. 1 and the Prophecy of Second Isaiah," *Tarbiz* 37 (1968) 105-32 (Hebrew). See also M. Fishbane, *Biblical Interpretation in Ancient Israel* (Oxford: Clarendon, 1985) 322-26. The study of the use of texts in other texts has come to be known as "intertextual criticism," whose impetus is in part founded on the work of the Russian socioliterary critic M. M. Bakhtin (see *The Dialogic Imagination* [ed. M. Holquist; Austin: University of Texas Press, 1981]). The most recent and arguably best example to date of intertextual work done on a large scale is Patricia T. K. Willey, *Remember the Former Things: The Recollection of Previous Texts in Isaiah 40–55* (SBLDS 161; Atlanta: Scholars Press, 1997). My goal, however, is not to demonstrate strict intertextual dependence among the creation traditions, but in a more general way to highlight the distinctive nuances among these traditions in order to discern their respective visions of moral order and community.

ments and their interrelated roles, as informed by the contextual setting, will serve as the point of departure. Consequently, I will address two inseparable and fundamental sets of questions regarding each and every creation account or collection of texts that constitute a discrete creation tradition.

1. *How* does a given text order the cosmos? Which elements and images of nature receive the most attention and how are they interrelated? What is humanity's position vis-à-vis nature? Such questions involve identifying the cosmic structure limned by the text and delineating the respective roles assumed by God, humankind, and the elements, the distribution and use of power, the source and extent of cosmic conflict, gradations of priority, and the center as well as the boundaries of creation. As the products of the ancients' moral imagination, each creation text or tradition depicts the created order in remarkably different ways, depending on what the authors intended to convey for their community's edification. This leads to the next line of inquiry.

2. *Why* is creation so ordered? The answer lies in examining creation's role within its larger literary and social context. To put it another way, how does creation set the stage for the unfolding divine-human drama that follows? This line of investigation is sensitive to both the larger literary context in which a particular account is embedded and the social and historical dynamics that were formative in the account's development. Such an inquiry leads to discerning the generative moral setting by which the network of relationships in creation is conveyed and made meaningful, constituting an ethos. It would admittedly be much easier to focus simply on the sociological or ideological roots of a given text or tradition. My aim, however, is more comprehensive and, I believe, relevant: to bring such questions of sociohistorical background and literary context into the larger purview of moral and theological discourse, first by discerning the normative values conveyed through the interrelated elements and characters of a given creation account in their natural, culturally defined, setting; second, by determining how such values are developed within the larger literary context (i.e., the Priestly and Yahwistic compositional layers,[116] the corpus of Second Isaiah, and the books of Proverbs and Job).

This particular mode of investigation has not been undertaken extensively because of the widespread tendency in modern scholarship to divorce

116. The literary boundaries of the Priestly and Yahwistic literary strata are drawn from those delineated by M. Noth in *A History of Pentateuchal Traditions* (tr. B. W. Anderson; 1972; repr. Chico, Calif.: Scholars Press, 1981) 17-19, 28-32). See also A. F. Campbell and M. A. O'Brien, *Sources of the Pentateuch* (Minneapolis: Fortress, 1993).

the creation mythos from its literary and cultural, specifically moral, context, its ethos. For example, the garden story is all too often treated as a self-contained episode apart from the patriarchal stories or from Israel's wanderings in the wilderness, and vice versa, within the sweep of the Yahwist's history. Much too frequently, Wisdom's play beside her Creator described in Prov 8:30-31 is analyzed apart from the larger moral context of the book of Proverbs. Puzzlement still surrounds the cavalcade of exotic beasts that populate the cosmic wasteland in Yahweh's answer to Job, although the key is to be found elsewhere in the book. For every contour and image of creation conveyed by the text for the reader's edification is a reason that is charged with moral significance.

An intrabiblical comparison of creation texts highlights their distinctive emphases and aims. Why do wild animals predominate in Yahweh's cosmology in Job 38–41, whereas the series of cosmological references in Second Isaiah highlights botanical images? The moral import of these animals in Job can be ascertained by examining their common roles within the evocative setting of the wilderness, as demonstrated elsewhere in the book and in the larger ancient Near Eastern context. Similarly, the significance of the botanical world in Second Isaiah is intimately tied to the ideology of royal gardening in the ancient Near East as well as to the overall message of redemption that the prophet announces on the eve of his community's release from captivity. Another case in point is the inordinate amount of attention given to the arable soil in Gen 2:4b–3:24 within the suggestive context of the garden in the Yahwist's account. The moral significance of land and agriculture in the Yahwist's history emerges when one examines their integral roles throughout the compositional layer of the Yahwist and in light of the social context of the monarchy and beyond. Wisdom's creation account in Prov 8:22-31 is, by contrast, modeled not after a garden but from a domicile set within a distinctly urban setting, a cosmopolis, which pervades the various instructive material that constitutes the book of Proverbs. Whereas the Yahwist finds mutual responsibility and work in God's primordial garden to be of crucial moral significance, wisdom stresses the value of play and its moral dimensions within God's cosmic household. To this mix of diverse settings and moral profiles is added the Priestly cosmogony, which limns creation as a cosmic sanctuary and espouses an ethic of holy rest and worship. To sum up, each of these creation texts stresses certain elements that thereby gain valuative significance, significance that comes into sharp focus only when one examines and compares their larger literary and social contexts. With each model of creation, a distinctive ethos is presupposed and an ethic is promulgated.

In this study, I have selected five creation texts or traditions that, relative to many other treatments of creation in the Old Testament, are fraught with the greatest amount of literary background. Two open the biblical canon: the so-called Yahwist's and Priestly versions of creation (Gen 1:1–2:3(4a) and 2:4b–3:24, respectively). Two other cosmologies are found in the wisdom literature: Job 38:4–41:26 and Prov 8:22-31. Each of these texts functions integrally in the larger literary space it inhabits, whether historical narrative, moral instruction, or poetic dialogue. Such is also the case with Second Isaiah (Isaiah 40–55 and related material), in which creation imagery is interspersed throughout this prophetic corpus with pointed rhetorical impact. In the prophet's case, cosmological discourse is not epitomized by any one particular text, but rather is conveyed by a series of texts that contribute to Second Isaiah's overall message. In all these cases, the creation accounts or traditions are not without relevance to the larger literary and cultural scope of the various biblical corpora. Indeed, they inform and confirm, shape and undergird, the larger rhetorical aims of the biblical authors and tradents.

Notably missing from this programmatic study, however, is any discussion of the creation psalms and their moral implications, a topic that well deserves an extended study in its own right. But for the purposes of this investigation, I have chosen those accounts that are laden with the most literary background in order to ascertain their respective moral ethoses with some degree of certainty. My hope is that they may serve as provocative case studies for future work on the role of creation in Scripture.

This study begins and ends with examining cosmological discourse. Unlike modern sociologists, biblical scholars are limited to ancient texts for investigating the moral dynamics of Israelite culture. The cosmic network of elements and characters articulates a constellation of interrelated values. Such formative values are codified in a number of imaginative ways, ranging from the metaphorical use of botanical images in Second Isaiah to the more subtle valuations with which certain structures and relationships are invested in the Priestly creation account. Through the deployment of images and literary structures, as well as wordplays, irony, allusions, and other rhetorical devices, the biblical cosmologists imaginatively designed their accounts in order to provoke moral reflection and faithful assent. In every case, the structures and features of the cosmos limn something of the moral contours of the ancient community. No presumptuous attempt is made in this study to subsume other major themes of Scripture, such as covenant and history, law and narrative, under some kind of cosmic ethos. My intent is much more modest: to reintroduce the discourse of creation in its various forms as simply one factor among many to be reckoned with in future studies of biblical ethics and theology. In its infatuation with covenant and history, biblical scholarship has until recently neglected the theological significance of creation, and has almost entirely forgotten that at the heart of creation's mythos is a moral ethos. To bring the moral contours of the cosmos into sharper focus, one must soar with the wings of the ancients' moral imagination to survey anew the wondrous realms of cosmos and community.

CHAPTER 2

It Was Good, It Was Hallowed: Integrity and Differentiation in the Cosmic Sanctuary

What sort of creative power is that which brings forth nothing but numbers and names?

Julius Wellhausen[1]

The ordering imagination is usually, among other things, a moral imagination.

Christopher Clausen[2]

The oppressive feeling that we don't have good luck, that God is not with us, that everyone is against us is an escape from responsibility and a disregard of reality. Things don't go well because we do things here hurriedly and in half-haste; this one chooses the cheapest offer without checking if it is the safest one; that one em-

---

1. J. Wellhausen, *Prolegomena to the History of Ancient Israel* (tr. A. Menzies and J. Black; 1885; repr. Gloucester, Mass.: Peter Smith, 1983) 361.
2. C. Clausen, *The Moral Imagination: Essays on Literature and Ethics* (Iowa City: University of Iowa Press, 1986) 6.

35

ploys a contractor who is willing to risk human life in order to save materials; this one signs that the bridge is usable without checking it out — all with "friendly negligence."

Yosef Lapid[3]

Located at the beginning of the biblical canon and, more specifically, of the Torah or Pentateuch, the Priestly account of creation in Gen 1:1–2:3(4a) commands an unassailably preeminent position. This cosmic overture to the entire canon is the literary and theological point of departure for all that follows, from creation to consummation. By virtue of its placement at the Bible's threshold, this quintessential creation story not only relativizes the other biblical cosmogonies interspersed throughout the Old Testament,[4] but also imbues all other material, from historical narrative to law, with cosmic background. Significantly, the tradents behind the cosmogony also preserved an extensive corpus of narrative, cultic, and legal traditions. Thus it is no surprise that something of a priestly ethos pervades the very structure by which the Priestly cosmologist(s) depicted the genesis of creation.

Compared to the Yahwist's anthropogony, the Priestly cosmogony reads more like a treatise than a narrative. It is in fact the most densely structured text of the biblical corpus, characterized by an intricate array of correspondences and variations.[5] Gen 1:1–2:3(4a) evinces a literary cohesion that bears certain theological and ethical implications. Suggestively absent is any hint of opposition or disruption in the cosmic process. Chaos, with a capital "C," has no place in this cosmic order, for creation is conducted decently and in order.

An Ethos of Order

As is often noted, the Priestly creation account reveals a complex network of correspondences established around a sequence of days and acts. Less noted are the well-delineated roles certain elements assume within the unfolding

---

3. Quoted from *New York Times* (July 18, 1997) A9, in reference to the collapse of the makeshift bridge at the Maccabiah Games in Ramat Gan, Israel, on July 15, which killed two Australian participants.

4. So J. D. Levenson, *Creation and the Persistence of Evil: The Jewish Drama of Divine Omnipotence* (San Francisco: Harper & Row, 1988) 100.

5. See W. P. Brown, *Structure, Role, and Ideology in the Hebrew and Greek Texts of Genesis 1:1–2:3* (SBLDS 132; Atlanta: Scholars Press, 1993) 1, 28-29, 81-83.

drama of this intricate structure. Both dimensions, structure and role, are integral to the ethos that characterizes the Priestly view of creation.

Structure and Sequence

The outline on page 38 highlights the sequential and interconnected structure of the Priestly creation account. Gen 1:1–2:3 is governed by a sequence of days that exhibit an internal correspondence, particularly Days 1-6, the so-called Hexaemeron. The left column (Days 1-3) presents a series of separations: light from darkness, sky ("firmament") from the waters, and land out of the waters. The right column (Days 4-6) describes the filling of these discrete domains: the celestial luminaries, aquatic and aerial creatures, and land-based animals as well as human beings. The daily progression reflects not so much a linear or evolutionary order as a coordinated one in which domains are delineated and populated. The sequence makes clear that the order of creation begins with the establishment of particular domains: sky, water, and land.

Internally, each day formally resembles the next through certain common literary features that include divine command ("And God said, 'Let . . .'"), execution formula ("And it was so"), fulfillment ("And God made X" or "And there was X"), approbation ("And God saw that it was good"), naming ("And God called . . ."), and day enumeration ("There was evening and there was morning, the X day."). Once these domains are established through formation and separation, life begins. Life is essentially characterized by mobility: aquatic and aerial creatures populate the waters and sky ("over the earth," v. 22; cf. v. 20), animals move about the land, human beings are commanded to fill and "subdue" the earth, even certain luminaries come to life, as it were, by governing the temporal domains of day and night. As part of the earth's established domain, vegetation is not included within the sphere of mobility or life within the Priestly *Weltbild*.

The correspondences between the two columns also highlight certain discernible variations among the domains and their occupants. In Days 5 and 6, for example, blessings, or more accurately commissions, are pronounced, addressed to both the aerial and aquatic creatures (v. 22), as well as to human beings (vv. 28-29). Yet the content of the blessings differs. In common is the command to "be fruitful and multiply" (vv. 22, 28a). Human beings are not distinct from the animals in this regard. Procreation is a blessing and a mandate for both animals and human beings, for their common commission is to populate their appropriate domains. (The land animals do not receive such a blessing be-

37

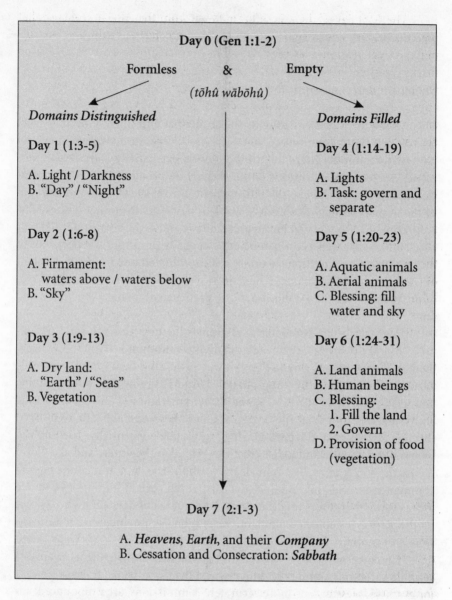

Day 0 (Gen 1:1-2)

Formless   &   Empty

(tōhû wābōhû)

Domains Distinguished   *Domains Filled*

Day 1 (1:3-5)   **Day 4 (1:14-19)**

A. Light / Darkness   A. Lights
B. "Day" / "Night"   B. Task: govern and
                                              separate

Day 2 (1:6-8)   **Day 5 (1:20-23)**

A. Firmament: A. Aquatic animals
   waters above / waters below   B. Aerial animals
B. "Sky"   C. Blessing: fill
                                              water and sky

Day 3 (1:9-13)   **Day 6 (1:24-31)**

A. Dry land: A. Land animals
   "Earth" / "Seas"   B. Human beings
B. Vegetation   C. Blessing:
                                              1. Fill the land
                                              2. Govern
                                           D. Provision of food
                                              (vegetation)

Day 7 (2:1-3)

A. *Heavens, Earth*, and their *Company*
B. Cessation and Consecration: *Sabbath*

cause they share the domain of land with human beings.) Human beings have, however, the added mandate or blessing to rule over creation, in particular over the animals of land, sea, and air (v. 28b). Such a governing role, too, is not entirely unique. Although the terminology is different, the celestial luminaries are also charged with the task of governing day and night (v. 18). What is unique to human beings is that their blessing integrates both procreation and rulership.

The final day of the account stands out from the six-day sequence that preceded it. Day 7 is categorically set apart, consecrated as sabbath. The culmination of creation is as much a day beyond creation as the introduction marks creation's preordered state. Day 7 and Day 0 bracket the account as a whole; the literary envelope they establish informs the aim and process of creation. Creation ("earth") begins as *tōhû wābōhû* (v. 2a), as formless, empty, and unproductive, without substance and direction.[6] Darkness and the deep are riveting representations of such an amorphous, precreated state. By its very nature, precreation is absolutely uninhabitable; it is unfillable. Conversely, formfulness is requisite for life. Creation's completion is characterized by differentiation and population: heaven and earth are established along with "all their company" (*kol-ṣĕbāʾām*, 2:1). Creation is at root a process of rendering formful and substantial ("filled") what was originally amorphous and empty, of establishing domains and their appropriate populace. Indeed, the two columns of temporal sequence address this dual state of cosmic lack, of formlessness and emptiness. The cosmos is given form through the establishment of discrete domains: day and night, sky, water, and land — the last deemed most important as the final domain established and the one that constitutes the dwelling place of humanity. Yet it all remains empty, a lifeless cosmic shell. With the sprouting of vegetation, conditions are ripe for life to flourish. The latter half of the six-day scheme describes the cosmos filled with innumerable entities, from luminaries to animals and human beings. The climax of the sabbath marks a homeostasis of activity, of a creation potent with life yet at rest from divine activity, parallel in some sense to the unordered and empty nature of precreation. Formed and filled, creation is complete. God is creation's formal and material cause.

Role and Relationship: The Stewardship of Creation

That the cosmos is the definitive result of divine activity, both word and deed, is often noted.[7] But that is only half the story. Divine activity introduces an intricate network of interrelationships in which both elements and life-forms assume crucial roles in the process and maintenance of creation.

---

6. The syntax highlights the static nature of precreation through the use of participles and a copula (1:2). The main clause begins in v. 3 with two finite verbs.

7. Distinctive of the Priestly cosmogony is the prominent focus on God's word, which constitutes a formal component in the account (*Wortbericht*).

"Inanimate" Elements of Creation

Creation is enlisted and coordinated not only by divine activity but also by particular elements at God's behest. These include earth, water, and light, the basic domains or elements of earthly life from the Priestly purview. Their participation in the creation process is rooted in the distinctive theological style with which the creation account is developed: creation by divine word or fiat. To be sure, God summons light into existence, the only instance that comes close to *creatio ex nihilo* (1:3).[8] More frequently, however, God's word sets the occasion for divine activity (vv. 7, 16, 21, 25). In a few notable instances, however, the divine summons is followed by fulfillment *apart* from any direct activity on God's part. In v. 9 God commands the waters to "gather together into one place in order to let the dry land appear. And it was so." Immediately thereafter, formulaic naming commences. No account of divine activity in gathering the waters is given. The waters *themselves* converge into a discrete body in order for the dry ground to emerge. God does not split the waters with a staff, but summons them with a word, and they obey.[9]

Similarly, the earth is summoned to sprout vegetation, or literally to "sprout sproutlings" (*tadšē'... deše'*, v. 11). Here verb and product are bound up in etymological identity. God's word is sufficient; there is no need for divine hands-on intervention. The power lies in the earth's fecundity, poised to fulfill the word and realize its own productive potential. It is in the earth's very nature to produce what it does, a bewildering variety of seed-bearing plants and fruit trees (v. 12). Similarly, the earth is later commanded to "bring

---

8. See also 1:7, 16, 27. Overall, however, the Priestly cosmogony does not exemplify a *doctrine* of *creatio ex nihilo*, "creation out of nothing." Syntactically, the first verse of Genesis is a dependent clause ("When God began to create the heavens and the earth . . .") rather than a complete sentence (i.e., "God created the heavens and the earth."). Indeed, the notion of *creatio ex nihilo* did not clearly emerge as a doctrine until the second century CE (G. May, *Creatio ex Nihilo: The Doctrine of "Creation out of Nothing" in Early Christian Thought* [tr. A. S. Worrall; Edinburgh: T. & T. Clark, 1994] 35-38, 62-84). The vigor and intensity with which both modern and ancient commentators have argued opposing positions betrays the fact that more than simply syntactical precision is at stake; deeply conflicting theological convictions underlie the various ways in which God is viewed in relation to the cosmos. For the Priestly author, however, the preexistence of chaos in no way intrudes on or limits God's transcendent character, but rather underlines the divine role as the creative *orderer* of the cosmos. Whereas God is comfortable with preexistent "chaos" in the Priestly cosmogony, many modern interpreters are not.

9. Cf. Tiamat's defeat by Marduk, who pierces the water monster's belly with an arrow and splits her apart in the Babylonian Epic of Creation, *Enuma elish* (IV.100-105, 136-39).

forth living creatures of every kind" (v. 24). The creation of these land animals is the result of combined activity of the earth and the Deity (v. 25).

Similar to the earth's production of land-based animals (v. 24), the waters
also bear a generative function when God summons them to produce swarms
of living creatures, or literally "cause to swarm swarming creatures" (yišrĕṣû . . .
šereṣ, v. 20).[10] As in the earth's case, the language is rhetorically precise and suggestive: the means of production is intimately linked to the product. Far from a
chaotic force, the waters are conceived as a positive and active participant in the
process of divine creation: God creates the "great sea monsters and every living
creature . . . that the waters produced" (v. 21).[11] In short, as objects of God's creative word, the earth and the waters are collaborators with God. By and large
God does not work de novo or ex nihilo, but *ex voce* and *per collaborationi*. As
W. H. Schmidt pointedly observes in relation to 1:11, "God's word . . . now ab-
dicates its creative power, i.e., the word now allows what has just been created to
be the origin of something new."[12] God's commanding performance in creation prompts also the positive performance of the elements.

The same can also be said of the luminaries in v. 15: "And let them be
lights . . . to give light" *(lim'ōrōt . . . lĕhā'îr)*. Like the earth and the waters, the
luminaries are assigned a function that corresponds to their internal nature.
In addition, two particular lights, the sun and the moon, are assigned the task
of ruling over the temporal domains of day and night. Light, earth, and water
actively participate in this methodical development of creation. Through the
divine word, God enlists them to contribute to the ongoing process of creation. Their work, as with all of creation, is deemed "good."

For the ancient cosmologist(s) who formulated this account, creation
need not have been "good." Particularly in the case of the waters, God could
have striven, more typically, as a warrior, rebuking,[13] defeating,[14] or at the

---

10. In this context, the verb *šrṣ* is best translated transitively (see Exod 7:28; Ps
105:30; as well as the LXX, Syriac, and Vulgate of 1:20). See Brown, *Structure*, 105-6n.25.

11. The earliest textual tradition probably pointed to the waters also generating
winged life, as indicated in the LXX (Brown, *Structure*, 25, 53, 115, 118, 128, 139-40). The
original text may very well have envisioned the *upper* waters having a hand in the creation
of the aerial creatures (1:7) in distinction from the creation of sea life from the waters below.

12. W. H. Schmidt, *Die Schöpfungsgeschichte der Priesterschrift* (WMANT 17;
Neukirchen-Vluyn: Neukirchener, 1964) 106. By contrast, C. Westermann attributes the
language only to the "steady monotonous style" of the Priestly author (*Genesis 1–11* [tr.
J. J. Scullion; Continental Commentary; Minneapolis: Augsburg, 1984] 124). Clearly, more
than dull consistency is at stake.

13. For example, Ps 104:6-7; Isa 50:2b.

14. Job 26:12; Ezek 32:2-6; Ps 74:13-14; Isa 27:1.

very least containing the forces of watery chaos.[15] Given the rich ancient Near Eastern background behind the so-called *Chaoskampf*, the archetypal conflict between the Deity and chaos, the Priestly cosmologist boldly divests all intimations of conflict from divine creation. From the amorphous deep in v. 2 to the rich bounty of sea life described in v. 21, including the "great sea monsters," the waters are drained of all potential hostility before creation even commences.[16] Nevertheless, they are not impotent or inert. The waters bear a life force that is altogether positive.[17] God is comfortable with "chaos," incorporating it constructively. For the Priestly cosmologist, only by the friendly convergence of divine and earthly powers can an enduring foundation for living creation be established. The dynamic movement of creation is not an indeterminate, open-ended process; stability is its goal.[18]

Life-Forms

Although not considered "life" proper by the Priestly tradents, vegetation plays a pivotal role in the created order. The natural produce of the earth, vegetation contains its own potential for regeneration: the bearing of seed is its common denominator (1:11-12). In addition, edible fruit is highlighted. As the final blessing makes abundantly clear, plants are for food; they provide necessary and sufficient sustenance for human and animal life (1:29-30).[19]

15. Jer 5:22; Prov 8:29; Ps 33:7.

16. While the question of whether the precreative deep (*tĕhôm;* v. 2) denotes inimical chaos is an open one, to assume an element of hostility in the precreative order simply on the basis of reference to *tĕhôm* in the circumstantial preface to creation is unwarranted. God's relationship to the deep perhaps holds the clue. God's breath or wind is described as "hovering *(mĕrahepet)* over the face of the waters" (1:2). The verbal parallel in Deut 32:11 and attestations of the root *(rhp)* from the Ugaritic Aqhat cycle (*KTU* 1.18.4.20-21, 31, 32) suggest the image of a bird hovering or soaring above the waters. In any case, translations that depict God's Spirit "raging" or "sweeping" across the waters simply do not fit in the verb's semantic field. What is chaotic in the beginning is the lack of order and completion.

17. The closest analogy is the pre-Socratic notion of *hylozoism,* the notion that the basic elements of the cosmos are capable of movement and therefore exhibit qualities of life (W. P. Brown, "Divine Act and the Art of Persuasion in Genesis 1," in *History and Interpretation: Essays in Honour of John H. Hayes* [ed. M. P. Graham et al.; JSOTSup 173; Sheffield: JSOT Press, 1993] 28).

18. See N. Lohfink, "God the Creator and the Stability of Heaven and Earth," in idem, *Theology of the Pentateuch: Themes of the Priestly Narrative and Deuteronomy* (tr. L. N. Maloney; Minneapolis: Fortress, 1994) 120-25.

19. The Priestly cosmogony assumes a vegetarian lifestyle for both animals and humans. Attempts to harmonize 1:29-30 with 9:2-5 are unconvincing. See Brown, *Structure,* 79-81.

The language of this final blessing signals a formal pronouncement of grant: "I hereby grant[20] to you all seed-bearing vegetation" (v. 29). The earth's plants constitute a bona fide blessing of abundance for the flourishing of life, not just for humans but for all living beings on the land.

As for all living beings, the account begins with the aquatic and aerial creatures, "swarmers" and "fliers" (v. 20). Their blessing is issued as a command: "reproduce, increase, and fill the waters in the seas, and let the birds multiply on the earth" (v. 22). Reproductive growth is their blessing, enabling them to populate their appropriate domains, filling the void. Of particular distinction are the "great sea monsters" (hattannînim haggĕdōlîm, v. 21).[21] They are simply mentioned as a matter of fact, without cause for concern, defensive or otherwise. Neither creatures of dreaded chaos nor the results of a divine blunder, these formidable aquatic creatures take their legitimate positions among the numerous species of marine life as members of good standing in God's creation.[22] Neither restricted nor contained, they too are permitted, indeed commanded, to increase and multiply.

From sea and air to land, animals of various kinds are created and empowered by blessing to proliferate. Diversity is part and parcel of the created order. Along with formlessness and emptiness, homogeneity is countered in the creative process. The universe is a thoroughly differentiated realm. No species is singled out for special treatment, except for one — humankind. Humanity's nature and role are set in stark relief in relation to the rest of creation, yet not without some measure of continuity. Like the birds and the fish, humanity is blessed with the potency of procreation. Human beings are commanded to "reproduce, increase, and fill the earth" (v. 28a). Yet there is more to this particular blessing, and its excess cuts to the heart of humanity's nature and role in creation.

Humankind's creation is introduced as a unique product of divine intervention, one that eschews any reference to the domains (v. 26).[23] Whereas the land-based creatures, from domestic to wild animals, are in part products of the land (v. 24), human beings are not. The opening command is "Let us make human beings in our image," not "Let the earth bring forth human beings." Unlike the Yahwist's anthropogony, the Priestly writer makes clear that the land is not the

---

20. Heb. hinnēh nātattî. The perfect form of the verb is declarative, signaling action simultaneous to verbal pronouncement.

21. Their fear-inspiring nature is underscored in Deut 32:33; Ps 91:13; Jer 51:34; Job 7:12; 74:13; Isa 27:1; 51:9; Ezek 29:3; 32:2.

22. Cf. Ps 104:26, which depicts the mighty Leviathan as God's "pet"; and 148:7, in which the sea dragons are called, along with the meteorological elements, to praise God.

23. Cf. Gen 2:7, which depicts the creation of primal man from the ground as a "groundling" or "landling."

source of human identity but only humankind's natural habitat (cf. 2:7). The land is humanity's secure place in the cosmos. Eminently land-based, human beings are, however, not "landlings";[24] they are rather "landlords." Fashioned in correspondence to God's image, they are in some sense corporeal godlings in that they are *like* God. Humanity's correspondence with God through the *imago Dei* is one of function and form, not substance.[25] Such language, at the very least, transfers the tasks and trappings of royalty and cult, the offices of divine representation and habitation, to humanity.[26] Often noted is the democratization of royalty in the creation account.[27] The Priestly author has imbued humanity with royal blessing and task in the world.[28] It is from this democratized royal context that the language of dominion and subjugation must be understood.

By virtue of their distinctive creation, human beings are uniquely commissioned to "rule" (*rādâ*) over animate life and to "subdue" (*kābaš*) the earth (1:26, 28). The first verb connotes royal control and power.[29] The second injunction could suggest that the earth is "an adversary to be pressed into service."[30] Admittedly, the Priestly account acknowledges that human life in the land cannot exist in effortless harmony with creation; it can flourish only by establishing some measure of control over the earth. The Yahwist's notion of forcefully and painfully working the soil as a consequence of the curse is regarded by the Priestly narrator as a noble exercise. Indeed, such control is first and foremost instrumental in making the land inhabitable for, or more literally "fillable" with, human life. Human beings must work *in* creation in order

24. This marks a stark difference with the Yahwist's presentation of the man's creation "out of the ground" (2:7).

25. P. A. Bird, "'Male and Female He Created Them': Gen 1:27b in the Context of the Priestly Account of Creation," *HTR* 74 (1981) 138-40, who draws from J. Barr, "The Image of God in the Book of Genesis — A Study in Terminology," *BJRL* 51 (1968) 11-26.

26. S. D. McBride Jr., rightly observes that the *imago Dei* of Genesis 1 has an inherently *sacral* as well as royal function ("Divine Protocol: Genesis 1:1–2:3 as Prologue to the Pentateuch," in *God Who Creates: Essays in Honor of W. Sibley Towner* [Grand Rapids: Eerdmans, forthcoming]).

27. See also Ps 8:5-8 (MT 6-9), in which the language of coronation is featured.

28. So Schmidt, *Schöpfungsgeschichte*, 139; H. Wildberger, "Das Abbild Gottes," *TZ* 21 (1965) 495-97; J. Van Seters, "The Creation of Man and the Creation of the King," *ZAW* 101 (1989) 341. For the relevant, particularly Akkadian, evidence, see Bird, "Male and Female," 140-44.

29. For example, 1 Kgs 5:4, 30; Isa 14:2, 6; Ps 110:2. The attestations of the verb in Lev 25:43, 46, 53 are significant in that they come from Priestly tradents who qualify the exercise of rulership over Israelite slaves as hierarchy without "harshness" (*perek*).

30. T. Hiebert, *The Yahwist's Landscape: Nature and Religion in Early Israel* (New York: Oxford University Press, 1996) 157. See Num 32:22, 29 (P), and Josh 18:1, which speak of the land "subdued" (*nikbĕšâ*) by God for Israel's occupation. See below.

for creation to work *for* human beings by providing sustenance and the means for their livelihood. Nevertheless, such a commission does not require exploiting the earth's resources, as the specific language of subduing might suggest. The Priestly author gives clear contextual clues that clarify and qualify this dominion over the earth.[31]

1. The hoarding of resources is implicitly forbidden in the Priestly account. Vegetation is granted to both humans and animals: "To every land creature and every bird of the air and every creature that moves on the ground, everything that has the breath of life in it (also) belongs every green plant for food" (1:30). The earth's edible resources are not the exclusive domain of humankind; rather, they are meant to be shared for the coexistence of all life.

2. There is no hint in the Priestly cosmogony that existence, including human existence, depends on predation or the death of animate life, a notion that is not introduced until Noah's postdiluvian blessing in 9:1-6. By contrast, the cosmogonic blessing conveys a subjugation without slaughter, a bloodless dominion. "Subduing" the earth is the distinctly human means of filling the land and maintaining constructive use of it. It entails the land's occupation and cultivation.[32]

3. Present are certain parallels between the divine and human roles in creation. God's creative word is tantamount to a royal or priestly decree, commanding the elements to bring forth their produce in the ongoing process of creation.[33] God is holy Lord over creation as much as human beings are God's representatives or surrogates, made in the divine image. As God is no divine warrior who slays the forces of chaos to construct a viable domain for life, so human beings are not ruthless tyrants, wreaking violence upon the land that is their home. By dint of command rather than brute force, the elements of creation are enlisted to fulfill the Deity's creative purposes. By dint of royal office, human beings have at their disposal the elemental forces of creation, including animate life, and are commissioned to harness them in order to ensure their flourishing on the earth. As there is no combat between God and chaos, so there is no mortal struggle between humankind and creation. The elements of cre-

---

31. By focusing almost exclusively on this one verse, W. Brueggemann characterizes the kerygmatic message of the Priestly writer, indeed creation itself, as one of conquest ("The Kerygma of the Priestly Writers," in Brueggemann and H. W. Wolff, *The Vitality of the Old Testament Traditions* [2d ed.; Atlanta: John Knox, 1982] 108-10).

32. See Lev 25:3 for the agricultural context of harnessing the land vis-à-vis the sabbatical year.

33. God's discourse is not an invitation but a command. For its Priestly background, see R. B. Coote and D. R. Ord, *In the Beginning: Creation and the Priestly History* (Minneapolis: Fortress, 1991) 51-52.

ation are conscripted to do what they do naturally. The same applies to humankind's dominion over the earth, exercised in the role of bearing God's image in and to the world. Although "subdue" remains the lexical definition for *kābaš*, its edge, sharpened in contexts of explicit conflict, is blunted by the irenic tenor conveyed in the Priestly account.[34] The royal rhythm of command and fulfillment discloses an ethos of order that requires effort but no weaponry. The sun and the moon do not govern by force but by oversight. To "subdue" the earth is to harness its powers and direct them. Such is the noble role of humankind; such is the domestic role of nature in this magisterial creation.

4. That human beings, males and females, are created in God's image suggests a level of *imitatio Dei* that comes to bear prominently on the institution of the sabbath in 2:1-3. God rested on the seventh day, having completed creation; so should the children of Israel, having concluded their weekly work (e.g., Exod 20:8-11; 31:12-17). For one full and pregnant pause in the temporal sequence, the exercise of royal dominion over creation is lifted and cosmic freedom carries the day, a fallow freedom. The cosmic institution of the sabbath imposes an absolute limit on divine and human (i.e., Israel's) activity. In that one moment creation recovers and rests apart from the exercise of dominion. As all creative activity ceases, so time itself is suspended. The seventh day marks both the earth's and God's restoration.

Ethos and Cosmos

A peaceable character pervades the Priestly cosmogony. All hints of conflict and opposition are effectively banished from this account. The elements of creation are poised to fulfill God's bidding at the drop of a word. Creation is gently yet decisively led to its fulfillment in a process of formfulness, an execution of separation and ful*fill*ment. Nothing lies outside God's creative direction and approbation, not even "chaos." For the Priestly cosmologist, "chaos" — technically a misnomer in the account (see below) — designates nothing more than formlessness, a static, amorphous state, tantamount to nothingness. Through divine word and deed, God imposes form and distinction by calling forth from this jumbled, undifferentiated mass the constructive powers of differentiation and provision.

---

34. Indeed, it is all the more blunted when one takes into account the other attestations of *kbš* in Priestly tradition, which suggest nothing more than occupying the land as a possession (Num 32:22, 29; Josh 18:1; see also N. Lohfink, "'Subdue the Earth?' [Genesis 1:28]," in idem, *Theology of the Pentateuch*, 9-11).

The process is the point. For every step of the creative process, formal approbation is rendered. The distribution and use of power cut to the heart of the Priestly ethos limned in this remarkably irenic cosmogony. First and foremost, God is creator of an order par excellence. Yet an omnipotent creator does not make a powerless and slavishly dependent creation. The basic elements of creation, as well as their respective inhabitants, also share a level of power that is altogether constructive when prompted by divine command. God's royal word calls forth, prompts, and brings to fruition the various potencies borne by these elements to engage constructively in the ongoing process of creation. Power is not divested from the cosmic arena but acknowledged and employed.[35] Moreover, there is no indication that God yields this power to the elements, somehow diminishing in some measure divine power or control over and in creation. Rather, God marshals by word and deed the respective powers already lodged within the domains and elements. Properly speaking, creation is not enabled by divine action;[36] it is rather incorporated into God's creative purposes. The cosmos is not, strictly speaking, empowered, but it is dignified through divine incorporation. The elements of creation are, in short, *ordained,* called to put forth what is necessary for the integral work of creation.

Any power that is properly delegated is granted in the form of a commission or blessing to certain luminaries and animal life. Absent is any indication that the elements once lacked power, creative or otherwise, as if they were originally inert. At the very most, God's world-shaping word activates what is already latent among the elements. What was genuinely lacking was the divinely set occasion to be called forth, the opportunity for the elements to contribute their potential products to the ongoing process of creation. The Priestly view of the cosmos is inherently dynamic and productive. At no stage does God energize, enable, or otherwise empower an erstwhile inert mass. God creates order out of "chaos" in part by drawing from and commanding its own creative dignity.

God does not rule over creation with a clenched or iron fist, wresting from or defeating chaos, but with an open hand to receive and direct the creative forces of a cosmos in progress. An arresting paradox comes to bear: although originally lacking form and substance, creation comes to contribute,

35. J. R. Middleton suggests, therefore, that divine creative activity is essentially rooted in love ("Creation Founded in Love: A Rhetorical Reading of Genesis 1:1–2:3," paper presented at the annual SBL meeting, Nov. 19, 1995). But such a love does not necessarily suggest self-risk.

36. Contra E. Elnes, "Creation and Tabernacle: The Priestly Writer's 'Environmentalism,'" *HBT* 16 (1994) 146; and Middleton, "Creation Founded in Love," 12.

under divine directive, to its own formation. Once they were lost but now they are formed: the waters and the earth realize their respective potentials as "seas" and "land," the systemic domains of life. At God's behest, they do what comes naturally. God prompts these elements of creation to participate *as they are able*.

The dynamics of blessing, too, highlight this ethos of cooperation. "Blessing activates the latent capacity [of reproduction] and directs it toward its goal."[37] The same can be said for much of the creative process as a whole. But in the particular blessing of reproduction, the Priestly writer stresses the self-sustainability of life. God "incorporates the means of perpetuity into the very design and constitution of the universe," thereby undercutting the rationale for fertility cults.[38] It is the earth, not Baal, that generates vegetation. Life creates itself through regeneration and procreation, actualized in blessing and not through the care or whimsy of the gods. The increase of species through procreation is a blessing without apology from the Priestly perspective.[39] Filling the earth is a mandated good. The replenishment of the species is a self-fulfilling blessing, from fish to human beings, male and female.

Gender within the Priestly worldview is not directly tied to the *imago Dei*.[40] Nonetheless, gendered identity, from animals to humans, embodies the potency of divine blessing. The differentiation of gender provides the necessary wherewithal to fulfill the Priestly commission: "Be fruitful and increase and fill the earth" (1:28). In short, creation is not radically contingent on divine intervention. Rather, the cosmos is interdependent vis-à-vis the Creator, and so also creation's constituent domains and elements in relation to each other.[41] The cosmic domains are separate and equal, yet adjacent and interdependent. They share a common formfulness in that each is created by similar movements of divine command, execution, fulfillment, and approbation. Earth and water respect each other's provenance as legitimate realms of reproductive life, blessed and empowered. Heaven and earth hold to their shared boundary, the "firmament" *(rāqîaʿ)*, finely hammered and thinned to infinite dimensions (1:6-7). As a natural development and growth of the power and diversity of life, the cosmos is a multiplex of discrete yet interre-

37. Bird, "Male and Female," 147n.
38. Ibid., 147.
39. The contrast with *Atrahasis*, in which human proliferation is conceived as a threat to the gods, could not be more striking.
40. Bird, "Male and Female," 129-59.
41. For a more systematic theological presentation of creation's interdependence, see M. Welker, *Schöpfung und Wirklichkeit* (Neukirchen-Vluyn: Neukirchener, 1995) 24; idem, "What Is Creation? Rereading Genesis 1 and 2," *TToday* 48 (1991) 62-64.

lated domains filled with swarming, creeping, soaring, breathing species — a pluralistic universe. Yet common order reigns. The Priestly cosmos is God's peaceable kingdom at work.

Beginning with light, creation for the Priestly author is not so much a big bang, an explosive contagion of power, as an orderly development.[42] The systematic structure and methodical movement of the text indicate, not coincidentally, an acute sensitivity to artistic form and balance, a literary style by which creative differentiation is rendered to an otherwise insubstantial glob of cosmos. The first creation literally sheds light on the process. The primordial presence of light introduces perception and separation into the erstwhile dark and undifferentiated mass. "God saw that the light was good" (1:4a). Henceforth, God perceives and renders divine approbation over every step in the careful process of cosmogony. What may seem dry and monotonous to the modern eye is in fact the inspired formation of a wondrous cosmic complexity. A creative "madness" lies behind the method. In the role of king, God is the consummate artisan,[43] wielding a verbal stylus to demarcate boundaries and tease out the inhabitable domains. God's word is a world-shaping word, and the cosmos is a thoroughly artistic product, constructed with the bricks and mortar of divine command and approbation. The finished product is a fully differentiated cosmic dwelling or ethos for all life.

The literary structure of the Priestly creation indicates a coordination of effort and order, resulting in an architecture of symmetry that presents a threefold correspondence among Days 1-6, thereby setting the seventh day in stark relief. Not fortuitously, the climactic seventh day is deemed holy, set apart from all other days, a day demarcated by the unique blessing of consecration. Whereas creation and its sequential unfolding are deemed "good," the last day is deemed "holy." A day unlike any other, the sabbath lacks the formal components by which the other days are formed. Absent are the familiar elements of command and fulfillment, execution and approbation. Like the veiled holy of holies of the tabernacle complex, this day stands apart from its surroundings. Yet it does not stand apart from God. Quite the contrary, day and Deity share common ground, separate from the world and joined in holiness. It is this day alone that God consecrates in order to rest, to cease all

---

42. See M. Welker, "Creation: Big Bang or the Work of Seven Days?" *TToday* 52 (1995) 180-87.

43. This is particularly clear in a comparison between Genesis 1 and Plato's *Timaeus* (Brown, "Divine Act," 20-32). M. Z. Brettler points out that the king in Hebrew Scripture was typically a builder and suggests that creation in the Priestly cosmogony is of a royal nature (*God Is King: Understanding an Israelite Metaphor* [JSOTSup 76; Sheffield: JSOT Press, 1989] 116-18).

activity on the ordained powers of life. Within a differentiated cosmos, the sabbath is the distinction above all others.[44] Creating temporal space for divine rest, the sabbath marks a scheduled indwelling of holiness, God's distinct domain.

Rest is the temporal analogue to dwelling. The psalmist, for example, has God pronouncing over Zion, "This is my resting place forever; here I will reside, for I have desired it" (Ps 132:13-14; cf. 1 Kgs 8:13).[45] Whereas the sanctuary or holy place *(miqdāš)* is the spatial domain of divine rest,[46] the sabbath is God's temporal dwelling place, a tabernacle in time.[47] Creation reflects temporally what the tabernacle reflects spatially, a separation of domains that culminates with temporal space for God to rest and dwell in. The correspondence between the completion of creation and the inception of rest is by no means unique to the Priestly account; Baal and Marduk also find their seats of rest upon the completion of temple and throne.[48] But for them, rest is wrought by victory over chaos. For God, rest is achieved by the successful coordination and methodical design of the cosmos, an artistic struggle, as it were, and nothing more.

With creation conceived as God's temporal sanctuary, it is only natural to speak of a cosmic ethos or habitation. Both process and product are crucial in identifying the ethos that pervades this creation. A stable creative order prevails in this cosmos, accomplished not through conflict and combat but by coordination and enlistment. Each domain, along with its respective inhabitants, is the result of a productive collaboration between Creator and creation. The final product is a filled formfulness. Form is achieved through differenti-

44. For the basic meaning of holiness as separation, see J. G. Gammie, *Holiness in Israel* (OBT; Minneapolis: Fortress, 1989) 9-13; J. Milgrom, "The Changing Concept of Holiness in the Pentateuchal Codes with Emphasis on Leviticus 19," in *Reading Leviticus: A Conversation with Mary Douglas* (ed. J. F. A. Sawyer; JSOTSup 227; Sheffield: JSOT Press, 1996) 65-67.

45. The Priestly narrative prefers, however, another term to denote divine dwelling: in place of *yšb* ("dwell"), as attested in Ps 132:14 and 1 Kgs 8:13, is Yahweh's "tabernacling" presence *(škn)* in the wilderness. See below.

46. See M. Weinfeld, "Sabbath, Temple and the Enthronement of the Lord — The Problem of the Sitz im Leben of Genesis 1:1–2:3," in *Mélanges bibliques et orientaux en l'honneur de M. Henri Cazelles* (ed. A. Caquot and M. Delcor; AOAT 212; Kevelaer: Butzon & Bercker; Neukirchen-Vluyn: Neukirchener, 1981) 501-2.

47. See A. Green's survey of Jewish literature on the identification of temple and sabbath in "Sabbath as Temple: Some Thoughts on Space and Time in Judaism," in *Go and Study: Essays and Studies in Honor of Alfred Jospe* (ed. R. Jospe and S. Z. Fishman; Washington, D.C.: B'nai B'rith Hillel Foundations, 1980) 287-305.

48. For the comparative material see Weinfeld, "Sabbath, Temple," 504-7.

ation, the mark of goodness. Whle differentiativg the various cosmic components, the process of separation, paradoxically, serves to hold the cosmic order together. Creation's "filledness" is achieved by the production of life.
From firmaments to land, boundaries maintain the integrity of each domain
as well as provide the cement that binds the cosmos as a whole. God's activity
is predominantly one of both separating and binding together.[49] This double
movement of creation is best described as differentiation, a kind of separation that also establishes a level of interdependence.[50] In short, creation is
characterized by *boundedness and boundness.*

Although not a product of the earth, as in the Yahwist's anthropogony,
the creation of humankind is also collaborative in nature: "Let *us* make humankind in our image" (Gen 1:26). It takes a heavenly council to raise humankind as much as it takes the coordination of the waters to allow the land
to emerge and to generate the swarming creatures. All in all, God is a collaborative agent. Enlisting the forces of creation, both earthly and heavenly, God
spearheads creation by forming and dignifying it by uttering commands,
sanctioning the results, blessing the means of regeneration, and consecrating
its completion in the sabbath. In that final act God ceases to impose further
order by withdrawing or separating from creation and, thereby, letting it go in
its own orderly goodness and creative continuation. Such is the way of cooperation and coordination, of boundedness and boundness, which provides
the stable context for life, divine and human, cultic and moral. Creation is the
final product of "form-filledness," the supreme good. Such cosmic integrity
or ethos, established by a creating God who calls forth and differentiates creation, informs and shapes the subsequent narrative and cultic corpus of the
Priestly tradents, as will be shown.

In addition, this cosmic ethos has all to do with creation's climax on the
seventh day. To exclude or downplay the final day from any discussion of the
Priestly ethos invariably results in distortion.[51] The cosmic ethos of the
Priestly tradents holds together a dual focus: creation's goodness, exhibited in

49. So also C. Plantinga, *Not the Way It's Supposed to Be: A Breviary of Sin* (Grand
Rapids: Eerdmans, 1995) 29.
50. See above and M. Volf's perceptive distinction between "differentiation" and
"separation" in *Exclusion and Embrace: A Theological Exploration of Identity, Otherness,
and Reconciliation* (Nashville: Abingdon, 1996) 64-65.
51. This is precisely the mistake Brueggemann makes in his analysis of the Priestly
message. By reducing the significance of the sabbath to the land, Brueggemann identifies
1:28 as the kerygmatic kernel in toto, which enables him to characterize the Priestly account as essentially a conquest tract ("Kerygma of the Priestly Writers," 109-10), despite
his caveat on p. 113.

the Hexaemeron, and God's holiness, evinced on the sabbath. Although goodness and holiness are separated by the temporal sequence of the Hexaemeron and the sabbath, they are also bound together. Holiness marks creation's completion. The relation between the holy and the good is particularly evident in that the number seven is a numerological motif that pervades the creation account, as is often noted.[52] Certain key words, for example, such as God (*'ĕlōhîm*, 35 times), "good" (*ṭôb*, 7 times), and "earth" (*'ereṣ*, 21 times), are attested in multiples of seven. The precreative section (1:1-2) renders a count of 21 words (7 words in v. 1; 14 words in v. 2), and 2:1-3 contains 35 words. Even the entire account of creation (1:1–2:3) features a total count of 469 (7×67) words. This is all to suggest that creation, even as a work in progress, reflects the goal of completion, embodied by the seventh day. The process bears its own teleology, for all of creation at work under divine initiative moves toward holy completion. As all creation is directed toward completion, completion sets the stage for consecration. Goodness and holiness, bounded and separate as they are, are also bound up in teleological correspondence, an integrity of temporal coherence. The primordial week, it turns out, is also a holy week.

Integrity down for the Count

With 2:3 the Priestly cosmogony concludes. Yet creation, in all of its variegated integrity, maintains a persistent role throughout the Priestly narrative and legislation, sustaining the course of right conduct and setting in relief the discrepancies of tragic conflict and sinful conduct among its inhabitants. Creation's integrity, reflected in the stewardship and interdependence of cosmogony, sets the stage for all that follows in the Priestly stratum of the Pentateuch. And the dramatic episode that immediately follows threatens to undo all that creation stood for "in the beginning."

Following the creation of the cosmos, the "generations *(tôlĕdôt)* of the heavens and the earth" (2:4a),[53] are the generations of human life, methodically conveyed in the genealogies dispersed throughout the Priestly narrative,

52. U. Cassuto, *A Commentary on the Book of Genesis, Part I: From Adam to Noah* (tr. I. Abrahams; Jerusalem: Magnes, 1961, repr. 1989) 14-15; Levenson, *Creation*, 67-68. For further bibliography and examples, see Brown, *Structure*, 100-101, 132-34, 239-40. The following examples are drawn from the MT.

53. This half verse from a Priestly hand — not necessarily the same hand that authored the cosmogony — most likely refers to the preceding material (1:1–2:3) given its cosmic scope, in contrast to the Yahwist's anthropogony that follows in v. 4b.

beginning with Adam (5:1). Their pervasive presence throughout the sweep of the Priestly narrative underlines the crucial import of humankind's creation as male and female (1:27; 5:2). Human proliferation on the earth is part and parcel of God's preeminent blessing of life (1:28), the fulfillment of the primal "great commission" (1:28).[54] This primal mandate is subsumed under the rubric of blessing and serves to drive universal history toward its fulfillment. Far from charting the growth of sin, as commonly argued from the Yahwist's account,[55] the succession of generations traces the progression of blessing on the earth. The ten-generational period that stretches from Adam to Noah (5:1-32) itself marks the distinct completion of an episode in human culture.

Identified as "righteous" and "blameless" or having integrity *(tāmîm)*, Noah stands at the cusp of a new era of human generations (6:9). Yet one need only go back to the seventh generation to find another righteous individual, Enoch, who is renowned for having "walked with God" (5:21, 24; 6:9). His years are numbered at 365, the shortest life span of any of these primal patriarchs, but also the most coherent. Enoch's years evince a temporal, cosmic orderliness that corresponds to his exemplary character. Indeed, Enoch is the Priestly author's answer to the Yahwist's Abel (4:1-10): Enoch is a favored individual who meets an untimely "death," not due to human violence but simply "because God took him" (5:24). The terseness of the language is fraught with suggestive significance. It could be that Enoch's short time spent on earth anticipates a distancing of human integrity from the "way of all flesh" (cf. 6:12). In addition, Enoch's life span serves as a sign of seasonal orderliness; his integrity matches that of the cosmos. In any case, Enoch's character stands apart from the inexorable progression of human blessing, a holy moment distinguished from the methodical fulfillment of genealogical blessing. Only Lamech, Noah's father, matches Enoch's age in significance, having lived to the ripe old age of 777 years. His life span marks the completion of the first human genealogy and paves the way for the appearance of Noah, the new *'ādām.*

The need for a new beginning is abruptly and tersely expressed in 6:11-12, whose language inverts the approbation refrain in Genesis 1. Instead of seeing that the cosmic state of affairs was good, stable, and filled with the blessing of life, God now perceives that "the earth was corrupt" *(šḥt)* and "filled with vio-

---

54. I refer to the primordial human blessing as such in light of W. Zimmerli's suggestive article, "The Place and Limit of the Wisdom in the Framework of the Old Testament Theology," *SJT* 17 (1964) 151-55 (repr. in *Studies in Ancient Israelite Wisdom* [ed. J. L. Crenshaw; New York: Ktav, 1976] 319-22).

55. For example, von Rad, *Genesis,* 108, 111-12; see Chapter 3.

lence" *(ḥāmās)* (6:11-13). Creation's goodness has been turned on its head. Instead of approbation, God finds only reprobation. Inseparably bound up, all of life and earth are afflicted. The choice of terminology, "corruption" and "violence," is deliberate. In addition to denoting moral turpitude, "corruption" can signify the ruin and destruction of cities and temples.[56] By overrunning the land, the corruption of life threatens to collapse creation itself.

As the antithesis of life and blessing, "violence" specifically targets the state of the living, the inhabitants of the earth, animal and human.[57] The proliferation of life, filling the earth, is no longer a blessing but a burden. The way of all flesh is no longer with God, as modeled by Enoch and Noah, but against God and creation. The earth has been subjugated by violence unbounded. Filling the land has reached a dead end. Together, "violence" and "corruption" subvert both the earth's structural integrity and the inhabitants therein, tearing away at life and its foundation. This is violence at its most unstructured and therefore wanton state. Violence and its accompanying effects make up the antithesis of creation's "goodness," carefully wrought by differentiation and coordination. Chaos has arrived, enveloping the earth and prompting its dissolution.

Divine judgment, consequently, reflects creation's downward slide into chaos. God's declaration to "destroy" all life from the earth means literally to "corrupt" *(šḥt)*,[58] taking the earth's corruption to its cosmic conclusion,[59] judgment by unbounded water. The earth's violence bears its own self-destructive reward. Chaos for the Priestly author is the natural consequence of corrupt conduct, which afflicts the earth like a virus, attacking its stability and demoralizing its integrity. Chaos is an eminently social phenomenon, but it is not uniquely human. Humans and land animals are bound up together in this hot zone of depravity, effecting complete moral anarchy, the outcome of unbounded predation. The deluge that follows is the final outcome and remedy.

Amid swirling social chaos and the breakdown of creation, Noah is commanded to build. He is a constructionist in a world on the brink of deconstruction. Indeed, the ark that Noah builds mirrors the three-tiered struc-

---

56. For example, Gen 13:10; 19:13, 29; Jer 6:5; Ezek 26:4; 43:4; Lam 2:5-6; Isa 1:4; Deut 4:25.

57. See also N. Lohfink, "Original Sins in the Priestly Historical Narrative," in idem, *Theology of the Pentateuch: Themes of the Priestly Narrative and Deuteronomy* (tr. L. N. Maloney; Minneapolis: Fortress, 1994) 106-10. Within the Priestly purview, "violence" denotes murder (Ezek 7:23). See J. Milgrom, *Leviticus 1–16* (AB 3; New York: Doubleday, 1991) 48.

58. Gen 6:13, 17; cf. vv. 11-12.

59. See the *BHS* emendation in v. 13.

ture of the cosmos: earth, sky, and firmament (6:16; 1:6-10). Noah's ark is a creation in miniature, designed to support the zoological diversity for which the cosmos was created. Noah's mission, like God's cosmic craftwork, is to construct an environment that preserves life for posterity, to gather two representatives of all animals, male and female, within the ark (vv. 19-20). Noah's family, all land animals (wild and domestic), and birds enter in reverse order of their creation (6:19-20; 7:13-14; cf. 1:20-27).

Moreover, God also commanded Noah to harvest the plants of the earth in order to sustain all life, as God granted to the first humans (6:21; cf. 1:29-30). As fulfiller of God's command, Noah is a life preserver amid divine judgment (6:17, 22). Noah's ecological mission grows out of the covenant of life that he receives in the end (v. 18). Noah is delivered from cosmic judgment and ensures the genesis of a new generation of life in toto. In his ark, he and his family dwell in peace within the microcosmos he has built; his family is one among many (cf. 8:19). Like creation itself, Noah's filled *oikos* or dwelling fulfills God's creative command: Noah "did all that God had commanded him" in bringing two of every kind (6:19-22), and the designated animals "went in as God had commanded them" (v. 16a).[60] Here, as in creation, the fulfillment of God's command is a collaborative effort.

"On that day" of Noah's six hundredth year, the cosmic boundaries between earth and water are dismantled from above and below, and creation returns to its primordial state (7:11; cf. 1:2), except for one crucial difference. Borne aloft by the cosmic waters is a tiny ship at sea, containing the culture of life (7:18), floating on the surface not unlike God's breath hovering over the waters prior to creation.[61] This return to "ground zero" day holds yet the seed of new creation, and it begins in a way similar to creation itself: a divine wind blows over the earth, the waters subside, and boundaries are reestablished (8:1b-2a).

Yet creation also begins with "remembrance" (8:1a). Noah and the animals in the ark constitute the link between the old and the new creations, between remembrance and promise, the dialectic of covenant. By the prospect of covenant (6:18), God cannot "forget," much less forsake, what was created in that initial week. By covenant, God must "remember," better yet honor, the divine handiwork of the past continued in Noah's microcosmic mission. In honoring the terms of the covenant, creation's undoing is arrested and the

60. The grammatical object is singular in the Hebrew, but likely denotes the animals collectively. In any case, Noah does not search out the animals to bring them into the ark; the animals take an active role in their own deliverance in populating the ark.

61. The LXX uses the same verb *(epipherō)* to describe God's Spirit and Noah's ark in relation to the waters for both 1:2 and 7:18.

tide begins to turn. In the seventh month, Noah's ark "comes to rest" (*wattānaḥ*, 8:4), but the waters have yet to return to their designated domains for the earth to dry out. That time is reserved for the first day of the first year of Noah's seventh century (v. 13a). The timing is critical: new creation commences once the old is put to rest.

When all is settled, life in its various forms proceeds out of the ark to populate a new earth. The "great commission" is recommissioned (9:1, 7). By bringing out the animals from the ark, Noah becomes the instrument of blessing for all the earth. But a new, disturbing element is introduced in God's recitation of the primordial blessing. The peaceful coexistence that once characterized creation as well as life in the ark no longer carries the day. God institutes human predation over the animals (vv. 2-6). Like the plants granted to humans in their blessing for nourishment (1:28-30), now the animals themselves are handed over for human consumption. For the Priestly author, predation has become part of God's regulation of human life[62] that takes account of the violence that once overcame the land.

Predation has become a necessary evil, for which the Priestly author gives no explicit explanation. Indeed, the question is not so much why human predation, but why *at this point* in the generations on the earth? Again, timing is crucial. Noah's world represents the contemporary world of the narrator, a world in which human beings occasionally sacrifice and eat meat, in addition to the fruits of the ground (cf. Lev 17:10-14). Yet the point of the Priestly narrative is that such a scenario was once *not* the case. That peaceful coexistence among the animals and humans once reigned has enormous ramifications for the Priestly tradents' contemporary world. Although lodged within the antediluvian realm of history, creation's peaceable ethos still generates a compelling, moral force.

In addition to granting the fullness of contemporary reality to Noah's world, the Priestly tradents win a hard-fought concession on behalf of the primordial world. Through the blood prohibition, human predation is firmly checked and contained: "Every moving thing that lives shall be food for you. . . . Only you shall not eat flesh with its life *(nepeš)*, that is, its blood" (9:3-4).[63] In granting humans the permission to eat flesh, animal life is still preserved and violence is regulated.[64] Blood replaces breath as the locus of life (cf. 6:17; 7:15). Consequently, by not ingesting blood, humans refrain

62. Cf. God's concession in the Yahwist's post-flood account, esp. 8:21.

63. See also Lev 3:17; 7:26-27; 17:10-14.

64. See R. D. Nelson's structuralist treatment of Gen 9:1-6 and Lev 17:10-1 in *Raising Up a Faithful Priest: Community and Priesthood in Biblical Theology* (Louisville: Westminster John Knox, 1993) 64-67.

from consuming life. To do otherwise requires a reckoning of capital punishment for both animals and humans (vv. 5-6). Despite whatever contradictions the modern reader may perceive in this Priestly injunction, the aim of the ancient author is clear: to regulate and control the bloodthirsty inclinations of the human heart that once threatened the very structures of the cosmos.[65] The Priestly tradents inject a note of ambiguity into the conventional practice of meat eating, construing carnivorism as a sign of alienation from the peaceful integrity by which creation was originally established. Noah's blessing is a legal remedy for the intractable nature of violence.[66] The severity of the punishment against murder is lodged squarely in the Priestly conception of the *imago Dei* (9:6; cf. 1:27; 5:1). The image of God is not permanently shattered by any fall from creation; human beings cannot escape their essential nature, but they can shatter God's image through wanton acts of violence. Humanity's created distinctiveness forms the very basis for this initial *tôrâ*, a prohibition against the willful taking of human life.

Thus the pronouncement of procreative blessing resurfaces on a drying landscape. But something more is declared: all the inhabitants of the ark are granted a covenant in perpetuity (9:8-17). In content, the covenant is a cease-and-desist order on God's part: "Never again shall all flesh be cut off by the waters of a flood" (9:11). God solemnly pledges that the boundaries set in place between earth and water shall prevail. There is no going back to the drawing board. Covenant entails God's unconditional commitment to remain true to creation's formfulness and integrity without destructive intervention, and its sign introduces a new element of creation, the rainbow. Framed in the sky, the cosmic bow is permanently hung, and so is all divine inclination to destroy.[67] Its aim is to convey "remembrance" of the covenant, that is, to ensure an honoring of its one stipulation, an overriding regard for life in all its forms. As the rainbow marks the aftermath of rain, so covenant marks the end of destruction and the beginning of blessing and order.

---

65. Again, cf. 8:21, which the Priestly author or redactor presupposes. For a similar conclusion regarding the biblical dietary laws, see J. Milgrom, "The Biblical Diet Laws as an Ethical System: Food and Faith," *Int* 17 (1963) 288-301 (repr. in idem, *Studies in Cultic Theology and Terminology* [SJLA 36; Leiden: Brill, 1983] 104-18). See also Gammie, *Holiness in Israel*, 11-12.

66. See T. Frymer-Kensky, "The Atrahasis Epic and Its Significance for Our Understanding of Genesis 1-9," *BA* (1977) 147-55.

67. For the military significance of the bow in Genesis 9 in light of *Enuma elish*, see B. F. Batto, "Creation Theology in Genesis," in *Creation in the Biblical Traditions* (ed. R. J. Clifford and J. J. Collins; CBQMS 24; Washington, D.C.: Catholic Biblical Association of America, 1992) 33-34.

Creation's ethos of boundedness and boundness is now established covenantally in a less than perfect world. As creator, God makes the first move to ensure that the cosmic order remains in place. The Priestly author suggestively lodges God's covenantal pronouncement in the larger setting of human blessing and order (9:1-7). Implied is that the divine initiative to refrain from overrunning creation by the flood serves as a model for covenantal conduct within the human realm, reflected in part by the previous injunction to refrain from devouring life (9:5-6). As much as the rainbow qua sign is a reminder to God of the covenant, it is also a public reminder to human beings of their response.[68] God's promise, unconditional as it is, is not without residual prescriptive force upon the Godlike stewards of creation, men and women. Human beings are to emulate the *covenanting* God. Indeed, this covenant with Noah and the animals points forward to future covenants in which both God's economy and the social order become particularized within Israel's own life. But for now, Noah dies after 950 years of righteousness with 150 days of nautical experience under his belt.

Will the Real Chaos Please Rise Up?

Creation and its dissolution from the flood, out of which a cosmic covenant emerges, present a theological envelope within the Priestly narrative. God began the formation of creation with a watery *tōhû wābōhû* (1:2), whose division makes possible the establishment of differentiated domains.[69] As creation's integrity or ethos is violated through unchecked violence, creation is (re)saturated by the flood. Prompted by violence run amok, divine judgment discloses a comparable means to rectify creation and return it to its precosmic state. Yet chaos, properly speaking, lies not in the deluge per se but in the flood's cause: violence and corruption, which have accompanied blessing's growth through

68. S. Niditch identifies three characteristics of "chaos" in Genesis: "formlessness," "homogeneity," and "timelessness," appropriate characteristics of pre-creation (*Chaos to Cosmos: Studies in Biblical Patterns to Creation* [SPSH; Chico, Calif.: Scholars Press, 1985] 12). If, however, chaos is to be defined as a state of affairs *inimical* to God's creative purposes, one must look elsewhere in the Priestly narrative.

69. For God's and the sign's role in the Noachic covenant, see M. V. Fox, "Sign of the Covenant: Circumcision in the Light of the Priestly *'ôt* Etiologies," *RB* 81 (1974) 570-73. Although the narrative clearly refers to *God's* remembrance, the public nature of the rainbow sign is not without social implications, first and foremost in conveying assurance of divine promise. For the relationship between memory and action, see B. S. Childs, *Memory and Tradition in Israel* (SBT 1/37; Naperville, Ill.: Allenson, 1962) 18-20.

the ten generations like a hidden parasite that in the end has overtaken its host, leaving God evidently no choice except to exterminate the carrier and wipe clean the earth.[70] Such is the Priestly justification: God takes the final step of bringing violence to its convulsive conclusion, a return to the formless void. Whence this social chaos came or how it emerged, the Priestly author gives no clue.[71] Indeed, the eruption of violence is as enigmatically abrupt in its genesis as it is all consuming in its scope. Internal to the Priestly narrative, a shock of tectonic proportions is registered between the creation of a perfect world filled with life in the beginning and creation's undoing by violence in Noah's time. What is clear, however, is that the state of the earth is directly attributed to the violence of life, the violation of the blessing of life, specifically the peaceful and orderly ideal embodied in the vegetarian lifestyle.[72]

The flood is creation's counterpart, a once perfect creation beset by a "perfect storm" at God's behest.[73] Both creation and deluge are complete in their scope and aim. Yet genuine, inimical chaos from the Priestly perspective is not to be found either in the beginning or in the aftermath but in the interim. If the deluge is to be considered a form of chaos, it is only of a derivative nature, one that mirrors social chaos. The flood has the focused aim of bringing creation back to the drawing board by means of a *controlled* cosmic meltdown, or more accurately, dissolution. Chaos, consequently, cannot be identified wholly with water, which remains a legitimate domain in the Priestly worldview. Rather, the Priestly author identifies chaos primarily with what has led up to this watery holocaust, namely violence run amok.[74] Embedded in the story of Noah is creation's antithesis, physically in the flood and morally in the social

70. Although Batto legitimately describes the Priestly cosmogony as a "perfect creation," he misidentifies the waters of the deluge as "a metahistorical force of evil," while also noting, correctly, that chaos has a human dimension (*Slaying the Dragon: Mythmaking in the Biblical Tradition* [Louisville: Westminster John Knox, 1992] 87). The Priestly author, however, lodges evil primarily within the realm of life, especially human life, a move also reflected in Priestly cultic legislation (see below).

71. Unlike the Yahwist's anthropology, which traces Cain's murder of Abel back to the primal disobedience in the garden.

72. See H. C. Brichto, "On Slaughter and Sacrifice, Blood and Atonement," *HUCA* 47 (1976) 20. Brichto appropriately translates ḥāmās as "lawlessness" in the Priestly context.

73. The quoted expression is borrowed from the title of S. Junger's gripping account of the monster gale that destroyed the "Andrea Gail" south of Nova Scotia on Oct. 28, 1991, during a routine fishing expedition (*The Perfect Storm: A True Story of Men against the Sea* [New York: Norton, 1997]).

74. Despite his emphasis on the import of violence in the Priestly narrative, Lohfink insists on identifying chaos wholly with water ("The Strata of the Pentateuch and the Question of War," in idem, *Theology of the Pentateuch*, 203).

chaos that gave rise to it. Unlike the cooperative domains of creation, the flesh of life constitutes the recalcitrant element. Life bears the potential for violence, and violence marks the violation of boundaries, an inundation of social chaos. Within the Priestly spatial worldview, the blurring of boundaries creates only dead space, and the watery conflagration is the final result and remedy of unbounded chaos. From human violence to cosmic deluge, chaos is that which dismantles established boundaries and assimilates domains that are designed to preserve and promote life *in all its plurality*.

As power is shared in the process of creation, so demoralizing chaos is shared in creation's dissolution, even by God, who takes the final step toward corrupting or ruining the earth with water. Yet a human family and the families of animals are spared in a ship that models creation in its paradigmatic form. Noah is creator and the one who fulfills commands in his role as life preserver, the instrument of blessing in a doomed world. To the extent that creation establishes an ethos of goodness, so Noah's righteousness bears cosmic significance. Noah models primordial stewardship by sustaining all of life in its representative forms. His "subduing" of the earth entails bringing together the animals of the earth into his zoological reserve, a floating speck of land, as it were. By fulfilling humankind's role as royal steward over creation (1:28), Noah is a beacon of righteousness in an ocean of anarchy. Noah exercises human dominion over creation by preserving the integrity and diversity of life.

The cosmic covenant established on an earth wiped clean of corruption marks a divine promise to refrain from such drastic and destructive measures ever again. As humankind's propensity for predation and violence is checked in the institution of the blood prohibition, so also God's inclination to rectify measures through destructive intervention is categorically renounced. God's covenant reestablishes the integrity of creation and ensures the efficacy of blessing. It "legitimates *God's* structures of creation for humankind, precisely those that belong to the natural world's capacity to sustain the matrix of history."[75] Earth is granted immunity from watery destruction; indeed, through God's honoring of the covenant, life is invested with an inviolable dignity that is prefigured in the very process of creation.

Creation and covenant are inextricably bound. It is no accident, then, that the first covenant of the Priestly narrative is unabashedly universal in scope. But from its cosmic breadth emerge particular implications for the human community. As God imposes a self-restriction, so humankind must restrict its propensity for violence and revere life even in carnivorous activity.

---

75. P. D. Miller, "Creation and Covenant," in *Biblical Theology: Problems and Perspectives* (ed. S. J. Kraftchick et al.; Nashville: Abingdon, 1995) 165.

Such culinary reverence includes regard for the very structures of creation, to which the dietary laws of Priestly legislation also attest (see below). By the inclusion of animals into God's cosmic covenant with Noah, the human family must include the animals within the circle of covenantal regard, for in blood resides life and in God's own image is found humankind's essential nature.

Covenant and Creation from Genesis to Sinai

Another ten generations unfold from Noah to Abram (10:1-7, 20-23, 31-32; 11:10-26). Like Noah, Abram opens a new chapter in the Priestly covenantal history, yet certain elements of creation's ethos remain. As the progenitor of a distinct people, Abram *separates* from his father in Haran (11:31) and from his nephew Lot in the land of Canaan, for "the land could not support both of them living together" (13:6, 11b). Abram and Lot part company, the former settling in the hill country of Canaan and the latter dwelling among the cities of the Plain (v. 12). A fiery holocaust ensues, thoroughly annihilating *(šḥt)* the cities of the Plain (19:29). Though outlawed cosmically by covenant, divine destruction is localized with regard to certain settings of human existence that are deemed hopelessly violent and corrupt (cf. 6:11-12). Amid the conflagration, Abram, like Noah, is remembered and Lot is rescued (v. 29). Though separated from Abram, Lot is bound to his uncle by "remembrance," established covenantally by God. God's covenant with Abram is prefaced by the statement of Sarai's infertility (16:1), which threatens to jeopardize the primordial blessing commissioned by the narrative earlier (1:28; 9:1, 7). As a provisional solution, Hagar the Egyptian is introduced as Sarai's substitute, and Ishmael is born (16:3, 15).

Amid such threat to blessing, God's covenant with Abram opens with a general exhortation: "Walk before me and be blameless" (17:1). Like Noah and Enoch before him, Abraham is to embody righteousness. Indeed, the slight shift in terminology, from walking "with" *('et)* God, as in Noah's and Enoch's case (6:9; 5:22), to walking "before" *(lpny)* God is significant. More than his primordial forebears, Abram is called to be the vanguard of integrity. As in Noah's case, the covenant promise is prefaced by a statement of the individual's integrity before God (6:9; 17:1), which makes possible its reception.[76] Likewise, the covenant that follows builds on the primordial blessing of life

---

76. As C. Westermann points out, the Abrahamic covenant requires *both* God's promise and Abraham's integrity (*Genesis 12–36* [tr. J. J. Scullion; Continental Commentary; Minneapolis: Augsburg, 1985] 256). See also S. McEvenue, *The Narrative Style of the Priestly Writer* (AnBib 50; Rome: Pontifical Biblical Institute, 1971) 145-78.

and procreation, but the grammar has changed. Abram's blessing is cast not in the language of command ("Be fruitful and . . ."), but in the language of promise: "I will make you exceedingly numerous" (17:2); "I will make you exceedingly fruitful" (v. 6). Moreover, the language of command has shifted from blessing to blamelessness. The primordial blessing was cast as a mandate (1:28), but with Abram, whose immediate situation has called the promise of progeny into question, the form of the mandate is filled with concrete, moral significance: Abram is to embody integrity (*tāmîm*, 17:1).

The content of God's covenantal promise, though based on the primordial blessing, gains particular social nuance for Abram: Abram is to beget a "multitude of nations" (*hămôn gôyim*, v. 4). Indeed, the promise is written into his new name as Abraham, "the father of a multitude." Not simply a "great nation," as found in the Yahwist's blessing (12:2), Abraham's royal blessing is given an *international* context. Similarly, Sarai is to "give rise to nations; kings of peoples shall come from her"; hence her name is changed to Sarah, "princess" (17:15).[77] In the Priestly worldview, the act of naming is crucial. In the cosmogony, the name introduces and formalizes new domains for life and governance (1:5, 8, 10). By their new names, the patriarch and matriarch have become founders of a new *cultural domain*, an international expanse that includes the birth and rise of kingdoms.

Abraham and Sarah are to "bear" a new land, and the result will be the transformation of Canaan (17:8). In its current state, the land of Canaan is simply an arena of sojourn or immigration, a foreign land (*māgôr*, v. 8) in which Abraham is a "stranger and alien" (*gēr-wĕtôšāb*, 23:4). Through God's covenantal word, however, the land is re-created into a "permanent possession" (*'ăhuzzat 'ôlām*, 17:8b). The fulfillment of God's covenant initiates a new creation, a new social context that is as distinctive as it is expansive. The blessing of progeny is meant to fill the landscape of Abraham's sojourns, turning it into a land of promise and possession. The Abrahamic covenant, in turn, sets the parameters for the character of a new community.

As the covenantal sign of the bow in the clouds was a new feature of the cosmos, so the sign of Abraham's covenant makes its mark in the landscape of human identity. Circumcision is the covenantal mark that furthers differentiation within humankind. Through this mark of separation, a covenantal community is formed "in the flesh" (vv. 13-14). By excising a part of the most vulnerable yet potent organ of the male anatomy, a community is formed from the mainstream of human life. With some measure of poetic justice, the male within the ancestral household who does not bear the incised mark of circum-

---

77. Indeed, her original name "Sarai" is simply an archaic form.

cision "shall be *cut off (wĕnikrĕtâ)* from his people" (v. 14). Yet the community to issue from Abraham's loins is surprisingly inclusive, as poignantly illustrated in Abraham's advocacy of Ishmael (v. 18).[78] Ishmael, too, is blessed with the trappings of nationhood; he is one of Abraham's multitude (v. 20).[79] Moreover, the covenantal promise is to include even slaves bought from any foreigner (v. 12). Such calculated inclusiveness anticipates the integrity of the land (see below) and presupposes the variegated goodness of creation. Despite their fixation on boundaries, the Priestly tradents are no nativists.

In short, Abraham's covenant is a covenant of distinction, graphically illustrated through the rite of circumcision. The result of his distinction is a peculiar solidarity with God: "I will establish my covenant . . . to be God to you and to your offspring after you" (v. 7). The covenant continues the primordial blessing of progeny in relation to a familial crisis: infertility has afflicted Israel's ancestral household (16:1a). Only after Abraham's circumcision can Sarah bear a child.[80] As with creation itself, differentiation ushers in the promise of new life. Even the sign of the covenant presupposes the blessing of progeny: "every male among you shall be circumcised" (17:12). But progeny is not the only thing at stake in this covenant. By circumcision a community is circumscribed; circumcision is the sign and signature of the Abrahamic covenant.[81] Separation from the mass of humanity entails a covenantal union with the Creator and a particular commitment of the community. Through circumcision, the cultural domain of community, like the natural domains of earth and water in creation, are incorporated into God's providential designs.

Circumcision is, moreover, an act of community formation that commences after creation itself is complete, for it is on the *eighth* day that the act occurs (v. 12a; Lev 12:3). Originally a rite of puberty or marriage, circumcision has been transferred to the realm of birth and creation.[82] The covenant of circumcision is a covenant of the community's circumscription. But unlike God's unopposed enlistment of the natural elements in creation, the recep-

---

78. Ishmael's inclusion is effected through Abraham's disbelief in God's blessing of progeny through Sarah.

79. Although Ishmael's descendants are called "princes" (*nĕśî'im*) and not "kings" (*mĕlākîm*), Abraham's son is not simply an afterthought, excluded from the covenantal circle, contra Fox, "Sign of the Covenant," 589.

80. For circumcision as a fertility rite, see R. G. Hall, "Circumcision," *ABD* 1.1026-27.

81. Cf. E. Isaac's argument that circumcision marks the *ratification* of a covenant ("Circumcision as Covenant Rite," *Anthropos* 59 [1965] 444-56). Although the evidence is skimpy, the description of circumcision as "signature" captures this possible nuance.

82. See Fox, "Sign of the Covenant," 591.

tion of the covenant "in the flesh" is not without a measure of imposition. Circumcision hurts! This excision marks the incorporation of a particular domain of "flesh," which is prone to chaos, having "corrupted its way upon the earth" (Gen 6:12). Circumcision serves to facilitate both the community's material existence through progeny and its cultural domain through pre-scription. In creation the waters are circumscribed in order for the land to emerge and provide for life; in circumcision the foreskin is removed to en-sure the progenital continuation of the community's existence. In circumci-sion a community is painfully created and a commitment of integrity is es-tablished: "Walk before me and be blameless, and I will make my covenant between me and you" (17:1b-2a). And it was so. Abraham did all that God commanded, circumcising the male members of his household, including Ishmael and his servants (vv. 23-26).

Equal to the promise of progeny, established by the covenant of circum-scription, is the Priestly focus on the domain of land in Genesis 23, first high-lighted in Genesis 1. Abraham does not lay claim to his covenantal land grant by force but by equitable negotiation. The negotiations over Sarah's burial site between Abraham and the Hittites of the land is a classic case of Semitic bar-tering, intense yet conducted decently and in order. Above the fray of fierce exchange is the protocol of hospitality: Ephron ben Zohar, the Hittite who owns the field of Machpelah next to Hebron, insists on giving the field to Abraham, whereas the patriarch insists just as vehemently on paying "the full price" for the field (23:7-11). Each commands the other to heed his offer (vv. 13, 15). But Abraham's persistence in the end wins out as Ephron slips the field's monetary worth into the negotiations while still insisting on handing it over to him: "What is that between you and me? Bury your dead" (v. 15). The patriarch has prevailed in his tenacity at purchasing the land fair and square. In so doing, Abraham has gained publicly and fairly a "possession" (*miqnâ lĕʿênê bĕnê-ḥēt*, v. 18) in the land of promise. Through this field, Abraham has gained a foothold in *filling* the land with his progeny, a land paid *in full* (*bĕkesep mālēʾ*, v. 9).

Fullness of payment promises fullness of progeny and fulfillment of Is-rael's destiny in the land (cf. 1:28). There is a profound irony in that Abra-ham's securing of the land is occasioned by the matriarch's death. The patri-arch's legal claim to the land begins with a burial site. Sarah's death marks the beginning of a series of burials that culminates with Jacob's internment (49:29-33; 50:12),[83] bridging the history of Israel's ancestral household and

---

83. The only exception is Rachel, who according to the Elohist is buried on the way to Ephrath (Bethlehem) and is memorialized by a pillar (Gen 35:21).

that of Israel's national liberation from Egypt. The Priestly history of the patriarchs and matriarchs serves to maintain, if not accumulate, Israel's claim
to the land.[84] Through the passing of each generation, reclamation of the
land accrues. Death is, ironically, instrumental for securing the blessing of
life and fruitfulness in the land. In short, Abraham's purchase of the burial
site marks the fulfillment of the land promise *pars pro toto*.[85]

In the fullness of the land, however, there remains marked differentiation.
Abraham's cultural domain remains distinct from the other inhabitants of the
land, most vividly illustrated in the tale of two brothers, Jacob and Esau. The
Priestly presentation of their relationship is admittedly colorless compared to the
dramatic suspense developed by the Yahwist's (and Elohist's) version. Jacob is the
obedient son of his parents who dutifully fulfills his father's charge (28:1-5, 7).
The Priestly agenda is transparent: Jacob's sojourn in Paddan-aram is no flight
but a quest to preserve Israel's ancestral bloodlines in the land of the Canaanites/
Hittites. As Rebekah complains, "What good will my life be to me if Jacob marries
. . . one of the women of the land?" (27:46). Israel must not be of the land but in
the land. Indeed, Esau has forced the issue by intermarrying two Hittites, making
"life bitter" *(mōrat rûaḥ)* for his parents (26:35). Such ethnic mixing is anathema,
for it blurs all distinction of Israel's ethnic identity. Endogamy is the material
means of preserving the integrity of Israel's cultural existence. As the cultural antithesis of his maritally inclusive brother, Jacob preserves God's covenantal blessing to be "fruitful and numerous" and "a congregation of peoples" (*qĕhal
'ammîm*, 28:3).[86] Sustained by the differentiated character of creation, *ethnos* and
ethos, for the Priestly narrator, overlap considerably.

As the patrilineal history, which extends from Abraham to Jacob, approaches Israel's own national history, the language of blessing persists, yet
not without some variation. Whereas Abraham was blessed as the progenitor
of a "multitude of nations," as his very name attests, Jacob (a.k.a. "Israel")
comes to be the father of a *qāhāl*, a "congregation," which for the Priestly
tradents carries cultic significance.[87] The language is even more suggestive in

---

84. See also W. Brueggemann, *Genesis* (Interpretation; Atlanta; John Knox, 1982)
195-97.

85. T. Pola, *Die ursprüngliche Priesterschrift: Beobachtungen zur Literarkritik und
Traditionsgeschichte von P^g* (WMANT 70; Neukirchen-Vluyn: Neukirchener, 1995) 308-9.

86. Here I do not follow the NRSV translation, "company," which levels out any distinction relative to Abraham's blessing to be a "multitude of nations" (Gen 17:8). The term
qāhāl bears a more technical and thus suggestive meaning that corresponds to the parallel
designation *'ēdâ*, "congregation," of Israel (e.g., Exod 16:1, 2, 9, 10; 17:1; 35:1, 4, 20). Of the
"multitude of nations," Israel is distinctly a congregation.

87. For example, Num 14:5; 16:3; 20:4; Lev 4: 13, 14, 21; 16:17.

the successive restatements of Jacob's blessing. At Bethel, God blesses Jacob with his new name Israel and charges him to "be fruitful and multiply; a nation and a congregation of nations *(qĕhal gôyim)* shall come from you, and kings shall spring from you" (35:11; cf. 17:4-6). In his last words to Joseph, Jacob recounts the Bethel blessing: "I am going to make you fruitful and increase your numbers; I will make of you a congregation of peoples *(qĕhal ʿammîm)* and will give this land to your offspring after you for a permanent possession *(ʾăhuzzat ʿôlām)*" (48:4; cf. 17:8; Lev 25:34). With the particular theme of the possessed land conjoined to the cosmic theme of human increase, embodied in the patriarchal blessing, Jacob's own blessing becomes constitutive of Israel's own genesis: Jacob is the eponym of a cohesive and distinct constituent of a land that is internally diverse: a "congregation of nations" among a "multitude of nations."

Such cultural distinction is underscored by Esau's reaction to Jacob's blessing in the latter's quest for a suitable spouse in the land of his maternal grandfather. Attempting to redeem his progeny and his status in the eyes of his father, Esau marries a daughter of Ishmael (28:9). But addition is no solution to preservation. Esau's descendants constitute a mixture of Canaanite and Egyptian bloodlines. By contrast, Jacob is the tabula rasa who bears the promise of the regeneration of distinction. The split between the brothers is, consequently, inevitable and necessary (36:6-8), mirroring the fateful split between Abraham and his nephew Lot (13:6), for in both cases "the land could not support them." Ethnic distinction is rooted in the land's sustainability. Division is necessary, as Esau moves to a distant land and is identified with Edom in the hill country of Seir (37:7-8). Yet the narrative keeps an eye on Esau's descendants, not out of suspicion or malediction, mixed though they are. That his genealogy is traced at all testifies to the continuation of divine blessing from the beginning (36:9-14). Fraternal parting is a mark of differentiation, not outright exclusion or abject condemnation. It creates space for Israel's claim to *fill* its own land with cultural distinction through a promise held by a deed paid in *full*.

Covenant, Creation, and Liberation

Israel's claim on the land, however, is not immediately realized. A major detour in the narrative is taken when Israel finds itself in Egypt. With Joseph's death, Israel's familial contours are consigned to past history (Exod 1:6). The age of the eponymous patriarchs and matriarchs is over, and the first steps toward nationhood are taken with a new generation. The people of the patri-

archs are now known as "the children of Israel" *(bĕnê yiśrā'ēl)*, Jacob's progeny. The transition is embodied in the fulfillment of one portion of the
blessing: "The Israelites became fruitful *(pārû)* and prolific *(wayyišrĕṣû)*, they
multiplied *(wayyirbû)* and grew exceedingly strong *(wayya'aṣmû)*, so that the
land was filled *(wattimmālē')* with them" (v. 7). The verbs augment the early
patriarchal blessings as well as amplify the Priestly "great commission" of
Gen 1:28. Indeed, the second verb, "proliferate" *(šrṣ)*, means literally
"swarm" or "abound," as attested in connection with the sea creatures (Gen
1:20, 21), the animals of the ark (8:17), and Noah's family (9:7). Israel's status
in Egypt is a command fulfilled, an actualized blessing.

There is, however, an incongruity: the land in which Israel resides is
Egypt, not Canaan; indeed, it is no land at all for Jacob's children; there is no
possession to be had in Egypt.[88] The second part of the blessing, which concerns inhabiting the promised land, remains a prolepsis, a work in progress.
Israel's blessing is, in fact, a bane on foreign soil. Filling a land that is not
theirs is tantamount to overrunning it, and the land in which they subsist has
taken formidable steps to subdue the people of the covenant, making "their
lives bitter" (Exod 1:14).[89] Henceforth the Priestly narrative has nothing
more to say about being fruitful and multiplying. Fulfilling the primordial
great commission is, in the end, only the preface to Israel's own vocation in
another land. Like the sabbath, which represents the culmination of and distinction from creation, Israel's destiny reaches beyond the blessings of self-
preservation. Israel's place is a land *and* an ethos.

Israel's subjugation takes the form of relentless labor. "With severity"
(bĕperek) the children of Jacob are pressed into service to carry out the king's
monumental and agricultural projects (1:13-14). Egyptian rule is characterized by a structured violence against another people,[90] a rulership that runs
counter to creation (cf. Gen 1:26-27). For example, the sabbath provision is
yet to be realized (cf. Exod 16:26; 20:8-11; 31:12-17). As the elements of creation were enlisted rather than wrested into servitude, so Israel's destiny must
be rooted in creative freedom "from the burdens of the Egyptians" (6:6). In
Egypt, Israel must bear the crushing burden of performing what is both alien
to their covenantal destiny and counter to the ethos of creation, the dignity of
place and restoration. Instead of willful obedience, Israel's response is plain-

---

88. The Yahwist's "land of Goshen" is not attested in the Priestly narrative in order
to underscore the crucial importance of the land grant of Canaan. Without any (immovable) possession in Egypt (Gen 47:27b), Israel is essentially landless from the start.

89. Heb. *wayĕmārĕrû 'et-ḥayyēhem;* cf. the similar language in Gen 26:35; 27:46.

90. The term *perek* bears connotations of oppressive and violent rule (Lev 25:43, 46,
53; Ezek 34:4). See also the Akkadian cognate *parâkum* in *AHw* 2.828-29.

tive groaning and protest to God (2:23b). As Israel's very nature is constituted by covenant, so Israel's liberation must begin with God's remembrance or honoring of the covenant (v. 24). Under Egyptian rule, both creation and covenant are compromised; indeed, God's very honor is at stake (see 14:4).

God's address to Moses, in which the name "Yahweh" is revealed (6:2-3), focuses directly on the blessing of the land, "a possession" (môrāšâ, v. 8; Deut 33:4; cf. Gen 23:18, 20; 17:8). Yet the fulfillment of this land blessing has gained a focus heretofore absent in the original covenantal blessing: "You shall know that I am Yahweh your God, who has freed you from the burdens of the Egyptians" (Exod 6:7b). Whereas the aim of the covenant has been for God to be Israel's God and for Israel to be God's people (Gen 17:7-8; Exod 6:7a), *acknowledgment* of God is tied specifically to Israel's liberation from Egypt. It is no coincidence, after all, that Moses' announcement to his people falls on deaf ears; with "stifled spirit" (qōṣer rûaḥ) they have not the capacity or historical precedence to appropriate such news and thereby acknowledge God (v. 9). Moreover, the Egyptians too "shall know that I am Yahweh" through Israel's release (7:5; 14:4b). With Yahweh's "outstretched arm and mighty acts of judgment," stifled spirits are released and hardened hearts are overcome. Such is the pedagogy of liberation.

The story of Israel's subsequent freedom from slavery serves to highlight Yahweh's indomitable power *over* human history and *in* creation. With Moses as intermediary and Aaron as spokesman, divine power is given depth and breadth. Through the protraction of the plagues, occasioned by Pharaoh's recalcitrant will, or "hardened heart," Yahweh's "signs and wonders" ('ōtōt, môpĕtîm) are gloriously "multiplied" (rbh, 7:3; 11:9; cf. 14:4). That Yahweh is indeed behind the king's intransigence is unambiguously clear (11:10; 9:12; 7:3; cf. 7:13, 22; 8:19 [MT 15]). Yet there is an expressed rationale behind such theological madness. The juxtaposition of Pharaoh's intractable resistance and the multiplication of the signs and wonders holds the key (7:3; 11:9). Without Pharaoh's stubborn resistance, the litany of wonders could not unfold. Because Pharaoh does not heed Israel's inevitable destiny, the plagues continue.[91] Indeed, they proliferate. For every step in Pharaoh's ossification, an opposite and greater wonder takes place. As it breaks in on Israel's history, the divine domain is to have its fill.

For the Priestly historiographer, the hardening of Pharaoh's heart testifies to the infinite expanse of Yahweh's sovereign power, which, like the pro-

---

91. See also B. S. Childs's distinction between the Priestly formulation of the hardened heart and the Yahwist's (*The Book of Exodus* [OTL; Philadelphia: Westminster, 1974] 171-73).

cess of creation itself, begins with calculated growth. For example, much of divine power is replicable by the magicians of Egypt in their "secret arts": the staff-turned-snake (7:8-13), the water-turned-blood (7:19-22), and the water-generated frogs (8:5-7). In the last two cases, the waters are employed to unleash ecological havoc by both Aaron and the magicians. Blood is a sign of Egypt's structural violence wrought upon the backs of slaves. A deluge of amphibians covering the land marks a decisive breach of the boundary between earth and water. Egypt has crossed the bounds of ethical propriety in its treatment of Israel. So creation, in response, is divinely directed to cross the bounds of its cosmic parameters.[92]

Yet Yahweh's power, as replicated by the magicians, is no gnostic exercise: Aaron's staff devours those of the magicians in the first wonder (7:12), portending the precedence of divine power over human machinations. When Aaron's staff is stretched out to strike "the dirt of the earth" (ʿăpar hāʾāreṣ), producing a plague of gnats over the land (8:16 [MT 12]), the magicians come up short for the first time and come to acknowledge Yahweh's irreplicable power, proclaiming, "This is the finger of God" (v. 19 [MT 15]). Perhaps it is no coincidence that it is this land-based display of power that establishes divine primacy over all other kinds of earthly powers, for the issue of the land is at stake in God's blessing and covenant. Cast in the air, dirt is again used, this time to bring about boils on both humans and animals, afflicting even the magicians (9:8-11). But what is not overcome is Pharaoh's heart. Indeed, overcoming an intransigent will is not the issue for the narrator, any more than overcoming Chaos is not germane to creation. Yahweh's directive activity in nature and society is absolute. The question is rather how long Yahweh plans to pack into Israel's formative history "signs and wonders," with Pharaoh's intransigence serving as their warrant. Even Pharaoh's hardened heart is "good" in that it points to divine handiwork or, more to the point, Yahweh's *filling* of human history. The end result is all the more pedagogically potent.

As blood throughout the land began the series of plagues, so blood is the sign of the final plague, the death of the firstborn. Like circumcision, blood on the doorposts and lintel of Israelite homes marks the distinction of the covenantal community. As in the case of the celestial bow, Yahweh is to "see the blood" on this "day of remembrance," passing over and sparing the households of Jacob (12:13). Yet distinction is not, prima facie, synonymous

92. For the reflections on the plagues as ecological disasters, see T. E. Fretheim, "The Plagues as Ecological Signs of Historical Disaster," *JBL* 110 (1991) 385-96; idem, *Exodus* (Interpretation; Louisville: John Knox, 1991) 105-12.

with exclusion. In developing this ritual of remembrance as a perpetual ordinance, the Priestly tradents stipulate: "If an alien *(gēr)* who resides with you desires to celebrate the Passover to Yahweh, all his males shall be circumcised; then he may draw near to celebrate it; he shall be considered a native *('ezraḥ)* of the land" (v. 48). The "congregation of Israel" *('ădat yiśrā'ēl)* embraces both aliens and natives alike (vv. 19, 47), for Israel is a sojourner in a foreign land. In its institutionalized form, the Passover is as inclusive as it is proleptic, anticipating permanent residence in a land yet to be inhabited and filled.

The means to that end is Yahweh's deliverance of Israel, creation-style. Unconvinced of Israel's holy destiny even after the final plague, Pharaoh senses that Israel's wilderness trek is aimless and takes aim to overcome the band of slaves once and for all (14:3). The pursuit is on and concludes at the sea, the locus of judgment as it was for "all flesh" in Noah's day. Accompanied by the promises of power, Israel has gone out "boldly," literally, with a "high hand" (14:8).[93] But with Pharaoh's warhorses snorting for the kill, the Israelites can only cry out (vv. 9-10). Yet forward into the sea they must go. And as in creation, the waters divide *(wayyibbāqĕ'û)* and the dry land emerges (v. 21b; cf. Gen 1:6, 9). With wall-to-wall water, Israel proceeds safely on dry ground. Pharaoh's army, however, is submerged in a deluge that marks the sea's return to its natural state. Only by God's power can Israel safely encroach *beyond* the land's natural borders for passage to its covenantally created destiny. The expressed purpose for the decisive conflict is Yahweh's desire to "gain glory over Pharaoh."[94] Divine glory is Yahweh's booty, as it were, reaped from Pharaoh's destruction; it is knowledge of divine sovereignty gained at a severe cost (v. 4). Yahweh's *Chaoskampf* is against Pharaoh and his army, not the waters of creation, which are merely the instrument of Israel's redemption and Egypt's judgment.

The deployment of divine signs and wonders continues with the introduction of manna and meat in the wilderness. As in the case of Pharaoh's heart, Israel's complaint serves as an occasion for another miracle: bread and meat in the wilderness, so that "you shall know that I am Yahweh your God" (16:12). Wondrous sustenance in the wilderness gains a temporal significance of cosmic proportions: in the alternation of evening and morning, Israel comes to know and behold Yahweh's glory (vv. 6-7). While meat comes in the evening, manna arrives in the morning (vv. 12-14). Despite their worst intentions, each Israelite gathers an equitable share, one omer apiece (vv. 17-18). In

---

93. The similarity between "high hand" (v. 8) and Moses' high staff (v. 16) is telling.
94. Heb. *wĕ'ikkābĕdā bĕpar'ōh* (Exod 14:17).

the wilderness the observance of the sabbath is introduced with its own temporal rhythm: six days of gathering and the seventh a "day of solemn rest, a holy sabbath to Yahweh" (vv. 22-23). As with the Egyptian plagues, the wilderness is a setting of signs. As a perpetual testimony to divine sustenance in a harsh landscape, an omer is to be preserved throughout Israel's generations, placed "before Yahweh," "before the testimony" (*hāʿēdut*, vv. 33-34; cf. v. 9).[95] It is at the conclusion of this account of the manna and the meat that the narrator jumps track slightly by having the testimony and the tabernacle already set before Israel's stay at Sinai. Like the sabbath institution, the tabernacle and the testimony have worked themselves into the narration before their proper time (cf. 25:16; 30:36), a narrative testimony to their solemn significance.

Sinai and Sanctification

The Priestly redaction of Exodus 19–24, the account of Yahweh's settlement on the mountain and the giving of the law, reveals much about the Priestly vision of Israel's identity in relation to its cosmic environs.[96] Indeed, what better place is there to survey Israel's role and mission in the world except on the Priestly pinnacle of Israel's formative history? The revelation of Israel's identity occurs prior to the tabernacle instructions and hence must be viewed in connection with them. At Sinai Yahweh proclaims Israel's identity vis-à-vis the international layout of the land in summary fashion (19:5b-6a):

> You shall be my treasured possession out of all the peoples.
>   **Indeed, the whole earth belongs to me** *(kî-lî kol-hāʾāreṣ),*
>   **but you shall be to me a priestly kingdom** *(mamleket kōhănîm)*
>   **and a holy nation** *(gôy qādôš).*

What is uniquely Priestly in this revelatory pronouncement, which cuts to the heart of Israel's identity, is highlighted in **bold**, beginning with the asseverative marker, "indeed" (*kî*, v. 5bβ). In contrast to the more provincial purview of the Deuteronomistic colon in 19:15bα, the Priestly redaction is more cosmic in focus. All the earth belongs to God, of which Israel is an integral

95. Frequently translated as "covenant" in Exodus, *ʿēdût* is not identical to *bĕrît* (Gen 6:18; 9:11-17; 17:2-21). See below.

96. The literary analysis of the Priestly redaction is perceptively conducted by T. B. Dozeman, *God on the Mountain: A Study of Redaction, Theology, and Canon in Exodus 19–24* (SBLMS 37; Atlanta: Scholars Press, 1989) 87-119.

71

part. Israel is to be a nation, a *gôy*, which establishes a measure of common ground with the surrounding peoples qua nations. Israel's distinction among the nations is its holiness, not an inherent quality but a goal to be sought.[97]

By embedding Israel's holy identity within the larger cosmic and international scope of its environs, the Priestly tradents nuance without leveling the rigid contrast established by the Deuteronomistic tradition elsewhere between the heathen nations *(gôyim)* and Israel, a "people" *('am)*.[98] By establishing a cosmic identity for Israel's distinctiveness, this Priestly redaction eschews the marks of cultural isolationism. Israel is not a cultural enclave, separated from the nations round about, but a nation and a kingdom set in positive relationship with the surrounding peoples. God's relationship, specifically in the act of consecration, holds the key to Israel's distinction, but it does not cut Israel off from the wider social and natural arena, which also belongs to God and thus is considered "good." That Yahweh's chosen people is commissioned to be a "kingdom of priests" is suggestive of a mediatorial, even cultic, role for this one people in relation to the cultures at large. As Thomas Dozeman observes, the Priestly vision of Israel at Sinai implicitly establishes an analogy between Moses as cultic mediator to Israel and Israel as cultic mediator to the nations, a conduit of blessing to the nations.[99] Israel's distinctive identity is in part defined by its distinctive relation, indeed mission, to the larger world.

Following the revelation of Israel's distinctive identity, the action on the mountain commences (24:15b-18). As a fiery cloud, Yahweh's "glory" *(kābôd)* settles on Sinai, covering the mountain for six days. On the seventh day, Moses is summoned (cf. Gen 2:1). Entering the cloud, Moses ascends the mountain and resides there for forty days. Like the burning bush of the Yahwist tradition (Exod 3:2), Moses as cultic mediator is unconsumed by the "devouring fire" of divine theophany (*'ēš 'ōkelet*, 24:17). The narrative imbues human and divine action with a structural symmetry: Yahweh descends on the mountain and "encamps" (*škn*, 24:16; cf. 19:20); Moses ascends the mountain to receive the divine commands that constitute the new community; and, like the sabbath, time stands still in this domain of moral communion. The meeting on the mountain ensues and what transpires is at base a blueprint for institutionalizing future encounters, for "routinizing"

---

97. Cf. Deut 7:1-6 (D) and Lev 19:2; 20:26; 21:8, 15; 22:9, 15 (P); Dozeman, *God on the Mountain*, 97-98. See below.

98. For example, Deut 7:6; 14:2; 26:18. See G. von Rad, *Das Gottesvolk im Deuteronomium* (BWANT 47; Stuttgart: Kohlhammer, 1929) 10n.5.

99. Dozeman, *God on the Mountain*, 141-43.

the fire of Yahweh, as time itself was routinized in creation by its fulfillment in the sabbath.[100]

Tabernacle, Testimony, and Creation

The series of instructions and the account of the tabernacle's construction mark
the pinnacle of the Priestly narrative in Exodus 25–40. At Sinai Yahweh legislates
a building program (25:1–31:17) that is then dutifully fulfilled (35:1–40:38). Despite some variation, command and fulfillment, as in the creation account, exhibit close correspondence; both are theologically integral to the narrative and
stylistically typical of the Priestly penchant for repetition.[101] Recalling the days of
creation, seven divine instructions are given, dominating the Priestly *tôrâ* (25:1–
31:17).[102] The verbal decrees are evidently matched by reference to a visual
model, a "pattern" *(tabnît)* or architectural blueprint, which Moses is shown on
the mountain (25:9, 40).[103] During his residence on the mountain, Moses receives instructions (24:16-18) for erecting a sanctuary *(miqdāš)* or tabernacle
(miškān), "so that [Yahweh] may dwell *(škn)* among them" (25:8).

---

100. Given the limited scope of his analysis, Dozeman's point that the divine action
of descending *(yrd)* and temporarily dwelling *(škn)* on the mountain offers a critique of
"past temple theology" is questionable, since it fails to account for the design and purpose
of the tabernacle that follows *(God on the Mountain,* 129-30; see also the more vigorous
presentation in T. E. Fretheim, "The Priestly Document: Anti-Temple?" *VT* 18 [1968] 318-
29). The episode on Sinai represents a *founding* event or ritual (see F. H. Gorman Jr., *The
Ideology of Ritual: Space, Time, and Status in the Priestly Theology* [JSOTSup 91; Sheffield:
JSOT Press, 1990] 54), a one-time event that prefaces the tabernacle construction, which is
designed to routinize without reducing God's presence among a people (see below).

101. As was typical of traditional historical scholarship, repetitions and variations
were judged as supplemental or secondary (e.g., M. Noth, who considered most of Exodus
35–40 as secondary *(Exodus* [tr. J. S. Bowden; OTL; Philadelphia: Westminster, 1962] 274-
75, 282). See, however, S. McEvenue, "Word and Fulfillment: A Stylistic Feature of the
Priestly Writer," *Semitics* 1 (1970) 104-10; idem, *Narrative Style;* idem, "The Style of a
Building Instruction," *Semitics* 4 (1974) 1-9; V. A. Hurowitz, "The Priestly Account of
Building the Tabernacle," *JAOS* 105 (1985) 21-30; P. P. Jenson, *Graded Holiness: A Key to the
Priestly Conception of the World* (JSOTSup 106; Sheffield: JSOT Press, 1992) 99-101.

102. See P. J. Kearney, "Creation and Liturgy: The P Redaction of Ex 25–40," *ZAW* 89
(1977) 375-87; Weinfeld, "Sabbath, Temple," 502n.5, 503n.1; R. Klein, "Back to the Future," *Int* 50 (1996) 266.

103. See also 26:30, which refers to the "plan" *(mišpāṭ)* that is shown to Moses, and
27:8: "They shall be made just as you were shown on the mountain." It is often assumed
that this "model" *(tabnît)* corresponds to a heavenly prototype, but such an assumption is
problematic (Hurowitz, "Priestly Account," 22n.4).

As the locus of holiness on earth, the tabernacle is to be Yahweh's dwelling among the children of Israel (see 40:34-38). But Yahweh's indwelling or "tabernacling" presence is not only the basis for the erection of the tabernacle; it is also the raison d'être of Israel's release from bondage: "I will dwell among the Israelites; I will be their God, so that they shall know that I am Yahweh their God, who brought them out of the land of Egypt so that I might *dwell* among them" (29:45-46). A comparison of the covenantal promise of land to the patriarchs with the land promises given to Moses is revealing.[104] In the revelatory address to Moses, Yahweh is identified as the God of both the exodus and the *eisodus,* the one to release Israel *out of* bondage and to bring Israel *into* the land "that I swore to give to Abraham, Isaac, and Jacob" (Exod 6:7-8). At Sinai, Yahweh is similarly identified as the author of the exodus (29:46), but instead of the so-called *eisodus* formula, an *eisoikus* ("indwelling") formula appears.[105] *Israel's habitation* in the land of "possession" is no longer at issue; what is of concern is *Yahweh's habitation* with Israel as a tabernacling presence.[106] The issue of dwelling per se is exclusively reserved for Yahweh within the Priestly historiography. Moreover, divine dwelling is intimately tied to acknowledgment of Yahweh as Israel's God. Indeed, the tabernacle or divine dwelling place serves as the testimony to God's habitation among a people and the fulfillment of Israel's stay at Sinai, analogous to the sabbath's place at the conclusion of creation. Like the cosmogonic process, the way in which the goal of Yahweh's indwelling is reached plays a critical role in the Priestly account of Israel at Sinai.

104. The Priestly narrative refers (or alludes) to the land promise in Gen 17:8; 23:4, 9, 18, 20; 28:4; 31:12; 48:4; 49:30; 50:12; Exod 6:4, 8. Absent in all of these citations is reference to Israel "dwelling" *(yšb)* in the land. Rather, Israel is given the land as a possession (*'ăḥuzzâ* [Gen 17:8; 23:4, 9, 20; 48:4; 49:30; 50:12] *miqnâ* [Gen 23:18]; *môrāšâ* [Exod 6:8]). The language of dwelling *(škn)* is lodged exclusively in the divine realm (e.g., Exod 24:16; 25:8; 29:45-46; 40:35). This is all the more extraordinary, given that the Yahwist regularly uses *škn* to describe humans living off the land (e.g., Gen 9:27; 16:12; 26:2; 35:22a).

105. See Pola, *Die ursprüngliche Priesterschrift,* 275-81, 286-90, 337-38, who from this comparison argues that the ending of the original Priestly narrative (P^g) is to be found in Exod 29:45-46, followed by the short concluding report in 40:16-17a, 33b.

106. For the meaning of *škn,* "to tent, encamp," suggesting temporary residence, see S. D. McBride Jr., "The Deuteronomic Name Theology" (Ph.D. diss.; Harvard University, 1969) 204-10; F. M. Cross Jr., "The Priestly Tabernacle," in *BAR* 1:224-27. Within the semantic field of the Priestly layer, the verb takes on the more technical sense of "tabernacling" (Dozeman, *God on the Mountain,* 127-31), which, however, does not preclude the sense of abiding presence (so T. N. D. Mettinger, *The Dethronement of Sabaoth: Studies in the Shem and Kabod Theologies* [ConBot 18; Lund: Gleerup, 1982] 90-97).

Congregational Construction

Yahweh's instructions begin with a call for voluntary contributions (25:2-7; cf. 35:5-9, 29). The Israelites, particularly those "whose hearts prompt them to give," are exhorted to give offerings of various precious metals, yarns and linens, animal skins, acacia wood, oil, spices, and precious stones. Yahweh's earthly sanctuary is neither cheap nor carelessly slapped together, but rather constructed from quality materials, matched by God's care in cosmogony. Not fortuitously, the cosmic domains of creation are represented in the tabernacle's constituent elements: metals, stones, and wood from the earth, water for ritual washing from the bronze basin (30:17-21), and lamps to render perpetual light (25:31-38; 27:20-21).[107] From these raw materials, a "sanctuary" or holy place (*miqdāš*, v. 8) is to be built, along with all its furnishings, including the priestly vestments.

The construction is spearheaded by the appointed chief artisans Bezalel of Judah and Oholiab of Dan, from the southern- and northernmost tribes (31:1-11). With their appointment, equal representation and investment in the construction of the tabernacle is achieved in the Priestly blueprint. As for the donors themselves, they are "softhearted," generous and willing to release a portion of their possessions for the common goal, in contrast to Pharaoh's hardened heart.[108] The enlistment of generous Israelites is sharply contrasted with the treatment the immigrant Israelites received in Egypt, where they were conscripted into Pharaoh's monumental building projects (1:13-14). Mortar and bricks are the materials of oppression compared to the freewill offerings of colorful yarns and acacia wood.

The following instructions begin with the holiest furnishing, the ark (25:10-22), and progress to the tabernacle itself (26:1-36), concluding with instructions for the altar, the outer court, and the lamp (27:1-21). Subsequently, the instructions for the priestly garments are given, along with the stipulations for the priests' consecration and offerings (28:1-29:46). The supplemental instructions in 30:1-38 include such furnishings as the incense altar, the bronze basin of water for ritual washing, and recipes for anointing oil and incense. As the architectural purview moves outward from the ark to the outer court, from the center to the periphery, the use of gold gives way to silver and finally to bronze as the metals of choice, denoting a gradation of holiness.[109]

107. The diversity of materials becomes all the more striking when one compares the materials of the sanctuary with those of the Yahwist's altar (Exod 20:22-26), which is constructed of arable soil (*'ădāmâ*) or field stones.

108. See particularly the expression *nĕdîb lēb* ("generous heart") in 35:5, 22.

109. See Jenson, *Graded Holiness*, 101-3. For example, gold is used to overlay the ark

75

As in creation, the Priestly ethos is evinced in part in the construction of the tabernacle: it is a holy edifice typified by differentiation and connectedness (e.g., 26:24). Ten curtains are used to demarcate this portable complex symmetrically. Fifty clasps of gold effectively "join the curtains to one another, . . . so that the tabernacle may be one" ('*eḥād*, v. 6). Similarly, the eleven curtains of goats' hair used for a tent over the tabernacle are joined together into "one" (v. 11). Curtains serve as boundaries to demarcate particular domains of holiness, the holiest one enclosing the "ark of the testimony" (vv. 33-34). As with any tent, particularly of such intricate proportions, the overall framework is made possible only by the firm placement, anchoring, and joining of each individual segment. With the outer curtains protecting the inner sanctum, any tear or loose fixture threatens the tabernacle's structural integrity, a stability established by a series of interlocking, segmented domains. Like creation, the tabernacle is characterized by symmetry, interdependence, and differentiation. Its structural integrity is a holy integrity of substance, sight, and smell, of holy "weight" *(kābôd),* vibrant color, and overpowering incense, a sensual holiness.[110]

It is only appropriate that the divine commands for this framework of holiness conclude with the ordinance of the sabbath, which corresponds directly to the climax of the Priestly creation account (31:12-17; Gen 2:1-3). Leading up to the sanctification of rest is the ordinance of leadership, established by the appointment of Bezalel and Oholiab (Exod 31:1-11). Bezalel in particular is "filled with the Spirit of God" (*rûaḥ 'ĕlōhîm,* v. 3; cf. Gen 1:2). Bezalel, Oholiab, and all the workers are endowed with skill or wisdom (*ḥokmâ*) for constructing the sanctuary. The stage is now set for the work to

---

(25:11) and the table (v. 24) as well as to construct the lampstand (v. 31); the water basin is constructed out of bronze (30:17), which is also used to overlay the altar of acacia (27:2).

110. For the integration of the senses of touch, sight, and smell, see Jenson, *Graded Holiness,* 107-11. Little is said, however, about what was *heard* in the Priestly cult. Y. Kaufmann suggested, consequently, that "the priestly temple is the kingdom of silence" (*The Religion of Israel* [tr. and abridged by M. Greenberg; New York: Schocken, 1960] 303; see also 110, 304-5, 309). See I. Knohl's nuanced discussion of silence in relation to the sacrificial act in *The Sanctuary of Silence* (Minneapolis: Fortress, 1995) 148-52; idem, "Between Voice and Silence: The Relationship between Prayer and Temple Cult," *JBL* 115 (1996) 17-30. Knohl argues that, owing to the Priestly caution against personalizing the Deity, petitionary prayer and praise were in principle eschewed within the inner temple precincts. Regardless of the precise extent to which speech may have been limited in actual cultic practice, silence corresponds well to the absence of divine speech on the seventh day (Gen 2:1-3), a more compelling reason, in my opinion, than the general concern over divine anthropomorphism for which Knohl argues. Silence during the act of sacrifice captures, in effect, a "sabbatical" moment in worship.

be done. Yet along with the instructions for the work comes a final ordinance, the sabbath, institutionalized as "a perpetual covenant" *(bĕrît 'ôlām)* and "sign forever" *('ôt hî' lĕ'ôlām,* Exod 31:16-17), which also establishes a temporal boundary as well as a point of completion for the work (vv. 12-17; cf. 39:43). Only here do the Priestly tradents use the formal term "covenant" *(bĕrît)* in the tabernacle legislation, highlighting the sabbath as the culmination of a continuum of covenants, beginning with Noah (Gen 9:8-17; 17:1-14). Sabbath observance has left its mark in various forms, from the Festival of Unleavened Bread (Exod 12:16) to the consumption of wilderness manna (16:22-23). Yet its *covenantal* climax marks a return to the very beginning, to creation itself.

Observance of the sabbath is deliberately correlated with God's work in creation, culminating on the seventh day, in which Yahweh "rested and was refreshed" *(šābat wayyinnāpaš,* Exod 31:17; cf. 20:8-11; Gen 2:1-3). As Yahweh blessed and consecrated the last day, setting it apart from all others, so Yahweh will consecrate Israel in its observance of that day (Exod 31:13). So ends Yahweh's instructions to Moses, concluding with the submission of the "two tablets of the testimony *(hā'ēdut),* tablets of stone, written with the finger of God" (v. 18).[111] God's finger carries the weight of both invincible power, displayed in the plagues of judgment against Egypt (8:18), and absolute authority, codified in Israel's charter for its existence.[112]

The litany of instructions in 25:1–31:17 finds its counterpart in the detailed fulfillment report in 35:1–40:33. Although some of the material in the latter is arranged in a different order,[111] the correspondences between word account *(Wortbericht)* and deed account *(Tatbericht)* are obvious. Fulfillment begins when Moses assembles the congregation of Israel and calls for freewill

111. The content of the tablets from the Priestly perspective is a matter of debate, since nowhere are the tablets referred to as "covenant" *(bĕrît;* e.g., 16:34b) as in the Yahwist's account (e.g., Exod 34:28). It is most likely, however, that the Priestly redactors simply presuppose the covenantal legislation of the Decalogue, as documented in Exod 20:1-17, which also reflects Priestly influence (e.g., vv. 8-11). By eschewing explicitly covenantal *(brt)* references to the tablets, the Priestly author effectively highlights the covenantal significance of the sabbath (Exod 31:12-17), in the same way perhaps that the seventh day in creation shifts the highpoint of cosmogony from the genesis of humankind to sabbath rest. For the implications, see below.

112. It is no coincidence that the Priestly narrator chooses the term "testimony" *('ēdût),* rather than "covenant," in part to stress that the tablets are the sole property of and charter for the *'ēdâ,* the "congregation" of Israel.

113. For example, the report on the bronze basin's construction follows the construction of the altar (38:8), whereas its instruction forms part of the supplemental material (30:17-21).

offerings from those of a "generous heart" (35:5, 22).[114] The response is over-whelming. As a freewill offering *(nědābâ),* from gold earrings to fine linens, the people provide an overabundance of raw material (v. 29; 36:3-4). Women in particular are highlighted in their spinning of yarn and goats' hair (35:25-26). These willing members of the congregation, women and men, contribute a surplus of such abundance that the artisans complain to Moses of a burden-some excess of material (36:4-5), prompting Moses to issue a restraining or-der: "So the people were restrained from bringing" (v. 6).[115] In the people's stewardship lies a sabbatical restraint.

Even here, the Priestly emphasis on boundaries predominates, striking an almost humorous note. The people have gone beyond the bounds of suffi-ciency. Enough is enough! By going overboard in their giving, the congrega-tion requires a measure of control. Excess, even in giving, is considered prob-lematic. This building project is thus no burdensome exercise demanded by an earthly king, Egyptian or otherwise. The tabernacle is not a fiscal black hole, gobbling up the people's resources and energies. Neither is it a white ele-phant, remote from and irrelevant to the community. Like creation itself, the tabernacle is an investment of the community in toto for the community in excelsis.

With the boundaries of the sabbath and stewardship in place, the work begins. Bezalel is acknowledged, again, for being "filled with God's Spirit . . . to devise artistic designs" (35:31, 32; cf. 31:3-4). Such spiritual endowment is artistic in scope. Both this man of Judah and Oholiab of Dan are filled with the aesthetic know-how to bring the tabernacle to its completion. With the construction of the outer court, a "tally of the tabernacle" *(pěqûdê hammiškān,* 38:21-31) is taken that lists the amount, value, and allocation of the precious metals contributed, as well as a census count, which details the half-a-shekel offering per head as a "ransom" or "atonement" *(kōper,* v. 26; 30:12, 15). In short, the tally documents the involvement of the community as a whole. With the manufacture of the Priestly garments, the tabernacle is completed, the commandments fulfilled (39:32, 42-43; cf. Gen 2:1-3).[116] Mo-ses inspects all the parts, noting that their work was completed "just as Yahweh had commanded," and blesses them (Exod 39:43). Such blessing is akin to God's final approbation of Gen 1:31.

With all the parts completed, what remains is setting up the tabernacle

114. Cf. similar language in 1 Chr 29:6-9; Ezra 2:68-69.

115. The Samaritan Pentateuch reads the verb *klh* instead of MT *kl',* suggesting an even tighter correlation with the sabbath (see Gen 2:1-2).

116. For a list of other formulaic parallels, see J. Blenkinsopp, "The Structure of P," *CBQ* 38 (1976) 280-83.

and positioning its parts. The process is highlighted by a special series of divine commands to Moses, which are fulfilled on New Year's Day of the second year of their release from Egypt, marked by the Passover celebration (Exod 12:2). In addition to his role as cultic mediator, Moses assumes the role of director by arranging all the constituent parts in their proper order, from placing the testimony in the ark to setting up the outer court. "So Moses finished the work" (40:33b). The final result, indeed the aim, is the filling of the tabernacle with Yahweh's *kābôd* or "glory," making entrance impossible even for Moses (vv. 34-35). The tabernacle has become Yahweh's domain, filled and fulfilled with impenetrable holiness.

Sanctuary Movement

The tabernacle's completion in 40:34-35 recalls much of what prefaced its introduction on the mountain in 24:15b-18.[117] On both Sinai and sanctuary Yahweh's glory dwells (24:16a; 40:35). Yet a startling discrepancy is evident in these two accounts of divine tabernacling. Whereas on the mountain Moses entered the cloud of glory to receive instruction, he cannot enter the tent occupied by the effulgence of divine presence. The clue to this contrast is found in a technical Priestly term, whose roots go back to creation itself: Yahweh's presence has "filled" *(mālē')* the tabernacle domain. Twice this is mentioned in 40:34-35. Materially, Yahweh's presence in the tent is of such concentration that human encroachment is impossible. The tent is filled impenetrably. Theologically, this domain of divine habitation is claimed as *Yahweh's own* for dwelling, like the differentiated domains of life in Genesis 1. The filling of a domain also entails its reclamation. Moreover, the divine glory that fills the tabernacle, comparable to the variety of life-forms that fill their respective domains in creation, is characterized by mobility. The tabernacle is God's home among a people homeward bound.

Israel at Sinai is the founding event that sets the stage for the transference of Yahweh's glory from mountain to sanctuary.[118] More than merely continuing what happened at Sinai,[119] the tabernacle *facilitates* Yahweh's glory in Israel's midst. The divine presence is preserved and routinized as it becomes efficacious on Israel's behalf. Like the temporal structure of cre-

---

117. See Dozeman, *God on the Mountain*, 130n.107, whose biblical citations are misnumbered. In his aim to contrast *škn* and *'lh*, Dozeman misses a more crucial contrast between these two accounts of divine indwelling (see below).

118. See also D. E. Gowan, *Theology in Exodus: Biblical Theology in the Form of a Commentary* (Louisville: Westminster John Knox, 1994) 183.

119. Contra Childs, *Exodus*, 540.

ation, divine activity finds its own, albeit variable, rhythm in relation to Israel's plight.[120] Indeed, the exigencies of the wilderness situation demand it, as made clear in the concluding account of the choreographed movement between Israel and its God (Exod 40:36-38). To be sure, Yahweh is by no means confined within the tabernacle; the cloud of glory ascends from the tabernacle at certain intervals. Yet this is no case of divine judgment, but merely a signal for the children of Israel to embark on another leg of their journey.[121]

The ascending and descending movement of divine glory dictates the itineration of a sojourning people, of Israel's work in the wilderness. Yahweh's departure from the tabernacle is no more a case of abandonment than Israel's departure is a matter of flight. The variable rhythm of divine movement transforms a painful trek through a wilderness of danger into a liturgical journey, a worshipful "work of the people." More specifically, Yahweh's tabernacling presence occasions Israel's rest in the wilderness. The rhythm of work and rest continues from both the divine and human sides. In short, the tabernacle is the domain of Yahweh's repose with Israel, as the "cloud continued over the tabernacle, resting on it" (Num 9:22). Signifying the sacramental and authoritative presence of God, the fire on Sinai has become the fire in the sanctuary.

This conclusive account of Israel's departure from Sinai sheds light on the nature of Yahweh's "dwelling" in the tabernacle. Much of the discussion surrounding this technical term has revolved around the issue of permanent versus temporary residence in the community.[122] Within the Priestly purview, however, the issue is not charged with the kind of metaphysical controversy modern scholars have made it out to be. By subsuming the old "tent of meeting" tradition[123] under the rubric of divine "dwelling" *(škn)*, the Priestly tradents forge a synthesis of divine action that is meant to give assurance of

---

120. See also Num 9:14-23, which refers to various lengths of time when the cloud was upon the tabernacle, "resting upon it" (v. 22).

121. It is precisely here that Dozeman's contention that the tabernacling presence of divine glory amounts to a critique of a temple theology breaks down. The dynamic movement of God's presence in relation to Israel's itineration in the wilderness, as well as at Mount Sinai, is literarily a necessary one meant to *assure* Israel of Yahweh's commitment and work rather than to attack any presumption of divine residence in the temple.

122. Two extremes are represented by Dozeman, *God on the Mountain,* 126-41; and Jenson, *Graded Holiness,* 112-14. The latter refers to the "permanent dwelling of God" in the tabernacle, whereas the former sees only transient residence. See also n. 106.

123. See Exod 25:22; 29:42-43. In both passages, the purpose of divine encounter is to speak or issue commands to a human audience, be it Moses or Israel.

Yahweh's continuing yet freely extended presence for the community — in short, God's covenantal commitment to Israel.

In 29:42-46 the language slides effortlessly from Yahweh's meeting "to speak" and to consecrate the tent and the altar (vv. 42-43) to Yahweh's dwelling to be "their God," prompting acknowledgment of Yahweh's pledge (vv. 45-46). Yahweh's dwelling with Israel is no more open to question than Yahweh's covenantal relationship to Israel is in doubt. All references to Yahweh's leave of the desert sanctuary are without critical force. Divine departure in the wilderness attests to the divine resolve to lead on Israel's behalf: "Whenever the cloud lifted from over the tent, the Israelites would set out; and in the place where the cloud settled down, there the Israelites would camp" (Num 9:17). Again, Yahweh's intermittent departures in no way imply a temporary residency. Quite the contrary, it is the *departure* that is deemed temporary, not Yahweh's dwelling. Yahweh's presence is kept firmly in view throughout Israel's journey. The cloud of glory never dissipates.

Nonetheless, to say that Yahweh's residence in the tabernacle is permanent is also a misreading, as if the cloud of glory were something *contained* in the tabernacle. Yahweh's "dwelling" *(škn)* is of a different nature from human habitation on the land *(yšb)*.[124] The Deity's relation to the tabernacle is a dynamic one, a mobile presence continually on the way, but never severed from the community, which follows Yahweh's lead (Num 9:20). To suggest that the Priestly notion of "dwelling" *(škn)* signifies the "tenuous character of divine presence" is itself tenuous.[125] There is nothing questionable about Yahweh's pledge to dwell with Israel in the wilderness or in any other context within the Priestly narrative. Yahweh's tabernacling presence with Israel connotes assurance without containment and mobility without the threat of abandonment. More broadly, it provides an assurance of accessibility to the Deity through the preservation and maintenance of the cult. As the tangible testimony of the cult, the tabernacle bears witness to Yahweh's commitment to a particular people. Indeed, the tabernacle houses just such a testimony, the two tablets (Exod 31:18; 16:34b). Whether permanent or impermanent residence, the tabernacle is unquestionably Yahweh's own as much as the community is Yahweh's people. By filling the tabernacle with the cloud of glory, the tabernacle has become Yahweh's personal property, a testimony to consecrated ownership.

124. Childs, *Exodus*, 540. But the fact that the Yahwist also uses *škn* to denote human habitation nuances this contrast.

125. Quotation from Klein, "Back to the Future," 271. Yet Klein goes on to talk of "permanence and stability" in relation to 40:34-35 (p. 272).

Yahweh's tabernacling with Israel matches Israel's tenting in the wilderness, an existence marked by mobility and accompaniment, which is in fact highly irregular (Num 9:20-22). "Whether two days, a month, or a longer time," the cloud and the camp would remain encamped before setting out. Such mobility reflects a temporal indeterminacy, for one would expect an established rhythm of six days on the road and a seventh-day encampment. Such is not the case, however, for the wilderness journey is, as in the Yahwist's landscape, a liminal one. The Priestly itinerary establishes spatial liminality from a distinctly *temporal* standpoint; an itineration of irregular intervals of rest and departure marks an interim period that points to the day when Israel can settle permanently in the land and Yahweh can find permanency in rest.

Divine dwelling from the (exilic) priestly perspective does not so much point backward in categorical judgment against Solomon's former temple as anticipate a new era in which a new and permanent edifice, superseding the former, provides the locus of rest for Israel and its God. Yahweh's tabernacling presence does not disqualify or even qualify the hope for permanent residence, divine or human. Yahweh's *kābôd* is in the end neither a free-floating, unpredictable vehicle of divine presence nor a static, inert substance, contained by the work of human hands. Yahweh's glory "dwelling" with a people is a palpable testimony of the divine freedom to *fulfill* the covenantal obligation to be Israel's God by *filling* the domain of the testimony (Exod 29:45; 40:34-35). Itself the replica of a divine model, the tabernacle is the model for new life and hope that exceeds the contingencies of a liminal landscape.

The Stewardship of Creation and Tabernacle

In addition to the *inclusio* between Sinai and sanctuary, the tabernacle account establishes a larger theological envelope within the sweep of the Priestly narrative. Many have noted certain similarities between the tabernacle and creation, suggesting that the completion of the tabernacle represents the climax and goal of Priestly historiography.[126] Whether or not the ending of an original Priestly narrative is to be found at the conclusion of the book of Exodus, a profoundly theological correspondence is established. Indeed, the

126. For example, Levenson, *Creation*, 83; B. Janowski, "Tempel und Schöpfung: Schöpfungstheologische Aspekte der priesterschriftlichen Heiligtumskonzeption," in *Schöpfung und Neuschöpfung* (ed. I. Baldermann et al.; JBT 5; Neukirchen-Vluyn: Neukirchener, 1990) 37-70; P. Weimar, "Sinai und Schöpfung: Komposition und Theologie der priesterschriftliche Sinaigeschichte," *RB* 95 (1988) 337-85; Brown, *Structure*, 208-14; Elnes, "Creation and Tabernacle," 148-52; Pola, *Die ursprüngliche Priesterschrift*, esp. 325-27.

construction of the tabernacle reveals much about the Priestly ethos of creation and vice versa.

Like creation itself, the process is in part the message. As creation was fashioned and unfolded systematically, so the tabernacle is constructed with great precision and care. Varying levels of creative agency are evident in the parallel accounts of creation and construction. In the cosmogony, the hierarchy of creative activity can be described in the following outline:

1. God: creator, command giver, inspector, blesser
2. Earth and waters: collaborative agents
3. Products:
   a. Light, firmament, luminaries, vegetation
   b. Life: animals and human beings[127]

In the Priestly cosmogony, the created order remains a creating order. Animals and humans are commanded to procreate and fill the domains; other objects of creation, though devoid of life *(nepeš)*, maintain certain established functions.

The breakdown of creative agency in the tabernacle's construction is more complex. Although never directly involved in actual construction, Yahweh remains at the head of the hierarchy of construction by maintaining the role of command giver. What Yahweh does create is a visual model or *tabnît* of the tabernacle. The constructive role is given to Bezalel and Oholiab, as well as those Israelites skilled in various forms of artistry. In varying degrees, these three agents take on the role of fulfilling the commands, issued by Yahweh and delivered by Moses. Bezalel in particular is endowed with the "Spirit of God," and therefore shares something in common functionally with the divine agent of creation (Gen 1:2). Indeed, his most common task is to "make" (*ʿśh*). Moses, too, as the deliverer of Yahweh's commands, assumes a partly "divine" role, especially as the one who "sees" the completed work and blesses the workers (Exod 39:43). In addition, Moses positions the constituent parts in their proper arrangement to set up the sanctuary. Finally, those Israelites of a "generous heart" are involved in the creative process, from weaving to setting stones. The levels of creative agency can be outlined as follows:

1. Yahweh: command giver and *tabnît* creator
2. Moses: command deliverer, inspector, blesser, arranger
3. Bezalel: creator, supervisor (along with Oholiab)

127. The outlines and discussion are adapted from Brown, *Structure*, 212-14.

4. Israelites: collaborative agents
5. Products:
   a. Tabernacle and its furnishings
   b. Dwelling place for Yahweh's glory

Like the earth and the waters, the Israelites as a whole are cast in the role of collaborative cocreators in the tabernacle's construction. In addition, Moses and Bezalel distinctively share in Yahweh's composite role evinced in creation, namely, of delivering and fulfilling commands, as well as beholding and blessing the product.

The result in both cases is a "form-filledness." In its proper arrangement and divisions, the tabernacle establishes a series of domains: the holy of holies (*qōdeš haqqŏdāšîm,* Exod 26:33), the holy place (*haqqōdeš,* 6:33; 29:30), and the court (*heḥāṣēr,* 27:9-19), which is also, in part at least, a "holy place" (*māqōm qādōš,* Exod 29:31), all together making up the "sanctuary" *(miqdāš)* or "tabernacle" *(miškān,* 25:8; 40:34).[128] Like creation, the tabernacle is structured by segmented form.[129] With its rich color, texture, and differentiated space, the tabernacle's formfulness, like creation's, points to a holistic vision of goodness, a structural and functional integrity. The sanctuary is a microcosm, "a world . . . ordered, supportive, and obedient."[130]

Inhabited by both God and the representatives of the congregation, the tabernacle is a cross-cultural domain. Human traffic in certain areas within the sanctuary is necessary in order to carry out the tabernacle's cultic func-

128. For a diagram and further explanation, see Jenson, *Graded Holiness,* 90-91.
129. Indeed, some coherence is evident between the differentiated character of the tabernacle, relative to its central location in the camp, and that of creation in its temporal and spatial order. From the central to the most peripheral domains, one can discern certain correspondences:

Creation	Tabernacle
sabbath	holy of holies
land	holy place
waters	court
celestial sphere	camp
"chaos"	wilderness

Although the degree of correspondence varies between each domain, evident is a marked progression from the crucial importance of holiness/sabbath and land/"holy place" to the more remote domains, concluding with those of "chaos" and wilderness, to which, not coincidentally, the "scapegoat" of the Day of Atonement service is sent (Lev 16:21-22; see below).
130. Levenson, *Creation,* 86.

tions. As inhabitants of sacred space, the priests bear a special role, which is underscored by the careful attention given to their garments (28:1-43; 39:1-31), as well as to their consecration (29:1-37; Lev 8:1-36). Their intimate relationship to holiness is evinced in their seven-day ordination period (Lev 8:33), similar to the seven-day atonement process for the altar's consecration (Exod 29:37). Laypeople, too, play a role in the sanctuary by presenting sacrifices for slaughter (e.g., Lev 1:1-17), yet are restricted to the court.

Human movement, including that of the priests, is carefully circumscribed within the sacred precincts. Free movement is reserved only for Yahweh's glory, which literally "fills" the sanctuary (40:34-35). Borrowing from the language of creation, this filling of cultic form generates life in this domain, without which the tabernacle would be an empty shell.[131] In addition, the filling of the tabernacle with Yahweh's glory signals the consummation of divine blessing. With the tabernacle serving as a holy reactor, glory is, as it were, the radioactive substance that generates blessing for all the people.[132] By whatever analogy, Yahweh's glory, lodged in the center of the camp, is the sine qua non of cultic existence.

The timing of divine dwelling is wholly intentional, for it transpires only after Moses has given his blessing (39:43) and completed his work (40:33b). From a temporal standpoint, the settling of Yahweh's effulgence corresponds in no small measure to the rest that commences after creation's completion (Gen 2:1-3). Thus Yahweh's dwelling (šākan) with Israel connotes a sense of repose within the larger Priestly narrative. As miškān, the tabernacle serves as the repository of divine glory. In the narrative sweep of the Priestly historiography, šākan is the spatial analogue to the temporal šabbāt. Together, they invest the Priestly ethos with rich, multidimensional significance. From a literary standpoint, climax is equated with center. As the day of rest represents the culmination of creation, Yahweh's habitation in the tabernacle establishes itself as the center of Israel's existence, represented by the camp that surrounds the tabernacle on all sides (Num 2:2-34). In conjunction with the creation story, Yahweh's dwelling with Israel takes on a measure of holy poignancy. With the completion of the tabernacle, Yahweh has finally come home to a particular people. Compared to the cosmogony of Genesis, the tabernacle account depicts the genesis of Yahweh's dwelling among a people, a holy ecology.

131. The only other instance in which the verb ml' ("fill") is employed in the tabernacle account to refer to divine "filling" is in connection with Bezalel's creative talents, which are the result of being filled with God's Spirit (rûaḥ 'ĕlōhîm; 31:5; 35:31, 33, 35 [with Oholiab]).

132. Cf. Gen 1:22, 28; Exod 39:43; Lev 9:22-23; Num 6:22-27.

As much as the tabernacle can be read in parallel with creation, so the former informs the latter and vice versa. Both share a common ethos. Similar to the construction of the tabernacle account, the Priestly cosmogony is an eminently *social* phenomenon, the grand result of careful and collaborative work between God and the elements or active domains, an enlistment and harnessing of latent cosmic powers called forth and ordained. As those generous of heart were beckoned to contribute to the tabernacle's construction, so the elements of creation are summoned to contribute to the ongoing process of cosmogony. One can thus speak of a "stewardship of creation," one that is by no means confined to humankind's ecological role. God's creation is as much the result of creation's stewardship as the tabernacle is the product of Israel's generous giving. The Priestly purview finds social and cosmic stewardship to be essential in reaching completion. God does not create ex nihilo any more than the tabernacle is created out of thin air by divine command. Constructive agents and forces are ordained and incorporated into the divine plan in both cases. This process of planned giving, as it were, bespeaks a rich and intricately complex vision of the world. The Priestly worldview treats the cosmos as a commonwealth, a federation of differentiated powers organized and harnessed for the common goal of life, be they natural or supernatural.

Creation governed by differentiation and cooperation establishes a cosmic cohesion that serves as the repository of life, but not for God's presence. Life, animal and human, is commissioned to fill the earth; God's effulgence, whether as cloud or fire, does not fill anything in cosmogony. It is reserved for another place, although its time was scheduled from the beginning as sabbath. As God has a word and a hand in the formation of creation, distance remains between divine transcendence and the created order. The bridge that connects cosmos and divinity is itself a relational concept: covenant. The observance of the sabbath "as a perpetual covenant" (Exod 31:16) concludes the series of tabernacle instructions and thus finds its parallel with Yahweh's tabernacling presence (40:34-38), which marks the fulfillment of the instructions. In the tabernacle, sabbath rest and divine dwelling embrace, and Yahweh has found a home in creation with a particular people. Yet that home is already temporally defined in cosmic creation: God rested on the seventh day (Gen 2:1-3; Exod 31:17). In sum, God's rest is given space in the tabernacle.

The sabbath is also given prescriptive force in the tabernacle account: "everyone who profanes it shall be put to death" (31:14b).[133] This is the first instance in the Priestly narrative in which the technical term "profane" or

---

133. For an examination of the sabbath injunction in Exod 31:13-17, see below.

"defile" *(ḥll)* is employed.[134] As a violation of holiness, profanation is the antithesis to sanctification. It is also the first time in the Priestly series of covenants that holiness is introduced. Whereas the Noachic covenant and its sign marked God's assurance never again to consign creation to destruction (Gen 9:9-15), and whereas the Abrahamic covenant and sign marked God's promise to establish a viable cultural domain for the patriarch's progeny and to be their God (17:4-8, 10), the sabbath covenant fills the particular cultural domain, Israel, with holiness (Exod 31:13b). Holiness is the pinnacle of the Priestly ethos. Whereas the Sinai instructions prescribe various means, from anointing oil to sin offering, for the consecration of the tabernacle, its furnishings, and its priests,[135] it is the covenantal observance of the sabbath that consecrates the people as a whole. As much as holiness is a matter of divine initiative, so is it also a matter of human observance: "Remember the sabbath day to keep it holy" *(lĕqaddĕšô,* lit. "to sanctify it"; Exod 20:8).[136] In all of these Priestly passages, God's rest on the seventh day explodes with emulative power: the sabbath is Israel's *imitatio Dei,* its cardinal virtue.

God's rest on the seventh day thus becomes a holy commission for Israel equal to the "great commission" of Gen 1:28. Work and rest, rule and release find a constructive equilibrium in Israel's vocation, as they have in God's creation of the cosmos. Indeed, the covenantal nature of the sabbath rest imbues all creation with covenantal nuance. Julius Wellhausen discerned a covenantal dimension to the Priestly cosmogony, but mistakenly identified it with the declaration of blessing in 1:28-30.[137] Yet he suggestively included within this alleged covenant the consummation of creation on the seventh day (2:1-3), which serves as a precursor to the covenant in Exod 31:12-17. In-

---

134. The term is otherwise found exclusively in the so-called Holiness Code of Priestly law: Lev 18:27; 19:8; 19:12, 29; 20:3; 21:6, 9, 21, 15, 23; 22:2, 9, 15, 32.

135. Aaron and his sons are consecrated through anointing to serve as priests (28:3, 41; 29:1, 33); the altar is consecrated through a sin offering (29:36-37); anointing oil is used for consecrating the tent and the ark, along with its furnishings and the priests (30:26-30; 40:9-15); divine agency is, of course, fundamentally instrumental for consecrating the tent of meeting, the altar, and Aaron and his sons (29:44).

136. See also Gammie, *Holiness in Israel,* 21-22.

137. Consequently, Wellhausen labeled the Priestly narrative as Q *(quatuor).* See J. Wellhausen, "Die Composition des Hexateuchs," *Jahrbücher für Deutsche Theologie* 21 (1876) 392 [repr. in *Die Composition des Hexateuchs und der historischen Bücher des Alten Testaments* [4th ed.; Berlin: de Gruyter, 1963] 1); idem, *Prolegomena,* 338-39, 385. Wellhausen included all of Gen 1:28–2:4 under "the covenant of Adam" (*Prolegomena,* 338) not simply the blessing, for which he has been routinely criticized. By regarding the sabbath as the "first sign" of the covenant, in parallel with Exod 31:12, Wellhausen accurately noted an intentional theological *inclusio* in the Priestly narrative.

deed, the entire sequence of seven days, culminating in the last, is referred to as a "sign forever" (*'ôt*, v. 17; cf. v. 15), whose purpose is Israel's sanctification (v. 13). The sabbath rest marks a communion of holiness, and sanctification is found in the refreshment. In the Yahwist's anthropogony, the primordial garden is the shalom before the "blessing." In the Priestly cosmogony, the seventh day marks the consecration before the covenant. The sabbath lies at the heart of the Priestly ethos.

In addition to informing each other, creation and tabernacle form perhaps the bookends of an original Priestly layer of Israel's formation,[138] or at least a magisterial *inclusio* that imbues everything within its narrative bounds with cosmic and cultic significance. Within this body of narrative material, three construction projects are referenced in the Priestly narrative: creation (Gen 1:1–2:3), mortar and brick service (Exod 1:13-14), and the tabernacle (35:1–40:38). It is the middle building project, distinctive in its terseness, that bears a markedly antithetical tone.[139] The corvée in Egypt is an exercise in ruthless imposition (*běperek*, 1:13-14), making the Israelites' lives "bitter" (*mrr*; cf. Gen 26:35; 27:46). But more telling is what is absent in the account. Lacking is the command-fulfillment correspondence. Nowhere is there the summons for voluntary contributions and the free exercise of naturally endowed talents. The work is severe, not fulfilling. Rest from labor is nowhere to be found. Oppressive work with brick and mortar is the ultimate foil for the aesthetic beauty and moral goodness that characterize the construction of both *kosmos* and *oikos,* creation and divine dwelling. The sabbath as *imitatio Dei* is also *liberatio hominis.*

With creation and tabernacle, divine rest and dwelling, bracketing this nadir in Israel's history, oppression in Egypt takes on added offense: it is both anticreational and antivocational in nature. Israel's vocation is to worship the tabernacling God, not construct monuments for an oppressive tyrant. In turn, the exodus or release from captivity bears an ultimate aim that is thoroughly creative in scope: that Yahweh may "tabernacle" or repose among the Israelites to be their God (Exod 29:45-46). Consequently, the aim of the exodus is to release Israel *from* oppressive labor *for* creative rest. Bound up with this holy rest is the acknowledgment of Yahweh as Israel's God (v. 46; 6:7). Indeed, such acknowledgment is well-nigh impossible in a situation characterized by unrelenting labor (6:9). While, from a general standpoint, leisure may be the cradle of culture, within the Priestly

---

138. So Pola, *Die ursprüngliche Priesterschrift,* 275-81, 286-90, 337-38.

139. See also Lohfink, "God the Creator," 132-33. Although not a product of the Priestly hand, the Babel project of Gen 11:1-10 is also an antitype. See Chapter 3.

ethos Sabbath rest is the basis for sanctity, Israel's cultic identity (19:5-6; 29:46; 31:13-17).

As divine repose is the expressed goal of the exodus (29:46), so Israel is to fulfill its destiny as a consecrated people by constructing the tabernacle and embodying the sanctified sabbath. The historical sweep of God's economy and the cosmic sweep of creative stewardship all lead to this unified goal in the Priestly narrative: the intersection of Yahweh's dwelling (25:8; 29:45-46) and Israel's habitation in the land (6:8), bound together in the sabbath observance. Whereas creation is called "good," rest is deemed "holy," the completion of goodness. Israel's release from burdensome work and Israel's creation of the tabernacle is ultimately for rest, both divine and human, the context of divine and human communion. The sabbath marks both the fulfillment of constructive work and the liberation from relentless labor. Sabbath is the goal of Israel's exodus, as it is for creation, a holy restoration.

Cult and Culture, Holiness and Goodness

With the cultic apparatus now in place, fashioned and properly arranged, making possible the habitation of God's glory in Israel's midst, proper arrangement and placement of the community naturally follow. With God's commanding presence now residing in the sanctuary, Israel becomes differentiated in a way that preserves an ethos of interdependence between God and the community. Like creation, the community is characterized by boundness and boundedness in relation to its creator.

Before the congregation can depart from Sinai to journey toward the land granted by Yahweh, the community is arranged according to tribe around the tabernacle in preparation for the trip. The tribe of Levi in particular is set apart or separated (bdl)[140] and appointed over the tabernacle (Num 1:50). By encircling the sanctuary, the Levites ensure a degree of separation between the community and the tabernacle, the community's center (2:17). As defined by the space they inhabit in relation to the sanctuary, their cultic role is twofold. On the one hand, their arrangement prevents divine wrath or plague from spreading out from the tabernacle and devastating the community in the case of desecration (1:53a; 8:19). On the other hand, as "guardians of the tabernacle of Yahweh," the Levites protect the sanctuary from encroachers (1:53b; 8:19).[141]

---

140. Num 8:14; cf. Gen 1:4, 6.

141. See J. Milgrom, "Encroaching on the Sacred: Purity and Polity in Numbers 1–10," Int 51 (1997) 243-44.

Thus the Levites act as a buffer for both sides, for God's holy presence and the common community. In addition, the Levites assume the special role of tending to the tabernacle by dismantling, carrying, and resetting it during Israel's journey (1:49-51).[142]

Of the Levites, the Kohathites are assigned a particularly holy role. They are to handle the most holy furnishings of the tabernacle, from the ark to the altars (3:31; 4:2). Consequently, theirs is a most dangerous business, for if they do not follow Aaron's lead when approaching the holy furnishings, they will die (4:17-20). Indeed, they are to handle the holy things only in transit, covering them with leather and blue cloth, without ever touching them directly (v. 15). As a whole, the Levites' vocation reflects the distinctive status of being Yahweh's personal property:

> I hereby take the Levites from among the Israelites as substitutes for all the firstborn that open the womb among the Israelites. The Levites belong to me. Indeed, all the firstborn are mine. When I killed all the firstborn in the land of Egypt, I consecrated for my own all the firstborn in Israel, both human and animal. To me they belong. I am Yahweh (3:12-13).[143]

In language reminiscent of the Priestly redaction of Exod 19:5b-6 regarding Israel's distinction from the nations in the land, the Levites are singled out as belonging to Yahweh, "unreservedly given" *(nĕtûnîm nĕtûnîm)* to Aaron and his sons (Num 3:9; 8:16).[144] They constitute a holy tribe of priests and sanctuary servants (3:1-10; Exod 6:16-20) in the same way Israel is a holy nation and kingdom of priests (19:6). As substitutionary representatives of the firstborn, each bears the mark of consecrated ownership. Yet the Levites are not completely severed from the larger community. They are a tribe among tribes, as Israel is a nation among other nations. Although the Levites are of a special class, assuming the unique role of ministering in Yahweh's dwelling,

---

142. Gammie suggests, uniquely, that the portable nature of the tabernacle might reflect an itinerant practice among the priests who ministered to the Israelites in exile (*Holiness in Israel*, 17n.13) a practice that, if true, would also include a Levitical role. Coote and Ord suggest that this practice was at least current in Palestine during the early postexilic period prior to the construction of the temple in 520-515 BCE (*In the Beginning*, 101).

143. See also 8:14-18; 3:45.

144. Diachronically, it is plausible that the Priestly redaction of Exod 19:5b-6 was drawn in part from the linguistic pattern that describes the Levites' consecrated status vis-à-vis the firstborn in Num 3:12-13 and related material. If so, the Priestly redaction of Exod 19:5b-6 suggests typologically that the Levitical tribe, in relation to Israel, serves as a model for all Israel in relation to the nations.

their service in the tent is also a service to the larger community in that they spare Israel from dedicating their firstborn in a consecration of death, whose precedent is found in the final plague in Egypt (Num 8:17; Exod 12:12-13).

Progenitally, the Levites remove certain obstacles from Israel's fulfilment of the universal commission to increase and fill the land (Gen 1:28).[145] Cultically, they serve to maintain the integrity of the sanctuary in its sojourn with Israel in the wilderness. Ethically, they serve as a paradigm of Israel's communion with God. The Levites constitute the liminal link between the holy priests and tabernacle furnishings, on the one hand, and the common folk, on the other. Their ministry is one of meticulous care and caution in sacred matters. The Levites are as much a grant to the community as they are a gift to Aaron and his sons (Num 8:19), for they help to maintain Yahweh's holy presence among a people. In short, the Levites are *bound* to the holy and the profane as much as they preserve the *bounds* of sacred space. They fail on both counts in the ensuing narrative.

Land and Liminality

With the cult fully established and the camp arranged around it, God's dwelling is finally accounted for and the issue of the land, last referenced in Yahweh's promise to Moses in Exod 6:8, returns to the fore. As the cloud lifts from the tabernacle, Israel sets out by stages, albeit irregular ones, from Sinai to Paran, while the Levites carry the dismantled sanctuary (Num 10:11-12, 17, 21). In the wilderness of Paran, Moses sends out tribal representatives to spy out the land that Yahweh is "giving to the Israelites" (13:2). Their mission is to inspect the land, but rather than beholding its goodness, they assess the land as categorically bad, both the terrain and its inhabitants, "a land that devours (*'ereṣ 'ōkelet*) its inhabitants" (v. 32).

The unfavorable report is ironically fitting within the Priestly purview. The clash of majority and minority reports discloses the Priestly stance toward the myth of chaos. Instead of expressing visual approbation, as God once esteemed creation,[146] most of the spies view the land as uninhabitable

145. As substitutes for the firstborn (3:12-13; 8:16-19) the Levites help to eliminate the need for sacrificing the firstborn male child in ancient Israel, while also transforming its significance. See J. D. Levenson, *The Death and Resurrection of the Beloved Son: The Transformation of Child Sacrifice in Judaism and Christianity* (New Haven: Yale University Press, 1993) 43-48.

146. In each case, sight and approval correspond in God's good creation: Gen 1:4, 10, 12, 18, 21, 25, 31.

for Israel. The formidable land is, like the wilderness,[147] unsuitable for settlement. The language employed in the report is especially telling: the spies liken the land to a voracious monster.[148] They have illicitly mythologized the land out of fear of the inhabitants' strength, claiming it to be unfit for, indeed a menace to, Israel's habitation, thus contravening God's primordial assessment of the land in its productive goodness (Gen 1:10, 12).

The contrast could not be starker between the spies' indictment of the land and the approbation given by Joshua and Caleb: "the land . . . is an exceedingly good land" (Num 14:7; cf. Gen 1:31).[149] Even the land's giant inhabitants "are no more than bread for us" (Num 14:9), recalling God's granting of the produce of the land to humankind (Gen 1:29). Violent subjugation is not even in the equation of occupation: "[Yahweh] will bring us into this land and give it to us, a land that flows with milk and honey" (Num 14:8).[150] The land of Canaan is deemed a good provider in every way for Israel; it is both *good* and *given* within the Priestly sphere of promise.

The spies' unfavorable report, however, contradicts these two dimensions. Their assessment of the land is exposed by Joshua's and Caleb's dissenting opinion merely as a monstrous mirage. The conflicting reports hinge completely on how the land is perceived. Within the larger scope of the Priestly worldview, the conflicting reports over the land reveals the Chaoskampf "myth" to be nothing more than a projection of fear — indeed, a failure of nerve. As in creation, chaos has no place in a land esteemed good. The goodness and "givenness" that pervade creation and Canaan's land effectively banish such fanciful flights of fear. Goodness necessitates trust in divine beneficence. The only alternatives are fear and rebellion (v. 9). Indeed, the spies' assessment hints at apostasy: the land's alleged appetite resonates with the holy fire that consumes all encroachers and apostates who would intrude upon God's domain (16:35; Lev 10:2). By refusing to enter the land, Israel has defiled its holy destiny. God's ensuing judgment suggests that such profanation can only be extirpated

147. Cf. Num 14:29, 32; Exod 14:3.

148. Lohfink notes that the spies describe the land essentially as an "earth-monster" ("Strata," 203), although such an image refers primarily to the imminent prospect of being defeated militarily by the land's inhabitants (14:3). Nonetheless, I would contend, more sharply, that the spies' unfavorable report aptly serves the Priestly polemic against *Chaoskampf,* as also evinced in Genesis 1. The minority report concerning the goodness of the land discloses all fears, socially based and mythologically construed, as wholly unfounded.

149. Heb. *ṭôbâ hā'āreṣ mě'ōd mě'ōd* (Num 14:7); *hinnēh-ṭôb mě'ōd* (Gen 1:31).

150. Absent in the language is any hint of war and victory. Cf. the Yahwist's version, which comes from the lips of Caleb in Num 13:30: "Let us go up at once and occupy it, for we are well able to overcome it" (*yākōl nûkal lāh;* cf. v. 31).

by the passing away of a whole generation, of those whose unfounded fear that their children would be taken as booty is inverted. Rather than be taken captive, their children are to occupy the land (Num 14:3, 31).

Following the crisis of the land is a crisis of the cult, provoked by Korah's rebellion in Numbers 16.[151] As the spies' report represents a failure of nerve to appropriate the goodness of the land, Korah's revolt represents a failure to revere the established boundaries of holiness. His company's complaint is that *all* Israel is holy,[152] that holiness is diffused (or diffusable) throughout the whole congregation, thereby dismantling all justification of a priestly oligarchy: "So why then do you exalt yourselves above the assembly of Yahweh?" The dispute over holiness reflects a contention over leadership (see 4:19-20). By his words, Korah, a Kohathite, seeks a community without distinction, a priesthood of all Israelites. Moses' rebuttal, however, equates the issue of democratized holiness with the chaos of sacrilege, which erases all social distinctions between the holy and the common. For Moses and Aaron, a distinction between who is holy and who is not is fundamental for the cultic community, for not everyone is "allowed to approach" Yahweh (16:5). For Israel's leaders, to democratize holiness is to desacralize it. The irony is that the Levites are allowed to approach, but in their complaint they "seek the priesthood as well" (v. 10). Moses charges Korah with duplicity and offers a test: he commands Korah and his cohorts to take up incense censers or firepans *(maḥtôt)*, which are reserved only for Aaron and his sons,[153] and to await a divine decision.

Soon enough, Korah and his assembly are separated from the congregation, not to enjoy the priestly prerogatives they sought but to be consumed by divine fire, a fitting fate for the mishandlers of fire (v. 35; cf. Lev 10:1-2).[154] In

151. As M. Noth correctly observed, "the Korah story is quite incongruously mixed up with the Dathan-Abiram story," the latter coming from the Yahwist's hand (*Numbers* [tr. J. D. Martin; OTL; Philadelphia: Westminster, 1968] 127-28).

152. Knohl suggests that the language of the complaint resembles the divine directive of holiness of the Holiness School, as found in 15:40 (*Sanctuary of Silence*, 81, 191-92; cf. 183n.43). In every cited case, however, a crucial difference is evident: the Holiness School views Israel's holiness as a goal — hence the use of the *waw*-consecutive or imperfect form of *hyh* — and not as a given, which Korah's company seems to presume. Korah's complaint bears more resemblance, theologically, to the Deuteronomic view of holiness as a property of the community (e.g., Deut 7:6; 14:2, 21). Although Knohl views this episode as a product of the Holiness School, not of the Priestly torah, Num 16:5-11 likely reflects rivalry over the Deuteronomic view of holiness, promulgated by the Levites.

153. Verse 17; see 16:40 (MT 17:4); 4:14-15; Lev 16:12; 1 Chr 6:49; 2 Chr 26:16-21; cf. Lev 10:1-2.

154. The reference to the earthquake in v. 32 originally applied to Dathan and Abiram in the Yahwist's narrative, not to Korah and his company, as found in the Priestly narrative.

their quest to desacralize holiness, Korah and his crew become the unwitting means for consecrating the censers, which constitute the altar's covering as a "sign" and "reminder" (*'ôt, zikkārôn;* Num 16:38, 40 [MT 17:3, 5]). The prohibition of outside encroachment is thus heightened by their failed quest (16:40 [MT 17:5]). The story of Korah's revolt solidifies the social distinction of holiness at a severe cost. The mishandling of the sacred censers entails death. The following episode involves the legitimate use of censers, which spares life (16:41-50 [MT 17:6-15]). At the prospect of the whole community becoming engulfed by divine wrath, Aaron stands "between the dead and the living," censer in hand, effecting atonement on the community's behalf (16:46-48 [MT 17:11-13]). "And the plague was stopped" (16:48 [MT 17:13]). The sacred censer illustrates both the dangerous and the life-giving dynamics of holiness. Through proper handling, this microcosmic fire of God is the bridge between the holy and the profane, between life and death. Through mishandling, it sanctifies the profane through death. Through proper use, the censer atones for the community, granting new life by mitigating the scourge of judgment.

Following these traumatic episodes and Aaron's vindication as head of the tribe of Levi (17:1-11 [MT 16-26]), the job description of the Levites and the priests are solidified, separate yet hierarchically joined: the non-Aaronide Levites are to serve the priests and perform the duties of the tent of meeting (18:3a); only the priests approach and handle the "utensils of the sanctuary" and the altar (vv. 3b, 5). The priests are further distinguished by the provisions they are to have. Reminiscent of the language of the primordial food blessing (Gen 1:29; 9:3), Aaron and his sons are granted their priestly due from the various offerings made to Yahweh, from the firstfruits of the land to the breast and right thigh of the firstborn animals (Num 18:8-19).[155] "All the holy offerings that the Israelites present to Yahweh I hereby give to you, together with your sons and daughters, as a perpetual due; it is a covenant of salt forever before Yahweh" (v. 19; cf. Gen 1:29).

This "covenant of salt" *(běrît melaḥ)*[156] formally underscores the perpetual and inviolable grant the priests are due in the sanctuary *(lěḥoq-'ôlām).*

---

155. The offering grant to the Aaronides opens with *'ănî hinnēh nātattî lěkā* (v. 8), almost identical to Gen 1:29. The verb of grant, *ntn,* is attested frequently throughout the passage, as is also the *lamed* of possession (e.g., Num 18:9, 11, 12, 13, 14, 15, 18, 19).

156. The salt refers to the Priestly custom of salting all sacrifices (J. Milgrom, *Numbers* [JPS Torah Commentary; Philadelphia: Jewish Publication Society, 1990] 154). Once salted, the sacrifice is transferred to the holy and thus to the priests' share. In the larger context, this covenantal grant parallels the grant of the land to the Israelites as a whole (v. 20; cf. Gen 17:8).

94

Their grant is unique, for it distinguishes the priests from the rest of the community, who are granted the land as their portion (Num 18:20). Aaron's "possession" (*ḥeleq* or *naḥălâ*) is Yahweh. Similarly, the Levites as a whole are not given any allotment of land (v. 24); their possession is the tithe as payment for services rendered in the tent, out of which a tithe is given to Aaron (vv. 21, 28). Like their fellow Israelites, the Levites, though they receive the tithe as their portion, must also give a tithe due Yahweh. The Levites remain betwixt and between, bound to both the holy and the common, and thereby serve as the cement of the community in communion with God.

Despite the pains taken to distinguish them in terms of service and privilege, both the priests and the Levites share much common ground. As members of the same tribe (so contended in the Priestly historiography), both the priestly and the non-Aaronide Levites are "insiders" of the sanctuary, although the movements of the latter are severely restricted relative to the former. The Levites are "joined" *(lwh)* to the priests in service to them as well as in service to the sanctuary (vv. 2, 4). In addition, neither the Levites nor the priests are to possess land, as their fellow Israelites are allowed to do. Their possession, like Yahweh's cultic possession, is the *fruit* of the land, plant and animal, the product of the land's occupation and cultivation by the community. Thus their role in the blessing of creation is not to "subdue" the land but to receive from it as a result of its cultivation. They reap the blessing of the land without having to work the land (cf. Gen 1:28, 29). The Levites are the landless blessed, for their vocation is to maintain God's dwelling in Israel's midst, but in so doing preserve Israel's place in the land. Along with the priests, the Levites ensure an abidance of holiness in the land. Their narrated failures only underscore the gravity of immanent holiness, both its distinctiveness and its relatedness to the land of Israel's existence.

Of Sin and Sanctity, Creation and Command

The curious incident at the "waters of Meribah" in Num 20:1-13, the site of Moses' sin,[157] uniquely captures something of the ethos limned vividly in the Priestly cosmogony. As one of the murmuring episodes, this vignette opens

157. See also Ps 106:33; Deut 32:51. Cf. Exod 17:1-7, which evidently comes from the Elohist's hand. For issues of redaction, see K. D. Sakenfeld, "Theological and Redactional Problems in Numbers 20.2-13," in *Understanding the Word: Essays in Honour of Bernhard W. Anderson* (ed. J. T. Butler et al.; JSOTSup 37; Sheffield: JSOT Press, 1985) 133-40; L. Schmidt, *Studien zur Priesterschrift* (BZAW 214; Berlin: de Gruyter, 1993) 45-72.

with the congregation's quarrel with Moses (and Aaron).[158] The land of the wilderness of Zin, they complain, is nonarable and consequently inhospitable for human life (v. 4). At the tent of meeting, Yahweh commands Moses to "take the staff and gather the congregation . . . and speak to the rock[159] before their eyes so that it yields its water" (v. 8). But Moses does not carry out what Yahweh had commanded. Instead, he strikes the rock twice with the staff, prefacing his actions with the question: "Listen, you rebels, from this rock shall we bring water for you?" (v. 10b). The discrepancies in the prescribed fulfillment have evidently gone beyond the boundaries of obedience, for Yahweh, despite the successful expulsion of water from the rock, indicts Moses and Aaron for mistrust and declares that they will have no role in Israel's *eisodus* (v. 12).

Shock over such a severe sentence and puzzlement over the nature of the crime invariably afflict the modern reader of this tale, "perhaps the most enigmatic incident of the Pentateuch."[160] Interpreters of this text, both ancient and modern, have made innumerable suggestions, from magic to self-doubt, regarding the nature and rationale of Moses' sin.[161] In any case, the obvious answer is disobedience: Moses and Aaron did not follow through on fulfilling the divine command as stipulated. But the question remains: What was the nature of the disobedience? Since a formal correspondence between command and fulfillment is crucial to Priestly style and ethos, the key must be in the discrepancy, which is found in Moses' specific failure to address the rock.

The command to "speak to the rock" may seem peculiar to the modern reader. Yet strong precedent to this is found in the Priestly creation account, which is structured around divinely given commands to particular domains and life-forms of creation (e.g., waters, earth, animals, humankind). Moses is specifically summoned to say something like "Let the rock bring forth water" or to employ the imperative in direct address. By adopting this mode of divine discourse, evinced in cosmogony, Moses is once again "made like God," as he was before Pharaoh (Exod 7:1). His role in the miracle making, underscored by the presence of the staff taken "from before Yahweh" (Num 18:9), is

158. For Aaron's lack of role, see W. H. Propp, "The Rod of Aaron and the Sin of Moses," *JBL* 107 (1988) 24-25.
159. Heb. *wĕdibbartem 'el-hassela'*. The command includes Aaron.
160. E. Arden, "How Moses Failed God," *JBL* 76 (1957) 50.
161. See the survey of scholarship in J. Milgrom, "Magic, Monotheism, and the Sin of Moses," in *The Quest for the Kingdom of God: Studies in Honor of George E. Mendenhall* (ed. H. B. Huffmon et al.; Winona Lake, Ind.: Eisenbrauns, 1983) 251-65; idem, *Numbers*, 448-56. See also Propp, "Rod of Aaron," 19, 22, 26.

to be Yahweh's mouthpiece, as he was in the tabernacle's construction. But instead of commanding the rock, Moses harshly addresses the people, verbalizing Yahweh's fulfillment report (20:8b) in the form of a question (v. 10b).[162] The formal discrepancies are critical for the Priestly narrator. Moses does not give the rock its discursive due and, in so doing, disparages both the people, whom he addresses, and Yahweh, whom he mistrusts.

By disobeying the divine instructions, Moses refuses to emulate Yahweh, whose own discourse effects creation, and thereby deflects attention toward himself and Aaron as the miracle makers,[163] while castigating his audience as "rebels" (*hammōrîm*, v. 10). Though attention is focused on the rock in Moses' discourse,[164] the rock is treated simply as an inert object and not as a collaborator in the creative enterprise of miracle making, which would have been acknowledged had Moses followed Yahweh's instructions. Moses thus rejects Yahweh's discursive power and the rock's compliance in creation. He rejects the creation by divine word and thus the *imitatio Dei* as the means of the miracle. For whatever reason, Moses refuses to mediate Yahweh's creative power. As in the Priestly cosmogony, divine authority and natural fulfillment work hand-in-glove. In this close correspondence between command and response, the created order, for all of its integrity and power, testifies to God's magisterial transcendence by virtue of its responsive obedience. Had Moses acted in accordance with Yahweh's holiness and in so doing acknowledged the integral power of the divinely created order by addressing the rock as Yahweh had commanded creation, due acknowledgment to the Creator would have been rendered. But such was not the case.

Striking *(nkh)* the rock was also not part of the command.[165] Indeed,

162. As it stands, the question can be answered either negatively or affirmatively. For affirmative answers to nonnegative rhetorical questions, see, e.g., 1 Sam 2:27; 1 Kgs 21:19; Jer 31:20. The overall context suggests that it be answered affirmatively (contra Schmidt, *Studien zur Priesterschrift*, 67-68; Propp, "Rod of Aaron," 22). Rather than expressing incredulity on Moses' part, the interrogative form is intended to convey astonishment to the congregation as well as maintain the harsh tone of address.

163. Schmidt identifies Moses' sin with his intent to demonstrate his powerlessness in bringing water out of the rock (*Studien zur Priesterschrift*, 66-72). This explanation, however, does not adequately take into account the accusation that Moses did not publicly mediate Yahweh's holy role in the miracle. Instead, Moses' discourse highlights his and Aaron's action, confirmed in beating the rock with the holy staff.

164. Along with the addition of the demonstrative particle *(zeh)*, the word order of Moses' question is striking. Attention is focused on the rock in such a way as to reduce the rock's role in the miracle.

165. With exclusive attention given to the possible implications of Moses' question (v. 10b), Sakenfeld treats v. 11a as secondary ("Theological and Redactional Problems,"

this is only the second case in the Priestly narrative in which a staff, most probably Aaron's,[166] is used to strike. Most frequently, the command is to "take your staff and stretch out your hand" (Exod 7:19; 8:5).[167] Preeminent striking, however, is reserved for Yahweh, who "strikes down" the firstborn in the land of Egypt.[168] That Moses strikes the rock twice only underscores his departure from the command.[169] It is not within the scope of Yahweh's command to beat the miraculous source of life-sustaining waters for the congregation. Moreover, the staff connotes holy presence before the congregation, as it had Aaron's holy precedence over the Levites in Num 17:1-11 (MT 16-26). To use the staff in such a violent manner is a sacrilege. In addition, double striking signals an impulsive display of anger that matches Moses' scathing address to the congregation: "Listen, you rebels. . . ." This episode at Meribah is primarily about Moses' sin; the people are not implicated.[170] There is, moreover, poetic justice in Yahweh's judgment: as Moses was charged to "bring out" (*yṣ'*) water from the rock to the congregation (20:8), which he failed to do properly, so Moses will not "bring in" (*bw'*) the congregation from the wilderness to the land given to Israel (v. 12; cf. v. 4). The rock was given to Moses to be addressed by discourse reminiscent of the Deity, not to be struck by dint of human force.

The story of Moses' sin remains enigmatic when it is read without reference to the Priestly view of nature as conveyed in the cosmogony. Yahweh charges Moses of not trusting "in me" (v. 12). Such trust would have been demonstrated by addressing the rock, as God had addressed the elements of creation, and awaiting its response, trusting that the rock would "obey." Instead, Moses takes matters into his own hands, castigating the congregation

---

148-49). See also the more expanded list of meanings behind the question in D. T. Olson, *Numbers* (Interpretation; Louisville: John Knox, 1992) 126-27. But the role of the rock is underscored in both the question and Moses' subsequent treatment of it.

166. See v. 9; 17:10-11; so Propp, "Rod of Aaron," 21-22.

167. The only other case of striking with a staff in the Priestly narrative is in the plague of gnats: Aaron is instructed to stretch out his staff and strike the dust of the earth (Exod 8:15 [MT 12]). The effect, however, is deleterious instead of salutary, as in the rock's case.

168. Exod 12:12, 13, 29; Num 3:13, 8:17.

169. Cf. Exod 17:5, 6, in which Moses is commanded specifically to strike the rock. The omission of striking in the command in the Priestly version is deliberate (so also E. W. Davies, *Numbers* [NCBC; Grand Rapids: Eerdmans, 1992] 205). The Priestly author has reshaped the tradition by associating Moses' striking with disobedience.

170. In this context, Moses' derogation of the congregation is unwarranted (so also Olson, *Numbers*, 128). The Priestly narrator has shifted, in effect, the theme of rebellion away from Israel to Moses himself.

and beating the rock. Trust in the rock's responsiveness in this context is tantamount to trust in Yahweh's power in creation. The indictment reads: "You did not trust in me to treat me as holy *(lĕhaqdîšēnî)* before the eyes of the Israelites" (v. 12a). Yahweh's holiness would have been publicly acknowledged had Moses obeyed by commanding, rather than beating, the rock.

The miracle of the rock cannot be considered apart from the Priestly view of miracles in general: miracles are "signs and wonders" to bring about acknowledgment of Yahweh's sovereignty.[171] Like the multiplication of the plagues in Egypt, Yahweh's wonder at the rock was to have its "fill" of Israel's formative history in the wilderness. Although the rock produced the water, it was not done in faithfulness, specifically by the faithful command of Moses, but rather by an undeterred grace on the people's behalf that overrode Moses' sin. Missing was simple trust in Yahweh's holy power *in* creation; hence Moses is not to share the sanctifying power that marks the completion of Israel's creation in the land.

The miracle at Meribah was meant to be a testimony to Yahweh's holiness and presence, not to Moses' aggrandizement. Moses did not evince such holiness; consequently, he cannot be present to bring his people into the land given to them. Although Yahweh will remain present with Israel, a successor is required to replace Moses: Joshua son of Nun (Num 27:18-20; Deut 34:9), who will be accountable to (lit. "stand before") the holy priest Eleazar (Num 27:21). By forsaking Yahweh's holiness, Moses must remain in Moab, overlooking the land of occupation, beholding the goodness of the land without partaking of Israel's rest-filled domain (Num 27:12, 13; Deut 24:1, 7).

Israel's Presence in the Land

Evidence of Priestly influence in the book of Joshua is a highly disputed matter among modern interpreters. Early inclinations to see evidence of a continuous Priestly recension in Joshua were undercut as a result of Martin Noth's monumental studies of the pentateuchal and Deuteronomistic traditions.[172] Recent

171. See Exod 7:3-5; 8:4, 17, 18.
172. "No traces of a coherent P narrative can be identified beyond Deut. 34. All that we find after Deuteronomy are isolated additions to older texts in the style and thought pattern of Priestly authorship. This is precisely the case also in the Book of Joshua" (M. Noth, *A History of Pentateuchal Traditions* [tr. B. W. Anderson; 1972; repr. Chico, Calif.: Scholars Press, 1989] 10). A contrasting view can be found in S. Mowinckel, *Tetrateuch-Pentateuch-Hexateuch: Die Berichte über die Landnahme in den Drei altisraelitischen Geschichtswerken* (BZAW 90; Berlin: de Gruyter, 1964), who attributes most

exceptions, however, include Joseph Blenkinsopp and Norbert Lohfink, who by the criterion of linguistic similarity find remnants of a Priestly narrative in Josh 4:19; 5:10-12; 14:1, 2; 18:1; 19:51.[173] Whether original to the Priestly narrative or evidence of Priestly supplementation to the Deuteronomistic narrative of Israel's occupation of the land, these verses merit consideration for determining an overall Priestly ethos of the Pentateuch.

These verses recount in typical Priestly fashion the establishment of the sanctuary (18:1) and the distribution of the land (14:1, 2; 19:51). Prior to this, a sabbath of sorts occurs in the cessation of the manna. The itineration of Israel in the wilderness is finished. Having crossed the Jordan, the Israelites are stationed at Gilgal, where they celebrate the Passover. Henceforth they eat "from the produce of the land," since the manna has ceased or "sabbathed" (5:11, 12). It is only appropriate that as the Passover inaugurated Israel's deliverance from Egyptian oppression it also inaugurates Israel's occupation of the land promised by Yahweh. As part of the promise, Canaan's crops are granted to Israel for its permanent livelihood in the land. The plants are theirs (cf. Gen 1:29).

So also is the land, which is distributed as an "inheritance" (naḥălâ) by lot (18:2). The conclusion of the distribution is given in 19:51, introduced in a similar manner: "These are the inheritances (nĕḥālōt) . . . distributed by lot at Shiloh before Yahweh, at the entrance of the tent of meeting. So they finished dividing the land." The language resembles Priestly style. This new generation of Israel does not charge in like marauders to subdue the land; taking possession of the land is done decently and in order. Dictating the allotments in the land, the sacred lot establishes the tribal divisions in the land with a holy, inviolable significance.[174] The Urim has taken the place of the sanctuary cloud, which has come to rest at Shiloh, now that the congregation is in the land. Israel is no longer on the move, from wilderness to wilderness, but in the land ready to differentiate itself geopolitically and fill the land according to the divinely ordained determinations.

---

of the latter half of the book of Joshua, in particular the tribal allotments (chs. 13–19) to a Priestly author.

173. Lohfink, "The Priestly Narrative and History," in *Theology of the Pentateuch*, 145n.29; Blenkinsopp, "Structure of P," 287-90, who suggests that 19:51 comprises the original ending of P (n. 62). Given the importance of land and Israel's occupation in the Priestly promises, I am inclined to treat these verses as authentic to an original Priestly compositional layer. I would also agree, however, that some of the original Priestly account of the occupation has been omitted in favor of other literary sources and influences. How much has been omitted is sheer speculation. Lohfink argues that only a brief report on Israel's occupation of the land, analogous to Exod 12:40-42, the Priestly narrative of the Exodus, was original to P ("Priestly Narrative," 145-46n.30).

174. Cf. Num 27:21-22.

Presupposed in Priestly material, the sanctuary remains stationary at Shiloh throughout the tribal allotments.[175] Yahweh's dwelling has finally come to rest, set up by Israel[176] and commemorating Israel's settled existence in the land.[177] With the erection of the tabernacle, the land lies "subdued" *(kbš)* before Israel (18:1). The juxtaposition is deliberate. The status of the land in some sense marks a fulfillment of the "great commission" of Genesis to "fill the earth and subdue it" (Gen 1:28). That the verb "subdue" *(kbš)* is used nowhere else in the Priestly material except in Gen 1:28 and Josh 18:1 underscores the latter's significance.[178] Israel's occupation of the land is a fulfillment of a universal commission for all humanity. As a consequence of Yahweh's "dwelling," now established in the land, Israel has found its own niche on earth. Not by blitzkrieg or by ban but by divinely ordained allotments is the land subdued. The land is not meant to be subdued by brute force any more than the rock in the wilderness was meant to produce water by being beaten. Such is the way of holiness in consonance with the productive goodness of creation. The land is to be received through the community's differentiated occupation.[179] Resistance from the land is nonexistent, for when surveyed from the Priestly high ground the land is as good as given. With the land divided, Israel's work is fulfilled *in principio* (19:51). Through the division of the land, Canaan is a land reclaimed and re-created for Israel's dwelling. On terrain differentiated by tribe and geography, bound and bounded, Israel's creation is made complete. As a land negotiated and once paid for generations earlier,[180] filling the land is the natural outcome.

So the extant Priestly narrative comes to rest with the issues of cult and

---

175. The canonical arrangement of the narrative material claims otherwise. The distribution of the tribal allotments begins at Gilgal, according to 14:6 in conjunction with v. 1, and moves to Shiloh, once Judah, Ephraim, and Manasseh are allotted territory (18:2). For the Priestly narrative in situ, however, Shiloh was the permanent spot for the distribution in toto.

176. Heb. *škn*, 18:1.

177. Cf. Josh 1:15.

178. See also Lohfink, "Strata," 200.

179. I agree in principle with Lohfink's argument that the Priestly use of *kbš* has more to do with occupying land than with overthrowing it by violence ("Subdue the Earth?" 9-11). In light of the Priestly renouncement of violence (Gen 6:11-13), occupation of the land must occur another way: by equitable distribution of allotments. To conclude, however, that the Priestly vision of the land occupation was pacifistic smacks of anachronism. The Priestly tradents do not envision a situation of peaceful coexistence with the inhabitants of the land; the latter must be evicted from the land by Yahweh as landlord (cf. Exod 14:26-28; Lev 18:24-25; 20:25).

180. Gen 23:9, 16-20 (see above).

land, Yahweh's dwelling and Israel's possession, finally resolved. The juxta-position of the sanctuary settled in the land and the land's established divisions reveals the larger narrative's dual thrust from Exodus onward. Yahweh's promise of land to Israel is given prominence in Exodus 6, as it was in Genesis 17 and 23. But attention to the land is suspended for the moment at the point of Israel's temporary residence at the foot of Mount Sinai. Here primary attention is devoted to Yahweh's tabernacling presence and related cultic issues (e.g., Exod 25:8; 29:46). Land as Israel's possession is not given explicit mention until departure is made from the mountain and the land is within sight (Num 13:1-26). From here on out, attention to cult and land alternate: conflicting reports over the status of the land are given and divine judgment is rendered (13:32–14:29); opposing views of holiness are aired with judgment executed (chs. 16–17).

The issue of land emerges again in the murmuring theme of Numbers 20, which provides background to Moses' refusal to acknowledge Yahweh's holiness (v. 12). Standing before the priest, Joshua is set apart from the congregation to maintain its direction toward the land after Moses' death (27:27; cf. Exod 14:3). Finally, the tabernacle is set up in the land, and the land is divided into tribal allotments. Although treated separately at certain points in the narrative, land and cult are given equal significance in the Priestly historiography.[181] Land is not relativized by cult or vice versa. Neither does one displace the other. Rather each accompanies the other throughout Israel's itineration, culminating in both Israel and the sanctuary finding their home in the land.

The connection is all the more vivid in Genesis. Creation completed leads to holiness established in the Priestly cosmogony. Israel's occupation of the land is creation's mirror image, as it were: Yahweh's holy dwelling established in the sanctuary leads to the establishment of Israel's land, divided and filled. The tabernacle is as much Yahweh's domain as the land is Israel's possession. Both land and cult, presence and occupation, lead to a greater goal: the acknowledgment of mutual identity between Yahweh and Israel. By re-

---

181. One cannot thus speak of the Priestly narrative's exclusive or "real goal" being "the presentation of regulations established at Sinai," as Noth claimed (*History of Pentateuchal Traditions,* 9). Nor can I agree with K. Elliger that despite the extent of the Sinai material in the Priestly corpus the real theme of P is not the cult but rather the land ("Sinn und Ursprung der priesterlichen Geschichtserzählung," *ZTK* 49 [1952] 129), a view that Lohfink seemingly adopts ("Priestly Narrative," 141-42; but cf. idem, "God the Creator," 129; idem, "Subdue the Earth?" 17). To the contrary, both land and cult are given equal weight and fulfilled in the Priestly narrative with the establishment of the tabernacle and the division of the land.

demption and the promise of land, Yahweh declares: "I will take you as my people and I will be your God" (Exod 6:7).[182] By dwelling with Israel in the sanctuary, "I will be their God." Yahweh pronounces a solidarity that Israel is to acknowledge fully (29:45-46). The covenant promise lives and breathes in occupied land and established sanctuary; it is fulfilled by filling both sanctuary and land with presence, both human and divine.

The Distinction of Holiness

The ethos of the Priestly tradition, however, does not conclude with the occupation of the land. Life does not end once the land is established and the tabernacle is stationed in it. Similarly, creation does not terminate on the sixth day; holiness embraces the seventh. A separate, but intimately related, corpus of Priestly tradition sheds further light on the moral context and praxis of Israel within the Priestly purview. Although set alongside the tabernacle account in canonical form, the holiness ethos laid out in Leviticus deals particularly with Israel's moral destiny *in* the land. Whereas the Sinai tabernacle account describes the holy integrity of Yahweh's dwelling, Leviticus, particularly the so-called Holiness Code,[183] stresses the integrity of the land, along with the sanctuary. Leviticus is to land as tabernacle is to cult.

Interspersed throughout the book, with a particular concentration in chs. 11 and 19–21, are references to Yahweh's incomparable holiness. Lev 11:44-45 is representative: "I am Yahweh your God; therefore, sanctify yourselves *(hitqaddîštem)* and be holy, for I am holy. You shall not defile *(lō'*

---

182. See also Gen 17:7-8.

183. The Holiness Code is traditionally considered to comprise Leviticus 17–26, although the literary boundaries are actually more fluid. Moreover, categorical distinctions have often been made in recent scholarship between the Priestly compositional layer of the Pentateuch and that of the so-called Holiness School (e.g., Milgrom, *Leviticus 1–16*, 13-51; Knohl, *Sanctuary of Silence*, 168-98). Irrespective of the redactional history of the book of Leviticus, however, my interest is in determining how these two layers are integrated to form a multifaceted view of holiness. That the literary deposits of these distinctive schools, despite numerous differences, are incorporated into a cohesive corpus of Priestly lore powerfully attests to the dynamic and compatible nature of holiness and moral praxis. With their different emphases, the Holiness Code and Priestly narrative and law exhibit more complementarity than conflict; hence all claims of independent status between the Holiness Code and the remaining material in Leviticus are questionable or in dire need of nuance. See V. Wagner, "Zur Existenz des sogennanten 'Heiligkeitsgesetzes,'" *ZAW* 86 (1974) 307-16; E. S. Gerstenberger, *Leviticus* (OTL; Louisville: Westminster John Knox, 1996) 18.

tĕṭammĕʾû) yourselves with any swarming thing that moves on the earth. For I am Yahweh who brought you up from the land of Egypt to be your God; you shall be holy, for I am holy."[184] Yahweh's self-proclamation of holiness frames an injunction that exhorts a life of holiness in general and restraint from eating "swarming" creatures in particular (see 11:29-31). Here and elsewhere, reference to Yahweh's holiness serves as the motive clause for Israel's praxis in the land. Holiness is the sine qua non of ethics in Leviticus. It involves fundamentally the establishment of distinctions and boundaries, physically and ethically. It is the foundation for a cosmic ethos.

Leviticus makes clear that the business of making distinctions is a holy enterprise conducted by the priests. As Yahweh addresses Aaron in 10:10-11: "You must divide *(ûlĕhabdîl)* between the holy *(hāqqōdeš)* and the common *(hahōl),* and between the unclean *(haṭṭāmēʾ)* and the clean *(haṭṭāhôr).* And you are to teach the people of Israel all the statutes that Yahweh has spoken to them through Moses."[185] As creation was the result of differentiation, so the priests continue this divine function by establishing distinctions for Israel. Indeed, to fail in this priestly enterprise "does violence" *(ḥms)* to and profanes Yahweh *(ḥll,* Ezek 22:26). The blurring of distinctions can lead only to chaos, a contagion of unrelieved impurity that overcomes prescribed restrictions and ultimately forces Yahweh, the Holy Dweller, to abandon sanctuary, as if the holy abode were a ship sinking into the depths of depravity (see Ezek 10:1-22). That which is holy is set apart from everything else. To profane is to transfer something or someone from the sphere of the holy to the realm of the common. The distinction of holiness is cosmically fundamental, for it is one that separates the seventh day from the preceding six in creation. In short, holiness marks the climax of creation and the genesis of Israel's ethics.

You Are What You Eat: The Priestly Kashrut

Distinguishing between the clean and the unclean has much to do with the business of boundary making. Cleanness connotes normalcy; impurity refers to something out of place or anomalous within the created order that must be avoided or rectified. Impurity and holiness represent antithetical states, although they share their distinction from the common. Casual contact with either realm is expressly forbidden. The dietary laws of Lev 11:2-43 vividly il-

---

184. See, e.g., Lev 19:2; 20:7-8; 22:32-33. Similarity in terminology suggests that Lev 11:44-45 belongs to the Holiness Code redaction of the book as a whole.
185. Cf. Ezek 44:23.

lustrate this principle of anomaly in various degrees. The Priestly tradents take pains to distinguish what is suitable food and what is unsuitable or out of bounds *for Israel*.[186] For example, fish that do not exhibit the typical qualities of fins and scales are considered unclean (11:9-11). Domestic animals that possess cloven hooves and ruminate set the standard for eating; thus the anomalous camels and rock badgers, which chew the cud but do not have the correct feet, are not staples for Israel; for the reverse reason, the pig is considered anathema (vv. 4-7). Modes of locomotion also set certain standards for appropriateness. The walking winged insects (v. 20) and the land swarmers (vv. 41-42) are considered unfit for the table. In both cases, the means of locomotion is appropriate to domains other than the land, namely, sky and water. Such animals are domain transgressors.

Another distinction can be identified in the variety of unsuitable birds listed in vv. 13-19. They are predominantly carnivores, a behavioral characteristic more appropriate to land animals and especially humans (cf. Gen 9:3).[187] Other distinctions, however, such as the exempted locusts (Lev 11:21-22), are ostensibly arbitrary in view of the cosmic template established in Genesis 1. The Priestly tradents do not give natural rationales for their distinctions. Nevertheless, that the classifications are informed, in part, by the prevailing structures of creation is critical.[188] The basic distinctions among the animals find their precedent in creation: land, water, and air creatures. Explicitly, the distinctions made within these domains serve to uphold a paramount distinction for the Priestly tradents — Israel's distinction in relation to the nations. The distinctions of domains in creation are the provenance of humanity's royal rule; the additional distinction between the pure and the impure is the provenance of Israel's priestly determinations. Yet the latter is drawn in part from the former, thereby advancing the database of differentia-

---

186. M. Douglas was the first to treat the laws in Leviticus from a structuralist standpoint in *Purity and Danger: An Analysis of the Concepts of Pollution and Taboo* (London: Routledge & Kegan Paul, 1966, repr. 1970) 41-57. For later modifications see B. J. Malina, *The New Testament World: Insights from Cultural Anthropology* (rev. ed.; Louisville: Westminster John Knox, 1993) 149-55; M. P. Carroll, "One More Time: Leviticus Revisited," *AES* 99 (1978) 339-46 (repr. in *Anthropological Approaches to the Old Testament* [ed. B. Lang; IRT 8; Philadelphia: Fortress, 1985] 117-26). Carroll sees culture's invasion by nature as the most basic criterion. For a favorable survey of these anthropological approaches, see P. J. Budd, "Holiness and Cult," in *The World of Ancient Israel: Sociological, Anthropological and Political Perspectives* (ed. R. E. Clements; Cambridge: Cambridge University Press, 1989) 282-90.

187. So Carroll, "One More Time," 121-22.

188. As Milgrom acknowledges, "The fact that Lev 11 is rooted in Gen 1 is of deeper theological import" (*Leviticus 1–16*, 47).

tion that promotes Israel's life in Canaan, distinguished from the existence of nations on earth.

Leviticus 20:24b-26 conjoins Israel's separation from the nations with the distinction made between clean and unclean animals.[189] "I am Yahweh your God who has distinguished *(hibdaltî)* you from the peoples. You shall therefore distinguish *(wĕhibdaltem)* between the clean animal and the unclean. . . . You shall be holy to me, for I Yahweh am holy. I have separated you from the other peoples to be mine." Israel's distinguishing among the edible animals within each cosmic domain reflects Yahweh's endowing Israel with unique, indeed potentially holy, distinction. By contrast, the peoples of the earth correspond to the unclean animals. Whereas the granting of *all* kinds of food in Gen 1:29 and 9:3 is operative and valid for the international realm, Israel must restrict its diet to preserve its distinction in the world. A holy people must eat only clean food; the unclean nations make no such distinction. Thus the category of the clean is itself a distinction that sets Israel apart from the nations. Internally, the diet distinctions figure critically in maintaining Israel's integrity as a community indwelled by God.

That certain criteria for Israel's distinguishing are drawn from the boundaries established at creation suggests that of all the nations on the face of the earth, Israel's identity corresponds in no small measure to God's creative intent in the beginning. Whereas the nations have legitimate claim over the abundant goodness of creation, only Israel can lay claim to the lion's share of Yahweh's holiness. The summons to be holy involves the creation of further distinctions within a realm deemed good. As the distinction of distinctions within creation, holiness lays the foundation for the further distinction between the clean and the unclean in Israel's domain.

You Are Where You Are: Purity and Atonement

The Priestly purview adds depth to the adage "Cleanliness is next to godliness." The converse also holds sway: Uncleanness is next to formlessness, the danger of impurity. Unrelieved contact with impurity has its final outcome in "defiling" *(ṭm')* the sanctuary (Lev 15:31). Separation from the unclean preserves the holy integrity of the tabernacle, the center of the community. Serious transgression of the boundary between the clean and the unclean, however, requires ritual restitution by sacrifice and sanctuary cleansing.[190]

---

189. See ibid., 689, 724-25.

190. For the infractions that required sanctuary cleansing, see John H. Hayes, "Atonement in the Book of Leviticus," *Int* 52 (1998) 6-7.

Atonement serves precisely this function, most ceremoniously expressed in the ritual of the high priest on the Day of Atonement. The elaborately ritualized movement specified on that day, a choreography of holiness, leads ineluctably to one stated goal: "Thus he [Aaron] shall make atonement for the sanctuary *(kipper ʿal-haqqōdeš)*,[191] because of the impurities of the people of Israel, and because of their transgressions, all their sins; and so he shall do for the tent of meeting, which remains with them in the midst of their impurities" (16:16).

To make atonement is to purge the sanctuary of impurities by blood, as demonstrated by the priest's ritualized activity at the altar: "He shall sprinkle some of the blood on it with his finger seven times, and cleanse it and hallow it *(ṭihărô wĕqiddĕšô)* from the impurities of the people of Israel" (v. 19). Within the sacred precincts, cleansing the sanctuary preserves its holiness.[192] Within the social domain of Israel, the atoning work of the priest has the rippling effect of cleansing the entire community: by making atonement for the sanctuary, the priest "shall make atonement for *(yĕkappēr ʿal)* the priests and for all the people of the assembly," not to mention for himself (vv. 33-34, 30).[193] The impurities that have accrued in the sanctuary over the year from willful transgressions are in turn banished to another realm, wholly separate from the community, into the wilderness, an act of deliberate dissociation that returns the dirt, as it were, of impurity to its proper place, outside the community (v. 21).[194] As in creation, the realm of the demonic has no place, literally, in the cultic community and, symbolically, in creation.[195] Chaos in the Priestly worldview is a relational construct, not a reified, much less deified, one. Chaos erupts when established boundaries collapse and when Is-

---

191. See the similar expressions in vv. 18, 20, 27, 33. For an illuminating study of the atonement ritual in the context of Priestly creation theology, see Gorman, *Ideology of Ritual*, 61-102.

192. For the purging function of atonement *(kipper)* see Milgrom, *Leviticus 1–16*, 1079-84.

193. Atonement for the priests described in v. 30 is also cast as a cleansing from all sins. Cf. 23:28 of the Holiness Code, in which the object of atonement is explicitly the people.

194. The Priestly legists refer to this outside, wholly separate, realm as "Azazel," more a domain synonymous with "wilderness" (v. 21) for the transference of impurities than the demon it denoted originally. See Milgrom, *Leviticus 1–16*, 1020-21, 1042-44, 1071-79. As noted above, a similar move is made in the demythologization of Chaos itself.

195. As Milgrom notes, Priestly theology consistently negates the demonic in contrast to ancient Near Eastern paganism: "With the demise of the demons [in Priestly theology], only one creature remains with 'demonic' power — the human being" (*Leviticus 1–16*, 43).

rael, in particular, finds itself in the realm of the impure; as a result, God is profaned. In short, through atonement both sanctuary and people are cleansed, and the boundary between the clean and the unclean, the holy and the profane, is reinstated.

In sum, atonement in the sanctuary and purity within the community have all to do with the maintenance of boundaries. In relation to the cosmic boundaries established at creation, Israel must discern its own boundaries to maintain its existence in the land and enable its moral life to flourish. Otherwise, Israel will compromise its holiness and lose its identity, theological and otherwise. By maintaining its internal codes of holiness, however, Israel can fine-tune a creation esteemed good in the beginning yet continually challenged by the threat of violence, of the chaos that erupts from the human heart.

Living in Integrity

One can view Israel's moral life, as prescribed in Leviticus, from three interrelated levels of existence: the individual in purity, the land in integrity, and the community in holiness. Each level derives from the priestly concern for living in holy integrity as defined by certain boundaries.

Living in Skin

To state the obvious, skin is the individual's essential boundary whose break signals a violation of physical integrity and a contagion of impurity. A bona fide skin disease constitutes a breakdown of the boundary, requiring priestly action and physical restoration. Acting as a diagnostician (but not as physician), the priest must determine what represents an authentic subversion of the skin, an affliction that "appears to be deeper than the skin" (*mar'ēh hannega' 'āmōq mē'ôr běśārô*, 13:3).[196] If the person is truly afflicted with a skin ailment, he or she is pronounced unclean. Having gotten under the skin, disease has infiltrated the self. The diagnostic time is seven days for the scaly-skin ailments (inaccurately referred to as "leprous" [NRSV]; vv. 3, 4, 5, 6, 26, 27, 31, 33, 50). The fate of the unclean person is life outside the camp (vv. 45-

---

196. See also vv. 18, 25, 30, 31, 34. Other diagnostic terms include "raw flesh in the swelling" (*bāśār ḥay baś'ēt*; vv. 10, 14-16) and "spreading in the skin" (*pāśâ hannega' bā'ôr*, vv. 5, 6, 8, 22). But once the skin is "covered" *(ksh)*, that is, made uniform, the person is declared clean (vv. 12, 13).

46). Once the person is cleansed or healed of the affliction, three purification rites are required in order to reintegrate the erstwhile impure person into the community, with atonement made on his or her behalf (14:20). With nothing foreign under the person's skin, that is, within the self, he or she is restored to the community.

Analogously, a house in the land of Canaan can also become afflicted with a "skin" ailment (*nega* *ṣāra'at*, 14:34), which requires priestly inspection during a seven-day interval in order to determine if the "disease" in the walls is "deeper than the surface" (*šāpāl min-haqqîr*, v. 37). Its cleansing is also marked by a purification ritual, similar to the first purification ceremony for the diseased person (vv. 49-53), and "atonement for the house" is fulfilled (*kipper 'al-habbayit wĕṭāhēr*, v. 53).

Other examples of physical breaches of the self or bodily impurity include mourning rites that involve gashing and tattooing the skin (19:28), trimming the beard (v. 27), carcass contamination (11:24-40), corpse contamination (Lev 21:11; 22:4b; Num 5:2b; 6:6-9; 19:18),[197] childbearing (Lev 12:1-8), emission of semen (15:2b-18), and menstruation (vv. 19-30), both normal and irregular (e.g., gonorrhea) in the last two cases. As Jacob Milgrom points out, they all share something in common from the realm of death.[198] Even skin disease is likened to the decay of a corpse, as in the case of Miriam's ailment (Num 12:12). Giving birth is an event that hangs precariously over the brink of death for both mother and child. Any breach of the skin points to the ever pressing threat of death.

Sexual intercourse — a necessary minor impurity for procreation — also involves a "breach" in personal boundaries and thus must be regulated to some degree (Lev 15:18). Much more serious are the illicit sexual unions, which warrant stern sanction by the Priestly legists, such as sexual union during menstruation, which transfers the woman's impurity to the man (15:24; 18:19; 20:18); incest in its various forms (18:6-18; 20:11-12, 17, 19-21); adultery (18:20; 20:10; Num 5:11-31); male homoerotic conduct (Lev 18:22; 20:13); and intercourse with animals (18:23; 20:15-16). The various cases that constitute incest and adultery threaten not only the integrity of the self but also that of the family and the larger community. Adultery defiles by violating familial boundaries and disintegrating communal bonds (18:20; 20:10). Incest dissolves the inner integrity of familial bonds that determine who belongs to whom within marital rela-

197. The priest and the Nazirite, both considered holy, are under severer restrictions because they can incur impurity simply by being in the vicinity of the corpse (Lev 21:11; Num 6:6). See also Ezek 44:26-27.

198. Milgrom, "Encroaching on the Sacred," 244.

tionships (e.g., 18:7-8) and who is off limits within blood relations (e.g., vv. 9-10). Sex with animals blurs all genetic distinction between the human and animal kingdoms. In both cases sexual separation is upheld through exogamy within the species rather than by endogamy within the family. By contrast, homoerotic behavior violates the differentiated genderedness of sexuality by establishing sexual union among those of identical gender, specifically male.[199] In such unions, sexual differentiation is leveled out. In sum, sexual union according to the Priestly perspective must preserve the balance between differentiation and integrity in relationship.

With the gendered community defined by inviolable bonds and boundaries, any compromise poses eminent social and, indeed, cultic danger. Such acts bring about defilement for all the parties involved, including the land (18:24-30; 20:22). Lev 18:26, 28 graphically describe the results of such defilement: "You shall keep my statutes and my ordinances and commit none of these abominations, either the native or the alien who resides among you . . . so that the land will not vomit you out (wĕlō'-tāqî') when you defile it (bĕṭāmma'ăkem), as it vomited out the nation that was before you."[200] A profound irony emerges in connection with the slanderous report given by the spies: "The land . . . is one that devours its inhabitants" (Num 13:32; cf. Lev 26:38). Living in skin has all to do with living in and off the land without being consumed on the one hand, or evicted on the other.

Living in Land

The land of Canaan is Israel's inalienable domain or inheritance, promised by covenant and fulfilled in occupation (Lev 20:24).[201] Moreover, it is an eminently distinct domain, a land distanced from Egypt and set apart from the myriad of the other nations (18:3; 20:23; 26:1-46). Canaan's physical distinction points to a crucial moral distinction. As Israel's domain, the land bears an integrity that corresponds to Israel's distinctive praxis, dissociated from

199. In light of the Priestly concern for procreation and holding onto the land as Israel's inalienable possession, homoerotic unions also constitute a waste of seed. See S. J. Melcher, "The Holiness Code and Human Sexuality," in *Biblical Ethics and Homosexuality* (ed. R. L. Brawley; Louisville: Westminster John Knox, 1996) 87-102, who suggests that the Priestly injunction against homoerotic conduct, as well as other forms of sexual behavior deemed deviant in Leviticus, stems from a basic concern over patrilineal inheritance of the land (p. 98).

200. NRSV; see also Lev 18:25; 20:22.

201. Cf. Gen 17:8, Exod 6:7. The Holiness Code thus exhibits deep ties with the covenantal land grant in Priestly narrative.

the pagan ways of the surrounding nations. Indeed, Israel's moral dwelling place or ethos is even distinguished from the purely physical domain of Canaan. "You shall not do as they do in the land of Egypt, where you lived, and you shall not do as they do in the land of Canaan, to which I am bringing you" (Lev 18:3). Israel's domain is defined by its praxis, a sphere of existence within yet distinct from Canaan that also claims Canaan as Israel's possession and dwelling. Thus to speak of Israel's land is to speak of Israel's distinctive ethos, Israel's dwelling in purity.

The intimate relationship between land and purity is most vividly brought into focus in chs. 18–26. Impurity in human relations results in defilement of the land, suggesting a kind of land sanctity that is matched elsewhere by the tabernacle: "Do not defile yourselves in any of these ways, for by all these practices the nations I am casting you out before you have defiled themselves. Thus the land became defiled, and I punished it for its sin *(wā'epqōd 'ăwōnāh 'āleyhā);* consequently, the land vomited out its inhabitants" (18:24-25).[202] Here land and people are inseparably bound. The land's integrity is a product of the community's integrity or purity. Through unrelieved impurity, both land and its inhabitants are defiled, and punishment is rendered against both land and people. Yet it is the land that has the expulsion right.

The effect on the land brought about by Israel's covenantal faithfulness (or lack thereof) is most graphically described in the series of blessings and curses in Leviticus 26. Parallel to creation's responsiveness to God's command in the creation of life, Israel's obedience fructifies Canaan's land with goodness (26:3-12), which includes fertility (vv. 4-5, 10), peace and security from hostile neighbors (vv. 6-8), the blessing of procreation (v. 9; Gen 1:28), and the assurance of Yahweh's dwelling in the land (Lev 26:11-12). In short, land is Israel's life, the product of Israel's salutary praxis. Covenantal disobedience, in turn, results in the land's dissolution (vv. 14-33): "I will break your proud glory, and I will make your sky like iron and the land like bronze. Your strength shall be spent to no avail, your land shall not yield its produce, and the trees of the land shall not yield their fruit" (vv. 19-20). Hardened by drought, the land, along with the sky, will become lifeless, like metal, impenetrable and nonarable.[203] The litany of woes continues: disease (vv. 16a, 25b), enemy invasion and occupation (vv. 16b-17, 25a, 32), wild animal invasion (v. 22), hunger (v. 26), cannibalism (v. 29), dispersion (v. 33a), and complete desolation of land and city (vv.

---

202. See also Lev 18:28; 20:23; Num 35:34; Deut 21:23.

203. The appropriate contrast with the dissolution of the earth by flood is deliberate (Gen 7:11). Both render the land impotent, yet by opposite means: deluge and drought, dissolution and desolation.

31-32, 33b). Also among the "curses" is an overcoming of Israel's once secure domain by external forces, cultural and natural: both the wild animals and Israel's enemies will ravage the land. Like creation's deluge, borders are overwhelmed and death is the inexorable result.

For the land itself, however, Israel's desolation effects the land's restoration: "The land shall be satisfied with[204] its sabbath years as long as it lies desolate while you are in the land of your enemies; then the land shall rest (*tišbat*) and be satisfied with its sabbath years. As long as it lies desolate, it shall have the rest it did not have on your sabbaths when you were living on it" (26:34-35). Cleared of apostate Israel, the land finally finds its sabbath, making up for the compromised sabbaths when occupied by Israel. The complex repetition of this passage leads to a damning indictment: along with disobeying Yahweh's commandments, ordinances, and statutes (v. 14), Israel has defied its own sabbaths. By spurning the divine decrees, Yahweh's own people have spurned the land, good and given (v. 43). Consequently, the land's relief can be achieved only by the land's relinquishment of Israel, a good riddance.

Yet the land cannot lie permanently at rest, in suspended animation as it were, any more than Yahweh is capable of permanently spurning Israel (v. 44). The covenantal curses conclude on a note of hope, recalling the land promised to the patriarchs (v. 42). By honoring this ancient covenant (Gen 17:1-22), Yahweh remembers the land and Israel makes amends (*rṣh ʾet-ʿāwōn*, Lev 26:43; cf. vv. 34-35). Yahweh's covenantal faithfulness and Israel's repentance are deliberately related. Yahweh's covenantal initiative sets in motion Israel's repentance in exile and return to the land, in short, the re-creation of a people. In this sense, the land finds its ultimate restoration or sabbath from the integrity of Israel's conduct *on* it. The issue of the land's rest and restoration informs the larger scope of the Priestly narrative. The land of Canaan is no wild frontier to be conquered by Israel.[205] Theologically, the land is a grant to be received, not the object of Israel's "manifest destiny." In this ethos of rest, the relationship between the land and its inhabitants is a reciprocal one based on divine ownership.

As the object of defilement and the subject of rest, the land bears a certain sanctity. In creation and covenant, sabbath rest denotes the sphere of holiness. Similarly, the tabernacle can also be the object of defilement, brought about, for instance, by sexual impurity (15:31), corpse contamination (Num 19:13, 20), and apostasy (Lev 20:3). Also, the entire camp can be defiled through contact

204. The verb *rṣh* connotes satisfaction as a consequence of full restitution (e.g., v. 41; 2 Chr 36:21). Israel also "satisfies" sin by making amends for it in exile (Lev 26:43).
205. Cf. Josh 11:23: "And the land had rest from war."

with the unclean (Num 5:1-4). Yet the land's "holiness," unlike the tabernacle's, is more implicit. Nowhere in Leviticus is the land proper called "holy" or "sanctified" *(qdš)*.[206] Instead, the priests and the congregation are most frequently the objects of sanctification (Lev 21:8, 15, 23; 22:9, 16, 32).

As Yahweh's dwelling, the tabernacle represents the quintessence of holiness. In comparison, the land's "holiness" is more a by-product, that is, derived from the integrity and (potential) holiness of its inhabitants.[207] What the land has is its integrity or purity, which like Israel itself must be maintained in the calling to be holy. In this sense, the land can be defiled by an impure people, as Israel's predecessors had presumably done to Canaan (18:26).[208] The land can also be defiled or polluted by the shedding of blood (Num 35:33-34). The land's "holiness" rests on the purity practiced by its inhabitants, who are called to be holy. Whereas holiness is the overarching goal or telos of Israel's life in the land, purity is its concrete embodiment. Both land and its people reflect this. The land is "good" (Num 13:32) and is implicitly holy as much as the inhabitants are potentially holy.

The integrity of the land also forms and informs Israel's relationships with the other inhabitants, particularly the alien *(gēr)*. The alien is a prominent figure in the Priestly communal landscape, an individual who is distinct from the congregation yet enjoys many of the rights, privileges, and responsibilities Israel enjoys as a holy community. Indeed, the alien is a test case of the Priestly concern with differentiation. In a nutshell, the *gēr* in Priestly law is a non-Israelite who has taken up permanent residence in the land. Yet, notably, the Priestly legists do not write off the *gēr*'s existence, as they do with the former inhabitants of the land who have been evicted from it (Lev 18:25; 20:23). Moreover, the resident alien is not a foreigner, who simply passes through or is living temporarily within the community and is prohibited from participation in the

206. Only parcels of land, or fields, are consecrated to Yahweh by their owners in Lev 27:16-24. Milgrom states that the most explicit statement regarding the sanctity of the land is found in 18:26-27; 20:2; 24:22 ("Leviticus," *IDBSup,* 544). Yet the technical terminology for holiness is found in none of these places. Indeed, holiness is reserved for Yahweh as an attribute, for the sanctuary as Yahweh's domain, and for Israel as a calling (19:2; 20:7, 26).

207. Knohl points out that the land's produce also exhibits "a kind of" holiness (*Sanctuary of Silence,* 188).

208. Although there is much to distinguish between the so-called Holiness Code, on the one hand, and the Priestly narrative and Torah, on the other, there is also much that is compatible, even logically congruent. The emphasis on the holy integrity of the land presupposes Israel's settled existence, whereas the Priestly narrative's emphasis on the tabernacle is expected within a historiography that primarily charts Israel's sojourns. Cf. Milgrom, *Leviticus 1–16,* 48.

holy festivals, such as the Passover (Exod 12:43, 48). Rather, the *gēr* is a bona fide resident of the land. As Yahweh addresses Moses, "You shall have *one* law for the alien and for the native" (*'ezrāḥ,* Lev 24:22),[209] legal parity for a culturally diverse land. Such juridical unity reflects the land's integrity, preserved and maintained by a holy community. This particular declaration is embedded in the stipulations regarding the application of *lex talionis* (vv. 15-22), which itself bridges social divisions endemic to any settled society.[210]

The book of Leviticus more broadly dictates ethical parity between Israelite and alien, providing a pointed rationale: "When the alien resides with you in your land, you shall not oppress the alien. As a native among you shall be the alien who resides with you;[211] you shall love the alien as yourself, for you were aliens in the land of Egypt: I am Yahweh your God" (19:33-34).[212] The virtually native status of the alien is grounded in Israel's own identity as an erstwhile oppressed people living in a foreign land (Exod 1:13-14; 2:23). Nativistic separation is overcome by shared identity, common ground that relativizes without erasing the distinction. Israel is not to incorporate the resident alien into oppressive service. To do so would be to repeat the sin of Egypt. Neither a true-blooded Israelite nor an anonymous slave, the alien remains distinct in the land of Israel.[213] More sharply, the critical status of the alien vis-à-vis Israel is reflected in Israel's very status in the land vis-à-vis God. In the stipulations regarding the Year of Jubilee, Yahweh declares, "The land shall not be sold in perpetuity, for the land belongs to me; with me you are but aliens and temporary residents" (25:23; cf. v. 35).[214] Not even Israel can lay absolute claim on the land; hence more is in common between the Israelite and the alien than meets the eye.

---

209. See also Num 15:15: "There shall be for both you and the resident alien a single statute, a perpetual statute throughout your generations; you and the alien shall be alike before Yahweh" (also vv. 16, 29).

210. The indefinite subject *'îš* ("anyone") is repeated throughout the passage (vv. 16, 17, 22).

211. The Hebrew word order is deliberate.

212. Ezek 47:22-23 is the only place outside the Priestly corpus in which the alien and the native are juxtaposed. Here the aliens are allocated land within the tribal territory in which they have settled. See C. Van Houten, *The Alien in Israelite Law* (JSOTSup 107; Sheffield: JSOT Press, 1991) 116.

213. I cannot agree with Van Houten that the resident alien is one who has become an "insider" in the community (*Alien,* 156). If so, the distinction in terminology would no longer apply. Lev 25:44, which sets the alien in parallel with the foreign nations from which slaves can be procured, is an embarrassing example. The alien's status in Israel's land is not so much a case of cultural assimilation as one of parity and differentiation.

214. The temporary resident, *tôšāb,* is another distinct class (Van Houten, *Alien,* 131).

On the one hand, the alien is permitted to observe the Passover (Exod 12:19, 48-49; Num 9:14)[215] and make offerings (Num 15:14-16; Lev 22:18). Particularly in the case of Passover observance, permission is granted without backhanded retribution if the alien chooses not to participate. The land is not defiled by the alien's negligence of the Passover. The permission to celebrate is akin to an invitation. An ironic freedom is extended in this permission: the alien is not bound to observe the one defining moment in Israel's history that bonds Israel to the alien. The Israelite, however, has no choice except to observe the Passover and is punished accordingly if negligent (e.g., Num 9:13). On the other hand, the alien, as a resident of the land, is required to observe the sabbath of the atonement by refraining from work (Lev 16:29) and to present burnt offerings at the entrance of the tent (17:8), as well as being prohibited from committing abomination, which would defile the land (18:26), from consuming blood (vv. 10, 12, 13, 15), from willful sinning (Num 15:30), from practicing apostasy (20:2),[216] and from blaspheming the Name (24:16). These prohibitive commands are shared by native and alien alike in the land. As a non-Israelite, the resident alien is given choice in the cultic life of Israel,[217] yet is fully bound by the prohibitions of holiness in order to maintain the purity of the land. The alien is a *virtual* native, alike but different.[218] In the land, Israel is commissioned to dwell as a distinct people. Yet the land and its inhabitants have found room for others, a partial pluralism.

This principle of distinction without exclusion finds its culmination in the love command given in Leviticus 19, the center of Priestly ethics. The juxtaposition of vv. 18-19, although belonging to separate units, is indicative of the larger ethos of Priestly theology: "You shall not take vengeance or bear a grudge against any of your people, but you shall love your neighbor as yourself:[219] I am Yahweh. You shall keep my statutes. You shall not sow your field

215. Provided the alien and his family are circumcised (Exod 12:48).

216. Presumably, the alien receives the benefits of purgation, like the Israelite on the Day of Atonement (v. 30, but cf. v. 33). See Num 15:25-26.

217. The choice, however, is of limited extent. For instance, only natives, not aliens, are mentioned in the Festival of Booths (23:42).

218. Natives can also slip into the category of "resident alien" by becoming financially dependent on their kin (25:35).

219. Heb. *wě'āhabtā lěrē'ăkā kāmôkā*. An often suggested alternative translation is: "You shall love your neighbor [who is] like you" (so, e.g., R. E. Clements, *Loving One's Neighbour: Old Testament Ethics in Context* [Ethel M. Wood Lecture; London: University of London Press, 1992] 25). Such a translation, however, would most likely require a separate clause (e.g., *'ăšer kāmôkā hû'*). See H.-P. Mathys, *Liebe deinen Nächsten wie dich selbst: Untersuchungen zum alttestamentliche Gebot der Nächstenliebe (Lev 19,18)* (OBO 71; Freiburg: Universitätsverlag; Göttingen: Vandenhoeck & Ruprecht, 1986) 9. Rather than

with two kinds of seed; nor shall you put on a garment made of two different materials." The well-known love command is embedded in a context of social containment. The neighbor is unequivocally a fellow Israelite, who is interchangeable with the moral subject as an object of love. Within the ethical sphere, the self and the neighbor are equivalent in moral worth and warrant. The equivalency of subject and object, of I and Thou, however, cannot extend to inherently different things, such as seeds or fabrics. The intermixing or leveling out of such distinctions is prohibited. Yet the love command, in virtually identical form, extends also to the alien (v. 34b): "You shall love [the alien] as yourself, for you were aliens in the land of Egypt: I am Yahweh your God." In short, Israel's ethos of distinction includes an ethic of parity.

Like the cosmic domains, separation is part of Israel's formation in the land. Indeed, from this standpoint the exodus from Egypt and the *eisodus* into Canaan represent essentially a pilgrimage of separation that marks the formation of an ethos of differentiation in Israel's history: "You shall not do as they do in the land of Egypt" (18:3). Assimilation is tantamount to enslavement. In the Year of Jubilee, Israel is specifically proscribed from ruling harshly *(lō'-tirdeh bĕperek)* over fellow Israelites who have had to sell themselves due to desperate circumstances (25:43, 46). They are counted not as slaves *('ebed)* but as hired laborers or tenants *(sākîr, tôšāb)*. The precedent is to be found in the exodus episode: "For to me the people of Israel are servants *('ăbādîm)*, my servants they are whom I brought out from the land of Egypt; I am Yahweh your God" (25:55). All Israelites are bound together in the defining moment of the exodus. For the Priestly legists, the exodus is the founding event of Israel's own ethos. Although designated by the same term in Hebrew, "slave" and "servant" could not be farther apart within the Priestly moral purview: "And I will walk among you and be your God, and you will be my people. I am Yahweh your God who brought you out of the land of Egypt, to be their slaves no more; I have broken the bars of your yoke and made you walk erect *(qômĕmîyût)*" (26:12-13).

The identity of the owner and the location of the slave/servant *('ebed)* make all the difference. To Yahweh belong servants who have been freed from the yoke of slavery. In Yahweh's land, "slaves" stand erect, while Egypt's "servants" are bent and broken (cf. Exod 2:23; 6:9). The exodus is a pilgrimage from slavery to servanthood, from landlessness to landedness, Israel's evolution toward liberation and moral integrity. In Israel's land, harsh rule is ban-

---

adjectival in force, the prepositional phrase is adverbial, by which the object "your neighbor" is set in parallel with the second person suffix, lit. "You shall love your neighbor as you."

ished. So also Yahweh's creation: there is no hostile force pitching for a cosmic fight that must be harshly suppressed; rather the cosmos is dignified by the temperate rule of sovereignty. Israel's conduct, in turn, must dignify the land and its diverse inhabitants, its home.

Living in Holiness

Informing and undergirding every prescription, holiness serves as the impetus and direction of Israel's moral life, the basis of Israel's distinction: "You shall be holy to me, for I Yahweh am holy, and I have separated you from the other peoples to be mine" (Lev 20:26). In the Priestly corpus, Israel's command to be holy is paramount (11:44; 19:2; 20:7, 26) and concomitantly Yahweh's act to sanctify a people (20:8; 22:32). Neither innate nor inaccessible, holiness is the distinctive domain of life created by Yahweh to be embodied or "filled" by Israel. As part of Yahweh's very nature, holiness is integral to Israel's unique destiny, an identity in the making. As in Priestly narrative, holiness bears in Leviticus both temporal and spatial dimensions, a sabbath and a sanctuary, a vocation and a moral sphere of existence.

It would be an understatement to contend simply that the seventh day was an important reference point in Israel's ritual observances.[220] The sabbath served as no less than the defining moment and temporal frame for ritual purity and festival. The seven-day period, or multiples thereof, marked a time of cleansing or purification required when living in skin was made vulnerable, as in the case of menstruation and giving birth (15:1, 12:2, 5); and the seven-year period, or multiples thereof, ensured Israel's integrity and existence in the land (25:2-34). Skin and house diseases required a quarantine of seven days.[221] For the individual, the ritual of cleansing involved a shaving of all hair on the seventh day and purification rites on the eighth day, the new day (14:9, 10-20). Seven times the cleansed person or domicile is to be sprinkled with blood (14:7, 51-52); seven times oil is sprinkled before Yahweh to consecrate the oil that is reserved for the cleansed person (14:16). The numerological significance of ritual is integral to the process of reintegrating the erstwhile unclean person or object back into Israel's fold, fully restored.

Restoration is also effected in the observance of the sabbath. The calendar of festivals in the Holiness Code begins with the sabbath stipulation

---

220. For a general treatment on the unique importance of the sabbath in Priestly lore and legislation, see Coote and Ord, *In the Beginning*, 84-86.
221. See 13:5, 26, 27, 31, 34, 50; 14:9, 38, 39.

(23:3), a prohibitive rest.[222] As in the various purgation observances, the seven-day period is, moreover, a formative element in the appointed festivals. For example, unleavened bread is to be eaten only for seven days with no occupational work performed on the first and seventh days, the holy convocations (*miqrā'-qōdeš*, vv. 6-8; cf. v. 3). The presentation of offerings, whether of firstfruits or of new grain, is conducted specifically on the day after the sabbath (vv. 11, 16). The Festival of Weeks commences on the day after the seventh sabbath (v. 15). In certain festivals, the sabbath day can migrate to other days. The day of holy rest is sometimes identified with the eighth day, as in the Festival of Weeks and the Festival of Booths (vv. 21, 36), as well as with the first day of the seventh month, as in the Festival of Trumpets (v. 23). The Festival of Booths in particular revolves around a seven-day period: seven days in the seventh month is reserved for rejoicing (v. 40). The tenth day of the seventh month is the Day of Atonement, a day of complete rest and "self-denial" (vv. 27-28, 32).[223]

The culmination of restoration is found in the sabbatical year, the annual extension of the weekly cycle of work and rest: "When you enter the land that I am giving you, the land shall observe a sabbath for Yahweh. Six years you shall sow your field, and six years you shall prune your vineyard and gather in their yield; but in the seventh year there shall be a sabbath of complete rest, a sabbath for Yahweh" (25:2b-3a). The sabbatical year is observed for the land's sake; the land is to lie fallow, free of any imposition of labor and open for consumption by slaves, tenants, livestock, and even wild animals (vv. 5-7). The sabbath transforms private land into an eminently public domain. This seventh year marks the complete cessation of subduing the land in order to restore it. Restoration is also key in another full extension of the sabbath, the Year of Jubilee, which is determined by "seven sabbaths of years." In the following year, or fiftieth year,[224] a time of liberty (*děrôr*, v. 10) was proclaimed. Israelites who had become indentured servants, due to dire circumstances beyond their control, were released (vv. 35-42); and land sold out of economic necessity anytime during the intervening years was restored to the original clan owners (vv. 8-12). Thus the Year of Jubilee marks the return of property to the rightful "owners" and an exodus of the "enslaved" back to their homes. The culminating sabbath of the Jubilee marks a leveling out, to some degree, of economic and social dispar-

222. Diachronically, vv. 2-3, 38 are most likely interpolations designed to give the sabbath pride of place in the calendrical listing.

223. Heb. *wĕ'innîtem 'et-napšōtêkem;* cf. 16:29.

224. Some scholars contend that it may actually have been the forty-ninth or seventh sabbatical year (C. J. H. Wright, "Jubilee, Year of," *ABD* 3.1025).

ities. As Yahweh proclaims, "With me you are but aliens and tenants" (v. 23b). Ownership is a relative concept.

As for the sabbath injunctions themselves in Priestly legislation,[225] Exod 31:13-17 is the most explicit in conjoining human and divine activity in a relationship of emulation. This passage is a compendium of sabbath instruction that gives evidence of systematic, literary structuring:

A	Sabbath sign: knowledge of sanctification	13
	B Holy to you	14a
	C Violation	14b
	D Sabbath of solemn rest	15a
	B¹ Holy to Yahweh	15a
	C¹ Violation	15b
A¹	Perpetual covenant and sign: work and rest in creation	16-17

The movement progresses from human prescription to divine description. Israel is directly addressed to observe the sabbath and appropriate its significance: "in order that you may know that I, Yahweh, am sanctifying you" (v. 13b). The penalty for working on the sabbath is death (cf. Num 15:32-36). The severity of the penalty reflects the solemn import of the observance: the sabbath is "holy to you." Analogously, the sabbath is "holy to Yahweh," a covenantal sign between Israel and its God (vv. 13b, 17a). The rationale behind the sign is spelled out at the conclusion of the injunction: Yahweh created for six days and then rested (v. 17).[226] Unlike the other covenantal signs of Priestly lore, Yahweh's creative activity is a reminder to Israel rather than to God. Consequently, all covenantal obedience on Israel's part stems in some sense from the sabbath observance. The divine act of creation and completion determines Israel's holy rhythm of work and rest.

Similarly, the sabbath injunction in the Decalogue of Exodus grounds the sabbath observance in the Creator's activity (20:8-11). Israel is enjoined to "keep it holy" (lĕqaddĕšô, v. 8). Work is prohibited on the seventh day, which includes Israelite, slave, livestock, and alien (v. 10). The rationale given is Yahweh's own creative activity: "For in six days Yahweh made heaven and earth, the sea, and all that is in them, but rested on the seventh day; therefore Yahweh blessed

225. Exod 16:23; 20:8-11; 31:13-17; 35:2-3; Lev 23:2b-3; cf. Num 15:32-36. Knohl assigns Num 29:9-10 and Gen 2:1-3 to the "Priestly Torah" (*Sanctuary of Silence*, 13-19, 67, 144n.80).
226. The *kî* clause in v. 17 is better read as causal (contra NRSV): "It is a sign between me and the Israelites, *for* Yahweh created . . ." (Fox, "Sign of the Covenant," 577).

the sabbath day and consecrated it" (*wayĕqaddĕšēhû*, v. 11).[227] Together, these injunctions in Exodus treat cosmogony as the fundamental basis to Israel's sabbath observance. As Yahweh consecrated this day apart from all other days, so Israel must consecrate it through their cessation from work.

The tie to Gen 2:1-3 is more than obvious. Contrary to Israel Knohl, who finds in the conclusion to the Priestly cosmogony a different provenance from that of the sabbath injunctions in Exodus, the similarity of language is unmistakable.[228] God created the heavens and the earth (Gen 2:1; Exod 20:11; 31:17); God both blessed and consecrated the seventh day (Gen 2:3; Exod 20:11); God rested (Gen 2:2; Exod 20:11; 31:17).[229] Within Priestly lore and law, the sabbath is intimately associated with God's creative activity. By refraining from work on the sabbath, Israel participates in the life of God. Of all the practices enjoined and commanded in the Priestly corpus, the sabbath observance constitutes the most powerful moral nexus between Israel's and Yahweh's identity; it is the prescriptive and ritual link between Yahweh's self-description, "I am holy," and Yahweh's command, "Be holy." Observance of the sabbath is the vehicle for and testimony to the consecration of a people.

In terms of its ethical significance, the sabbath's *blessing* plays a crucial role, a fact easily overlooked by the attention given to the sabbath's holy consecration among interpreters. God not only hallowed but also blessed the sab-

227. Note the *inclusio* of consecration that opens and concludes the sabbath command (vv. 8, 11) and marks, as in 31:13-17, a rhetorical movement from human prescription to divine description.

228. Knohl states that Gen 2:1-3 does not mention the name "sabbath" and lacks "any command forbidding the performance of human labors" (*Sanctuary of Silence*, 18). To conclude, therefore, that the cosmogony is of a different provenance is a most tenuous use of the argument from silence. First, the sabbath commands in Exodus are reserved exclusively for Israel, not for humanity in general. Thus the presence of prescriptive language for the seventh day in Gen 2:1-3 would not make sense, given its universal scope. Second, the lack of the name "sabbath" in the cosmogony is rendered inconsequential by the fact that God is described as "sabbathing" on the seventh day (Gen 2:2-3). The use of the formal name is tied directly to its prescriptive language, reserved for Israel. Given his criteria for delineating Holiness School theology, Knohl would be more consistent in arguing that Gen 1:1–2:3 is a product of the Holiness Code. By assigning different provenances, Knohl concludes that whereas the Holiness School forbids labor, Priestly legislation does not, citing Num 28:9-10. Yet this passage focuses exclusively on the provision of priestly sacrifices and is not concerned with the occupational work of Israelites in general. For example, Aaron bears the duty of replacing and arranging the tabernacle bread on the sabbath, according to the Holiness Code (Lev 24:8).

229. The slight variations in language, particularly in describing divine rest (*npš*, Exod 31:17; *nwḥ*, 20:11) are not sufficient warrants for assigning a provenance different from that of the cosmogony.

bath. As life itself, the seventh day is an object of blessing (Gen 1:22, 28). In the former case, filling the appropriate domains of sea and land with life fulfills the role of blessing, the ongoing activity of procreation. Analogously, by blessing the final day of creation, Yahweh assigns an ongoing, creative function to the sabbath (Gen 2:3; Exod 20:11). Much of Priestly law, in essence, fills out the significance of the sabbath's blessing for Israel. Sabbath restores both the land and a people in the ongoing task of moral living. Consequently, the sabbath day is by nature open-ended, bereft of temporal closure, in contrast to the other days of creation (cf. Gen 2:3), yet filled with moral force, as evinced in the cult's ongoing maintenance. In the sabbath, time stands still, emptied of human manipulation and rife with divine communion. In the blessing of the sabbath, Israel is distinctly blessed with the ongoing task of moral conduct in the world.

In sabbath is lodged the locus of ethical order, from Aaron's unceasing arrangement of the sanctuary bread every sabbath day "as a commitment of the people of Israel, as a covenant in perpetuity" (24:8), to Israel's own "self-denial" on the sabbath. In sabbath is the measure of self-restraint and service. As the sanctuary is the defining center of the community in the wilderness and the land, so the sabbath is the defining moment of ritual and conduct. Through the cessation of common activity, the sabbath generates a holy community in its temporal life. Cosmically, the sabbath is God's temporal space. Ethically, it is Israel's domain, as much as the land is Israel's dwelling place. In Lev 25:2 an indelible link is forged between the land's rest and Israel's exodus, a journey from enervating labor to constructive rest. As Yahweh's glory fills the sanctuary, so Israel embodies the sabbath rest. Signified by the sabbath, holiness is Israel's domain in communion with its creator. In the sabbath, Israel fills the domain of the holy. Like the tent of meeting, the locus of the divine/human encounter, the sabbath is the meeting point between prescription and praxis, consecration and blessing.

An Ethos of Restoration: Identity and Integration

> The absence of boundaries creates nonorder, and nonorder is not
> the end of exclusion but the end of life.
>
> Miroslav Volf[230]

The final arrangement and presentation of Priestly lore and legislation into a coherent corpus of narrative and law no doubt functioned crucially for a peo-

230. From *Exclusion and Embrace: A Theological Exploration of Identity, Otherness, and Reconciliation* (Nashville: Abingdon, 1996) 63.

ple set to restore its community in a land once lost.[231] Having been landless in exile, the children of Jacob, as in Egypt, must muster the social and theological capital to form and reform Israel's identity back in the land. The land of the exile, Babylonia, had set the stage for a profound transformation of the community's identity, as was necessary for its own survival in exile. As Daniel Smith has argued in his sociological study of the exile, the Priestly emphasis on order and separation constituted a survival strategy for preserving Israel's distinct identity.[232] Identity and distinction were forged in response to the dangers of assimilation in the land of exile. On foreign soil, Babylonian incorporation of the exilic community galvanized the development of Priestly lore as both protest literature and survivalist's guide. On native land, potentially corrosive conflict with those who remained or settled in the land during the intervening years crystallized Priestly tradition. In Judah the new homecomers were faced with the immediate challenges of integration and formation of the community's identity. Such were the root concerns of the Priestly tradents.

From a sociological standpoint, the construct of the alien represents a concerted effort among the Priestly tradents to maintain both distinction and integration in the land. Most likely representing the indigenous person, spared from exile and firmly planted in the land, the alien in Priestly law represents an ethical resolve to accord similar rights and privileges, in many cases, to "erstwhile Israelites" who had not undergone the trauma of the exile, a quintessentially formative experience for the Priestly tradents.[233] By no means were the aliens written off as foreigners to be driven off the land.

231. The date of the Priestly tradition, both the Holiness Code and narrative, remains a matter of some dispute. I refer to the bibliographies presented by Dozeman, *God on the Mountain*, 87n.1; and Brown, *Structure*, 246 nn. 102, 104. See more recently the review of scholarship in Joseph Blenkinsopp, "An Assessment of the Alleged Pre-Exilic Date of the Priestly Material in the Pentateuch," *ZAW* 108 (1996) 495-518. Much of the linguistic evidence marshaled in support of a preexilic dating, as championed by Kaufmann and more recently by Milgrom and Hurvitz, has been successfully questioned by Blenkinsopp.

232. D. L. Smith, *Religion of the Landless* (Bloomington, Ind.: Meyer Stone, 1989), esp. 10, 80-81, 140-43.

233. Contra H. Cazelles, who contends precisely the reverse by identifying the gēr or "alien" with the returning exiles and the 'ezrāḥ, the "native," with the indigenous of the land ("La mission d'Esdras," *VT* 4 [1954] 131-32). See the criticisms of Van Houten, *Alien*, 151-55. Rendering gēr as a *Prosylet* ("convert"), Mathys, moreover, identifies the 'ezrāḥ with the exiles *during* the exile, those who "had lost the land and hoped to return" (*Liebe deinen Nächsten*, 45). The respective identities were clearly maintained during the restoration period, during which Priestly legislation was finalized. That the Priestly legists were able to reverse the "plain senses" of these terms testifies to their ideological innovation.

Priestly legislation was aimed at resisting, even protesting against, such temptation. Priestly legists forged a solid bond of identity between the exiled Jews and resident aliens, lodged squarely in the exodus and lived out in the sabbath (Exod 20:10; Lev 19:34; cf. 25:23). Yet the alien remained admittedly second class, and this is where the moral imagination of the Priestly legists ultimately falls short. Within the Priestly landscape, one is hard-pressed to find full parity, much less a reunion, in the occupation of Canaan. Nevertheless, from an ethos characterized by differentiation and integration, cosmically discernible in creation, the Priestly tradents impart a credible and compelling context for the (re)formation of Israel's moral identity in their restoration program for the community.

Distinction without Exclusion

From cosmogony to cult, the Priestly ethos places a high premium on Israel's distinction in the land of its dwelling and in the sanctity of God's dwelling. Separate from the nations, Israel was to be a "priestly kingdom and a holy nation" (Exod 19:6). Continually cleansed from the impurities of human sin, both willful and unwitting, Yahweh's dwelling was maintained through an intricate system of atoning or purgation rituals designed to ensure Yahweh's presence among a people. In the Priestly landscape, holiness is Israel's prescribed essence ("Be holy") as it is Yahweh's described nature ("I am holy"; cf. Exod 6:2). Holiness is the core of Yahweh's and Israel's distinction. As holiness sets God off from creation, it also demarcates Israel from the pagan nations around it. The distinction of holiness is framed cosmically in creation on the seventh day and exemplified morally in Israel's embodiment of purity.

Leviticus 20:24-26 makes pointedly clear that the business of distinction making within the created order is the essence of Israel's culture crafting. Here Yahweh reiterates the promise of Israel's land as the rightful domain of Israel's distinction from the nations. Israel's cultural domain in the land consequently provides the grounds for establishing further distinctions, namely, between the pure and the impure, a distinctly holy enterprise (v. 26). Making distinctions is uniquely Israel's commission, parallel to filling the land as humanity's general commission. Whereas all of humanity is blessed with the cultural task of filling and cultivating the earth for its livelihood, Israel is blessed with the holy mission of cultivating purity and distinguishing it from what is impure. By fulfilling its destiny, Israel wholly identifies its culture with its cult.

THE ETHOS OF THE COSMOS

The making of distinctions establishes Israel's own domain, the domain of purity, in which to live faithfully in the land of Yahweh's sanctuary. Both discerned and created, purity is uniquely Israel's moral space. On the one hand, purity is informed by the larger structures of the cosmos, as revealed in the diet laws. Impure animals are likely to be boundary crossers that exhibit peculiar characteristics alien to the behaviors and qualities typical of their natural domains. Impurity is essentially unnatural and a differentiated creation serves as a template for making such distinctions. On the other hand, purity is by no means static, much less dead, space: the community's purity is generated by moral living in consonance with Yahweh's dwelling in their midst and Israel's dwelling in a derived "holy" land. Purity is inherent in creation as much as it is established by Israel's conduct in accordance with Yahweh's holy decrees. Israel's journey toward distinction, toward establishing and filling its proper domain, is the driving force behind Israel's unfolding history from the Priestly perspective.

In the hands of the Priestly historiographer, the exodus marks a journey from exile to ethos, a founding event that takes on potent and polyvalent significance in Priestly legislation. Israel's exodus from Egypt is not simply an emancipation from bondage, but a distinction out of disarray, form from chaos. From the context of the cult, Israel's enslavement in Egypt was a near fatal exercise in assimilation. Like the earth amid the deluge, the land of Egypt was awash with chaos. Here was a land without barriers, filled with structured violence brought about by the enslavement of a people. Here also was a land in stagnant time, where no hope of sabbath rest could take root, and thus no hope for the dignity of distinction in a foreign land. The absence of such dignity was an affront to Israel's identity, indeed, a crime against humanity for any bearer of the *imago Dei*.[234]

As much as the exodus is the journey from Israel's landlessness to landedness, it is also Yahweh's quest for a dwelling place among a people. In the middle of the wilderness, Sinai marks the transference of glory from mountaintop to inner sanctum. From exodus to *eisoikus*, Yahweh settles with a people on their *eisodus*. God's indwelling defines a people as particular, nothing short of holy, the quintessence of distinction. The filling of sacred space with sacred substance is the end and goal of Israel's cult. God both consecrates the sabbath and graces the tabernacle with divine presence, with *doxa* (glory). Divine indwelling enables Israel to dwell in a land of release and

---

234. Again, the moral imagination of the Priestly tradents falls short by not taking a more rigorous stand against enslavement in their own land (cf. Lev 25:44-46).

abundance, in a perpetual sabbath as opposed to relentless oppression, a land of completion and not chaos. As far as "chaos" is from form, the distinction between Egypt and Canaan is cosmically distanced. Yet a paradox is evinced in the contrast. Israel is not released for absolute self-determination, for such is to wander aimlessly in the wilderness with the certain fate of death in a perpetual state of liminality (cf. Exod 14:3).

In the founding event of the exodus, Israel is released from slavery to servanthood, from bondage to a high-handed people in allegiance with a gentle-handed God, who ensures the integrity of all who live off the land, both alien and Israelite. Yahweh's indwelling also furthers the divine distinction, for God, the Creator, separate from the cosmos, has become Yahweh, Israel's identified God (Exod 6:2), separate from the nations. God has chosen to capitalize on the sabbath rest by filling it with a particular people. Israel's distinction vis-à-vis the cosmos is this: Israel inhabits the sabbath "space," signified spatially by both the tabernacle and the land. The sabbath is distinctly Israel's domain.

Yet the contours of Israel's distinction, as well as Yahweh's, are not as rigid or exclusive as they would appear. By inhabiting the domain of holiness, Israel itself has crossed from the common to the holy. Similarly, Israel's priests ritually crossed the boundary between the profane and the holy, not casually but with utmost care, lest the violence of violation break out. Ritual was the means of restoring the integrity of boundaries that delineated purity and holiness in time and space. Yet as much as a holy priest remains a person, bounded by skin, a holy nation is still a nation in need of a domain. Israel's distinctiveness is thus an immanent one, evinced *in* the world, not over and against it. Israel's relationship to the land reflects God's relationship to the cosmos. God's creative power is evinced not by flexing a strong and outstretched arm against the recalcitrant forces of chaos, but by calling forth and collaborating with the elements of creation, both created and preexistent. The creation of the cosmos reflects the sovereignty of a different order, unlike that of Marduk or Baal.

That Yahweh chooses to dwell with a people rather than reside exclusively in the heavens, utterly detached from messy worldly affairs, testifies to the natural immanence of holiness, a separation from within. For the Priestly tradents, the immanence of God's holiness evinces a nonoppressive hierarchy. That the Priestly worldview reflects a social hierarchy is undeniable; what is remarkable, however, is that the tradents take pains to distance such a hierarchy from all hints of oppression and violence,[235] lessons learned in the deluge

---

235. Cf. the pairing of violence and oppression *(ḥāmās, šōd)* in Ezek 45:9.

and the exodus. This nonoppressive hierarchy can be seen in a number of examples, beginning, as noted above, with creation.

God creates not by brute force but with great care. The human task of subduing the earth does not pit humanity against nature, but reflects a working *with* nature through cultivation and occupation, through promoting and harnessing creation's integrity. Moses' sin is as much the beating of the rock as it is his contempt for Yahweh's command. Abraham's possession of the land comes about through open and fair negotiation, a price paid in full. The non-Aaronide Levites are joined to the priests in the common task of maintaining the sanctuary's holy integrity on Israel's behalf. Humans and animals share in common the land as the source of their mutual livelihood. The aliens of the land share with Israel a common identity. Such distinctions reveal a larger integrity founded on distinctions without lapsing into exclusion or apartheid.[236] The Priestly ethos of differentiation can sustain the hope for reconciliation. For the Priestly tradents, separation without integration breeds contempt and fear, as well as generates a hierarchy of violence; differentiation engenders integrity, an immanence that is both apart from and involved in the wholeness of creation. Creation without differentiation is either chaos or nothing at all. Uniformity is tantamount to the unformed.

Integrity without Inclusion

Israel's distinction is part of a larger integrity that binds Israel to Yahweh, its creator, and to the cosmos. The cosmos itself is formed with a structural integrity or stability in mind. Therein lies creation's "goodness" (*ṭôb*). The success of creation is confirmed by the optimal life its inhabitants can secure from their respective domains, including the nations throughout the land, of which Israel is a member.[237] The goodness of creation is comprehensive in scope: as an approbative expression "it is good" marks the successful completion of creation in stages and as a whole. The final approbation accounts for the entire cosmos in all its integrity, both aesthetic and instrumental. Creation exhibits an exquisite, variegated beauty as well as a fully functional in-

236. *Apartheid* is Afrikaner for "apartness." See also Gammie's appropriate references to the former political ethos of South Africa and to racial segregation in the U.S.A. as representing potential dangers of the Priestly principle of separation in contemporary political contexts (*Holiness in Israel*, 13). I would contend that Priestly theology is sufficiently nuanced to safeguard such distortions (see below).

237. See Lohfink, "God the Creator," 125-35.

tegrity in providing for life. The world has value; it is endowed with goodness wrought by a process that affirmed creation's dignity through separation and interdependence, analogous to the construction of the tabernacle. In short, creation's goodness is evinced in its stewardship. Diversity within appropriate bounds is a mark of goodness or integrity, which holds it all in balance.

In ethical parlance, the earth's goodness, its *ordo bonorum*, provides the essential "premoral" grounding for Israel's moral ethos.[238] In bestowing cosmic approval to creation, God in effect steps back to survey its wondrous intricacy and integrity. By stepping back to gain a bird's-eye view of the cosmos,[239] God initiates a movement from creation's goodness to the domain of holiness. Within the seven-day scheme, creative activity is the necessary preface to holiness, and holiness marks the completion and culmination of creation. Similarly, Israel's distinctive ethos marks in part a stepping back from creation and allowing God's good creation to inform its ethic of holiness. This ethos of holiness is specific to Israel among the nations as it is peculiar to God in creation.

From the soil of creation's *ordo bonorum* emerges Israel's own moral life, an *ordo sanctorum* from which the *ordo caritatis*, or love ethic, derives (Lev 19:18, 34).[240] Yet Israel's internal ethic of impartial love has cosmic grounding: all humankind is created in God's image. The self and the other share in common the divine image (Gen 1:26-27). To love the neighbor as one's self is to love the other who is created like one's self, a fellow human being, yet conceivably different, as in the alien's case. As the bearer of God's image, Israel lives out of this domain of holiness, a moral sphere that is in fact endemic to all humanity. It is to the Priestly tradents' credit that God's holiness bears an anthropological correlate. Such is the cosmic grounding of Israel's distinctive ethic. Israel's ethos, distinctive as it is in concrete form, encompasses a cosmic expanse. Although fundamentally distinguished, the cosmic order of goodness and Israel's order of holiness are tightly interrelated. Holiness points unequivocally to the integrity of distinction.

Within cosmogony, the blessing of holiness is essential to creation and

---

238. I draw from L. Janssens's article, "Norms and Priorities in a Love Ethics," *Louvain Studies* 6 (1977) 207-26, esp. 210-18. Although he does not deal with creation theology per se, much of what he says about "pre-moral values" pertains to the Priestly valuation of creation.

239. Cf. Gen 1:2, in which God's Spirit or breath is likened to a hovering bird.

240. See also Deut 10:19. The NT repeats the love command no less than eight times (Matt 19:19; 22:39; Mark 12:31, 33; Luke 10:27; Rom 13:2; Gal 5:14; Jas 2:8) and expands the definition of "neighbor," a move already anticipated in the Priestly "inclusion" of the alien.

not a disconnected appendix. As Israel's land requires rest and restoration from cultivation during the sabbatical year, so creation, by extension, requires a homeostasis in order to preserve its life-sustaining integrity. In this sense, creation's integrity depends on holiness, a stabilizing and restorative force in the world. Only implicit in the tabernacle material of Priestly tradition (Josh 18:1), the cosmic role of holiness in relation to the establishment of the land is boldly delineated in rabbinic sources. In the midrash *Pesiqta of R. Kahana*, for example, the completion of the sanctuary, Yahweh's dwelling, is inextricably tied to creation: "Before the sanctuary was erected, the world shook; [but] from the moment the sanctuary was erected, the world was firmly established."[241] The establishment of Yahweh's dwelling place finalizes creation, and a sabbath stasis is reached. Within Priestly tradition, the erection of the tabernacle at Shiloh established a land ready to be occupied.

More broadly, sabbath is possible only when creation has fulfilled its role in sustaining life, a mark of divine blessing (Lev 25:21; Exod 16:22). The sabbath, in turn, restores the land in its blessing function, preserving its holy integrity. The Priestly cosmologist makes clear, however, that it is not Yahweh's task to require all of humanity to abstain from work; rather, it is Israel's task to embody the sabbath rest as a testimony to and for the land Israel possesses. In all of creation, the sabbath is uniquely Israel's niche. It is also the space generated by Israel's moral activity from within. Holiness is both Israel's dwelling and activity. Within this moral sphere or ethos, Israel is called to a life of *imitatio Dei;* by such a life holiness is generated for Israel. Cultically, this entails advancing the realm of the holy into the realm of the common and, in turn, diminishing the realm of impurity through the conduct of purity.[242] Holiness is a wholly ethical realm, both generated and given, lived out and lived within. In Priestly parlance, holiness is the space that requires Israel's filling and expansion.

The integrity of creation has much to do with the Priestly vision of community. The Priestly cosmogony issues an historical word on target, addressed to the particular community, Israel; hence it was intended to play a crucial role in the reformation of the community's identity in the land.[243] It is

241. P. Schäfer, "Tempel und Schöpfung: Zur Interpretation einiger Heiligtumstraditionen in der rabbinischen Literatur," *Kairos* 16 (1974) 132.

242. See Milgrom, *Leviticus 1–16,* 732; idem, "Changing Concept," 72.

243. Biblical scholars have been occupied by and large with delineating the mythological, particularly Babylonian, influences that have allegedly come to bear in Priestly tradition. The danger in comparative research, a legitimate and informative enterprise to be sure, lies in identifying the Priestly message of creation in exclusive relation to *Enuma elish,* for example, as if Gen 1:1–2:3 were addressed primarily to the Babylonian

highly significant that the creation account locates a positive place and role for each and every differentiated segment of the created order, from sea monsters and reptiles to men and women. Nothing is subdued or forcibly pushed into position; rather, creation is accomplished through active collaboration and cooperation. Recalcitrance and chaos have no place in this cosmos of compliance. Creation offers a model of stewardship that is also reflected in the sanctuary's construction. Cohesion reached through the kind of collaboration by which all elements and segments of the cosmic order are incorporated, rather than castigated, pervades this Priestly vision of cosmos *and* community. Stability and balance together form the space necessary for Israel's own formation.

Creation thus offers both a cosmic prolegomenon and program for a community's formation, characterized by distinction and integrity. For a community struggling to restore its identity, the Priestly account of creation is particularly apt. That nowhere in the cosmogony are opposition and conflict even registered suggests a cosmic idealism that is rhetorically strategic. In the hands of the Priestly cosmologist, chaos is banished from the created order with the mere stroke of a stylus, put to rest, as it were. Rather than reifying, much less deifying, chaos as a necessary evil of cosmogony, Priestly tradition embeds chaos within the matrix of life itself, particularly human life, not as a necessity but as an ever present possibility. Chaos is violence run amok. It denotes the human violation of prescribed boundaries that foster the stability of community, a social contravention based on fear of and contempt for Yahweh's created order, in short, a desecration of creation and community.[244] As much as chaos is an eminently social phenomenon, so also is cosmogony for the Priestly tradents.

Far from the typical combativeness of many creation accounts, the Priestly cosmogony positively constructs a network of interdependent relations that function in a harmonious and cooperative order. Opposition and conflict are, at best, nonexistent, or, at worst, deliberately bypassed. Perhaps the Priestly cosmogony marks an early, hopeful attempt at reforming Israel's postexilic identity. It may very well have marked an irenic new beginning in Israel's formation in the land before opposing forces became so pronounced as to require an explicit program of vindication and vilification, as can be found in Ezekiel 40–48, wherein a hardening of social boundaries is evident

---

mythographers. The latest example of reading the Priestly cosmogony almost exclusively through the lens of Babylonian myth can be found in Batto, *Slaying the Dragon*, 73-101. For further sociological presuppositions and implications, see Brown, *Structure*, 230-34.

244. Again, see Gen 6:11-13; Num 13:32; 14:7-9.

and the "foreigner" is explicitly excoriated.[245] But whether from naive confidence or from battle-worn hope, the Priestly cosmogony establishes a powerfully utopian vision of community. In a period in which internal conflict invariably accompanied each and every effort toward social reform, it is to the Priestly tradents' credit that they affirmed the *friendly* convergence of diverse and potentially divergent powers as the most secure foundation for a stable and holy reformation of Israel's identity. If Israel's internally turbulent history under Persian rule transformed, in the end, an originally irenic program of social formation into an exercise in clench-fisted control, then the Priestly cosmogony remains an imaginatively ideal testimony for future generations.

It is also for future generations that the Priestly restoration program leaves a legacy of guarded caution regarding the dangers of unchecked inclusion.[246] For all of the Priestly emphasis on integrity, cosmic and communal, inclusion is not part of the equation; indeed, it is tantamount to the violence of assimilation. Inclusion bears a distinctly dark side in the eyes of the Priestly authors. Pushed to its extreme, inclusion is all consuming when it comes to the point of erasing boundaries and leveling out distinctions that are integral for cosmic and communal integrity. If the exodus account says anything within the larger scope of the Priestly purview, it is that inclusion can lead to enslavement. The Israelites had fulfilled part of the primal great commission by successfully proliferating in great numbers in Egypt (Exod 1:7), yet they were without a land and thus bereft of the dignity of distinction. Ruthless labor was their plight, and any hope for true formation in this land of chaos was not to be had. Enslavement was Egypt's assimilation program, transforming a distinctly covenant people into an anonymous labor pool.

On a far grander scale, the Priestly flood story recounts earth being filled with the toxic mass of violence, precipitating an all-encompassing deluge as the earth's final remedy. Violence is the subversive power of radical indeterminacy, directionless and deconstructive, that aims at extinguishing life itself in its all-embracing sweep. For the ancient tradents, chaos was the logical extreme of inclusion, the embodiment of nonorder. For Croatian theolo-

---

245. Foreigners *(běnê-nēkār)* in Ezekiel's restoration program perhaps overlapped with the resident alien in Leviticus (e.g., Ezek 44:4-9; cf. Isa 56:3a, 6-8). By contrast, the "foreigner" *(nēkār)* as a sociological category receives scant attention in Priestly lore (only in Exod 12:43; Lev 22:25). The Levites, too, receive a more unwelcome reception in Ezekiel (44:10, 12-13). For a careful analysis of the purpose and redactional complexity of Ezekiel 40–48, see S. S. Tuell, *The Law of the Temple in Ezekiel 40–48* (HSM 49; Atlanta: Scholars Press, 1992).

246. An illuminating work that pointedly exposes the dangers of an unnuanced ethos of inclusion is that of Volf, *Exclusion and Embrace,* esp. 57-98.

gian Miroslav Volf, the Priestly tradition finds penetrating contemporary relevance.[247] Nonexclusionary boundaries are the outward manifestations of social dignity and worth. When violated, oppression is the ultimate result. The Priestly insistence on the necessity of establishing boundaries even within the land counters, for example, the modern Zionist appeal to an "undivided Jerusalem," which seeks to sustain an oppressive order of control in Israel today.

The Priestly ethos is found in the fine balance between integration and distinction, a tightrope the biblical tradents themselves fell from on occasion. An all-embracing goodness encompasses creation, the arena of sustenance for all life. From the side of Israel's distinction, creation requires respect for, without calling for the inclusion and leveling out of, the numerous nations that dwell on it. Yet the cosmos also has room for Israel's distinctive dwelling place, the domain of holiness, created and cohabited by God. As a people among peoples, Israel finds its home by offering a home for its creator, a move that bridges a seemingly insurmountable separation. Yet there in the sanctuary, the center of community, Yahweh dwells with a people in order to claim them.

A snippet of Priestly redaction that points to Israel's place in the sociocosmic order bears repeating: "Indeed, the whole earth belongs to me, but you shall be to me a priestly kingdom and a holy nation" (Exod 19:5b-6). A holy nation among many nations, Israel is called to a life of holiness that places it in a distinctive *and* positive relationship to the earth's integrity in all its plurality, for community and cosmos belong to the same creator. As the tabernacle serves to generate blessing for the community, so Israel as a priestly kingdom and sabbath community ultimately serves as a conduit of blessing to the nations. Like the Levites' call to service on behalf of the larger community through its ministry in the tent,[248] Israel's distinction includes maintaining and furthering the integrity of creation through its uniquely holy role. In the end, Israel's calling is a testimony that God's glory is to encompass all the earth,[249] that the tabernacle, filled with God's effulgence, is the microcosmos of things to come, so that all may know that Yahweh is creator.

From separation emerges identity, and integration marks the self's maturity. Contextually, the Priestly vision of community may not have fully reached a consistent and complete vision of cosmic integrity and nonexclusionary boundaries, but it has most certainly paved the way for a letter

247. Ibid., 63-64.
248. Num 3:12-13; see above.
249. For example, Pss 57:5, 11; 72:19; 108:5; Isa 6:3.

written centuries later to a deeply divided Christian community to make the bold claim that through Christ, in whom "the fullness of God was pleased to dwell" and by whom "all things hold together," reconciliation has embraced the cosmos, as in the beginning (Col 1:17-20).

CHAPTER 3

"From the Dust of the Ground," from "Bone of My Bones": The Ethos of the Garden Mythos in Genesis 2:4b–3:24

There is therefore no possibility of drawing a sharp line between the will-to-live and the will-to-power.

Reinhold Niebuhr[1]

If men spit upon the ground, they spit on themselves.

"Chief Seattle"[2]

---

1. R. Niebuhr, *Moral Man and Immoral Society: A Study in Ethics and Politics* (New York: Charles Scribner's Sons, 1953) 42.

2. Although frequently ascribed to the most famous leader of the Susquamish tribe, whose oration in 1854 was allegedly published in the *Seattle Sunday Star* on Oct. 29, 1887, by Henry Smith, this quote actually comes from screenwriter Ted Perry in the 1972 film *Home*, about ecology. I use it not only to highlight the distinctive relationship between the ground and the primal man depicted in the Yahwist's creation story, but also to illustrate how a Native American figure of almost a century and a half ago has become "ecologized" in modern popular culture (see M. Jones Jr., "Just Too Good to Be True: Another Reason to Beware of False Eco-Prophets," *Newsweek* [May 4, 1992] 68).

As is often noted, the so-called Yahwistic account of creation (Gen 2:4b–3:24) differs remarkably from the Priestly cosmogony that precedes it (1:1–2:3[4a]). Whereas the latter begins with an "empty" mass of water and darkness, 2:4b-5 depicts an arid landscape devoid of vegetation and rain. God's first act from the Yahwist's account is not the creation of light (1:3) but that of a man (2:7). Only thereafter does vegetation spring forth (vv. 8-9). These two creation stories of differing historical contexts and ethical aims, though tightly linked, begin on opposite ends of the cosmic spectrum, as it were. Whereas the Priestly account concludes the six days of creation with the creation of the human race, the Yahwist begins with anthropogony. Whereas the Priestly account is thoroughly cosmic in scope, the Yahwist recounts, in essence, the genesis of culture.

In the Garden

Whereas culture is rooted in cult from the Priestly perspective, culture begins with agriculture in the Yahwist's narrative. The centerpiece of the Yahwist's creation is a parcel of arable land in Eden. This garden not only serves as the literary point of departure for the larger narrative that extends from Genesis to Numbers, but also informs the structure and meaning of the Yahwist's epic as a whole. While many have described the garden story as something similar to "a true *mythos,* a parable of the human situation,"[3] few have explored the garden's distinctive ethos in relation to the Yahwist's larger historiographic work. Within the primordial setting of the garden, the author limns a moral context or setting that persists throughout the narrative's panoramic sweep from primal community to Israelite culture. Indeed, the garden holds the key to the meaning of Israel's history, as presented by the Yahwist, and that key can be found in the dramatic layout of the garden story itself, which consists essentially of two scenes, 2:4b-25 and 3:1-24. The structure of the first scene of creation can be outlined as follows:

3. C. Meyers, *Discovering Eve: Ancient Israelite Women in Context* (New York: Oxford University Press, 1988) 79. Meyers takes an etiological approach to myth, drawing from the Roman historian Sallust (1st century BCE), who defined myth as something that "happens every day" (ibid., 80). More helpful has been the move to explore the "myth" as part of the Yahwist's "rationalized" history (J. Van Seters, *Prologue to History: The Yahwist as Historian in Genesis* [Louisville: Westminster John Knox, 1992], esp. 128-29). Both approaches to the Yahwist's anthropogony, however, lack any substantive discussion of moral ethos in the Yahwist's creation account.

Cultivating the Garden Community

I. Setting the Stage 2:4b-9
   A. Land of lack 2:5
      1. No pasturage 2:5aα
      2. No field crops 2:5aβ
      3. Reason 2:5b
         a. Lack of rain 2:5bα
         b. Lack of a man to till the ground 2:5bβ
   B. Underground stream to water the ground 2:6
   C. The man created from the ground 2:7
   D. The garden 2:8-9
      1. The man's placement 2:8
      2. Yahweh's cultivation of the garden 2:9
II. The Four Rivers of Eden 2:10-14
III. Setting: Vocation and Community 2:15-25
   A. Vocation 2:15-17
      1. The man's placement and vocation 2:15
      2. Interdiction 2:16-17
   B. Community 2:18-25
      1. First attempt 2:18-20
         a. Creation of animals from the ground 2:19
         b. The man's response: naming 2:20a
         c. Verdict: failure 2:20b
      2. Second attempt 2:21-23
         a. Creation of woman from the man 2:21-22
         b. The man's response 2:23
            (1) Eureka! 2:23a
            (2) Naming 2:23b
      3. Etiology of marriage 2:24
      4. Pre-"cultural" status 2:25
         a. Lack of clothing 2:25a
         b. Lack of shame 2:25b

As the outline indicates, the plot is driven largely by a series of lacks, a sequence that moves effortlessly from agricultural to cultural deficiencies: vegetation (v. 5), rain (v. 5), cultivator (v. 5), helper (v. 18), clothing, and shame (v. 25).[4] Except for the last two items, which are addressed in the following

4. On lack and supply as defining the structure of Genesis 2–3, see T. Boomershine,

chapter, whenever a lack is identified, the narrative recounts the steps taken to meet it.

Similar to the way in which other ancient Near Eastern creation accounts begin, the stage is set for the unfolding of creation with a negative accounting of the primordial state of affairs: there was no vegetation, for there was no rain and no man *('ādām)* to till the ground *('ădāmâ)*. The narrator describes not a preexistent chaos but a landscape devoid of the material conditions for subsistence familiar to both author and audience. The lack of vegetation is mentioned twice in parallel fashion. As Theodore Hiebert has noted, field crops *(śîaḥ haśśādeh)* and pasturage *('ēśeb haśśādeh)* for stock breeding are specifically identified, reflecting a mixed agricultural economy.[5]

In somewhat reverse order, the narrator addresses these lacks in the landscape. Instead of rain,[6] an underground spring is described in v. 6 that would saturate the land,[7] and the stage is set for the first creation, the man, *hā'ādām* (v. 7). With his creation from the ground *('ădāmâ)*, the conditions are now ripe for planting a garden (v. 8). A state of narrative equilibrium is reached when the man is placed in the garden to tend and keep it (v. 15) until Yahweh issues a prohibition (v. 17). While not disruptive in itself, the interdiction raises the possibility of transgression and precludes closure of this first section.[8]

The narrative enters a new phase with the identification of another deficiency, that of a "helper" (v. 18). Her creation receives the lion's share of literary attention, spanning no less than six verses (vv. 18-23). Yahweh first creates animals from the ground *('ădāmâ)* to satisfy the man's need, but the man's response requires the Deity to return to the drawing board (v. 20b). In a second undertaking Yahweh creates a living being from the man and the result is a woman, prompting this time an exultant approbation from the man (v. 23). The woman is a success and is appropriately named *'iššâ*, having been created from the male *('îš)*. The narrative concludes, but does not end, with a descrip-

---

"The Structure of Narrative Rhetoric in Genesis 2–3," *Semeia* 18 (1980) 113-29; J. Galambush, "*'ādām* from *'ădāmâ, 'iššâ* from *'îš*: Derivation and Subordination in Genesis 2.4b–3.24," in *History and Interpretation: Essays in Honour of John H. Hayes* (ed. M. P. Graham et al.; JSOTSup 173; Sheffield: Sheffield Academic Press, 1993) 33-46.

5. T. Hiebert, *The Yahwist's Landscape: Nature and Religion in Early Israel* (New York: Oxford University Press, 1996) 37.

6. Rain proper is not mentioned again in the Yahwistic compositional layer until Gen 7:4, in which Noah is informed of Yahweh's intent to flood the earth from on high.

7. Heb. *'ēd* is most likely related etymologically to Akk. *edu* or *id* (Sum. *id*), both of which can denote an underground swell or spring. For a discussion of the alternatives, see H. N. Wallace, *The Eden Narrative* (HSM 32; Atlanta: Scholars Press, 1985) 73-74.

8. Galambush, "*'ādām* from *'ădāmâ*," 37.

tion of their communal life together that indicates two distinctly cultural lacks: nakedness and shamelessness.

Of God, Ground, and Gardening

In addition to Yahweh Elohim, three important characters come to the fore within the plot: the ground (*'ădāmâ*), the man (*'ādām, 'îš*), and the woman (*'iššâ*). Each is bound up with the other in unique and crucial ways. One need only note the similarity of terminology with respect to the three earthly characters: *'ādām*, the man, is created out of the ground or soil, *'ădāmâ* (2:7); the female, *'iššâ*, is formed from the flesh and bone of the male, *'îš* (2:21). These phonetical, possibly etymological, connections are developed in the course of the narrative to designate nothing less than the respective roles, relationships, and identities of these protagonists.

The ground is the first to appear (v. 5). Its role in the narrative is to produce vegetation. Yet it initially lies dormant; consequently, the first lack to be identified is the ground's "need" for rain and an *'ādām* to work it. Not to be identified with the more general term "earth" (*'ereṣ*), the *'ădāmâ* denotes the specifically arable land.[9] The ground is what the man is to cultivate, literally "work" or "serve" (*'bd*, 2:5; 3:23). It is the object of the man's role, his vocation. The connection between the man and the ground is bone-deep, for the ground also serves as the raw material for his genesis (v. 6). Quite in contrast to some Mesopotamian accounts that required the slaughter of a god to fashion the first human being,[10] the irenic simplicity of the man's creation in the garden is striking.

The description of human creation reads literally: "Yahweh Elohim formed the man out of dirt from the ground" (*hā'ādām 'āpār min- hā'ădāmâ*, v. 7).[11] Dirt or fine soil (*'āpār*) — usually translated "dust" (NRSV)[12] — from

9. Hiebert, *Yahwist's Landscape*, 34-35.

10. Cf. *Atrahasis* (Old Babylonian version) I.208-10, 224-30, in which the god Awilu (a play on the Akkadian word for "man") is slaughtered so that the "same god and man were thoroughly mixed in the clay" (tr. B. R. Foster, *Before the Muses: An Anthololgy of Akkadian Literature* [2 vols.; 2d ed.; Bethesda: CDL Press, 1996] 1.167-68); *Enuma elish* VI.28-38, in which the rebellious god Qingu is slaughtered, from whose blood humanity is created (Foster, *Before the Muses*, 1.384).

11. Grammatically, the description of the man's genesis features a double object: dust or soil serves as the accusative object of material, and "ground" is the prepositional object. The former object also denotes the man's identity (Gen 3:19b).

12. The reference to the subterranean waters moistening the land precludes the image of dust, which *'āpār* can connote in other contexts.

the ground suggests that the man is a particularly refined object taken from the ground, in subtle distinction from the animals, which are created simply "from the ground" (*min-ha'ădāmâ*, 2:19).[13] This first living object of divine craftwork, akin to the work of a potter,[14] is a man of the soil (cf. 3:19, 23). His origin bespeaks his identity: as a "groundling"[15] he is a product of the ground and is bound to it in vocation. Nevertheless, the relationship between man and ground is not simply one of dependency. As the *'ādām* is a product of the *'ădāmâ*, the fertility of the *'ădāmâ*, is a product of the *'ādām*'s work. By tilling the soil, the man sustains himself and the soil realizes its productive potential. Far from one-sided, the relationship between the soil and the first human is naturally mutual, indeed symbiotic.

Although the arable land is the source of vocation and sustenance for this primal farmer, it is significant that Yahweh is depicted as the first cultivator, both of the garden and the primal community. In the role of landowner, Yahweh plants a garden in the *'ădāmâ* and plants the man within the garden to maintain it (2:8, 15). The man is not commanded to plant, but commissioned to "tend and keep" what has already been planted (v. 15). This primal garden is of supernatural origin, the product of God's green thumb, and the man is the tenant commissioned to secure and maintain this oasis of order.[16] As for its composition, this "garden" is in fact an orchard of various fruit trees, including the fig (vv. 9, 15; 4:7), all for the man's sustenance. The land is tilled not for God's nourishment but for the man's.[17] Compensation for his work is the free reign he is granted over the produce of every tree in the garden, with one notable exception: "You shall not eat of it" (2:17). Cast as a divine prohibition, a primal *tôrâ* is promulgated. Although the man has virtually free reign, the orchard is still "Yahweh's garden" (13:10). This interdiction is at base an ecological prohibition. It is within the space between the com-

13. Given the rocky nature of the highlands of Canaan, fine soil is a rare commodity.

14. The verb *yṣr* is frequently attested in descriptions of pottery making (2 Sam 17:28; Isa 29:16; Jer 18:2-4). Job, too, ascribes to God his being fashioned from clay (Job 10:8-9).

15. The English word "human" also reflects the Hebrew pun: the word comes from a theoretical Indo-European root *(ghum)* meaning "earth" (Meyers, *Discovering Eve*, 82).

16. As R. B. Coote and D. R. Ord point out, "to keep" *(šmr)* the garden connotes more than simply upkeep but also guarding and watching over the garden. I would disagree, however, that such a function is exclusively royal, as they imply (*The Bible's First History* [Philadelphia: Fortress, 1989] 54).

17. Cf. *Atrahasis* (Old Babylonian version) I.vii, which identifies humankind's role to "feed people and sustain the gods"; and III.v, which likens the gods to flies gathering over the protagonist's postdiluvian offering.

mission and the prohibition that the man's vocation — indeed, part of his very identity — is to be found: to work the ground but not reap its entire bounty.

The man's vocation is, like that of his Mesopotamian and Egyptian descendants, to irrigate. The *'ādām* of the garden is no dryland agriculturist but an irrigation farmer.[18] Such an occupation is suggested by both the reference to the primordial spring in 2:6 and the extended interlude that follows in vv. 10-14, which describes a primordial river source issuing "out of Eden to water the garden." Eden is the source of the four great rivers of the known world. Free of the vicissitudes of rainfall, the grove is watered by this archetypal river. Eden is the mythic source of the "'life-arteries' of all lands of the earth,"[19] including Mesopotamia and Egypt.[20] In both regions, irrigation depends on an extensive network of canals to distribute river water onto the arable soil. Such canals are the "lifelines of the land," in the words of a Mesopotamian poet.[21]

Hiebert suggests that the imagery is drawn directly from the oases of the Jordan Valley, citing Gen 13:10 as evidence.[22] Such may very well be the case, but the Yahwist does not admit to it. Hiebert's cited verse, which describes Lot's amazement over the choice land of the Jordan, is cast in the form of a simile: "the whole region of the Jordan . . . was entirely irrigated like the garden of Yahweh, like the land of Egypt." The land of Egypt and Yahweh's garden are juxtaposed, and therein lies the force of the analogy.[23] The Yahwist envisions a distant time in which the southern Jordan Valley, comparable to the Nile Delta, was the envy of the region. Regardless of Eden's location, the Yahwist limns Eden's garden as an archetypal ecosystem comparable to those

18. See the distinction in Hiebert, *Yahwist's Landscape,* 36-37; Meyers, *Discovering Eve,* 47-63.

19. C. Westermann, *Genesis 1–11* (tr. J. J. Scullion; Continental Commentary; Minneapolis: Augsburg, 1984) 216.

20. The "Gihon," the name of the second river, most probably includes the Nile, even though the river is described as "flowing around the whole land of Cush" (v. 13). In this context, Cush refers to the land south of Egypt (Ezek 29:10; 2 Kgs 19:9), which brings the narrative purview closer to the actual source of the Nile without naming it as such.

21. *Atrahasis* (Old Babylonian version) I.22, 24 (tr. S. Dalley, *Myths from Mesopotamia: Creation, The Flood, Gilgamesh, and Others* [Oxford: Oxford University Press, 1989] 9).

22. Hiebert, *Yahwist's Landscape,* 52-53.

23. Hiebert confuses metaphor with factual data for locating the garden of Eden somewhere in the Jordan rift valley. The Yahwist does not make a "comparison of the Garden of Eden to the Jordan Valley" (*Yahwist's Landscape,* 54), but precisely the reverse! Cf. Coote and Ord's contention that the garden terrain of the Yahwist bears distinct Mesopotamian parallels (*Bible's First History,* 50-51).

of the powerful cultural centers of the ancient Near East, which were free of all reliance on capricious rainfall. For the Yahwist's audience, the garden is essentially out of place in the highlands in which Israel took root; its physical contours are alien to the harsh landscape of the hill country of the Levant.[24] The southern Jordan Valley, the Yahwist contends, was once such a lush ecosystem, an Egypt in miniature, but that was then.

Regardless of the actual (or mythic) geography on which Eden is based,[25] the man's vocation is unambiguously clear: he is an irrigationist, working the ground in order to channel and distribute the constant groundswell of subterranean water. Nowhere is there indication of a life of idle ease for the man. As dramatically illustrated in the opening tablet of *Atrahasis*, irrigation work can indeed be quite toilsome. The lower-class gods, the Igigu, were forced by the senior Anunnaki to dig out canals and clear channels, prompting a rebellion and eventually the creation of the human race as substitute workers. The gods plead with the mother goddess Mami (Nintu, *Belet-ili*), "Create a mortal that he may bear the yoke! Let him bear the yoke, the work of Ellil, let man bear the load of the gods!"[26]

Eden's garden, too, is no land of idleness; human existence, from the very outset, is defined in terms of work. Nevertheless, keeping the garden is far from burdensome, particularly in contrast to life outside it (3:17b-19). Compared to the harsh hill country of Canaan, which required backbreaking work to produce orchards, the garden is a farmer's delight (2:9).[27] Yet something is awry with regard to the kind of work the man is commissioned to perform. Unlike his divine counterparts in the Mesopotamian pantheon, the man does not complain or rebel; rather, Yahweh perceives that he needs "help" and responds with continuing creation. Unlike the Deity of the Priestly tradents who renders official approbation over everything created, the God of the Yahwist does not hesitate to criticize the current, incomplete state of divine handiwork: "It is not good" (*lō'-ṭôb*, v. 18a). Like the arid land with which creation began, something

24. Cf. Deut 11:10-11, which describes the land Israel is about to occupy as very different from Egypt, "where you sowed your seed and watered it with your feet, like a garden of vegetables; but the land which you are going over to possess is a land of hills and valleys, which receives water by the rain from heaven."

25. More likely, "Eden" does not refer to any specific location but rather is meant to evoke the sense of "delight" (*'dn*; cf. Ezek 36:35; Joel 2:3).

26. *Atrahasis* (Old Babylonian version) I.195-97 (tr. Dalley, *Myths from Mesopotamia*, 15).

27. Sustaining orchards in the highland environment was made possible only through terracing, which required an enormous amount of energy (O. Borowski, *Agriculture in Iron Age Israel* [Winona Lake, Ind.: Eisenbrauns, 1987] 15-18; Meyers, *Discovering Eve*, 59-60, 84).

is lacking. The possibility of community remains an empty prospect. Yahweh's self-proclaimed mission is to find a "helper" *('ēzer)*,[28] one who can support the man in his labor of leisure and offer companionship. What is wrong about the present arrangement, Yahweh observes, is the man's aloneness *(lĕbaddô)*. This "helper" must be his companion and counterpart, not his servant,[29] one who can join the man socially as well as vocationally.

So the search is on for a partner fit for the man, his match. Yahweh provides for the man's need in a way that allows him to contribute to the ordering of his world. All manner of animals are created from the ground *('ădāmâ)*, and the man is free to determine their respective roles. It is significant that the animals are brought to the man; the man is not led to their own habitations for his response. The garden is thus thoroughly anthropocentric in its cultural topography. By naming the animals, the man defines them as, for example, domestic or wild.[30] In this process, Yahweh is not so much experimenting[31] as granting the man the freedom to determine the roles of these new creatures. Yahweh brings them to him "to see what he would name them" (v. 19), and the man, through the exercise of language,[32] places these animals in relation to the agricultural setting in which he himself has been placed, incorporating them into his divinely ordained vocation and livelihood. Naming the animals marks, no doubt, the beginning of animal husbandry. The man is as much the master of domestic animals "out of the ground" as he is the harvester of the plants "out of the ground" (2:9).

Yet no corresponding partner can be found.[33] There is a certain irony here: the man and all the animals share, literally, common ground. Yet despite their

---

28. The term is used frequently to describe God in the role of deliverer from Israel's adversaries (e.g., Exod 18:3; Deut 33:7; Ps 20:3).

29. Westermann's observation is apropos, though overstated: "The words 'a helper fit for him' refer ... [not] to the help which she could offer to the farmer. Any such limitation destroys the meaning of the passage. What is meant is the personal community of man and woman in the broadest sense — bodily and spiritual community, mutual help and understanding, joy and contentment in each other" (*Genesis 1–11*, 232). Within the Yahwist's social purview, the "helper" includes both vocational support and community for the man.

30. Note the threefold classification employed in 2:20. What is usually translated "animal of the field" *(ḥayyat haśśādeh)* comprises the wild animals who presumably are free to come and go with respect to the garden. Note the identical description of the serpent in 3:1.

31. So C. L'Heureux, *In and Out of Paradise* (New York: Paulist, 1983) 17.

32. On the relationship between language and ordering, see G. von Rad, *Genesis* (tr. J. H. Marks; rev. ed.; OTL; Philadelphia: Westminster, 1972) 83.

33. That the man finds no "helper" among the animals precludes linking human identity with certain animals, as one might find in royal identifications with particular predators, like the lion (see Chapter 4), as well as elevating certain domestic animals, like the ox or ass, to the level of human worth.

shared pedigree, no animal "corresponds" to the man (kĕnegdô),[34] none about which the man can say, "with me" ('immādî, 3:12). The man remains the first-born of the soil; he alone bears his namesake "groundling." As part of the populace of the garden, some of the animals can render service to the man, but they cannot provide community. There is no "man's best friend" in the animal world. For that, the man needs a counterpart and he must discover it for himself, literally from within himself.

Yahweh's second undertaking is a complete success. In the same manner of presenting the animals, Yahweh places the new candidate before the man, eliciting a cry of jubilation from him. Not from the ground but from the man is the woman fashioned. Her genesis establishes a qualitative distinction from the animals, which share "common ground" with the man. Yet she is not wholly alien to this "groundling." She and the man share common flesh and breath. The woman is not another ground-based animal, either to serve the man or to inhabit the fields outside the garden. Her derivation from the man is celebrated not for her subordination but for her shared equality and essence with him: "bone of my bones and flesh of my flesh" is she (2:23). The man's jubilant cry is the eureka of kinship.[35] He knows her as his own. Nevertheless, the woman is not identical to the man; she is not another 'ādām fashioned from the soil. The man shares something in common with the animals and the plants that the woman does not share. With her creation gendered life is introduced.

The woman is cut from a different cloth, namely, from her complement, the man. Yet by virtue of her creation from him the man recognizes something different about himself. By giving up part of himself, he gains a new aspect of his identity, his 'îšness or maleness, in relation to the woman ('iššâ). This new identity, however, does not replace or displace his other identity.[36] He remains an 'ādām throughout the course of the narrative, tied inextricably to the ground of his being.[37] Together, the primal man and woman remain

34. As Meyers points out, the prepositional phrase at the end of 2:18 means "opposite" or "corresponding to" (Discovering Eve, 85).

35. Cf. Gen 29:14; Judg 9:2; 2 Sam 5:1; 19:13-14.

36. Contra J. Rosenberg, who contends that the man's new "name" vis-à-vis the woman is a renouncement of his earlier name 'ādām (King and Kin: Political Allegory in the Hebrew Bible [Bloomington: Indiana University Press, 1986] 58). Gen 2:25 testifies against any such displacement.

37. Gen 3:17, 20, 22, 24, but cf. 3:6. Contra P. Trible, who argues that the shift in terminology from 'ādām to 'îš signals a material change in identity from an androgynous creature to the male counterpart of 'iššâ (God and the Rhetoric of Sexuality [OBT; Philadelphia: Fortress, 1978] 97-99). See the criticisms of B. S. Childs, Old Testament Theology in a Canonical Context (Philadelphia: Fortress, 1985) 189-91; Galambush, "'ādām from 'ādāmâ," 35-36.

'ādām and 'iššâ (2:25), similar but different.[38] As a character of complexity in the story, the man bears a dual identity dependent on his relational status: his "maleness" is evinced in his relationship to the woman; his "groundedness" is revealed in relation to the soil from which he was created. Moreover, these different sides translate into differing roles: as 'îš he is the woman's companion; as 'ādām he is a tiller of the soil.

There is a profound paradox in the creation of the woman: to supply the man's lack, Yahweh takes something from him. By lacking part of his side, the man finds completion in the woman. As the ground needed a tiller to realize its productive potential (2:5), so the man ostensibly needed a companion to fulfill his divinely ordained task of tending the garden. Yet much more is at stake, of course, when it comes to gendered relationships, as the narrator makes indisputably clear. "A helper fit for him" denotes personal community in its most basic sense. The explanatory note in v. 24 invests the garden story with etiological force by construing the narrative as the precedent and rationale for marriage: creation by separation establishes a binding force for union, one that involves separation between generations ("man" and "father"), as it entailed the detachment of the man's rib from himself. The consummation of marriage marks a return not to some primal state of sexless fusion but to an originative state of intimate community. It is the rediscovery of shared identity. Climaxed in the man's jubilation, the narrative attests that sexual union is not simply an isolated ecstasy; it is the fruit of mutual service and companionship. In the context of marital concord, sex bears a certain pedagogy: it is the joyous discovery zone of kinship.

With the fashioning of the woman, creation appears completed. Yet a note of ambiguity is introduced at the end of this first scene. The primal couple lack both clothing and shame (v. 25), as if the narrator were reminding the reader that the world of the garden lies vastly remote from the immediate world of cultured life. Although pointedly unnatural within the immediate world of the narrative, shame from a cultural perspective is the natural reaction to being exposed. As much as the garden is remarkable in its uniqueness for an audience subsisting in the hill country of Canaan, so the couple's naked and unashamed lifestyle is exceptional, free from a culture defined by honor and shame.[39] Life within the garden is essentially for-

38. Note M. P. Korsak's appropriately literal translation of 2:25: "The two of them were naked, the groundling and his woman they were not ashamed" (*At the Start: Genesis Made New* [New York: Doubleday, 1993] 7).

39. Borrowing from recent anthropological studies, treatments of honor and shame within the biblical context have become nothing short of voluminous, e.g., S. M. Olyan, "Honor, Shame, and Covenant Relations in Ancient Israel and Its Environment," *JBL* 115 (1996) 201-18; the collected essays in *Honor and Shame in the World of the Bible* (ed. V. H.

eign to life outside it. For an audience peering in from the outside, two lacks still require attention: lack of clothing and lack of shame. Positively, the couple is entirely at ease with their nakedness. Yet the specific mention of shame's absence implies a temporary state.[40] Like the mythical geography of the garden, the lacks of shame and clothing disclose an ethos that is out of place within the public arena of cultured life, for clothing and honor are nothing less than emblems of civilized society.[41]

Yet there is a place within culture for such lacks: this primal ethos is recaptured, as v. 24 suggests, in those most intimate moments when husband and wife are joined in consummation. Culture consigns the lack of clothing and shame exclusively to the private realm. However remote this realm is, it drives a new generation to cleave *from* the preceding one and to cleave *to* its own. From a cultural perspective, Eden may exist only as a "private" garden, yet its alluring power governs the inexorable rhythm of separation and union among the generations. In this one dimension of cultural life, the private realm wields a powerful precedence over the public. In short, the Yahwist imagines a distant time in which human relationships were publicly free from the determinations of contemporary culture, a haven in which loving social intercourse was uncircumscribed by civility. Sexual union is at once the most private and the most primordial of human acts, and shame's absence in the garden is striking only in a world fraught with its presence. By virtue of this lack, the couple exemplifies an innocent antithesis to contemporary culture. But that too can be remedied.

Expulsion from the Garden

Genesis 3 is the second scene of the anthropogony, without which the first scene would remain by and large irrelevant to the Yahwist's view of culture. As

Matthews and D. C. Benjamin; *Semeia* 68 [1994] 1-61); M. Bechtel, "Shame as a Sanction of Social Control in Biblical Israel: Judicial, Political, and Social Shaming," *JSOT* 49 (1991) 47-76; D. Daube, "The Culture of Deuteronomy," *Orita* 3 (1969) 27-52; M. A. Klopfenstein, *Scham und Schande nach dem Alten Testament* (ATANT 62; Zurich: Theologischer Verlag, 1972). Frequently cited anthropological resources are the collected essays in J. G. Peristiany, ed., *Honour and Shame: The Values of Mediterranean Societies* (London: Weidenfeld & Nicholson, 1966); and in J. G. Peristiany and J. Pitt-Rivers, eds., *Honor and Grace in Anthropology* (Cambridge: Cambridge University Press, 1992). For further citations, see Olyan, "Honor, Shame," 202-3nn.4-5.

40. Galambush, "'*ādām* from '*ădāmâ*," 38.

41. Cf. the character of Enkidu, the primitive man of the wild, who is acculturated by the prostitute Shamhat and clothed appropriately. See Dalley's translation of tablet II.ii (*Myths from Mesopotamia*, 59).

S. Niditch rightly observes, with Genesis 3 the garden story reveals itself to be a "tale of emergence" from ideal to reality.[42] The plot can be outlined as follows:

The Desiccation of Community

I.	The Serpent	3:1-5
	A. Description	3:1a
	B. Conversation with the woman	3:1b-5
II.	The Tree of Knowing Good and Evil	3:6-7
	A. Description	3:6a
	1. Good for food	3:6aα
	2. Attractive	3:6aβ
	3. Instructive	3:6aγ
	B. Woman's response	3:6bα
	C. Man's response	3:6bβ
	D. Result	3:7
	1. Awareness of nakedness	3:7a
	2. Remedy: filling a lack	3:7b
III.	Confrontation with Yahweh	3:8-13
	A. The couple's reaction: fear	3:8-10
	B. The man's objection: blame of the woman	3:11-12
	C. The woman's objection: blame of the serpent	3:13
IV.	Divine Curse	3:14-19
	A. Against the serpent	3:14-15
	1. Curse of mobility	3:14
	2. Enmity with the woman and her offspring	3:15
	B. Against the woman	3:16
	1. "Labor" pain	3:16a
	2. Desire and subordination	3:16b
	C. Against the man	3:17-19
	1. Curse of the ground: toil	3:17-19a
	2. Return to the ground: death	3:19b
V.	Life of Curse	3:20-24
	A. Man's name for the woman: Eve	3:20
	B. Divine provision for clothing	3:21
	C. Expulsion from the garden	3:22-24

42. S. Niditch, *Chaos to Cosmos: Studies in Biblical Patterns of Creation* (SPSH; Chico, Calif.: Scholars Press, 1985) 25-43.

1. Reason: the tree of life   3:22
2. Return to tilling the *ground*   3:23
3. Cordoning off the garden   3:24

Several characters that figure prominently in the plot are drawn from the previous chapter. Yahweh Elohim, the man, and the woman remain central. In addition, the "character" of the ground concludes the garden story (3:23), as it had marked its beginning (2:5). As in the previous chapter, the narrative focuses on how these characters interrelate. What drives the plot now is not so much the filling of genuine needs as the filling of falsely perceived needs, which results in a breakdown and reconfiguration of relationships. The scene opens with the introduction of a wholly new character.

Encroachment and Expulsion

The serpent comes from a class of animals already identified; it is a *wild* animal (2:19, 20). As such, the serpent's domain is not limited to, or even at home in, the ordered garden. The serpent is the creaturely other, inhabiting the outskirts of human habitation. As a rule, the animals of the wild can bear a threat to human life. The presence of wild animals frequently signifies the desolation of human habitation, for they populate what human beings have abandoned.[43] From a cultural standpoint, the realms of human and wild life are considered mutually exclusive. That the serpent is sharing the same space with the woman within the garden (let alone conversing with her!) is itself highly anomalous. The wild and wily serpent is an encroacher, but a unique one, for it holds the distinction of being the craftiest of its kind (3:1), a paragon of disingenuity.[44] The term that denotes the serpent's superlative distinction, *'ārûm*, signals an ingenious wordplay with the description of the cou-

43. For example, Zeph 2:14 (emended according to LXX), 15. See Chapter 5 below.
44. The Hebrew expression *'ārûm mikkōl* denotes the serpent's superlative nature. The root *'rm* in its various forms can denote something either positive or negative, depending on the context. Within Proverbs, it denotes prudence and a shrewd sense (e.g., Prov 1:5; 8:5, 12; 12:23; 15:5; 19:25). Elsewhere, however, this virtue is more a vice, connoting craftiness and scheming: Saul describes David as subversively cunning (1 Sam 23:22); God's enemies devise crafty plans against Israel (Ps 83:4); the wise are guilty by their craftiness (Job 5:13; 15:5); the killer who acts in malice deserves death (Exod 21:14); and the Gibeonites trick Joshua into sparing their lives (Josh 9:4). In all these cases, premeditated scheming captures the sense of *'ārûm*. See also M. V. Fox, "Words for Wisdom," *ZAH* 6 (1993) 159-60.

ple's nakedness (*'ărûmmîm,* 2:25). While identical in consonantal spelling, in view of the singular form of the latter, the two terms could not be more different in signification. The couple's nakedness suggests complete innocence and harmony; by virtue of its cunning the serpent introduces alienation and dissolution into the garden community.

The serpent's narrative role is to create an ostensible lack from the perception of the protagonist. With subversive cunning, it initiates a conversation with the woman by posing an absurd question or statement:[45] "God said, 'You must never eat of any tree of the garden.'" If what the serpent suggested were true, the human citizens of the garden would starve. The serpent's outrageous query serves as a hook to engage the woman, and her response does not regurgitate the prohibition; indeed, she makes it all the more stringent: even to *touch* the tree will result in death (3:3). Undeterred, the serpent suggests that she and her man still lack something, namely, the facility of discerning judgment[46] and its accompanying divine status: "when you eat of it, your

---

45. It is not at all clear whether the serpent is posing a question or a statement, since the verse lacks the interrogative particle. For translating the serpent's discourse as a statement, see J. T. Walsh, "Genesis 2:4b–3:24: A Synchronic Approach," *JBL* 96 (1977) 164 (repr. in *"I Studied Inscriptions from before the Flood": Ancient Near Eastern, Literary, and Linguistic Approaches to Genesis 1–11* [ed. R. S. Hess and D. T. Tsumura; SBTS 4; Winona Lake, Ind.: Eisenbrauns, 1994] 362-82). Cf. E. A. Speiser, *Genesis* (AB 1; Garden City, N.Y.: Doubleday, 1964) 21. Either way, the serpent's discourse requires a counterstatement.

46. The merism "good and evil" (*ṭôb wārāʿ*) is frequently taken to denote universal knowledge. See Wallace, *Eden Narrative,* 121-29, who cites the similar expression in 2 Sam 19:36 as evidence. The context of this passage, in which Barzillai the Gileadite addresses King David, suggests, however, a distinctly Epicurean slant: "I am eighty years old. Can I discern what is pleasant and what is not *(haʾēdaʿ bên-ṭôb lĕrāʿ)?* Can your servant taste what he eats or what he drinks? Can I listen to the voice of singing men and singing women?" Given his old age, Barzillai laments of losing all sensation of pleasure, indeed the capacity for enjoyment, but general knowledge is not the issue here, particularly since he had enough sense to decline King David's invitation! To dilute the merism to a level of general knowledge overlooks the particular context of Barzillai's discourse and, for that matter, that of the serpent in Gen 3:5. More helpful are the parallel expressions in 2 Sam 14:17, 20, in which David is exhorted by the woman of Tekoa to do the right thing. She praises the king for "discerning good and evil" (*lišmōaʿ haṭṭôb wĕhārāʿ,* v. 17), and later praises him for "knowing all things that are on the earth" (*lādaʿat ʾet-kol-ʾăšer bāʾāreṣ,* v. 20). From this one could contend that the merism denotes comprehensive knowledge; but assumed throughout the woman's discourse is that such knowledge, however wide ranging, is intended for deciding the best course of action in a moral or political dilemma. Discerning judgment remains the issue. (For a discussion of the close parallel in Deut 1:39, see below.) See the criticisms against a universal reading of the merism by W. M. Clark, "A Legal Background to the Yahwist's Use of 'Good and Evil' in Genesis 2–3," *JBL* 88 (1969) 270-78, which Wallace passes over with only a cursory paragraph (*Eden Narrative,* 118).

eyes will open, you will be like gods knowing good and evil" (3:5).[47] The serpent promises elevated, indeed transcendent, standing in the garden.

Doubt and distrust are engendered not by the serpent per se but by the free act of gazing on the arboreal wonder.[48] By insinuating that Yahweh's prohibition is arbitrary, the serpent prompts the woman to reevaluate the tree's prohibitive status in the garden. She perceives the tree as "good" (*ṭôb*) for food, a "delight" (*ta'ăwâ*) to the eyes, and "desirable for gaining wisdom" (*neḥmād . . . lĕhaśkîl*). Far from being amoral attributes, the tree's qualities are deemed worthy of appropriation. A genuine temptation is at work. On the one hand, the tree displays a sensuous, irresistible attraction. On the other hand, its alluring quality lies in the eyes of the beholder. Despite her protestation in 3:13, the serpent did not trick the woman into eating the fruit; it only prompted her to reconsider the tree's worthiness for consumption. What the woman perceives about the tree are eminently worthy things in and of themselves: basic sustenance, delight, and effective wisdom, in short, a taxonomy of goodness (*ṭôb*). As she reaches out to appropriate this goodness, the woman in effect adjudicates the life that Yahweh has ordained for the primal couple as deficient, as lacking in some regard. She partakes and hands some of the fruit to the man, who has been with her all along (3:6b). Curiously, the narrator mentions her eating the fruit without any change of perception until after the man also has partaken (see below).

Once both have eaten, certain results ensue. As the serpent foretold, their eyes are opened, but rather than becoming gods, attaining new heights of self-empowering knowledge, the couple become acutely aware of their naked vulnerability (*'êrummîm*, 3:7; cf. v. 22), reaching only a partial knowledge at best. Consequently, the man and woman cover themselves with fig leaves, a pathetic attempt at clothing. Their situation is perceived as all the more desperate when they hear the "voice" of Yahweh strolling through the garden (v. 8). As they tried to hide their nakedness before each other, they now hide behind trees in fear before an inquiring God. But their location in the garden is precisely what gives them away. The question "Where are you?" indicates not so much divine ignorance as the couple's culpability. Their disobedience has led them to become invisible and vulnerable in the garden. The garden of delight has become the garden of dread, and their newly found fear initiates a

47. The acculturation of the primitive man Enkidu in the Epic of Gilgamesh causes him to become wiser and, in the words of Shamhat the prostitute, "become like a god!" (Standard Babylonian version, I.iv; Dalley, *Myths from Mesopotamia*, 56).
48. To claim, as does Rosenberg, that the tale's central action is "man's victimization by beast, as in *Gilgamesh*," overreads the role of the serpent and effectively ignores the wealth of literary attention given to the tree and its description (*King and Kin*, 63).

tragic sequence of blame. The woman is excoriated by the man for offering the fruit. The woman, in turn, blames the snake for deceiving her. The serpent, however, is left without rebuttal.[49]

The resulting threefold curse introduces a world that is painfully familiar to the narrator's audience: the snake's slithering movement and the fear and hostility it engenders (v. 14), the woman's labor and pain of childbirth (v. 16), and the toil necessary for dryland farming (vv. 17-19). The curse in effect transports the couple (and the serpent) into the real world of conflict and hardship, the realm of culture and danger. The relationships between the characters that populated the irenic setting of the garden are disrupted and reconfigured.[50] Whereas the woman and the serpent enjoyed free intercourse in the garden, enmity now reigns.

The woman must suffer pain *('iṣṣābôn)* in pregnancy *(hērôn)* and in bearing children (v. 16a).[51] Yet, despite her agony, the *'iššâ's* desire for her namesake, her husband *('îš)*, remains intact (intensifies?), even though her husband will be a domineering *'îš*, one who will "rule over" her *(yimšāl-bāk,* v. 16b).[52] Such is the life of curse. Whereas mutual support and joy

49. D. N. Fewell and D. M. Gunn suggest perceptively that the absence of the serpent's rebuttal, which "stops the sequence of blame from becoming a cycle," is deliberate, for the serpent's alibi no doubt would have implicated God in the couple's disobedience. How the serpent would have responded, if given the chance, must remain lodged in the readerly imagination ("Shifting the Blame: God in the Garden," in *Reading Bibles, Writing Bodies: Identity and the Book* [ed. T. K. Beal and D. M. Gunn; London: Routledge, 1997] 17). Indeed, the serpent would have only needed to say, "I only spoke the truth!" in order to present a technically credible defense (see below).

50. See Galambush, "*'ādām* from *'ădāmâ*," 33-46.

51. Meyers argues that *'iṣṣābôn* in the first line denotes physical labor and is not related to pregnancy and childbearing (*Discovering Eve*, 99-105; idem, "Gender Roles and Genesis 3:16 Revisited," in *The Word of the Lord Shall Go Forth: Essays in Honor of David Noel Freedman in Celebration of His Sixtieth Birthday* [ed. C. L. Meyers and M. O'Connor; Winona Lake, Ind.: Eisenbrauns, 1983] 344-46; repr. in *A Feminist Guide to Genesis* [ed. A. Brenner; FCB 2; Sheffield: Sheffield Academic Press, 1993] 118-41). Such a reading, however, ignores the internal parallelism of the first line, specifically the correspondence between "pregnancy" and "labor," as well as the external parallelism with the second line, which is linked with the etymologically related *'eṣeb* ("agony"), whose prefixed preposition, *bĕ*, Meyers must translate in the sense of accompaniment. On the one hand, Meyers is correct in noting that *'iṣṣābôn* need not be reduced simply to the pain of pregnancy, given its attestation in the man's curse and in the other cases she cites. On the other hand, the term, given its context, is not unrelated to pregnancy and childbearing. The woman's "labor" includes all her work on behalf of her household in her pregnant condition, causing even simple tasks to be intensely burdensome.

52. Whereas Meyers argues against any reductionistic rendering of the first line of the curse, she reduces the language of domination to that of the man's prevailing will over

characterized the primal relationship, the conflictive dynamics of domination, already in full swing with the man's blame of the woman in v. 12, now prevail. The curse bears the fruit of blame. Simply put, "while the woman's relationship to the man is characterized by desire, the man's relationship to the woman is characterized by rule."[53] Through the curse her mate has become her master. In short, the complementary relationship between the woman and her substance of origin, the man, is wholly disrupted. In the world of curse, origin no longer indicates complementarity and mutual joy but domination and pain.

Equally dramatic is the cursed relationship between the ground (*'ădāmâ*) and the man (*'ādām*). The man's curse is also the ground's curse (v. 17b). Once bonded by mutual need — the man needed the ground for his vocational livelihood and sustenance, and the ground required a tiller to fulfill its productive potential — they have become alienated. Yet like the woman's desire for her husband, the man's vocation does not change; he must still "till the ground from which he was taken" (v. 23). What has changed is the soil's produce and the means of eliciting it. Instead of yielding luxuriant fruit trees, the ground is destined to produce thorns and thistles, as well as some grain, but only after much toil. The man's work shares common ground with the woman's labor: both are fraught with pain and toil. As the woman (*'iššâ*) is painfully bound to her husband (*'îš*), the *'ādām* is painfully tied to the *'ădāmâ*. His service to the soil has become a crushing burden; the soil is now his master. As the man was taken out of the ground in his genesis, now he must return to it in his death, for he is "dirt" and to "dirt" he shall return (v. 19). The couple's disobedience has introduced not just the element of alienation, but also an ontology of bondage. Relationships between human beings and their environment are now based on power and control, as a matter of survival. As the man has been thrust into the harsh environment of the highlands of Canaan to eke out his existence, the woman is transported into the painful world of familial hierarchy and childbearing.

Julie Galambush notes perceptively, "The narrative simultaneously renders, reflects, and accounts for a world in which women and men have the potential for mutuality but instead live in antagonistic relationships of domina-

---

the woman's reluctance to become pregnant and bear children (*Discovering Eve*, 115-16). To the contrary, pregnancy and bearing children were highly prized in ancient Israel, as evinced, for example, in the family episodes in Genesis (e.g., Gen 16:1-6; 19:30-38; 29:31–30:24; 38:1-30).

53. P. A. Bird, "'Male and Female He Created Them': Gen 1:27b in the Context of the Priestly Account of Creation," *HTR* 74 (1981) 158.

tion and subordination."[54] The same can also be said of the relationship between the 'ādām and the 'ădāmâ. The mutual, symbiotic relationship the man once had with the land has become disrupted. Only with painful exertion can the man bring forth produce from the soil, from a ground that no longer yields to, indeed welcomes, his advances.

The soil's intractable nature exhibits unyielding hostility. The man must through great effort force the soil to yield its produce in the ground beyond the garden, a land from which he too was taken and to which he is driven back (v. 23). In order to subsist off the land, the man must subdue it (cf. 1:28). On the one hand, there is an enforced limit to the man's power: barred from the tree of life by the cherubim and flaming sword, the man cannot take back the garden, regardless of the amount of force he can muster. On the other hand, the couple is not driven out defenselessly from their irretrievable oasis of order. Yahweh provides them clothing for the harsh environment that they are to face, far surpassing their pathetic attempt at covering themselves (3:21; cf. v. 7b).[55] Yahweh remains divine provider, even in a godforsaken land. So begins the acculturation of the first community.

Before taking stock of what the couple must face outside the garden, it is necessary to recapitulate the moral dynamics conveyed by the Yahwist's garden anthropogony.

The Geo-Ethical Landscape

The topography of the garden and its environs is grounded in the 'ădāmâ. Whereas the earth ('ereṣ) encompasses the whole land, only a portion of the earth is deemed fit for human tilling, habitation, and work. The "ground" is the scene of human origin and community; in short, it is a social arena. This 'ădāmâ is the eminently habitable land, which includes the garden but extends beyond it (cf. 2:9 and 3:23). The couple's expulsion from the garden was not an expulsion from arable soil per se to an arid wasteland, but from a blessed 'ădāmâ to a cursed 'ădāmâ. As a consequence of the curse, the garden becomes inaccessible to the couple, yet it still assumes a crucial place on the "ground."

54. Galambush, "'ādām from 'ădāmâ," 45.
55. According to Rosenberg, the provision of animal skins for clothes and the man's choice of partner are the two instances in which culture "invades" the garden (*King and Kin*, 63). Granted, the former instance marks a decisive move toward culture as known by the Yahwist; the latter, however, is of a different class: within the garden, gendered harmony provides the basis of a "precultural" community.

Life outside the garden is fraught with pain and power. As a matter of survival, arduous force is required to obtain the desired results, whether in bearing children or in producing crops. Compared to the ease and security of the irrigationist, dryland agriculture is inherently burdensome and risky, owing to the capriciousness of rainfall and the unreliability of the soil. The well-irrigated garden is an apt symbol of abundant provision and security; dryland farming is the practice of subsistence, a labor of pain.[56] In both agricultural contexts, however contrastive, the man's vocation, indeed his "home," is with the plants of the ground. As much as the man comes from the ground, the ground remains part of himself.

The harsh landscape of the cursed 'ădāmâ reflects the harsh realities of relationships: strife, alienation, and painful "returns," the woman to the man (3:16) and the man to the ground (v. 19). As the gender relationships are not immune from the ravages of domination, the produce of the earth has to be beaten, as it were, out of the recalcitrant soil. Yet it is unclear in this harsh landscape who is master over whom. The man must force the soil to yield its produce in order to "serve" the soil. The woman possesses the unrivaled power to bear new life, indeed to produce a "man" (4:1), for she is Eve, "the mother of all living" (3:20). Yet she is named and "ruled over" by the man. Such is this new life of curse, a life of subsistence off a land of meager resources and fraught with hierarchy, conflict, and tragedy.

Knowledge and Wisdom

The critical turn of the garden plot comes when the woman succumbs to the alluring tree in the middle of the garden. What she perceives and what subsequently transpires drive the narrative to its tragic conclusion. The taxonomy of goodness ascribed to the tree by the woman in 3:6 mirrors as well as intensifies the qualities attributed to the garden in general. In 2:9 the garden grown from the ground is described twofold: it is a "delight to the sight" *(neḥmād lĕmarʾeh)* and "good for food" *(ṭôb lĕmaʾăkāl)*. By contrast, the woman perceives the particular tree of the knowledge of good and evil in threefold fashion (3:6). Like the trees surrounding it, the tree in the middle of the garden is "good for food" *(ṭôb . . . lĕmaʾăkāl)*, but what follows in the description marks a heightening of intensity: the tree is regarded as a sheer "delight to the eyes"

56. For a concise description of what was involved in dryland agriculture in the hill country of Canaan, in contrast to irrigation farming, see Meyers, *Discovering Eve*, 47-61.

(ta'ăwâ-hû' lā'ênayim).[57] There is an irresistible aesthetic quality to this one tree that surpasses all others in the pleasant grove. Finally, the tree is "delight-fully conducive to make one wise" *(nehmād . . . lĕhaśkîl).*[58] The language of visual delight ascribed to all the trees is given a distinctly sapiential nuance in this final attribution. Taken together, these three attributes convey an advancement from material sustenance to aesthetic appreciation and edifying wisdom, a progression of discernment. This tree allegedly promises to make the journey from perception to sagacity a pilgrimage of delight.

The key to understanding the tree and its fruit within the larger context of the narrative is found in the final attribution. Despite recent translation attempts to divest the expression of sapiential meaning,[59] it is clear from the context that the tree denotes wisdom of a special sort, given its very title. Indeed, the arboreal image elsewhere in biblical tradition serves as a riveting symbol of wisdom:

> [Wisdom] is a tree of life to those who grasp her;
>   those who hold her fast are called happy (Prov 3:18).

57. The term *ta'ăwâ* can be positive or negative, depending on the context. In Ps 38:10 (MT 9), it denotes a deep longing for deliverance. In Prov 11:23, it denotes the noble desire of the righteous (see also 19:22; 10:24). At the opposite extreme, it can denote lust for something (Pss 10:3; 112:10; Prov 21:25, 26). Its particular nuance depends entirely on the object and subject.

58. The verb *śkl* in the hiphil can take on a wide range of meanings, from ponder and consider (e.g., Isa 41:20; 44:18) to gain insight, display prudence or skill, and prosper (e.g., Jer 9:23; Pss 94:8 [in parallel with *bîn*]; 2:10; 36:3 [MT 4]; Prov 17:8). In its various cognate forms, the root *śkl* is part of the stock vocabulary of Proverbs (e.g., 16:23; 21:11; 10:5, 19; 14:35; 15:24; 17:2; 19:14). Indeed, the Hiphil stem assumes a certain pride of place in the introductory catalogue of virtues in Prov 1:1-6: "to gain effective instruction" *(lāqahat mûsar haśkēl, v. 3).* Throughout its various attestations, the term denotes a pragmatic form of wisdom that is powerfully effective for the one who employs it.

59. Taking his cue from H. Gunkel, S. Mitchell omits this final attribute as too complex for the Yahwist's simple literary style, and thus consigns it to the work of a glossator (Mitchell, *Genesis* [New York: HarperCollins, 1996] 7, 124). But the complex literary style is evident only in the English translations; the Hebrew maintains an almost poetic symmetry for all three clauses. Rather than deleting the clause entirely, the LXX, along with the Vulgate, evidently smoothed its translation by omitting the subject "tree" and treating the disputed verb *śkl* (Hiphil) as a synonym for *ta'ăwâ,* "delight." Similarly, R. Alter renders the verb *śkl* as simply another verb of perception: "the tree was lovely to look at," while admitting that this is a rare use of the verb in the biblical literature (Alter, *Genesis: Translation and Commentary* [New York: Norton, 1996] 13). By contrast, Korsack's recent translation retains the sapiential nuance: "the tree was attractive to get insight" *(At the Start, 9).*

The fruit of the righteous is a tree of life,
    but violence takes lives away (11:30, NRSV).

Hope deferred sickens the heart,
    but a desire fulfilled is a tree of life (13:12).

A healing tongue is a tree of life
    but perverseness in it breaks the spirit (15:4).

For the tradents of proverbial wisdom, the tree signifies both wisdom and prosperity or shalom (Prov 3:17b). It evokes ḥokmâ (Greek sophia) herself, who offers longevity in her right hand and riches and honor in her left (3:16).[60] That the alluring description of the tree from the woman's point of view begins with "good" is itself telling. The serpent had promised divine discernment between "good and evil"; the woman perceives the tree's fruit to be "good." In short, the tree is an icon of goodness, aesthetic and otherwise. But how far it is distinctly moral and edifying in its goodness is another issue.

Despite the tree's sapiential connection in proverbial wisdom, the Yahwist does not make the kind of singular identification of the tree with wisdom as the sages of Proverbs do. For one thing, the narrative in its final form posits two trees, the tree of knowledge (Gen 2:9, 17; cf. 3:5) and the tree of life (2:9; 3:22, 24). Most scholars view the latter tree as an addition to the story.[61] But what some may deem secondary from a traditio-historical perspective is of crucial significance in the narrative's received form. Regardless of the historical development of the text, two trees emerge as equal enticements for the couple (3:6, 22): the tree of life, associated with sagacity and prosperity in proverbial wisdom, and the tree of knowledge. Given the widespread usage of the former by the ancient sages, the latter tree is most likely the result of the

60. For the possible mythic associations of woman with wisdom, see Meyers, *Discovering Eve*, 91. I would add that there may also be an inherent connection between man and immortal life (and its loss), as one finds in the characters of Gilgamesh and Adapa.

61. So, e.g., D. Carr, who deems Gen 2:9b; 3:22, 24 as "remnants of a separate source or later redactional addictions" that can be easily bracketed out for discussion ("The Politics of Textual Subversion: A Diachronic Perspective on the Garden of Eden Story," *JBL* 112 [1993] 583). So also O. H. Steck, "Die Paradieserzählung: Eine Auslegung von Genesis 2,4b–3,24," in *Wahrnehmungen Gottes im Alten Testament: Gesammelte Studien* (TBü 70; Munich: Kaiser, 1982) 41-45 (reprinted from Biblische Studien 60; Neukirchen-Vluyn: Neukirchener Verlag, 1970, 46-52). If pressed to give a diachronic reading of the text, I would suggest, going along with K. Budde's original theory, that the Yahwist edited and expanded an original tale in which there was one forbidden tree that remained unspecified except for the fact that it stood in the middle of the garden (cf. 3:3, 11; see Westermann, *Genesis 1–11*, 212-13).

Yahwist's literary cultivation.[62] Its presence bifurcates wisdom to suit the dramatic development of the story, and in so doing introduces a critical, indeed polemical, dimension not found in the wisdom literature.

By splitting *sapientia* into knowledge, on the one hand, and life, on the other, the Yahwist drives a wedge deep into the heart of wisdom. In wisdom, according to the sages, is found the inner unity of knowledge and life, of instruction and blessing, and to rend them asunder would bankrupt sapiential discourse, rendering the grand promises of wisdom null and void. Yet the Yahwist does just that. Life is wrenched from discerning knowledge. Together, knowledge and life constitute the quintessence of wisdom, but separated in the hands of the Yahwist, knowledge loses all efficacy for the characters within the Yahwist's primordial world. Only the tree of life can confer the power of life, yet it is barred from the man (3:22-24).[63] Without it, the tree of knowledge offers only shame and misery. In the garden of delight, the Yahwist wields an ax.

Moreover, the Yahwist implants in the very description of this tree a veritable trap. Through the eyes of the woman, the Yahwist characterizes the tree as conducive for effective knowledge *(śkl)*, that is, for gaining the kind of wisdom that leads to, among other things, prosperity and happiness. The kind of knowledge with which the Yahwist describes the tree is eminently instrumental in nature, a knowledge of means for attaining desired ends, the requisite know-how for mastering life. The tree represents a form of intellectual capital that can function in self-serving ways, depending on the aim of the wielder of wisdom. The serpent promised divine status for the couple, and so in the hope of a self-apotheosis the woman reaches out and takes it

---

62. That the "tree of the knowledge of good and evil" is nowhere else found in the biblical corpus yet remains central to the Yahwist's account, in contrast to the "tree of life," suggests that the tree of knowledge, rather than the tree of life, was the Yahwist's innovation (so also E. Kutsch, "Die Paradieserzählung Genesis 2–3 und ihr Verfasser," in *Studien zum Pentateuch: Walter Kornfeld zum 60. Geburtstag* [ed. G. Braulik et al.; Vienna: Herder, 1977] 11-13, 22-24). As I will show, both named trees are elaborations that are essential to the thrust of the narrative. The "tree of life" does not simply serve as a reminder of an alternative version of the garden story, contra Westermann, *Genesis 1–11*, 212-13.

63. The expression *ḥay lĕʿōlām* ("life forever") may be more hyperbole than a clear reference to eternal life proper. At any rate, a similar sense of immortality is used in proverbial wisdom: "righteousness delivers from death" *(ṣĕdāqâ taṣṣîl mimmāwet*, Prov 10:2b; 11:4); "the righteous are established forever" *(ṣaddîq yĕsôd ʿôlām*, 10:25). Wisdom herself is described as offering not only honor and riches but also "long life" *(ʾōrek yāmîm*, 3:16). (For a different reading of the theme of immortality in Genesis 2–3, see J. Barr, *The Garden of Eden and the Hope of Immortality* [Minneapolis: Fortress, 1993] 14-20). Imparting eternal or simply long life, the tree of life in Genesis is associated with wisdom in Proverbs.

(*lqḥ*, 3:6). Such knowledge is a thing to be grasped and manipulated, a knowledge without trust in Yahweh's beneficence.

The irony is that what the woman perceives as irresistibly good leads directly to nothing good in any immediately apprehensible way. Partaking the fruit in violation of the interdiction may suggest a lack of discernment, as might be confirmed in the proverb: "Desire without knowledge is not good, and one who moves too hurriedly misses the way" (Prov 19:2 NRSV). The woman's desire, in disregard of the divine command, led to disobedience, as if she had been ignorant of the interdiction all along. Yet had the tree truly imparted moral discernment and conferred what the woman thought it would, she would have chosen in a discerning way. Indeed, the same proverb can be marshaled in support if translated more accurately: "A life *(nepeš)* without knowledge is not good," as her gaze contemplatively lingers on the tree before partaking. Succumbing to the sensuous delights of wisdom, according to the sages, is itself a discerning act.[64] To the credit of the Yahwist's sense of dramatic nuance, the woman's actions can be argued both ways, as commendable or as shortsighted.

Yet what is decisively clear from the Yahwist's perspective is that the fruit of the tree was, to put it mildly, a disappointment. It did not deliver as promised.[65] The paradoxical function of the serpent's promise is critically revealing. On the one hand, the serpent's assurance actually is confirmed on one level: the couple's eyes are opened, they become "like God, knowing good and evil" (see Gen 3:2), and they do not "die" upon eating the fruit. On the other hand, the serpent's discourse with the woman is deceptive to its core. The serpent begins the conversation with a patently false claim aimed at engaging the woman. The serpent's promise, though technically truthful, is dubious in light of the debilitating effects of the couple's partaking: their knowledge gained from the tree, far from effecting apotheosis, engenders their sense of vulnerability, including an acute awareness of their mortality, as well as a disruption of their relationship with God, all confirmed by their fear over Yahweh's "voice" (3:8). Not lying outright, the serpent has told the truth without telling the full truth, a "truthful" ruse. For the Yahwist, the serpent is the embodiment of wisdom at its most

64. As is often noted, the character of wisdom in Proverbs is deliberately profiled with erotic imagery, a prominent rhetorical feature of sapiential discourse (e.g., Prov 4:6; 5:15-19; 7:4).

65. C. M. Carmichael perceptively notes the similarity between the Yahwist's pessimism toward wisdom and that of Qohelet in Ecclesiastes, who associates the consciousness of toilsome labor with wisdom ("The Paradise Myth: Interpreting without Jewish and Christian Spectacles," in *A Walk in the Garden: Biblical, Iconographical and Literary Images of Eden* [ed. P. Morris and D. Sawyer; JSOTSup 136; Sheffield: JSOT Press, 1992] 50-54).

subtle, reprehensible, and thus dangerous form.[66] The serpent's collusion rests, at root, in its presentation of the tree of knowledge as the tree of life, as the promise of apotheosis fully reified in botanical form.

The inefficacy of the tree's fruit is mirrored by the tree of life, whose literary presence does not resurface until the end of the narrative (3:22, 24). In the body of the narrative, the tree of life is out of sight, out of mind. Had both trees been grafted into one, the results of appropriating the fruit would have been much different. But that is not the Yahwist's story.[67] As it stands, the tree of the knowledge of good and evil, without the accompanying tree of life, offers only a partial, damning knowledge, an awareness of a further lack. The tree of knowledge, split apart from the tree of life, lacks the efficacy of shalom, which is already a given in Yahweh's garden. By contrast, wisdom addresses her audience by issuing the invitation, "Whoever finds me finds life" (Prov 8:35a). In the Yahwist's anthropogony, the couple partook and found the ravages of death. In light of the injunction, the couple's grab for wisdom was an outright betrayal of trust.

The Breakdown of Community

The aftermath of ingesting such knowledge is devastating. Intimacy is replaced by fear and alienation, and eros is contaminated.[68] The fruit has soured the couple's life together and their communion with God, and the anthropogonic narrative has turned full circle, leaving the primal couple to fend for themselves in a

66. For ancient Near Eastern connections between the serpent figure and wisdom, see K. R. Joines, "The Serpent in Gen 3," *ZAW* 87 (1975) 4-9; idem, *Serpent Symbolism in the Old Testament* (Haddonfield, N.J.: Haddonfield House, 1974) 21-26.

67. The closest ANE analogue is the scene from the Epic of Gilgamesh in which the protagonist has in his grasp the plant of life, whose power to rejuvenate is divulged by Utnapishtim, yet through failure of nerve postpones ingesting the plant so that he can try it out on an elder, before losing it to a snake (tablet XI). If the Yahwist had wanted to compose a story more akin to this Babylonian parallel, the result would have had the woman holding the fruit in her hands but tragically failing to consume it. The actual tragedy, however, is lodged precisely in the ingestion. That there are two trees in the story plays into the Yahwist's stinging critique of wisdom. See also Ea's trickery in preventing the sage Adapa from obtaining immortality from Anu (Dalley, *Myths of Mesopotamia*, 184-88).

68. See A. J. Hauser, "Genesis 2–3: The Theme of Intimacy and Alienation," in *Art and Meaning: Rhetoric in Biblical Literature* (ed. D. J. A. Clines et al.; JSOTSup 19: Sheffield: JSOT Press, 1982) 20-36 (repr. in *I Studied Inscriptions*, 383-98); Trible, *God and Rhetoric*, 105. Drawing from both Hauser and Trible, Carr makes a similar statement, but is compelled to develop it almost exclusively from a diachronic perspective ("Politics of Textual Subversion," 587).

land devoid of irrigation (cf. Gen 2:5). Their living environment is desiccated, and so also their community. From their newly found knowledge, they gain a perspective that recognizes their nakedness for what it is as culturally defined, an object of shame and a subject of vulnerability.

Throughout the biblical literature, the exposure of genitalia and buttocks was considered eminently dishonoring. Next to death itself, naked flight was deemed the worst form of defeat (Amos 2:16; Isa 20:1-6). One telling example of such degradation is the story of the shameful treatment of David's emissaries, who are sent to Hanun, the new king of the Ammonites, to practice *ḥesed* or covenantal loyalty (2 Sam 10:2).[69] Hanun's courtiers, however, suspect the purity of David's motives, so they shave off half the beard of each of David's ambassadors, cut off their garments "in the middle at their hips," and expel them (v. 4). Such exposure prompts great shame (v. 5), so much so that David allows them to remain in Jericho for their beards to grow back before permitting them to return to Jerusalem. Such an unconscionable act on the part of the Ammonite king prompts subsequent military conflict (vv. 6-19).

Another example is David's dance before the ark of Yahweh,[70] which elicits a scathing rebuke from his wife Michal (2 Sam 6:20): "How the king of Israel honored himself *(nikbad)* today, uncovering himself *(niglâ)* today before the eyes of his servants' maids, as any vulgar person might shamelessly uncover himself *(kĕhiggālôt niglôt)!*"[71] In her sarcastic reprimand, Michal unveils much about a culture rooted in honor and shame: exposure is anathema, for it embodies shame of the basest kind. Moreover, she injects a sexual undertone, which David ironically plays on in his response: "It was before Yahweh . . . that I have danced before Yahweh. I will make myself yet more contemptible *(nĕqallōtî)* than this, and I will be abased *(hāyîtî šāpāl)* in my own eyes; but by the maids of whom you have spoken, by them I shall be held in honor *('ikkābēdâ)*" (vv. 21-22). David's repeated reference to being "before Yahweh" is revealing. His joyous abandonment and virtually naked innocence before the ark indicate a privileged communion with Yahweh. Similarly, the primal couple's nakedness was once a condition for intimacy and communion (Gen 2:24-25). In the garden the first man and woman were continually "before" God.

Once shame is introduced, however, the couple hide from Yahweh's presence, feeling exposed, vulnerable, and alienated. Dishonor follows disobedience, and the man and woman now perceive themselves as threatened

---

69. See Olyan's extended discussion in "Honor, Shame," 212-13.

70. See also Chapter 6.

71. Olyan describes this example as ironical, but it is more sarcastic in tone ("Honor, Shame," 213n.37).

before Yahweh and even by each other. The sequence of events acknowledges that shame is an eminently public phenomenon, which explains why the effects of the forbidden fruit were not evident until *both* the man and the woman had partaken. Together, the primal couple feel exposed before each other and Yahweh, hence the immediate attempt to cover themselves, however pathetically, and hide among the trees at the sound of Yahweh's presence. The narrator presents a subtle irony in the description: the couple literally "hears Yahweh Elohim's voice" *(šmʿ ʾet-qôl YHWH ʾĕlōhîm)*, as the Deity casually strolls through the garden (3:8). With a slight change in the consonantal spelling, the clause could easily read: "They hearkened to the voice" of Yahweh (*šmʿ lĕqôl;* cf. 3:17a), that is, they obeyed God.[72] Rather than prompting moral adherence, Yahweh's "voice" now inspires terror.

The issue at stake is obedience: Yahweh curses the man for having "hearkened to the voice of your wife" (3:17). The implication is that the man did not obey Yahweh's verbal decree. The man and the woman henceforth "hear" Yahweh's voice differently. Yahweh is now perceived as an invasive threat rather than as a beneficent provider and source of moral guidance. The narrator indicates this lamentable change of perception, from welcome to dread, adherence to shame, with an artful variation of a stock literary expression.

Another masterful wordplay is found in the root letters that ironically link the serpent and the couple together, *ʿrm,* which can denote cunning (3:1) or nakedness (2:25; 3:7, 10, 11), depending on the context.[73] The narrator teases the reader, particularly the ancient one, with the range of meanings for each context. Is there a sense in which the serpent, as the most cunning of the wild animals, is also the most "naked"? Perhaps the serpent is as shameless in its trickery as the couple is innocent of their nakedness.[74] Furthermore, that the serpent is an animal traditionally associated with *wild* life, that is, life outside the cultivated garden, suggests a brazen disregard for appropriate boundaries, particularly between the human and the wild. With the serpent, shamelessness assumes its conventional abject nuance. As for the primal couple, the man and the woman become shamefully cognizant of their nakedness after partaking of the fruit (3:7). The objects of the serpent's cunning, they have gotten wise to the snake (3:13). But it is too late. The couple's awareness of their nakedness comes at the price of shame, the fruit of knowledge. In a garden far away, exempt from the despoilments of shame and fear, the couple

72. Specifically, the direct object marker is replaced by the preposition.

73. In proverbial wisdom, the root is considered in a positive fashion, even though elsewhere it can denote craftiness (Job 5:12; 15:5; Ps 83:3 [MT 4]). See Brown, *Character in Crisis,* 26; Fox, *Words for Wisdom,* 158-59.

74. Galambush, "'ādām from 'ădāmâ," 38.

lived in a land of delight and fulfillment, a garden of shalom. In their grab for self-transcending knowledge, the couple were left with self-degrading awareness. With the onset of shame, the outcome of disobedience, relationships born of mutual freedom and intimacy become shackles of bondage.

Amid the ironies and wordplays,[75] one thing is startlingly clear within the unfolding drama of the Yahwist's anthropogony: the primal couple disobeyed Yahweh's prohibition. There was nothing wrong about the tree proudly standing in the center of the garden; that its fruit was taken in disobedience, however, was another thing. By partaking of the fruit, the couple had assessed their life in the garden as deficient. From the narrator's perspective, however, the real deficiency was evinced in the couple's lack of obedience. The Yahwist has carefully set up the story in order to bring about a fateful collision between divine command and the quest for wisdom.[76] The optimistic world that prevails in classical wisdom is not reflected here. The Yahwist submits in dramatic form a scathing critique of wisdom's ethos. The lure of wisdom was occasioned by the serpent's cunning and the perceived need for self-improvement or gain. The serpent, itself a boundary breaker, promised an apotheosis, an advancement from the adherence to determined good to the self-determination of good.

As an anthropogony, the Yahwist's account of the garden imagines a world set apart from familiar experience, apart from the confinement of culture and divine punishment. Life in the garden is no drudgery of the gods. But neither is it a vacation for the man. It is a vocation. As keeper of the garden, the man is given a liberal dose of freedom to organize his world in relation to the animals and plants. He is given free reign over all the trees, except one, and therein lies the rub. This land, remote as it is, is not a land devoid of commandment. Life before Torah is still *shema*;[77] obedience must reign even in this blissful landscape. This garden of delight is not a realm of fantasy and escape from moral accountability. It is rather the province of the Yahwist's moral imagination, a land of fulfillment and failure, full of provision and rife with lack, that has all to do with the formation of community and culture.

---

75. For a survey of other, more subtle wordplays, see B. J. Stratton, *Out of Eden: Reading, Rhetoric, and Ideology in Genesis 2–3* (JSOTSup 208; Sheffield: Sheffield Academic Press, 1995) 166-67.

76. Meyers's attempt to dissociate the act of partaking from the tree of wisdom from any notion of sin, claiming that the first sin does not occur until Cain's murder of Abel, neglects the incontrovertible role of divine command in both scenes (*Discovering Eve*, 87). Both the primal couple and Cain disobey by failing to resist temptation.

77. As noted earlier, the Yahwist employs the root *šmʿ* ("hear" or "obey") in various ways to highlight the couple's disobedience.

The ecology of the garden reflects an ethos within which divine law is pitted against self-procured wisdom.[78] Law establishes a setting in which mutual harmony, abundant provision, and constructive freedom can flourish. Yet, as the ancient narrator is quick to point out, self-determination has its limits within the scope of the law. Without adherence to this primal *tôrâ*, which establishes certain limits of human activity, freedom exceeds its grasp and harmony is replaced by hierarchy. Life outside the garden is cursed with painful wrenchings and returns, yet the garden still persists, although no longer maintained by the man. By recounting this drama of anthropogony, the Yahwist has deposited the garden into the cultured reader's moral imagination. The garden's existence remains in the land or *'ădāmâ*, albeit barred by the cherubim. Nonetheless, in those fleeting moments of mutual bliss and fulfillment in which the exercise of force is forsaken, an occasional slip by the flaming sword is possible, an access that the Yahwist does not entirely obstruct (2:24)[79] and one that the author of the Song of Songs immeasurably widens:

> A garden locked is my sister, my bride,
>   a garden locked, a fountain sealed.
> Your channel is an orchard of pomegranates with all choicest fruits,
>   henna with nard, nard and saffron, calamus and cinnamon,
>   with all trees of frankincense, myrrh and aloes,
>   with all chief spices —
>
> a garden fountain, a well of living water,
>   and flowing streams from Lebanon.
> . . . .
> Let my beloved come to his garden,
>   and eat its choicest fruits.
> I come to my garden, my sister, my bride.
>   (Cant 4:12-15, 16b–5:1a, NRSV)[80]

---

78. Cf. Isa 5:21; 29:13-14; Jer 8:8-9, which castigate the wise, and Deut 4:5-8, which claims that true wisdom and discernment come only from observing the "statutes and ordinances" of Moses. See L. Alonso-Schökel, "Motivos sapienciales y de alianza en Gn 2–3," *Bib* 43 (1962) 301-2; Carr, "Politics of Textual Subversion," 592.

79. See the survey of some recent interpretations of the so-called "Fall" in the garden story that suggest a less fatalistic reading of the couple's disobedience in W. Sibley Towner, "Interpretations and Reinterpretations of the Fall," in *Modern Biblical Scholarship: Its Impact on Theology and Proclamation*, ed. F. A. Eigo (Villanova, Pa.: The Villanova University Press, 1984) 53-85.

80. The discussion of whether the author of the Song of Songs intended to redeem the garden of Eden story (so Trible) or was simply unaware of any "fall" (so Fox) remains

What the Yahwist leaves open for the imagination, the love poet conveys in evocative detail. The poet identifies the garden, sealed from outside threat, with the young woman herself (cf. 6:2).[81] Both the poet and the narrator, however, envision a setting, an ethos, in which the notions of honor and shame, hierarchy and domination, are thrown into question, transcended, or at the very least relativized.[82] The garden's ethos can be embodied by reaching a "second naïveté,"[83] a level of imaginative appropriation in which the conventional codes of hierarchy, honor, and shame, all rooted in the exercise of power, are suspended yet never permanently overcome in the public arena. Sexual union within marriage thus need not be another harbinger of pain and power in a land of curse. That the Yahwist institutionalizes marriage *prior* to the curse (2:24) suggests that marriage bears the promise of mitigating a curse-filled existence. Marriage offers the opportunity to recultivate Eden within the hearth and home of human existence.

It is not fortuitous, then, that life outside the garden begins with the man "knowing" his wife (4:1), a union that apprehends, however dimly, a glimpse of life within the garden, yet whose outcome now invites pain and strife. As Genesis 4 makes all too clear, the painful wrenchings that characterize life outside the garden become all the more intense, indeed, a matter of life and death. Yet all is not lost. As Yahweh clothed the fig-draped couple before their expulsion from the garden, so Yahweh has a few gracious surprises in store for this family's exile from the garden.

---

moot. One thing, however, is clear: from the Yahwist's standpoint, the intimacy evoked in the terse phrase "naked and were not ashamed" (2:25) implies mutual sexual awareness on the part of the couple. Consequently, lovemaking within a marital context for the Yahwist — unlike in the Song of Songs — recaptures in some form the ethos of the garden. For the possible connections between Eden and the garden setting for lovemaking in the Song of Songs, see Trible, *God and Rhetoric*, 161; F. Landy, "The Song of Songs and the Garden of Eden," *JBL* 98 (1979) 513-28; M. Fox, *The Song of Songs and the Ancient Egyptian Love Songs* (Madison: University of Wisconsin Press, 1985) xxv, 283-87.

81. Fox, *Song of Songs*, 286.

82. See D. Bergant, "'My Beloved Is Mine and I Am His' (Song 2:16): The Song of Songs and Honor and Shame," *Semeia* 68 (1996) 36-37, who identifies the various ways in which this book transcends the codes of honor and shame.

83. I shamelessly borrow the phrase from P. Ricoeur's hermeneutical discussion in *The Symbolism of Evil* (tr. E. Buchanan; Boston: Beacon, 1960) 351-52. Ricoeur refers to this level of interpretation as an act of "sympathetic imagination," the basic aim of phenomenology (p. 19). See below.

Outside the Garden

What am I to do? This is my career. I can't continue getting butted like that. I've got children to raise. I've got to retaliate. Look at me! Look at me! I'll go home and my kids will be scared of me.

Mike Tyson[84]

The garden sets the stage for what follows in the Yahwist's epic by establishing a model of moral valuation: relationships characterized by mutuality, harmony, blessing, and most critically, obedience are esteemed good. This ethos has the mythic and cosmic backing to serve as a paradigm with which all that subsequently transpires can be compared. The Yahwist has divulged the profound depths of his moral vision by using the garden as the setting and foil for human disobedience. The geo-ethical contours of this lush parcel of land remain prominent as the Yahwist recounts the next generation of the primal family.

Life outside the garden begins in procreation. The man (*'ādām*) "knows" Eve. Indicated by the man's climactic approbation in 2:24, the couple "knew" each other intimately in their mutual sharing within the garden as *'îš* and *'iššâ*, naked and unashamed, apart yet joined together. Now, however, the man knows the woman from a different perspective, as the "mother of all living," and conception follows as well as the pain of childbirth. The Yahwist need not declare this outright in narrative form, for it is now a given part of reality as defined by the woman's curse (3:16). What the narrator does highlight is Eve's remarkable declaration: "I have created a man (*'îš*) with Yahweh,"[85] a declaration of creative partnership with the Deity. Cast out of the garden, the man and woman are not left to fend for themselves. In that moment of supreme vulnerability and pain when the balance of life and death hangs by a thread, Eve gives birth to Cain and attributes her success to Yahweh. Eve's declaration would have made more

---

84. June 28, 1997, after Tyson was disqualified in his fight with Evander Holyfield for having bitten off part of the latter's ear (*New York Times*, June 30, 1997, C5).

85. Heb. *qānîtî 'îš 'et-YHWH*. Much has been made over the precise nuance of the preposition *'et*. For a discussion of the suggested alternatives, see Westermann, *Genesis 1–11*, 290-91. The use of the preposition here denotes the sense of assistance (e.g., Gen 21:20; 26:24; 39:2; so also the LXX and Vulgate of Gen 4:1). U. Cassuto, along with Westermann, suggests the sense of "together with" or "equally with" God's creation of man (Cassuto, *A Commentary on the Book of Genesis, Part I: From Adam to Noah* [tr. I. Abrahams; Jerusalem: Magnes, 1961, repr. 1989] 198-99). Such a sense would be more explicit had Eve given birth to an *'ādām* rather than an *'îš*. Divine assistance, like Yahweh's clothing the primal couple and protection of Cain, seems more in keeping with the tenor of the narrative.

sense, perhaps, if she had said: "I have created a man (*'îš*) with the groundling (*'ādām*)." But a simple lesson in the birds and the bees is not the point here. Despite the painful reality of Eve's curse, Yahweh provides support in the struggle for life and ensures that the human family will not become extinct in a curse-filled land, even though each generation must return to "dirt."

The Ontology of Violence

As the narrative progresses, the reader encounters both familiar and new elements. Cain, whose name is drawn from the folk etymology given by the mother ("creation"), is a "ground tiller" (*'ōbēr 'ădāmâ*, 4:2), like his father (3:23).[86] Abel, whose name can denote "emptiness" (*hebel*), is a "sheepherder" (*rō'ēh ṣō'n*). One can only imagine what kind of maternal pronouncement would have rendered such a name as Abel's. Yet in keeping with his name, any explanatory discourse regarding his birth is simply not meant to be. From a poetics perspective, Abel is a virtual stick figure before Cain's passionate and complex character. Within the purview of the narrative, Abel is a powerless figure in a land of curse. In a terrain riddled with the exercise and abuse of power, Abel, apropos to his name, invites only disaster. Outside the garden nature abhors a vacuum.

Many modern interpreters have understood the story of Cain and Abel as an etiology of two ethnically distinct cultures represented by the farmer, on the one side, and the shepherd, on the other. But as Hiebert points out, these two sons and their respective vocations typify a family living off the Mediterranean highland regions, a harsh landscape that required both cultivation and herding for the household's survival.[87] The story recounts a conflict generated by an archetypal rivalry not between shepherds and farmers but between siblings.[88] The violence that ensues is kept within the family.

The setting is established when Cain, in keeping with his profession, is described as bringing an offering from "the fruit of the ground" (4:3).[89] In disjunctive sequence,[90] Abel offers the firstlings of his flock. Arising naturally,

---

86. The absence of the definite article, and thus of the direct object marker, in v. 2b serves as a vocational epithet like "sodbuster" in describing the farmer. A similar case is found in the description of Abel's vocation.

87. Moreover, animal husbandry is implied in the man's naming of the animals in 2:19-20.

88. Hiebert, *Yahwist's Landscape*, 38-40.

89. The reference is *minḥâ*, which is used in a general sense, unlike in Lev 2:1-16.

90. Heb. *wayyābē' qayin . . . wěhebel hēbî' . . .* (vv. 3-4).

the competition for divine favor is undeclared, yet enmity is about to take root in the ground outside the garden. In sharp contrast, the model of relational harmony embodied in the garden creates space for reimagining the moral dilemma and for identifying an alternative: an equity of favor extended to both Cain and Abel. On the one hand, Yahweh is in part the culprit, playing a decisive role in preserving the ethos of the curse, rather than of blessing, by rejecting Cain's gift. On the other hand, the seemingly arbitrary nature of Cain's rejection and Abel's approval is illusory.[91] As conflict is built into the very morphology of kinship relationships, so the rejection of the ground's firstfruits is featured in the moral topography of the Yahwist's landscape. Outside the garden, Cain presented an offering from the fruit of the *cursed* ground that was, as a result, deemed unworthy.[92] The cursed ground is the bane of Cain's vocation in more ways than one. In a land of lack, enmity and competition find fertile opportunity to reign.

The cursed ground and its unacceptable fruit, however, remain only in the background of what follows. Indeed, there is no indication that Cain sinned at all by offering a deficient sacrifice, even though Abel wins Yahweh's favor. The matter-of-fact recounting of Yahweh's disregard for Cain's offering precludes any moralistic reading.[93] The narrative spotlight focuses on Cain's reaction: inflamed with rage, "his face falls," he is frustrated and discontented (4:5b). After rhetorically questioning Cain, Yahweh issues a stern warning: "If you do well, then there is lifting up; but if you do not do well, at the door lies sin, a croucher; for you is its desire, but you must master it." Despite the wealth of translation problems, some general sense can be made. The "lifting up" refers to the lifting up of Cain's face and can also connote Yahweh's favor. But if Cain cannot change his attitude and conduct, then a far more terrible danger lurks at the threshold. In short, Cain is not culpable for offering a deficient sacrifice, for the conundrum provoked by Yahweh's rejection occurs primarily in order to determine what Cain will do next (cf. 2:19), and therein lies his responsibility.

The term "croucher" is commonly used of animals. It can refer, for ex-

91. The LXX fills the moral gap by claiming that Cain did not cut up his sacrifice properly, perhaps not unlike the trick Prometheus played on Zeus. See M. S. Enslin, "Cain and Prometheus," *JBL* 86 (1967) 88-90; J. W. Wevers, *Notes on the Greek Text of Genesis* (SBLSCS 35; Atlanta: Scholars Press, 1993) 54-55.

92. See G. A. Herion, "Why God Rejected Cain's Offering: The Obvious Answer," in *Fortunate the Eyes That See: Essays in Honor of David Noel Freedman in Celebration of His Seventieth Birthday* (ed. A. B. Beck et al.; Grand Rapids: Eerdmans, 1995) 52-65; F. A. Spina, "The 'Ground' for Cain's Rejection (Gen 4): *ʾdāmāh* in the Context of Gen 1–11," *ZAW* 104 (1992) 319-32.

93. See Spina, "The 'Ground' for Cain's Rejection," 322.

ample, to lions (Gen 49:9), dragons (as a metaphor for Pharaoh in Ezek 29:3), and leopards (Isa 11:6). "Sin" is cast as a predator. That a wild animal is crouching is not in itself noteworthy; it is merely resting. But that the beast is inclined at the door of Cain's domicile is a frightful prospect indeed! One slight disturbance and this "doorstep demon"[94] is suddenly aroused.[95] For fear of stirring up this wild creature, Cain is made a prisoner in his own home. Yahweh issues a mandate for controlling this creature that echoes the curse directed to the woman in Gen 3:16b. The language of painful return is now applied to a crouching creature, which, if aroused, will dominate (i.e., possess) Cain. Cain's only option is to exert a valiant effort to master the sin, to domesticate this ominous specter from the wild. The apparition lurking at the threshold is the beast within. As much as Cain's father must master the land to yield its produce, Cain must master himself.

Cain fails. He "rises up," as if he were the one "crouching," and kills his brother.[96] The intense language of pathos that characterized Cain's reaction over Yahweh's rejection of his sacrifice, as well as Yahweh's subsequent warning (vv. 5b-7), is left behind in the ensuing narrative (v. 8). The narrative, supplemented by other textual versions, eschews all lurid description of Cain being overcome with rage or possessed by a demonic spirit. Rather, it reports Abel's murder in dry, premeditated fashion. Immediately following the account of his emotional trauma, the vignette of Abel's death reveals Cain as a calculating criminal. Much is left unsaid in the narrative: Cain's dark and turbid impulses give rise to cold calculation; his predatory beast within is the source of premeditation. By mortally dominating Abel, Cain has allowed "sin" to dominate him. Yahweh's psychological probe of Cain's emotional trauma suggests that the situation need not have transpired the way it did. Kinship harmony can still prevail, but only through self-control.

Yahweh confronts Cain in the same way Yahweh confronted the primal couple in the garden: Yahweh asks, "Where?" Location is all important in the Yahwist's moral landscape: the man and the woman hiding among the trees; Abel's body left in the field. Yahweh's query this time is not concerned with the addressee's location, as in the case of the couple's whereabouts (3:9b), but Cain's brother's. Unlike the garden story, Cain does not launch into a confes-

---

94. Scholars generally acknowledge that the figure is in some way connected to an Assyrian description of a demonic *rabīṣum* (so H. Kaupel, *Die Dämonen im Alten Testament* [Augsburg: B. Filser, 1930] 77; Speiser, *Genesis*, 33; Westermann, *Genesis 1–11*, 299).

95. Cf. Gen 49:9, which likens Judah to a crouched lion ready to be aroused.

96. Although the language of Abel's murder is cast in typical Hebrew prose (*wayyāqom . . . wayyahargēhû*), Cain's "rising up" connotes special significance in light of the language of "crouching" immediately preceding.

sion but instead fabricates an alibi by professing ignorance, coupled with the impertinent retort, "Am I my brother's keeper?"

Much has been made of Cain's rhetorical question as indicating an ideal configuration of relationships in which human beings are each other's "keeper" (*šmr*). In truth, however, Cain's insolent response is technically correct: he is not his brother's guardian. As Paul Riemann has demonstrated in an often overlooked article, nowhere is such language actually used in biblical tradition to describe human beings attending to others.[97] Only God is the "keeper." Cain wins the technical point, but loses the battle, however, for he cannot apply the expression in such a way as to disclaim all form of fraternal responsibility.[98] Cain's cunning, like the serpent's, is a "truthful" ruse. As with any battle of wits, Cain overstates the issue in order to acquit himself. Nevertheless, Cain is responsible for his brother in much the same way as the first man and the woman were responsible for each other in their kinship relationship of support or "help" (*ʿzr*, 2:18). Although each member assumes different roles and vocations within the family system, mutual support and responsibility are nonnegotiable items for the primal family's survival. They are ethical mandates prefigured in the garden.

Like his father, the firstborn Cain is a "tiller of the ground," and so it is a matter of poetic justice that the ground's "mouth" testifies against him, if his own mouth will not. In Yahweh's words, the blood of the slain Abel "cries out to me from the *ʾădāmâ*," the ground (3:10). The language of Yahweh's indictment is telling. Shed by Cain's hand, Abel's blood cannot be contained (v. 11b) but slips, as it were, through his fingers to be caught by the gaping mouth of the *ʾădāmâ*. As *ʾādām* was "taken" from the *ʾădāmâ* and is eventually to return there, Cain has violated the ground by making it "take" back his brother.[99] More than just the scene of the crime, the ground actively bears witness to this fratricide by serving as the receptacle of Abel's blood. It opens its mouth to receive the blood of the victim, not to "swallow" the evidence,[100] but to "take it in" *(lqḥ)*, preserve it, and give it voice.

With a masterful stroke of irony, the Yahwist employs the stock lan-

97. P. A. Riemann, "Am I My Brother's Keeper?" *Int* 24 (1970) 482-91.
98. Westermann refers to Genesis 37–50 to highlight the ambiguity of Cain's retort (*Genesis 1–11*, 304).
99. A. J. Hauser, "Linguistic and Thematic Links between Genesis 4:1-16 and Genesis 2–3," *JETS* 23 (1980) 301-2.
100. The Yahwist could have easily used another verb, such as *blʿ*, to indicate a literal swallowing (cf. Num 16:30-32), but that would have implied a suppression of evidence rather than its unveiling.

guage of the earth "swallowing up" *(bl')* life with its mouth,[101] and turns the ground into a preserver of life and justice. By "taking in" Abel's life-blood, the ground takes on the juridical role of witness.[102] Significant is that the "voice" *(qôl)* of Abel's blood sets Yahweh's implementation of justice in motion. Although Abel's body is out of sight from the narrator's selective purview, the dead brother's "voice," which has been entirely silent until now, is deafening. As noted above, the voice or sound of a main character has figured prominently in the Yahwist's narrative heretofore: the man disobeyed Yahweh by listening to the "voice" of his wife in disobedience (3:17a); Yahweh's "voice" inspired dread in the human inhabitants of the garden (3:8). Now Yahweh hears the "voice" of the victim's blood issuing from the ground's mouth, demanding redress. The accusation cries out from the blood, but the blood is held in the "mouth" of the ground. By preserving the evidence in its "mouth," the ground finds its own voice as a juridical witness.

As the ground plays a decisive role in Yahweh's indictment, so it also figures prominently in Yahweh's punishment of Cain, as it did for Cain's father (3:17-19). The tiller of the ground continues to lead a life of curse. By way of intensification, it is now the man who is cursed "from the ground" (v. 11a), whereas in the primal man's punishment the ground was cursed "because of you" (3:17). Given the close connection between man and land, the interchange is a natural one. Moreover, Cain's curse plays on the prepositional relationship with the ground: as man was created "from the ground" *(min-hā'ădāmâ,* 2:7), so he is now cursed "from the ground" (4:11a). Given its repeated appearance throughout the anthropogony and beyond, the prepositional phrase is a veritable cliché in the Yahwist's stock vocabulary. In Cain's curse, the preposition is a double entendre: Cain is cursed *from* the ground, in the sense of being driven away and alienated (v. 14a).[103] He is also cursed *because* of it (v. 11b).[104]

The result is the land's impotence in Cain's hand: the *'ădāmâ* refuses to yield to Cain its produce *(kōaḥ,* lit. "strength"). Cain has killed Abel and, in so doing, the life of the land. Perhaps here a clue to the significance of Abel's

101. Many of the biblical references to the earth swallowing up its victims point to the story of the revolt of Korah, Dathan, and Abiram: Num 16:30, 32, 34; 26:10; Deut 11:6; Ps 106:17. See also Exod 15:12, which recounts God's cosmic battle against the forces of Pharaoh. In addition, earth as an instrument of death echoes the Ugaritic deity of death, Mot, who is described as devouring Baal in his mouth *(KTU* 1.5.I.5-7; II.3-5; 1.6.II.22-23).

102. For nature's role as witness in legal contexts, see Chapter 6.

103. This would involve the common separative use of the preposition *min*.

104. Here one should not exclude the causal use of the preposition.

name is offered: the blood of the empty figure who embodied "nothingness" has effectively annulled the soil's fecundity. The connection is thick with irony: the ground cannot "give to [Cain] its strength" because the manslayer has shed the blood of his powerless brother Abel. The impotent figure of Abel has attained powerful significance in his death. As the object of Yahweh's favor, Abel is a martyr of blessing; as the victim of Cain's bloodthirsty retribution, he is a martyr for justice. The blood-soaked ground is the occasion for Cain to be driven by Yahweh from the *'ădāmâ*, the soil of his sustenance (v. 14), into the vast domains of the "earth" *(hā'āreṣ)*.

It is understandable for Cain to object that his punishment is tantamount to a death sentence. Curiously, he does not complain of vainly scavenging a barren wasteland to die from starvation, as one might assume from the content of Yahweh's curse; rather, Cain objects to the prospect of being killed by anyone who might encounter him as a fugitive and wanderer. Cain's exile is not from the human community per se. Driven from the ground, Cain is exiled to a social domain devoid of refuge and rife with violence, a realm of a social anarchy infinitely remote from the harmonious order of the garden.[105] As a fugitive and wanderer *(nā' wānād)* bereft of all citizen rights, Cain is an alien in a hostile land (v. 14). The state of the land thus reflects the moral state of communal existence. Fertile soil is the ground of justice and right relations.

Cain's objection prompts, however, a startling change of plans in Yahweh's wielding of justice. As in the couple's being clothed before having to face the harsh life outside the garden, Yahweh grants Cain protection from the hostile environment he is about to face. A mark is placed on Cain to protect him from retributive slaughter; the message behind the mark wields a compelling threat of deterrence: the perpetrator of Cain's death will suffer "sevenfold vengeance" *(šib'ātayim yuqqām, v. 15)*. As in the garden, Yahweh lays down a law (cf. 2:17).[106] Cain is cast out as an outlaw yet remains under the protection of a divine ordinance. The statute is designed to stem the

---

105. Cain's curse and alienation from the land of provision to a life of wandering could be compared hermeneutically to being banished to a drug-infested inner-city community in which an ethos of violence prevails. This "code of the street," as urban sociologist E. Anderson identifies it, reflects a subculture in which the rare commodity of "respect" must be secured through intimidating displays of power in order to deter the ever present potential for harassment and violence ("The Code of the Streets," *Atlantic Monthly* [May 1994] 81-94). It is no coincidence that Cain himself is the first city builder, prefiguring ironically the archetypal city of refuge. Cain's city anticipates, however, urban centers that are anything but safe havens (see below).

106. For other examples, see Gen 26:11; 31:33; 44:9-10; Exod 19:17b.

downward cycle of blood vengeance that would be set in motion upon the victim's death at the hands of a murderer. By promulgating such a law, Yahweh pledges to be Cain's kin in his alienation from the land and from the Deity. As for the particular form of the sign, the narrator leaves it to the reader's imagination. Claus Westermann cites a rabbinic tradition that God gave Cain a dog as his companion — perhaps a pit bull.[107]

Properly equipped to be a *nād,* a wanderer, Cain settles in the land of Nod *(nôd).* Wandering and settling are not excluded from the narrator's perspective on Cain; together they denote a rhythm of disruption. Cain is driven outside the cultivable land *('ădāmâ),* which can sustain permanent settlement, into a vast, formidable terrain *('ereṣ-nôd)* in which settling is at best a temporary endeavor. Such a wasteland is incapable of sustaining permanent settlement; neither can it sustain an enduring social order, for Cain must enter the menacing land with nothing less than the divine backing of retributive force simply to survive. Here is where alienation proper is introduced: Cain goes "away from Yahweh's presence" (v. 16).

The narrator suggests that arable soil and divine presence are coextensive. Yet Cain sets out into the wasteland wearing the protective armament of divine deterrence, an ordinance intended to check further violence through the exponential rise of violence. Within the larger sweep of the Yahwist's narrative, the painful and coercive exertion with which the first generation was cursed has risen ineluctably to the level of violence in the second generation. Evicted from the *'ădāmâ,* Cain, unlike his parents, can never return. The march of time from one generation to the next is marked by a movement from painful bondage to wrenching alienation, a procession made inevitable by the introduction of an "ontology of violence,"[108] a reality that for the Yahwist is basic to the advancement of antediluvian culture yet fundamentally opposed to the garden's ethos.

The Descent of Culture

Cain's eviction from the sustained and settled life in the *'ădāmâ* and his entrance into the land of "wandering" open a new chapter in this family saga. Whereas his parents, as recent exiles from the garden, conceived and raised

107. *Berakot Rabba* 22:12; Westermann, *Genesis 1–11,* 313.
108. P. Berger's analysis of violence as the foundation of any political order is apropos in Cain's case, but does not preclude the Yahwist's imagination from positing alternative forms of social existence, as evidenced in the garden story (*Invitation to Sociology: A Humanistic Perspective* [Garden City, N.Y.: Doubleday, 1963] 69).

their children on the arable yet less-than-reliable soil, Cain, as the first exile of the 'ǎdāmâ, sets in motion the emergence of a new generation, pushing the social paradox of 2:24 to its extreme: engendered life through marital union also entails separation. For Cain, such separation is an eviction from the habitation of the previous generation. So far, each successive generation, by dint of moral violation, extends itself to progressively less hospitable and thus less habitable regions. Cain begins a new generation on essentially nonarable terrain, the "earth" ('ereṣ) minus the rich soil of the 'ǎdāmâ, which for the cursed Cain refuses to yield its strength.

Alienated from the land and his identity as a "soil tiller," Cain takes on the new role of city builder, a vocation by default (4:17). Drawing from the early work of Karl Budde, Westermann emends the end of the verse to read "and he called it [the city] Enoch, after his own name."[109] With this slight textual change, Westermann's text attributes to Enoch, not Cain, the founding of the city. Since textual precedent is entirely lacking for such a corrective measure, however, Westermann actually broaches the traditio-historical background of the verse rather than its textual development.[110] Simply put, it is more likely that the Yahwist has intentionally recast an ancient tradition of the founding of Enoch by identifying its founder explicitly with the condemned figure of Cain. Cain both fathers Enoch, his son, and founds Enoch, the city. He has sired a city. Bypassing all logic, the Yahwist's moral imagination revels in the profound irony of depicting Cain as both wanderer and founder of this emblem of civilization. The city that Cain built is a monumental achievement that comes at a price. Given his punishment as a wanderer, the city is Cain's refuge[111] but also a harbinger of misery. Hiebert notes the division of opinion among interpreters regarding the Yahwist's esteem for the city, either as a favorable achievement of civilization or as an evil place built by the first murderer, and argues for a neutral status.[112]

The status of the city ('îr) from the Yahwist's perspective is fleshed out in the later narrative, but even in this early episode it is clear that the city bears both guilt and redemption by association. Cain, this man of extremes, condemned yet protected, wielder of death yet spared for life, is inseparably bound up with this crown of culture. The Yahwist's manipulation of tradition indicates a thoroughly ambivalent attitude about the city, rooted in the city's drive toward collective power, yet intended as a refuge from violence in Cain's

109. Westermann, *Genesis 1–11*, 322, 326-27.
110. The likelihood of such a discrepant tradition is furthered by the connection of the name Enoch and its connotation as "founder" (Westermann, *Genesis 1–11*, 327).
111. Cf. Num 35:9-34; Deut 4:41-45; 19:1-13; Josh 20:1-9.
112. Hiebert, *Yahwist's Landscape*, 42.

case. The formidable hunter Nimrod is the founder of the mighty cities of Mesopotamia (10:8-12); the city walls of Babel contain a dangerous coalescence of collective power (11:1-9); Sodom and Gomorra are forever linked by the corrosive effects of sexual violence. All bear Cain's legacy.[113] The city itself is neither the pit of human depravity nor the shining light on the hill; it is the highly ambiguous, rather than blandly neutral, emblem of culture, a construct of extremes.[114]

The Yahwist's frame of reference is eminently rural, as Hiebert ably demonstrates. Agriculture reigns supreme as the material setting of the overall narrative, and it is by that very reason that the city is something of a *Fremdkörper* (foreign body) in the Yahwist's landscape. The building of cities lies beyond the realm of Israel's particular history, which is to be traced through another lineage.[115] Suggestive is the striking dearth of references to tilling the soil, the fundamental vocation of primal man, within the taxonomy of culture that follows Cain's settlement in the land of "Wandering" (4:1-22).[116] Six new generations proceed uninterrupted, with the last, Lamech's progeny, reaching the apex of social diversification in the antediluvian era: Jabal, a sort of vocational hybrid of Cain, the wanderer, and Abel, the pastoralist, is a seminomad "living in tents and possessing livestock"; Jubal is a patron of the musical arts; and Tubal-cain is a blacksmith (vv. 20-22).[117] The arts, technology, and seminomadic pastoralism become the defining branches of an increasingly diversified cultural milieu, all coming from the last and struggling farmer of the primeval age, Lamech.

The legacy of Cain lives on in the character of Lamech; he is Cain redivivus and multiplied. Lamech confesses to his two wives of manslaughter and augments Cain's protective mark elevenfold (vv. 23-24). What the Romantic Hebraist J. G. Herder called the "song of the sword," Lamech's taunt is intended to intimidate as much as Cain's mark was designed to deter. Lamech's weapon, however, is not his sword; it is his threat of disproportionate retribution against anyone who seeks to exact vengeance over his killing of a young man *(yeled, 'îš)*. As Westermann aptly notes, the Yahwist's placement

---

113. See G. Wallis, "Die Stadt in den Überlieferungen der Genesis," *ZAW* 78 (1966) 133-48.

114. Cf. M. Fishbane's perceptive but overstated assessment of Cain's city in *Text and Texture: Close Readings of Selected Biblical Texts* (New York: Schocken, 1979) 27.

115. Westermann, *Genesis 1–11*, 327.

116. Not until 5:29 is there any reference to farming, which is cast as a cursed profession.

117. See Hiebert's rendering of the description of Tubal-cain's profession (*Yahwist's Landscape*, 44).

of this "braggart song" at the conclusion of the Cainite genealogy indicates that as human culture advances, so the possibility of mutual destruction increases.[118]

What is not usually noted, however, is that the Yahwist deliberately places the song within a familial context. More than simply preening in the presence of his two wives, Lamech twice commands the attention of Adah and Zillah: "hear my voice" (šĕmaʿan qôlî), "listen to my word" (haʾzēnnâ ʾimrātî). The first command echoes similar shema phraseology attested earlier in the larger narrative. Whereas the voice of Yahweh strolling in the garden inspired dread in the primal couple through no divine fault (3:10), Lamech's message intends to spread fear. Why Lamech specifically addresses his wives is another matter, however. His fearsome boast is meant to address any and all potential enemies who would entertain the prospect of exacting vengeance against Lamech for the death of the young man. For Lamech to direct his terror-inspiring taunt to his wives is curious and suggests an additional dynamic at work, one that threatens to tear the fabric of his household at its seams.

By placing Lamech's boast within the setting of the family, the Yahwist draws suspicion on the kind of relationship Lamech has with his two wives. Is Lamech intimidating his wives into submission so as to preclude any attempt of implementing blood vengeance against him by their hands? That Lamech identifies his victim specifically as a "youth" (yeled, derived from the verb "to bear" [4:1, 17]), hints ever so subtly at the possibility of child slaughter. If so, the Yahwist has moved the level of violence from fratricide to near infanticide of Oedipal proportions.[119] If not, the stress on the victim's youth is striking, indicating a harrowing, lopsided exchange of violence between an adult and a youth.[120] Moreover, the familial setting only heightens the suspicion of corrosive conflict from within the family and between generations. Finally, in contrast to the establishment of Cain's protective mark (4:15), the fact that

---

118. Westermann, Genesis 1–11, 337.

119. Indeed, a rabbinic midrash on this passage, cited by Rashi, contends that Lamech's song refers to his killing of both Tubal-cain and Cain (Tanḥuma 12b). Furthermore, the midrash has the generations between Cain and Lamech swallowed up by the earth and Lamech's wives refusing to bear him any more children. See D. Steinmetz, "Vineyard, Farm, and Garden: The Drunkenness of Noah in the Context of Primeval History," JBL 113 (1994) 203n.24.

120. See P. D. Miller's analysis of the "parallelism of degree" in "Yeled in the Song of Lamech," JBL 85 (1966) 477-78. As Miller indicates, the killing of a child would warrant greater revenge than the killing of an adult. The audacity of Lamech's boast is in his turning the multiplication tables around on his behalf.

Lamech himself is the one who proclaims retributive protection without reference to divine backing indicates a conspicuous godforsakenness in his discourse. In any case, multiplied vengeance closes the Cainite genealogy. For the Yahwist the Cainite line marks the nadir of human existence, if not a complete dead end.[121]

The narrative returns abruptly to the primal generation to recount the birth of one more son, one who replaces Abel (v. 25). The "vacancy" embodied and left by Abel is now filled with new life. Like her proclamation over Cain in 4:1, Eve attests to Yahweh's hand in successful childbearing. Seth is the product of divine "establishment" (*št*). He too bears a son and, as the first man to name a child, calls him Enosh ("man"). From the naming of a son, the narrative moves to the calling on Yahweh's name, and a new stage in human history is inaugurated, one in which worship of *Yahweh* is established long before Israel comes on the scene (cf. Exod 3:14-16; 6:2-3).

Noah: Moral Man in Immoral Society

Noah found a vine which was expelled from and left the Garden
of Eden and its clusters with it; he took from its fruit and he ate,
and he desired them in his heart, and he planted from it a vineyard on the earth.[122]

Pirqe Rabbi Eliezer 23

From the Sethite line rather than from the Cainite lineage within the Yahwist's narrative comes forth Noah, the only one of his generation to find favor "before Yahweh" (6:8; 7:1). But before warranting such approbation, Noah is given his name with the accompanying pronouncement by his father in 5:29: "This one will bring us relief (*yĕnaḥămēnû*) from our work and from

---

121. Much depends on how the Yahwist's narrative, in its original form, connected Noah genealogically to the previous generations. The extant and mostly Priestly genealogy of Gen 5:1-32, the "*Toledot* of Adam," identifies Noah as a son of Lamech through the insertion of the Yahwistic genealogical note after 5:28. In the Yahwist's narrative, however, it is likely that Noah was originally connected to the Sethite line begun in 4:25-26 (contra Westermann, *Genesis 1–11*, 359-60; cf. H. N. Wallace, "The Toledot of Adam," in *Studies in the Pentateuch* [ed. J. A. Emerton; VTSup 41; Leiden: Brill, 1990] 24-29). In their final form, chs. 4–5 distinguish between a Cainite Lamech, who increases human violence, and a Sethite Lamech, who foretells the mitigation of the land's curse. Noah falls squarely into the latter lineage.

122. From Steinmetz's translation in "Vineyard, Farm," 193.

the painful labor *(mē'iṣṣĕbôn)* of our hands, from the ground *(min-hā'ădāmâ)* that Yahweh has cursed." Once again, the cursed ground emerges at a critical juncture in the plot. Noah's father utters a hope-filled pronouncement that his son will provide relief from the painful labor with which human existence has been cursed vis-à-vis the soil. Poetically, *'ădāmâ* or "ground" is set in parallel with "work" *(ma'ăśâ)* and "painful labor" *('iṣṣĕbôn;* cf. 3:16a, 17b), all governed by the same preposition. Noah is destined to alleviate the pain of labor and, consequently, to mitigate the primal curse leveled against the first man of the ground (v. 17). Noah's appearance will usher in a new age of comfort or respite; his presence is alleviative. It is no coincidence, then, that Noah himself is described as a "man of the ground" *('îš hā'ădāmâ,* 9:20; cf. 2:7). His identity is rooted in his vocation as a viticulturist in the postdiluvian age, but already some comparison with his primal ancestor is evident in this birth announcement. Noah is the new Adam who will usher in a new age of existence. For Lamech's generation, however, the respite Noah provides is the flood, perhaps the "greatest irony" of the narrative.[123]

Like his Mesopotamian counterparts Utnapishtim and Atrahasis, Noah is renowned for his righteousness (cf. 6:8; 7:1; cf. also 6:9 [P]; Ezek 14:14, 20). As the single recipient of divine favor, the figure of Noah is set in stark relief against the rampant turpitude that afflicts the human race (Gen 6:5-6). The Yahwist's *Leitwort* that characterizes this hopeless generation is "evil" *(ra'* or *rā'â,* v. 5), a moral depravity that cuts to the very marrow of rational thought and "imagination" *(yēṣer).* The Yahwist's "evil" connotes a psychosocial depth that is matched by the pathos of the garden tragedy and that of Cain's condition (4:6). The impulse to grasp and dominate has come to rule every facet of human thought and conduct, a holistic wickedness, seemingly irredeemable and irreversible. The beast within has overcome the human self. Yahweh's reaction to this reprobate race resonates with language reminiscent of Noah's character, the human race, and the soil: "Yahweh was sorry *(wayyinnāḥem)* that he had made humankind on the earth and it painfully grieved him *(yit'aṣṣēb)* to his heart" (6:6). The depravity of human hearts has painfully pierced Yahweh's heart as much as the curse has provoked the pain of labor on human beings (3:16, 17; 5:29). Ironically, Yahweh shares the pain of humans. But whereas such agony prompts the longing for comfort in humans, it leads to their destruction for Yahweh.[124] Furthermore, Yahweh's reaction is a sorrow that can be assuaged only by Noah, who bears the promise of comfort *(yĕnaḥămēnû,* 5:29). Given the similar terminology, sorrow and relief bind Yahweh and Noah together. The re-

123. Wallace, "Toledot of Adam," 29.
124. Ibid., 28.

175

calcitrant soil that engenders grief for human beings is metaphorically reminiscent of a recalcitrant humanity that engenders unrelievable sorrow in Yahweh's heart. The curse of the ground has come full circle.

Yahweh's resolve to destroy life also resonates with an earlier episode. Yahweh intends to wipe out *(mḥh)* all life "from the face of the ground" (*mē'al pĕnê hā'ădāmâ*, 6:7; 7:4). This phraseology has so far been used only in Cain's objection that Yahweh has effectively driven him off the face of the earth (4:14). Yahweh's resolve is the banishment of banishments. From Adam to Cain, humanity has suffered a series of cosmic setbacks that have forced humans into progressively less habitable areas, from the garden to the wasteland. Now Yahweh is ready to push humanity once and for all into the sea.

Unlike the Priestly account of the flood, the Yahwist's story does not limn a massive effulgence of water from above and below, bringing about a virtual reversal of creation (cf. 7:11 [P]). Rather, a prolonged cloudburst saturates the "dry land" (*ḥārābâ*, v. 22) for forty days and nights, causing the water level to rise and bear the ark above the earth (v. 17b). This is the first mention of rain since the passing reference to the ground's lack in 2:5 prior to humankind's creation. The only mention of water heretofore has been that of the subterranean waters saturating the *'ădāmâ* (2:6). Humanity's banishment from the well-irrigated garden has forced reliance on the capriciousness of rainfall. In a harrowing turn of poetic justice, Yahweh causes it to rain on the dry land to the point of destroying everything "in whose nostrils is the breath of life" (7:17b). The intent is to wipe out all life from the surface of the earth as a way of cleansing, even replenishing, the earth.[125]

For the Yahwist, the cradle of life is found between two extremes, the deluge and the dryness. The balance between the two establishes the conditions for human flourishing. When Noah sees that "the face of the ground" is drying (7:13b), he knows life is ready to begin anew and offers sacrifices of thanksgiving. The world began with one extreme and with the exception of the populated ark, all "breathing" life ceases in the opposite extreme. Nevertheless, the curse of the flood is not without its salutary consequences, for by it the land is refreshed and replenished for full productive potential. Through humankind's destruction and the land's replenishment, justice is served. From the perspective of the dry *'ădāmâ* (cf. v. 22), the flood is too much of a good thing! With the ground more than satisfied, human culture is wiped clean for a second chance. Marking a new beginning in history, the Yahwist's flood is the watershed of humanity's continuing genesis, nothing less than a

---

125. See the verb *mḥh* in 2 Kgs 2:13; Prov 30:20; Isa 25:8.

moral evolution. Noah is the new "man of the soil," of the ground refreshed and poised to yield its strength to the tiller.

Man of the Soil

Noah stands alone in a culture of wickedness. The Yahwist unequivocally identifies Noah as righteous (*ṣaddîq*) in a generation that is rotten to the core (7:1). As for the contours of Noah's righteousness, the Yahwist is terse: "Noah did all that Yahweh had commanded him" (7:5). This is no empty formulaic statement, for it captures the very heart of the garden's ethos: the couple was given a command but failed to carry it out (2:16-17). By contrast, Noah is the consummate command fulfiller.

The dark and turbid thoughts that characterize Noah's generation are outwardly reflected in the exponential rise of violence embodied by Cain and his descendant Lamech. This escalation progresses through a cycle of temptation (e.g., the tree of the knowledge of good and evil, "crouching" sin), disobedience (grasping the fruit, fratricide), and curse. Consequently, the garden and its ethos become increasingly remote in the Yahwist's social landscape. With Noah, however, the cycle is broken and the garden is retrieved, at least in vestigial form. As Yahweh "saw" the heart of the matter, that "the evil of humankind was great" (6:5), so Yahweh "sees" Noah's righteousness (7:1). Although one person's righteousness cannot save an entire generation, any more than nine righteous individuals can prevent Sodom's destruction.[126] Noah's righteousness is efficacious for a *new* generation. Noah's pleasing offering prompts Yahweh to pronounce a promise (8:21): "I will never again curse (*lĕqallēl*) the ground on account of humankind, even though[127] the imagination (*yēṣer*) of the human heart is evil from youth, nor will I ever again destroy every living creature, as I have done."

Serving as the conclusion to the flood story, Yahweh's pledge recalls the language of 3:17 and 6:5-8.[128] Yahweh promises never to "curse" (*qll*) the ground again. Although the verb for "curse" is different from the one used previously in the narrative (*'rr*, 3:14, 17; 4:11), the sense is essentially the

---

126. For whatever reason, Abraham does not barter with Yahweh to less than "ten righteous men" (Gen 18:32).

127. The *kî* clause of v. 21 is more likely concessive than causal.

128. See the survey of recent opinions in Westermann, *Genesis 1–11*, 455-57.

129. See the paired juxtapositions of both verbs in Gen 12:3 and Exod 22:27.

130. BDB, 886. The root *qll* in the Qal can denote dishonor (1 Sam 2:30; see Olyan, "Honor, Shame," 205n.11).

same, except with an added nuance:[129] Yahweh acknowledges that the land has been violated, literally "made contemptible,"[130] through the primordial curse and, paradoxically, through the flood. Yahweh's pledge relieves the soil of its curse without entirely overturning the curse, which is mitigated but not abrogated.[131] The garden thus is neither regained nor entirely forfeited. Although the land is relieved, it does not return to its primordial well-watered state to bear another pristine garden. Thorns and thistles remain. Yahweh's self-pledge is focused on the potential of the primordial curse to set in motion the land's inevitable destruction, the complete cessation of producing anything (cf. 4:12). Indeed, the poem that follows highlights *in nuce* the agricultural seasons as perduring marks of the land's endurance and thus its fertility (8:22).[132] The land will continue to produce thorns and thistles, but its edible produce will never cease.

Also striking is that Yahweh's vow does not stem from a new anthropology; the old one, fraught with violence and dark imaginings, is acknowledged as intractable and irredeemable (v. 21). With the simple stroke of divine fiat, the Yahwist irreversibly turns what was previously depicted as intolerable into something inevitable and ultimately acceptable.[133] The change occurs in Yahweh's heart, not in the human heart. Yahweh does not create a new man. Noah is, rather, the best the human race can offer, and he is good enough. Yet something has changed in the natural order, requiring nothing less than the holocaust of the flood to bring it about. Yahweh's pledge is not the lament of resignation. Through the curse of the flood, the soil is paradoxically regenerated and the consequences are not lacking in the social realm. As a "man of the soil" (9:20), Noah reconstitutes the primordial connection between man and ground.[134] His offerings prompt a divine guarantee: Yahweh ensures the inviolable status of both the soil and humanity. Together, soil and humanity bear a new integrity as a consequence of the flood, one that the Priestly author finds as the basis for the first covenant (9:8-17). As the new Adam, Noah plants a vineyard.

131. Given the poetic parallelism, Wallace wants to reduce the "curse" attested in 8:21 to the flood, which as he admits would be unique in the Yahwist's narrative ("Toledot of Adam," 26.).

132. See Hiebert, *Yahwist's Landscape*, 45-48.

133. A. F. Campbell and M. A. O'Brien, *Sources of the Pentateuch* (Minneapolis: Fortress, 1993) 97n.17.

134. By contrast, Steinmetz contends that the relationship between the soil and man is altogether severed in the figure of Noah ("Vineyard, Farm," 196). The divine pledge makes clear, however, that both soil and humankind share in common the guarantee of divine protection.

Eden's Access Denied

Before Noah leaves behind the legacy of Yahweh's promise to uphold the productivity of the land and the flourishing of human life, the Yahwist recounts the puzzling incident of Noah's drunkenness and curse (9:20-27). Like previous generations, the human family from which the earth is peopled (9:18-19) is entangled in a moral crisis. Many interpreters, beginning with Hermann Gunkel, treat the story as an originally independent legend that largely serves as an etiology of Canaan's subservient status in the land (9:25-27; cf. 10:6).[135] There is, however, another crucial level of interpretation evident from the larger sweep of the Yahwist's historiographic work.

This strange postdiluvian tale finds its point of departure echoing certain themes from the garden story. As Adam was the first human agriculturist, so Noah is the first viticulturist, literally the "first [to be] a man of the soil" (9:20).[136] It takes only a quick narrative leap to find Noah, having partaken of the fruit of his labors, lying naked in a drunken stupor in his tent. Whereas the fruit of the tree of good and evil engendered a "higher" level of awareness in the primal couple, Noah's cultivated yield induces only unconsciousness. The grape is in effect the inversion of the "apple."[137] Both, however, yield self-degrading results. The man and woman desperately sew fig leaves for cover and hide in fear of Yahweh's presence. There in his tent lies Noah naked, unashamed and unaware, indeed, unconscious. The theme of nakedness, as in the garden story, is of crucial significance. Ham, Noah's son and father of Canaan, "sees" his father's nakedness (v. 22), and the tale lurches forward to its conclusion in Noah's curse against his son's progeny.

Many contend that the verb "to see" in this context connotes homo-incestuous rape.[138] Such a claim, however, only detracts from the explicit dynamics of the narrative evident in light of the garden story. The verb recalls

135. H. Gunkel, *Genesis,* (8th ed.; HAT 1; Göttingen: Vandenhoeck & Ruprecht, 1969) 78-83; See Westermann's discussion in *Genesis 1–11,* 490-91.

136. Heb. *wayyāḥel nōaḥ 'îš hā'ădāmâ.* Cf. Gen 10:8; see Spina on the grammatical structure of v. 20, particularly the function of *ḥll* (Hiphil), in "The 'Ground' for Cain's Rejection," 329.

137. Although the fruit from the forbidden tree is never identified, popular culture has envisaged an apple.

138. For example, Steinmetz, "Vineyard, Farm," 199; A. Phillips, "Uncovering the Father's Skirt," *VT* 30 (1980) 38-43; Niditch, *Chaos to Cosmos,* 52-53 (with some nuance); cf. others cited by Westermann, *Genesis 1–11,* 488. Those who argue for such a claim cite the interchangeability of the verbs "see" and "uncover" found in Leviticus 18 and 20 (e.g., 20:17). The Holiness Code, however, does not necessarily fall within the semantic field of the Yahwist's narrative.

the garden scene in which the man and woman partake of the forbidden tree and their eyes are consequently opened to realize their nakedness (3:7). As a result, shame invades the innocent privacy of the garden. The couple can no longer endure their nakedness, much less allow Yahweh to see their exposed state. Likewise, Ham violates Noah's privacy by apprehending his father's nakedness and, rather than covering him up, goes public by telling his brothers. Therein lies the unforgivable sin: Ham exposes Noah's nakedness for all his familial world to behold. Fortunately, Ham's brothers act appropriately, never laying their eyes on their father but properly covering him up with all due respect to their progenitor.

Contrary to popular opinion, the story revolves not around the evils of alcohol, but around the response of Noah's sons, in the same way the story of Cain and Abel focuses on Cain's reaction to his rejected offering rather than on any particular reason behind the rejection. Noah is not morally implicated in his unconscious state, lying uncovered under the cover of privacy, in the same way that Cain is not cursed for having offered an unfavorable sacrifice (4:5).[139] Ham is the one who bears the curse, having failed in his honorable duty as a son. He has exposed his father's nakedness before the public arena of shame. Privacy is its own cover, however. In Noah's impenetrable stupor, nakedness itself bears no shame until it is beheld and consciousness is regained.

Once Noah discovers ("knows") Ham's sin, he curses Canaan, Ham's son, while blessing Ham's two brothers (9:25-26). The curse introduces a hierarchy heretofore foreign to primal families: Shem and Japheth are blessed with lebensraum, while Canaan must serve his brothers (vv. 25-27). Eviction from the arable land is no longer an option, as it was for Cain. The next most severe penalty is servitude to one's kindred. Looking forward, Noah's curse is a veritable prophecy of Israel's dominant status in the land of Canaan. Looking backward, Noah has taken over the divine role of curse pronouncer (cf. 3:16-19). As Yahweh planted the first garden and uttered curses against its inhabitants, so Noah plants his vineyard and utters both curse and blessing. As Devora Steinmetz points out, Yahweh recedes in the background while Noah acts as an autonomous moral agent.[140]

Yet another level of comparison is warranted — namely, between the respective settings of the primal couple's disobedience and Noah's drunkenness. Indeed, the garden lies in the background of Noah's action as much as

139. Contra Steinmetz, who refers to Noah's "loss of knowledge" as his "sin" ("Vineyard, Farm," 207).
140. Ibid., 200.

180

the cursed ground lies behind Cain's failure to secure Yahweh's favor in his offering (4:4-5). The Yahwist describes Noah's planting (9:20) in similar fashion to Yahweh's cultivation of the garden (2:8). Noah's planting is a "reenactment" of divine cultivation.[141] Consequently, some level of correspondence is established at the very outset. The result is a vineyard vignette, a garden story set between culture and curse. Although Noah's agricultural world lies on this side of the flood, without the primordial garden as a backdrop this earthy tale would lose its profundity.

Compared to the garden story, Noah's inebriation and nakedness mark an abortive effort to return to the garden's womb, an attempt that does not implicate Noah per se, but whose results are considered nonetheless pathetic. Indeed, inebriation in the Yahwistic narrative can serve the legitimate function of casting off cultural inhibition for a greater good, as illustrated in the story of Lot's daughters, who get their father drunk in order to have intercourse and thereby "preserve offspring" (19:34). Drunkenness can also set the stage for lovemaking (Cant 5:1). Again, of what moral condemnation there is, Ham, not Noah, shoulders the blame.

Yet Noah's drunkenness under the cover of darkness is at best a sorry means for recapturing an agricultural paradise. Escapism is not the way, and Noah's vineyard is not the garden. Noah's vineyard is at best only a truncated garden, as much as Noah's family is only an incomplete household, ostensibly lacking a female companion or "helper." The wife's absence in this vignette is suggestive. Although Noah is a "man of the soil," an *'îš* inextricably related to the ground, he is also an *'îš* without an *'iššâ* in this tale. If there is any hope of returning to the garden's bliss, however fleetingly, it cannot be done alone, much less through loss of consciousness. Noah's stupor indeed recalls the "deep sleep" (*tardēmâ*, Gen 2:21) that overcame the primal man prior to the woman's creation, but it is rather a foil for a failed attempt to recapture primordial bliss, an attempt that leads to self-degradation. Adam's sleep set the occasion for the creation of intimate community; Noah's stupor marks a regression toward numbing isolationism. As noted in Gen 2:24, the Yahwist signals a way of regaining access to the garden of delight, to this realm of shameless intimacy, through the bond of marital love that cultivates mutual worth. Whether from violence or invasive sight, the garden is ever on the verge of desiccation in the harsh cultural landscape. Yet it can perennially be replenished from the well of moral imagination in acts of responsible and mutually edifying union. Noah's vineyard is at once an instructive and failed attempt in this new era of human history.

141. See Hiebert, *Yahwist's Landscape,* 50.

Culture Revisited and Relativized

The so-called Table of Nations in Gen 10:1-32, whose Yahwistic layer comprises vv. 8-30, recounts the rise of nations and peoples to explain existing cultural relations that populate the Yahwist's contemporary world. In comparison to the Yahwist's earlier narrative, noteworthy is the emergence of cities by the mighty warrior and hunter, the grandson of Ham, Nimrod, who founds the great cities of Babylonia and Assyria (vv. 10-11). Like Cain, the cursed city builder, Nimrod is a man of violence, a warrior no less (*gibbōr*, v. 8). Yet the power that Nimrod wields is channeled in a culturally constructive form. An expert in the hunt, Nimrod bears a distinctly royal stature. As reflected in ancient Near Eastern iconography and royal annals, hunting wild game was considered the preeminent task of the king, a test of royal prowess in battle.[142] In Nimrod's case, as often presupposed in ancient Near Eastern royal accounts, subduing the wild was a culture-making act, one that secured space for human habitation. The mighty urban centers of Mesopotamia attest to Nimrod's formidable reputation.

As indicated by Peleg's name ("Division," 10:25), the earth remains divided by the proliferation of cities, lands, and peoples, all descendants of the divided family of Noah. The scattering of people is also described in another way, as the Yahwist indicates in this final installment of the "primeval history," the etiology of Babylon (11:1-9). This urban tale is unique within the Yahwist's purview, since it departs from the narrative's heretofore primary focus on the family. Consequently, one wonders whether this story is more an insertion than an invention of the Yahwist.[143] But this story bears significant linkage to the primeval garden story. Whereas Noah's vineyard proves to be an inadequate analogue to the primeval garden, the story of the tower of Babel in 11:1-9 is the garden's outright antithesis.

The spreading populace depicted in 10:6-32 is reversed, albeit temporarily, in the voluntary concentration of peoples recounted in the following chapter. The overall effect is abrasive; while the genealogies systematically recount the progress from families to peoples and nations gradually extending to the far corners of the known world, the following chapter suddenly has them all regrouping in one locale. Something highly amiss is at work. The peoples gather and settle in Shinar, the formidable land of Mesopotamian culture (cf. 10:10-12) and take it upon themselves to build the archetypal ziggurat-city (11:4).

---

142. For evidence and literature, see Chapter 6.

143. Further evidence is the literary tension with Nimrod's founding of Babel in 10:10.

The intent, however, is not to honor the patron God, the ostensible aim of any ziggurat worth its mortar, but to honor the builders by "establishing a name" for themselves (v. 4).[144] Naming has assumed crucial significance from the garden onward: the man freely names the animals (2:19) and the woman (2:23; 3:20); Eve names Cain and Seth (4:1, 25) as testimonies of Yahweh's involvement; and Lamech names Noah with hopeful promise (5:30). In each case, divine activity figures either in the activity behind the naming or in the name's actual significance. In this tale of hubris, however, the activity of naming is for the first time construed not as bestowal but as a self-reflective act, to make "a name for ourselves." Possessing a great name is frequently associated with royalty and divinity.[145] As a monumental memorial to its founders, this metropolis pushes human culture to its heroic excess: a collective self-esteem so exalted and top-heavy with pride that it crumbles under its own weight. As a foil to the simple, irenic "garden club," planted by Yahweh and tended by the man, is the heroic attempt at building an "egopolis."

It all starts innocently enough, like viewing the tantalizing tree of the garden from a distance. An initial invitation is extended to develop building materials (11:3), which would be expected of any urban project. Once the materials are set, however, a second invitation is issued to construct a towering city, and only then is abject self-ambition articulated (v. 4). The unity of human discourse ("Come, let us . . . ," vv. 3, 4) reflects undivided initiative and contrasts sharply with the discourse of commandment in the garden ("you may . . . , you shall not . . . ," 2:16-17). Yet like the expulsion of the man from the garden (3:22-23), the towering heights of the escalating city bring down a divine preemptive strike. Echoing 3:22, Yahweh expresses concern that nothing can be withheld *(bṣr)* from humanity's collective reach (11:6b). The issue of power and apotheosis once again come to the fore, as they had with the tree of life in the garden. There it was the individual man who momentarily had within his grasp the fruit of life; on the plain of Shinar, a collective populace has within its reach the porthole to heaven. In both cases the reach of human grasp is at stake. Similarly, expulsion from all possibility thereof is the result. In short, the tale of Babel recounts humanity's attempt to cultivate with brick and mortar the towering tree of life.

The confusion of language sets the stage for this forced diaspora, "so that they will not understand *(šmʿ,* 'hear') one another's speech" (v. 7). Throughout the primeval story, "hearing" is more than simply auditory re-

---

144. For other examples of "making a name," see Isa 6:12; Jer 32:20; Neh 9:10; cf. Gen 12:3, in which God promises a great name for Abraham.

145. For example, 2 Sam 7:9, 23; 8:13; 1 Kgs 1:47.

ception; it conveys commitment and obedience. Understanding each other's language is not itself the problem. The unity of language is simply the occasion for the emergence of a collective coalescence of power that can breach the heavenly realm, as it were. The Yahwist recounts the misguided attempt at cementing social cohesion through the marshaling of social capital of monumental proportions. But the end result is a linguistic diversity by default. For the Yahwist, multiculturalism is a divine check on collective pride as much as the divinely ordained age limit in the antediluvian period was intended to arrest the growth of heroic power (6:1-4). The name finally given in this abortive affair bestows an ironically unwelcome renown, one that attests to abject failure and social dissolution, for the erstwhile dwellers of "Babel." So ends the Yahwist's primeval epic or, more accurately, anti-epic.[146]

The Garden and the City

The garden and the city in the Yahwist's primeval history represent two poles of social existence. The simple harmony and unabashed innocence of the garden setting by and large transcend, or more accurately "prescend," the cultural norms of power and honor. The preeminent city pushes the dynamics of power and pride to their logical conclusion, self-ruin. Much of the Yahwist's epic is spent in establishing the "egopolis" and the garden as unattainable extremes: both are ostensibly barred from human access by either linguistic confusion or cherubim and flaming sword. But they do not remain out of sight, out of mind from the Yahwist's purview, for together they expose the prideful and frequently violent excesses of human culture, as well as highlight the glimmers of hope for harmony and moral integrity, all set in unmistakable relief vis-à-vis the garden and the city.

The Yahwist's view of culture cuts to the heart of the narrative's thrust, as Robert Di Vito and others have demonstrated. Drawing from Westermann and David Damrosch, Di Vito argues that the Yahwist's epic represents a "desacralization" of culture: "J's stories depicting the progress of civilization make no mention at all of a divine origin of the arts of cattle breeding, horticulture, or metallurgy," as one finds in various Mesopotamian myths.[147] God

---

146. See R. A. Di Vito, "The Demarcation of Divine and Human Realms in Genesis 2–11," in *Creation in the Biblical Traditions* (ed. R. J. Clifford and J. J. Collins; CBQMS 24; Washington, D.C.; Catholic Biblical Association of America, 1992) 53-56; D. Damrosch, *The Narrative Covenant: Transformations of Genre in the Growth of Biblical Literature* (San Francisco: Harper & Row, 1987) 134.

147. Di Vito, "Demarcation," 51.

in no way depends on human labor and has no "need" of humanity, Di Vito repeatedly points out.[148] All in all, the Yahwist's epic is an "unabashedly negative assessment of human civilization and cultural progress."[149]

Di Vito is only half right, however. First, horticulture within the Yahwist's narrative world does bear divine precedent (2:8, 15; 3:23). On a more basic, methodological level, Di Vito's observations end up black-boxing culture, encasing it with brick and mortar. The Yahwist's point is that the ideal of human culture is not to be contained within casemate walls or identified with the heroic heights of honor and self-empowerment. The Yahwist is not a cultural curmudgeon, although he is a cynic with regard to the power and the pride that allegedly drive human civilization upward and onward. Culture per se is not vilified; rather, it requires direction. The Yahwist provides a riveting vision of normative relations cultivated in the garden and sustained throughout the primeval narrative as both a foil and a source. Granted, the Yahwist's assessment of urban culture is predominantly negative; city life is profiled as a sort of anti-garden.[150] Nevertheless, a nuanced critique rather than a categorical rejection of culture is proffered. The towering city of Babel, as presented, is a larger-than-life city, an archetype that no earthly city can ever achieve, for it lies in ruins.

Instead of the city, the Yahwist prefers the family to bear the promise of genuine community, whether it is the primeval one, nurtured and sustained by the mythic garden, or the patriarchal one, challenged and torn on the rocky ground. Yet given the prevailing "focus on the family," the Yahwist concedes that a full return to the garden of delight is well-nigh impossible, for cultural consciousness and power are intractable factors of human existence, and drunkenness is a sorry attempt at reentry. The human inclination for self-determined discernment and the reality of the curse together mark a point of no regression. By outwardly barring Eden's entrance, the Yahwist maintains an ideal of culture without succumbing to naive idealism. By quashing the human "egopolis," the Yahwist retains a realism about culture without being fatalistic.

Though barred from human encroachment, the garden still informs. In as much as its ethos is defined by the integrity of agricultural and familial relations, the garden generates moral alternatives for human existence within the tragic tug and pull of social conflict. On the one hand, Cain's murder of

---

148. Ibid., 51, 53.

149. Ibid., 54.

150. Cf. Reinhold Niebuhr's reference to Augustine's condemnation of the city "as a compact of injustice" (*Moral Man and Immoral Society*, 70).

Abel appears inevitable within the prevailing realities of curse and power, but Yahweh confronts Cain in the heat of the moment with an alternative solution aimed at preserving the integrity of kinship ties. On the other hand, Noah is an exceptional example of righteousness in a culture rife with wickedness; consequently, his vineyard flourishes on the replenished soil. Yet even he cannot re-create Eden. As paradoxes abound in the tangled web of relations set in high relief by the garden, so also is God's role surprisingly complex.

Yahweh's clothing of the couple is the primal act of culture crafting. Cain, the murderer damned from the land of sustenance, is protected in a land of anarchy. Such paradoxes of failure and grace are grounded in free choices. The garden reminds the reader outside and the characters within that their choices need not go the way of destruction and curse. The confrontational address "What have you done?" evinces genuine dismay on the part of God (3:13; 4:10). The pain of childbirth and the soil's thorns and thistles remain, but so does the freedom of choice granted the first man in naming the animals and partaking of the garden's fruit, the freedom to order the world either equitably or unjustly. The curse does not rigidly restrict the range of moral possibilities, but it does require, as in Cain's case, greater effort to ensure a right course of action. Indeed, the curse finds its own limitation in the figure of Noah as much as Noah discovers an incompleteness in his righteousness. As "a general pointer towards future events,"[151] the hope-borne relief pronounced by Lamech over Noah's birth remains operative and keeps the garden's ethos in sight within the realm of moral imagination and conduct.

In the panoramic sweep from garden to city, the Yahwist limns and sustains a twofold ethos of moral existence, a primal paradigm for human existence, even culture:[152] (1) the harmonious interdependence of human relations, modeled after the mutual kinship of gendered life in the garden; and (2) the fruitful symbiosis between humankind and the land, modeled by the first man and, to an extent, by Noah. The Yahwist makes clear that both dimensions carry the weight of divine precedent and depend on obedience. These two dimensions of integrity not only negatively assess but also constructively address the panoply of relations that will come to bear on Israel's ancestral development later in the Yahwist's narrative. Between the extremes of pristine garden and self-glorified city, Israel must find its own moral niche in the Yahwist's rugged landscape.

151. Wallace, "Toledot of Adam," 27.
152. Or "Urmodell des Menschseins" (A. Ganoczy, *Schöpfungslehre* [Leitfaden Theologie 10; Düsseldorf: Patmos, 1987] 17-18).

The Garden and the *Gēr*

Although the author of Israel's first historiographic compendium seems to take delight in posing moral conundrums for the protagonists in Israel's "family history" (Genesis 12–50), the Yahwist is no moralist. Acting both deceitfully and righteously, the patriarchs are far from being paragons of virtue, yet they are not condemned. They are blessed, not cursed, and like Noah, they are wielders of blessing and curse. In addition, their foreign neighbors, from the morally indignant pharaoh (12:18-20) to the blessing-giver Melchizedek (14:18-20), are not without a certain measure of integrity. Other than the men of Sodom, the inhabitants that populate the Yahwist's foreign terrain are scarcely vilified. Israel's ancestral household lives by and large off the land in covenantal coexistence with its neighbors. The Yahwist is thus no nativist.

Their foibles notwithstanding, the patriarchs and matriarchs of Israel bear the hope for a blessed community in a world fraught with conflict and coercion. Despite their trickery and failures, they do not come under the scourge of judgment, for they are, the Yahwist makes repeatedly clear, the bearers of blessing. For these saintly sinners who comprise Israel's ancestral heritage, outright condemnation is suspended in order to sustain the hope that is laid on them of establishing a morally credible community in the land. In accepting these blemished patriarchs and matriarchs, the Yahwist points forward to the final result, Israel's moral *telos* in a land that mirrors human history's *protos* in the garden. Blessing, which drives Israel's history to its consummation, is the means of return to an integrity of land and community, the two inseparable elements of the garden's ethos.

Yahweh's command to Abraham to separate from his kindred and family opens a new chapter and serves literally as the point of departure (12:1b-3).[153] "Go from your country and your kindred and your ancestral house to the land that I will show you, so that[154] I may make of you a great nation, bless you, and make your name great. So be a blessing![155] I will bless those who bless you, though I will curse anyone who demeans you.[156] In you all the families of the earth shall acquire blessing."

153. Abraham's departure from land and kin, however, is anticipated by the Priestly layer in Terah's uprooting of his family from Ur to migrate to Canaan (11:31).

154. The purpose clause is indicated by the series of prefixed cohortatives that make up v. 2, with one notable exception.

155. Not often noted is that the verb *hyh* is imperative in form, which imbues the language of blessing with prescriptive force. This rare construction is also found in Isa 19:24 and Zech 8:13.

156. For the syntax of this peculiar clause see P. D. Miller Jr., "Syntax and Theology in Genesis XII 3a," *VT* 34 (1984) 472-76.

Like Noah, but unlike the primal couple, Abraham obeys. Consequently, the patriarch receives a reputation of *tôrâ* obedience, of unwavering adherence to the commandments, statutes, and law of God (26:5).[157] Abraham is promised land, empire status, and a great name, themes that resonate with the primeval period of the Yahwist's history as well as point forward to universal fulfillment (12:3).[158] Equally so, he is mandated to embody such blessing. What Abraham receives and is charged to embody is a full taxonomy of blessing that links Israel's ancestral heritage with Israel's national history. Abraham's family ushers in a new beginning in the power and promise of blessing, prefigured in the garden and subverted in the primal couple's curse.[159] Sarah, too, figures integrally in the embodiment of blessing. Unlike Noah, whose wife is absent as he fulfills his vocation as a viticulturist, Sarah is ever present in Abraham's sojourns. She is not at home waiting and weaving while Abraham is out voyaging or foraging. The patriarch and matriarch form an inseparable pair in this journey of blessing, one that will eventually bring Israel back to the entrance of the garden. But for the time being, the fullness of blessing highlights the patriarch's lacks yet also explodes with moral force: "Be a blessing!" Blessing constitutes Abraham's marching orders.

Abraham sets himself apart from the urban-minded mass of humanity portrayed in the tower of Babel story by receiving rather than grasping the prospect of name and fame (v. 2; cf. 11:4). As others have noted, Abraham's blessing is royal in nature.[160] The royal blessing of national status is transferred to the head of the ancestral household.[161] Royal ideology is not "democratized," properly speaking,[162] but it is "familialized," that is, lodged within the family rather than in the court. As the progenitor of a "great na-

---

157. Gen 26:5 most likely comes not from the Yahwist but from a later Deuteronomist.

158. For the latter see von Rad, *Genesis,* 154, 159-60.

159. H.-P. Müller, "Segen im Alten Testament: Theologische Implikationen eines halb vergessenen Themas," in idem, *Mythos — Kerygma — Wahrheit: Gesamelte Aufsätze zum Alten Testament in seiner Umwelt und zur Biblischen Theologie* (BZAW 200; Berlin: de Gruyter, 1991) 237, 245 (repr. from *ZTK* 87 [1990] 1-32). Noting that the language of blessing proper is not used in the Yahwist's primeval history, H. W. Wolff identifies Gen 12:1-4a as the key passage for understanding the Yahwist's overall message and narrative arrangement, climaxing with the conclusion of Balaam's third oracle in 24:9, which echoes Gen 12:3 ("The Kerygma of the Yahwist" [tr. W. A. Benware], in W. Brueggemann and H. W. Wolff, *The Vitality of Old Testament Traditions* [2d ed.; Atlanta: John Knox, 1982] 41-66 [repr. from *Int* 20 (1966) 131-58]). As will be demonstrated, however, this central oracle also recalls, not coincidentally, the ethos of Eden, the archetype of blessing.

160. For example, G. Garbini, *History and Ideology in Ancient Israel* (tr. J. Bowden; New York: Crossroad, 1988) 79; Van Seters, *Prologue to History,* 256.

161. N. C. Habel, *The Land Is Mine: Six Biblical Land Ideologies* (OBT; Minneapolis: Fortress, 1995) 120-21.

162. So Van Seters, *Prologue to History,* 256.

tion," Abraham's royal status is not attained, however, at the destruction of "all the families of the earth," but in his blessing them. In Abraham's case, royal domination, if not eschewed, is at least nuanced by blessing, the leitmotif of the Yahwist's history.[163] Noteworthy is that the exogenous peoples are described at the outset as extended "families" (mišpēḥōt) rather than nations (gôyim) or peoples ('ammîm). The family of Abraham, including nephew Lot (13:1), share a familial structure with the peoples of the earth at this particular juncture of history.

Opening the Abrahamic promise is the essential issue of land. "Ground" is specifically mentioned in connection with the "families of the 'ădāmâ" in 12:3 (NRSV "earth"). With the patriarchal history in full swing, "land" ('ereṣ) and "ground" ('ădāmâ) become by and large interchangeable. Both terms can denote arable land because now even the earth can bear Yahweh's blessing through Abraham.[164] It is the destiny of Abraham's family to dwell in a far land that Yahweh has chosen for him to develop into a great nation. Such land, cultivated with Abraham's "seed," is to generate blessing.

Susceptible to famine, however, the land provides no blessing in its current state (v. 10), and Abraham and Sarah are forced off the land "to sojourn" (lāgûr) in Egypt. Abraham is a gēr, not one of the landless poor, scavenging the land, but a man of means in search of new land, in short, an immigrant or "resident alien."[165] Outside his promised land, Abraham becomes embroiled in a moral dilemma: for fear that the Egyptians will kill him to possess her, he encourages his wife, who is "beautiful in appearance" (yĕpat-mar'eh, v. 11), to lie about her marital status by telling the authorities that she is Abraham's sister. Indeed, the ruse is a clever half-truth, for Sarah is in fact Abraham's half sister, having the same father (see 20:12).[166] Like the serpent's use of cunning, the deception lies more in what is omitted than in what is said. Once the ruse is discovered, Pharaoh berates Abraham, adopting a tone similar to that of Yahweh's address to the primal family's failure in the garden: "What is this

163. See Gen 18:18; 22:17-18; 26:1-3, 12-33, 27:27-29; 28:14; 30:27, 30; 39:5; 41:55-57; Exod 12:31-32; Num 24:9.

164. For 'ădāmâ see Gen 19:25; 28:14, 15; 47:18, 19, 26. But see Hiebert's attempt to delineate the difference between 'ereṣ ("land") and 'ădāmâ ("arable soil") in Yahwist's Landscape, 88. Gen 12:3, however, blurs the distinction.

165. Habel, Land Is Mine, 118-19, who draws from F. Spina, "Israelites as gērîm, 'Sojourners,' in Social and Historical Context," in The Word of the Lord Shall Go Forth, 321-35.

166. For the complexities of endogamous patrilineal relationships, see N. Wander, "Structure, Contradiction, and 'Resolution' in Mythology: Father's Brother's Daughter Marriage and the Treatment of Women in Genesis 11–50," JANES 13 (1981) 75-99; M. E. Donaldson, "Kinship Theory in the Patriarchal Narratives: The Case of the Barren Wife," JAAR 49 (1981) 77-87.

you have done to me?" (v. 18; cf. 3:13; 4:10). In the meantime, Abraham has enriched himself, presumably from the gifts he received from the Egyptian court while Sarah was a member of Pharaoh's harem.

The narrative contours of the primeval garden reside deep in the structure of this tale about the "ancestress in danger" (12:10-20). Textual allusions to the primeval story abound.[167] A brief reference outside the story helps to set the stage for such a comparison: Egypt is comparable to the well-watered "garden of Yahweh" (13:10). The couple enters an agricultural paradise. The theme of tempting beauty associates Sarah with the forbidden tree (12:11, 14; cf. 3:6). As a consequence of their physical allure, both the tree's fruit and Sarah are "taken" (3:6; 12:15), resulting in a violation of established boundaries: the marital bond between Abraham and Sarah is breached, as was the primal prohibition regarding the tree's fruit. Abraham and the serpent, moreover, find common ground in their use of cunning: both play the role of the trickster (3:1-5; 12:12-13).[168] In addition, Sarah participates fully in Abraham's ruse as much as the primal man partakes of the fruit handed to him by the woman. Divine action also plays a major role: Yahweh afflicts the household of Pharaoh with "great plagues" (12:17); Yahweh curses the primal man's household (3:16-19). In both cases, expulsion is the final response.

The story of the sojourn in Egypt exhibits, however, an intermixing of roles that precludes any linear, allegorical correspondence to the garden myth. Pharaoh takes on the divine role of expelling the family. Moreover, the well-deserved reprimand comes from the human agent, Pharaoh, not Yahweh, whose plagues are instrumental in uncovering the ruse. Here is a case of a plague with a double edge: it convicts Pharaoh in his violation of the marital bond as well as Abraham in his role as deceiver. Abraham must face Pharaoh's indignation with his tail between his legs. In detecting the ruse, Pharaoh comes to knowledge (cf. 3:7). As a result of his deceit, Abraham heightens his material status, despoiling Pharaoh's hospitality (12:16).

Who is to blame in this seemingly simple tale of deceit? Scratch the sur-

---

167. To my knowledge, no one has argued extensively for explicit linkage between this tale and the garden story. To the contrary, Cassuto views the former as a prolepsis of Israel's sojourn and exodus in Egypt (*A Commentary on the Book of Genesis, Part II: From Noah to Abraham* [tr. I. Abrahams; Jerusalem: Magnes, 1964, repr. 1992] 334-37) an interpretation that does not exclude mine, for there is nothing to prevent this vignette from serving double duty within the larger scope of the Yahwist's narrative, whose larger structure is shaped by the garden story (see below).

168. For an extended explication of the role of the trickster in Israel's ancestral history, see S. Niditch, *Underdogs and Tricksters: A Prelude to Biblical Folklore* (San Francisco: Harper & Row, 1987) 23-69.

face and the answer is as enigmatic as the tale itself: no one and everyone. Unlike the serpent's trickery, Abraham's collusion is motivated by genuine fear. Is Abraham's fear for his life justified? Indeed, it is. The only other case of royal adultery recorded in biblical tradition is one that resulted in the husband's murder (2 Sam 11:1-25). Outside his future homeland, Abraham must live by his wits in order to survive. He is wise as a serpent, and he is by no means a dove. His ruse is morally dubious, provoking a pharaonic ire of divine proportions (Gen 12:18; cf. 4:10). Yet Abraham's deceit is at least understandable through his fear in a rugged land of aggression and danger. His lie is a necessary evil aimed at sparing his life and thereby preserving the promise of progeny. In allowing for some justification in Abraham's behavior, the Yahwist nonetheless refrains from letting the patriarch off the hook. With a terseness designed to pique the reader's imagination, the Yahwist portrays Sarah's induction into Pharaoh's harem as an unconscionable arrangement. With Sarah imprisoned in Pharaoh's palace, Abraham's ruse would have backfired, not in his own death, but in losing Sarah as wife and "helper" in the blessing of progeny and great-nation status. Nowhere in the narrative is mention made of Abraham's concern over that prospect. Instead, the Yahwist simply recounts Abraham's material enrichment as a consequence of Sarah's abduction. By preserving his life, Abraham places Sarah at risk and thereby puts all hope for blessing in jeopardy. Only divine intervention can rectify matters and force the narrative back to the prospects of blessing. More than simply a deus ex machina, Yahweh's role in this tale of entanglement is both subtle and decisive, salvaging the blessing yet also provoking the conundrum at the outset, perhaps to see what the patriarch would do (cf. 2:19).

With Pharaoh as adulterer, Abraham as deceiver, and Sarah as accomplice, moral ambivalence is for all to share. Yet no one is vilified or condemned outright, unless it is Abraham before Pharaoh's outrage. Yet Abraham is not cursed; he is simply expelled from a land to which he does not belong. The critique of Abraham is a subtle one. Abraham is not glorified in his role as trickster. One-upmanship, much less moral triumph, is not within the scope of this tale. Escaping by the skin of their teeth, Abraham and Sarah are driven back to where they belong so that the prospect of blessing can take root in the land in which they were meant to reside. Abraham is not so much the cunning hero, eponymous or otherwise,[169] as the entangled patriarch, whose actions are thoroughly ambiguous, morally and otherwise.

In short, the dynamics of the garden tale are played out in subtle and complex ways with the effect of heightening the moral discrepancies of the

169. So Habel, *Land Is Mine*, 118.

principal protagonists. The garden is a foil for the land of Egypt. Despite the fertile security of the Delta basin, the land of the Nile is also a land of preeminent power and danger. Egypt is an inversion of Eden. The garden's ethos invests this tale, in both its structural and textual correspondences, with moral ambivalence. The history of human failure repeats itself in the land of Egypt, but in a way that also bears hope. The reader can breathe a sigh of relief with the Deity's intervention, for it sustains the promise of blessing amid conflict and peril. Hope rests on the divine pledge of blessing and more broadly on Yahweh's continuing activity in the entanglements of human history. But such hope also emerges from the fray: that Abraham is exposed for his moral failings without divine denunciation leaves open the prospects of something better, of a place on which moral dilemmas and deceptions need not encroach. Without the ghost of the garden looming in the background, this tale of sojourning in a foreign land would be quite different, perhaps of a glorified trickster who triumphs over Egypt's evil empire. Yet to pose the issue in this way is unfair, for the contours of the garden story are so deeply implanted in this tale of deceit and expulsion that they cannot be uprooted. Intimations of the garden's ethos, its physical and moral dimensions, imbue the tale with a moral pointedness from which even Abraham, the obedient patriarch, is not immune. The obedient patriarch has suffered a crisis of trust and failed.

So the couple is ejected from the land of the Nile back to their homeland. Indeed, this land stretching between the desert and the hill country becomes a scene of strife (rîb, mĕrîbâ) between Abraham and his nephew Lot (13:7, 8), the future father of Moab and Edom. More living space is needed, so Abraham proposes an amicable separation, allowing Lot to choose the land in which to dwell. The basis for this separation is the simple acknowledgment from Abraham that "we are kindred" ('aḥîm, v. 8). Kinship is appealed to for equitable sharing and peaceful relations. Lot's gaze longingly settles on the plain of the Jordan, "well watered everywhere like the garden of Yahweh, like the land of Egypt" (v. 10). Like the fruit of the tree, this tempting facsimile of Eden is there for the taking. To his credit, Abraham gives it up. By letting go of all claim to this ostensibly preferable stretch of land, Abraham has chosen correctly, as confirmed by the following reiteration of the divine promise that the remaining land will be populated by Abraham's offspring, made "like the dirt of the earth" ('āpār hā'āreṣ, v. 16). The promise recalls the language of anthropogony, but with an added nuance:[170] the stuff out of which primal man was created is given a collective dimension within the context of bless-

---

170. Cf. 'āpār min-hā'ădāmâ (2:7). Again, "earth" and "ground" ('ereṣ and 'ădāmâ) within the Yahwist's patriarchal history are practically synonymous (see above).

ing.[171] Yet quantity is not the only point. Given the expression's primordial background, the governing verb (*śym*, "put," "establish") connotes a creative nuance with the sense of (trans)forming or fashioning.[172] Through Abraham, Israel will be created from the ground up, as was the first man.

Any similarity between the garden of Yahweh and the plain of Jordan, however, rests on appearances alone. This well-watered garden is actually a jungle of depravity, for a city lies in its midst and its name is Sodom, whose inhabitants were "wicked, great sinners against Yahweh" (13:13). The story of Sodom need not be repeated here, except to highlight its ironic affinities with the primeval story. Echoing the cry from Abel's blood (*ṣōʿăqîm*, 4:10), the "outcry" (*zĕʿāqâ, ṣĕʿāqâ*) against Sodom does not reach deaf ears, suggesting that once again the ground is coated with the blood of the slain (18:20, 21). The men of Sodom desire to "know" Lot's angelic guests through violence (19:5), yet in their savage grasp for "knowledge" they are struck with blindness (v. 11; cf. 3:7). Lest they be consumed in the city's punishment, Lot and his family are forcibly expelled from Sodom (19:16; cf. 3:23). Finally, Yahweh rains down destruction, not a deluge of water but a holocaust of fire, destroying the entire plain, including the arable soil (*ʾădāmâ*, 19:23). Such punishment surpasses anything previous. Only in this story is the level of divine tolerance breached, made painfully clear in the barter scene over Sodom's fate between Abraham and Yahweh (18:16-33). Even in this case Abraham fulfills his role as blessing giver, interceding on Sodom's behalf. Yet Sodom's situation is irredeemable.

In the account of the city's destruction, the mythic contours of the garden are set against the once lush physical contours of the southern river valley. Everything is perverse behind the succulent foliage of Jordan's plain: violence replaces harmony and the arable soil becomes a salt-infested wasteland. Such is Sodom's legacy.[173] Despite erstwhile appearances, Sodom is a desiccated garden from the roots up. Things are not always what they seem in the Yahwist's moral landscape. The lure of the garden's ethos must lie elsewhere.

---

171. See also 28:14, which contains the identical expression to convey the expansive range of Jacob's progeny.

172. For example, Mic 1:6; Exod 4:11; 14:21; 1 Sam 8:1; Isa 54:12.

173. For Sodom's moral legacy, see Ezek 16:49: "This was the guilt of your sister Sodom; she and her daughters had pride, excess of food, and prosperous ease, but did not aid the poor and needy." Ezekiel's reference to Sodom's structural violence in a land of plenty parallels the Yahwist's reference to sexual violence in a facsimile of paradise.

Ethos and Kinship

As in the primeval history, the primary focus of Israel's ancestral heritage is on family and land relations. The strife between Lot and Abraham portends an array of relational challenges that Israel's ancestral household faces.

Marital Relations

When the primal man discovers his mate and match, he proclaims their mutual kinship as "bone deep" (2:23). The Yahwist's subsequent narrative comprises three generations of patriarchs and matriarchs: Abraham and Sarah, Isaac and Rebekah, and Jacob and his two wives, Rachel and Leah.[174] Yet their marital relationships are less than harmonious. The contrast becomes all the more striking when one takes account of the prevailing cause of so much marital discord: the blessing of progeny. The promise of progeny is itself a bone of contention within the marital relationship. For example, Abraham and Sarah feud over Hagar's status as surrogate mother within the patriarchal household (16:1-6). As Abraham's wife and "sister," Sarah is a rival of sibling proportions. To resolve the conflict, Abraham must concede Sarah's control over Hagar: "Your slave-girl is in your power; do to her as you please" (16:6 NRSV). Yet this is no resolution, for Hagar must flee from Sarah's harsh treatment (16:6b-14). At a higher pitch, the two wives of Jacob, sisters Leah and Rachel, fight bitterly over who can produce the most children from their common husband. Acrimonious competition over Jacob's seed is reflected even in the names of his children. The success of Rachel's maid at producing a second son for Jacob elicits the following gloat over her sister in the naming of Naphtali: "With mighty wrestlings I have wrestled (naptûlê 'ĕlōhîm niptaltî) with my sister and have prevailed" (30:8; cf. 32:22-32). Levi, Leah's third son, is named in the hope that "my husband will be joined (yillāweh) to me" rather than to her rival sister (29:34). In both Sarah's and Jacob's wives' cases, competition and jealousy are the destructive consequences of the patriarchal blessing.[175] The blissful joining of man and woman has become a battlefield of contention and manipulation outside the garden.

174. Joseph's wife, Asenath, however, receives only scant attention in Genesis (41:50) and is evidently absent from the Yahwist's narrative.

175. See N. J. Cohen, "Sibling Rivalry in Genesis," *Judaism* 32 (1983) 331-42.

Fraternal Relations

Marital and kinship relations are inseparably related within the garden. The first man's jubilation over the discovery of his companion/counterpart is cast in the language of kinship (2:23). So also is Laban's discovery of his nephew Jacob (29:14). As with the marital relationship, kinship relations are inextricably bound up with the blessing of progeny and land, a source of both contention and promise.[176] The theme of kinship rivalry and its moral implications finds its most pronounced treatment in the Jacob cycle (25:19–35:22).

Jacob, Trickster in Transition   The twin sons of Isaac begin as jostling rivals within Rebekah's womb, portending the intense struggle of two nations of unequal power (25:22). Esau, the firstborn, is named for his reddish and hirsute appearance (*'admônî, śē'ār,* v. 25), representing the region of Edom and his country Seir. Jacob's collective reference, "Israel," is given later in the narrative; for now he is named for his grip on Esau's heel (*'ăqēb,* v. 26), a name that will prove apt when Esau complains that he was "supplanted" or cheated (*'āqab*) by his brother (27:36). The contrast between the names is striking: Esau is named for his external appearance; Jacob is named for his personal behavior. In short, Jacob's very name denotes rivalry in the most manipulative, "grasping" form. Yet he is also the bearer of Israel's blessing and identity. How a duplicitous, conniving hero can be the bearer of Israel's identity, the father of the twelve tribes, is the crux that drives the Jacob cycle. Blind Isaac's penetrating question cuts to the heart of the matter: "Who are you, my son?" (27:18).

Reminiscent of Cain's and Abel's respective vocations, Jacob and Esau are distinguished. Esau is a skillful hunter, an *'îš śādeh,* literally a "field man" (25:27). Jacob is an *'îš tām,* literally a "moral man."[177] As a hunter, Esau traffics with the wild, hunting the "beasts of the fields." Jacob, however, prefers the domestic life, "living in tents" (cf. 4:20). The tight juxtaposition of Esau and Jacob in this one verse imbues their respective descriptions with the sense

---

176. Fishbane, *Text and Texture,* 60.

177. So also S. D. Walters, "Jacob Narrative," *ABD* 3.600. See the use of *tām,* translated "blameless" (NRSV), in Job 1:1, 8; 2:3a. The nominal cognate *tummâ* in Job 2:3b denotes "integrity." While admitting that *tām* implies "more of a moral status" in all other contexts, Ronald S. Hendel interprets the term as a reference to Jacob's preference for culture, "mild man" that Jacob is (*The Epic of the Patriarch: The Jacob Cycle and the Narrative Traditions of Canaan and Israel* [HSM 42; Atlanta: Scholars Press, 1987] 112, 128). Given the contrast between Jacob and his brother of the wild, such cultural nuance may be implied but in no way brackets out the moral issue of Jacob's character, which is central to the cycle. Moreover, mildness is not a vocation.

of vocation. Jacob is meant to be a moral man as much as Esau is a skillful hunter. English translations of v. 27b, however, dilute Jacob's vocation (KJV "plain," NRSV "quiet," NJPSV "mild"), but Jacob is described unambiguously in terms of moral commendation and vocation. Yet Jacob hardly acts in exemplary fashion: he barters with Esau to secure his *bĕkōrâ*, his inheritance rights as firstborn (25:29-34) and, in collaboration with his mother, steals the blessing *(bĕrākâ)* of the firstborn from his father (27:1-29).[178] In the latter episode, it is the mother, Isaac's wife, who initiates the ruse (cf. 12:11). She literally commands Jacob: "hear my voice" (*šĕmaʿ bĕqōlî*, 27:8). Her word is *shema*. But Jacob is clearly an accessory to the crime. He is a "smooth man" (*ʾîš ḥālāq*, 27:11), a double entendre that denotes not only Jacob's skin, in contrast to Esau's hair, but also his deceptive speech (cf. Prov 5:3; 26:28). In his cunning, Jacob is as slippery as a snake.[179]

Yet where is the "moral man" in all this? Although the narrative does not shy away from depicting his less than blameless character, Jacob, like Abraham before him, is not roundly condemned for his behavior. No divine punishment is exacted. Instead, the Yahwist lets the consequences of Jacob's deceptive character run their course, lowering Jacob into the den of strife. Once Esau discovers his brother's ruse, Jacob must flee for his life and from the land of his birth. It does not get easier in the land of his mother's home, where the deceiver becomes the deceived. Jacob's character could not be more ambivalent. A "moral man" is yet to be found in this sordid cycle. This designation of Jacob early in the narrative can only be proleptic. Jacob's moral character is a work in progress, the object of Yahweh's subtle craftwork. In short, Jacob's integrity is his vocation, and he begins as a problem apprentice.[180]

To forestall the murderous outcome of sibling rivalry, Jacob flees to Haran, the home of Rebekah's brother. In his flight he receives a pronouncement of blessing from Yahweh at Bethel (28:13-15) that recalls and conflates Abraham's blessings in 12:2-3 and 13:14-17. Jacob will receive both land and progeny "like the dirt of the earth" (cf. 13:16; 2:7) and

---

178. As Walters points out, "birthright" and "blessing" in Hebrew "not only sound alike but are visually similar" (*ABD* 3.601). The narrative suggests an equivalency: Jacob's blessing as the dominant nation is based on his gaining the firstborn status at Esau's expense.

179. An ironic reversal is, however, evident: Jacob is a man of culture, "living in tents" (25:27), whereas the serpent is an animal of the wild, like Esau (3:1).

180. See also E. Davis's analysis of Jacob's integrity as part of his moral education in "Job and Jacob: The Integrity of Faith," in *Reading between Texts: Intertextuality and the Hebrew Bible* (ed. D. N. Fewell; Louisville: Westminster John Knox, 1992) 205.

through him and his descendants "all the families of the earth shall be blessed" (28:14b; 12:3). The new element, required in Jacob's flight from home, is the promise of divine accompaniment (28:15). As Jacob's moral status is a pressing question, so also is the issue of the land, for in fleeing from his brother Jacob is abandoning the land of promise, thereby placing the blessing in jeopardy.[181] As the blessing of Isaac's progeny is the source of strife, so the blessing of the land serves as the resolution: Jacob shall return and populate the land Yahweh has granted him, but it will require fraternal reconciliation. Yahweh's promise to Jacob at Bethel elicits a new knowledge of Yahweh's presence in his midst (28:16): "Surely Yahweh is in this place — and I did not know it!" By his profession of ignorance, Jacob admits that his own wily wisdom has met its limits. Inextricably tied to Yahweh's promise of his return to the land, Jacob's moral transformation has begun.

In the land away from home, Jacob meets his match in his uncle Laban. Laban's profession of kinship to Jacob, complete with embraces and kisses, has as much to do with duplicity as it does bloodlines (29:13-14). Laban is, after all, the wily brother of the mother of deception. Collusion is set in motion when Laban invites Jacob to serve him with wages, "because you are my kinsman" (lit. "my brother," 'aḥî). A verbal agreement is negotiated, and the games begin with uncle and nephew warily circling each other to see who can outwit whom. Jacob is the first to take a fall, duped on the very night of marital consummation. Laban substitutes his older daughter Leah for Jacob's true love Rachel, and in the heat of the moment and under the cover of darkness, Jacob is caught unawares. There is poetic justice in the deception: Jacob's grasp of Esau's rights of primogeniture got him Laban's firstborn daughter.[182] There is also a larger irony at work: deception has entered the bed chamber. While the marital ruse perpetrated by Isaac and Rebekah was discovered in the midst of intimate "play" by the peeping king Abimelech (26:6-11), Jacob, the perpetrator of ruses, gets tricked at his own game in the heat of consummation.[183] Deception has encroached on

---

181. Walters, "Jacob Narrative," 602. Walters, however, overstates the case by claiming that like Esau spurning his birthright, Jacob has "spurned the Abrahamic promise." Jacob's flight is a necessary one, prompted by the machinations of his mother (28:42-45). The theme of blessing in jeopardy is one already encountered in 12:10-20. There the blessing of progeny was the issue.

182. Walters, "Jacob Narrative," 603.

183. Jacob's sojourn in the motherland and the deception he faces from his uncle indicate an ironic culmination of the theme of ruse making on foreign soil, as attested in the Yahwist's "ancestress in danger" stories (Gen 12:10-20; 26:1-11*). Indeed, Jacob's fi-

the private garden of delight. In his desire to know Rachel, he comes to know her sister unawares. Jacob consequently assumes the role of plaintiff by uttering the familiar formula of complaint: "What is this you have done to me?" (29:25; cf. 26:10; 12:18). When Jacob accuses his uncle of deception, Laban appeals to local custom, and Jacob serves Laban another seven years to marry the apple of his eye.

Although nothing is resolved morally or otherwise, blessing continues to operate while the screw continues to turn. Jacob gets the upper hand by enriching himself with Laban's flocks through a magical ploy (30:31-43), after Laban professes to Jacob that "Yahweh has blessed me because of you" (v. 27; cf. v. 30) and subsequently tries to cheat him. Laban's proclamation, aimed at retaining Jacob's services at whatever cost, echoes the divine promise extended to Abraham in 12:3. Jacob has become a blessing to Laban. Amid the scheming plots, blessing inexorably begins to fill the jagged crevices of broken relationships. The final deception occurs when Jacob and his wives set out toward Jacob's home while Laban is occupied with shearing sheep (31:1-22). The scene opens with Yahweh commanding Jacob: "Return to the land of your ancestors and to your kindred" (v. 3; cf. 12:3). Like the primal man's relationship to the ground to which he must return (2:7; 3:19), it is in the land of Canaan that Jacob's identity and vocation are to be developed. He does not return, however, to a land of cursed existence: his "curse," as it were, has been the twenty years of hard service under his sly uncle (31:36a-40). Rather, Jacob must return to a land where reconciliation with his kindred can be found, where Jacob can dwell redeemed and reconstituted as the credible bearer of God's blessing.

When Laban catches up with the refugees, the familiar charge of deception is leveled against Jacob. Jacob responds with a pronouncement of fear, reminiscent of his father's rationale behind his ruse before King Abimelech (26:9, 7). Like Abraham before him, Isaac was afraid to identify Rebekah as his wife for fear of his own life. Jacob's response, however, marks a subtle turnaround: his fear is for the sake of his two wives rather than for his own life (31:31). Compared to the first "ancestress in danger" story, Jacob's response indicates a surprising move toward integrity. The story of Abraham's immigration into Egypt gave no indication of patriarchal concern for Sarah and her induction into Pharaoh's harem (12:10-20). Likewise, Isaac's fear in Gerar is expressed solely in selfish terms (26:7). By contrast, Jacob expresses

---

nal confrontation with Laban is characterized by a genuine fear over the fate of his two wives, a reversal of his forefathers' fear for their own lives as motivation of the ruse (31:31; see below).

his concern for Rachel and Leah. Admittedly, Jacob's motives are not altogether altruistic, but the fact that Jacob cannot stand to part from his wives, whereas his forefathers could, indicates a significant moral step over the first patriarch's ruse. Citing his own conscientious service in defense (31:38-40), Jacob, the "smooth man," is turning into a "moral man."[184]

So begins the movement toward reconciliation between Laban and Jacob, formalized by a covenant, with Yahweh serving as guarantor and a boundary established to prevent one from encroaching on the other's land (31:46-53a). But such reconciliation between nephew and uncle is mere child's play compared to the reconciliation of two brothers. Jacob's rapprochement with Esau is fraught with great suspense and mystery. Jacob fears that Esau has prepared to attack him with four hundred men (32:6) and takes appropriate defensive measures. Jacob's desperate prayer to Yahweh bespeaks a measure of genuine piety, even though it is spoken from the battle trenches, as it were (vv. 9-12). Most significant is that Jacob is no longer devising a ruse to escape his brother's clutches. Rather he has cast himself entirely on the efficacy of Yahweh's promise made at Bethel (28:13-15). Jacob is no longer the vanguard of deception but the supplicant of grace.

The outcome is a wrestling match at the Jabbok ford that is cloaked in mystery. Jacob wrestles with a man and wrenches from him a blessing and a new identity (32:29): "You shall no longer be called 'Jacob' but 'Israel' (yiśrā'ēl), for you have striven (śārîtā) with God and with men and have prevailed (tûkāl)." Acknowledged without apology is Jacob's way of life, as one constantly grasping. In his striving, Jacob has persevered, gaining birthright, blessing, and wealth. The event conflates every instance in which Jacob has struggled with his kin, be it brother, father, wives, or uncle (cf. 30:8). Yet such acknowledgment of Jacob's way of life is not a tacit endorsement of his lifestyle. Like Abraham, Jacob's striving has consistently gotten him into hot water, only to escape by the skin of his teeth. The stranger who wrestles with him is thus every person, and most concretely Esau, against whom Jacob has played the trickster, and in the end, God. Yet Jacob and his opponent are more than rivals; they are wrestling partners in the fullest sense. The verb "strive" (śrh) can also mean "persist."[185] For all his bad timing and conceit, Jacob has also persisted with Yahweh by relying on the promise of land and divine accompaniment.[186] As a result, he is morally empowered, but not without severe cost.

184. Walters, "Jacob Narrative," 604.
185. See BDB, 975.
186. The nuance of accompaniment is pronounced in Yahweh's promise to Jacob: "Look, I am with you" (28:15).

Jacob names the wrestling venue Peniel ("God's face"), explaining, "I have seen God face to face, and yet my life is preserved" (32:30b). Jacob perceives the match as nothing short of a revelation about himself, his patron God, and ultimately his brother (33:10).[187] This story is the closest Jacob ever comes to assuming heroic status. Yet it comes at a crucial cost: Jacob must limp away from the match, more vulnerable than when he started. By refusing to let go of the blessing (32:26b), Jacob is at once victorious and wounded. He continues as a grasper of blessing, but no longer at the expense of kin and people. Rather the blessing is appropriated to his own hurt. The wrestling match was a victory in his blessing and a moral triumph in his wounding. Jacob is no hero; he remains a work in progress. He began as a thoroughly ambivalent character yet finds himself on the way to reformation as he now crosses over to the land of blessing.

Jacob's moral status is a blessing in progress and culminates in his meeting with Esau. Jacob approaches his brother as a supplicant, a striking contrast to the "grasper" who helped engineer the loss of Esau's birthright and blessing.[188] As Jacob has grown up, so also has Esau, offering forgiveness and kindness (33:12, 15). But full reconciliation between brothers is not to be had within the Yahwist's scope: Esau offers to accompany Jacob on his journey, but Jacob graciously declines and agrees to meet his brother in Seir, Esau's country. Yet Jacob never gets there; instead, he journeys for a short distance to a small site on the Jabbok, presumably limping all the way, and settles (33:17). In any case, by returning to his land and reconciling, at least partially, with his brother, Jacob fulfills his vocation as an *'îš tām*, a man of integrity. Integrity was Jacob's vocation as much as hunting was that of Esau, "the man of the field," and farming was that of the primal man, the man of the ground. As the bearer of both blessing and integrity, inseparably related, Jacob qua Israel has fulfilled his mission.

Joseph, Victim of Innocence Although himself transformed, Jacob leaves a legacy of strife and deception with the surrounding peoples: by deceit[189] the sons of Jacob avenge Dinah's rape and kill all the males of the city of Shechem. No longer the "grasper," Jacob laments their abominable actions (34:30). Similarly, internal dissension is provoked when Jacob extends to Joseph favorite-son

187. Although 33:10 is usually relegated by source critics to the Elohistic source, the wrestling match described by the Yahwist would not be complete without the reference to Esau's face looking like the "face of God."

188. In the Elohist's variant of the story, Jacob actually offers Esau back his blessing (*bĕrākâ*, 33:11). See Fishbane, *Text and Texture*, 51-52.

189. Heb. *bĕmirmâ*, 34:13; cf. 31:20.

200

status, setting in motion, as with Abel's favored sacrifice, a cycle of strife and violence among Jacob's sons (37:3a-4). Only Judah's appeal to mutual kinship stops Joseph's brothers from killing him outright (37:26-27), a partial mastery, at best, over their deep enmity against Joseph. Whereas Jacob was the culpable victim who became enslaved in Laban's land, Joseph is the innocent victim who rises to power in Egypt as Pharaoh's right-hand man. Joseph's unassailable character is the fruit of Jacob's transformed integrity.

Like Jacob, Joseph performs a ruse against his brothers, but one that does not implicate him so much as test the moral mettle of his brothers. By stepping into the breach to bear the blame and become Joseph's slave in place of the youngest brother, Benjamin (44:18-34), Judah prompts Joseph to divulge the ruse and disclose himself to his brothers. Judah's integrity has passed the test for all. Echoing Jacob's blessing from Isaac (27:28), Pharaoh offers the "fat of the land" to Jacob's family, and Joseph sends his brothers off to his aging father with gifts as well as with the parting words, "Do not quarrel along the way" (46:24).[190] The book of Genesis closes with the settlement of Jacob's family, the culmination of integrity, and the consummation of reconciliation (50:15-21).[191]

Kinship with the Land

As with fraternal and marital relations, relationship with the land is of utmost concern for the Yahwist. As the 'ādām was placed in the garden and commissioned to till the 'ădāmâ as part and parcel of his identity, so Israel's ancestral family is commanded to reside in the land of Canaan to embody their moral and national identity, to fulfill their destiny. For every patriarch who enters the stage of the Yahwist's epic, the divine blessing of land and progeny is extended.[192] In addition, the blessing of land thrusts the ancestral family into contact with other social groups. For example, the blessing of land is materially channeled through Jacob's father, Isaac (27:28), bringing him into a potentially conflictive relationship with those outside his household. Isaac's

190. Once again, a younger son is singled out for special treatment: Joseph lavishes gifts on Benjamin (v. 22).

191. Cf. the position offered by G. W. Coats, "Another Form-Critical Problem of the Hexateuch," in *Narrative Research on the Hebrew Bible* (ed. M. Amihai et al.; *Semeia* 46 [1989] 69-71). Coats contends that the Yahwist "undercuts the account of reconciliation," which I find unconvincing (p. 71).

192. The one exception is Joseph, who is not an ancestor of Israel but the eponymous hero of two particular tribes. For Abraham, the promise of blessing came to include a solemn covenant (Gen 15:12-18).

character stands out as one who is able to secure the land through negotiation, work it, and thereby reap the land's blessing. After the unfortunate incident in Gerar (26:1-11),[193] Isaac attempts to settle in Philistia, sowing seed and reaping "in the same year . . . a hundredfold" (26:12). The narrative sequence is telling: blessing materializes after Isaac works the land (26:13). Reminiscent of the primal man's tilling, Isaac, the blessed patriarch, performs his work on the ground and reaps accordingly.

Isaac's Philistine neighbors do not like his unprecedented prosperity in the land, however, and Abimelech expels him (v. 16; cf. v. 11; 12:20). Isaac's subsequent settlements reap similar conflictive results, specifically over water rights (26:19-21), until one well is dug and called Rehoboth ("Room"), a testimony to securing sufficient territory (v. 22). Nevertheless, the ancestral blessing is pronounced elsewhere, at Beer-sheba (vv. 24-25). There too a striking narrative sequence unfolds. While Isaac's servants are digging a well, Abimelech approaches and invites Isaac to enter into a covenant of peaceful coexistence (v. 29). A meal is shared to seal the covenant, and Abimelech, along with his cabinet, depart in peace. Only then does the narrative report the jubilant discovery of water, giving Beer-sheba its name (v. 33). Through covenant, Isaac has found his home.

The divine pronouncement to Isaac earlier in this remarkable narrative forges a direct link between blessing and obedience to *tôrâ* ("to my voice, my charge, my commandments, my statutes, and my law," 26:4-5). Isaac's subsequent actions, along with their accompanying consequences, establish a matrix of obedience, occupation of the land of blessing, prosperity, and peace,[191] all fruits of the garden's ethos. Like Noah before him, Isaac bears the possibility of cultivating a new Eden in the land of promise and its concomitant blessings. But an enduring appropriation of the garden and its ethos is yet to be had. Through Isaac's progeny, sibling strife and deception invade his familial garden, and it takes nothing short of Jacob's moral transformation to rekindle the hope of reestablishing an oasis of order (see above).

193. This third story of the "ancestress in danger" (Gen 26:1-11; cf. 12:10-20; 20:1-18 [the Elohist's version]) finds Isaac and Rebekah deceiving King Abimelech, who uncovers their ruse by discovering the couple in the heat of conjugal "play," true to Isaac's name (26:8). M. E. Biddle has noted that all three stories depict the patriarch as the vehicle of blessing and curse for the nations vis-à-vis 12:3 ("The 'Endangered Ancestress' and the Blessing for the Nations," *JBL* 109 [1990] 602-11).

194. Walters, "Jacob Narrative," 601.

Exodus and Ethos

Owing to the cycle of strife and famine, Jacob's family finds itself in Egypt, admittedly in the best of conditions: Jacob's family is offered the "best of the land of Egypt" (45:18). Although Jacob's household is separated from its own land, Israel's home away from home in Egypt is Goshen, situated somewhere in the eastern Delta.[195] Israel is never to forget its true home, as Jacob's (Israel's) dying wish to be buried with his ancestors in the land of Canaan makes poignantly clear (49:29-30). Beyond the Jordan, "Israel" is buried before a great company of Egyptians and "Israelites," together raising "a very great and sorrowful lamentation" (50:10a).

Such poignant solidarity was not to last, however. A pharaoh who did not know Joseph ascends the throne and resolves, like the wily serpent in the garden, to deal "wisely" (ḥkm) with Israel in the land (Exod 1:10), and the hope for the homeland becomes all the more urgent for Israel. Whereas the Israelites once found peace and prosperity in the land of Goshen, they are now forced to build supply cities for the new king (1:11), a perversion of the primordial vocation to till and keep the soil.[196] For Israel, the curse of Egypt is the crushing burden Pharaoh afflicts on the children of Jacob, like the accursed ground lording its unyielding power over the exiles of the garden. Both the cursed soil and the land of Egypt limn an ontology of bondage. Moreover, primordial fratricide has now turned into male infanticide (v. 22). Compared to the fleshpots of oppression, Israel's distant homeland is described in none too glorious terms: "a land flowing with milk and honey."[197] At one point in Israel's journey back to the land of promise, the height of irony is reached when a complaint is leveled against Moses for having driven Israel "out of a land flowing with milk and honey to kill us in the wilderness," a geo-ethical confusion that proves fatal (Num 16:13, 31-34).

Egypt, the cultural center of the south, has turned into the hub of chaos. Not only is Israel oppressed under Pharaoh's heavy hand, conflict erupts from within (Exod 2:13).[198] Egypt's desolation is nowhere more dramatically illustrated than in the series of plagues Yahweh sends upon the land. Terence Fretheim aptly describes these plagues as ecological catastrophes that bring

195. For the issues of location, see W. A. Ward, "Goshen," *ABD* 2.1076-77.

196. Cf. 1 Kgs 5:13-18 (MT 28-33), which describes Solomon's levy of Israelites for his monumental building projects.

197. Heb. *'ereṣ zābat ḥālāb ûdĕbāš*, Exod 3:8, 17; Num 13:27; 14:8; 16:14.

198. Moses is dismayed over two Hebrews fighting but does not hesitate to kill an Egyptian (2:11-13).

about a reversal of creation.[196] Yet within the Yahwist's purview, they also bear another function: setting the distinction between Israel and Egypt in stark relief by distinguishing the land of Goshen, the site of Israel's settlement, from the larger land of the Nile.

In the series of ecological catastrophes or "plagues" that follow, it is no accident that the Nile is the first to go, polluted with blood and rendered undrinkable (7:14-18, 20b-21a, 23-25).[200] The Nile was Egypt's prime source of agricultural sustenance in a land of little rainfall. This river of rivers made Egypt the environmental haven "of the world" within the Yahwist's geographical scope (Gen 41:57). The bloody Nile is thus an apt symbol of Egypt's moral ruin. All similarities with the "garden of Yahweh" (Gen 13:10) are effectively deconstructed by this first plague. Indeed, as a consequence of the Nile's pollution, the inhabitants of the land must adapt to a practice of dryland existence by digging wells for water (Exod 7:24; cf. Gen 26:18-23), geographical justice from the Yahwist's hand. The Nile's blood testifies to the structural violence wrought upon Israel in the same way that the blood-soaked ground was a stark testimony to Cain's crime (Gen 4:10). The bloody Nile is, in short, the scene of Egypt's crime against humanity.

The land of Goshen, however, remains unscathed throughout the series of plagues. By divine decree, the land of Goshen is "set apart" (*wĕhiplētî*, Exod 8:22 [MT 18]) in the third plague; Yahweh makes a distinction *(wĕhiplâ)* between the livestock of Israel and that of Egypt in the fourth (9:4); hail does not touch the land of Goshen in the fifth (v. 26); Israel is granted light while all of Egypt is plunged into darkness in the seventh (10:23); and in the death of the firstborn, not even a "dog shall growl at any of the Israelites . . . so that you may know that Yahweh makes a distinction between Egypt and Israel" (11:7; cf. 12:23). Immune from environmental catastrophe, Israel's land is a haven in hell, a bastion of blessing in a land of ecological curse. By contrast, Egypt is stripped of all vegetation by the sixth plague of locusts: "nothing green was left, no tree, no plant in the field, in all the land of Egypt" (10:15). The ecological distinction between Israel and Egypt is potent with pedagogical significance: "I will set apart the land of Goshen, where my people live, . . .

199. T. E. Fretheim, "The Plagues as Ecological Signs of Historical Disaster," *JBL* 110 (1991) 385-96. See also his commentary *Exodus* (Interpretation; Louisville: John Knox, 1991) 105-12.

200. M. Noth regarded the last clause of v. 17 ("and it shall be turned to blood") and v. 20b as Priestly redactional bracketings (*A History of Pentateuchal Traditions* [tr. B. W. Anderson; 1972; repr. Chico, Calif.: Scholars Press, 1981] 30n.105). See Campbell and O'Brien, *Sources of the Pentateuch*, 136n.102. But such a separation of these clauses from the Yahwistic unit of vv. 17-20 is artificial.

so that you may know that I Yahweh am in this land" (8:22 [MT 18]; cf. 9:7). Such knowledge finally softens Pharaoh's heart and sends Moses and his people away, but not without a special request: "And bring a blessing on me too!" (12:32). So Moses and his company leave the chaos of Egypt to occupy the land of blessing and order to conduct authentic worship and recapture the ethos and telos of their existence.[201]

Between Chaos and Ethos

The wilderness, however, lies formidably between the Israelites and the promised land. Israel's experience in the desert is essentially a liminal state of existence, at once negative and positive, dangerous and creative, a state of transition.[202] The wilderness is a land between curse and blessing, between chaos and order. This land of geographical liminality has its social consequences as well. The wilderness is a scene of contention and complaint.[203] Moses himself is a man vexed and betwixt; he is literally caught between the people's constant complaints over the hardship of wilderness living and Yahweh's irrepressible wrath, which is ever poised to destroy them (e.g., Num 11:10-15). Yet Yahweh also provides.

It is only in the Yahwist's larger geo-ethical landscape that the significance of manna in the wilderness can be understood. This "bread of heaven" (Exod 16:4) is anything but that. Far from being a miraculous blessing of abundance, manna is better understood as Yahweh's stopgap measure for quieting the people's subversive murmurings in a liminal land: "The rabble among them had a strong craving" (11:4); so begins the account of manna in the post-Sinaitic wilderness. Desire breeds discontent, and the results are mutiny under Moses and disobedience against Yahweh. The people regard manna as woefully deficient in comparison to the sumptuous smorgasbord of meats and vegetables to which they were accustomed in Egypt (11:4b-6). Most likely a form of excrement from insects,[204] manna so perceived by the wandering Israelites is a sorry means of

---

201. The tie between the land and Israel's ethos is even reflected in the issue of cultic practice. When Pharaoh suggests to Moses that he sacrifice to God within the land, Moses objects that the sacrifices his people intend to offer are by nature "offensive to the Egyptians," hence the need to leave Egypt in order to conduct genuine worship (Exod 8:25-26).

202. See R. L. Cohn's suggestive study in *The Shape of Sacred Space: Four Biblical Studies* (AARSR 23; Missoula, Mont.: Scholars Press, 1981) 7-23; Hiebert, *Yahwist's Landscape*, 124.

203. See the studies of G. E. Coats, *Rebellion in the Wilderness* (Nashville: Abingdon, 1968); and V. Fritz, *Israel in der Wüste* (Marburger theologische Studien 7; Marburg: Elwert, 1970), which stress the negative side of the wilderness traditions.

204. See J. C. Slayton, "Manna," *ABD* 4.511.

living off the land: "There is nothing at all but this manna to look at," complain the people (11:6). But that is the point. On the one hand, manna is meant to fill only nominally the people's hunger without tempting them to take up permanent residence in the wilderness. On the other, such a means of nominal sustenance must be enticing enough to prevent them from immediately returning to the house of bondage as a matter of survival.

More importantly, however, the partaking of manna bears a pedagogical function: it enables the community to practice observing in this meager land the law of the sabbath in the land of plenty (16:4-5, 22-30). That the sabbath is promulgated *before* Israel receives formal instruction through the law proper at Sinai (32:21) underlines the special significance of this holy ordinance for the Yahwist. In the wilderness, the sabbath law is conceived by Yahweh as a "test" to see "whether they will follow my *tôrâ*" (16:4). They fail, but receive only a mild scolding from Moses (vv. 27-29; cf. Num 11:33-34). As in the case of Yahweh's prohibition in the garden, the sabbath ordinance imposes a limit on human grasping. Both the forbidden tree and the sabbath day are set apart from human activity as tests of obedience. Yet, in contrast to the abundant provision of the garden, manna is nothing more than liminal food for a liminal people in a liminal land, and it takes nothing less than a monumental concession on Yahweh's part to grant the Israelites meat, which comes with a vengeance: "Therefore Yahweh will give you meat, and you shall eat . . . not only one day . . . but for a whole month — until it comes out of your nostrils and becomes loathsome to you" (Num 11:19-20). Liminality is an arena of extremes; balance is not to be found in the wilderness.

The problem with manna broaches a larger issue that is prominently featured in the Yahwist's landscape: the mountain of Sinai. From the deliverance at the sea to the murmurings in the desert, Yahweh assumes the role of patient caregiver, doggedly providing on Israel's behalf. For each request and complaint, Yahweh immediately provides, whether it is the sweet waters at Marah (Exod 15:22-25) or water from the rock at Massah and Meribah (17:1-7). Yahweh is constant in forbearance up until the foot of the mountain. There, certain limits are established: "Any who touch the mountain shall be put to death" is the divine decree, so holy is the mountain (19:12a). But holiness is not the only issue. The decree echoes Eve's recitation of the "law" before the serpent: "You shall not touch it, or you shall die" (Gen 3:3b). Like the tree of the knowledge of good and evil, the mountain of God is not a thing to be touched, much less grasped.[205] Yet

---

205. The Yahwist characterizes the people, apart from Moses and Aaron, as ever on the verge of transgressing the boundary between mountain and desert. The choice of language is revealing: the people are threatening to "break through" *(prṣ)*, a term that can also

something from the mountain is offered to the community for its appropriation. Unlike the fruit of the tree, the two tablets of stone, given by God, are to be received.

Sinai marks an irreversible turning point in Israel's journey through the desert: Israel is no longer a people of needs to be met, and Yahweh is no longer simply their patient provider. The community has now received its ethos in codified form. Through the granting of the law, Israel has assumed all rights, privileges, and, most importantly, responsibilities pertaining to a covenant people, and Yahweh can now expect covenantal obedience. It is only after the Israelites have received the law and departed from the mountain to resume their trek that their murmurings are met with judgment. Ushering in an age of responsibility, Sinai is Israel's bar mitzvah.[206] As noted above, the post-Sinai example of the contested manna is a case in point, resulting in a plague that wipes out all "who had the craving" (Num 11:33-34). But it only gets worse from there. Dissension arises when Moses' own siblings, Miriam and Aaron, question the authority of Moses, the humblest man "on the face of the earth" (12:2-3). Yahweh's response exposes the complaint for what it is, a rebellion of discontent (vv. 6-8), and afflicts Miriam with skin disease.

The complaint of complaints, however, comes from the sons of Eliab, Dathan and Abiram, who accuse Moses of planning to kill his people by bringing them into the wilderness, *out of* "a land flowing with milk and honey" without a comparable substitute (16:13b). As noted above, their complaint rests on a geo-ethical confusion that is, at best, only half right. The wilderness is no land of blessing, but Egypt, despite all appearances to the contrary, is no such land either. The brothers' subversive reasoning prompts Moses to establish a test comparable to the contest of Elijah and the prophets of Baal (1 Kgs 18:20-40): "This is how you shall know that Yahweh has sent me to do all these works. . . . If these people die a natural death, or if a natural fate comes on them, then Yahweh has not sent me. But if Yahweh creates something new and the ground opens its mouth and swallows them up, . . .

---

mean tear down and destroy or remove something, such as an altar (Judg 6:25; 1 Kgs 18:30), evoking the striking image of a mountain in shambles at the hands of the rabble (cf. the ruins of the Babylonian ziggurat in Gen 11:8). Israel is characterized as an unruly mob (cf. Exod 32:25). Moreover, a telling motivation is disclosed: the people intend to "break through to Yahweh to *look*" (19:21). The reference to sight is paralleled in Eve's longing gaze at the forbidden tree (Gen 3:6).

206. See J. A. Wilcoxen's illuminating study on the thematic differences between the pre- and post-Sinai wilderness episodes in "Some Anthropocentric Aspects of Israel's Sacred History," *JR* 48 (1968) 344-48.

then you shall know that these men have despised Yahweh" (vv. 29-30). Yahweh follows suit and the ground swallows the rebels up, families and all. Yahweh, indeed, has "created something new" for a wandering people, an ethos that holds Israel accountable for its rebellious deeds, one that both convicts and shapes a community according to *tôrâ*. Like the ethos of the garden, the law from the mountain encounters disobedience and prompts divine judgment, fundamentally shaping Israel's mythos.

The juxtaposition of the garden and the mountain elicits a powerful irony: whereas the primal couple impulsively grasped for wisdom from the forbidden tree in transgressing Yahweh's decree, Israel, by their rebellions in the wilderness, refuses to appropriate the law and the land, whose produce is equal to Eden's (see below). Curse, on the one hand, and judgment, on the other, are the consequences. Yet the law also holds the potential of terminating the judgment by anticipating the good life in a land in which no one is "empty-landed" (Exod 34:19b) and from which the "firstfruits of the ground," unlike Cain's gift (Gen 4:3), can be offered to Yahweh (Exod 34:26a). The curse is reversed in the land of plenty, which is inseparably bound up with the law. The law is not a wilderness ethic, a survivalist's code for nomadic existence in the howling desert. Through covenant, Israel is homeward bound. The law from the mountain anticipates blessing in a land of settlement. As will be shown, the garden, in turn, finds its telos in this vehicle of blessing.

The final judgment in the wilderness is one that requires the extinction of an entire generation, with a few noteworthy exceptions. The damnable sin is a failure of nerve to rise up and "take the land" given by Yahweh to Israel (Num 13:30). Spies are sent out to survey the lay of the land of promise and to return with some of its fruit (v. 20). They return with grapes, pomegranates, and figs, produce worthy of an agriculturist's paradise (vv. 23, 27).[207] Yet the formidable inhabitants and their fortified towns dissuade most of the spies from offering a counsel of occupation. Caleb, however, issues a minority report, claiming that the land is there for the taking (v. 30). Siding with the majority, the people express their desire to return to Egypt (14:1), and Yahweh is consequently ready to lower the boom. Through Moses' pleas for leniency and divine reputation (vv. 13-19; cf. Exod 32:11-13), however, a compromise is reached: the present generation, having disobeyed Yahweh's "voice," must die out, leaving its children as beneficiaries of the land (Num 14:22-23a). The period of forty years in the wilderness aims to purge Israel as much as the flood purged the earth of wickedness, and, as in Noah's case,

207. Cf. Gen 3:7; 9:20; Cant 4:13-15.

there is one exemplary character from the masses destined to partake of the fruits of the land. Caleb is lifted up as the paragon of obedience; he and his descendants are granted the right to take the land (v. 24). The scene that follows Yahweh's pronouncement is filled with a pathos comparable to the final, wrenching scene in the garden (Gen 3:7-13): the Israelites attempt to take the land on their own, but to no avail. Moses warns them: "Why do you continue to transgress the command of Yahweh? That will not succeed" (Num 15:41). Tantamount to suicide, the people of judgment attempt to possess the land of their ancestors by force, and the people of the land come down and rout them.

This tragic turn of events is a travesty of justice from the Yahwist's perspective, but one that is not unprecedented. Through the law and the blessing, inseparably related, Israel was given the chance to reclaim the land of blessing in which their ancestors once lived. The ramifications become clearer in light of the garden story. The primal couple was judged for illegitimately taking from the tree. Yahweh's primal *tôrâ* was transgressed. With their newfound knowledge, they were expelled from the garden to eke out their existence in a land of curse. History repeats itself in the story of Israel in and out of Egypt, but the dynamics have changed. Israel leaves the land of curse, Egypt, whose similarity to the garden is superficial only, and in the godforsaken wilderness receives the *tôrâ*, which anticipates — indeed, permits — reentry into the land of blessing. With their new-found knowledge, Israel has the opportunity to take the land of their ancestors. By appropriating the law, this "grasping" is not only legitimated but mandated. They appropriate the land by appropriating the law, and they can fulfil the law only in the land of blessing. A synoptic comparison of the two chains of narrative sequence that govern the respective plots of the garden and the exodus/wilderness stories underlines their correspondences. See the chart on page 210.

The two columns of narrative sequence, admittedly simplistic in arrangement, highlight certain subtle parallels and inversions between the garden and the exodus/wilderness stories. The story of the garden progresses by and large from the inside out, from the blissful garden to the curse-filled land. The story of the exodus advances in the opposite direction, from a land plagued by curse (Egypt) to the land of blessing (Canaan). At least this is the ideal. A detour, however, is taken in Numbers: Israel disobeys in the wilderness by desiring to return to the land of bondage, thereby refusing to take the land of blessing, given by Yahweh, and to appropriate the law that anticipates such a land. It is in this larger sequence of narration that the function of the wilderness traditions for the Yahwist comes clear: the wilderness marks the time in which Israel desires to return

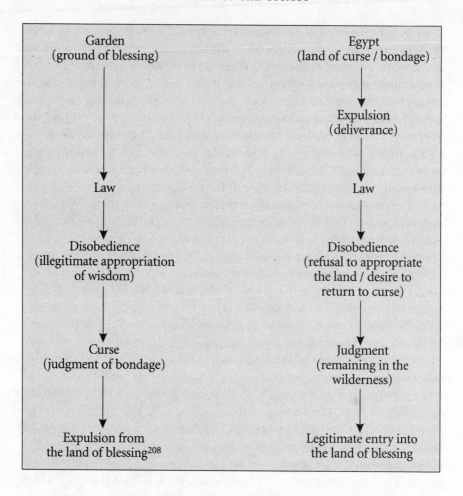

to the life of curse.[209] By refusing to claim their land and destiny, Israel reveals itself to be a community infatuated with curse, lusting for the bondage of Egypt — expressed in terms of culinary delight (Num 11:4b-6) — in the same way that the primal couple was attracted to the bondage of wisdom, the fruit of knowledge.

For the Yahwist, there is no moral middle ground between curse and

208. One could go further with the garden column. The "curse" of the flood serves to distinguish Noah from his generation as much as the plagues serve to distinguish Israel from Egypt.

209. See also A. F. Campbell, *The Study Companion to Old Testament Literature* (OTStudies 2; Wilmington, Del.: Glazier, 1989) 104-5.

blessing, between bondage and freedom, and yet for the dramatic sake of Israel's history, there is. The wilderness is the land of judgment, itself a purgatorial state of existence. The community is judged to remain in a liminal land, between curse and blessing, for another forty years. Although the reverse expulsion or deliverance from Egypt, the land of curse, is heretofore incomplete, the story of Israel in the wilderness does not end in complete failure, trapped in a land of judgment. Unlike Cain, Israel is not condemned to subsist off a liminal land, never to return to the 'ǎdāmâ. The chain of sequence that leads from obedience to occupation remains an ever potent possibility. As the telos of settled existence, the blessing of land remains intact, ever awaiting Israel's appropriation. The generational purge is designed to set the stage for a fresh start at reentry. The offspring of the old generation is destined to separate completely from their forebears in order to be joined to the land of Canaan (cf. Gen 2:24). This land of promise is the community's consummation.

As an aside from the Yahwist's narrative, it is noteworthy that the Deuteronomist describes this new beginning in the Mosaic memoirs of Israel's journey from Sinai to the Transjordan (Deut 1:1–4:43). The new generation consists of the children "who have not known today good and evil" (lō'-yādě'û hayyôm ṭôb wārā', 1:39). Of all the merismic formulations of "good and evil," this one is the closest to the Yahwist's description of the forbidden tree in Genesis 2.[210] For the Deuteronomist, this expression denotes the age of accountable discretion (cf. Isa 7:15). As children in the wilderness, the new generation is without the "knowledge of good and evil" and thus cannot be held accountable for Israel's rebellion. They were too young to appropriate the law given at Horeb/Sinai and are therefore not culpable for Israel's disobedience in the wilderness. They are innocent until proven guilty, for they enjoy the grace of late birth, as it were. This "knowledge of right and wrong" in the context of Israel's rebellion is the harbinger of judgment, as much as the forbidden tree was the precursor of curse for the disobedient couple. The lack of such knowledge in the same context is a reprieve, indeed a blessing poised to catapult a new generation into the land. In short, the Deuteronomist perceives what is implicit in the Yahwist's narrative: a return to the blessing of innocence and communal integrity. This new and innocent generation signals the need for a fresh appropriation of the law of Horeb/Sinai on the plains of Moab, with the previous generation, dead and gone, serving as the negative example.[211]

210. So also Clark, "Legal Background," 274.
211. Within the larger pentateuchal narrative sequence, Deuteronomy marks a second promulgation of tôrâ for a new generation in order to constitute this new Israel as

Eden Recultivated

What precisely is Israel's destination beyond the wasteland, according to the Yahwist? A revealing clue is given, as one might expect, near the end of the epic (at least in its received form), in the final contest between curse and blessing (Numbers 22–24). Balaam, a pagan seer,[212] is hired by Balak, king of Moab, to curse Israel into a weakened state, for "they are stronger than I; perhaps I shall be able to defeat them and drive them from the land" (22:6). Balak echoes Pharaoh's fear (Exod 1:9-10): Israel's power has become dangerously excessive, posing a threat to the kingdoms of the earth. Counteractive measures are required: enslavement and infanticide, as in the case of Egyptian hegemony, or curse and expulsion, Moab's stratagem. Yet it all comes to naught: Balaam is compelled to bless Israel. He cannot "go beyond the command of Yahweh" (Num 22:18). Any prospect of curse is thwarted by divine constraint: Balaam, the master of malediction, becomes the purveyor of blessing.

The way the narrative recounts Yahweh's compulsion on Balaam in the so-called tale of Balaam's ass is noteworthy vis-à-vis the garden story. The donkey sees the angel with a drawn sword blocking Balaam's journey with the Moabite officials to curse Israel (22:23). Balaam strikes his beast of burden on three occasions, attempting to force it to keep to the way, but to no avail. The animal eventually speaks, and Balaam's eyes are opened to behold the angel with the drawn sword before him, prompting a profession of sin (v. 34). The angel allows Balaam to continue his journey, but with the proviso that he "speak only what I tell you to speak" (v. 35). This tale is more than a humorous incident about a talking animal and a surprised seer. It is the mirror image of the garden story. Whereas the talking serpent lured the primal couple into disobedience that resulted in their banishment from the garden, barred by a flaming sword, the donkey prevents Balaam from being killed by the sword-drawn angelic guardian.[213] That the divine guardian permits Balaam in his obedience to continue on his way rather than sending him back home is highly significant. Balaam is about to enter a vision that far surpasses that of any angel. Indeed, through his perceptual powers Balaam models the right confluence of obedience and knowledge:

---

landed and just community. See S. D. McBride Jr., "Polity of the Covenant People," *Int* 41 (1987) 229-44.

212. For background information on this enigmatic figure, see M. Barré, "The Portrait of Balaam in Numbers 22–24," *Int* 51 (1997) 255-67; J. Milgrom, *Numbers* (JPS Torah Commentary; Philadelphia: Jewish Publication Society, 1990) 469-76.

213. So also Coote and Ord, *Bible's First History*, 293.

"the oracle of the man whose eye is clear, the oracle of one who hears the words of God, and knows the knowledge of Elyon, who sees the vision of Shaddai, who falls down, but with his eyes uncovered" (24:16). Inverting the epistemology of disobedience, as demonstrated by the primal couple, is Balaam, the pagan seer, whose knowledge is founded on humble obedience, on *shema*, yet whose eyes are open (cf. Gen 3:5, 7). What Balaam sees is nothing short of the Yahwist's vision of the land as Eden, the ethos of Israel's telos (Num 24:5-9).

5 How fair are your tents, O Jacob,
   your encampments, O Israel!
6 Like palm groves that stretch out,
   like gardens beside a river,
   like aloes that Yahweh has planted,
   like cedar trees beside the water.
7 Water shall flow from their buckets,
   and their seed shall have abundant water.
   Their king shall be higher than Agag,
   and their kingdom shall be exalted.
8 God who freed them from Egypt
   is like the horns of a wild ox for them.
   They shall devour enemy nations and break their bones.
   They shall crush their arrows.
9 They crouch, they lie down like a lion,
   and like a lioness; who dares rouse them?
   Blessed is everyone who blesses you,
   and cursed is everyone who curses you.

The oracle, commonly considered an example of early Hebrew poetry and dated earlier than Balaam's two previous oracles, is probably not the free invention of the Yahwist but was, nonetheless, incorporated by the Yahwist into the narrative for a particular purpose.[214] The blessing opens with an ascription of beauty or goodness *(ṭôb)*[215] to Jacob's encampments and moves immediately to the lush image of a grove of various trees, planted by Yahweh and watered by a river, a veritable Eden,[216] and concludes with a cross refer-

214. For a sampling of the various approaches to and theories about dating the Balaam oracles, see D. Olson, *The Death of the Old and the Birth of the New: The Framework of the Book of Numbers and the Pentateuch* (BJS 71; Chico, Calif.: Scholars Press, 1985) 154-55.

215. See Gen 3:6; 24:16; Cant 4:10.

216. For the correspondence with Edenic images, see H. Rouillard, *La péricope de Balaam (Nombres 22–24): La prose et les "oracles"* (Ebib 4; Paris: Gabalda, 1985) 356-68.

ence to the Abrahamic blessing in Gen 12:3.[217] Three trees are identified, two of which are unique ecologically in the setting depicted in the oracle: the cedar, which does not grow beside rivers, and the aloe, which is not indigenous to Israel.[218] This taxonomy of trees envelops Balaam's garden with a mythic aura. Water is an equally prominent image in Num 24:6-7, mentioned no less than four times; "river" (*nāhār*, v. 6a) "water" (*mayim*, vv. 6b, 7a), and "abundant water" (*mayim rabbîm*, v. 7aβ). The last reference introduces a mixed metaphor: abundant water will be provided for Israel's "seed" or progeny.[219] The series of poetic images marks a shift from flora to human fauna that escalates in intensity as well as in social significance. In light of the larger movement of the oracle, the irenic landscape of the well-watered garden changes into the aggressive image of a raging lion (v. 9a). Indeed, the sequence of water and botanical images anticipates such a shift: the "abundant water" can also denote surging power,[220] and the reference to "seed" denotes a new generation. Replenishing the soil with "abundant water," a veritable flood of blessing, enables the seed of a kingdom, no less, to take root. Water is harnessed to sustain the royal images that follow, from exalted king to ox and lion. As blessing, the surging water with which Israel's seed is irrigated serves to sustain life and confer power.

The oracle moves effortlessly from garden to kingdom, from peace to power. In the poetic hyperbole of prophetic oracles, Israel is Eden recultivated. The "gardens beside a river" are more than simply a "reminder" of an Eden of the remote past.[221] Eden has in fact materialized among Israel's tents. Balaam's oracle is prophetic in the sense that securing Israel's share of a land yet to be occupied is held firmly in view (cf. 24:17). Israel's future empire springs forth from the soil of settled existence, not from a wilderness of aim-

217. Wolff noted this deliberate reference to the patriarchal blessing but failed to develop the larger relationship between the images of Eden and the blessing ("Kerygma of the Yahwist," 62).

218. See E. W. Davies, *Numbers* (NCBC; Grand Rapids: Eerdmans, 1995) 269. In addition, the word for "aloes" (*'ăhālîm*, v. 6) appears to be an intentional pun on "tents" (*'ōhālîm*, v. 5).

219. Scholars are split over whether the "seed" is to be taken literally to denote botanical life or figuratively to denote human progeny (see Davies, *Numbers,* 270). Milgrom adopts the idiosyncratic translation of "root" (*Numbers,* 204), but if such a meaning were intended, one would expect the more typical *šōreš.* Within the larger movement of the unit, I take v. 7a to be transitional; thus "seed" is a double entendre in this context. Otherwise, the reference to kingdom immediately following in v. 7b is too abrupt.

220. See the survey of H. G. May, "Some Cosmic Connotations of *Mayim Rabbîm,* 'Many Waters,'" *JBL* 74 (1955) 9-21.

221. So Milgrom, *Numbers,* 204.

less wandering. The garden thus fulfills Israel's destiny in the land of blessing. More remarkable, however, is that Balaam portrays Israel's encampment in the wilderness *as* a garden, not journeying toward one. Jacob's tents in the threatening wilderness constitute the garden of delight. Like Isaac sowing seed amid the Philistines, Israel holds the seeds of the garden. With prophetic eyes, Balaam sees the encamped community as the epitome of Eden. As the harbinger of blessing, wandering Israel bears the garden on its shoulders as much as it carries the tablets of the law in its itineration. Israel's new generation embodies the garden planted by Yahweh, and from it a kingdom is to spring forth in the land. Israel is the "national equivalent of the garden of Eden."[222] Israel is granted not only the gift of discernment through *tôrâ* but also the gift of life through the land. Yet, as Balaam's blessing makes graphically clear, blessing is ultimately lodged within the community, even in a wasteland.[223] The unity between knowledge and life, cultivated by the sages and rent asunder in the garden, is joined together in the law. This too is Yahweh creating something new.

Nevertheless, moral failure raises its head for the final time. Following the sublime vision of Israel's flourishing as the Edenic garden, Israel's apostasy in the highlands of Peor is all the more abominable (25:1-5). In the same way the irenic state of the garden serves as a foil for the couple's disobedience and curse, the blessing announced by Balaam sets Israel's tragic failure at Peor in the sharpest possible relief.[224] Yet Israel's blessing is not forfeited, since the final apostasy also marks the complete extinction of the first generation, paving the way for a new entry into the land. What is required is a purge of the community, a pruning of the garden. So ends the extant sweep of the Yahwist's epic.

The Garden and the Kingdom:
The Yahwist's Socioliterary Setting

Balaam's oracle presents Israel from both internal and external perspectives. Internally, Israel embodies the garden and with it the blessings of abundance and equity. The garden is Israel's ethos, its "dwelling." Externally, however, the garden's ethos goes only so far. Israel is a raging lion

222. Coote and Ord, *Bible's First History,* 295-96.
223. As Müller points out, the recipient of blessing is always human or divine in the biblical traditions ("Segen im Alten Testament," 224).
224. Olson, *Death of the Old,* 162.

ready to devour the nations. Israel's external relations are characterized by dominance and aggression. No true kinship is to be had with Israel's neighbors. As the Yahwist was reluctant to embrace the prospect of complete reconciliation between Jacob and Esau,[225] so the narrator recounts the resistance Israel faces from Edom in its wilderness trek (Num 20:19-20). All in all, the Yahwist refrains from extending the garden's ethos, its setting of kinship mutuality and harmony, as embodied, for example, by Joseph and his brothers, beyond the particular contours of Israel's own identity. Domination characterizes Israel's relations with the families qua nations of the earth. Yet the Yahwist provides some justification for this formidable picture of hegemony. The context of Balaam's curse provides the crucial setting for the language of power with which his oracles, particularly the third and fourth, are rife. Moab seeks Israel's destruction from the land. The rich agricultural language ascribed to Jacob's encampment in the third oracle suggests that Israel in the wilderness is like a fruit waiting to be plucked. Like the forbidden tree, Israel cannot be seized without dire consequences, a point that the prophet Jeremiah makes in his own recounting of the wilderness tradition: "Israel was holy to Yahweh, the firstfruits of his harvest. All who ate of it were held guilty; disaster came on them, says Yahweh" (2:3). Unlike Abel, Israel cannot be the martyr of blessing but rather its champion. Israel's kingdom marks no less than the triumph of blessing. In a land of conflict, social existence is established only by the extension of power; and such power, from the Yahwist's standpoint, is the fruit of blessing. Like Cain's mark, blessing is Israel's protection.

Yet qualification is also evident from the Yahwist's pen. As the patriarchs, particularly Isaac, modeled an ethos of covenantal coexistence and blessing with their neighbors in the land,[226] Israel's national destiny is to bring about blessing for "all the families of the earth" (Gen 12:3; 18:18; 28:14;

---

225. Gen 33:12-17 (see above).

226. The contrast between Balaam's oracle and the patriarchal narratives is striking. As bearers of blessing, Israel's ancestral families do not attain dominance in the land but rather find peaceful coexistence in the land through covenant making. (See, e.g., the covenant between Abimelech and Isaac in Gen 26:26-33; Habel's discussion of "immigrant theology" in *Land Is Mine*, 115-33). By contrast, Moses and the Israelites meet only stiff resistance in the land of Canaan. With ancestral families developing into nations, the Yahwist presupposes in Balaam's blessing the rise of political power in the land. As a family, Israel's ancestors could by and large live peaceably among foreigners; as a nation, Israel must dominate the land for its own survival. Yet the concept of international blessing is by no means jettisoned in the latter case.

cf. 30:27).[227] Blessing remains the conduit of kinship, through which its sustaining waters, admittedly, can only dribble to a world fraught with conflict and coercion. Israel's garden is a kingdom in a less than perfect world, for it takes nothing short of a kingdom to preserve the garden and impart its blessing. As the primal man was the guardian (*šmr*) of the garden (Gen 2:15), so Israel must protect its community and habitation.

That the oracle moves fluidly from garden to kingdom suggests something of the Yahwist's social location. The monarchy is not a relic of history for the Yahwist, but a vibrant institution, indeed, a telos of patriarchal blessing (Gen 12:3). Yet the Yahwist does not subsume the garden under the kingdom. To the contrary, the kingdom arises organically out of the garden, like a towering cedar, whose king is "higher than Agag" (Num 24:7).[228] The difference is all the more striking in the case of the primeval garden. There, no ascendancy to power takes place; only a failed attempt is recounted. The primal couple's grab for knowledge and power result in self-degradation and exile rather than self-preservation, much less self-apotheosis.[229] Ostensibly, 'ādām is no majestic royal figure either in or out of paradise. If any royal connections underlie his character in the garden, the primal man is, at most, a stripped king. More accurately, he is, at the very least, an ordinary farmer from beginning to end.[230] For the Yahwist, hunters and warriors are the stereotypical candidates for royalty (see Gen 10:10-11). The "groundling's" vocation does not change outside the garden: he is to till and keep the soil in whatever state it is. Nevertheless, from the garden a kingdom can

227. For a thorough study of the syntactical and semantic issues surrounding the patriarchal blessing, see Wolff, "Kerygma of the Yahwist," 41-66. For more general treatments, see C. Westermann, *Blessing in the Bible and the Life of the Church* (tr. K. Crim; Philadelphia: Fortress, 1978) 29-33, 49-59; C. W. Mitchell, *The Meaning of BRK "to Bless" in the Old Testament* (SBLDS 95; Atlanta: Scholars Press, 1987) 29-78, 165-67; Müller, "Segen im Alten Testament," 220-51.

228. Cf. Num 23:21b, which refers to God as Israel's king.

229. Since wisdom is frequently associated with kingship and governance in biblical tradition (e.g., 1 Kgs 3:4-28; 4:29-34; 10:1-13; Prov 1:1; 8:14-16; 10:10, 13; 20:26, 28; 25:1-7; 28:2-3, 15-16; 29:2, 12, 14, 16; 30:27-31; 31:1-9), the Yahwist's critique of wisdom naturally extends to royal ideology as the purveyor of wisdom. See W. Brueggemann's analysis of the ideological connections between wisdom and the court in "The Social Significance of Solomon as a Patron of Wisdom," in *The Sage in Israel and the Ancient Near East* (ed. J. G. Gammie and L. G. Perdue; Winona Lake, Ind.: Eisenbrauns, 1990) 117-32.

230. See Hiebert, who cites Ezek 28:12-19 and Gen 1:26-28 as possible influences on those interpretations that see the 'ādām exclusively as a royal figure (*Yahwist's Landscape*, 61, 187n.92); and Van Seters's comparative observations in *Prologue to History*, 120-21. Cf., e.g., Coote and Ord, who describe Adam as a "sweatless figure" in the garden and thus a king (*Bible's First History*, 50).

be cultivated. The garden is indeed a forceful reminder of Israel's roots, and woe be to the king who forgets.[231]

The Yahwist is fully aware that agricultural practice and monarchic policy can conflict. As Oded Borowski notes, "an agrarian society cannot survive when a large portion of its labor force is engaged in activities away from home and is not available to attend to agricultural activities which have to be performed daily."[232] Borowski identifies two events in Israel's history in which agricultural concerns were the driving force behind social movements that checked the extension of royal power: the rebellion against Rehoboam, whose father, Solomon, had conscripted Israelites to implement the king's monumental building projects (1 Kgs 5:13-15 [MT 27-29]). Such forced labor would have interrupted necessary agricultural activities.[233] In addition, the social uprising that gave rise to Jehu's purge of the Omride dynasty had its roots in a particular patch of land: Jehu leaves the body of the Omride king Jehoram in Naboth's vineyard as a sign of poetic justice and proclaims: "'As surely as I saw yesterday the blood of Naboth and the blood of his sons,' says Yahweh, 'I will requite you on this plot of ground'" (2 Kgs 9:26). In both cases, the severance of land and people, of individual and property, is considered anathema.[234] For the Yahwist, it is nothing short of a violation of human integrity and identity.

As noted earlier, the Yahwist's cultural suspicion is aimed primarily at the city. Enoch, Babel, Sodom, Pithom, and Rameses are all, in the Yahwist's mind, urban centers founded on collective ambition and oppression in various degrees. Once an agriculturist, the condemned Cain was forced to become an urban culturist. More than any other social context, the city poses the prospect of transgressing the divinely ordained limits established for the flourishing of human life, the result of which is death or scattering. Admit-

---

231. In suggesting that the Yahwist's narrative was written in part to criticize the excessive concentration of royal power (cf. Gen 11:1-9), I am in fundamental disagreement with Coote and Ord's contention that J is merely a private document from David's reign aimed at reaching out to bedouin bands between the border of Palestine and Egypt (*Bible's First History*, 31-35). I find the elements of dissension and reform too pronounced to settle for royal, even Davidic, "authorship."

232. Borowski, *Agriculture in Iron Age Israel*, 9.

233. Borowski suggests that the leader of the rebellion and first king of the northern kingdom of Israel, Jeroboam, was more sympathetic to Israel's agricultural needs, given his new date for the celebration of Sukkot (*Agriculture in Iron Age Israel*, 9n.25).

234. For a perceptive treatment of the similar importance of land in prophetic discourse, see J. G. Mays, "Justice: Perspectives from the Prophetic Tradition" in *Prophecy in Israel: Search for an Identity* (ed. D. L. Petersen; IRT 10; Philadelphia: Fortress, 1987) 149-51 (repr. from *Int* 37 [1983] 5-17).

tedly, the garden, too, is not immune to such transgression. Human conduct is the crux. Yet the Yahwist clearly casts his lot in favor of the agrarian setting: it is from the fine and fertile soil that human identity was fashioned and Israel's ethos is to flourish. A kingdom cannot be built on a wasteland or on the backs of those who work the soil. Internally, a kingdom is cultivated from the abundance of the soil and not at the expense of the community's "social capital." Indeed, it is from such abundance that Israel qua kingdom can bless the nations of the earth. Agriculture, the Yahwist claims, is the backbone of Israel's culture, the ground of the kingdom, and it would be a moral triumph, no less, to have a king who "loved the soil" (cf. 2 Chr 26:10).

The Paradigm of Paradise: Ethos and Ethics

It is commonly assumed among biblical scholars of various stripes and interests that the central issue of the garden story is etiological in nature. Carol Meyers's treatment of the Yahwist's anthropogony is typical: the narrative "holds up the ephemeral state of Eden for a brief glimpse and then brings the humans at last into the real world. Why must this be so? Why must humans experience harsh reality? The narrative provides an etiological response to the precariousness of Israelite life."[235] But that is only half the story. The mythos of the garden also upholds an ethos that maintains an enduring presence, hovering above the fray and at the same time residing deep within the tales of entanglements. The tensions and turns in the narrative, from Cain's curse to Balaam's blessing, reflect the various ways in which the morphology of the Eden myth performs in human history. For example, without the garden the moral pathos of Noah's vineyard or Abraham's sojourn in Egypt would be diluted, if not compromised. In these cases, the garden is at once critical and instructive; it presents a paradox of hope and judgment, a moral baseline that eschews moralism. As the new "man of the soil," the righteous Noah brings comfort to toilsome existence from the ground up, yet his consummate abilities at viticulture cannot beat a path back to the primal garden. As an ironic antidote to the tree in the middle of the garden, the fruit of Noah's vines brings about shame through loss of consciousness, whereas the forbidden fruit elicits shame by gaining consciousness. Noah's solitary attempt to enter the garden is deemed pathetic at best. Cultural regression is not the route.

By receiving the threefold blessing of land, progeny, and nationhood,

---

235. Meyers, *Discovering Eve*, 84. See also Van Seters, *Prologue to History*, 129; Ricoeur, *Symbolism of Evil*, 232-35.

Abraham, the obedient patriarch, is also introduced as a new Adam who bears the promise of reversing the curse of expulsion. Yet he sojourns in the land of the Nile and there reveals his duplicitous side in this Egyptian Eden by jeopardizing both his wife and the blessing, while enriching himself, a veritable perversion of life in the garden. More extreme is Lot's choice to live among the Sodomites in the valley that resembles "the garden of Yahweh," which is laid waste by depravity and judgment. In both cases, appearances of the garden in the harsh landscape are cruel mirages, yet the garden's spirit, its ethos, remains an ever present hope. Such is prominently the case with Jacob, whose return to the land of blessing and birth, his destiny, is an integral part of his pilgrimage as a "moral man," a trickster in transition.

As the Yahwist makes painfully clear, there is no enduring access to Eden in these locales and times. Egypt is not Israel's home, neither is Sodom or for that matter Haran, for both are cultivated by codes of deceit and oppression alien to the life, prefigured in the garden, to which Israel is called in covenant. The garden cannot flourish except on Israel's covenantally constituted soil. Eden must be homegrown. By linking the garden to Israel's settlement in the land, the Yahwist boldly claims that of the countless families of the earth only Israel carries the ethos of the garden into the realm of history to be planted in Canaan's soil. The garden is Israel's ethos, its God-given dwelling for the flourishing of community.

From a material standpoint, humanity's role in the garden is preeminently agricultural. It is the man's primal vocation; his very identity is bound up with the ground. The ecological implications for our modern industrial age are significant, even revolutionary, as Ted Hiebert aptly points out.[236] Although the Yahwist's respect for the land most certainly exceeds ours in many ways, the author of the epic is admittedly no environmentalist in any modern sense. The Yahwist is at root a historiographer[237] and is thus more concerned with the genesis and formation of Israel's national character, its faith and conduct, in short, its cultural and religious identity. When the plow and seed-drill are put to the soil, the task of culture making, even kingdom building, commences and a moral ethos is ready to be cultivated.

In a very basic sense, the soil coheres with the community: by working and preserving the soil, "to till it and keep it" (Gen 2:15; 3:24), the primal family preserves and cultivates itself. Moreover, the ground testifies against

236. Hiebert, *Yahwist's Landscape,* 140-62.
237. For a helpful discussion of history and historiography in biblical and ancient Near Eastern traditions, see J. Van Seters, *In Search of History* (New Haven: Yale University Press, 1983) 1-7, 227-48; idem, *Prologue to History,* 9-44, particularly his view of history as "national tradition" (pp. 34-38).

any breach within the community by preserving rather than swallowing up the blood of the victim (4:10-11). When Cain feigns ignorance over his brother's murder by asking sarcastically, "Am I my brother's keeper?" (4:9), the murderer convicts himself for having forced the ground to receive his brother's blood, rendering the soil impotent in his hands. Cain has abrogated his responsibility as a productive and caring member of the primal family; he has violated the bond of kinship. Similarly, when Laban forces Jacob into service with only slave wages and deceptive promises, he has deceitfully undermined his own proclamation of kinship with his nephew. In the garden, the man's relationship to the soil and to his companion reflects a moral coherence of the community that also coheres with the environment. The man's kinship is with both his companion and the ground, with community and vocation, all inextricably related to his identity. As much as the primal woman is defined as "helper" in relation to the man — that is, as an equal partner for support, commitment, and affection — so the community is configured to promote such values as the fruits of blessing.

As embodied by the human inhabitants of the garden, the Yahwist imparts a high and holistic view of work that cuts to the very core of human identity. In the soil lies not only nature's inviolable dignity, but also and more concretely humanity's. When humanity is alienated from the soil, for whatever reason, through curse, corvée, or royal covetousness,[238] the land lies fallow and the community becomes morally stagnant, indeed violated. It is no accident that central to the Yahwist's history is the portrayal of Israel's ancestral household living off the land. The community, indeed the kingdom, began as a family farm, for therein lies the most familiar form of kinship with the soil and community. From the dirt of the soil, the man proceeds inexorably to the bone of his bones, from ground to woman, from genesis to community. Yet Israel's ethos is by no means limited to family values; its mission of blessing is to "all the families of the ground (*'ădāmâ*)" (Gen 12:3), an international shalom. While the Abrahamic promise of land is realized in Israel's occupation of the land of Canaan and the kingdom is the realization of the blessing of "great nationhood," the international blessing, for the Yahwist, remains to be fulfilled in Israel's telos.

In the beginning was an ethos, formed in Eden's womb and nurtured by a dialectic of freedom and commandment. As the primal couple was granted free reign over the garden, they were also given an interdiction, a primal *tôrâ*.

---

238. The story of Naboth's vineyard (1 Kgs 21:1-29) is a classic example of royal covetousness that violates familial land inheritance (v. 3).

On the one hand, freedom is defined within certain limits and presupposes the possibility of violating such limits: the primal couple's grab for divine autonomy, the Shinarites' encroachment on the heavenly realm (Gen 11:1-9), Israel's potential to transgress the boundary of holiness (e.g., Exod 19:12-13a; 20–23). On the other hand, freedom is nurtured through the equitable abundance of provision. Whether in the garden or in the wilderness, God provides, making possible an integrity embodied in community. As an icon of blessing, Eden represents not only an enduring trust in the beneficence of the earth but also a resilient faith in God as provider, whether as garden cultivator, blessing giver, or covenant maker. As the garden story passionately illustrates, genuine community requires the meeting of needs; community is formed by addressing certain lacks. Yahweh recognizes the man's need for a companion and creates a host of living beings until the man can identify his match. The correspondence of need and fulfillment, lack and provision, drives the garden story onward. In provision, the man is granted the freedom to select his match and discover for himself the profound joy of community in its most intimate form. The man is as free in determining the nature of community as the Creator is doggedly persistent in creating it for him. Such divine tenacity carries over for sojourning couples in the land and even for the rabble in the wilderness.

Yet genuine needs must be distinguished from false ones. In gracious provision comes responsibility. Although a necessary condition, the material abundance of blessing is not sufficient for Israel's ethos to take root. By issuing a prohibition in the garden, the Yahwist stresses the primacy of law over wisdom, of community over material blessing or beauty. Wisdom, however delightfully edifying in form, lends itself all too easily to manipulation; it is something to be grasped and subsumed rather than received and appropriated. Indeed, the appropriation of law for the Yahwist safeguards the community from the temptations and dangers of wisdom. The grab for wisdom comes from a false need, one that undermines the community yet is authentically human. The Yahwist's view of humanity is neither naive nor fatalistic. The human sphere is not a freedomless zone, but a tangled mass of competing impulses and needs on which the person is free to act or not act. The primal couple, out of choice from a perceived lack, partook. Yahweh counsels Cain over his need to find a way to restore himself without violence, a destructive, false need over which Cain must gain mastery. By contrast, divine command or *tôrâ* is life sustaining, promoting right relations and self-control. Like the forbidden fruit, obedience leads to knowledge, but of a kind that apprehends not human vulnerability and curse, but God and blessing: "show me *your ways*, so that I may *know* you and *find favor* in your sight,"

Moses petitions Yahweh before the divine "goodness" *(ṭôb)* is revealed to him (Exod 33:13, 19).[239]

Noah, Abraham, Isaac, Jacob, Moses, Caleb, and even the pagan Balaam all obey God. "Listening to Yahweh's voice," they are all practitioners of *shema*, and therein lies their righteousness. Abraham's obedience, in particular, permits him to exercise his freedom in contexts fraught with moral dilemmas. That his behavior is sometimes questionable, however, is not a matter of *tôrâ* commandment per se but of a larger ethos, an integrity of being that is equally mandated: "Be a blessing" (Gen 12:2). Jacob, the "grasper" himself, is transformed from a "smooth man" into a "moral man," thereby filling the ethical gap left vacant by his forebears, particularly Abraham, and *tôrâ*. Integrity has become Jacob's (Israel's) vocation as much as tilling the soil was the first man's. Both require arduous cultivation. In the person of Jacob, the blessing of the land fits hand in glove with the power of integrity. Israel fulfills its destiny as a community of integrity not by grasping wisdom through cunning for its own enrichment but by appropriating the law and the ethos for its instruction, the *tôrâ* that descends from the holy mountain and the ethos that springs forth from the garden.

Throughout the family history, the Yahwist refrains from giving a blanket approval on the "knowledge" used for self-determination, the fruit of "wisdom." Quite the opposite, wisdom's deleterious effects are discerned from the various displays of cunning, from the serpent's to the patriarchs', which lead inexorably to further entanglements and potentially tragic results. The proclivity to take matters into one's own hands, whether out of fear, suspicion, or wanton self-gain, remains authentically human. Yet not all deceptive initiatives are inherently bad: Tamar's ruse in playing the temple prostitute is morally legitimated in the face of Judah's neglect of levirate responsibility (Gen 38:26). Through subterfuge, Tamar's father-in-law comes to acknowledge his sin of omission. Similarly, Joseph's deception effectively tests the moral mettle of his brothers and helps to achieve reconciliation in the end. In both cases, cunning is employed to highlight and resolve egregious violations of communal integrity.[240]

Given the moral ambivalence and complexity of the human creature, the Yahwist crowns his ethical vision with divine commandment. But it is

239. Admittedly, Exod 33:1-23 is disputed source critically. Noth sees it as "a conglomeration of secondary accretions" (*Pentateuchal Traditions*, 31n.114). Others, however, see vv. 12-23, at least, as Yahwistic, given the consistent use of the name "Yahweh" (e.g., Hiebert, *Yahwist's Landscape*, 169).

240. It is telling that these stories come near the end of the Yahwist's patriarchal history, whereas earlier incidents of subterfuge are by and large ambivalent.

to the credit of his moral imagination that the Yahwist also cultivates an ethos from the ground up: it is in the garden, the ground of shalom, that *tôrâ* finds its moral context, its dwelling. Israel's mission is to appropriate this context, the land of blessing, to fulfill the law. Israel needs the land in order to fulfill its ethical vocation as much as the land is in need of the community to realize its productive potential. The symbiosis of community and soil remains a constant in the Yahwist's national purview beyond the primal garden.

Through cultivation, a richness of moral living emerges from the soil that establishes as well as extends beyond the domain of codified law. In the Yahwist's geo-ethical landscape, the garden stands behind the mountain of the law, or perhaps resides at its pinnacle.[241] In either case, life within the garden is the embodied example, the glorious pattern to which the law points, an integrity within community and with the environment. Law plays a necessary and crucial role in the historical saga of Israel's formation as a covenantal community. As such, the law's function is not merely to condemn. On the contrary, *tôrâ* offers an entrance into the garden that can be crossed only through a life of obedience. Although *tôrâ* does not exhaust the garden's ethos, it does offer the opportunity to unlock the garden's entrance for the community as much as adherence to the primal *tôrâ* permitted the couple to remain within the pastoral setting.

The Yahwist's *tôrâ* points to and presupposes this ethos of integrity: the erroneously called "decalogue" of Exod 34:11-26 moves freely between matters of worship and agriculture. Sabbath is mandated even during plowing and harvest (v. 21); "the best of the firstfruits of your ground you shall bring to the house of Yahweh your God" (v. 26). As with the two trees of the garden, Yahweh exerts sole prerogative over certain produce of the land. The impulse of the exodus is to attain the ground of right worship (Exod 7:16; 9:13). As with the ethos of the primeval mythos, law was an integral part of life in the garden. Law is not simply a "necessary evil" or a post hoc development as a consequence of the curse. Its roots are also found in the pristine integrity of the garden. Law serves as the linchpin of integrity for the Yahwist: adherence to the interdiction points to an integrity of trust both in God as sufficient provider and in the human partner as the sufficient source of community. Disobedience, signified by the grasping of wisdom, marks a betrayal of such trust. The ethos of the garden places law in its proper context, determining it

---

241. The latter is suggested in Fishbane's perceptive comparison of the garden mountain and Sinai, using Moses' encounter with the burning bush at the foot of the mountain as a linchpin (*Text and Texture*, 113-14).

as an instrument of liberty and the means of integrity: "You may freely eat of every tree of the garden, but . . ." (Gen 2:16); "Let my people go, so that they may worship me" (Exod 9:13).

Lodged deep in the shadows of archetypal memory, the imagery of Eden retains its powerful hold over the Yahwist's cultural consciousness, over his moral imagination, offering glimpses of redemption in a landscape marred by possessiveness and pride. On a cultural terrain ever shifting from the quakes of international conflict and conquest, the garden provides a stable dwelling for social existence. On the rugged ground of Canaan's hill country, the Yahwist beckons the community to reenter and embody the garden, to return home and obey. As exemplars of ambivalence, of moral failure and triumph, Israel's ancestors could only intimate in various degrees the life of Edenic integrity, while falling short of embodying it fully. Indeed, they only bore the promise. But with Israel's ancestors long dead and the establishment of the kingdom in firm sight, the time is ripe to embody the blessing, to claim the land and its ethos as a moral triumph and mission for the world's sake — so the Yahwist claims for his community.

Without the blessing, the garden appears only as an impossible ideal, blissfully remote from the constant struggles for dominance and control or from the obsessive quests for primacy and honor. In the garden, all intimations of violence, manipulation, and even shame are banished. Eden is a haven for integrity. Yet the garden does not remain floating like a disembodied spirit, ethereal and out of reach. The Yahwist could easily have depicted a "hanging garden," one suspended inaccessibly above the fray of tragic human existence. Instead, the Yahwist has God planting the garden firmly on the ground, in the same soil from which the man himself was fashioned. The author of the epic boldly claims that despite humanity's successive separations from the garden, the garden still provides the tangible setting for renewal and redemption. The garden, to reverse a well-known phrase, is the "possible impossibility."[242] Israel is called on to embody the garden, and the means to such embodiment is the power of blessing, which beginning in Gen 12:1-3 "ex-

---

242. Cf. R. Niebuhr's moral paradox: "the vision of a just society is an impossible one, which can be approximated only by those who do not regard it as impossible" (*Moral Man and Immoral Society*, 81; also 82, 34-35, 266). The phrase "impossible possibility," employed first in his *Interpretation of Christian Ethics* (New York: Harper, 1935), denoted for Niebuhr the unattainable ideal of realizing the self-negating ethic of love within the complexities of the national and international contexts. For an illuminating discussion of the differences between Niebuhr's and K. Barth's use of this phrase to denote the unreality of sin, see J. Bettis, "Theology and Politics: Karl Barth and Reinhold Niebuhr on Social Ethics after Liberalism," *Religion and Life* 48 (1979) 53-62.

tends through the patriarchal stories like a red line."[243] That thread marks nothing less than a path to Israel's moral destiny "back to the future" in the garden. Similarly, the prophet Malachi makes the claim: "'All nations will count you blessed, for you will be a land of delight,' says Yahweh of hosts" (Mal 3:12). In short, the possibility of the garden is not an unattainable ideal for the Yahwist. The garden's ethos retains an ontology that emerges out of divine blessing, which itself bears both moral force and gracious provision. The garden is an elusive ideal in the land of curse, but within the domain of blessing, Eden becomes palpably real.

To return to the Genesis garden, to the land before shame and beyond culture, involves a moral advancement, not a regression, a reawakening, not a reversion to an unconscious state. Israel, much less human culture, cannot return by reversing consciousness, as the Yahwist makes clear in Noah's case. Nevertheless, a path can be beaten to the garden by reaching a "second naïveté," by appropriating an ethos nurtured in the garden, borne aloft by blessing and risen from the ravages of curse.[244] Eden is no longer accessible in its pristine immediacy. The flaming sword remains. Moreover, the "first naïveté" of the garden was the primal world, a world devoid of cultural consciousness. The Yahwist does not call his community back to a precultural state in which everyone is naked and unashamed. Yet the Yahwist does call Israel to a life in which individuals are genuinely acknowledged as subjects of worth and objects of respect and care. The garden remains an integral part of the Yahwist's moral imagination, informing and shaping Israel's destiny and conduct in the land. In short, the garden remains barred from grasping and unreachable by regression. But it does remain free for appropriation, at least partially so. Balaam's blessing is no fanciful dream.

What makes such appropriation possible is blessing, which denotes the transference of the powers of life, from fertility to dominion and divine favor.[245] As Eden was the archetype of blessing, so is it, according to the Yahwist, also blessing's consummation or telos. Thus blessing brackets the bulk of the Yahwist's historical narrative. Driven by blessing, Israel's deliver-

---

243. Von Rad, *Genesis*, 165.

244. Again, I find Ricoeur's hermeneutic useful. In the Yahwist's hands, the garden is a powerful symbol whose immediacy is lost after the couple's exile but whose formative influence can still be felt and even appropriated. In Ricoeur's own words, the "second naïveté" is "the mode of 'as if'" (Ricoeur, *Symbolism of Evil*, 19).

245. For blessing as "transference of power," see Westermann, *Blessing*, 52-53. See also the survey of the various benefits of divine blessing in Mitchell, *Meaning of BRK*, 62-78, 165.

ance and journey is unwaveringly oriented toward the fulfillment of bless-ing.[246] Moreover, the Yahwist imbues this blessing of power with moral nu-ance. Blessing is prescriptive; it connotes the power for integrity, and it is Balaam's blessing that propels Israel back to Eden. Perhaps the driving ques-tion for the Yahwist is not so much what the precise contours of this integrity are, to which the law points, as where such integrity can flourish, the "ground" of *tôrâ*. Again, Yahweh's initial question to the disobedient couple in the garden ("Where are you?") is primary.

For the Yahwist, integrity dwells on the bedrock of justice, on the ground that preserves the blood of the victim, such as Abel's, to cry out and require restitution. It dwells wherever potential enemies are joined together, reconciled, and share a meal. Such is the "consummation" of covenant. Integ-rity flourishes wherever one welcomes the other, not out of conquest or de-ception but out of mutual need, respect, and love. The garden's ethos plants itself wherever one looks into the face of a stranger and recognizes the other as oneself or as God (Gen 2:23; 32:30; 33:10). As limned in the garden and re-established by covenant, communion, divine and human, is the fundamental context in which integrity flourishes. Eden offers hope for a return, however painful or triumphal, to communion. Integrity emerges within the arena of right relationships and can be shared by means of blessing with all the fami-lies of the earth as much as the primal parents of humankind embodied it, however fleetingly. Israel's telos is a witness to humanity's integrity. Even Esau matures, Abimelech initiates a covenant, and Balaam blesses, all for Israel's sake, if not for the sake of the world. Far from being an arena of hopeless de-pravity, the world too can share in the integrity of shalom, recalling a time in which all peoples once "invoked the name of Yahweh" (4:26). The shalom of the garden, as the originative blessing for an original humanity, can only point to a time in which "the princes of the peoples gather as the people of the God of Abraham" under Yahweh, the cosmic king (Ps 47:8-9 [MT 9-10]), an era in which Israel is to be "a blessing in the midst of the earth, whom Yahweh of hosts has blessed, saying, 'Blessed be Egypt my people, and Assyria the work of my hands, and Israel my heritage'" (Isa 19:24-25).[247] Yet the

246. Westermann's rigid demarcation between blessing and deliverance breaks down, at least, in the Yahwist's epic (*Blessing*, 28). Eden's garden and its fulfillment por-tended by Balaam is just as miraculous a manifestation of blessing as Israel's exodus is a miraculous manifestation of deliverance. Furthermore, Israel's deliverance from Egypt, just as Abraham's and Sarah's expulsion from Egypt (Gen 12:10-20), is for the cause of em-bodying blessing in the land of promise.

247. For the universal scope of Israel's blessing, see also Jer 4:1-2; Zech 8:13, 23; Acts 3:25; Gal 3:8.

Yahwist is no more a "naivitist" than he is a nativist. Israel's God wields the power to curse those who would curse Israel (Num 24:9; Gen 12:3).

Nevertheless, as boldly as the Yahwist points to the world's potential integrity and Israel's definitive role within it, he critiques himself and his imagination falls short. The final series of blessings in the Yahwist's epic brazenly mixes irenic and violent images, of aloes and lions, symbols of peace and domination.[248] Despite the Yahwist's expansive claims, the garden's parameters remain by and large confined within Israel's national boundaries. Within the garden tyrants and lions have no place, while shalom and integrity do. Yet Israel is no insulated community cut off from the larger cultural milieu, from the ground of human existence. Israel has a blessing to share with the world so that the nations "may know that I Yahweh am in this land" (Exod 8:22 [MT 18]) and that they be taught *tôrâ* and peace (Isa 2:2-4). When the garden's tendrils embrace the world, even the "wolf and the lamb shall feed together, and the lion shall eat straw like the ox" in the banquet of blessing (Isa 65:25).[249] Transplanting the rich soil of the primordial garden, the author of Revelation envisions a cosmopolis of paradise, not a garden per se but a city in which the tree of life stands and whose leaves "are for the healing of the nations" (Rev 22:2). As much as Israel's ethos partakes of humanity's *protos*, Israel's *telos* is to be shared by the nations. Through blessing the world reaps a harvest of reconciliation; by blessing the chaos of curse is transformed into an oasis of order.[250]

---

248. Num 24:5-9 (see above); see also vv. 17-19; 23:24.

249. The following colon states, however, "but as for the serpent — its food shall be dust!" Even this prophet of the restoration could not imagine all the inhabitants of the land blessed and transformed (cf. Isa 11:6-9).

250. See Müller's discussion of the world-structuring power of blessing, "Segen im Alten Testament," 246-48.

CHAPTER 4

"I Am about to Do a New Thing": *Yahweh's Victory Garden* *in Second Isaiah*

As the years went by and age overtook her, there was something comical yet touching in her bedraggled appearance on this awesome occasion . . . her studied absorption in the implausible notion that there would be yet another spring, . . . sitting there with her detailed chart under those dark skies in the dying October, calmly plotting the resurrection.

E. B. White[1]

My friend, we have cut down the towering Cedar whose top scrapes the sky.

Enkidu[2]

1. E. B. White, "Introduction," in K. S. White, *Onward and Upward in the Garden* (ed. E. B. White; Toronto: McGraw-Hill Ryerson, 1979) xix.
2. Tablet V of the Epic of Gilgamesh, translated by M. G. Kovacs, *The Epic of Gilgamesh* (Stanford: Stanford University Press, 1989) 46.

A s the Yahwist transports Israel across the wilderness to the garden of promise on the wings of an old seer's blessing, an unnamed prophet of the exile ("Second Isaiah") pulls Israel back to the wilderness with the cord of judgment to lay claim to a different kind of garden. The rhetorical landscape on which the prophet stands is a smoldering, barren wasteland, a land of judgment and fire,[3] a scene that recalls at least two related harrowing scenes: (1) Historically, it recalls the conflagration of Jerusalem conducted by the Babylonian captain of the guard, Nebuzaradan (2 Kgs 25:8-11; Isa 64:11); and (2) literarily, this desolate terrain recalls the terrifying scene of devastation with which "First Isaiah" opens: a land desiccated and devoured by foreigners, cities burned with fire, and besieged Zion left as a mere lean-to, the most fragile of shelters (Isa 1:7-9).[4] The resulting wasteland[5] is the concrete manifestation of cosmic chaos or *tōhû*, to which the prophet frequently refers.[6]

Yet this lifeless landscape is not destined to remain so. Yahweh is not to be sought in an empty wasteland (*tōhû*, 45:18-19). The desolate terrain provides merely the backdrop for an imminent transformation that conjoins images drawn from culture and horticulture,[7] to reshape the contours of the exilic community on the eve of its deliverance. Such a dramatic transformation of nature is set within the larger cosmic framework: Yahweh is poised from on high as the consummate creator without rival, whose hands have "stretched out" (*nṭh*) the heavens above (40:22; 42:5; 45:12; 48:13; 51:13)[8] and

---

3. Isa 42:24-25; cf. 1:5-7; 9:18-21; 34:9-10; 64:10-11.

4. This opening scene in the book of Isaiah is usually thought to describe the aftermath of Sennacherib's invasion of Jerusalem's environs in 701 BCE. See, e.g., J. T. Willis, "An Important Passage for Determining the Historical Setting of a Prophetic Oracle — Isaiah 1.7-8," *ST* 39 (1985) 158-62; C. Seitz, *Isaiah 1–39* (Interpretation; Louisville: John Knox, 1993) 32; but cf. E. Ben Zvi, "Isaiah 1:4-9, Isaiah, and the Events of 701 BCE in Judah: A Question of Premise and Evidence," *SJOT* 5/1 (1991) 95-111; J. H. Hayes and S. A. Irvine, *Isaiah, the Eighth-Century Prophet: His Times and His Preaching* (Nashville: Abingdon, 1987) 72-73.

5. Heb. *ḥorbâ* ("waste place"; 44:26; 49:19; 51:3) or *šōmēmâ* ("desolate"; 49:8, 19). Related terms include *midbār* ("wilderness"; 40:3; 41:18-19; 43:19-20; 50:2; 51:3), *yĕšîmôn* ("desert"; 43:19-20), *yabbāšâ* ("thirsty"; 44:3; cf. the cognate in 40:7-8, 24), *'ereṣ ṣîyâ* ("desert"; 35:1; 41:18; 53:2), and *ṣāmē'* ("thirsty land"; 44:3).

6. Of all the biblical corpora, Second Isaiah contains the highest concentration of this term. See Isa 34:11; 40:17; 40:23; 41:29; 44:9; 45:18-19; 49:4; cf. Gen 1:2; Jer 4:23; Isa 24:10; 29:21; 59:4. This chaos of dryness and desolation referred to by the prophet is the material opposite of the watery "chaos" limned in Gen 1:2.

7. The agricultural scene of 55:10-11 notwithstanding, the prophet draws his botanical images primarily from the realm of horticulture (see below).

8. Cf. 54:2-3, in which the tent imagery corresponds to the resettlement of Zion. Also cf. 51:16, in which the MT has the heavens planted (*nṭ'*) rather than spread out (*nṭh*),

"laid the foundation" *(ysd)* of the earth below (48:13; 51:13, 16) to create something new.[9] What happens between heaven's vault and the earth's firmament in Second Isaiah is the focus of this chapter.

Creation's Germination

Surveying the images and elements of creation, one need not look far to find numerous references to plant growth in Second Isaiah. Rich with metaphors and images drawn from the realm of horticulture, the prophet's discourse limns a remarkable range of botanical diversity — from the lowly brier (55:13) to the most majestic of trees, the cedar of Lebanon (41:19; 44:14) — unmatched anywhere else in biblical literature, Second Isaiah contains a veritable catalogue of flora, without much fauna (cf. 43:20). Yet this semantic field, rich as it is, remains by and large neglected in standard studies of creation theology. For example, Carroll Stuhlmueller's otherwise exhaustive treatment of Second Isaiah's creation vocabulary entirely ignores this dimension of the prophet's portrayal of *creatio continuata*.[10] Such neglect is understandable. Most students of biblical creation have tended to focus on creation references from the top down, that is, from the perspective of divine activity subduing the dark and dangerous forces of chaos or commanding structure from formless mass. To be sure, the prophet draws from these perspectives too, but Second Isaiah's creation theology emerges primarily from the ground up, as it were. Typical neglect of this dimension is ironic, since the botanical realm forms the indispensable basis for the prophet's worldview and ethos. Two examples will suffice to demonstrate the deliberate link between divine act and plant growth forged by this prophet of the exile.

First, in 42:9 the prophet employs a standard verb for germination, *ṣāmaḥ*, to refer metaphorically to Yahweh's new creation. At the climax of the first "servant song" Yahweh declares that whereas the "former things"

---

either a clever wordplay or the result of textual corruption. Given the lack of textual variants, except for the Peschitta, I opt for the former. See n. 171.

9. The architectural image coheres with that of the temple in 44:28 and 54:11. Elsewhere, the earth's genesis is described as spread or stamped out (*rqʿ*; 42:5; 44:24; Ps 136:6; cf. Isa 40:19 [gold overlay]; Exod 39:3 [plates of gold]; Num 16:38-39 [MT 17:3-4] [hammered plates]).

10. C. Stuhlmueller, *Creative Redemption in Deutero-Isaiah* (AnBib 43; Rome: Pontifical Biblical Institute, 1970) 209-29. So also B. C. Ollenburger, "Isaiah's Creation Theology," *Ex Auditu* 3 (1987) 54-71. R. A. Simkins's comprehensive work provides only a cursory glance at the botanical references in Second Isaiah (*Creator and Creation: Nature in the Worldview of Ancient Israel* [Peabody, Mass.: Hendrickson, 1994] 104-5, 149, 242).

(hāri'šōnôt) have come to pass *(bā'û),* "new things" *(hădāšôt)* are now declared before they "sprout forth" *(ṣāmaḥ).* The prophet could have easily employed a colorless parallel to the verbal root *bw'* ("to come") in the second colon, such as *hāyâ* or *yāṣā',* to describe the imminent arrival of the "new things." Rather, the author chose to use a distinctively botanical referent.[11] Similarly, in 43:19 the "new thing" *(hădāšâ)* that Yahweh announces is something that sprouts onward and upward *(ṣmḥ)* for immediate apprehension by the prophet's audience. In this case, Yahweh's "new thing" involves the reversal of the natural elements of earth and water that played such significant roles in the exodus: whereas a dry way once split the mighty waters that extinguished Pharaoh's army (43:16), river paths now cut through the parched wasteland to provide drink to Israel, prompting praise even from jackals and ostriches (43:20-21). Again, the divinely created new thing is described primarily in terms of botanical growth.[12] Yahweh's *hădāšâ* is a decisively new act of creation. That it is described as sprouting out of the soil in no way diminishes, rhetorically or theologically, the creative force of divine action.

Second, the most dramatic correlation between divine activity and botanical growth occurs in 55:10-11.

10 For[13] as the rain and the snow descend from heaven
      and do not return there
          unless[14] they have saturated the land,
          causing[15] it to produce and sprout forth,
          giving seed to the sower and food to the consumer,
11 so my word that issues out of my mouth
      shall not return to me,
      that is, return empty,

11. See Gen 2:5, 9; Pss 104:14; 147:8; Isa 42:9; 43:19; 44:4; 45:8; 55:10.

12. The only other substantive use of *hădāšâ* in Second Isaiah occurs in 48:6; v. 7 describes them as "created now" *('attâ nibrĕ'û).* The preference for the technical verb *bārā'* suggests a certain parallel with *ṣāmaḥ,* thereby confirming the crucial significance of the latter verb.

13. The introductory *kî* sets this passage within the larger framework of repentance and return (vv. 7-8), suggesting that the "return" of Yahweh's word (v. 11) is bound up with the return of Yahweh's people (vv. 7, 12).

14. Contra R. J. Clifford's translation, the conjunction *kî-'im* introduces an exceptive rather than adversative clause (*Fair Spoken and Persuading* [New York: Paulist, 1984] 189-90; but cf. GKC §163cd. The tense change in vv. 10aα-β and 11bα confirms the exceptive use of the conjunction (see Gen 32:27).

15. The series of three *wĕqāṭal* forms denote action simultaneous to or immediately following the land's saturation *(hirwâ).*

> unless[16] it has accomplished that which I have purposed,
> succeeding in the thing for which I sent it.

The language of agriculture is part of a larger meteorological scenario that corresponds to the creative potency of divine discourse. Yahweh's word is likened to precipitation from the heavens refreshing *(rwh)* the thirsty land.[17] The word of the Deity is as much an enlivening word for nature as it is a sustaining one for Jacob and Zion.[18] The earth testifies to the potency of the divine word through what it produces to sustain human life (v. 10b). As the precipitation enables the ground to produce life *(yld* and *smh)*, so also the divine decree, the analogy claims. The apodosis in v. 11 is left vague regarding the tangible results of God's word. The goal of Yahweh's word is not given specific content in this extended simile; it is left hanging on the parallel horticultural imagery conveyed in the protasis. Whatever Yahweh's purpose is,[19] it is intimately bound up with the fructification of the land.

Of note in this passage are the striking references to the forward and returning movement that characterize the meteorological and discursive realms: precipitation descends and returns in analogous fashion to Yahweh's word, which issues forth and returns filled. Such language is unique to the meteorological realm. What is meant by precipitation "returning" *(šûb)* to the heavens? From simple observation, precipitation is a one-way event. (The evaporative cycle was not common knowledge among the ancients.) Given the parameters of the analogy, the "return" of precipitation is equated with the fructified land. The simile acknowledges that the cosmos is ordered by Yahweh such that precipitation is not without its salutary effect on the soil, enabling life to flourish in return for such provision. Water is not wasted on the parched ground in the di-

---

16. As in the previous verse, this clause is also exceptive. The new variable is the addition of the word "empty" *(rêqām)*, which implies that the divine word is to return filled, as opposed to empty (see below).

17. The only other use of this verb in Second Isaiah is in 43:24, in which Yahweh complains of Jacob's neglect in "satisfying" him with the fat of sacrifices. The verb is set antithetically to *yg'*, "to weary." Consequently, the verb signifies, along with the physical image of watering, the sense of refreshing and sustaining the weary.

18. Cf. the reference to the servant's discursive power to sustain the weary in 50:4. For the translation issues, see A. Laato, *The Servant of YHWH and Cyrus: A Reinterpretation of the Exilic Messianic Programme in Isaiah 40–55* (ConBOT 35; Stockholm: Almqvist & Wiksell International, 1992) 123.

19. The term that denotes divine purpose, *ḥāpaṣ*, is related to the noun *ḥēpeṣ*, which comprises the actions of both the servant (53:10) and Cyrus (44:28; 46:10-11; 48:14). The only other instance of this noun in Second Isaiah occurs in the description of the gloriously restored Jerusalem, whose walls are to be laid with "precious stones" *('abnê-ḥēpeṣ)* in 54:12.

vine economy of creation (cf. Job 38:24-27). Furthermore, precipitation is part of a cycle within a cycle: the agricultural cycle brings about this cycle of precipitation. So also the divine word: Yahweh's utterance is no futile exercise, for it cannot be thwarted from its intended purpose. Yahweh's word does not return "empty," but is "filled" to completion (cf. Isa 40:2).[20] Like the rain that restores the land, the divine word enlivens and sustains a people for a particular purpose. The return is the result.

Yet this language of going forth and returning, though naturally complementary, remains striking within the contexts of divine discourse and precipitation. The stress of the analogy falls on the adverb "empty" *(rêqām)*. This pivotal term recalls cultic regulations regarding annual festivals: "No one shall appear before me empty-handed" (Exod 23:15; 34:10; Deut 16:16). To appear before God involves offering a portion of one's produce, crop and animal, with which the worshiper has been blessed. Part of that bounty is, in effect, returned to God. For the prophet, the return that is characterized by the fructification of the land and the accomplished word takes on cultic significance: it is an offering to Yahweh for the rain of blessing and the gift of sustenance.

In addition, the adverb is employed in situations of conflict and crisis.[21] Most explicit is David's eulogy over the deaths of Saul and Jonathan. In 2 Sam 1:22 Saul's and Jonathan's military successes are praised: "From the blood of the slain, from the fat of the mighty, the bow of Jonathan did not turn back *(nāšôg)*, nor the sword of Saul return empty *(rêqām)*." Returning empty-handed is tantamount to defeat. By contrast, the "filled" sword is one accompanied by the spoils of victory. Given its use noted above, *rêqām* in Isa 55:11 subtly imbues the agricultural cycle with the dynamics of campaign and conquest. In so far as Yahweh's discourse must not return empty, Yahweh's word is, like Saul's sword, a weapon, and the booty is the bounty. The plunder is the harvest of agricultural produce and accomplished purpose: the sustenance of a people.

It is perhaps not fortuitous that this complementarity of movement that so characterizes the analogy established in Isa 55:10-11 helps also to shape the formal literary contours of a roughly contemporaneous historiographical work, the Neo-Babylonian Chronicles, which duly recorded the international triumphs, failures, and successions of the Babylonian kings from 747 to 539 BCE, from the reign of Nabunasir to the Persian conquest of Babylon by Cyrus. A. K. Grayson notes that Chronicles 1–7 exhibit similar characteristic phrases for battle, defeat,

20. The word for fill, *ml'*, can in fact denote completion and accomplishment (Gen 29:21; Lev 8:33; 12:4, 6).

21. God promises that Israel will not leave empty-handed from Egypt (Exod 3:21). Jacob proclaims that if God had not been on his side, his uncle would have dismissed him empty-handed (Gen 31:42).

retreat, and death.[22] In addition to Grayson's list, however, there is also a typicality of language that serves to frame practically each year of each king described, particularly in Chronicles 3–6.[23] Each entry lists the regnal year — even the day and month in many cases — along with the military and political affairs of each successive Babylonian king.[24] With few exceptions, an entry opens with reference to the king mustering *(dekûm)* his army, going forth to a given geographical location for battle *(alākum ina PN)*, and concludes with his return to Babylon *(ana mātīšu târum* or *ana Bābili^{ki} târum)*, sometimes with plunder, sometimes in defeat.[25] Such repetitive language provides a literary template for conveying information about the military engagements of the king in chronographical fashion. In effect, these verbs of movement establish a rhythm for each regnal year described. Moreover, such language contributes to the generic description of royal character: each king, for a given year, either succeeded or failed militarily, not to mention cultically. Success at war typically resulted in the capture or return of cultic images.[26] Otherwise, an empty return was the lamentable result.[27]

22. *ABC*, 8.

23. In Chronicle 1, foreign kings such as Tiglath-pileser III dominate the entries; consequently, the language describing their reigns is different. In Chronicle 2, Nabopolassar in his early years begins to take center stage, although the king of Assyria still dominates; hence the language can only begin to approximate that found in Chronicles 3–6 (see Chronicle 2.22, 24, 28). Chronicle 7 describes the exceptional — and politically disastrous — case of Nabonidus. Yet the language echoes the standard language of previous chronicles: Nabonidus remains in Tema, not marching anywhere (ii.6, 11). He is impotent vis-à-vis the king of Anshan, Cyrus. Having defeated the army of Akkad at Opis, Cyrus captures Babylon simply by "entering" the city *(īrub;* iii.16, 18), after which the gods of Akkad "return" *(itūrū;* 21-22). See also i.7 and ii.1. See S. Sykes, "Time and Space in Haggai-Zechariah 1-8: A Bakhtinian Analysis of a Prophetic Chronicle" (Ph.D. diss.; Union Theological Seminary in Virginia, 1997) 78-84.

24. For background discussion see J. Van Seters, *In Search of History: Historiography in the Ancient World and the Origins of Biblical History* (New Haven: Yale University Press, 1983) 79-91.

25. See, e.g., Chronicle 3.1, 8-9, 16, 30, 32, 27, 53, 57, 58, 65; Chronicle 4.1, 4, 5, 14, 19, 26 (returning in defeat); Chronicle 5, obverse, 15-16, 20; reverse, 5, 7, 9, 10, 16, 20; Chronicle 6.3-34, 26-27.

26. For example, Chronicle 1.iii.2-3; Chronicle 2.16-17; Chronicle 3.8-9. The quintessence of cultic failure is embodied by Nabonidus, Babylon's last native king. Chronicle 7 observes no less than four times that while Nabonidus remained in Tema, Nabu "did not come to Babylon" *(ana Bābili^{ki} ul illiku)* and Bel "did not come out" *(ul ūṣa;* ii.5-6, 10-11, 19-20, 23-24). The king's stay at Tema corresponds to the cessation of the Akitu festival. It is not until Nabonidus's last regnal year, when he is recorded to be royally active, that the Akitu festival resumes (7.iii.5-12).

27. See 2.24, 27-28 and 3.96, as well as Grayson's comment on the expression *mimma ul ilqû* on 2.27 *(ABC,* 89, 218).

Yahweh's character, similarly, is reflected in this productive back-and-forth movement of divine discourse in Second Isaiah. The circuitous tour of the divine word is imbued, however subtly, with the language of military success. It should be no surprise, then, to find the character of the divine warrior behind such language. Elsewhere, Yahweh's word musters the heavenly bodies for battle (40:26b; 48:13). The rhythm of going forth and returning with the plunder of accomplished purpose characterizes this efficacious movement of divine discourse, speech that issues forth as a royal edict, whether to stir up the king of Anshan or, like rain, to refresh the land. On the surface, the prophet eschews the traditional language of storm theophanies. The divine warrior's conduct is not expressly likened to the violent flash and thunder of storms that set the earth quaking and quivering;[28] rather, Yahweh's word is compared to the seasonal regularities of rain and fertility. The effects are nevertheless no less precipitous.

The prophet draws on the example of the frequently torrential rainy season that extends from winter to early spring to illustrate this efficacious movement of divine discourse.[29] This is a time when earthly monarchs and armies are typically at rest, awaiting the arrival of spring in order to (re)extend control over the land for profitable return.[30] Royal success is marked by exacting tribute, asserting control, and, if necessary, razing garrisons and cities by conflagration.[31] Yahweh's word, which is no less mobile, is no scorched-earth policy, however. To the contrary, the divine edict, which tours the land while earthly armies are at rest, satiates the land with life-giving sustenance.

The coincidence is at least curious that Cyrus enters Babylon[32] in the late fall (the third day of Marheshvan [October/November]), just prior to the onset of the early rains, to proclaim peace. Soon thereafter and throughout the rainy season, the gods of Akkad (Babylonia) are returned to their rightful places,[33] having been gathered illegitimately by Nabonidus, according to Per-

28. For example, Hab 3:3-15; Judg 5:4-5; Nah 1:3-5; cf. Isa 42:13-15.

29. The climate of Babylonia, similar to Judah's and in contrast to Assyria's, is a study of contrasts, from the hot dry weather during late spring–early fall to the sometimes violent downpours during the late fall–early spring.

30. See 2 Sam 11:1a. The Neo-Babylonian Chronicles feature the kings mustering and marching during the months from Nisan (March/April) to Tishri (September/October) and returning by Marheshvan (October/November) or Kislev (November/December). Only on occasion does the Babylonian king march out in the months of Kislev and Tebet (December/January), as in the case of Nebuchadrezzar in Chronicles 5, rev., 6, 9, 11, 14, 25.

31. See Chronicles 3.71; 4.3, 10; 6.18-20.

32. Cyrus's army entered Babylon earlier on the 16th day of Tishri without a battle.

33. From Kislev (November/December) to Adar (February/March). See Chronicle 7.18, 21-22. See also Cyrus's own proclamation of peace and cultic restoration in the Cyrus Cylinder (ANET, 316).

sian propaganda.[34] Whether by historical chance or by strategy, Cyrus broke the back of Babylon and immediately embarked on a campaign to restore Babylonia cultically and economically just as the rains began to pummel the ground. Coincidence or not, the Divine Warrior's successes, couched in the language of agriculture, are no less sweet. In both cases, rain marks the onset of restoration, and for the prophet historical time corresponds to agricultural time. Moreover, any mention of conflict is lacking in this compendium of divine discourse (as also in the account of Babylon's conquest), yet the circuitous tour of Yahweh's word is no less a victory campaign whose plunder is the germination of life.[35]

This movement of divine discourse spills over into 55:12-13, wherein a similar complementarity of motion is conveyed. Instead of Yahweh's word, the prophet's audience now becomes the subject (and object) of movement. "In joy you shall go out and in peace you shall be led." This too is no less a victory march, although all hints of opposition are lacking. The people are met not by the clash of enemy swords but by the peals of creation's praise. Like the rain and the word, the people's foray is also a return, no less a homecoming. The comprehensive description of Yahweh's efficacious word began with reference to the earth's fertile production (v. 10) and it ends with a garden, cleared of thorns and briers, as a perpetual memorial to Yahweh's victorious word (v. 13b).[36]

As this sample survey indicates, botanical references and images assume a prominent position in the prophet's discourse on creation. When Yahweh speaks, new things sprout up from the barren ground of history. Moreover, such language contributes a crucial dimension to the prophet's rhetorical strategy. The prophet repeatedly calls Israel to perceive and respond to Yahweh's decisively new word of redemption, and yet it is a word that is as familiar as seasonal plant growth. By describing divine discourse with botanical metaphors, the prophet effectively naturalizes his call to action for his audi-

---

34. Nabonidus's gathering of the gods aimed at reasserting control over the land as well as preventing Persian power from spoliating the divine statues. See M. Weinfeld, "Cult Centralization in Israel in the List of a Neo-Babylonian Analogy," *JNES* 23 (1964) 202-12; P.-A. Beaulieu, "An Episode in the Fall of Babylon to the Persians," *JNES* 52 (1993) 241-61.

35. See the references to the extinction of opposition in 41:11-12 and 51:13.

36. As B. F. Batto has pointed out, such language is redolent of the Noachic covenant set forth in Gen 9:8-1 ("The Covenant of Peace: A Neglected Ancient Near Eastern Motif," *CBQ* 49 [1987] 191n.14). This Priestly passage designates the bow in the clouds as the sign of God's oath *(běrît ʿôlām)* never again to cut off life from the earth (9:14-17; cf. Isa 54:9-10). But the primary subject of the sign in Isa 55:12-13 is the grove of cypresses and myrtles, not the mountains and hills.

ence, a call that reverses divine judgment and ushers in a new age of release and restoration, in short, a word in season. To refuse to acknowledge this new word is, the prophet implies, as unnatural as living in a wasteland, tantamount to letting the land lie fallow, to wasting a word in an already wasted land. Yahweh is not sought in *tōhû* (45:19). Conversely, to respond to Yahweh's word is to grasp the plow's handle and not look back. What is to emerge out of the soil to alter irrevocably the combined fate of Jacob and Zion is the topic at hand.

The Fruits of Creation and Community

Second Isaiah is replete with images drawn from the botanical realm. The selective survey that follows highlights the intimate connection the prophet establishes between community and nature, specifically culture and horticulture, in order to convey a new ethos for a reconstituted community.

Withering and Flourishing: Isaiah 44:1-5

Beginning with ch. 40, the first reference to botanical growth is found in vv. 6-7, one that explicitly identifies grass (*ḥāṣîr*) with flesh (*bāśār*, v. 6) or people (*'ām*, v. 7). The point of the simile is to highlight the transitory nature of human life and, in particular, the people's capacity for covenantal loyalty (*ḥesed*) or faithful constancy.[37] As the grass and the flower wither away before the god-awful sirocco,[38] so also the people's faithfulness amid the heat of judgment. What remains is Yahweh's word, ever operative and efficacious (v. 8). The correlation between grass and human life is further developed in the following section, wherein the rulers and princes are turned into *tōhû* or nothingness (*'ayin*, v. 23). The following verse describes these unfortunate rulers in a manner similar to the fate of all flesh described in 40:6-7: they are scarcely planted before Yahweh blows them away as stubble (v. 24).

It is all a foil, however, for the scene of luxuriant growth depicted in 44:1-5. Jacob, Yahweh's servant, is addressed with the oracular formula of assurance (*'al-tîrā'*, v. 2), followed by an extended causal clause in vv. 3-5. It is within this formulated reason that certain floral images spring to life. The

37. See J. D. W. Watts, *Isaiah 34–66* (WBC 25; Waco: Word, 1987) 78.
38. God's breath (*rûaḥ*) in this context denotes the execution of judgment already fulfilled (40:2).

238

prophet weaves together natural and human categories of reference, the warp and woof of Yahweh's redemptive work. The movement begins with the realm of nature (v. 3a), moves to recorded speech (v. 3b), then back to nature (v. 4), and concludes with human discourse (v. 5). The initial shift in v. 3 from the natural to the human level is cast in parallel fashion: Yahweh will pour *(ysq)* water on the thirsty land and in like manner pour Spirit and blessing on Jacob's descendants. In start contrast to Yahweh's withering *rûaḥ* in 40:7 and 24, Yahweh's Spirit is likened to the refreshing rain that restores the arid land to heightened fertile capacity.[39] Implied is that the land thirsts for water as much as Jacob's "seed" stands in need of regenerative redemption. Both experience a severe condition of want, and their fates are bound up together. At stake is the flourishing (or extinction) of a people, for which the arena of nature sets the stage.

The results are staggering. From the once parched soil sprout forth willows *('ărābîm)* and tamarisks(?). The latter species probably denotes the evergreen *tamarix jordanis,* which once lined the banks of the Jordan in plentiful groves.[40] The former *(salix acmophylla* or *salix alba)* is a streamside tree that today thrives along the fresh waters of the Jordan in contrast to the similar Euphrates poplar *(populus euphratica),* which is more tolerant of salt water.[41] An equally evocative image of luxuriant growth occurs in Ps 1:3 (cf. Ps 92:12 [MT 13]). Here the psalmist juxtaposes the unspecified tree (the pious) and the chaff (the wicked) driven away by the wind (1:4). The comparison also holds within the larger rhetorical context of Second Isaiah's message (Isa 40:7, 24). By establishing such a contrast, the psalmist suggests an equivalency be-

39. The connection between "Spirit" and "water" is all the more striking in that the verb *yāṣaq* ("pour") is nowhere else attested in biblical literature to have "Spirit" as its object. Anointing oil for priests and kings is often the verb's object (Gen 28:18; Exod 29:7; Lev 8:12, 15; 21:10; 1 Sam 10:1; 2 Kgs 9:6).

40. The MT *běbēn ḥāṣîr* ("in between grass") is distinctly unhebraic and indicates textual corruption. The poetic parallelism would suggest that the simile in the second colon applies also to the first, hence D. Winton Thomas's *(BHS)* graphic emendation of the afformative preposition (from *bě* to *kě*). I take MT *bēn* to denote a particular species of tree, most probably a tamarisk, given the Aramaic and Arabic cognates, and consequently render *ḥāṣir* (or *ḥāṣôr*) adjectivally as "evergreen" (so also J. M. Allegro, "The Meaning of *byn* in Isaiah xliv. 4," *ZAW* 63 [1951] 154-56). In addition, since *'ēšel* commonly denotes the leafless tamarisk *(tamarix aphylla)* and, perhaps, the Nile tamarisk (Gen 21:33; 1 Sam 31:13), I have in mind the *tamarix jordanis* as the best candidate for the enigmatic term. See F. N. Hepper, *Illustrated Encyclopedia of Bible Plants* (Grand Rapids: Baker, 1992) 64, 68, 74.

41. See the discussion in M. Zohary, *Plants of the Bible* (Cambridge: Cambridge University Press, 1982) 131; Hepper, *Illustrated Encyclopedia,* 71-72. Hepper contends that the Euphrates poplar is denoted in Isa 44:4.

tween flowing streams and *tôrâ* (Ps 1:2): as trees depend on rivers in the desert for sustenance, so the blessed depend on Yahweh's law for guidance and happiness. Such is the sustaining power of *tôrâ*.

The metaphorical connection between law and water may also be presupposed, however vaguely, in the Isaianic passage: as Yahweh's law has served as Israel's constitution, so the "downpour" of Yahweh's Spirit will reconstitute the new Israel. In any case, the flowing streams in the desert enable not only botanical growth but also the community of faith to flourish. Jacob's progeny will proclaim, in oral and written form, their fidelity, indeed, their absolute belongingness, to Yahweh. As holy objects are inscribed with Yahweh's name (*qōdeš laYHWH*),[42] so individuals will label themselves as belonging to Yahweh.[43] The result is an imputing of corporate holiness under the rubric of divine ownership.[44] The image of Yahweh's Spirit being poured out, as in the pouring of oil, also suggests a dissemination of holiness. Within the prophet's purview, the formula "belonging to Yahweh" connotes nothing less than a transfer of ownership, analogous to the case of an emancipated slave handed over to God in the form of temple service.[45] This instance of *paramonē*[46] (the granting of freedom for service to God) accords well with the prophet's language of release and liberty elsewhere.[47]

In short, Israel's progeny will not only increase and flourish but be sanctified as a holy people, reclaiming, in effect, Yahweh's conditional promise that Israel will be both a "treasured possession" and "a holy nation" (Exod 19:6; cf. Isa 61:6). These two dimensions of corporate status, holiness and ownership, are inseparable. In addition, the blessing of progeny — so prominent in the patriarchal promises in Genesis — is conjoined with this blessing of corporate holiness. Regardless of whether an open incorporation of new members into the holy community is suggested here,[48] unmistakably clear is

42. Zech 14:20-21 refers to horse bells and cooking pots inscribed with the words "Holy to Yahweh" (*qōdeš laYHWH*). The same words are inscribed on an ornament on Aaron's turban (Exod 28:36-38).

43. Although the significance of writing specifically on the palm of the hand is unclear, the act is nonetheless akin to that of inscribing an object.

44. A similar sense of corporate holiness is reflected throughout Deuteronomy (e.g., Deut 7:6; 14:2, 21; 26:18-19).

45. See the ancient Near Eastern parallels offered by M. Weinfeld, *Social Justice in Ancient Israel and in the Ancient Near East* (Minneapolis: Fortress, 1995) 118-20.

46. The related Greek verb means "to attend and serve" (ibid., 119n.90).

47. For example, 42:7; 43:1-7; 45:13; 46:12-13; 48:20-21; 51:5, 8; cf. 61:1-2.

48. See Stuhlmueller, *Creative Redemption*, 130-31. For a counterreading see A. Wilson, *The Nations in Deutero-Isaiah: A Study on Composition and Structure* [ANETS 1; Lewiston, N.Y.: Edwin Mellen, 1986] 84-85.

the claim that future generations hold the power to reconstitute corporate Israel by acknowledging their identity as Yahweh's own. The identification of the well-watered garden is complete: Jacob/Israel is the stated goal of God's cultivation, an oasis that bears the name of Yahweh.[49]

The Taxonomy of Community: Isaiah 41:17-20

Whereas Isa 44:1-5 features two kinds of tree growth, 41:17-20 depicts no less than seven species.[50] As in 44:1-5, the prophet weaves together human (41:17, 20) and botanical (vv. 18-19) referents, but here with greater focus on the latter. The section opens with a particular characterization of Israel as poor and needy, specifically, parched with thirst (v. 17). Their need is met by Yahweh's proclamation to provide an abundance of water on the "bare heights" (šĕpāyîm, also 49:9) and "valleys" (v. 18). As a result, the desert is transformed into a swamp and spring. Compared to 44:1-5, the presence of water here is all the more pervasive: the pool has replaced, or resulted from, the flowing streams. The fertile result is a forest of remarkable biodiversity. Yahweh intends to plant seven distinguishable varieties of trees, all coexisting in the transformed wasteland.

It is not fortuitous within this taxonomy of trees that the majestic cedar ('erez; cedrus libani) is listed first, a mountain tree that requires much precipitation and grows normally at an altitude between 4,600 and 6,000 feet.[51] It is not indigenous to the desert.[52] The highly valued wood of these "trees of Yahweh" (Ps 104:16) was used in the monumental construction of the temple and palace (1 Kgs 6:9-20; 7:26; Isa 9:10 [MT 9]).[53] The Cilician fir (Abies cilicica), a similar coniferous tree associated with the flora of Lebanon (bĕrôš, sometimes translated "cypress"), is often mentioned with the cedar as temple building material (1 Kgs 9:11; 2 Kgs

49. Cf. 55:13 and see below.
50. The number seven may be of significance within the Masoretic tradition, particularly when compared to the other versions. See Watts, Isaiah 36–66, 100.
51. By contrast, Jerusalem ranges from 1,970 feet (Kidron Valley) to, at most, 2,740 feet (French Hill) above sea level.
52. Zohary, Plants, 115, 104-5; Hepper, Illustrated Encyclopedia, 26-27.
53. Cedar and cypress were the woods of choice among the Assyrian kings for their monumental building projects, both temple and palace (e.g., AR 1.324 [A.O.86.1004.6']; AR 2.57 [A.O.87.11.20'-21']; AR 2.227 [A.O.101.2.56-57]). Mount Amanus and the Lebanon range were major sources of cedar (e.g., AR 3.47 [A.O.102.8.41']; AR 3.51 [A.O.102.10.i.26-28]; AR 3.54 [A.O.102.iii.39-45a]).

241

19:23; Zech 11:1-2).[54] Indigenous to the Sinai, the acacia *(šiṭṭâ; acacia raddiana)* was used for constructing the desert tabernacle (Exod 26:15). Unlike the other trees, it grows naturally in the desert.[55] The leafy-tree myrtle *(hădās)*, which requires more water than the acacia to flourish, was used for the construction of lean-tos during the Festival of Booths (Neh 8:15).[56] Also used for such cultic construction, as well as for the two cherubim and doors of the temple's inner sanctuary (1 Kgs 6:23, 31), was the Aleppo pine *('ēṣ šemen)*, the only pine native to the highlands of Canaan and probably the "majesty of Carmel" in Isa 35:2.[57] The cypress *(tĕ'aššûr; cupressus sempervirens)*,[58] erroneously translated "box tree,"[59] is attested elsewhere in Isaiah as a wood to be used to "beautify the place of [Yahweh's] sanctuary" (60:13). Unlike the cedar, the cypress is native to Israel.[60] Finally, the *tidhār*, either the plane *(platanus orientalis)* or laurustinus *(viburnum tinus)*, grows naturally on Mount Carmel and is included in 60:13 as building material for the sanctuary.[61]

An unnatural diversity is the key to this taxonomy of trees. For all of his expertise in botany, Michael Zohary must ask with some degree of perplexity why the acacia, a tree native to the desert and frequently found in the Negev, is to be brought to a place that already abounds with them, to which he offers no answer except to say that identifying plants in Isaiah is a difficult task.[62] Indeed. Nevertheless, the following reason can be given: Isaiah's taxonomy reaches beyond natural conditions that allow for the growth of one kind of tree in the desert but cannot sustain the kind that prefers a much higher, moister altitude. The prophet limns a biodiversity that is nothing short of phantasmic: some trees are native to the desert; others not, as in the case of the cedar and fir, both of which are associated with the Lebanon mountain range.

A clue to the purpose of this botanical catalogue is found in 60:13, which repeats verbatim the latter half of the list (41:19b), adding the "glory of

---

54. Zohary, *Plants*, 106-7.

55. Ibid., 116; Hepper, *Illustrated Encyclopedia*, 63.

56. The myrtle also constitutes the pristine grove featured in Zechariah's first vision (Zech 1:8, 10, 11).

57. Zohary, *Plants*, 114.

58. Attested only in Isa 41:19; 60:13; Ezek 27:6.

59. Hepper, *Illustrated Encyclopedia*, 31; Zohary, *Plants*, 14.

60. I. Jacob and W. Jacob, "Flora," *ABD* 2.805.

61. Identification is uncertain. See Zohary, *Plants*, 12; Hepper, *Illustrated Encyclopedia*, 73-74; Jacob and Jacob, "Flora," 806.

62. Zohary, *Plants*, 116.

Lebanon," and connects the various species with the place of Yahweh's sanctuary. Although the myrtle, acacia, and Aleppo pine of 41:19a are more native to Canaan, in contrast to the cedars of Lebanon, all are used for the purpose of cultic construction, whether it be temple, tabernacle, or booth. Such materials as the cedar and the fir need no longer be imported, the prophet envisions; all will be cultivated together in a fantastic botanical garden homegrown on Zion's erstwhile wasteland. In short, to borrow from a possibly later interpreter of Second Isaiah,[63] the glory of Lebanon along with the majesty of Carmel[64] and Sharon[65] will take root in the barren desert to reveal Yahweh's glory (Isa 35:2).[66] The resulting grove, incomparable in its diversity, is cultivated by an incomparable Gardener (40:12-13; 44:7), whose glory is unveiled in Zion's restoration.

Although this catalogue of tree species is extensive, two species are strikingly absent, the oak ('allôn or 'ēlôn) and the terebinth ('ēlâ or 'ayil).[67] Occasionally paired together, these trees were associated with worship (e.g., Gen 13:18 [originally singular]; Josh 24:26). For example, the Yahwist's veneration of oak trees is clearly evident in the patriarchal narratives. At both Shechem and Hebron, the oak tree is the natural setting for theophany (Gen 12:6; 13:18; 18:1).[68] Twice Abraham witnesses an appearance of Yahweh at the oak of Moreh at Shechem (12:6; 18:1). Yet such arboreal association with Yahwistic worship was vehemently questioned by some prophets, including Isaiah.[69] The unnamed prophet of the exile seems to have followed his predecessor's disdain for these majestic trees, given their use in popular religious

63. See C. R. Mathews's treatment of Isaiah 34–35 in response to Odil H. Steck's redactional investigation (*Bereitete Heimkehr: Jesaja 35 als redaktionelle Brücke zwischen dem Ersten und dem Zweiten Jesaja* [SBS 121; Stuttgart: Katholisches Bibelwerk, 1985]) in *Defending Zion* (BZAW 236; Berlin: de Gruyter, 1995) 120-79.

64. As suggested above, the "majesty of Carmel" most likely refers to the Aleppo pine or the Laurestinus, but need not be confined to it. See Hepper, *Illustrated Encyclopedia*, 24-25.

65. The "majesty of Sharon" could refer to either the Tabor oak or the carob tree (*ceratonica siliqua*). See Zohary, *Plants*, 33, 63; Hepper, *Illustrated Encyclopedia*, 23, 123-25.

66. As Mathews notes, the subject behind the plural "they" in 35:2c is grammatically tied to the wilderness and dry land. Yet in light of 40:5 ("all flesh") on which Isaiah 35 evidently depends, the antecedent appears to be human beings (*Defending Zion*, 120). Given the prophet's metaphorical use of botanical images, these referents are not mutually exclusive.

67. See the distinction made by Zohary, *Plants*, 108.

68. See Theodore Hiebert's discussion in *The Yahwist's Landscape: Nature and Religion in Early Israel* (New York: Oxford University Press, 1996) 107-9.

69. For example, Hos 4:13; Isa 1:29-30; 57:5; Ezek 6:13; cf. 1 Kgs 14:23-24; Jer 2:20; 3:6, 13.

practice.[70] For example, Isa 1:29-31 renders harsh judgment on those who cultivate terebinths (*'êlîm;* cf. 17:10-11). They shall, the prophet inveighs, become like the trees themselves, and wither away for lack of water and be burned like tinder (1:31).[71]

Isaiah's successor has composed his taxonomy with care and precision. The diverse forest profiled in 41:19 serves as a sharp antithesis to Isaiah's pagan groves. Isaiah refers to such terebinth gardens as having been chosen *(bḥr)* and cultivated by human hands (1:29). Second Isaiah's grove is described as planted and watered by Yahweh alone (41:19), the outgrowth of Jacob's redemptive choice (44:3). Elsewhere, this garden serves as a "name" and "everlasting sign" to Yahweh (55:13b), a reminder of Yahweh's covenantal faithfulness to Zion over and against First Isaiah's pagan grove, a tragic testimony to Jacob's faithlessness. For the Yahwist, the oak can legitimately serve as a medium of revelation; for the Isaianic school, it is the transformed wilderness (35:2; 41:20) and, by extension, all flesh (40:5), that receives and transmits Yahweh's glory.[72] In short, this remarkable arrangement of trees figures as the crowning result of Yahweh's restorative word, of a victory for life.

In summary, despite the tentative identification of several of these trees within Second Isaiah's taxonomic list, a wide spectrum of biodiversity is clearly discernible, one that ranges from the nonnative cedar of Lebanon to the homegrown desert acacia tree. It is a sacred grove that surpasses in variety anything humanly possible. Why the catalogue stops at seven species is anyone's guess. Perhaps it is meant to suggest holy completion. The list easily could have extended itself to eight within its poetic parameters. The bicolon of v. 19a lists four species, beginning with the cedar and concluding with the Aleppo pine, in 3 + 3 meter; v. 19b, however, catalogues only three, but retains the identical accentual count. In place of the "missing" species is the adverb *yaḥdāw*[73] at the end of the verse, which serves to highlight the striking coexistence of these species.

---

70. See S. Ackerman's discussion of Isa 57:5 in *Under Every Green Tree: Popular Religion in Sixth-Century Judah* (HSM 46; Atlanta: Scholars Press, 1992) 102-3, 152-53.

71. Third Isaiah (chs. 56–66), however, reverses the images by referring to all those who mourn in Zion as "terebinths of righteousness, the planting of Yahweh" (*'êlê haṣṣedeq matta' YHWH;* 61:3). In light of the condemnation in 57:5, the prophet's positive use of a tree traditionally associated with apostasy *may* signal the prophet's specific inclusion of faithful foreigners into the Yahwistic cult (e.g., Isa 56:6-8).

72. In both 35:2c and 41:20, the subject of the "seeing" can either be the flora or a nonspecified cast of human beings.

73. Of note is that this term denoting corporate existence and activity finds its highest concentration in Second Isaiah (14 occurrences in 16 chapters).

Similarly, the following bicolon (v. 20a) positions the same adverb in the identical position. But the antecedent has shifted: no longer the trees of the grove, rather the *human* subjects, the "poor and needy" of v. 17, will "together" *(yaḥdāw)* discern Yahweh's creative work. The luxuriant grove is a reflection of a people gathered and reconstituted, of Zion restored.[74] When Yahweh proclaims to Zion, "You are my people" (51:16), their precise identity remains an open question. At the very least, embraced are the descendants of Jacob gathered from the ends of the earth, and not simply from Babylon.[75] The striking diversity of the garden could also reflect a mixed constituency that comprises both natives and foreigners, those who specifically have *not* come forth "from the loins of Judah" (48:1).[76] The prophet, however, never quite reaches the level of explicitness as does his prophetic successor ("Third Isaiah") in 60:10-16. There Yahweh's garden is bracketed by divine declarations of foreigners *(běnê-nēkār)* and nations *(gôyim)* entering into Zion's service. Coupled with 56:1-8, which refers to foreigners joining themselves *(lwh)* to Yahweh (v. 6), it becomes clear, in later Isaianic tradition at least, that the biodiversity of the garden reflects the ethnic diversity of the community.[77] At the very least, such diversity in this transplanted garden limns the return and coexistence of the dispersed who have survived on foreign soil. As the original Eden was the home for all humanity, so now this new Eden holds the promise as the hearth for all peoples (51:3).

74. Indeed, in a presumably contemporaneous passage, the reforestation of Lebanon marks Israel's restoration (Isa 29:17).

75. For example, 43:5-7; 45:22; 49:6.

76. See the corrected reading *mimmě˓ê* for MT *mimmê* ("waters") suggested by *BHS* (cf. 48:19).

77. The continuing debate over whether Second Isaiah encouraged proselytism or espoused national imperialism appears irresolvable (cf. Isa 44:5; 45:22-23; 51:4-5). What can be said is that categories of universalism and exclusive nationalism do not apply; they are two extremes that lack unambiguous support in the text. Like God's creation, the nations find their immediate relevance, indeed their raison d'être, in relation to the particular community of Israel and not in and of themselves. The prophet perhaps finds it strategic to address the pressing crises of his community (e.g., assimilation, conflict, despair) through the rhetoric of indirection, that is, through reference to nations and nature ostensibly external to the particular domain of his community, much like Catholics and Protestants of Northern Ireland today discussing the distant struggles between Jews and Palestinians in order to effect reconciliation and common cause among themselves. Again, not until Third Isaiah does one find the floodgates of Zion fully opened to the Gentiles. Yet even in Third Isaiah, as with his predecessor, Zion is by no means deconstructed but remains the locus of salvation that is extended to the *gôyim* (cf. Isa 19:18-25). See the survey and discussion in M. Brett, "Nationalism and the Hebrew Bible," in *The Bible in Ethics: The Second Sheffield Colloquium* (ed. J. W. Rogerson et al.; JSOTSup 207; Sheffield: JSOT Press, 1995) 153-57.

The expressed goal of the garden's cultivation is "so that they may together perceive and know, realize and understand that the hand of Yahweh has done this" (41:20). Such language recalls, Claus Westermann points out, "the language of the old songs of victory" of God's salvific intervention.[78] Yahweh's outstretched hand wields both the sword of victory and, as it were, the stylus of creation.[79] This dual dimension of Yahweh's handiwork is not the result of some newly learned ambidexterity on the part of the Deity. These two modes of divine action were inseparably connected long before the exilic prophet came on the scene.[80] Moreover, the sword and the stylus are not the only tools of choice; the simple garden spade is also found in Yahweh's hand. Yahweh's planting of Israel is an image firmly rooted in the ancient conquest traditions.[81] Yahweh's garden-grove is no mere "pleasant planting" (cf. 5:7); it is a victory garden,[82] one that is to yield a harvest of justice and righteousness.[83]

What is also striking about the final purpose clause of 41:20 is the accumulation of verbs denoting perception that conclude the passage: "see" (r'h), "know" (yd'), "realize" (śym), and "understand" (śkl), a veritable taxonomy of cognition. Three out of these four modes of apprehension are found within the setting of the Yahwist's garden in Eden. In the primordial garden, the woman sees (r'h) that the tree of the knowledge of good and evil was edible, visually appealing, and conducive for gaining wisdom (śkl, Gen 3:6). I have argued that the Eden narrative thrusts a stake into the heart of sapiential ideology,[84] and, to be sure, the exilic prophet also takes a dim view on the wise (Isa 44:25; 47:10). But knowledge is everything for Second Isaiah. Interspersed throughout the prophet's oracles is the injunction to look and see, to understand and acknowledge Yahweh's creative work and glory (e.g., 40:26;

78. C. Westermann, *Isaiah 40–66* (tr. D. M. G. Stalker; OTL; Philadelphia: Westminster, 1969) 81.

79. For example, Exod 13:14, 16; Deut 4:34; Pss 17:14; 28:5; 44:2-3 (MT 3-4); 75:8 (MT 9); 92:4 (MT 5); 109:27; 111:7; 136:12; 138:8; 144:7.

80. For example, Pss 74:12-17; 89:8-13 (MT 9-14); 135:5-11; 136:12.

81. For example, Exod 15:16-17; Num 24:5-9; Pss 44:2 (MT 3); 80:8-16 (MT 9-17); Isa 60:21.

82. The phrase "victory garden" was coined in the United States during World War II when American citizens were urged to reserve part of their land to raise food for themselves. I am using the phrase, however, to refer to victory as a fait accompli. For the ancient Near Eastern background, see below.

83. Cf. 32:15-18; 33:5; 45:8. All in all, God's handiwork is celebrated comprehensively for the justice it engenders: "The works of [God's] hands are faithful (*'ĕmet*) and just (*mišpāṭ*)," intones Ps 111:7. See below.

84. See Chapter 3.

48:6; 49:18; 51:6; cf. 35:2b; 40:5). Like the tree in the midst of Eden, Yahweh's victory garden imparts a certain kind of wisdom, but not the kind that requires ingestion and results in vulnerability and shame (Gen 3:7-10). The prophet has deliberately ejected all fruit from this sacred grove.[85] The kind of knowledge imparted by this forest is meant to empower and shape a new community. This knowledge is founded on an acknowledgment of the divine cultivator, whose majestic grove offers credible proof of redemptive power. The variegated composition of the grove suggests the germination of a diverse people formed and reformed by Yahweh. This victory garden is thus no mere oasis in the desert or a promised way station for liberated exiles; it is nothing less than the nursery of a nation.

Many of the prophet's predecessors and contemporaries similarly likened Israel to a sapling destined either to flourish or to wither away and be burned.[86] This anthro-botanical grove serves as a powerful symbol of the dispersed, transplanted and reunited, forming the garden of the new Zion and recovering the flora of Eden itself, Yahweh's first garden (51:3). But the "fruit" of the new Zion is its wood. With the mighty cedar at the top of the list, Yahweh's new grove is redolent of the timbered temple. The garden symbolically serves as a natural "temple grove," the ancient counterpart of the modern "cathedral grove," a cliché used to describe old-growth forests that inspire veneration.[87] The prophet's sacred grove is intended to evoke acknowledgment of Yahweh's redemptive power.

The prophet, however, does not convey this arboreal wonder for its material utility, for providing the necessary building material for the temple's restoration. Indeed, nowhere does the prophet mention such timber felled and used for temple construction.[88] The symbolic power of the grove is more far reaching; its planting is the very founding of Israel's new identity. As the chisel is forbidden to touch the unhewn stones of the "altar of the earth" (Exod 20:24-25), so the intervention of human artifice must never find its way into this forest. This temple is a natural. It is garden-grown yet fortified with human presence and praise.[89] And woe be the one who takes an ax to the grove!

85. Whereas the Yahwist depicts Eden as a luxuriant orchard (Gen 2:9, 16-17), the prophet recasts it in the form of a variegated forest (cf. Isa 51:3).

86. Examples include Amos 9:15; Jer 32:41; 11:16-17; Isa 5:5-6, 27:6; Hos 14:5-7. See Simkins's discussion in *Creator and Creation*, 103-5.

87. See S. Schama, *Landscape and Memory* (New York: Knopf, 1995) 13.

88. The temple's reconstruction is mentioned only once (44:28).

89. Cf. Isa 51:1, in which the prophet likens his audience to ashlars for the temple's foundation (cf. 1 Kgs 5:17-18; 6:7).

It is no coincidence, then, that First Isaiah indicts Sennacherib for having felled the cedars of Lebanon (Isa 37:24). The destruction of Lebanon's forest is a testimony to the emperor's prowess in destroying cities (v. 27), as he mocks the "Holy One of Israel" (v. 23). In a dirge celebrated over the Babylonian king's defeat, the cypresses and cedars of Lebanon exult, "Since you were laid low, no one comes to cut us down" (14:8). It was traditional of Assyrian kings to boast of their imperial prowess by describing their destruction of Lebanon's remote forests. More than simply providing raw material for royal monumental projects, the destruction of the natural forests was a sign of royal vigor and ruthless control over the Mediterranean seaboard. In addition, attacking kings typically took pains to raze the royal orchards of an enemy king, as part of the convention of ancient Near Eastern besiegement,[90] a practice expressly forbidden by Deuteronomic legislation (Deut 20:19-20). The peoples of the land, like the forests of the earth, were at the mercy of a victor's foreign policy. Similarly, the prophet makes clear that *Waldsterben ist Volksterben*, that the forest's destruction can prefigure the destruction of a people.

The Roots of Royal Gardening

There is, however, another side to royal botanical activity. The ancient Near Eastern despot not only destroyed gardens and forests of far-off lands in order to demonstrate his royal prowess; he also cultivated them at home.[91] Botanical gardens described in the royal annals are fraught with ideological significance. Fundamentally, they served the symbolic purpose of asserting the king's reign over his kingdom. Assyrian kings took special pride in their agronomic prowess. For example, Tiglath-pileser I boasts of his internationally renowned green thumb: "I took cedar, box-tree, Kanish oak from the *lands over which I had gained dominion* — such trees which none among previous kings, my forefathers, had ever planted — and I planted (them) in the orchards of my land. I took rare orchard fruit which is not found in my land (and therewith) filled the orchards of Assyria."[92] The kind of orchard the king cultivated

---

90. For example, Shalmaneser III's defeat of the rebel Marduk-bel-usate (*AR* 3.30 [A.O.102.5.iv.5a]); Shamshi-Adad V's siege of the city Nemetti-sarri (*AR* 3.190 [A.O.103.2.iii.35']); Tiglath-pileser III's destruction of the cities of King Mukin-zeri (Calah Summary Inscription 7.23-24).

91. For general discussion, see A. L. Oppenheim, "On Royal Gardens in Mesopotamia," *JNES* 24 (1965) 328-33; D. J. Wiseman, "Mesopotamian Gardens," *AnSt* 33 (1983) 137-44; M. Hutter, "Adam als Gärtner und König," *BZ* 30 (1986) 258-62.

92. *AR* 2.26 (A.O.87.1.vii.17-27 [italics mine]).

was stocked with an abundance of diverse botanical species transplanted from various conquered lands. Moreover, the cultivation of orchards was integrally related to urban restoration.[93] Sargon II prides himself in his simultaneous ability to restore towns and plant orchards, setting "out plants in waste areas where a plow was unknown in (all the days) of former kings."[94] The planting of orchards in uncultivated areas testified to the unprecedented might and wisdom of the current king vis-à-vis his predecessors.

The most detailed account of a royal garden or orchard among the Assyrian royal annals is in the so-called Banquet of Ashurnasirpal II inscription, which recounts the lavish banquet celebrating the renovation and dedication of the Calah palace.[95] After listing the various woods — eight kinds — used to renovate the palace, Ashurnasirpal then lists at least 41 varieties of trees, from cedars to various fruit trees, that he saw and presumably transplanted in his resplendent orchards in Calah, while marching through the lands as a conquering hero.[96]

Assyrian gardens were intimately associated with palace and temple. Tiglath-pileser I describes his palace garden in Nineveh beside the Ishtar temple as an integral part of his royal residence: "I planted a garden for my lordly leisure. I excavated a [canal] from the River Husir (and) [directed it] into this garden. . . . Within this garden I built a palace, . . . I portrayed therein the victory and might which the gods Assur and Ninurta, the gods who love my priesthood, had granted me."[97] The king's palace serves, in effect, as a victory hall of fame for the king's heavenly patrons, Assur and Ninurta.

Both Sennacherib and Esarhaddon[98] are wont to describe their palace parks, which they liken to the natural mountain groves.[99] One mountain frequently named, Mount Amanus, was renowned for its cedars and thus was a frequent destination of Assyrian kings for supplying their monumental building projects.[100] Similarly, Lebanon with its towering cedars was regarded as a prototype for temple gardens: an Assyrian text describes a temple park as "the

93. For example, the restoration of Calah by Ashurnasirpal II (*AR* 2.252 [A.O.101.17.v.1-7]; *AR* 2.222 [A.O.101.1.iii.135]).

94. Cylinder Inscription (*ARAB* 2, §119). See also his "Letter to Assur," (*ARAB* 2, §160), which recounts the restoration of Ulhu.

95. *ANET,* 558-60.

96. *AR* 2.290 (A.O.101.30.36b-52).

97. *AR* 2.55 (A.O.87.10.71-74); cf. *AR* 2.27 (A.O.87.1.vii.17-27).

98. *ARAB* 2, §698.

99. *ARAB* 2, §368; see also §§376, 414.

100. For example, Ashurbanipal's use of the "immense beams of cedar and cypress, the produce of Mount Amanus and Mount Lebanon" to complete Esagila's roof (*ROB,* 201 [B.6.32.2.58-60]). See also *ARAB* 2, §§367, 388.

Garden of Plenty, the image of Lebanon."[101] Even the parks, modeled after their mountainous sources, were used to supply timber.[102] Sennacherib refers to his parks in Nineveh as veritable tribute from his conquered territories: "Above the city and below the city I laid out parks. The wealth of mountains and all lands, all the herbs of the land of Hatti, myrrh plants, among which fruitfulness was greater than in their (natural) habitat, all kinds of mountain vines, all the fruits of (all) lands, herbs and fruit bearing trees I set out for my subjects."[103] Common was the boast that the trees and plants of the royal orchards thrived better in their transplanted condition than in their natural habitats.[104] The royal victory gardens not only testified to the king's victories over foreign lands but also to the king's prowess for improving nature.

The pharaohs equally prided themselves in their horticultural abilities. Ramses III opens his testimony to the peace and security he obtained for his kingdom with a reference to his fructifying accomplishments throughout the land: "I planted the whole land with trees and verdure, and I made the people dwell in their shade."[105] The gardens of the Egyptian royal annals are frequently tied to the temple. Ramses III repeatedly mentions the great groves and arbors (lit. "places of chambers of trees")[106] that surround his temples.[107] Regarding the restoration of the Horus chapel, he states: "I made to grow the pure grove of thy temple."[108] Such temple groves were considered the gardens of particular gods, property that figured in their estates, which included everything from cattle to towns.[109]

Like the Assyrian kings, the pharaohs had a penchant for imported plants. Like the parks modeled after Mount Amanus and Lebanon within the Assyrian palace precincts, the far-off land of Punt became a paradigm for Egyptian temple groves. Somewhere along the Eritrean/Ethiopian coast and frequently described as the "land of the god," mysterious and exotic Punt was a favorite trading expedition spot for the female pharaoh Hatshepsut. Particularly prized were the "trees of green incense,"[110] the precious resins of myrrh and frankin-

---

101. *ANET*, 110. Ezek 31:8 describes Lebanon as the "garden of God." See the discussion with accompanying iconography in O. Keel, *The Song of Songs* (tr. F. J. Gaiser; Continental Commentary; Minneapolis: Fortress, 1994) 169-71.

102. For example, *ARAB* 2, §415.

103. *ARAB* 2, §399.

104. For example, *ARAB* 2, §§402, 403.

105. *ARE* 4, §410.

106. *ARE* 4.115n.e, 264n.a.

107. *ARE* 4, §§194, 215, 217, 220, 262, 264.

108. *ARE* 4, §272.

109. For example, estates of Re (*ARE* 4, §280) and Ptah (*ARE* 4, §337).

110. J. A. Tyldesley, *Hatchepsut: The Female Pharaoh* (London: Viking, 1996) 146.

cense needed for the manufacture of incense. Striking is that not only were supplies of incense taken from Punt but also living trees that could be transplanted in the gardens of the temple of Amen. In the scenes of her magnificent Deir el-Bahri temple, around thirty trees or parts of tree are depicted in rich detail.[111] One inscription refers to "31 fresh myrrh trees, brought as marvels of Punt for the majesty of this god Amen, lord of Thebes; never was seen the like since the beginning."[112] This grove from Africa transplanted in the temple precincts of Amen is literally a Punt in miniature: by the command of the great god Amen, her "father," Hatshepsut establishes for him "a Punt in his house, to plant the trees of God's-Land beside his temple, in his garden, according as he commanded. . . . I have made for him a Punt in his garden."[113]

Hatshepsut's successor and stepson, Thutmose III, perhaps inspired by, if not set to outdo, Hatshepsut's horticultural prowess,[114] constructs a new temple at the east end of the Karnak complex, his "Festival Hall," behind which is a small room, his "Botanical Garden," which depicts the flora brought back from Syria during his twenty-fifth year.[115] The inscription of Thutmose's third campaign featured in this unique chamber refers to the reliefs as the "plants which his majesty found in the land of Retenu. All plants that grow, all flowers that are in God's-Land [which were found by] his majesty when his majesty proceeded to Upper Retenu, to subdue [all] the countrie[s], according to the command of his father, Amon, who put them beneath his sandals."[116] This particular horticultural endeavor is expressly associated with Thutmose's conquest of Syria. This recessed, botanical chamber is an enduring symbol of his victories "put before my father Amon, in this great temple of Amon, a memorial forever and ever."[117]

To sum up, gardens in ancient Near Eastern royal historiography served to bear witness to the significant achievements of the king. They were the "natural" signs of restoration, both urban and cultic, as well as of victory over foreign lands. Such rich background sets in relief the powerful significance of the prophet's envisaged garden. With garden spade in hand, Yahweh is ready to plant a victory garden to mark the reconstitution of a people in a land once

111. Ibid., 148.

112. *ARE* 2, §272.

113. *ARE* 2, §295.

114. For the alleged animosity between Hatchepsut and her stepson see the most recent, albeit debatable, discussion in Tyldesley, *Hatchepsut*, 216-27.

115. P. A. Clayton, *Chronicle of the Pharaohs* (London: Thames and Hudson, 1994) 110.

116. *ARE* 2, §451.

117. *ARE* 2, §452.

cursed. The restoration of a desiccated land and a devastated community is no mean feat; it takes nothing less than a warrior king to "set out to build a city in the desert, in the wasteland" — so asserts Shalmaneser IV with self-congratulatory flair.[118]

The Anti-Garden: Idol Manufacture in Isaiah 44:9-20

Contrary to the horticultural prowess of earthly kings, the prophet's visionary grove is established exclusively by Israel's God and is thus off limits to human artifice. As confirmation, human work on wood is mentioned only in association with the production of idols in Second Isaiah. The felling of trees is described in excruciating detail in the satire of the idol makers of 44:9-20, a passage embedded within an international trial scene.[119] Though the holm tree(?)[120] and oak are also mentioned (44:14), the cedar[121] gains the spotlight as the one the carpenter plants and patiently cultivates, only to be cut down, half of which is used for the fire for fuel and the other half fashioned into an idol (vv. 14-17). The indictment that concludes the prose sets the ironic tone at an even higher pitch (vv. 18-20). In contrast to 41:20, 44:18-19aα profile a taxonomy of ignorance. Here the light of understanding is all but extinguished for the artisan. Not only is the process of idol manufacture enervating, as in the case of the ironsmith (v. 12; cf. 41:6-7), but it is also an exercise in self-delusion and, ultimately, self-destruction (44:20).[122] The final product assumes human form (*tabnît 'îš*, v. 13), as much a thing of beauty as a premonition of human frailty and death.

Curiously, the process of production is told in reverse. The satire begins with the final product (v. 13b) and then recounts the steps that led to it in some-

118. *AR* 3.242 (A.O.105.2.10-11).

119. It is usually assumed that 44:9-20, along with the other passages on idolatry (40:18-20; 41:5-7; 46:5-7), is secondary. Yet despite being frequently regarded as prose, the text in *BHS* is formatted as poetry. Indeed, the section does exhibit poetic parallelism in chiastic fashion (e.g., vv. 12ab, 13a). Moreover, the highly variable prosody of this passage is not unprecedented elsewhere in Second Isaiah (e.g., 41:1-10). In addition, the nonsequential movement of the drama precludes a strictly prose setting. See R. J. Clifford, "The Function of Idol Passages in Second Isaiah," *CBQ* 42 (1980) 460-64.

120. Heb. *tirzâ*. Clifford translates it as "ilex" ("Function of Idol Passages," 461).

121. I read the *Ketib* of v. 14b as *'erez* instead of *'ōren*.

122. Clifford claims that v. 20 is an insertion, since its judgmental tone is "out of harmony with the restrained ironic narration of the passage" ("Function of Idol Passages," 463). Such a judgment fails to account for the conclusive position of the verse, serving as an answer to v. 17bγ. See also Wilson's criticism in *Nations*, 175-76.

what haphazard fashion. But there is perhaps a reason behind this chronological madness. Instead of the narrative sequence immediately returning to the point of origin after v. 13 (i.e., back to the planting of the cedar, v. 14b), there is an intervening step. For emphasis, the narrative singles out the felling of the cedar before describing its planting and growth. The reader moves immediately from the final product, an *imago hominis,* to the destruction of the tree, which supplies the raw material. Idol manufacture entails first and foremost arboreal destruction. The jarring effect is heightened when following the reference to the flourishing cedar, carefully planted and nourished by the rain, the narrative immediately consigns it to the fire to warm the artisan.

This back-and-forth movement between the burning wood and idol manufacture drips with irony. The artisan is unable to see the absurdity of idol production vis-à-vis the burning of cedar wood for cooking food (v. 19). The irony comes to a head with the concluding statement, "He feeds on ashes" (v. 20).[123] Here two opposing actions, one life-sustaining and one life-deluding, are collapsed together. Idol manufacture offers only a diet of destruction, one that inexorably saps the life out of the artisan unawares (cf. v. 12), rendering him lifeless (lit. "nothing," *tōhû,* v. 9). Although the artisan cries out to his polished block of wood for deliverance (v. 17b), the consequence is the opposite. "He cannot save himself," concludes the narrator in v. 20. The idol is simply a projection of himself, ostensibly a glorious figure (*tip'eret 'ādām,* v. 13) but unveiled as pathetic and lifeless, an object of shame and destruction (vv. 11, 17b, 20). The road to self-destruction thus begins when the ax is taken to the tree.[124] The cedar's destruction adumbrates the destruction of those who use its wood to practice idolatry.

If Richard Clifford is correct that the larger unit of 44:6-22 presents a trial scene in which the idol makers represent the nations with their idol witnesses,[125] then certain explosive international implications are to be discerned from the satire. Idolatry is a death trap for the nations, Israel not excluded. As a tree is cut and burned, so is the life of the manipulator of dead wood drained away, his cognitive senses rendered useless, reduced to mirroring his product, dull and lifeless. The contrast with Yahweh's garden could not be more marked. The carpenter's activity in cultivating his grove only to cut it down to create

123. *rō'eh 'ēper;* cf. Gen 18:27; Job 42:6. Although the verb refers to tending herds, it can also denote feeding and grazing (Gen 41:2, 18; Isa 30:23). The use of the term here verges on the metaphorical, as attested in Prov 15:14, and can connote identity by association (Prov 13:20; 28:7; 20:3).

124. It is no coincidence that the description of idol manufacture is prefaced with a reference to the ironsmith's ax (v. 12; cf. v. 14; Deut 20:19).

125. Clifford, "Function of Idol Passages," 463.

idols confirms his blindness and ignorance. It is, in the end, a violation of worship and, no less, a rape of reason. Yahweh's victory garden, on the one hand, serves as the locus of enlightenment, a display of redemptive power designed to awaken the senses to new heights of understanding and authentic veneration (41:20),[126] while testifying of a people sustained and flourishing. The grove of idols, on the other hand, is nothing but a nursery of nonsense, the tragic testimony of a *senseless* waste of life for both the cultivation and its cultivator.

In the Garden: An Ethos of Righteousness and Justice

In addition to understanding and knowledge, joy and thanksgiving over both Jacob's vindication and Zion's restoration comprise the harvest of Yahweh's garden (51:3). As the parched wasteland constitutes the common ground between a dispersed people and Zion,[127] so Yahweh's victory garden marks their mutual restoration and reunion. But more than thanksgiving and joy are harvested from this garden. Isaiah 45:8 specifically identifies salvation *(yeša')* and righteousness *(ṣĕdāqâ)* sprouting out of the ground.[128] Similarly, in 32:15-18 the wilderness is transformed into a "forest" and "fruitful field" *(ya'ar* and *karmel)* in which righteousness *(ṣĕdāqâ)* and justice *(mišpāṭ)* dwell.[129] The results of this "indwelling" are peace and security *(šālôm)*.[130] The images are unmistakably similar to 45:8; the only difference lies in the precise relationship between the garden metaphor and its tenor: whereas the fertile field in First Isaiah provides a secure habitation for righteousness (32:18), the fertile habitation in Second Isaiah is identified with righteousness (45:8). Either way, the garden produces a communal ethos in which righteousness and justice find firm rootage.

Throughout the book of Isaiah, "righteousness" *(ṣĕdāqâ* or *ṣedeq)* and "justice" *(mišpāṭ)* are either poetically paired in parallel cola or, on occasion, tightly juxtaposed to form a hendiadys or linguistic whole.[131] Such poetic

126. Cf. 42:16, 18-20, in which Israel is depicted as the blind and deaf servant. As noted above, perception plays a crucial role in the prophet's rhetorical arsenal.
127. See 43:19-21; 51:3.
128. See also Isa 61:11, which likens righteousness *(ṣĕdāqâ)* and praise *(tĕhillâ)* sprouting forth *(ṣmḥ)* before the nations like the shoots of a garden.
129. For similar language see 1:21.
130. Curiously, Batto ("Covenant of Peace," 201-10) overlooks this central passage in his discussion of the covenantal motif of the planting of peace (cf. Ezek 34:25-30; Hos 2:18-25; Lev 26:3-6; Zech 8:12).
131. For example, in synonymous parallelism: 5:16; 28:17; 32:16; 56:1; 59:9, 14; as a hendiadys: 9:6; 33:5. See Weinfeld, *Social Justice,* 25-39.

correspondence is not as pronounced in Second Isaiah, however. Nevertheless, this lack of literary correlation need not suggest that "righteousness" has severed all ties with the semantic environment of "justice," thus assuming an entirely different meaning. To the contrary, the inner unity between justice and righteousness is carefully preserved in Second Isaiah, for it is precisely their interrelationship that is transformed in new ways, as will be seen. But first it is necessary to discern the peculiar significance of ṣedeq in Second Isaiah. It appears that this prophet of the exile has increased the term's repertoire of meaning without digging up and discarding the semantic groundwork laid by his prophetic predecessor. One illustrative example is found in 51:4-8, which opens with tôrâ and mišpāṭ conjoined in parallel fashion (v. 4). The related term ṣedeq — frequently rendered "victory" or "vindication" in the Cyrus material[132] — is then introduced in the following verse in conjunction with yešaʿ ("salvation," v. 5).[133] Others have noted this particular nuance with which Second Isaiah imbues ṣedeq.[134] The root's association with military victory certainly predates the prophet.[135] Yet this is hardly an exclusive nuance for the prophet, for ṣedeq also bears clear affinities to tôrâ and mêšārîm ("equity") elsewhere (e.g., 42:21; 51:7; 45:19).

On another front, tôrâ and yešaʿ are bound up together in 51:4-5 by virtue of their common predicate: they both "issue forth" (yāṣāʾ). As salvation has gone forth, eminently victorious, so will Yahweh's tôrâ, eminently efficacious. It is no surprise, then, to find in v. 7 tôrâ and ṣedeq brought together as qualities to be appropriated in the will and heart.[136] The circle is now complete: Yahweh's salvation is juridically binding and Yahweh's tôrâ is decisively salvific. The inclusively fluid meaning of ṣedeq, as demonstrated from the various placements of the term, prevents any attempt to separate law from liberation and liberation from law.[137] In the garden, an ethos of righteousness is cultivated whose fruits are release *and* restoration, salvation *and* moral constitution. Moreover, salvation (yĕšûʿâ) is conjoined with ṣĕdāqâ in vv. 6 and 8 in a context of perdurability

132. For example, 41:2, 10; 45:13.

133. Several Greek manuscripts add the metaphor of light, consonant with v. 4, thereby establishing a clear correspondence between tôrâ and ṣedeq.

134. S. Blank, *Prophetic Faith in Isaiah* (New York: Harper & Bros., 1958) 152-56; Wilson, *Nations,* 105-6.

135. Cf. ṣĕdāqôt in Judg 5:11; Mic 6:5; see F. Crüsemann, "Jahwes Gerechtigkeit im AT," *EvT* 36 (1976) 427-50.

136. Ps 119:142 and Isa 51:7 also relate righteousness (ṣedeq) to tôrâ.

137. In addition, the frequently suggested distinction between ṣedeq and ṣĕdāqâ, one abstract and the other concrete in meaning, does not hold for Second Isaiah. For a survey of the literature, see Weinfeld, *Social Justice,* 34n.31.

not found in First Isaiah yet sustained in 59:16-17, 61:10, and 63:1.[138] This language of permanence, which stands in sharp relief to the description of creation's passing away (v. 6) and social conflict (v. 8), occurs in two other related passages. In 40:8 Yahweh's word endures, while the grassy fields wither away. In 54:10 Yahweh's covenantal love for Zion (ḥesed) remains everlasting, a bĕrît šālôm ("covenant of peace") whose precedent is found in the Noachic oath (v. 9). What endures beyond creation is Yahweh's redemptive word of justice and salvation, the fruits of covenantal commitment.

As for ṣedeq or ṣĕdāqâ, "vindication" is an appropriate translation that bridges the various poetic correspondences, particularly in light of the prevailing jurisdictional language and form that characterize the prophet's discourse. Righteousness connotes the triumph of right and justice in a legal proceeding, whether it be over the nations, their gods, or individual contenders. Given their wide semantic range, ṣedeq and ṣĕdāqâ presume a triumph not limited to liberation. Israel's triumph is for the cause of justice and righteousness, indeed, for the sake of Yahweh's name (48:9; 52:5-6). It is the moral triumph of redemption that shall put to shame all who have questioned Yahweh's purpose within the international court of contention (45:24-25).

The Servant and the Shepherd

Perhaps it is no coincidence, then, that mišpāṭ and ṣĕdāqâ or ṣedeq, the harvest of Yahweh's victory garden, find their historical ramifications played out in two separate yet interrelated figures: Yahweh's shepherd, Cyrus, who brings about divine ṣedeq (41:2, 10; 45:13), and Yahweh's servant, Israel, who implements Yahweh's mišpāṭ (42:1, 3, 4). Together, they embody the two sides of royal reign, a bifurcation of royal character. On the one hand, Cyrus assumes the role of Yahweh's victorious arm subduing the nations. He is Yahweh's pet warrior unmatched in power and skill (41:21-29; 45:1-7), an invincible raptor (46:11) who imparts a swift and terrible justice on the nations, his feet scarcely touching the path of his campaigns (41:3). Cyrus is, in essence, the Blitzkrieger of Yahweh's righteous might (45:24). He is to bring about the kind of victory that vindicates Yahweh's redemptive purpose for Israel (41:2, 10; 45:13), which leaves no choice but to break the might of Babylon (45:2; cf. 47:1-15) as forcefully as Pharaoh's army was "quenched like a wick" (43:17).

By contrast, Yahweh's servant quenches no wick (42:3); he displays no such spectacular might. Indeed, he suffers from a justice gone awry (mēʿōṣer

138. See also 46:12-13.

256

ûmimmišpāṭ, 53:8). Yet he is commissioned to bring forth *mišpāṭ* and *tôrâ* to the nations (42:1, 3, 4). Such justice is implemented not through might but through the endurance of suffering (42:2-3; 53:11). Yet as Cyrus was aroused in *ṣedeq* (45:13), so Yahweh calls servant Israel in *ṣedeq* (42:6). Cyrus and servant find their common bond in the multidimensional role of righteousness. While Yahweh's shepherd captures the lion's share of righteous judgment to execute on the nations, Yahweh's servant receives the arduous, even punishing, task of extending justice to the ends of the earth (49:4-6). One inaugurates Yahweh's righteousness by force; the other cultivates it through patient suffering.

Both dimensions of righteousness, deliverance and justice, are integral to Yahweh's purpose, particularly in a world in which royal authority and authoritative guidance, righteous power and just teaching, were rent asunder by the experience of exile, when imperial rule was in the hands of foreigners. Despite the ostensible severance, however, the prophet strains to hold both justice and deliverance together in a remarkably nuanced way. As the focus on Cyrus fades from view after 48:12-15 and the servant comes to share a greater portion of the rhetorical spotlight in 50:4-11 and 52:13–53:12, the functional relationship between these two figures becomes further clarified.

Commensurate with Israel's vindication, Yahweh's judgment against the nations and their idols levels out, in effect, the uneven political landscape in order to allow Israel's justice, its ethos, to flourish. Yahweh's message of comfort, transmitted through a chain of commands to the heavenly council in 40:1-11,[139] calls for clearing away the rocky terrain (vv. 3-4). But not everything is flattened. The transformed topography sets in high relief the one mountain remaining, the high mountain that daughter Zion is summoned to ascend (v. 9). As the executor of Israel's vindication, Cyrus serves to clear the way by subduing the nations (45:1-2). Consequently, space is made so that Zion can spread out like a tent to possess the nations (54:3), as Yahweh spreads out the heavens like a curtain (40:22; 44:24; 48:13; 51:13).

The prophet is not saying, as Millard Lind suggests in his otherwise perceptive article, "that the politics which tries to control by coercion is ineffective in terms of the continuity of community."[140] Rather the prophet finds co-

---

139. See C. Seitz, "The Divine Council: Temporal Transition and New Prophecy in the Book of Isaiah," *JBL* 109 (1990) 193-206.

140. M. C. Lind, "Monotheism, Power, and Justice: A Study in Isaiah 40–55," *CBQ* 46 (1984) 435. Drawing from S. Mowinckel, Lind introduces an artificial tension between the "power politics" of Cyrus and Yahweh's "creative power of word-event" (p. 439). Part of Yahweh's creative power is in calling Cyrus to tear down nations in order to make room for Israel's restoration (Isa 44:28; 45:1-7, 13).

ercion through Cyrus's conquests to be supremely necessary not only for Israel's restoration (44:26-27; 45:13) but also for Yahweh's universal *mišpāṭ* (45:22-23), promulgated by the servant (42:1, 3, 4; 50:4). The intrinsic connection between the coercive force of judgment — what Lind disparagingly refers to as violent power politics[141] — and the ethos of the servant's discourse is best illustrated in the third servant song (50:4-11), in which the speaker refers to the assurance of a vindicator (*maṣdîq*, v. 8a) in the face of adversity (vv. 8, 11), as well as to his vocation as teacher (v. 4). Moreover, the servant proclaims to have a hand in the fiery demise of his enemies (v. 11)! Here the vocational distinction between the shepherd and the servant is blurred.

Nevertheless, the servant's role does not end in self-vindication. His vocation is established, in part, through suffering and patient endurance. For illustration, the poet chooses only two images, the lamb (53:7) and the sapling (*yônēq*, 53:2). The latter resonates with much of the prophet's botanical imagery elsewhere. Unlike the cedar in Yahweh's mighty grove, the servant is a frail root in dry ground (*ṣîyâ;* cf. 41:18b), without form (*tō'ar*) or majesty (*hādār*, 53:2).[142] The antithesis to Eden's alluring tree of wisdom (Gen 3:6), this young plant is utterly undesirable in appearance.[143] Yet the servant is equally a repository of knowledge, of wisdom gained by hardship and humiliation (Isa 53:7, 11a), of knowledge that powerfully imputes righteousness (v. 11b).[144] The servant's vocation is realized by two related modes of agency: (1) through self-sacrifice, by serving as the silent object of abuse, the servant effects the righteous status of the nations; and (2) through Yahweh's power the servant will be exalted to unprecedented heights of international glory, much to the astonishment of the nations (52:13; 53:12). The frail sapling shall flourish.

In short, the figures of the servant and the shepherd embody the variant shades of Yahweh's redemptive purpose for Israel and the nations: victory, vindication, righteousness, and justice. The interrelational nature of their respective vocations is most vividly represented, dare I submit, within the botanical realm. The series of divine commands in 45:8, which constitutes part

141. Lind, "Monotheism," 439.

142. The latter term can be applied to themes relating to royalty and agriculture (e.g., Ps 21:5 [MT 6]; Lev 23:40).

143. The suggestive language of Isa 53:2b, with its (negative) concentration on sight (*r'h*) and desire (*ḥmd*), bears striking correspondence to the description of the "tree of the knowledge of good and evil," whose desirable appearance is described as irresistible (Gen 3:6).

144. Lit. "make many righteous," according to the Masoretic accentual division.

of — or is inserted into — the extensive swath of Cyrus material from 44:24 to 45:13, depicts a scene of rain and regeneration. The heavens shower *ṣedeq* on the parched land, so that *yešaʿ* and *ṣĕdāqâ* can sprout forth from the soil.

Given his association with the victory of righteousness (41:2; 45:13), Cyrus is the *ṣedeq* that comes like a swift, torrential rain, washing away oppressing nations that have desolated Israel's cultural terrain. This downpour of vindication satiates the parched ground, thereby enabling *ṣĕdāqâ* and thus justice to germinate and flourish (45:8). Justice and right order can find no place to flourish without the rocky terrain forcibly leveled and inundated with life-giving water. Elsewhere in biblical literature of royal provenance, the figure of the king is likened to both the sun and the rain.[145] It is not fortuitous, then, that Cyrus, as *ṣedeq*, is likened to precipitation, enabling the community to flourish. The servant is the plant that represents the community (53:2), requiring patient cultivation.[146] Elsewhere, this servile figure is likened to light, a light to the nations (42:6; 49:6), the orb of justice to the peoples (51:4).[147] Again, the shepherd and the servant represent two sides of the royally imprinted coin, yet they are presented as discrete figures with different, yet fully compatible, missions. Whereas the former comes swiftly as a torrential downpour, the latter arrives in the ever persistent movement of rising and setting and in the gradual development of botanical growth. To return to 55:10-11, Cyrus is, in short, Yahweh's commissioned weapon, the royal word that marches out to clear and prepare the soil for the transplanting of Yahweh's people. In "return," the community is cultivated, and that cultivation is the task and testimony of the servant.

The Contours of the Cultivated Community

The moral contours of this righteousness that sprouts forth from the soil are never detailed by the unnamed prophet. Already noted is the remarkable biodiversity of the righteous grove. As for the ethical character of the community, only allusions are made at various points, suggesting that in terms of *tôrâ* teaching, the prophet does not consider himself an innovator but one commissioned to fashion new skins for vintage wine. Nowhere is a *new* covenant officially proffered, as in Jer 31:31-34. The prophet's interest in the traditional

---

145. For example, Ps 72:6 (corrected); Prov 19:12; Job 29:23-25; 2 Sam 23:3-4. See M. S. Smith's discussion of the royal roots of solar imagery in "The Near Eastern Background of Solar Language for Yahweh," *JBL* 109 (1990) 29-39.

146. Cf. the servant's arduous labors in 49:4.

147. The sun god in Mesopotamia, Šamaš or UTU, was also the god of justice and righteousness.

norms of cultic purity and conduct is clear in Gen 43:22-28. As Jacob is debili-
tated by despair, so Yahweh, through cultic neglect, has become burdened by
Israel's sins (vv. 22-24). The venerable tradition of cultic purity is crucial for life
outside captivity: Zion's captive children are ordered both to depart and to pu-
rify themselves (52:11; cf. 48:20). Zion, in turn, will admit only the circumcised
and the clean (52:1). The prophet's vision of community grows directly out of
tôrâ teaching, which, along with *mišpāṭ*, emanates as a light to the peoples
(51:4-5). For the prophet, history demonstrates that disobedience to *tôrâ* has
resulted in Jacob's plunder and captivity (42:24). Consequently, Israel's release
entails a commensurate restoration of its covenantal conduct.[148] Second Isaiah
lays the groundwork for a new enactment of Israel's social charter, one governed by equity and justice, that is, righteousness.[149]

The prophet roots Israel's restoration in the soil of Yahweh's covenantal
commands (48:18). Yahweh's repetitive self-pronouncements correspond to
traditional *tôrâ* guidance and piety.[150] Not unrelated is the prophet's concern
for the proper invocation of Yahweh's name, particularly in oaths (48:1; cf.
Exod 20:7). "Truth" *('ĕmet)* and "righteousness" *(ṣĕdāqâ)* provide the norms
of propriety and have everything to do with the confession of Yahweh's sovereignty over the nations' idols (cf. Exod 23:13). In addition, the prophet's depiction of Jacob as imprisoned and impoverished discloses an urgent concern
for the equitable treatment of the most vulnerable in society (41:17; 42:7;
49:9-10; 55:1), one that reflects both prophetic and royal, not to mention
Deuteronomic, provenance.[151] In the exodus, Israel's self-identity was forged
on the anvil of oppression, providing thereby a powerful impetus for treating
its own destitute with equity and mercy.[152]

Second Isaiah envisions the contours of the restored community shaped
by *tôrâ*, both cultic and constitutional, hence the invitation to the covenantal
feast in Isaiah 55.[153] What is notably new is the prophet's recasting of the royal
covenant, already adumbrated in the frequently used term borrowed from the
field of botany with which this study began, *ṣāmaḥ,* "to sprout forth," the
prophet's *terminus technicus* for the germination of a new creation and thus a

148. The intervening years of exile is of little concern for the prophet. The exile represents at best a liminal period of judgment that gives way to a new beginning of cultic and
covenantal restoration.

149. See 42:1, 3, 4; 50:10; 51:1, 7; cf. Deut 16:20-21.

150. For example, 43:11; 44:6, 8; 45:14b; 46:9b; 47:8, 10; cf. Deut 4:35, 39; 5:6; 32:39.

151. For example, Psalm 113; 1 Sam 2:2, 7-8; Deut 10:18-19; 24:17-22; Isa 61:1-9.

152. For example, Exod 23:9; Lev 19:34; Deut 10:19.

153. For the Deuteronomic connections to this chapter, see W. Brueggemann, "Isaiah 55 and Deuteronomic Theology," *ZAW* 80 (1968) 191-203.

new community. Outside Second Isaiah, the language of botanical growth is frequently tied to the Davidic monarchy.[154] Such language connotes the sure resurgence of royal power. For example, Ps 132:17 refers to the dynastic horn of David "sprouting up" (ṣāmaḥ). Ezekiel foretells of the day in which a royal horn will sprout up for Israel (29:21). Second Isaiah's contemporary, Jeremiah, describes David, the executor of justice and righteousness in the land, as a "righteous sprout" (ṣemaḥ ṣaddîq, 23:5; ṣemaḥ ṣĕdāqâ, 33:15).[155] Zechariah employs the image of the "sprout" or branch (ṣemaḥ) to acknowledge the rise of Yahweh's royal servant Zerubbabel (3:8), whose very name ("shoot of Babylon") is consonant with such imagery.[156]

Building on Jeremiah's metaphor of the "righteous sprout," Second Isaiah reconfigures royal righteousness (ṣĕdāqâ) to incorporate the whole community. Although Zion is not "deconstructed," David is. The one righteous sprout of David is now extended and democratized to comprise all of Zion's children in the same way that the prophet collectivizes the covenantal grant of David in 55:3-5. Similarly, in Yahweh's sacred grove stands not one tree but a multitude of trees that together bear witness to Yahweh's redemptive power (41:20; 44:5). The sapling of the servant, too, is representative of corporate Israel.[157] With the fulfillment of judgment, Yahweh's ancient covenant with David (2 Sam 7:4-14) enables all Israel to bear witness to the nations. The new community is David redivivus as much as Yahweh's victory garden is Eden recultus. Indeed, they are one and the same.

154. Much is made of the reference in Isa 11:1 to "shoot" (ḥōṭer) and "branch" (nēṣer) issuing from, respectively, the stump and roots of Jesse. That the botanical language is different in Second Isaiah may well reflect Jeremianic influence, particularly if Isa 4:2-6 (cf. ṣemaḥ in 4:2) is a later addition. The specialized verb for growth in 11:1b (prh) is used in 45:8b to describe the earth bearing salvation (yeša').

155. The latter text of Jeremiah shifts the focus of the conferred titular name ("YHWH is our righteousness") from the royal figure to Jerusalem. Such a move from the individual to the community is one that Second Isaiah makes all the more explicit by making corporate the Davidic covenant in 55:3-5.

156. Cf. Zech 6:12. The metaphoric use of ṣemaḥ is also documented in a third-century BCE Phoenician royal inscription in connection with the term ṣdq (KAI 43.10-11), meaning either "legitimate heir" (so C. L. Meyers and E. M. Meyers, Haggai, Zechariah 1–8 [AB 25B; Garden City, N.Y.: Doubleday, 1987] 202-3) or "righteous shoot," i.e., an heir who will act righteously (so S. E. Loewenstamm, Comparative Studies in Biblical and Ancient Oriental Literature [AOAT 204; Kevelaer: Butzon & Bercker; Neukirchen-Vluyn: Neukirchener, 1980] 212-13; Weinfeld, Social Justice, 60).

157. For example, 41:8 and 49:3, in which Israel is identified as Yahweh's servant. See the most recent discussion of Laato, who, drawing from H.-J. Hermisson, argues that the servant figure represents two different Israels, one disloyal and one ideal (Servant of YHWH, 35).

261

Again, the prophet does not convey in great detail the moral shape or ethos of the restored community. The force of the prophet's rhetoric is focused elsewhere, primarily on demonstrating that the time is ripe for sowing, now that the rain clouds of Yahweh's vindication are brewing on the horizon. Unlike a modern-day meteorologist, this prophet scans the heavens not to predict but to announce the storm that will rain down Yahweh's new reign of righteousness. Far from inspiring dread, the storm that transforms the wilderness is meant to dispel all fear.[158] The fructified desert is the tangible sign and result of Yahweh comforting Zion's wastelands (Isa 51:3). In the recultivated Eden, fear is permanently expelled, and with it all opposition and conflict (e.g., 41:11-13).

What is the content of this fear that the prophet so strenuously tries to allay? Given the intimate association between Yahweh's assurances and the desert's transformation, such fear is first and finally the fear of the community's utter dissolution, of the garden's desiccation as a result of divine abandonment or limitation (40:27). Whereas First Isaiah uttered judgment against those who cultivated pagan groves, namely, that they would wither away (Isa 1:30), his predecessor assures Zion that it will flourish. To the idolatrous nations Yahweh comes either as a sirocco to wither the grass and desiccate the land (40:22-24; 44:15)[159] or as a downpour sweeping away all oppression to set in motion the growth of life, the cycle of ṣedeq (45:8; 55:10). To Zion, Yahweh comes as gardener, whose life-giving water nourishes and refashions a people who were once nourished in Yahweh's womb.

For the exilic prophet, the botanical realm is a window into the political realm. The regeneration of the land constitutes nothing less than Zion's revival. The prophet is not, as is sometimes assumed, merely urging the exiled in Babylon to embark on a hazardous wilderness journey with the promise of an oasis planted in the howling wasteland to sustain them along the way.[160] The prophet explicitly acknowledges the wilderness tradition three times (48:21; 43:20; 49:10),[161] but imbues it with the language of cultivation (43:19,

158. See 40:9-10; 41:10, 13-14; 43:1, 5; 44:2; 51:7; 54:4. In a related tradition, Isaiah 35 opens with the panoramic view of the blossoming desert and moves immediately to a call to strengthen those incapacitated by fear (35:3-4).

159. The sequence of nature's destruction found in 42:14-17; 50:2-3; 51:9-10, which includes the desiccation of vegetation and rivers, highlights the divine warrior's role, as embodied by Cyrus in leveling out the political landscape and thereby vanquishing all opposition for the sake of Israel's restoration (cf. 44:27-28).

160. See, e.g., W. H. Propp, *Water in the Wilderness: A Biblical Motif and Its Mythological Background* (HSM 40; Atlanta: Scholars Press, 1987) 103-5; Simkins, *Creator and Creation*, 242.

161. The wilderness accounts in Exod 17:1-7 and Num 20:2-13, in which water plays a miraculous role, say nothing of a transformed wilderness.

ṣmḥ), overshadowing it with the towering cedars of the new garden, of a wilderness transformed. In so doing, that ancient desert journey is extended to its proper destination, the mountain of God, not Sinai but Zion, from which Yahweh's *tôrâ* shall emanate (Isa 2:3b). The wilderness is thus no *terra intermedia*,[162] but it is a *terra reformanda*, a land poised for transformation, a community ready for reformation. Eden's recultivation in 51:3 is no temporary provision or mere way station for the elect on their way to Zion. To the contrary, all streams lead to Zion (49:10b), for the well-watered grove *is* the newly restored Zion, Israel's goal and Yahweh's destination. What sprouts forth from the soil is a reunited people, vindicated and transplanted, called to bear witness to all the world.

Whereas the uplifted signal *(nēs)* in 49:22 may very well serve as a royal sign of liberation, that is, a symbol of freedom to signal the release and return of Zion's children,[163] it is merely provisional when compared to the grove that is expressly called Yahweh's everlasting sign at the conclusion of the prophet's discourse (55:13). In place of a pole or tree, which in Hittite law signaled freedom to particular cities, the prophet unveils a luxuriant grove as an enduring memorial to the permanence of liberty, to the binding and perdurable nature of Israel's vocation of holiness.[164] Second Isaiah's message is thus both soteriologically and aretogenically oriented,[165] designed to shape the moral identity and conduct of a restored people.

What fruit, then, is born from the witness of a land fructified and a people restored? Or, to cast the question theologically, what returns to Yahweh, whose purposeful word has been sent forth (55:11)? Something does return by way of confirmation of an accomplished mission. As a word is sent out, so a word must return, one that confirms the realized goal of Yahweh's redemptive activity on behalf of Jacob and, indeed, of all the nations (45:22-23).[166] Water is gratuitously poured out in the desert to give drink not only for God's chosen people but also for the wild animals of the *tōhû* ("wilderness"), "so that they may declare [Yahweh's] praise" (43:20-21). In solidarity with Israel,

162. So Mathews, *Defending Zion*, 125, 129.

163. So Weinfeld, *Social Justice*, 14-15, 103-7.

164. See the important discussion of the biblical concept of liberty in S. D. McBride Jr., "The Yoke of Torah," *Ex Auditu* 11 (1995) 1-16.

165. Derived from the Classical Greek *aretē*, meaning excellence or virtue, this newly coined term has been introduced to highlight the ethical dimensions of soteriology and the pastoral dimensions of doctrine. See E. Charry, "Academic Theology in Pastoral Perspective," *TToday* 50 (1993) 101-2n.15.

166. The apparent difference between 45:22-23 and 55:11 is deceiving, since the content and results of that word are spelled out in no uncertain terms in 45:23b.

all of nature resounds with the peals of praise.[167] Here nature finds its true fulfillment: it provides a cosmic model for Israel's response to Yahweh's redemptive work, a paradigm of praise. Reclaiming the purpose of covenantal law, Yahweh's praise and glory constitute the essential goal of Israel's redemption (43:7, 23; 48:9-11). Sacrifices of praise and honor, of bounty and booty, accompany the word that returns to God from "battle," from having watered and raised a veritable blue-ribbon garden of victory, the new "city of righteousness" ('îr haṣṣedeq, Isa 1:26). It is to this end, then, that the unnamed prophet of the exile, by the proverbial sweat of his brow, sets out to cultivate his community (32:13).

"Plotting the Resurrection": The Old and the New

Second Isaiah's view of creation is a *creatio continuata* with a vengeance: "From this time forward I make you hear new things, hidden things that you have not known. They are created now, not long ago; before today you have never heard of them" (48:6b-7a). The prophet revels in the surprising nature of Yahweh's ongoing work in creation. More than an event in the primordial past or a continued state of preservation, creation for the prophet is the arena of divine innovation, rife with novelty and renewal, a cosmos as open-ended as God is freely sovereign. Not locked into timeless and static categories, creation is eminently historical; it will never be the same once God is finished redeeming Jacob, and neither will Zion.[168] As Gerhard von Rad is famous for noting, creation and redemption are virtually synonymous for the prophet.[169] Both nature and culture are poised for transformation. Nature is in need of redemption as much as Israel requires a new genesis. As Yahweh's judgment on Israel is inseparably tied to the land's desolation, so Israel's redemption is closely associated with the land's fructification. Such is the new thing Yahweh promises to Israel within the conflictive world of nations and nature.

Yet the dynamic nature of divine innovation is steadfastly covenantal in scope and structure. "Blessed shall you be in the city, and blessed shall you be in the field," begins the Deuteronomic list of covenantal blessings (Deut 28:3). Field and city, culture and nature, are recipients of God's blessings,

---

167. See the hymn of victory in 42:10-17, esp. vv. 10-12.

168. See Ollenburger's perceptive discussion of the historical, providential nature of biblical creation in "Isaiah's Creation Theology," 54-71.

169. See Chapter 1.

contingent on Israel's fulfillment of the commandments and decrees that God charged Israel to observe in the land (6:1). Among the myriad of blessings is the guarantee of rain in due season (28:12). Conversely, when the covenant is breached, "Yahweh will change the rain of your land into powder, and only dust shall come down on you from the sky until you are destroyed" (28:24). The prophet of the exile clearly operates within this covenantal ethos when he announces the completion of Israel's service and the commencement of a new age of restoration and comfort (Isa 40:1-2; 49:13). Although Israel failed the stipulations of both cult and covenant (42:24-25; 43:22-28), the age of punishment has been fulfilled, making way for their attendant blessings.

The tension between the old and the new, between tradition and the unprecedented, is most starkly established in the prophet's diverging calls to remembrance and dismissal. In connection with the exodus tradition, on the one hand, the prophet enjoins his audience *not* to "remember the former things or consider the things of old" (43:18).[170] On the other hand, he exhorts transgressors, specifically idolaters, to "*remember* the former things of old" (46:9a). One injunction deals with the recovery of covenantal faithfulness (46:9b), the other with the manner of impending deliverance (43:19b-20). As for the latter, Yahweh's deliverance will be unprecedented, yet still very much related to the past. The dry path that allows for safe passage through the mighty waters but is submerged to extinguish Pharaoh's army "like a wick" (cf. Exod 15:10) serves as a foil for what the prophet is about to announce.

The formidable waters that were once parted for the safe travel of fleeing refugees now serve as the life-sustaining path through the threatening desert. No longer a threat, water is the source of deliverance, even of guidance, to the returning exiles, whereas the dry land presents an obstacle to overcome. To make matters even more convoluted, no foreigner king will be in hot pursuit to reclaim his illegitimate hegemony over God's chosen people. Instead, a new royal foreigner, Yahweh's anointed shepherd, will effect the release of a captive people, paving the way for their restoration. In this new age of liberty, the elements of nature and nativism are reversed, and the prophet's source of appeal to such divine innovation is a natural theology in which God

---

170. C. Seitz interprets the "former things," particularly in conjunction with the prophet's negative command, as reference to "Isaiah's judgment proclamation" (*Zion's Final Destiny* [Minneapolis: Fortress, 1991] 201). But an injunction to dismiss the previous period of judgment and punishment does not cohere with the immediate context of 43:14-21, which recounts the passage through the Reed Sea, an event of miraculous deliverance (vv. 16-17).

remains free to create what God will, unthwarted by human objection (45:9-13) and unshackled by tradition.

Despite repeated reference to the unprecedented nature of divine intervention, the prophet reminds the new Israel of its roots, of the rock from which they were hewn and of Abraham and Sarah who bore them (51:1-2). These roots go back even farther, the prophet claims, for the character of this new community is stamped with the contours of primordial creation: as Yahweh stretched out the heavens above, so will Zion's curtains be spread out to encompass, and thereby restore, even the most desolate areas (54:2-3). Similarly, Zion is to be recultivated as the heavens have been "planted" (51:16).[171] Similarly, as the solid foundations of the earth were laid, so those of the new Jerusalem, of the temple in particular, will be firmly established (44:28; 54:11). With welcoming arms, Zion greets returning Jacob and becomes the hostel of Israel's habitation, the source of covenantal life, and the ideal reflection of a world that was created not as an empty wasteland (*tōhû*, 45:18-19) but as the cradle of life and order (*ṣedeq*; cf. 48:1; 51:1). As the earth was created to produce life in abundance, so Zion is replanted as a holy garden, diverse and ever verdant.

Oblivious to our modern distaste for mixed metaphors, this prophet of the exile does not think twice about conflating images of nature and culture, those of garden and city. But then such evocative rhetoric finds its precedence in the Yahwist's planting of Eden and its embodiment in the Davidic kingdom.[172] The prophet has recultivated that garden for a new age with new effect. The recultivated garden is the righteous city Zion, where people can once again flourish, a habitation in which people can sink their roots deep into the fertile soil of covenantal integrity. For Isaiah, such discourse, which begins to break the bounds of ethnicity and nationality, is meant to glorify Israel's creator. It is for the city's sake that the showers of justice shall again water the urban wasteland. The rain must pummel and clear away the parched, rocky terrain of international conflict and brutality, as well as satiate Jacob's deprivation, whose thirst is for righteousness. Therein lies the victory. With the land inundated with the waters of justice, the prophet is not oblivious to the plumbing. Therein lies the covenant.

Drawn from the royal grant, the covenant's perdurability is contrasted with the evanescent power of earthly rulers. Yahweh's covenant requires the vanquishing of all princes and rulers with the exception of Cyrus. Their demise, too, is firmly rooted in Yahweh's creative capacity: princes and rulers

171. The MT is favored as the *lectio difficilior*.
172. See Chapter 3.

shall revert to *tōhû*, like grass withering before Yahweh's breath (40:22-24). By contrast, Yahweh's covenant with Israel is everlasting and reconfigures the international arena so that all the nations will come to rely on the glorified Israel for their source of cultural and moral sustenance (55:3-5). As a "light to the nations" (42:6; 49:6), this covenant assumes international, even cosmic proportions, superseding even creation itself. Though earth and heaven may vanish, Yahweh's righteousness remains (51:6, 8). Yet Yahweh's covenantal liberty still requires a ground on which to stand, and that ground is Zion, the garden of righteousness.

Although the specifics of covenantal loyalty are only alluded to in Second Isaiah, as mentioned above, the one blatantly direct course of human action to which the prophet repeatedly refers is set within the context of human creativity. Here one can find some resonance with the Priestly cosmogony, which portrays the creation of the cosmos in correspondence to the construction of the tabernacle.[173] With the prophet, however, the relation between divine and human creativity is one of ironic contrast rather than of correspondence, for the human product is idolatry.

Again, the prophet revels in describing the process of idol manufacture. In addition to 44:9-20, other passages are dispersed throughout the prophetic corpus. What they have in common is the detailed descriptions of various artisans constructing an idol with wood and various materials. The finished product is established as immovable (40:20; 41:7). The passage 41:6-7 is particularly telling. Here each contributor encourages the other by exhortation and, in one case, approbation: "It is good" (*ṭôb hû'*, v. 7). Empowerment and approbation are inextricably related (cf. Genesis 1). Nonetheless, the product is nothing, Yahweh proclaims (Isa 41:24), its creators being merely human; indeed, they too have become *tōhû* (44:9-11). The product is the producer, and vice versa. The true and sole source of strength comes from Yahweh, as made clear in the very next passage: "Do not fear, for I am with you; do not be afraid, for I am your God; I will strengthen you, I will help you, I will uphold you with my victorious right hand" (41:8-10; cf. 35:3-4). In reality, the prophet claims, idol manufacture is an enervating enterprise (44:12).

Try as they might to mimic divine activity, the idol makers are doomed to failure. Neither a rock of stability nor the arm of deliverance, the immovable idol is in fact a crushing burden on its worshipers. In a satire of the Babylonian procession of the gods, the prophet exposes the fallacy of idol worship. Fellow Israelites who worship idols are likened to beasts of burden, weary from bearing their lifeless load (46:1-7). Borne aloft in regal pageantry, the

173. See Chapter 2.

images of Marduk and his son, Nabu, require backbreaking work, and all for nothing. Such is the oppression of assimilation Israel suffers in a foreign land, requiring a new exodus toward the recovery of true worship. Idolatry is revealed for what it is, the most insidious form of self-demoralization (46:6-7). As the basis of aniconic worship, Yahweh's incomparability is the very foundation of human dignity.

Much in contrast to these burdensome loads, the God of Zion is far from immobile. Yahweh is the bearable lightness of being: "I have made, and I will bear; I will carry and will save" (46:4). Yahweh's pronouncement moves fluidly from creation to redemption. The problem with idols is that they can *not* move; by contrast, free and decisive movement characterizes the Rock of Israel's salvation. Only a God on the move can redeem a people and propel them homeward. Full of unflagging energy, this God does not rest or enjoy the sabbath (40:28). As Yahweh's people are stuck in the rut of hopelessness and fear, their world too is construed as impassable, barren of new possibilities and bereft of human dignity.

Yahweh's "new thing," God's creation of a new community, breaks the cycle of despair that is engendered by reading Israel's historical tradition as an obituary, as a compendium of Israel's fall into the pit of judgment, or of a people cast into the barren wasteland, the haunt of jackals (Mic 1:3; Job 30:29; Isa 13:22). Lifeless is the land of lamentation. As the desert is barren, so the judgment appears final and permanent. But as the judgment is lifted, so the wilderness is fructified, recultivated by the Creator, and the howls of lamentation are displaced by the praises of both wild animals and humans (Isa 43:20-21). The wasteland is cultivated, and with cultivation comes acculturation. A community is restored.

With the cedars towering above the land, this grove planted by Yahweh is as impregnable as it is lofty. This new Zion will no longer be the fodder for foreign kingdoms, whose goal is to fell the lofty trees in order to flex their imperial muscle over lands hinder and yon.[174] Relationships have radically changed: a foreigner is now a friend; an enemy king is Yahweh's messiah (45:1); lamenting jackals offer praise; and the mighty waters guide a delivered people. Nature and nativism are overturned, and woe to anyone who dares to question Yahweh's new ordering of life and community (45:9-11)! That Yahweh can create anew, even in unprecedented ways, suggests that *creatio continuata* is ever potent with new possibilities, of new configurations of relationships that in the end must enhance all honor and praise due Yahweh's sovereign name.[175]

---

174. See, e.g., 2 Kgs 19:23.
175. See F. M. Cross, "The Redemption of Nature," *PSB* 10 (1989) 102-3.

Although the prophet's envisaged community is a new creation, its ethos is venerable. The redeemed Israel is not created with an instantaneous flash out of the blue, but is cultivated in due season. Onward and upward grows this garden planted by Yahweh and tended by those whose primordial vocation is to "till and keep" the soil (Gen 2:15). The gardeners are the covenant keepers. The prophet understood well the art of gardening, of seasons and weather patterns, of the germination of blessing and the blight of judgment, all to cultivate the contours of a new covenant community that can bear the blessing and teach the ways of Israel's Creator to the world.

CHAPTER 5

"Rejoicing in His Inhabited World":
Wisdom's Playhouse in Proverbs

Over the waves of the sea, over all the earth, and over every people and nations I have held sway. Among all these I sought a resting place; in whose territory should I abide?

Sirach 24:6-7, NRSV

Wisdom is at home in the heart of the discerning.

Proverbs 14:33a

A frequently neglected text in many general treatments of creation theology and, more so, of biblical ethics,[1] Prov 8:22-31 marks the pinnacle of

---

1. On the one hand, any mention of Proverbs 8, or even the book of Proverbs, is lacking in such general treatments on biblical creation as O. H. Steck, *World and Environment* (BES; Nashville: Abingdon, 1980); R. A. Simkins, *Creator and Creation: Nature in the Worldview of Ancient Israel* (Peabody, Mass.: Hendrickson, 1994); J. Barr, *Biblical Faith and Natural Theology* (Oxford: Clarendon, 1993). But cf. A. M. Wolters, *Creation Regained: Biblical Basics for a Reformational Worldview* (Grand Rapids: Eerdmans, 1985) 26-27. Probing the relationship between order and wisdom, R. E. Murphy is not alone in his resigned assessment that Wisdom's role in creation "remains unclear" ("Wisdom and Creation," *JBL* 104 [1985] 5). On the other hand, the most comprehensive and recent treatments of creation's role in Wisdom's ethos fail to integrate fully the depth and range of specifically *moral* reflection evinced in the worldview of Proverbs: L. G. Perdue, *Wisdom*

Wisdom's discourse regarding creation and herself in chs. 1–9.[2] In this passage, Wisdom's persona recounts her own experience of creation as established by Yahweh, her creator. Wisdom's reflections on cosmogony are part of a larger unit, 8:1-36, that aims to convey her moral character and power to the "immature" (*pĕtā'yim*, v. 5). Her discourse is both self-justifying and evocative; its purpose is to persuade potential followers to welcome her and, consequently, acquire the facility for moral discernment. Wisdom's aim is to instill in the "listening heart," or discerning intellect, nothing short of a cosmic conscience. Her account of creation serves both to justify her moral worth to the community and thereby to impress on her audience the primacy of her ways, as she was the first of Yahweh's creative "way" (8:22). In short, Wisdom's witness to Yahweh's creative performance is designed to generate a distinctly moral outlook on behalf of her audience. The moral contours of creation, as limned by Wisdom, and their role in the general sapiential discourse of Proverbs constitute the focus of this chapter.

Wisdom's Place and Role in Creation

In Prov 8:22-31, Wisdom speaks explicitly of her relationship to Creator and creation:[3]

22 **Yahweh had me**[4] in the beginning of his (creative) way,[5]
the earliest of his works of yore.

---

and Creation: The Theology of Wisdom Literature (Nashville: Abingdon, 1994) e.g., 79-80, 93-94, 100, 121-22; D. Bergant, *Israel's Wisdom Literature: A Liberation-Critical Reading* (Minneapolis: Fortress, 1997) 83-85, 104.

2. For Proverbs 1–9 as the product of the final, postexilic editing of the book of Proverbs, see C. Camp, *Wisdom and the Feminine in the Book of Proverbs* (BLS 11; Sheffield: Almond, 1985) 233-39. Linguistic, thematic, and structural evidence for such editing is presented in Harold C. Washington, *Wealth and Poverty in the Instruction of Amenemope and the Hebrew Proverbs* (SBLDS 142; Atlanta: Scholars Press, 1994) 111-33. C. Maier offers a succinct survey of the issues and approaches in *Die "fremde Frau" in Proverbien 1–9: Eine exegetische und sozialgeschichtliche Studie* (OBO 144; Freiburg: Universitätsverlag Göttingen: Vandenhoeck & Ruprecht, 1995) 19-23.

3. For readability, I have highlighted in boldface those portions of the poem that refer explicitly to Wisdom's character.

4. Heb. *qānānî*; for similar uses of the verb in other creative, including procreative, contexts, see Gen 4:1; 14:19, 22; Deut 32:6; Ps 139:13. The verb can also denote acquisition or purchase (e.g., Prov 1:5; 4:5, 7; Exod 21:2; see B. Vawter, "Prov. 8:22: Wisdom and Creation," *JBL* 99 [1980] 205-16). The colloquial choice of translation opts for the former sense. See also the use of *hyl*, "to give birth," in vv. 24, 25.

5. Heb. *derek* can connote both path or direction, including God's (Deut 2:27; Ps

272

23 Of old I was **woven**,[6] from the beginning,
    before the earth's inception.

24 When the deeps were not, I was **engendered**,[7]
    When the wellsprings were not yet ladened with water,

25 When the mountains were not yet anchored;[8]
    In advance of the hills,[9] I was **brought forth**.[10]

26 Before he had made the earth abroad[11]
    and the first clods of soil,

27 When he established the heavens, I was there.
    When he circumscribed[12] the surface of the deep,

28 When he secured the skies,
    and stabilized[13] the springs of the deep,

29a When he assigned the sea its limit,
    lest the waters would transgress his decree,

77:19 [MT 20]), and behavior (e.g., Prov 2:8; 3:6, 23; 4:26; 5:8, 21; 10:9; 11:50). Wisdom, too, has her path (3:17; 4:11; 8:32; 9:6; cf. Isa 40:14).

6. The Masoretic reading derives the verb from *nsk*, meaning "to pour out," as with libations (e.g., Exod 30:9; Isa 30:1), "to weave" (Isa 25:7; 30:1), or "to install" (only Ps 2:6, which refers to the king established on Zion). *BHS* proposes *nĕsakkōtî*, from *skk*, meaning either "to cover" (e.g., 1 Kgs 8:7; Exod 40:3) or "to weave" (Ps 139:13; Job 10:11). I opt for the latter, agreeing with G. A. Yee that Ps 139:13 offers a suggestive parallel to Prov 8:23, wherein *qnh* parallels *skk*, suggesting the context of gestation ("The Theology of Creation in Proverbs 8:22-31," in *Creation in the Biblical Traditions* [ed. R. J. Clifford and J. J. Collins; CBQMS 24; Washington, D.C.: Catholic Biblical Association of America, 1992] 89n.8). From either *nsk* or *skk*, the meaning to "weave" as a metaphor for gestation makes the best contextual sense. See also *HALAT*, 3.712.

7. Heb. *hôlālĕtî*, from *hyl*, can denote birth (e.g., Isa 51:2; Job 39:1; 15:7; Ps 51:5 [MT 7]).

8. Cf. Job 38:6.

9. The preposition *lipnê* carries temporal force in parallel with *bĕṭerem*.

10. See n. 7 above.

11. I treat *'ereṣ wĕhûṣôt* as a close-knit pair, a virtual hendiadys (cf. Job 5:10).

12. Lit. "engraved a circle" *(bĕhûqô hûg)*. The root *hqq* can denote the act of inscribing (Isa 30:8; Ezek 23:14; Job 19:23) or that of prescribing by decree (Deut 33:21; Isa 33:22; Prov 31:5). The description refers to the containment of the deep by the horizon, similar to the sea in Prov 8:29a (cf. Job 26:10; 22:14). The verb is also attested in Prov 8:29b with reference to the earth's foundations "carved out," which also connotes prescriptive force.

13. In light of several textual versions, I emend the verb, as proposed by *BHS*, to *bĕʿazzĕzô*, in parallel with the previous verb. The Masoretic reading resulted from a transposition of the last two consonants.

29b-30aα When he carved out the foundations of the earth,
I was beside him growing up.[14]

30aβ-b I was his delight day by day,[15]
playing[16] before him every moment,

31   playing in his inhabited world,
delighting with the offspring of *'ādām.*

Wisdom's so-called hymn of self-praise is artistically shaped to stress her place and role in creation. The beginning and end of the passage describe Wisdom's character in relation to the cosmos. The first two verses disclose her intent in launching into this litany of creation: to establish her antiquity, indeed preexistence, relative to the rest of creation (vv. 22-23). Primordial through and through, Wisdom was Yahweh's preeminent and first creative act. Her litany concludes with her distinctly active role in the cosmos (vv. 30-31).

The intervening verses focus on Yahweh's activity in cosmogony with only occasional self-references to Wisdom's observing presence. Her associ-

14. In agreement with M. V. Fox ("*'Āmôn* Again," *JBL* 115 [1996] 699-702), I read *'āmôn* as the infinitive absolute of *'mn,* "to support" or "nourish" (e.g., 2 Kgs 10:1, 5; Est 2:7, 20b), which serves in context as an adverbial complement. (For other options see R. B. Y. Scott, "Wisdom in Creation: The *'Āmôn* of Proverbs VIII 30," *VT* 10 [1960] 213-22; and most recently C. R. Rogers, "The Meaning and Significance of the Hebrew Word *'mwn* in Proverbs 8,30," *ZAW* 109 [1997] 208-21). The verb frequently functions as a substantive in its active participial forms, denoting a nurse, male or female, with a sucking child (Num 11:12; Ruth 4:16; 2 Sam 4:4; Isa 49:23). It can also convey the sense of being established or assured (2 Sam 7:16; Isa 22:23, 25; 33:16; Jer 15:18). Many scholars propose a passive participle in Prov 8:30 for the consonantal form (*'āmûn*), suggesting the image of a dependent child (cf. Isa 60:4). But the grammar would require the feminine, rather than masculine, form. Given the difficulty of a masculine passive form whose subject is feminine Wisdom, Rogers is compelled to suggest, not originally, an accusative of state whose antecedent is Yahweh. Such a move, however, is unnecessary when one recognizes the disputed term as a true infinitive whose subject remains Wisdom. As Fox points out, the same verb in Est 2:20b is also an infinitive absolute with intransitive force. Moreover, the larger context tips the scale. Given the absence of any hint of creative role assigned to Wisdom, as suggested in the common translation of "master worker" or "craftsman," coupled with the theme of joy immediately following, the image of Wisdom maturing from "infancy" fits the overall context best. See also the verbal parallel between Prov 8:30aα and 30aβ.

15. Plural of intensity. The *BHS* emendation is unnecessary; cf. Jer 31:20: *yeled ša'ăšu'îm* ("child of delight").

16. The verb *śḥq* can denote laughter or play (see below).

ation with creation is thus more than simply temporal; such could easily have been expressed simply with the first two verses. The nature of creation in relation to Wisdom discloses something of the sapiential message the sages intended to impart in Proverbs, an ethos[17] that captures both the heart of Wisdom's role and that of her listeners, a moral context in which both Wisdom and follower can "grow up." Although modesty is not her virtue, Wisdom's litany is more than a hymn of self-praise.[18] Establishing her legitimacy, Wisdom's reflections on creation also convey a sense of place for her identity and conduct, her character and her "play," as well as that of her disciple (see vv. 32-36). Her final words suggest that her discourse is, in the end, an ode to joy.

The Character of Creation

Similar to the Yahwist's creation account, Wisdom's litany opens with the realm of nonexistence ("not yet"), beginning with the waters' absence (v. 24). The heights and depths of creation, the deep and the mountains, are included in this litany of lacks (vv. 24-25). Concluding the first strophe (vv. 22-26), the creation of the earth's soil is mentioned, setting its importance in relief. The following section describes Yahweh's fashioning of the cosmic domains identical to those in the Priestly cosmogony (Gen 1:1–2:3): heaven (sky), the waters, and the earth (Prov 8:27-29b). The deep is circumscribed, along with the sea; the sky is secured; and the subterranean springs are stabilized. Last and most importantly, the earth's foundations are established (v. 29b).

Unlike the Priestly account of creation, Wisdom's litany does not depict an altogether perfect creation. An element of danger lurks within the created order. Of the domains Wisdom identifies in her account, the waters receive the most attention. Beginning with the absence of water, Wisdom's account

17. Again, *ethos,* from the Greek, denotes "dwelling place" or context that allows for the cultivation of the moral life in consonance with the moral vision imparted by the texts in question (see Chapter 1). The most extensive investigation of Wisdom's ethos in Proverbs can be found in P. J. Nel, *The Structure and Ethos of the Wisdom Admonitions in Proverbs* (BZAW 158; Berlin: de Gruyter, 1982), a useful study that is, however, hampered by a lack of focus regarding the term, sometimes employed to mean Sitz im Leben (pp. 79-82), other times used to denote a pedagogical theory and ethical context (pp. 83-127). Although restricting himself only to the admonitory form in Proverbs, Nel correctly notes the important place of the created order in Wisdom's ethos (pp. 110-115).

18. Cf. Perdue, *Wisdom and Creation,* 89-90.

later refers to limits being imposed on the watery depths and the sea (vv. 27b, 28b, 29a). The heavenly vault circumscribes the sea; the sky (lit. "clouds") is made firm like a roof to prevent collapse from the waters above; the wellsprings are strengthened in order to hold the waters below; and the geological foundations are shored up lest the earth sink into the watery depths. Water assumes a double role: it is both life-giving and life-endangering. An unbounded sea marks a trespassing on the land and a transgression of divine command (v. 29a). Comparable to the Priestly cosmogony, divine discourse plays a markedly formative role in creation, but the object and manner of such discourse could not be more different. For the sages, Yahweh's word functions as a restraining order, a negative injunction in sharp contrast to the methodical series of positive commands found in Priestly lore.[19] As the sole object of Yahweh's decree, water is proscribed and prescribed. Chaos is thereby contained.

The ground, in turn, is referenced at certain critical junctures in Wisdom's ode. The soil's formation is underscored at the conclusion of the first strophe (v. 26). Similarly, the earth's foundations receive strategic attention at the culmination of creation before Wisdom recites her activity (v. 29b). They are also formed with a degree of prescriptive force,[20] firmly established to serve as the base for the habitation of life and to withstand the cosmic pressure of watery chaos. With humankind as the principal object of her affections, the inhabited ground constitutes the safe domain of Wisdom's "play."

The sequence of Wisdom's account does not seem to be governed temporally. All that is crucial in the timing is Wisdom's priority: she is first and foremost of all creation. Everything else falls into place thereafter, situated and secured. Indeed, Wisdom's account is characterized more by space than by time. The "day by day" of v. 30 merges differentiated time into a continuous stream of sapiential jubilation during and after the formation of creation. In the place of God's *timing*, emphasized in the Priestly account, is an inordinate interest in divine *activity*. Pronounced are Yahweh's incomparable abilities in constructing the cosmos: shaping, establishing, supporting, and stabilizing. God is the consummate architect, sinking the pillars of the mountains and etching an impenetrable circle around the deep. Bedrock and horizon mark the inviolable boundaries of the cosmos. With the skies shored up and the deeps contained by deed and by word, the cosmos becomes a bastion of security and, consequently, Wisdom's play-

19. Gen 1:3, 6, 9, 11, 14, 20, 22, 24, 26, 28.
20. See n. 12 above.

ground,[21] or more accurately, playhouse. *Creatio ex nihilo* is not an issue for Wisdom, but *creatio ob salutem* is.

Wisdom in Creation: Eyewitness and Player

Wisdom's own genesis is of an entirely different order. Like the creation of light in the Priestly cosmogony (Gen 1:3), Wisdom's genesis precedes all else. She is not constructed like an edifice, but "woven," as in gestation (Prov 8:23; cf. Ps 139:13).[22] In Wisdom's genesis, Yahweh plays not the architect but the weaver and, more prominently, her progenitor. Wisdom's creation is described by metaphors of conception and birth; she is "woven," engendered, and brought forth, born by Yahweh. Throughout cosmogony, Wisdom grows up (Prov 8:30a). She is a child of God, embraced by divine delight. Such is her identity, wide-eyed and full of awe as Yahweh goes about the business of creating. Her presence is passive in the sense that she does not assist Yahweh in constructing the cosmos. Yet she does play an active role, founded precisely on the discursive act of recounting creation. Wisdom witnesses. She uncovers creation by recounting its story to her audience.

Moreover, Wisdom remains by Yahweh's side, delighting daily in divine presence and workmanship. She is receptive to Yahweh's affections as much as she is the purveyor of delight for humankind. Indeed, Wisdom's mirth conveys an approbation of joy for both creation and Creator. Like the Priestly sabbath rest, Wisdom's play in the cosmos marks the completion and purpose of creation.[23] Yet unlike the climax of the Priestly cosmogony, Wisdom's mirth is not confined to any single day. Her unbounded joy both signals Yahweh's victory over chaos and renders approbation at each step in the stabilizing process. Her play is supported by creation, made firm and safe. With creation in place, re-creation begins and continues ad infinitum, presupposing and preserving creation's security. By dint of Yahweh's commanding presence and architectural prowess, the cosmos is in effect "child-proofed" for Wisdom; and like the sabbath day, Wisdom's play is without closure.

Wisdom's play before Creator and in creation is fraught with cosmic

---

21. So also B. Lang, *Wisdom and the Book of Proverbs: An Israelite Goddess Redefined* (New York: Pilgrim, 1986) 79.

22. See n. 6 above.

23. Contra G. M. Landes, "Creation Tradition in Proverbs 8:22-31 and Genesis 1," in *A Light unto My Path: Old Testament Studies in Honor of Jacob M. Myers* (ed. H. N. Bream et al.; Philadelphia: Temple University Press, 1974) 288-89, who contends that the motif of joy has no correlation in the Priestly cosmogony.

background. Much more than simply affectionate revelry between parent and child,[24] Wisdom's activity represents the climax of creation and communion with Yahweh. Both "delight" and "play" characterize her relationship with Yahweh and her relationship with creation. Wisdom plays before Yahweh and she plays in and with Yahweh's living world. Moreover, she is the object of the Deity's delight as much as humankind is the object of Wisdom's mirth. Delightful play thus binds Wisdom to both the divine and human spheres, not in a relationship of servile dependence — Wisdom is not Yahweh's codependent — but in the freedom of interdependence. Precisely in this way she is a "living link."[25] Having a foot in both worlds, Wisdom exudes a joy, potent and vital, that embraces the transcendent and immanent realms of existence. Yahweh and creation are bound together by Wisdom's elation, by a celebration of Yahweh's creative activity through Wisdom's re-creative response.

Wisdom's play is polyvalent in other ways as well. The closest biblical parallel to "playing before" Yahweh is found outside the Wisdom corpus. When the ark of Yahweh was transferred from Baale-judah to Jerusalem in order to consolidate royal power over the fledgling unified nation, David and "all the house of Israel were dancing before Yahweh" (*měśaḥăqîm lipnê YHWH*) in the festive procession (2 Sam 6:5; see v. 21). Such cultic "play"[26] involved music making and ritual dancing "before Yahweh" (v. 14).[27] Marked by frenzied motion and rapturous cacophony, the scene depicts a joyous victory celebration[28] performed before the divine throne, a spectacle of cultic

24. Many interpreters remain at this level of sentiment without exploring the distinctly moral implications of Wisdom's play, e.g., Perdue, *Wisdom and Creation*, 91; cf. W. P. Brown, *Character in Crisis: A Fresh Approach to the Wisdom Literature of the Old Testament* (Grand Rapids: Eerdmans, 1996) 38-39.

25. The expression is borrowed from Scott's demonstrably false definition of *'āmôn*, which, however, captures well Wisdom's relational activity in the larger context ("Wisdom in Creation," 222). R. E. Clements's description of wisdom as the "inalienable bond that unites the creative intention of God with the experienced working of the world" is apt (*Wisdom in Theology* [Didsbury Lectures, 1989; Grand Rapids: Eerdmans, 1992] 155).

26. Drawing from Judg 16:25-26, 2 Sam 12:17, and Exod 32:6, J. M. Sasson defines *měśaḥăqîm* as "play-acting" ("The Worship of the Golden Calf," in *Orient and Occident: Essays Presented to Cyrus H. Gordon on the Occasion of His Sixty-Fifth Birthday* [ed. H. A. Hoffner; AOAT 22; Kevelaer: Butzon & Bercker; Neukirchen-Vluyn: Neukirchener, 1973] 155-56).

27. MT *dāvid měkarkēr běkol-'ōz lipnê YHWH.* The verb *krr,* "to whirl about," is equivalent to *śḥq.* An anti-scenario of such cultic celebration can be found in Exod 32:6, in which Israel "revels" (*wayyāqumû lěṣaḥēq*) before the golden calf.

28. For possible military connotations, see C.-L. Seow, *Myth, Drama, and the Politics of David's Dance* (HSM 46; Atlanta: Scholars Press, 1989) 91-97.

ecstasy that could easily be read as sexual profligacy, as did David's Saulide wife (v. 20). By virtue of Wisdom's position before God, sapiential play suggests a cultic performance of sorts.[29] But that may not be all. As Michal read David's performance before the ark as a promiscuous display, "play" can assume an erotic nuance. For example, King Abimelech discovers Isaac with Rebekah in the midst of foreplay or intercourse (yiṣḥāq mĕṣaḥēq 'ēt ribqâ, Gen 26:8).[30] Yet play can also be as innocent as two children playing together (Gen 21:9). Similarly, "delight" (root ś") can be shared between parent and child, as in the case of Zion with her people and God with Ephraim (Isa 66:12; Jer 31:20).

Significant for Proverbs 8, the last three citations demonstrate that the motifs of play and delight impart a sense of *familial* belongingness. Gen 21:8-10 is particularly apt. When Sarah observes Ishmael, the child of the Egyptian Hagar, "playing" with her own son Isaac, she bitterly complains to Abraham: "Throw out this slave woman with her son, for the son of this slave woman shall not receive any inheritance along with my son Isaac" (v. 10). In Sarah's eyes, the ostensibly innocent play between two children was an insufferable transgression, an encroachment on her familial domain. Ishmael's play was illicit, for in Sarah's restrictive view it violated the boundaries of the bêt 'āb, Abraham's "paternal house."[31] The intensely personal relationship between Yahweh and Wisdom is first and foremost the fruit of an inviolable familial relationship. Wisdom's play is the natural and appropriate response to the formation of the cosmic domicile, the bêt YHWH.[32] Safe and secure, creation

---

29. R. Stecher argues that Wisdom's play is *exclusively* cultic ("Die persönliche Weisheit in den Proverbien Kap. 8," *ZKT* 75 [1953] 435-37). Any discussion of Wisdom's cultic play is curiously lacking in L. G. Perdue's otherwise comprehensive treatment in *Wisdom and Cult* (SBLDS 30; Missoula, Mont.: Scholars Press, 1977).

30. Heb. śḥq and ṣḥq are etymologically identical. The latter spelling is the result of assimilation (Seow, *Myth, Drama,* 96n. 49).

31. To resolve a similar situation of childlessness, Rachel gives Jacob her handmaid Bilhah, "so that she may bear upon my knees" (Gen 30:3). In contrast to Ishmael's plight, Bilhah's firstborn, Dan, is fully incorporated into Jacob's growing bêt 'āb. For a general description of the bêt 'āb, see most recently S. Bendor, *The Social Structure of Ancient Israel* (JBS 7; Jerusalem: Ben Zvi Press, 1996) 45-204; and the collected essays of C. Meyers, J. Blenkinsopp, J. J. Collins, and L. G. Perdue in *Families in Ancient Israel* (ed. L. G. Perdue; FRC; Louisville: Westminster John Knox, 1997), which trace the social development of the family from ancient Israel to early Judaism. For the Mesopotamian legal contexts for resolving the problem of childlessness in the paternal household, see T. Frymer-Kensky, "Patriarchal Family Relationships and Near Eastern Law," *BA* 44 (1981) 211-12.

32. I am not suggesting, however, that creation is here depicted as a temple ("the house of Yahweh"), as is apparent in the Priestly cosmogony or is sometimes suggested of Wisdom's house in Prov 9:1 (see below).

is Yahweh's established household wherein Wisdom is familialized by her intimacy with Yahweh and human beings are socialized through her play. In the household of God, Wisdom is the archetypal kin to human beings (Prov 7:4), and joy is the inheritance she extends to humankind (see below).

Delight and play are as multidimensional in meaning as the relationships described in v. 30 are manifold. Yahweh's delight in Wisdom is thoroughly parental; any nuance of the erotic is at most subtle, if not peripheral.[33] In any case, such divine pleasure is considered unabashedly innocent and morally potent. Similarly, Wisdom's activity before Yahweh is that of a child, freely laughing and playing, dancing and singing, in joyous rapture over the securing of creation and the intimacy of divine communion. Wisdom's delight with human beings reflects Yahweh's delight with darling Wisdom. As the agent of delight, directing her affections to the "sons of Adam" *(bĕnê 'ādām)*, Wisdom is the grand mediatrix[34] of divine joy to the earth's human inhabitants. In her play with the inhabitants of creation, Wisdom assumes the role of mother and lover on behalf of her audience, the male recipients of sapiential instruction (see below). Wisdom will prove to be man's greatest match and companion for life, so the sages exhort, the quintessential "helper as his partner" (Gen 2:20).

Creation in Context

Given its mythological undertones and unclarity, Wisdom's creation litany has been examined all too often apart from the moral context or sapiential ethos conveyed throughout Proverbs 1–9 and, indeed, the book as a

---

33. A possible hint of sexual nuance, however, could be argued in light of the reference to Wisdom "growing up" before God (v. 30aα). With Wisdom's maturity, an erstwhile parental relationship could evolve into an erotic one. Indeed, some have suggested that the relationship in popular religion between "Yahweh and his Asherah," as attested on two pithoi from Kuntillet ʿAjrud (cf. the inscription from Khirbet el-Qom), figures as part of the mythological background of this text (so M. D. Coogan, "Canaanite Origins and Lineage: Reflections on the Religion of Ancient Israel," in *Ancient Israelite Religion: Essays in Honor of Frank Moore Cross* [ed. P. D. Miller Jr. et al.; Philadelphia: Fortress, 1987] 118-20; but cf. O. Keel and C. Uehlinger, *Göttinen, Götter und Gottessymbole* [QD 134; Freiburg: Herder, 1992] 237-82). If so, such a relationship, however, would serve more as a foil than as support for the relationship between Yahweh and *sophia*. The sages have transformed a possibly sexual relationship between Yahweh and a consort into a parental one.

34. The term is drawn from B. K. Waltke, "Lady Wisdom as Mediatrix: An Exposition of Proverbs 1:20-33," *Presbyterion: Covenant Seminary Review* 14 (Spring 1988) 1-15.

whole.[35] Many consider the cosmological discourse of 8:22-31 as simply another way of demonstrating Wisdom's unassailable authority over creation and human life.[36] Consequently, some even find the image of Wisdom's play in creation as unfitting for the larger context of the chapter, as does R. B. Y. Scott:

> The fact is that the thought of Wisdom as a child playing is not really congruous with the total context in Prov. viii, and this suggestion, based on the metaphors of birth and play, is superficial. The first part of the chapter and the peroration in verses 32-36 appeal to men to listen to Wisdom because of her primacy in creation, which is expressed as *priority* in sequence. For this high claim to grave authority the imagery of a *gay, thoughtless childhood is inappropriate.*[37]

To regard Wisdom's litany as simply a way of demonstrating her "priority in sequence" is only half the story, but to find her play as embarrassing is a whole other story! As noted above, the very description of creation functions integrally in Wisdom's ethos and ethic, her context and conduct as play. Containing chaos, Yahweh establishes a fundamentally secure space that proves conducive for Wisdom's activity. Fashioned and solidified, creation is Wisdom's domicile to practice joy. Although not the "self-revelation of creation," as Gerhard von Rad argued,[38] Wisdom possesses deep ties to creation. Creation figures necessarily in Wisdom's character, enabling her to exercise her role before God and human beings. As limned by the poet, creation is essentially Wisdom's playhouse, the formative context and setting in which Wisdom matures as player

---

35. A representative example is found in the recent introduction of J. Blenkinsopp, *Wisdom and Law in the Old Testament: The Ordering of Life in Israel and Early Judaism* (New York: Oxford University Press, 1995), who discusses the book of Proverbs and its ethic in one chapter and the special case of Prov 8:22-31 in a separate section (pp. 18-45 and 157-62, respectively). But given the book's unitary editing, a product of the "Restoration community" of the early Persian period that, like the Priestly material, also incorporated older material (Washington, *Wealth and Poverty*, 114-33), one must account for wisdom's play in creation within the overall context of Proverbs.

36. For example, K. A. Farmer, *Who Knows What Is Good? A Commentary on the Books of Proverbs and Ecclesiastes* (ITC; Grand Rapids: Eerdmans, 1991) 52-53; Blenkinsopp, *Wisdom and Law*, 160-61; Bergant, *Israel's Wisdom Literature*, 85.

37. Scott, "Wisdom in Creation," 218-19 (italics mine). See also H. Ringgren, *Word and Wisdom: Studies in the Hypostatization of Divine Qualities and Functions in the Ancient Near East* (Lund: H. Ohlssons, 1947) 102.

38. G. von Rad, *Wisdom in Israel*, tr. J. D. Martin (Nashville: Abingdon, 1972) 144-76. Cf. S. Terrien, "The Play of Wisdom: Turning Point in Biblical Theology," *HBT* 3 (1981) 137; Murphy, "Wisdom and Creation," 9.

and moral agent. Indeed, play and moral conduct are inseparable, and one cannot be compartmentalized from the other, developmentally or otherwise. From the poet's perspective, Wisdom's play is morally and cultically evocative. As the preeminent model of moral conduct, Wisdom plays eternally. She is at once laughing child and moral agent, the beginning and fulfillment of creation. In the moral worldview of the ancient sages, Wisdom is the consummate *player* and her followers are called to a life of *imitatio sapientiae*.

The efficacy of Wisdom's play is already grasped in her instruction to would-be disciples in the following section (8:32-36).

32 And now, sons, listen to me:
  Happy are those who keep my ways.

33 Hear instruction *(mûsār)* and be wise, do not be negligent.

34 Happy is the one who hears me,
  watching my gates day by day,
  keeping watch over my doorposts.

35 For whoever finds me finds life and obtains favor from Yahweh.

36 But the one who bypasses me *(wĕḥōṭĕʾî)*[39] does violence *(ḥōmēs)*
  to his own life,
  and all who hate me love death.

This concluding passage does not simply mark a return to 8:1-21,[40] as if Wisdom's cosmic ode in vv. 22-31 were merely a detour in her discourse. Wisdom's exhortation to the good life follows naturally from her ode to joy in vv. 22-31.[41] Wisdom's advice to her "sons" begins to reap the moral substance of her play within the inhabited world. Wisdom's delight is imparted to those who would follow her amid the highways and byways of human intercourse. They are esteemed happy *(ʾašrê)*, blessed with the fullness of life and joy (vv. 32, 34). Happy is the one who zealously welcomes Wisdom's instructions, vigilantly watchful for her. Wisdom commands the attention of her disciples to impart advice crucial for moral conduct and well-being. As the first of Yahweh's "way," Wisdom reveals her way be-

39. The verb *ḥṭʾ* figures prominently in the nomenclature for sin (e.g., Num 27:3; Deut 19:15; 2 Kgs 10:19; Amos 5:12).

40. So Perdue, *Wisdom and Creation*, 91.

41. As Nel avers, "The whole of Chapter 8 is a poetic unity and an artistic creation in form and content beyond compare" (*Structure and Ethos*, 33).

fore her audience (*drk*, vv. 22a, 32b), the way of righteousness and justice (v. 20; 1:3b).[42] She commands her listeners to be wise through the appropriation of instruction, and like her priestly counterparts who enjoin Israel to be holy (e.g., Lev 20:7-8), joy is Wisdom's sanctifying power to impart. To hear and heed Wisdom is to discern the cosmic reverberations of her mirth. As reciprocal virtues of moral conduct, play and discipline (*mûsār*) are the warp and woof of Wisdom's ethos.

The same themes of blessing, creation, and security are also found in Prov 3:13-26.[43] The first section of this extended passage is framed by two beatitudes, as found also in 8:32, 34. "Happy is the one who finds Wisdom and the one who acquires understanding. . . . The one who holds her is esteemed happy" (3:13, 18b). Within this unit, Wisdom's incomparable value is assessed: "Her income is better than silver, . . . more precious than jewels." She is the ultimate desire (v. 15), for she holds in each hand the keys to longevity and prosperity (v. 16).[44] A fitting climax to Wisdom's efficacy is her identification with the "tree of life," a figure found elsewhere in Proverbs and in the Yahwist's anthropogony.[45] With this symbol Wisdom confers the fullness of life or *šālōm*, peace and prosperity (v. 17b). The tree of life recalls the garden of abundant blessing, which for the sages is eminently accessible. One need only "lay hold of her" (*maḥăzîqîm bāh*, 3:18). The metaphors are mixed, for the same verb is used to describe the seductive embrace of the adulteress

---

42. Justice (*mišpāṭ*), righteousness (*ṣĕdāqâ, ṣedeq*), and equity (*mêšārîm*) constitute the distinctly moral virtues promulgated in Proverbs 1–9. See Brown, *Character in Crisis*, 23-25.

43. For the unit's poetic integrity, see R. J. Clifford, *Creation Accounts in the Ancient Near East and in the Bible* (CBQMS 26; Washington, D.C.: Catholic Biblical Association of America, 1994) 179.

44. Here Wisdom most closely resembles Ma'at, the Egyptian goddess of truth and justice, who is portrayed holding a staff in one hand and the *ankh* sign in the other (see C. Kayatz, *Studien zu Proverbien 1–9* [WMANT 22; Neukirchen-Vluyn: Neukirchener, 1966] 104-5, including the obverse photograph). Despite the significant differences between Ma'at and Wisdom, certain similarities stand between the two in terms of their moral performance in the divine and human worlds. Both represent justice and are associated with play in the heavenly realm (see O. Keel, *Die Weisheit Spielt vor Gott* [Freiburg: Universitätsverlag; Göttingen: Vandenhoeck & Ruprecht, 1974], esp. 63-67). For a more cautious treatment of the comparative issues and alleged parallels, see M. V. Fox, "World Order and Ma'at: A Crooked Parallel," *JANES* 23 (1995) 31-48, who correctly observes that Ma'at does not denote order as such but "the force that creates and maintains order, namely justice/truth," which finds its closest parallel to the Hebrew *mêšārîm* (p. 41). For the Egyptian background, see M. Lichtheim, *Ma'at in Egyptian Autobiographies and Related Studies* (OBO 120; Freiburg: Universitätsverlag; Göttingen: Vandenhoeck & Ruprecht, 1992) 19-37.

45. Prov 11:30; 15:4; cf. Gen 2:9; 3:22. See Chapter 3.

46. Cf. Prov 4:13; Neh 10:30.

(7:13).[46] Wisdom's disciples come to the tree not to pluck or to fell but to cleave tightly in order to reap the benefits she offers. Wisdom is the primordial tree-turned-lover for the disciple (cf. 4:5-9).[47] She is the disciple's companion and sustainer. The knowledge and life that Wisdom offers are inseparably bound up, never to be rent asunder.

Following Wisdom's arboreal image is her role in creation, as found in the so-called little cosmogony of 3:19-20.[48]

> Yahweh by wisdom founded the earth,
>> establishing the heavens by understanding.
> By his knowledge the deeps burst open,
>> and the clouds drop dew.

Here wisdom is not the fully developed, personified character encountered in 8:1-33. Wisdom is rather identified with Yahweh's discerning judgment and skill ("his knowledge") by which creation is fashioned. Not a moral subject in her own right, wisdom is identified with God's intellect at work in creation, essentially instrumental in scope and purpose. Far from being incomprehensible and chaotic, Yahweh's cosmic handiwork gives evidence of craft and calculation, of intelligent workmanship and discernible design. The earth and heavens are securely established; even the unruly deeps "burst open" *(bq'),*[49] but only at Yahweh's discretion to fertilize the earth (3:19).[50] Any threat from the waters, actual or potential, is nonexistent. What is at issue contextually is wisdom's moral efficacy as grounded in creation, that is, the role and rationale of blessing that Wisdom offers to those who find her.[51] That creation itself gives evidence of Wisdom guarantees her efficacy on behalf of those who would follow her. She is both the tree of life and the design of creation, the means and end of blessing.

Wisdom's instrumental role in creation is the public, indeed cosmic,

---

47. The goddess Asherah, too, was symbolized by a tree (Deut 16:21) or wooden pole as her cult object (e.g., 1 Kgs 14:15; 16:33; 2 Kgs 17:16; 21:3, 7). See J. Day, "Asherah in the Hebrew Bible and Northwest Semitic Literature," *JBL* 105 (1980) 385-408.

48. Relative to its context, this unit was most likely independent in origin, but came to be placed in its present position in order to underscore the means and warrant of Wisdom's efficacy on the son's behalf.

49. Cf. Gen 7:11, which employs the same verb to describe the beginning of the flood in the Priestly compositional layer. Intertextually, the sages have put a positive spin on the cosmic deluge by stressing the restorative role of the waters on the earth's behalf and, by extension, humanity's.

50. Cf. Gen 2:6; 7:11; Prov 8:27, 29; see Clifford, *Creation Accounts,* 180.

51. See also Clifford, *Creation Accounts,* 179; E. Otto, *Theologische Ethik des Alten Testaments* (TW 3/2; Stuttgart: Kohlhammer, 1994) 166-67.

sign and seal of Yahweh's assurance of *šālôm* for the "son," who constitutes Wisdom's implied audience.[52] By donning prudence and foresight,[53] the instrumental attributes of Wisdom (v. 21), the son can walk securely and enjoy the good life, immune from the sudden panic and onrushing storm that can beset the wicked (vv. 23-25); the Creator is the source of the son's confidence in right conduct and his victory over the dangers and attractions of moral chaos (v. 26). Yet such security is also the result of certain virtues having been *cultivated,* hence the father's admonition to appropriate the virtues of common sense. Through the appropriation of wisdom, a life of security and blessing unfolds. By wisdom, Yahweh constructs the cosmos, securing it with order so that even the subterranean waters find their fructifying role in the domain of human habitation. By wisdom, the moral self fashions and inhabits a world of order in which virtue can flourish.

An orderly world is a secure world, the sages stress, on both the cosmic and individual planes. Yahweh's cosmos mirrors the ethos, or ethical space, of the moral agent; in both frames of reference, human and divine, local and cosmic, moral soundness and security prevail. The particular virtues of prudence and foresight, taking on a life of their own, serve as guardians and shields for the young student of wisdom on the path of life (2:7, 11-12). They keep the errant youth's path straight, his conduct uncompromised. That path, the "way of the good," is both his and Wisdom's making. As the metaphor of righteousness, the way or straight path imbues the moral will with a direction, a teleology of moral conduct.[54] Right conduct ensures the agent's "abiding in the land" (v. 21).[55] Fashioned by God and inhabited by Wisdom's followers, the environment of life, this existential world of moral agency, is as

52. The son is the conventional audience for most of the discourse in Proverbs 1–9 (e.g., 1:8, 10; 2:1; 3:1, 11, 21, 4:1 [plural], 10, 20; 5:1, 7 [plural], 20; 6:1, 20; 7:1, 24 [plural]; 8:32 [plural]). Ethically, his character represents the addressed moral self, the "interpellated" subject (C. A. Newsom, "Woman and the Discourse of Patriarchal Wisdom: A Study of Proverbs 1–9," in *Gender and Difference in Ancient Israel* [ed. P. L. Day; Minneapolis: Fortress, 1989] 143).

53. Heb. *tušîyâ ûmĕzimmâ.* Both terms denote resourcefulness or competence, which ensures success (e.g., 2:7; 1:4). See M. V. Fox, "Words for Wisdom," *ZAH* 6 (1993) 161-65. On the instrumental virtues of wisdom in general, see Brown, *Character in Crisis,* 22-33.

54. The metaphor of the "way," as an indicator of conduct, is designated by four words in Proverbs 1–9: *derek* (e.g., 2:20; 3:17; 4:11; 5:8, 21; 8:13, 32), *'ōraḥ* (2:8, 15; 3:6; 9:15), *ma'gal* (2:9, 15, 18; 4:11; 5:26), and *nĕtîbâ* (1:15; 3:17; 7:25; 8:2). For the motif of the two opposing ways in Proverbs, see N. C. Habel, "The Symbolism of Wisdom in Proverbs 1–9," *Int* (1972) 131-57.

55. The verbs *škn* ("to dwell") and *ytr* ("to remain") are employed.

much the human subject's making as it is Yahweh's creation. By keeping on the straight path, the son is led to fulfilled dwelling in the land. The exercise of virtue marks the agent's *eisodus* into an ethos, the blessed "abode of the righteous" (3:33).

Chaos in Context

The dwelling of the righteous, like the cosmos, is an impregnable domain, sound and secure, a sanctuary of cultivated virtue (cf. 1:33). By likening the moral agent's world to a refuge, the sages betray a pressing concern about the challenges and dangers that their community faces in order to flourish. They do not mince words in identifying the particular dangers, which, like the watery depths contained by divine decree, are ever pressing upon the community's life. Whereas the way of the wicked is likened to dark chaos (*'ăpēlâ*, 4:19; cf. *ḥōšek* in 2:13), the path of the righteous is the "light of dawn, increasing in brightness until full day" (4:18), the light associated with the inbreaking of divine justice and salvation but attained through the cultivation of moral conduct.[56] Righteousness bears a palpable effulgence; it is Wisdom's glory, as it were, settling in the domain of moral activity. Chaos is its antithesis, and it raises its head in two interrelated forms, according to the sages, in violence and strangeness.

Chaos of Violence

It is no accident that the book of Proverbs begins its discursive movement[57] with a father's warning to his son about the dangers of fiscal greed (1:10-19).[58] Intent on undermining the father's authority, certain "sinners" (*ḥaṭṭā'îm*) attempt to lure the son into their savage schemes for quick profit (v. 10). They

---

56. The morning light is indelibly associated with divine deliverance and epiphany (e.g., Isa 17:14; Pss 46:5 [MT 6]; 88:13 [MT 14]; 90:14; 143:8). See J. Ziegler, "Die Hilfe Gottes am Morgen," in *Alttestamentliche Studien: Fr. Nötscher zum sechsigsten Geburtstag* (ed. H. Junker and G. J. Botterweck; BBB 1; Bonn: Hanstein, 1950) 281-88; B. Janowski, *Rettungsgewissheit und Epiphanie des Heils* (WMANT 59; Neukirchen-Vluyn: Neukirchener, 1989).

57. The first seven verses of Proverbs serve as the book's programmatic introduction, much like a purpose statement in a course syllabus. For an examination of its aim and structure, see Brown, *Character in Crisis*, 23-30.

58. As Newsom points out, v. 19 reveals the central concern of the father's discourse ("Woman and Discourse," 145).

revel in their strength to cause bloodshed, ambushing the innocent and stealing their wealth (vv. 11, 16), and they invite the son to join in their predatory life-style as an equal partner (vv. 13-14). Their greed for gain is, like Sheol's appetite, insatiable and destructive (v. 12). Depicted by the father as ruthless predators, these entrepreneurs of violence are in fact the son's peers. Vying for his attention, these enemies of the people entice the son to share in their marauding gang. Their "ethic" is attractively egalitarian: "Throw in your lot among us; we will all have one purse" (v. 15). But it is only a veneer that attempts to cover over an ethos of violence.

The father's discourse is pedagogically effective: he uncovers their sham by taking his son firmly by the hand and leading him to view the gang's enticements from a larger, critical perspective. He compels the son to step back and look at the bigger picture, to move from the ethic to the ethos, to the larger context in which the ethic is shown, in fact, to have no place. As it turns out, their egalitarianism is devoid of equity.[59] From the larger community's perspective, there is nothing equitable in their sharing, for it feasts on the blood of their victims. Yet, as the father clinches his argument, their ethic evinces poetic justice: they shall all meet their own destruction fair and square by ambushing themselves and cutting their own throats! Having appropriated the father's perspective, the son is secure and wiser for it. He is like the knowing bird that, rather than rushing into the snare, can look knowingly on from distance as the net is baited in vain (v. 17; cf. 7:23). The admonition of 3:31-32 sums up the father's message:

> Do not envy the violent and do not choose any of their ways,
>> for the perverse are an abomination to Yahweh,
>> but the upright are in his confidence.
> The Lord's curse is on the house of the wicked,
>> but he blesses the abode of the righteous. (NRSV)

By intervening on his son's behalf, the father establishes a "collective efficacy," a means of informal social control that ensures a sense of familial community, an ethos designed to protect and prevent the son from getting lured into the attractions of rapacious self-gain.[60] In short, such discourse aims at con-

---

59. "Equity" *(mēšārîm)* is a crucial and eminently moral virtue for the sages, denoting fair judgment and judicious speech (1:3; 2:9; 8:6; 23:16; Pss 9:8 [MT 9]; 58:1 [MT 2]; 75:2 [MT 3]; 96:10; 98:9; 99:4).

60. The terminology is borrowed from the recent sociological study of R. J. Sampson, S. W. Raudenbusch, and F. Earls, "Neighborhoods and Violent Crime: A Multi-level Study of Collective Efficacy," *Science* 277 (Aug. 15, 1997) 918-24. Their study suggests

taining the chaos of violence. By heeding the father's warnings, the son discerns his home as a moral refuge, a haven of integrity immune from the perilous schemes of unbounded greed, and a boundary, in turn, is imposed on social chaos. The son is to remain in the abode of righteousness.

The juxtaposition between the father's warning and Wisdom's discourse that follows (1:20-33) suggests a level of continuity, a shared goal. While the father reins the son back into the refuge of righteousness, the home, Wisdom beats a path to the busiest corners to address her audience, the "immature" (*pĕtāyim*, vv. 20-23). Whoever they are, the immature are evidently on their way to sharing the fate of those vilified by the father. In her diatribe, Wisdom proclaims that she will laugh at their calamitous end, at the panic that will seize them like an onrushing storm (v. 27). Like the son's voracious peers, those who have rejected Wisdom shall be "sated with their own devices," eating "the fruit of their way" (v. 31; cf. vv. 12-13, 19). Wisdom's message is simple and direct: "Waywardness[61] kills" but virtue makes for secure dwelling (vv. 32-33).

Chaos of Strangeness

A more prominent source of moral danger identified by the sages is the so-called "strange woman."[62] To the son she is, in gender and in character, the quintessential other. To Wisdom she is quintessentially evil, the anti-*sophia*. Similar to the father's protection of the son from his peers, Wisdom plays a salvific role for the son who is confronted by the other woman. By appropriating wisdom, the father promises the son that he "will be saved from the strange woman (*'iššâ zārâ*), from the foreign woman (*nokrîyâ*) with her smooth words, who forsakes the partner of her youth and violates her sacred covenant (*bĕrît 'ĕlōheyhā*), for her house leads down to death and her paths to the shades" (2:16-18; see also 6:20-24). She is the archetypal adulteress and covenant breaker, the embodiment of chaos that threatens to overwhelm and dissolve all familial structures.

---

that, in addition to poverty, informal social control (e.g., the "monitoring of spontaneous play groups among children, a willingness to intervene to prevent acts such as truancy and street-corner 'hanging' . . . , and the confrontation of persons who are exploiting or disturbing public space") is negatively associated with variations in violence (p. 918). Their statistical data suggest that such collective efficacy "remained a robust predictor of lower rates of violence" (p. 923).

61. In context, *mĕšûbâ* refers to "turning one's back" to wisdom and moral "backsliding," as suggested in the parallel to *šalwâ* ("ease," "complacency") in v. 32b.

62. Heb. *'iššâ zārâ, nokrîyâ*; 2:16; 5:3, 20; 6:24; 7:5; cf. 23:27-28.

In stark contrast to the abode of the righteous, the strange woman's dwelling is the facade of Sheol. Those who enter are "disappeared," never to regain the "paths of life" (v. 19; 5:3-6). On a less mytho-horrific note, the son is warned not to darken her doorway, lest he hand over his "sufficiency to others" (*la'ăḥērîm hôdekâ*, 5:9), to "strangers" (*zārîm*) who will divest the self, once enslaved to an "alien" (*nokrî*), of the wherewithal for self-sufficiency (v. 10). Engagement with the strange woman leads to the alienation of wealth and self.[63] As the son's peers threaten the familial community with their violent grab for profit, the strange woman threatens both the hearth and society by robbing the self of material integrity and moral identity.

The danger of "strangeness" is the danger of demoralizing dependency, which leads to loss of self. To "bind yourself to a stranger" (*zār*) is forbidden, for it is tantamount to enslavement (6:1). Within such a relationship of inequity, strangeness signals the disintegration of neighborly relations, for the stranger is in fact identified with one's neighbor (*rē'ekā*). Without a balance of socioeconomic power among neighbors, victimization reigns, like a gazelle or bird trapped in the hand of a hunter (v. 5; cf. 1:17; 7:22-23). Whether by death or by enslavement, the embrace of the stranger entails the demise of the self, an object of shame and dishonor. The one who has entered the door of the stranger's house can only lament: "I am utterly ruined in the public assembly" (5:14). By rejecting discipline, the self suffers the ravages of moral decay and dissolution, public humiliation and death (5:11, 14). Within the context of sexual chastity, discipline commutes life-sustaining vigor, indeed joy, in the wholesome celebration of eros with the "wife of [one's] youth." She is the true and intimate neighbor; in her the purity of equity lives and breathes. She is the full and legitimate partner in the play of life.

The stranger thus can be potentially anyone who disrupts the balance of power among neighbors. As the consummate stranger, the "other woman" offers only a love affair with death. The mother[64] recounts for her son an episode she witnessed from her window of a "young man without sense" taken in by this femme fatale. The strange woman is akin to a predator scouring the streetcorners in search of prey (7:12-13, 22-23). Her eyelashes are her weapons (6:25); her smooth woods and kisses are her bait (7:13, 21; 5:3). Mimicking the unscrupulous peers who attempt to lure the son into their violent cause (1:11), the adulteress issues her own invitation: "Come, let us take

63. For the monetary ramifications, see Washington, *Wealth and Poverty*, 165-66.

64. The speaker in Proverbs 7 is more likely the mother than the father (so A. Brenner, "Proverbs 1–9: An F Voice," in idem and F. van Dijk-Hemmes, *On Gendering Texts* [Biblical Interpretation Series 1; Leiden: Brill, 1993] 120).

our fill[65] of sex until morning; let us delight ourselves[66] with love" (7:18). Like the murderous youths, the strange woman lures the youth to his doom, like a stag in a trap (v. 23). As the father enabled the son to view the thrill of highway robbery as ultimately suicidal, the mother reveals the love of the strange woman to be a necrophilia.

Together, the parents exhort the son to appropriate their commandments and reproofs in order "to preserve [him] from the evil woman (*'ēšet rā'*), from the smooth tongue of the alien woman" (*nokrîyâ*, 6:24). Whereas a prostitute's fee is a loaf of bread, the victim's own life is the prize and prey of the adulteress (v. 26). The strange woman is, in fact, no foreigner from a distant land;[67] she is the woman next door, the neighbor's wife (*'ēšet rē'ēhû*, v. 29). Yet her ways and her identity are cut from a different cloth, for she has forsaken "the partner of her youth" (2:17). Her "foreignness" is exemplified in her waywardness: she has a house but no home (7:11), and so remains outside any familial ethos. She is a rover and a wanderer, not to mention an importer

65. The verb *rwh* refers literally to drinking or saturating (Prov 5:19; Ps 65:10 [MT 11]; Isa 55:10), suggesting a connection with the peers' invitation to "swallow" (*bl'*) the innocent, like Sheol, and to "fill" (*ml'*) their houses with wealth (Prov 1:12-13).

66. The root *'ls* also connotes the sense of taste (Job 20:18).

67. Attempts to prove that the "foreignness" of the adulteress is essentially cultic are strained and unnecessary for understanding what is at stake in the sages' rhetorical worldview (e.g., G. Boström, *Proverbiastudien: Die Weisheit und das fremde Weib in Spr. 1–9* [LUÅ 1/30/3; Lund: Gleerup, 1935] 42-52, 103-55; W. McKane, *Proverbs* [OTL; Philadelphia: Westminster, 1970] 338; J. Blenkinsopp, "The Social Context of the 'Outsider Woman' in Proverbs 1–9," *Bib* 72 [1991] 462-67). See the persuasive critique of C. Camp, who argues that the adulteress is cultically a bona fide Israelite, although sociosexually a deviant vis-à-vis the family structure ("What's So Strange About the Strange Woman?" in *The Bible and the Politics of Exegesis: Essays in Honor of Norman K. Gottwald* [ed. D. Jobling, P. L. Day, and G. T. Sheppard; Cleveland: Pilgrim, 1991] 17-31, esp. 21-23, 27, but cf. 28; see also Maier, *Die "fremde Frau,"* 177-214). The issue of ethnicity, however, is an open question. Making sense of the contentious issues of land, wealth, and exogamy in Proverbs, Washington argues that the stranger represents those women who did not belong to the former exilic community, the *gôlâ*, which was reestablishing itself in the Judean province (*Wealth and Poverty*, 165-66; idem, "The Strange Woman of Proverbs 1–9 and Post-Exilic Judean Society," in *Second Temple Studies*, vol. 2: *Temple and Community in the Persian Period* [ed. T. C. Eskenazi and K. H. Richards; JSOTSup 175; Sheffield: JSOT Press, 1994] 217-43), which may prove to be too simplistic a distinction, given the complexity of evolving social relationships during the early Second Temple period. The sages suggest that the stranger is anyone outside the familial balance of power and moral sphere of existence or ethos. Despite Washington's attempts to distance adultery from strangeness ("Strange Woman," 227), it is clear that the "strange woman" either has forsaken or is about to forsake her marriage covenant (2:16-19; 6:24-36; 7:19-20; as also implied in 5:1-23; 7:4-5). Therein lies most crucially her status as an outsider.

of Egyptian linens.[68] The danger she represents lurks just outside the door; to touch her invites self-destruction. The strange woman is the watery chaos that laps at the threshold of the self, threatening to submerge the self. As Yahweh contained the deeps by decree to establish a cosmic haven for Wisdom's play, so the sages establish by all means of forceful rhetoric, from indictment to graphic narrative, a boundary between the youth and the married woman to prevent a fatal attraction.

The sages portray the relationship between the adulteress and the male subject as a form of demoralizing bondage. She is depicted as a ruthless predator. The youth is the unwitting victim, death's helpless prey. Unlike Wisdom's play, erotic as it is edifying, the strange woman's seductive powers only dominate and enslave. The male is the helpless victim, engulfed by the alien woman's discourse and ultimately by the yawning maw of Mot, the Canaanite god of death.[69] Yet he remains fully responsible for his fate. His powerlessness is due to his culpable lack of sense or discernment of the consequences of the stranger's deadly embrace (ḥăsar-lēb, 6:32; 7:7), as well as his lack of discipline or self-control ('ên mûsār, 5:23). In his ignorance, the youth is blinded both to the husband's wrath, whose single-minded purpose is to exact revenge, and, more broadly, to the punishing consequences of public shame. By succumbing to the other woman, the youth has violated both the husband and the larger community,[70] who, in turn, will seal the "victim's" fate in his love affair with death (6:32-35). While the ignorant youth traverses from life to death, the adulteress remains ever the embodiment of chaos and wellspring of forbidden desire. Whereas the stranger stalks her prey, the moral agent diligently searches and discovers Wisdom as a lost lover.

Eros and Ethos

True eros can be found only with Wisdom, the sages vigorously claim.[71] Within the safety of her cosmic domicile, Wisdom's play imparts both delight

68. Prov 7:11, 16. That she imports fabric may seem incidental until one compares her with her counterpart in Prov 31:10-31, who diligently manufactures her own (vv. 13, 19, 21, 22, 24). This "woman of worth" ('ēšet-ḥayil), the son's ideal spouse, is portrayed as a consummate producer of textiles.

69. McKane, Proverbs, 287-88.

70. Nothing, however, is said of the consequences for the strange woman's violation, for she remains mythically larger than life, the very instrument of death.

71. The erotic dimensions of Wisdom fit hand in glove with her personified status in Proverbs 1–9. In the older literary strata found in Proverbs, the language of sexuality as-

and discipline, foreplay and foresight. Such "virtues" are received, however, only at the moral subject's initiative. Unlike the strange woman, who lurks at every dark corner to ambush the unsuspecting, Wisdom waits in the public square to be found by her would-be followers. To initiate a relationship with her, it is incumbent on the moral self to be the subject rather than the object of the seductive embrace. In the direct words of a parental sage, "Get wisdom; get insight!" (4:5).[72] Through the appropriation of wisdom, a world of security and responsibility is unfolded for the listening heart. Those who join themselves to wisdom (3:18) must cleave to the parental precepts of wisdom's familial ethos (4:4),[73] a pedagogical reversal of the Yahwist's etiological note on marriage in Gen 2:24.

The imperatival language of the parent mirrors the benefits that Wisdom imparts: "love her" (Prov 8:6); "prize her" (v. 8); "guard her" (v. 13b); "embrace her" (v. 8); and "keep my commandments and live" (4:4; 7:2; cf. 8:32). Wisdom, in turn, will "keep," "guard," "exalt," and "confer honor on" her students (4:6, 8; cf. 6:23).[74] Life is not only the substance of parental command to the son but also Wisdom's prize for her lover (v. 13b; 8:35). Although conditioned entirely on the agent's initiative, the relationship between Wisdom and the moral self is mutual, edifying, and, so the sages evocatively suggest, intensely passionate. In the words of Wisdom herself, "I love those who love me" (8:17). Wisdom's disciple is not a sex slave or prey but a full and responsible participant in sapiential lovemaking. Wisdom's play is fair.

Wisdom, moreover, is no stranger; rather, she is to be addressed as "sister" and "intimate kin"[75] (7:4), terms of endearment that profile her as a bona fide member of the family. That she is a constant topic of parental discourse attests to her familial nature, most concretely expressed in the father's discourse of 5:15-20. The son's spouse incarnates Wisdom's familial eros, a relationship that by any other standard might be considered incestuous.

---

sociated with Wisdom is virtually absent. For a brief survey of Wisdom and eros in Proverbs 1–9, see R. E. Murphy, "Wisdom and Eros in Proverbs 1–9," *CBQ* 50 (1988) 600-603.

72. Heb. *qĕnēh ḥokmâ qĕnēh bînâ*. The verb *qnh*, "acquire" or "create," is potent with moral significance.

73. The verb *tmk* ("to hold fast") is attested in 3:18 and 4:4.

74. Suggestively missing is any language of Wisdom's embrace of her student. The act of embrace connotes initiative, whether the self's embrace of Wisdom (4:8; cf. 5:20) or the strange woman's embrace of the wayward youth (7:13). Wisdom is exclusively embraced, never embracing. She is responsive only at the *initiated* affections of her follower. Otherwise, the ethical force of her relationship with her student would be lost.

75. See the same term *mōdā'* in the Qere of Ruth 2:1.

15 Drink water from your cistern,
      flowing water from your well.

16 Should your springs be dispersed abroad,
      (like) water channels in the streets?

17 Let them be for you alone,
      and not for sharing with strangers.

18 Let your fountain be blessed, and rejoice in the wife of your youth,
      a lovely doe, a graceful hind.

19 May her breasts satisfy you constantly,
      with her love may you always be intoxicated.

20 Why should you be drunk, my son, with a strange woman,
      and embrace the bosom of a foreigner?

The relationship between son and spouse is conveyed through the image of water, a potent symbol that signifies sustenance and fertility. The wife's "water" frames the passage (vv. 15, 18a, 19b-20) as much as the husband's "water" fills part of the poetic body of the unit (vv. 16-17, 18a). Like the deeps that fertilize the earth (3:20), the wife is the source of sexual sustenance, the son's own "cistern" (5:15). She is the fountain of life and the embodied source of wisdom.[76]

Her husband, too, is a water source, whose streams are to flow only to her (vv. 16-17). Otherwise, the father warns, the son's springs will dissipate to the streets and strangers (vv. 16-17), and so also his life, for from the man's heart "flow the springs of life" (4:23).[77] Adultery only drains the life of the self.[78] By contrast, the symbol of the flowing fountain is a potent image of water that embraces both husband and wife (5:18).[79] Shared among these two sources, water is mutually given, received, and, as a cistern holds water, con-

---

76. See Prov 1:23; 13:14; 16:22; 25:26.

77. On a purely physical level, the issuance of springs and water channels signifies semen (McKane, *Proverbs*, 319). But similar language in 4:23 suggest a wider, more ethically nuanced reading.

78. The rhetoric suggests that adultery leads, inter alia, to impotence.

79. Common interpretation holds that the "fountain" or "spring" (*māqôr*) in v. 18a refers exclusively to the woman, as evinced in similar images in v. 15 (*bôr, bě'ēr*) and supposed linear parallelism in v. 18b (e.g., McKane, *Proverbs*, 319). But the explicit association of water imagery with the husband in the prior two verses also designates the male as a source of water.

tained in joyous matrimony (v. 18b).[80] Reserved for them alone, the vehicle of life and erotic joy must not flow beyond their relationship. So also their passionate abandonment: only from the wife must the husband become "always intoxicated"[81] and satisfied with her breasts (vv. 19-20). Only in faithful matrimony is Wisdom's "play" enacted. Within marriage, the waters are harnessed and bound by Wisdom to create new life and refresh one's own, but by breach of marriage they are unleashed with a destructive force that dissipates the self and destroys the familial community.

The father's counsel to the son makes pointedly clear that Wisdom is familialized within the covenant of marriage. She cannot be had by any other means. Nevertheless, Wisdom serves as the vital link between the family and the larger world for the moral subject. Like the strange woman, Wisdom is not bound to the home (cf. 7:11); she can be found in the most public of places within the city, in the centers of human interchange, imparting her instruction.[82] Wisdom and the strange woman share the common domain of the city. But their paths, the sages make clear, never cross. Whereas Wisdom revels in her public persona, the strange woman operates undercover at night (7:9). Wisdom's ways are straight and righteous; the stranger's habits are crooked and treacherous. Wisdom's ethos encompasses not only individual and family values but also those values indispensable for the larger community. She freely transverses all realms of social intercourse, from private to cosmic. Her world is a cosmopolis.[83] Her ways include communal concord and right relations between neighbors (3:27-34). More broadly, by Wisdom all "kings reign, and rulers decree what is just" (8:15, 16). She embodies not only those virtues that are instrumental for the individual, such as prudence and discretion, but also those that are in-

---

80. Similar to Cant 1:4, the imperative "rejoice" is concretely embodied in the activity of lovemaking (G. A. Anderson, *A Time to Mourn, a Time to Dance: The Expression of Grief and Joy in Israelite Religion* [University Park: Pennsylvania State University Press, 1991] 36).

81. The verb *šgh* has the broader meaning of going astray, but is used occasionally to connote drunkenness (Isa 28:7; Prov 20:1).

82. See Prov 1:20-21; 8:1-3; cf. 7:12.

83. Representing the final stage(s) of the book, Proverbs 1–9 and 31:10-31 effectively shift the socioliterary context from that of agriculture, as evinced in the earliest forms of proverbial wisdom (C. Westermann, *The Roots of Wisdom: The Oldest Proverbs of Israel and Other Peoples* [tr. J. D. Charles; Louisville: Westminster John Knox, 1995], esp. 120-21), to that of urbiculture. For an analysis of the city in Proverbs, see R. N. Whybray, "City Life in Proverbs 1–9," in *"Jedes Ding hat seine Zeit . . .": Studien zur israelitischen und altorientalischen Weisheit* (ed. A. A. Diesel et al.; BZAW 241; Berlin: de Gruyter, 1996) 243-50.

herently moral and essential for the society at large: "righteousness, justice, equity," the precepts of the covenantal community.[84] Socially, Wisdom is the bridge between family and community. Theologically, she is the link between the Creator and the moral self. Pedagogically, Wisdom is found where discipline and delight embrace.

Delight and Discipline

As the crown of creation, Wisdom's delight in the human race is mirrored in Yahweh's delight in Wisdom (8:30b-31), a delight she imparts to her disciples in the form of beatitudes that acknowledge the virtues of discipline and diligence.[85] Wisdom's blessing is the fruit of her disciple's vigilance, the reward for being ever at her doorstep, stationed at her dwelling, and, ultimately, inhabiting her ethos. In her domain, Wisdom's values dwell in and guard the self. Moreover, the values of joy and discipline are inseparably linked. The parental sage exhorts the son to "rejoice in the wife of your youth," while observing that the wicked "die for lack of discipline" (5:18, 23). The nexus between delight and reproof reaches the level of apotheosis in the parental instruction of 3:11-12:

> My son, do not reject Yahweh's discipline
>   or be weary of his reproof,
> for Yahweh reproves the one he loves,
>   as a father [reproves] the son in whom he delights (*yirṣeh*).

Harsh as it may seem, discipline is the vehicle of parental love, one that inculcates values necessary for moral living. Like Wisdom's delight imparted to her disciples, Yahweh's "tough love" leads ineluctably to the joyful status of Wisdom's followers: "Happy are those who find wisdom and those who get understanding" (3:13).

As the fruit of desire, however, delight or joy is not an ultimate end, for it can also be misdirected. Those who forsake the upright paths and walk in darkness "rejoice (*śmḥ*) in doing evil and delight (*gyl*) in evil's depravity" (2:14). The flip side to the proclivity toward wickedness is the re-

---

84. Heb. *ṣedeq, mišpāṭ, mêšārîm;* 1:3; 8:6, 8, 20. See Brown, *Character in Crisis,* 25-26.
85. See above. The beatitude formula can also be found in 14:21b ("Happy are those who are kind to the poor"); 16:20b ("Happy are those who trust in Yahweh"); 20:7 ("Happy are the children who follow [the righteous]"); 28:14a ("Happy is the one who is in constant dread" [see below]); 29:18b ("Happy are those who keep the law").

jection of discipline, as poignantly conveyed in the lament of the demor-
alized adulterer: "Oh, how I hated discipline and my heart despised
reproof" (5:12). Delight and contempt, joy and hatred, represent opposite
poles of the will. Their respective objects — the seductive stranger, on the
one hand, and wholesome Wisdom, on the other — undermine or determine the will's integrity. Any middle ground is excluded, for the object of
desire reflects one's ultimate concern, which defines the morphology of
the self. To "desire [the stranger's] beauty" is to be enslaved, captured by
her eyelashes (6:25). Conversely, moral freedom rests on a single-minded
love for Wisdom.

For the sages, all moral conduct boils down to the integrity of discourse,
the revealer of character and the medium of appropriating virtue. Discourse
is the exchange currency of social intercourse and the vehicle of socialization.
Whereas the stranger's lips seductively "drip honey" (5:3), Wisdom's words
are noble and right (8:6). The adulteress invites the senseless youth, "Come,
let us take our fill of love until morning; let us delight ourselves with love"
(7:18; cf. 1:11). Wisdom announces to the naive youth, "Come, eat of my
bread and drink of the wine I have mixed" (9:5). The "foolish woman"[86] offers a counterinvitation with an added allure, "stolen water" and "concealed
bread," ill-gained provisions that satisfy only the dead (vv. 17-18). The question of whose invitation to accept, Wisdom's or the strange woman's, is a matter of life and death.

As a credit to their pedagogical ingenuity, the sages successfully lodge
the rigors of wisdom within an ethic of self-fulfillment. Happiness is both the
fruit and ground of discipline, the exercise of play, the sages suggest. As
Yahweh established creation by "firming up" the elements vis-à-vis the watery
chaos, the exercise of virtue secures the self from the moral dangers that lie
within and beyond one's hearth and home. Through wisdom a dwelling of
delight is fashioned that transforms one's domicile into a cosmopolis and the
cosmos into an *oikos*.[87]

---

86. Despite her variant title, the "foolish woman" (*'ēšet kĕsîlût*, v. 13) figures inte-
grally in the composite character of the strange woman (G. A. Yee, "'I Have Perfumed My
Bed with Myrrh': The Foreign Woman [*'iššâ zārâ*] in Proverbs 1–9," *JSOT* 43 [1989] 55, 67;
Maier, Die *"fremde Frau,"* 256-57).

87. See also the suggestive comments of L. G. Perdue, "The Israelite and Early Jewish
Family: Summary and Conclusion," in Perdue, *Families in Ancient Israel*, 178-79.

Joy and the Art of Community Formation

Prefacing the book as a whole, Proverbs 1–9 concludes with the character of Wisdom having "built her house," "hewn[88] her seven pillars," and prepared a lavish banquet for her guests (9:1-6). This final episode of Wisdom's activity is fitting. She concludes her work by creating her own domicile, setting a precedent and model for all home building, as evident in 24:3-4:

> By wisdom a home is built,
>   and by understanding it is established;
> By knowledge the rooms are filled[89]
>   with all precious and pleasant riches. (NRSV)[90]

Interpreters have labored hard to determine the significance of Wisdom's house with its seven pillars in 9:1, suggesting, inter alia, the model of a temple or its literary replacement.[91] One would expect to find, however, Wisdom engaged in cultic activity or the like, which is nowhere in evidence. The slaughtered animals and mixed wine are the products of Wisdom's abundant hospitality, not solemn worship. In building her house, Wisdom has established once and for all the symbolic parameters of her ethos or dwelling. Wisdom has matured[92] and she has built the archetypal home, expansive and complete,[93] a bastion of hospitality and security, like creation itself.[94] Like

---

88. So MT *ḥaṣĕbâ*. The LXX and Peshitta, along with the Targum, suggest *hiṣṣibâ* (Hiphil of *nṣb*), "set up." The former is, however, the *lectio difficilior*.

89. Heb. *yimmālĕ'û*. Cf. the sinners' expressed intent to "fill *(nĕmallē')* our houses with booty" (1:13).

90. See also 14:1; 24:27.

91. See the discussion in McKane, *Proverbs*, 362-63; P. W. Skehan, "The Seven Columns of Wisdom's House," in *Studies in Israelite Poetry and Wisdom* (CBQMS 1; Washington, D.C.: Catholic Biblical Association of America, 1971) 9-14 (revised from *CBQ* 9 [1947] 190-98); idem, "Wisdom's House," in ibid., 27-45 (revised from *CBQ* 29 [1967] 162-80); Washington, *Wealth and Poverty*, 124-25. For a unique reading of the text that, however, cannot be supported textually, see J. C. Greenfield, "The Seven Pillars of Wisdom (Prov. 9:1) — A Mistranslation," *JQR* 76 (1985) 13-20.

92. See the translation of 8:30 above.

93. The significance of the *seven* pillars suggests a sense of cosmic completion. Cf. B. Lang, "Die sieben Säulen der Weisheit (Sprüche IX 1) im Licht israelitischer Architektur," *VT* 33 (1983) 488-91.

94. Indeed, 24:3-4, cited above, is stylistically very similar to the "little cosmogony" of 3:19-20. In both *Tatberichte*, Wisdom plays a cognitively instrumental role in construction, whether it be the cosmos, on the one hand, or the domicile, on the other. In both, realms of security and abundance are established.

Yahweh, Wisdom has an "edifice complex." Modeled after the cosmic home, Wisdom's *oikos* is a testimony to the inherently *constructive* nature of moral conduct.

As Yahweh finds delight in Wisdom continually "beside him" (8:30), Wisdom finds her delight with humans in the setting of table fellowship, playing the role of gracious host. Although her handmaids comb the town to summon one and all to the sapiential banquet, Wisdom's invitation carries one stringent condition: "Forsake immaturity[95] and live; walk in the way of understanding" (9:6). Wisdom's invitation is as gracious as it is directive. Not all manner of characters can enter through her door.[96] The hopelessly recalcitrant are barred, counted as intruders into her domestic, well-ordered world, where abundance prevails and the dinner conversation is edifying.

Entering Wisdom's house is the consummate act of moral appropriation (9:4-6). By contrast, darkening the strange woman's domicile ensures only self-destruction (7:27). On the one hand, by gaining entrance into Wisdom's domain, the moral self, in turn, is entered and sustained by Wisdom. As the father foretells, "Wisdom will enter your heart and knowledge will give pleasure to your palate" (2:10).[97] On the other hand, by setting foot into the stranger's house the self is snared and pierced by an arrow like a hunted animal (7:23). The contrast between these two opposing figures lies precisely in their domestic settings. The nature and location of their respective dwellings, their ethoses, has all to do with the direction, conduct, and outcome of the moral self. Whereas Wisdom's home is the fundamental setting for the nurture and sustenance of the moral self, the other woman's domicile renders only dissolution and death for the self. While Wisdom's *oikos* reflects the integrity and sustaining power of creation, wherein life-giving water is mutually shared and contained (5:15-20), the stranger's household reaches down into the depths of death where chaos reigns (7:27; 9:18). The latter's house is a trapdoor into the abyss. Whereas chaos is the stranger's *oikos*, the cosmos is reflected in Wisdom's ethos.

In Wisdom's home, the nature and quality of offered food is highlighted. Her "slaughtered animals" are not her human victims, as in the stranger's case (see 7:22), but part of an edifying banquet for her guests (9:2). Wisdom's feast is the scene of two complementary movements in the formation of character, of en-

95. I take *pĕtā'yim* to be an abstract (masculine form) plural of *petî*, as found in Prov 1:22.

96. Exclusion from Wisdom's domicile reflects a realistic assessment of the moral dynamics of association (e.g., "Whoever walks with the wise becomes wise, but the companion of fools suffers harm" [13:20]).

97. Heb. *nepeš;* so also McKane, *Proverbs*, 283.

298

trance and ingestion, and what follows in the maxims of 9:7-12 is essentially Wisdom's main course, food for the wise.[98] The person addressed in these snippets of proverbial instruction is one who has accepted Wisdom's invitation and has come to partake in the banquet of insight. From these maxims, the guest is given instructions on how to handle sapiential discourse, specifically concerning whom to address and not to address. The "scoffer" and the "wicked,"[99] when corrected,[100] will only react in anger (vv. 7-8a). The lesson to be learned is the futility of instructing the incorrigible. Not only is it a waste of time, it can be harmful. By contrast, the wise "will love you" for such reproof (v. 8). "How happy is the one whom God reproves," intones Eliphaz in Job 5:12. To give to the wise, who never cease to gain from instruction,[101] marks the pinnacle of pedagogy. The student has entered into the company of the wise and has become a teacher, Wisdom's host, charged to help others in the sapiential quest, a journey on which the teacher too must continue. To correct the wise is an equal-opportunity right among the company of colleagues. In short, enlightened and effective discourse is the staple of Wisdom's banquet and the edification of delight.[102]

98. Scholars commonly assume that vv. 7-12 betray a textual intrusion by disrupting the invitational tone of Wisdom's address in vv. 4-6 (e.g., Lang, *Wisdom and the Book of Proverbs*, 87-89; McKane, *Proverbs*, 368). Be that as it may, there are indications of logical development in the overall flow of discourse. McKane identifies "incorrigibility" as the overarching theme of this passage but fails to account for the profile of the addressed character ("you") in these general maxims, which is that of the advanced student of Wisdom who is instructed on the nature of edifying discourse.

99. Within the sapiential worldview, the "scoffer" *(lēṣ)* and the "wicked" *(rāšāʿ)* represent the hopelessly intransigent. The former, in particular, is incapable of discipline and delights in deriding *(lyṣ)* the wise and despising knowledge (1:22; 13:1; 15:12). "The scoffer seeks wisdom in vain, but knowledge is easy for one who understands" (14:6). Thus avoidance of the scoffer is the rule of thumb (Ps 1:1). Embodying strife, the scoffer must be banished in order to achieve peace in the community (Prov 22:10). His punishment is an object lesson for the "immature" *(petî, 19:25).*

100. Verb *ykḥ;* cf. Prov 3:12; Job 5:12.

101. See also Prov 1:5, in which the wise, in addition to the immature, constitute the implied audience of Proverbs. In 1:4-5 the overarching pedagogical movement of chs. 1–9 (+ 31:10-31) is disclosed: that of the moral self from ignorant youth to responsible adult and sage.

102. Eating and sapiential discourse are intimately associated in Proverbs and elsewhere in the wisdom corpus: "Does not the ear test words as the palate tastes food?" (Job 12:11); "The lips of the righteous feed many, but fools die for lack of sense" (Prov 10:21); "from the fruit of the mouth one is filled with good things" (12:14a); "From the fruit of their words good persons eat good things" (13:2a); "The righteous have enough to satisfy their appetite, but the belly of the wicked is empty" (13:25, NRSV); "Pleasant words are like a honeycomb, sweetness to the palate *(nepeš)* and health to the body" (16:24; see 24:13-14). But cf. 25:16, 27. See also 13:4, 25; 15:1; 17:1.

While Yahweh fashioned the cosmos, Wisdom was at the Creator's side, witnessing the handiwork and "growing up" (8:30a). Now, as an architect herself, Wisdom creates her own domain within the secured expanse of God's creation, a world of her own making to be inhabited by her receptive followers. As Yahweh cordoned off the waters from creation (8:29), so Wisdom bars the incorrigible, the "scoffer," from setting foot in her home (9:6, 7-8). Secured from the chaos of moral recalcitrance, Wisdom's hearth is the haven for the educable, and the domain of her delight. In her house the world is "self-proofed" for the willing subject. As hostess, moreover, Wisdom cannot withhold instruction anymore than a lover can withhold affection. Her table is graciously set for moral reflection and conduct. Her fête is the fruit of her love, the labor of her play. Nurturing and commemorating the successful appropriation of instruction, Wisdom's feast is a victory banquet for the moral self.

The Play of Discipline

In her examination of Wisdom as metaphor, Claudia Camp comments on Wisdom's play: "Play is fundamentally liminal deconstructive activity. For Wisdom, it takes place at the heart of the interaction between God and humans, and, thus, at the heart of the theological endeavor."[103] Camp rightly stresses the central feature of play in the divine/human encounter, mediated by Wisdom in creation. Play is the medium of sapiential delight, an active engagement in appropriating and exercising Wisdom's values and virtues. Play is liminal in that it cannot be contained exclusively within one realm or another, for it is by nature interactive; solitary "play" is an oxymoron.[104] The sages, however, steer clear of any "deconstructive" play. To the contrary, Wisdom's play is considered quintessentially edifying and life-giving, play with a purpose. She does not tear down in order to build up; her attention is focused not so much on the intransigent, the "scoffers" and the "fools" who have already cast their lot in declining discipline (cf. 1:22-26), as on the naive and open-minded, the "immature," who still have a fighting chance to appropriate her instruction and values.[105] Rejection is reserved for the former, for they

103. C. Camp, "Woman Wisdom as Root Metaphor: A Theological Consideration," in *The Listening Heart: Essays in Honor of Roland E. Murphy* (ed. K. G. Hoglund et al.; JSOTSup 58; Sheffield: JSOT Press, 1987) 58-59.

104. Solitary existence is considered ethically suspect by the sages: "The one who lives alone is self-indulgent" (18:1a). By contrast, friendship is highly prized (e.g., 18:24).

105. The *petî* ("immature individual") is open to either instruction or folly (Prov 9:4, 16) and naively believes everything (Prov 14:15).

have categorically rejected Wisdom, but the joy of play is accorded the latter as the fruit of maturity.

Wisdom's engagement with her followers is recognized as play from a particular perspective. As the father enables the son to step back and witness the self-destructive conduct of his peers, however enticing and egalitarian their invitation may appear, Wisdom's activity in and with the inhabited world is perceived as play from a cosmically comprehensive perspective. The sages contextualize the erotic dimensions of sagacious play within the faithful domicile of marital bliss. To Wisdom's neophyte, the appropriation of Wisdom may seem anything but playful. Sapiential instruction can seem arduous and harsh to one tempted by immediate gratification and gain, but her lasting benefits outweigh any hardship that moral appropriation might initially entail.[106] Although Wisdom is first introduced as a veritable prophet, hurling indictments against her detractors and the immature (1:20-33), sternness gives way to joy, Wisdom's delight in engaging the willing student. Rather than exhorting him to suffer Wisdom's rebukes, the father advises his son first and foremost to find Wisdom, the incomparable treasure that she is, and to embrace her as his long-lost lover (4:5-9). For those who intend to keep her, Wisdom's rebukes are recognized for what they are, open and constructive expressions of affection (3:12; 8:3).[107] In the collegial community of Wisdom's dwelling, mutual edification reigns and "iron sharpens iron" (27:17).

The Play of Discourse

Edifying discourse lies at the heart of the sapiential enterprise. Measured against the seductive and deadly utterances of her evil counterpart, Wisdom's discourse is profiled as fundamentally constructive. The discourse of Wisdom's nemesis is like a "deep pit" that engulfs the living, carrying them to Sheol (22:14; cf. 23:27; 30:16, 20). The opening of the mouth is the threshold of the heart and the window to one's character, the sages repeatedly claim.[108] "The mouth of the righ-

106. Cf. Sir 4:17-18, which posits a two-stage *paideia*. Wisdom first leads her children along "tortuous paths," "tormenting them with her discipline." Once they have proved themselves, Wisdom "will come straight back to them again and gladden them." The sages of Proverbs place relatively greater emphasis on the latter stage.
107. "Like a gold ring or an ornament of gold is a wise rebuke to a listening ear" (25:12); "A rebuke strikes deeper into a discerning person than a hundred blows into a fool" (17:10); "Better is an open rebuke than hidden love" (25:7, NRSV).
108. In proverbial wisdom, intelligence and discourse are bound up: "The lips of the

teous is a fountain of life, but the mouth of the wicked conceals violence" (10:11, NRSV). Life and death, creation and chaos, have their roots in discourse.[109] "With their mouths the godless destroy their neighbors, but by knowledge the righteous are delivered" (11:9); "By the blessing of the upright a city is lifted up, but by the mouth of the wicked it is overthrown" (v. 11, NRSV).[110] Blessing and efficacious knowledge are the fruits of wise discourse.

For the sages, edifying discourse is not a matter of quantity. Indeed, a proliferation of words is counterproductive and ethically suspect: "When words are many, transgression is not lacking, but the prudent are restrained in speech" (10:19, NRSV). Unenlightened discourse is reckless by nature. The cacophony of chaos, careless discourse dispenses only calamity and dissolution to both agent and audience,[111] but salutary is an economy of speech. To underscore the importance of restrained speech, the ancient sages playfully blur the boundaries between opposite character types: "Even fools who keep silent are considered wise; when they close their lips, they are deemed intelligent" (17:28, NRSV).[112] Whereas foolish speech unleashes a veritable deluge of discourse that creates only strife and destruction (18:6), spareness of words bespeaks an abundance of knowledge (17:27).

Moreover, such discursive restraint reflects integrity of character and an edifying spirit: "Whoever belittles another lacks sense; a discerning person remains silent" (11:12). What comes in and goes out of one's mouth are equally crucial: the image of a wide-open mouth invites self-destruction, whereas guarded lips that bar the intrusion of worthless "food" or thought preserve life (13:3; 10:32). The former connotes an insatiable appetite to one's own detriment (13:4, 25), for what goes in can come out: "Like a dog returning to its vomit is a fool who reverts to his folly" (26:11). Thus it is with a modicum of ambiguity that the anonymous sage compares discourse to water: "The words of the mouth are deep waters; the fountain of wisdom is a gushing stream" (18:4a); "The beginning of strife is like letting out water; so stop before the quarrel

---

righteous know what is acceptable, but the mouth of the wicked [know] what is perverse" (10:32). See also 10:20; 17:20.

109. "Death and life are in the power of the tongue, and those who love it will eat its fruits" (18:21, NRSV). See also 12:6, 18, 25; 15:1, 2, 4, 7; 26:27.

110. "The words of the wicked are a deadly ambush, but the speech of the upright delivers them" (12:6, NRSV).

111. For example, 10:11; 17:20; 18:6, 7.

112. Jerzy Kosinski's modern parable *Being There* (New York: Bantam, 1985) finds its moral premise in this ancient proverb. Elsewhere, the sages revel in underscoring the incongruity between the fool and fine speech (e.g., 17:7; 26:7; 29:20).

breaks out" (17:14). The mouth can discharge a cataclysmic deluge or a refreshing stream, as can the waters of creation.[113]

The yawning chasm that separates the wise from the foolish is reflected by their verbal performance. Consequently, the manner of speech, its style and execution, is considered critically important. Much of Proverbs is concerned not only with *what* is said but, more so, *how* it is packaged. Form and content are inseparably related in sapiential rhetoric. Authentic discourse, according to the sages, reflects the unity of beauty and truth, of knowledge and rhetorical elegance, the polished product of life-enhancing play. The restrained and reflective discourse of the wise, in short, shapes moral direction:

> With patience a ruler can be persuaded;
>   and a soft tongue can break bones (25:15; cf. 16:21).

> A soft answer turns away wrath,
>   but a harsh word stirs up anger (15:1).

> A gentle tongue is the tree of life,
>   but perverseness in it breaks the spirit (15:4).

> Rash speech is like sword stabs,
>   but the tongue of the wise brings healing.
> Truthful lips endure forever,
>   but a lying tongue lasts only a moment (12:18-19).[114]

The tongue of the wise is commended for both the integrity that directs it and the salutary results it produces. From the mouth of the righteous, a moral world is fashioned and secured. The sagacious utterance conjoins elegance with truth in an aesthetic of conciseness. The proverb attests to the literary terseness of sapiential discourse, a precision in form designed to be both rhetorically arresting and morally evocative.[115] In its appropriate context, the proverb is a word on target, and "a word fitly spoken is like apples of gold in a setting of silver" (25:11, NRSV).[116]

In short, the sapiential word is a world-producing word. By stepping back to see the forest for the trees, the reader of Proverbs finds that the

---

113. For example, 3:20; 8:29 (see above).

114. The above citations reflect the NRSV.

115. For a suggestive analysis of the proverb's rhetorical function in biblical narrative, see C. R. Fontaine, *Traditional Sayings in the Old Testament* (BLS 5; Sheffield: Almond, 1982).

116. In the mouth of a fool, however, such discourse is lame and hurtful, like a limp leg or a "thornbush wielded by a drunkard's hand" (26:7, 9).

discourse of the wise has wrought a world inhabited by extreme polarities of character, the wise and the foolish, the rash and the restrained, the mature and the naive, in short, a veritable cavalcade of scoundrels and heroes, of losers and victors, in the sapiential quest. The world of the sages is characteristically dualistic, a rhetorical setting intended to be pedagogically provocative in the task of imparting instructions for moral conduct to young and old alike. The sapiential world is a world fraught with potential danger but secured by the counsel and conduct of Wisdom (11:14).

The Socioliterary Context: Conflict and Conciliation

The divided literary world of Proverbs mirrors, in part, the historically conditioned world in which issues of land, possession, and marriage were matters of utmost concern. Such was the social context of the postexilic period, one of corrosive tension between the returned exiles, the *gôlâ*,[117] and the residents in Judah or the "peoples of the land(s)," who had escaped the formative experience of Babylonian captivity.[118] As the exiles began to return and reestablish themselves, conflict over land ownership was inevitable.[119] During this tumultuous period, a family was more than simply one social unit among others; it was the source of survival within the fray. Familial contours were forged on the anvil of social conflict, fashioned from the discord and division between nativist exiles and a "Canaanite" Israel.[120] For the former exiles, a stable and endogamous household was the cornerstone of the restored community in the homeland. Reclaiming the land required the preservation (or revision!) of the family lineage, along with its accompanying inheritance rights.[121] Consequently, an "ideology of [genealogical]

117. See Ezra 4:1; 6:16, 19-20; 8:25; 10:7, 16.

118. See Ezra 3:3; 9:1-2, 11; 10:2, 11; Neh 9:24, 30; 10:31-32.

119. See Ezek 11:15-17. For a succinct overview of the conflictive situation, particularly in relation to the problem of exogamy, see Blenkinsopp, "Social Context," 467-73; Washington, "Strange Woman," 232-38.

120. The true Israel came to be identified with the exilic community (e.g., Ezra 1:11; 2:1; 9:4; 10:6; Neh 7:6), whereas the residents of Judah were excluded from the covenant community as veritable Canaanites. See Washington, "Strange Woman," 232; H. G. M. Williamson, "The Concept of Israel in Transition," in *The World of Ancient Israel: Sociological, Anthropological and Political Perspectives* (ed. R. E. Clements; Cambridge: Cambridge University Press, 1989) 155.

121. See Ezra 2 and Nehemiah 7, which recount the failure of certain families to prove their patrilineal ties to the land. Some resorted, however, to genealogical revisioning

descent"[122] helped to define the boundaries of the legitimate family — Israel in miniature.

Out of this world fraught with division and strife, the sages fashioned a dualistic worldview that polarized the familial and the strange. With the land as a central issue of contention, Yahweh's establishment of the cosmic domain is a cosmogony of reclamation: the containment of chaos and the establishment of a cosmic home for safe and secure dwelling. Moreover, the creation of Wisdom initiates a movement of genealogical descent: Yahweh's relationship to Wisdom is essentially parental. Wisdom, in turn, addresses her followers as her own children (8:32). Her pedigree thus defines the familial identity of her followers over and against those who have succumbed to the strange woman, who has no home (7:11), and are consequently "cut off from the land" (2:22).

Yet in this sapientially bifurcated world, there is surprisingly a measure of common ground. Such is the case with a socioeconomic polarity, the great divide between the rich and the poor, categories that no doubt overlapped in some measure with the *gôlâ* community and the impoverished indigenous population of Judah.[123] Although the destitute are sometimes castigated and wealth is intimately associated with virtue, blessing, and wisdom in proverbial discourse,[124] poverty does not warrant the kind of condemnation one might expect. "It is better to be poor and walk in integrity than to be crooked in one's ways even though rich" (28:6; cf. 19:1). "The rich person is wise in self-esteem but a discerning poor person sees through the pose" (28:11, NRSV). The inclusive contours of right character reach beyond the social stigma of poverty. Normative character is not to be monopolized by any particular class. Moreover, the character of Wisdom informs and critiques social standards that maintain rigid economic distinctions.[125] Frequent are the injunctions to care for the poor and acknowledge their rights (*dîn dallîm*, 29:7).[126] Most pointedly

---

in order to distance themselves from the "peoples of the land(s)" and become included in the *gôlâ* community (Washington, "Strange Woman," 233-34).

122. Washington draws from cultural anthropologist M. Sahlins ("Strange Woman," 243).

123. For a comprehensive study on this topic, see R. N. Whybray, *Wealth and Poverty in the Book of Proverbs* (JSOTSup 99; Sheffield: JSOT Press, 1990). See also B. W. Kovacs, "Is There a Class-Ethic in Proverbs?" in *Essays in Old Testament Ethics (J. Philip Hyatt, In Memoriam)* (ed. J. L. Crenshaw and J. T. Willis; New York: Ktav, 1974) 171-89; J. D. Pleins, "Poverty in the Social World of the Wise," *JSOT* 37 (1987) 61-78.

124. For example, 6:6-11; 8:18; 10:4-5, 15; 13:18, 21; 22:13; 24:30-35; 26:13-16; 27:23-27.

125. See 13:7, 11; 18:23.

126. For example, 13:23; 14:21; 21:13; 22:22-23; 28:3, 27; 31:9.

is the common ground shared between the socioeconomic classes established in creation:[127]

> The rich and the poor meet together:[128]
> Yahweh is the maker of them all (22:2).

> The poor and the oppressor meet together:
> Yahweh gives light to the eyes of both (29:13).

Because Yahweh has created the inhabitants of the earth in toto, a rapprochement between the divided classes is integral to the divine handiwork. Parallel in language, these two proverbs cast Yahweh in the role of creator and imparter of wisdom, giving "light to the eyes."[129] Through the God-given power of imaginative discernment, the poor and the oppressor can see eye-to-eye as bona fide children of a creator God and as equal players in Wisdom's household. Such common ground is potent with moral force: "Those who castigate[130] the poor insult their Maker" (17:5a); "Those who oppress the poor insult their Maker; but those who favor[131] the needy honor him" (14:31). Oppression is a distinctly unnatural act, an affront to the Creator and a violation of the created order. Yahweh's creative role is infused with judicial character in 22:22-23:

> Do not rob the poor because they are poor,
> or crush the afflicted at the gate;
> for Yahweh will take up their case[132]
> and rob[133] of life those who rob them.

The divine roles of prosecutor/judge and creator/restorer are tightly interrelated in Proverbs. Lodged in the sapiential order is a binding force connecting the polarities of social power and status, the rich and the poor, tyrants and subjects, that is grounded in creation by a common Creator and

127. See also H.-J. Hermisson, "Observations on the Creation Theology in Wisdom," in *Israelite Wisdom: Theological and Literary Essays in Honor of Samuel Terrien* (ed. J. G. Gammie et al.; Missoula, Mont.: Scholars Press, 1978) 45.

128. Heb. *nipgāšû*, which connotes a mutual encounter. See also Ps 85:11.

129. Cf. Prov 20:12 ("The hearing ear and the seeing eye, Yahweh has made them both").

130. Verb *l'g*, which denotes absolute derision (Job 22:19; Ps 44:13 [MT 14]).

131. Verb *ḥnn* (Ps 37:21, 26; Prov 19:17; 28:8).

132. Heb. *yārîb rîbām*, distinctly legal terminology.

133. The verb *qb'*, although rare (only here and in Mal 3:8, 9), corresponds in some intensified sense to *gzl* in the previous verse, hence the identical translation of the verbs.

made discernible by Wisdom. Wisdom's play in the inhabited world is as encompassing as it is directive. Excluded are the scoffer and the wicked, who in the end reveal themselves to be more literary foils than real and rounded characters: pedagogically useful, strangely remote, and ultimately without substance.

Wisdom at Home: The Ethos of *Sophia*[134]

The character that rounds out the book of Proverbs is the so-called woman of worth or valor *('ēšet-ḥayil)* in the acrostic poem of 31:10-31, identified as a heroic hymn.[135] Her effusively detailed description suggests that she is Wisdom incarnated within the household, the familial embodiment of Wisdom.[136] As in Wisdom's account of Yahweh's acts of creation in 8:22-31, deed outweighs discourse. Nowhere is the valiant woman given direct speech. Instead, things are said *about* her in direct discourse (vv. 28-29). While her words are identified with those of Wisdom (v. 26a), her hands, rather than her mouth, receive the lion's share of attention. But this is no loss. Like words whose meanings are determined by linguistic convention, her actions, as grounded in social convention, communicate with equal impact. Comparable to Wisdom's discourse, the woman's deeds also convey a crucial aspect of Wisdom's ethos: "Wisdom *(ṣôpîyâ)*[137] are the ways of her household" (v. 27). Wisdom's dwelling is identified with the woman's home.

By her willing hands and discerning judgment, this woman of wisdom provides abundantly for her household, from food and clothing to liquid assets. She is the economic engine of her household, the *bêt 'ēm* or "mother's house," the feminine counterpart to the *bêt 'āb* or *bêt 'ābôt*, the "paternal estate."[138] Comparably, the maternal household is a nonrestrictive domain for

134. I use the Greek translation of "wisdom" (Heb. *ḥokmâ*) in this context, given the wordplay in 31:27 (see below, n.137).

135. See A. Wolters, "Proverbs XXXI 10-31 as Heroic Hymn: A Form-Critical Analysis," *VT* 38 (1988) 446-57.

136. For the importance of this poem to the book as a whole, see T. P. McCreesh, "Wisdom as Wife: Proverbs 31:10-31," *RB* 91 (1985) 25-46.

137. The participle of Heb. *ṣph* ("keep watch") is a deliberate play on the Greek word for wisdom, *sophia* (A. Wolters, "*Ṣôpiyyâ* [Prov 31:27] as Hymnic Participle and Play on *Sophia*," *JBL* 104 [1985] 577-87).

138. As C. Meyers points out, although the precise expression is not found in the book, Prov 31:15, 21 (2x), 27 refer to "her house" *(bêtāh)*. Reference to the "mother's house" is attested in Gen 24:28; Ruth 1:8; Cant 3:4; 8:2. ("'To Her Mother's House': Considering a Counterpart to the Israelite *bêt 'āb*," in *The Bible and the Politics of Exegesis: Es-*

its primary inhabitant. "She is like merchant ships; she brings her food from far away" (v. 14).[139] Whereas she imports her food from far-off lands, this woman of the house manufactures all manner of fabric, for domestic use and for export.[140] The garments she produces establish her household as solid and safe (v. 21); "power and majesty"[141] are her own clothing (v. 25).[142] Girded with strength and equipped with powerful limbs (v. 17), she is a veritable warrior on the domestic front; her house is an impregnable fortress.[143]

Yet domestic as it is, the valiant woman's domicile is not a gated household, shut off from the outer world. Her door is flung open on behalf of the community as much as her lips are parted wide to deliver wisdom and covenantal teaching, the "law of faithfulness" (tôrat-ḥesed, v. 26).[144] This woman of wisdom has familialized tôrâ. Reaching out to grasp the spindle, she also extends her hand to the poor and needy (vv. 19a, 20b).[145] Her children and spouse also depend on her. As wife and mother, the woman of worth is based at home. As provider, she brings in food from afar and exports her wares to the same extent. To both the poor and the spindle[146] her hand extends, to grasp and to hold.[147] Her household comprises the grand central stations of the larger community, the marketplace and the city gate, on the domestic level (vv. 23,

---

says in Honor of Norman K. Gottwald on His Sixty-Fifth Birthday [ed. D. Jobling, et al. Cleveland: Pilgrim, 1991]) 17-32). Missing from Meyers's study, however, is the identical expression, "her house," employed in the context of the strange woman's domicile (7:8, 11, 27), a foil for the woman of valor's household (see above).

139. By contrast, the husband of the "strange woman" is most likely a merchant (7:19-20).

140. See 31:14, 18, 19, 21, 22, 24.

141. Heb. 'ōz-wĕhādār is an ascription of royal power: Pss 8:6; 21:6; 29:4; 96:6; 104:1; Ezek 27:10.

142. It may not be completely fortuitous that the description of Wisdom's creation by Yahweh employs the metaphor of weaving, which would establish a "genetic" association between Wisdom and the "woman of worth" (8:23).

143. In this sense, the "woman of worth" can be rendered "the woman of valor." See the examination of military language noted by Wolters, "Proverbs XXXI 10-31 as Heroic Hymn," 453-54.

144. The latter expression likely includes covenantal law, in addition to parental instruction (cf. 1:8; 28:4). The tôrâ associated with the mother is also found in 1:8; 6:20, 23. See Washington's suggestive treatment of "law" in Proverbs (Wealth and Poverty, 129-33).

145. The same verb šlḥ is found in both cola.

146. The common translation "distaff" for kîšôr in v. 19a is likely erroneous. See A. Wolters, "The Meaning of Kîšôr (Prov 31:19)," HUCA 65 (1994) 91-104, who suggests that a doubling spindle is designated.

147. The close parallel between v. 19b (verb tāmak) and v. 20a suggests that more than an impersonal or patronizing assistance to the poor is meant.

31). Her house is not an enclave but a base of operations, and the same can be said of her gender.[148] She is merchant and household head, warrior and cultivator. Like Noah, she plants a vineyard (v. 16; cf. Gen 9:20). As a warrior, she laughs in the face of adversity (v. 25), as does Wisdom (1:26; 8:30-31). Her character, Wisdom in the home and in the flesh, both bends and binds the genders. Her domesticity is magisterial; her combat is the labor of love. Open yet protected, her household is a domain of security and delight.[149]

"Fearful" Play

The moral profile of *sophia* in the home concludes on an unmistakably theocentric cadence in the same way the taxonomy of virtues profiled in 1:2-7 is rounded out with the theme of the "fear of Yahweh" (31:30b; 1:7).[150] A theological leitmotif in sapiential discourse,[151] divine reverence defines *sophia's* conduct and discourse. As the most basic and cardinal of virtues, "fear" is the default drive of moral conduct: it commands avoidance and hatred of evil (3:7; 8:13) and, conversely, the love of goodness and instruction (15:33). Its elevated status is matched by its moral potency to create a credible ethos. As the source of confidence and security (19:23), divine reverence establishes a veritable refuge (14:26; cf. 18:10). Like Wisdom herself, such "fear" is the "fountain of life" (14:27), enriching and prolonging the quality of life (10:27; 19:23; 22:4). Far from connoting terror, "fear" is for the sages the *technicus terminus* for the salutary nexus between trust and obedience in God

148. I am indebted to Mary P. Boyd for calling my attention to the thorough mixing of feminine and masculine attributes in the figure of the valiant woman.

149. Her family and community praise her and esteem her happy ('*šr*, v. 28a; *hll*, vv. 30b, 31b).

150. Standard treatments of the theme include J. Becker, *Gottesfurcht im Alten Testament* (AnBib 25; Rome: Pontifical Biblical Institute, 1965); S. Plath, *Furcht Gottes: Das Begriffe jr' im Alten Testament* (AzT 2/2; Stuttgart: Calwer, 1962). Within wisdom literature, see Nel, *Structure and Ethos*, 97-100; J. Marböck, "Im Horizont der Gottesfurcht: Stellungnahmen zu Welt und Leben in der alttestamentlichen Weisheit," *BN* 26 (1985) 47-70.

151. Attempts to lodge this theme exclusively in the final stage(s) of the book's literary development are not convincing (e.g., McKane's "Class C" in *Proverbs*, 8-22; idem, *Prophets and Wise Men* [SBT 1/44; Naperville, Ill.: Allenson, 1965). Contra McKane, see Perdue, *Wisdom and Creation*, 79; idem, *Wisdom and Cult*, 229-30n.29; F. M. Wilson, "Sacred and Profane? The Yahwistic Redaction of Proverbs Reconsidered," in *Listening Heart*, 313-34. The motif of divine reverence, and more broadly religious piety, is evenly dispersed throughout the book and is conveyed in various literary forms: e.g., 1:7, 29; 2:5; 3:7; 8:13; 9:10; 10:27; 13:13; 14:2, 16, 27; 15:16, 33; 16:6; 19:23; 23:17; 24:21; 28:14; 29:25; 31:30.

THE ETHOS OF THE COSMOS

(19:23; 13:13). Instead of paralyzing the subject, the "fear of Yahweh" mobilizes and directs the moral self.[152] Divine reverence is both *Ehrfurcht* and *Freude*, reverence and revelry, the source of joy and of responsibility.[153] By dint of moral imagination, the sages have re-created the meaning and purpose of fear.[154]

As Wisdom was the beginning *(rē'šît)* of God's creation (8:22), so the "fear of Yahweh" is the beginning *(tĕḥillat, rē'šît)* of knowledge (9:10; 1:7), creating a domain of trust and security for the moral self.[155] The cosmic conscience Wisdom imparts is a theocentric conscience. In Wisdom's ethos, fear of the world is displaced by trust in the Creator (29:25). Such divine "fear" is the root of joy: "Happy is the one who is in constant dread *(mĕpaḥēd tāmîd)*, but one who is hard-hearted *(maqšēh libbô)* will fall into catastrophe" (28:14). As it stands, the first colon sounds oxymoronic, but, again, the ancient sages had a far different concept of "fear" from that found in modern or other ancient, even biblical, renderings. The "dread" to which the sages refer is defined by what follows in the second half. A pliant heart is the antithesis to Pharaoh's hardness of heart, motivated in part by the fear of Israel's presence in the land (Exod 1:9-10). The proverbial allusion to Pharaoh as the archetypal example of recalcitrance is underscored by the following two proverbs, which critically assess the "wicked ruler" and the "cruel oppressor" (Prov 28:15-16). The "dread" esteemed by the sages is the human subject's openness to the divine will and exercise of obedience, nothing short of a covenantal allegiance to Yahweh (see 31:26b). As "slavery" was reconstrued by the Priestly tradents to denote the liberating integrity of "servanthood,"[156] the "fear of Yahweh" marks for the sages an exodus of the will, from fear of the world to reverence of and obedience to Yahweh, a "fear" that banishes all fear (3:25).

Divine reverence negates a cosmic fear that construes the world as eminently insecure, a dwelling or ethos in which chaos rules. By contrast, Wisdom's world is one of abundant provision and blessing, a world in which "new growth" inevitably sprouts and sufficient food is available to nourish

152. Cf. Exod 14:31; Deut 4:10, 34; 5:4-5, 24-29, which treat fear as a natural and normative response to God's dramatic intervention. Particularly in the Deuteronomic ethos, fear denotes obedience to God as evinced in law, interchangeable with covenantal love (Deut 10:12).

153. For fear as a source of joy, see Prov 28:14; Sir 1:11-13; and below.

154. For more terror-inspiring notions of fear as dread *(pḥd)*, see Deut 28:66-67; Isa 12:2; Job 3:25; 4:14.

155. For godly fear as the *Ausgangspunkt* for wisdom, see Otto, *Theologische Ethik*, 162-65.

156. For example, Lev 25:42-43, 55; 26:12-13. See Chapter 3.

one's household (27:25-27). Godly fear reflects a deep piety characterized by an unshakable faith in a gracious Creator and a secure creation, an assurance that a life led by wisdom is an eminently successful one.[157] In their cosmic paranoia "the wicked flee when no one pursues, but the righteous are secure as a lion" (28:1). The deluded sluggard cries out, "There is a lion in the streets!" (26:13; cf. 22:13). Such worldly fear, the sages suggest, motivates immoral conduct, from the oppressive policies of tyrants to the senseless behavior of lazy fools. Sapiential fear is a bold fear, the source of moral valiancy that overcomes all failure of nerve. That is not to say that the wise blissfully have no (worldly) fear. Divine reverence is not the kind of naive trust by which the immature unknowingly head toward danger at their own expense (22:3). The wise simply know better and act accordingly (14:16).

Divine reverence also displaces all fear of the other in the sense that the former casts exclusive allegiance on Yahweh and subverts the enticements of "strangers."[158] Fear of Yahweh empowers the individual to resist the seductive wiles of the archetypal stranger (7:6-27), of necrophilia personified. Regardless of the complexity with which the strange woman's character is portrayed, none can match the depth and profundity of Wisdom's character, which freely assumes the roles of stern prophet and frolicking child, of counselor and lover.[159] Wisdom's vastly complex character attests to the limitless array of moral resources she has at her disposal to secure and protect her followers from all challenges that would compromise or defeat them, particularly the paralyzing attractions of the evil stranger. Like the psalmist who relies on the sufficiency of Yahweh's protection before his enemies, the wise shall "fear no evil" (Ps 23:4), assuming a posture that indicates moral allegiance as much as it does confidence. The seductive fear of the Other, however, is both a trust in and an intellectual commitment to the familial.[160] Misplaced reverence is a

157. See also Perdue, *Wisdom and Creation*, 79; Marböck, "Im Horizont der Gottesfurcht," 54-59. The book of Job, however, questions this connection between moral integrity and success.

158. Nevertheless, the point of the mother's teaching in Proverbs 7 is to instill in her son a certain xenophobia, as it were, of the strange woman. But, again, such fear is not immobilizing but one that underscores the absurdity of engaging with the stranger, thus empowering the moral agent for resistance.

159. For example, Blenkinsopp suggests that Wisdom's character is essentially derivative of that of the "Outsider Woman's" persona ("Social Context," 466-67). But the remarkable range of roles that Wisdom covers in Proverbs 1–9 suggests that she is much more than simply a "reverse mirror image" (p. 466).

160. Cf. Ps 111:10, which similarly states that "the beginning of wisdom is the fear of Yahweh" yet underscores Yahweh's mighty acts of redemption and the divine *mysterium tremendum* (vv. 2-9).

love affair with strangeness and death; authentic reverence acknowledges the transcendent within the familiar. Therein lies the sages' most profound play on the theme of fear: the holy and awesome Other is revealed in the intimate and edifying joy of one's most familial kin, Wisdom. The exercise of fear sustains the frolic of Wisdom's play. Sapiential fear is relaxed reverence in the presence of God, the constructive side of rest.

Integrative Play

The bookends of Proverbs, chs. 1–9 and 31:10-31, have aimed at naturalizing Wisdom and lodging her within a domestic world that also embraces the larger community, the city, and, indeed, the cosmos. Unlike her archenemy, who is also competing over the son's allegiance, Wisdom is the archetypal kin and friend (7:4). She is the spousal paradigm for his maturity. Wisdom's ethos, more broadly, is familialized for a community constituted by *tôrâ*, by justice, righteousness, and equity (1:3; cf. 28:4, 7, 9). The family and the community are thus bound together in "collective efficacy."[161] The link is embodied by a transcendent, eminently moral figure that intervenes on behalf of her children and sustains the moral life of the community. In so doing, Wisdom familializes the world, a world made *ecu*menical in which rich and poor, household head and impoverished outcast can meet together, and chaos is diminished.

As Wisdom's play constitutes her mode of interaction with Creator and creation, so the moral self's engagement with the world is informed by Wisdom's recreation. The one who fears Yahweh is the one who exercises virtue, remaining in the secured and stable world of Wisdom's ethos. "The wicked are overthrown and are no more, but the house of the righteous remains" (12:7).[162] Wisdom's play is not carefree, for lack of restraint ushers in the fool's demise (14:6), and lack of self-control is like a "city breached, without walls" (25:28). But neither is her play, and thus her follower's, simply an act of "subordination" to the created order.[163] To be sure, Wisdom is not an autonomous agent, an independent deity in her own right, but neither is she Yahweh's slave. She is God's playing child, not some static or abstract order. As Roland Murphy observes rhetorically, "who has ever sued for, or been pursued by, order, even in the surrogate form of a woman?"[164] Wisdom's engage-

161. See n. 60 above.
162. See also 10:25, 30; 11:4, 6.
163. So implies Nel in his claim that the ethos of wisdom is one of "humble subordination to the divine and created order" (*Structure and Ethos*, 112).
164. Murphy, "Wisdom and Creation," 9.

ment with Yahweh and the inhabited world is as passionate as it is informed. She is God's prime witness and partner. Her ways are recreative within a relationship of reciprocity. Unleashing chaos is fool's play (*śĕḥôq*, 10:23), but wise conduct is literally "child's play" to the discerning, both a calling and an avocation, the wellspring of joy[165] and the way of integrity.[166] As the irrepressible moral agent, Wisdom confers fervent life to the one who exercises virtue.

Wisdom's Encompassing Household

As Yahweh's "firstborn," Wisdom plays an integral role in creation in more ways than one. Her primordial "age" is proof of her unmatched pedigree, but her evocative identity emerges most definitively through her play in and with creation, creation conceived not simply as primal beginning but as the arena of continually lived experience,[167] of *personal* engagement and responsibility, of levity and love. Her play builds on and continues the divinely established security of the inhabited world. Her engagement with both Creator and creation establishes the distinctly moral sphere for human beings, one built on the essential goodness of creation and fashioned for the nourishment of the moral life. Instead of planting a lush garden of blessing in the land of myth, Wisdom builds a solid house of abundance in a gritty city. Wisdom's base of operations encompasses a distinctly urban setting. Her house is her moral domain, finely constructed from the raw materials of creation and established for the exercise of moral conduct and discourse. From her house, she reaches out to the community to sustain and direct it, inviting and cajoling citizens to cross the threshold of her domicile and enter into the world of Wisdom.

By no means antithetical to cultic practice, Wisdom's house is the familial counterpart to the Priestly temple, the spatial domain of holiness.[168] Wisdom's hearth is a distinctly moral domain as much as the tabernacle is Israel's

165. See also 10:28; 12:22; 17:22.
166. For example, "To get intelligence *(qōneh-lēb)* is to love oneself; to keep understanding is to prosper" (19:8).
167. See Murphy, "Wisdom and Creation," 5-11.
168. Of note is that Sir 24:8-12, dependent on Proverbs, explicitly identifies Wisdom with Zion, the home of the "holy tent" in which Wisdom ministers before the Creator (v. 10). The connection between cult and wisdom in Proverbs is not one of identity, however, but of analogy or juxtaposition: sapiential play before God is comparable to the faithful worship of God; both are linked by the practice of reverence, which manifests itself in both the home and the cult.

distinctly holy space. Both house and temple, hearth and tabernacle, are established in a creation made secure and good. Indeed, they are the climactic acts of ongoing creativity conceived back "in the beginning." Wisdom's eyewitness account of creation supplements the Priestly cosmogony by personalizing the process of a differentiated cosmogony and turning the cosmic temple into a cosmic household. By her play before God, Wisdom familializes the Priestly cult. Wisdom tabernacles in the family as God's glory dwells in the temple, and she is no more confined to the hearth than Yahweh is contained within the holy děbîr, the inner sanctum. God dwells among an entire people, Israel; Wisdom roams a sprawling city. As God finds rest by dwelling in the temple, so Wisdom's joy is fulfilled within the household, welcoming and hosting her disciples. Her altar is her table; her slaughter is her sacrifice. But again, Wisdom's household is no critical replacement for the cult any more than David's dance before the ark was meant to displace the sacrificial system; Wisdom's hearth is simply the cult's complement in a socially complex society.[169] Wisdom's mirthful play exists side by side with Aaron's solemn ministry. Her play is integrative, mediating common ground between tôrâ and cult on a well-plastered floor. Holiness and play, glory and wisdom, the ethics and hypostases of the Creator, find their intimate association enlivened by a doting father and a firstborn child.

Wisdom's house extends potentially to all. Her cosmic role rests on an imaginative and moral vision, a heightened level of moral discernment that encompasses all creation, only to be shortchanged, admittedly, by an inability to see the vision through the fray of social conflict and convention, by a failure to see beyond the "strangeness" of a human being and discern his or her intrinsic value rather than demonize his or her character.[170] Yet the sages cannot be charged with flagrant inconsistency, for underneath creation's firm footing lurk the turbid waters of chaos, contained by divine discourse yet ever pressing upon the cosmic oikos. Admittedly, the sages were quick, indeed too quick, to see such chaos fully manifested by certain human characters, from the wicked fool to the deadly adulteress, all foils for the follower of Wisdom. Moreover, Wisdom's ethos encourages the kind of exclusive elitism that all too easily slices up humanity into dualistic compartments.

Yet Wisdom's play with the populated world is evocatively complex. It embraces certain polarities of social life such as the rich and the poor, bring-

169. Such an observation coheres well with Clements's observation that wisdom represents "an intensified moralising" of the efficacy of worship (*Wisdom in Theology*, 163-64).

170. For further discussion, see Bergant, *Israel's Wisdom Literature*, 96-105.

ing them together as full players within the household of Wisdom, on the common ground of moral integrity. Wisdom is the consummate bridge builder, linking family and community as part of her household as well as humankind and God as part of Yahweh's household. Connecting heaven and earth by her revelry of reverence, Wisdom extends her kinship to the world. Such is Wisdom's boldness, reaching out and bridging the chasms that divide and threaten to engulf human existence. Such is Christ's temerity in ministering to sinners, including the adulteress:[171] "I have come to call not the righteous but sinners" (Matt 9:10-13; Mark 2:15-17; Luke 5:30-32). As Wisdom incarnate, Christ implodes and extends the familial contours of Wisdom's ethos: when the crowd points to his family standing outside, Jesus responds, "Who are my mother and my brothers? . . . Here are my mother and my brothers! Whoever does the will of God is my brother and sister and mother" (Mark 3:31-35).[172] In the household of God are many rooms (John 14:2).

Wisdom's engagement with the world is recreational and constructive. Whether in the face of adversity or in the space of security, Wisdom continues to play, preserving as well as re-creating the human world by her moral mirth. Far from the corrosive mischief that causes strife and alienates neighbor from neighbor,[173] Wisdom's frolic is passionately edifying, cohesive and binding, an ethos of discipline and an eros for life. Both the beginning and the end of the quest for coherence, Wisdom's play marks a victory over those forces that threaten to dismantle the integrity of creation and community as well as continues the struggle to preserve and employ those powers that can reestablish a world of good.

As Wisdom plays, so must her followers. Never aimless or static, *imitatio sapientiae* is directive and purposeful. In its purest form, moral play is not reckless but respectful and edifying, valuing and rejoicing in the other without fear or prejudice. Such conduct is at once self- and covenant fulfilling. Bold without presumption and faithful beyond submission, the revelry of reverence is fair and free. In Wisdom, the moral agent is a self-discriminating and self-reliant subject who must decide on his or her own whether to educate the foolish; there are legitimate reasons for either course of action (Prov 26:4-5). In Wisdom's mansion there is sufficient room to maneuver. Fearless and edifying play in Wisdom's world is the reverential dance

---

171. John 4:1-42; 7:53–8:11.

172. Cf. Mark 10:28-31, in which Jesus refers to the radically enlarged family of faith.

173. "Like a maniac who shoots deadly firebrands and arrows, so is one who deceives a neighbor and says, 'Am I not just joking *(měśaḥēq)?*'" (Prov 26:19).

before the Creator. As the towering mountains and the great abyss are part of creation, Wisdom teaches that the height of ecstasy and the depth of responsibility are one and the same.

CHAPTER 6

"Ask the Animals and They Will Teach You": Job's Carnival of Animals

What a singular brute feat of outrageous fortune: to be born to citizenship in the Animal Kingdom. We love and we lose, go back to the start and do it right over again. For every heavy forebrain solemnly cataloging the facts of a harsh landscape, there's a rush of intuition behind it crying out: High tide! Time to move out into the glorious debris. Time to take this life for what it is.

Barbara Kingsolver[1]

I killed a *nahiru,* which they call a "sea-horse," in the midst of the sea.

Tiglath-pileser I[2]

Not commonly associated with any model or doctrine of creation comparable to what can be found in Genesis, Isaiah, or Proverbs, the book of Job is nonetheless rife with creation imagery. One need not look far to find it. Job's first poetic discourse is loaded with cosmological images: light, darkness, clouds, water, and mythic creatures (3:3-26). Similarly, Yahweh's climac-

1. B. Kingsolver, *High Tide in Tucson* (New York: HarperCollins, 1995) 16.
2. *ARAB* 1 §302.

tic response to Job is populated with similar phenomena borrowed from the realms of cosmology, meteorology, and zoology (chs. 38–41). This literary envelope suggests that the book of Job has everything to do with how the world is to be perceived from an intensely global perspective. As the victim of divine abuse, Job can only view the cosmos sliding inexorably into chaos. As creator and alleged perpetrator of such abuse, Yahweh discloses the cosmic expanse as a complex work of aesthetic and moral import. One cosmos, yet two remarkably opposing moral worldviews frame the bulk of the book. As if that were not enough, sandwiched between this cosmo-poeic clash are the friends' polemically charged appeals to tradition designed to put both Job and God in their proper place. Simplistically put, at least three discrete global perspectives are evident just within the poetic portions of this book: Job's, his friends', and Yahweh's.[3] The book of Job stokes the flames generated by the clash of wildly divergent moral perspectives about the world.[4]

Given the book's creation-oriented framework (chs. 3, 38–41), one scholar has assessed the intervening cycles of dialogue in chs. 4–31 as digressive in the way they introduce issues of justice and guilt into the plot, matters foreign to the real theme of creation.[5] Such a view, however, overlooks the ample supply of creation themes and images liberally dispersed throughout the cycles of dialogue. Creation images are marshaled and presented by all participants in one way or another to score points in the debate over Job's moral status. Indeed, much of the tension behind the deliberations is produced precisely by the collision of moral worldviews that the participants themselves impart.[6] The center of the book is, thus, no detour at all. In Job the issues of creation and justice, of morality and cosmology, are inseparably intertwined, and this is no artificial linkage. The separation of cosmos and ethos is a modern bifurcation.[7] The tragedy of Job's own life, nothing less

---

3. Not to mention Elihu's perspective (chs. 32–37), whose voice is inserted at a later stage in the book's development.

4. From a hermeneutical perspective one could say that the disturbing genius of Job lies in its thoroughly phenomenological outlook. The book of Job highlights the multifarious character of contextualized experience by giving full voice to the wildly differing perceptions of Job, the friends, Elihu, and finally, Yahweh, yet not without some sense of resolution.

5. See E. Good, *In Turns of Tempest: A Reading of Job* (Stanford: Stanford University Press, 1990) 212-13.

6. See M. Tsevat's illuminating discussion of their respective positions in "The Meaning of the Book of Job," *HUCA* 37 (1966) 73-106 (repr. in idem, *The Meaning of the Book of Job and Other Biblical Studies* [New York: Ktav, 1980] 1-38).

7. See Chapter 1. A classic example in modern biblical scholarship can be found in F. M. Cross's assessment of the message of Job: "It repudiated the God of history whose

than a travesty of justice as perceived by Job, is characterized by global chaos. The protagonist views the created "order" through the prism of existential crisis and finds it to be etched in the blood of a crime scene. Job's world is inescapably a *perceived* world, rife with moral outrage.

Job's world is also an imaginative world, as painful as it is inspiring, full of unspeakable predicaments and exotic beasts, a fantasy in the richest sense. But it is no flight of fancy, some charming or deranged daydream intended to titillate the reader's curiosity. Neither is Job's fantasy an exercise in self-aggrandizement.[8] Job's fantasy is driven by a peculiarly profound logic designed to bring Job to the brink of repentance (42:1-6) and his community to the threshold of transformation (42:11). The poet's imagination is potent yet purposeful, for it is in the business of reforming the moral worldview of tradition. Job is about a community's moral formation, about the radical reorientation of particular values that have proved less than helpful in an age of crisis.[9] Moreover, the poet's imagination is geared not simply to recover or develop a

---

realm is politics, law, and justice.... The Lord of history failed to act.... The transcendent creator spoke" (Cross, *Canaanite Myth and Hebrew Epic* [Cambridge: Harvard University Press, 1973] 344). Noteworthy is the unnecessary polarity Cross presupposes between justice, lodged within the realm of history, and creation. As the wisdom literature clearly indicates, history does not have a monopoly on the matter of justice. See Y. Hoffman's discussion of the prevalent theme of recompense in the book of Job (*A Blemished Perfection: The Book of Job in Context* [JSOTSup 213; Sheffield: Sheffield Academic Press, 1996] 222-63).

8. D. J. A. Clines describes the book of Job as essentially a rich man's fantasy ("Deconstructing the Book of Job," *BR* 11/2 [1995] 32). He comes by this in part by adopting Frederic Jameson's position that all texts are designed to repress social conflict and thereby maintain the status quo (p. 35). Such a view, however, excludes the possibility that Job might bear revolutionary implications vis-à-vis even the elite, learned class.

9. Many scholars place the composition of the book in the time of Israel's exile (587-535 BCE), despite the fact that concrete historical references are entirely lacking. The linguistic evidence suggests that the prose tale in its final form is no older than the sixth century BCE (A. Hurvitz, "The Date of the Prose Tale of Job Linguistically Reconsidered," *HTR* 67 [1974] 17-34). It is entirely possible, however, that the work as a whole was finalized later in the postexilic period with this period of dislocation and suffering in mind. One possible corroborating factor is the stress on the *familial* setting in Job, a feature typical of postexilic literature (e.g., Proverbs 1–9; 31:10-31; see C. Camp, *Wisdom and the Feminine in the Book of Proverbs* [BLS 11; Sheffield: Almond, 1985] 233-38). Noteworthy is that Job is characterized by superlative, even royal, attributes, yet he remains a patriarch of his household, unlike the protagonist of the much later pseudepigraphical *Testament of Job*, who is king of Egypt. Given its plausible postexilic setting, one could say that Job is not unlike many contemporary writings emerging today and no doubt well in the future that can be considered "post-Holocaust" treatments of theology and culture. Viewed in this way, Job is a "postexilic" reading of the world.

plethora of mythological metaphors[10] or to multiply ad infinitum options for thought and conduct. Rather, it is focused on the task of transforming character, both Job's and the community's, and the (re)construal of creation is the indispensable means for attaining this goal.

The poet's imagination is quintessentially a *moral* imagination, one that is about the task of broadening and reshaping the moral horizons of character. But its role is not primarily to recast abstract concepts and principles. Imagination finds its niche in the book of Job by remaining on the level of concreteness. Specifically, the poet's imagination populates a world with surprises, with images and creatures drawn from nature, the likes of which Job has never considered. It is an imagination run wild. An utterly alien world imposes itself on Job, a world not simply defined by the loss of possessions and status, but one filled to the brim with wondrously strange phenomena (chs. 38–41). From lions to Leviathans, from onagers to ostriches, these denizens of the wild dominate Yahweh's response to Job and thus serve, somehow, as the climax of the book and the denouement of Job's transformation. They present Job with a new, unprecedented moral vision. Yet among modern readers seeking solutions to the perplexing problems of theodicy, these elusive figures have been a source of puzzlement, disappointment, and even scandal.[11] How these exotic beasts of nature serve to resolve Job's case against God and reorient the praxis of the reading community is the focus of this chapter. In order to assess their crucial role in Yahweh's response to Job, one must start back at the beginning and survey the creation, particularly animal, imagery employed in the story's dramatic development.

The Topography of Patriarchy: The Prologue

The prose introduction sets the stage by defining Job's character and his social world, both of which become undermined in the ensuing discourses. Job

---

10. See L. Perdue's metaphorical treatment of Job in *Wisdom in Revolt: Metaphorical Theology in the Book of Job* (BLS 29; JSOTSup 112; Sheffield: Almond, 1991); idem, *Wisdom and Creation: The Theology of Wisdom Literature* (Nashville: Abingdon, 1994) 123-92; and my review of the latter work in *Int* 50 (1996) 64-66.

11. For example, J. G. Williams regards Yahweh's response as "poor theology" ("Job and the God of Victims," in *The Voice from the Whirlwind: Interpreting the Book of Job* [ed. L. G. Perdue and W. C. Gilpin; Nashville: Abingdon, 1992] 222). For a sample survey of interpreters who have taken offense at Yahweh's allegedly evasive answer to Job, see L. Alonso-Schökel, "God's Answer to Job," in *Job and the Silence of God* (ed. C. Duquoe and C. Floristan; Edinburgh: T. & T. Clark, 1983) 45.

is, in part, defined by his possessions; they contribute significantly to his su-perlative distinction throughout the Orient (1:3). The list of his possessions begins with Job's family, namely, his ten children, and extends to his eleven thousand domesticated animals (sheep, camels, oxen, and donkeys), not to mention countless servants. Job has built a family qua empire, and he sits on a veritable throne over a kingdom for which, like any judicious king, he feels himself ultimately responsible.[12] Such is evident in his almost obsessive rou-tine of conducting early morning offerings on his children's behalf in case they have cursed God during the feast days (1:5). Both Job's possessions and his actions constitute tangible confirmation of his unassailable integrity (*tummâ* or *tām*) as preeminent patriarch over his household, prompting God to pronounce his unrivaled status in all the land (1:8; 2:3). Befitting his emi-nence, Job is a man of unprecedented blessing, hard evidence for the satan to challenge Yahweh (1:10). In the satan's own words, Job's possessions have "broken out over" or "overrun" the land *(pāraṣ bā'āreṣ).*[13] As Job's wealth has transgressed the land, as it were, so Yahweh has violated all sense of equity in favoring Job.

The systematic destruction of Job's familial kingdom begins with the spoliation or elimination of Job's flocks and herds. Every item listed in Job's catalogue of possessions in 1:3 is taken away, from oxen to camels (2:14-17). Foreigners invade Job's land, divine fire consumes his flocks, and a destruc-tive wind from the desert collapses his children's house, killing them all (2:19). In short, Job suffers a localized holocaust. His familial fortress is sys-tematically destroyed from beyond and from above. Like invading foreign ar-mies, forces from divine and desolate provenances, from the heavens and the desert, have encroached on Job's fiefdom and decimated it. The protective wall of blessing, the fence of his gated community, has been breached (cf. 1:10). Such is the divine "touch" (1:11). Once his possessions have been re-moved, the second wave of attack is equally invasive, reaching now to flesh and bone (2:5-7). Once the king of his house, Job now sits on an ash heap, be-reft of the trappings of patriarchy: ownership, honor, and stature.

12. It is no wonder that the later *Testament of Job* casts Job as king, specifically over Egypt (cf. 19:9; 29:25).

13. The NRSV "increase" is too tame a rendering of the verb *prṣ*. Although the verb is attested only here in the prose, the poet employs it in 16:14, along with its nominal cog-nate, to liken Yahweh's treatment of Job to a military onslaught. The satan's observation thus suggests that Job's amassment of worldly goods is having a deleterious effect on the land. Job is, in effect, "besieging" the land with his wealth. Moreover, the test in 1:13-19 is described as a siege against Job's familial fortress from outside and above.

The Dawn of the Dead: Job's First Discourse

As is commonly recognized, Job's first words in ch. 3 signal a complete turnaround in his character and worldview.[14] Having rebuked his wife for urging him to "curse God and die" (2:10), Job is now frightfully full of malediction (3:1). Job imprecates his life and, by extension, all creation. His birthday curse is cast in such a way as to evoke the dissolution of the created order, to drag it all down with him into the pit of deep darkness. Yet in that hole of hell exists a liberating new order. For Job it is a breath of fresh air.

Images of light and darkness prevail throughout Job's first discourse. Like the separation of day from night, which initiates the process of creation (Gen 1:3-4), Job's genesis is cast in dual form: the day of his birth and the night of his conception (Job 3:3). Job, however, condemns both elements: gloom and doom are called on to overcome day and night (vv. 4-6), reverting the primordial distinction that is the basis of life into undifferentiated chaos. Job calls forth the complete reversal of creation, all in order to snuff out his own life. Deep darkness[15] is described as a predator, ready to pounce and destroy (vv. 5-6), an apt symbol of insatiable death. Merging the particular and the universal, Job construes his death wish as the threshold through which creation itself meets its dissolution, emptied of the light of life and filled with dark despair (2:7, 9).[16]

This horrendous evocation of chaos gives vent to Job's own moral outrage against the misfortune that has befallen him. As he himself will later testify, Job has become the victim of God's abusive whim (7:12-15; 9:17-19, 30-32; 10:16-17). Such personal injustice underlies the motivation to have all of creation plunged into eternal darkness.[17] As Job's very life unravels, so must also the world. The dissolution of the cosmos is a punishment designed to fit the crime. Indeed, Bildad's words are quite on target when he derisively questions Job, "You who tear yourself in your anger — shall the earth be forsaken because of you?" (18:4a).

To call forth creation's antithesis, Job chooses the mythic image of Levi-

14. R. D. Moore, "The Integrity of Job," *CBQ* 45 (1983) 17-31.

15. The poet piles up numerous synonyms for darkness that serve as epithets for death. Cf. Job 10:21-22.

16. Cf. 38:7; 41:18 (MT 10).

17. See the similar situation of cosmological shutdown in Combination I of the Balaam Texts from Deir 'Alla (P. K. McCarter Jr., "The Balaam Texts from Deir 'Alla: The First Combination," *BASOR* 239 [1980] 49-60; J. A. Hackett, *The Balaam Text from Deir 'Allā* [HSM 31; Chico, Calif.: Scholars Press, 1980]; M. Barré, "The Portrait of Balaam in Numbers 22–24," *Int* 51 (1997) 254-66.

athan (3:8), a creature of chaos. Next to Job himself, this is the only reference to a living creature in his execration of the cosmos. No wonder, for the arousal of this monstrous creature provokes the very demise of the created order. As day and night are cursed,[18] overcome by Job's fulminations, so Leviathan is awakened from the watery depths of its habitation. Whoever is skilled enough, indeed bold enough, to rouse this untamable beast is one who is well versed in the science of cursing, of defying both creation and Creator. In his impassioned death wish, Job, the victim of forces unseen, flirts with mythic powers beyond his control by exhorting the predacious darkness to seize and destroy, and Leviathan to subvert, the cosmos (vv. 4-6). Leviathan is chaos personified; Job, the master of malediction, is the perpetrator of chaos. The irony runs deep with these two strange bedfellows, locked not in mortal battle but in an unholy partnership to deconstruct the world (cf. 7:12).

The subversion of creation does not, however, result in anarchic ruin. The collapse of the created order is merely prefatory to Job's plaintive question regarding his survival in the birth canal (3:13). He imagines a radically different form of existence, one without trouble and fear, as inclusive as it is liberating. Job envisions existence in Sheol as one that encompasses all walks of life, both great and small. There in the "house appointed for all living" (30:23), true community is to be found: kings and counselors equal to slaves and prisoners, all in fellowship together. Social divisions are erased, and the inhabitants of Sheol enjoy the eternal blessings of freedom. Job yearns for the "democracy of the dead." Although he holds an initial fascination with the rich and ruling elite (3:14-15), the final focus of Job's attention is directed toward the enslaved (vv. 18-19) and their release from servitude in death. Job, once the wielder of wealth, can now identify with those who forever have lacked material means. On the one hand, the prospect of death unleashes a host of imaginative possibilities for communal existence, stripped of hierarchy and unburdened of responsibility. Job even hints of liberation for the wearied powerful (v. 17). On the other hand, life, to which Job must return in fear and trepidation, is bereft of any alternative. Life, not death, is the limiting foil. Chaos is the great liberator.

Job's subversion of creation in ch. 3 is by no means unrelated to the blissful depiction of death given in the latter part of his discourse. Chaos and death are a natural fit. What is remarkable, however, is the dramatic move-

18. The Hebrew of 2:8 reveals a remarkable wordplay not reflected in the NRSV. See M. Fishbane, "Jeremiah iv. 23-26 and Job iii 13: A Recovered Use of the Creation Pattern," *VT* 21 (1971) 160, who treats the verse as a magical wordplay.

ment from the predation of chaos to the quiet serenity of egalitarian fellow-ship. Chaos serves to erase all form and structure associated with life and community on this side of existence. For Job, this is indeed salutary, even lib-erating. Chaos has paved the way to freedom; it packs a revolutionary wallop. As the subversive instrument that disrupts and breaks down the cosmos, chaos ushers in new possibilities of social existence. The ancient sages long equated social upheaval with cosmic upheaval. Prov 30:21-23 is an exemplary case:

> Under three things the earth quakes;
> under four it cannot endure:
> > when a slave becomes king,
> > > when a fool is glutted with food,
> > when an unloved woman marries,
> > > when a maid succeeds her mistress.

Conversely, the cosmic order reflects a durable social order in which each person knows and retains his or her place. A reconfiguration of such a so-cial order, however, is precisely what death holds for Job. The prospect of death galvanizes Job's moral imagination in his quest for relief and rest. Death is the repository of dreams; indeed, it offers unprecedented wis-dom.[19] Only in death can Job reside in such a community of equals, one so radical in its orientation that only predatory chaos can clear away the cos-mic clutter and set the stage for a new morphology of community. Only in the land of the dead, stripped of all stratification, can freedom and equality reign, so Job imagines. The dissolution of the cosmic community is ulti-mately its rehabilitation.

Although turgid with bitter malediction and incalculable despair (Job 2:9-10), Job's discourse in ch. 3 unveils an unprecedented moral vision. The topography of patriarchy is leveled out. Gone are Job's possessions: animals, servants, and children. All that remains are the ominous creatures of chaos, darkness and Leviathan. These monsters, however, do not perturb Job; he en-lists them to help him attain the goal for which he passionately yearns, the re-spite of death and the communion it offers. Yet something does strike dread in Job's heart, and it comes as an insurmountable obstacle in his journey to-ward blissful rest. "Trouble" *(rōgez)* has come (3:26; cf. v. 17). Assuming nei-ther the form of terrifying beast nor the guise of predatory darkness, "trou-

---

19. In Job 3:21-22 the yearning ("digging") for death and the joy of finding it, as if it were a buried treasure, ironically resemble the quest for wisdom (e.g., 28:1-19, 22; Prov 3:13-18; 8:18-19).

ble" comes in the arrival of Job's friends,[20] ready to offer "consoling" advice (2:11-13). To Job they are veritable wolves in sheep's clothing, breathing violence, not comfort. Job exhibits no fear toward the grotesque creatures of chaos; his dreaded adversaries are human.

In the Cauldron of Contention

Job's maledictive plea for death, which demands the reversion of creation to precreative chaos, establishes a foil that actually adumbrates its resolution. Many of the elements introduced in his verbal discharge reappear with an ironic vengeance in Yahweh's response at the book's conclusion (chs. 38–41): for example, creation, death, light and darkness, Leviathan, Job, God. As noted earlier, the theme of creation introduced in Job's cosmic curse finds its match in the final discourse, a cosmic blessing of sorts. What is not often noted, however, is how the intervening chapters help to set the stage for the litany of creation that is unfolded in the final chapters. The friends do not embark on a tortuous detour that eventually comes back full circle to Job. To the contrary, the resulting clash of viewpoints they provide contributes indispensable counterpoints and connections to the book's discursive climax, the cosmos as revealed by Yahweh. As Job enters the whirlpool of disputation, there is much to learn before Yahweh's final disclosure.

Casting the First Stone

Eliphaz begins the spiral of confrontation with appropriate deference (4:2-4), but quickly cuts to the chase: Job has sinned and must receive the restorative discipline of divine reproof. Such is the fate of all humankind. The Temanite constructs his argument by contrasting the righteous, sovereign might of God (5:8-16) with the contingent status of earthly, particularly human, creation (4:17-21). His argument opens with the case of the wicked and their certain demise (vv. 8-9), and then takes a surprising turn, abruptly moving from the human to the animal realm (vv. 10-11). Whereas the wicked are described by a twofold verbal reference — they "plow iniquity" and "sow trouble" — the following figure is designated by no less than five different names.

---

20. Positioned at the conclusion of Job's lament, the reference to "trouble" serves as the transition to Eliphaz's discourse, which marks the first volley in the heated cycle of deliberations between Job and his friends.

The imposing figure of the lion is thus no mere afterthought in Eliphaz's argument. This predator is revealed to be an eminently contingent creature, utterly disposable in the hands of God, however noble and fearsome it might be to others, particularly to humans (e.g., Prov 30:30).

No explicit reason, however, is given to validate the lion's extinction, as in the case of the wicked. Rhetorically, the case of the lion concludes the unit on the wicked (Job 4:7-11) before Eliphaz addresses the tragic frailty of the human condition (vv. 12-21). It appears that lions and humans share at least one thing in common, contingency. By divine action the lions' teeth are broken and tent cords are plucked up (vv. 10, 21). Given its reputation as a ruthless predator, the lion is an exemplar of the universal scope of creation's contingency, so also God's messengers in v. 18. In addition, the king of beasts serves as an apt transition to Eliphaz's main point regarding humanity's general contingency (vv. 17-21). All humanity faces a glass ceiling of capacity vis-à-vis God: absolute righteousness and might are held only in God's hands. In short, Eliphaz begins his argument with Job by citing specific cases of moral culpability that warrant divine punishment, and concludes the first part of his argument with a graphic description of universal contingency. The figure of the lion, which suffers guilt by association with the wicked, serves as the transition.

Characteristic of Eliphaz's discourse is his constant oscillation between the particular and the universal conditions of the human creature (cf. 5:1-5, 6-7). In ch. 5 Eliphaz moves from imprecating the fool (vv. 2-5) to describing all humankind as a "troublesome" breed ('āmāl, v. 7; cf. 4:8; 3:17, 26). Yet nature is not to blame for this permanent blemish. "Misery" and "trouble" do not sprout out of the soil like thorns and thistles, for God is the one who irrigates the soil with life-giving rain (v. 10). Rather, these twins of travail are uniquely human characteristics. Nevertheless, like the plants of the field, God sustains those who commit themselves to the Creator, including the mournful and the poor (vv. 10-11, 15-16; cf. Prov 16:3), while uprooting the schemes of the wise and mighty (Job 5:12-14) like thistles and thorns. Whereas Eliphaz earlier painted a dismal picture of the human condition, a no-exit situation, he now suggests a way out for some: the embrace of discipline (v. 17).

Eliphaz has danced deftly around the human condition, with its concomitant predicaments and possibilities, in order to put Job on the fence between doom and redemption. To his credit, Eliphaz tries to inject Job with hope (vv. 19-26), but in so doing must push Job to the brink of moral compromise, to the doorstep of bad company. If only he would repent and welcome his suffering as divine discipline, then his redemption would commence. The rosy picture that Eliphaz paints in his concluding statements in

vv. 19-26 overturns, almost point by point, all that he has said previously concerning the imminent demise of culpable human beings (4:8, 19-21; 5:2-5). But he adds one thing more: Job will enter into a covenant of peace with the wild animals,[21] indeed with all of nature (5:22-23), if he will only accept his predicament as the Deity's corrective reprimand. Associated with destruction and famine, the animals of the wild will no longer inspire fear and vulnerability for Job (v. 22).

Such language evokes a venerable prophetic tradition that augurs a covenant of eschatological proportions, one that ushers in prosperity and peace with all of nature.[22] This legal leitmotif bears association with the Noachic covenant.[23] In Ezek 34:25-30 such a covenant requires the permanent eviction of all wild animals from the land. But Eliphaz's visionary covenant suggests a fellowship of peace with the beasts of the field rather than their expulsion.[24] Although Job will regain his position as the unsurpassed owner of flocks and herds (5:24b), this covenant of peace is more than simply a reestablishment of Job's lebensraum; the covenant is not implemented at the expense of his natural environs. To be sure, the trappings of peace include secured social status. Yet Eliphaz's promise, however fleetingly presented, envisions a global communion that bridges the chasm between civilized friend and wild foe.[25] Eliphaz offers a vision of concord, of reconciliation no less, between nature and culture. By offering such a promise, Job's first friend-turned-foe adumbrates Yahweh's own resolution of Job's case, which commands respect for and empathy with the wild (see below). For Eliphaz, the lion and Job shall lie down together in shared misery and ultimately in collective redemption.

Job the Hunted

Eliphaz's sweet vision, however, falls on deaf ears. Job's misery overrides all blessed testimonies, exposing them as false hopes. To Eliphaz's depiction of

21. Although the formal expression "covenant of peace" is not attested, covenant (bĕrît) and the verb šlm ("live in peace") are set in parallel positions.

22. For example, Hos 2:18-25; Isa 54:10; Ezek 34:25; 37:26. See B. F. Batto, "The Covenant of Peace: A Neglected Ancient Near Eastern Motif," CBQ 49 (1987) 187-211.

23. See Isa 54:9-10 and Batto, "Covenant of Peace," 190-91.

24. Likewise, Hosea's covenant does not stipulate such banishment, but rather lists the animals as genuine partners in the covenant (Hos 2:18-25).

25. Rhetorically, reference to this covenant, particularly from the mouth of Eliphaz, sets in motion an ironic dynamic: Job's civilized friends turn out to be his foes, whereas the denizens of the wild ultimately become his friends and instructors (cf. 12:7; 30:29).

Job the restored, Job presents himself as the one besieged. Skewered by the "arrows of Shaddai" (6:4), Job begins a tortuous self-examination vis-à-vis an unscrupulous God and an unjust creation. Although the provoker of chaos (3:3-10), Job adopts the posture of victim, insistent on his helpless state, and asks rhetorically whether his strength is that of stones and bronze (6:12). Job is no monstrous opponent for God to manhandle. He is no paragon of chaos, no veritable Leviathan, to warrant such abuse (7:12). To God, Job is the lion's prey (10:16).

With his own misery serving as a prism, Job constructs a particular cosmology that revels in the divine art of annihilation; an anti-cosmology is the result. In 9:4-10 Job brackets his cosmology with seemingly deferential statements regarding God's inscrutable wisdom. God is "wise in heart" (v. 4) and "beyond understanding" (v. 10). Such acclaim is also a vexing source of puzzlement, for nowhere does a normative rationale enter into Job's cosmic picture. Mountains are overturned, the earth's foundations are shaken, the sun is suppressed from rising, stars are destroyed, and watery chaos is defeated (vv. 5-8). All are testimonies to God's invincible strength (v. 4). But where is wisdom in this? Job asks. There is no method behind the madness here, only raw, uncontrolled wrath. Job makes clear that God's anger is devoid of moral backing, contrary to the reproaches and judgments of the prophets.[26] God's behavior remains morally unaccountable, all the more so in light of Job's particular situation. Job's innocence is irrelevant in the grand scheme of things, for it cannot stay God's hand (9:15, 19-20). God is an indiscriminate thug, who even controverts the administration of justice (9:24). Moral distinctions do not color the landscape of providence. The social order "is all one" (9:22a), an amorphous mass of moral subversion due to God's tyrannical rule. The world of mountains and monuments, of nature and culture, of the wicked and the upright, finds common ground only in the brunt of divine anger.

A similar depiction of the deconstructive God at work is found in Job's anticosmology in 12:13-25, a harrowing portrayal of creation and culture descending into cosmic anarchy. Whereas 9:4-10 focused exclusively on the elements of creation and their contravention, ch. 12 highlights the social order and its demise. With a perfunctory nod of deference, Job prefaces his creation mythos with an acclamation of divine wisdom and strength (vv. 13, 16). But similar to 9:5-9, Job turns the latter attribute against the former: divine might does not make right. What is the wisdom in tearing away at creation without

26. See A. J. Heschel's trenchant examination of divine wrath among the classical prophets in *The Prophets* (1962; repr. in 2 vols.; New York: Harper & Row, 1975) 2.59-78.

any foresight of mending it? God tears down, but does not build up (12:14; cf. Jer 1:10). God desiccates the land and floods it in a convulsive rage of destruction (Job 12:15); God enlarges nations only to destroy them (v. 23). Again, cosmos and culture are united in a seamless web drawn taught. As the waters are drained from the land, so wisdom is permanently withheld (vv. 15a, 20, 24-25). From kings to counselors, sages to judges, God deprives of wisdom those who have earned it the most (vv. 17-21, 24-25; cf. Prov 8:15-16). To God's credit, the high and mighty are overthrown, but cosmic justice is not served unless the lowly and oppressed are concomitantly lifted up (cf. Job 5:15-16; 1 Sam 2:4-8; Luke 1:51-54). Praise is not conjured, only dread and indignation. Job holds God accountable for a world that has spun off its moral axis, for overwhelming it with such impenetrable darkness that even the enlightened must wander "in a pathless waste" (Job 12:22, 23-25; cf. 3:23). Chaos has no direction, either spatial or moral (*tōhû lō'-dārek*, 12:24).

Bracketed by two anticosmologies, Job launches into God with heedless fury. Job unbound confronts an insufferable God. Turning Psalm 139 on its head, Job reminds God that he is a wondrous creation, formed with great care and intimate precision (Job 10:8-11; cf. Ps 139:13-16).[27] Yet as the fiber of his very being, physical and moral, unravels, Job accuses God of abject abandonment, of an egregious breach of loyalty *(ḥesed)* that was established at the moment of conception (Job 10:12). Job regarded his conception as bearing the signature of lifelong covenantal commitment to his well-being and to the development of his moral constitution. But God has reneged on this covenant in utero. Like all the earth dissolving in darkness, Job begins his descent into the "land of gloom" (vv. 21-22). The state of the cosmos hangs in the balance with Job's fate.

In the Violent Pursuit of Wisdom

To his friends, Job's dark musings present an unconscionable affront, for Job's newfound knowledge controverts the accumulated sagacity of the past sapiential tradition by drawing from the veracity of his experience and that of nature. Bildad's plea that Job reconsider the wisdom of the ancestors (8:8-10), whose influence, by dint of tradition, is borne by successive generations, is disputed by Job's appeal to another font of wisdom: nature. In 12:7-12 Job launches a counterattack against his friends' employment of tradition to force

27. See W. P. Brown, "*Creatio Corporis* and the Rhetoric of Defense in Psalm 139 and Job 10," in *God Who Creates* (Grand Rapids: Eerdmans, forthcoming).

him to admit his guilt. "Ask the animals[28] and they will teach you; the birds of the air, and they will tell you; [ask] the plants[29] of the earth and they will teach you; and the fish of the sea will declare to you" (12:7-8); so Job begins his assault on wisdom's traditional ethos.

Often noted is the savage parody that pervades Job's final speech in this first round of debate.[30] Job begins with biting sarcasm as he makes a caricature of his friends' discourse (12:1-2), yet the following verses disclose serious accusations and commitments on the part of Job (vv. 3-6): Job insists he is equally qualified in the business of wisdom (v. 3), thus his observations about the world and his predicament are solemnly legitimate (vv. 4-6). What follows in vv. 7-8, then, is not simply a sarcastic imitation of the friends' previous discourse.[31] Job's appeal to nature as the font of wisdom is not, as Robert Gordis maintains, "an ironic citation of his Friends' view."[32] Job may very well be imitating the type of sapiential speech that is rife with stern appeals for remedial learning, as in Bildad's speech (8:8-10). Yet Job's sarcastic entreaty comes with a difference: his appeal to nature is intended to contravene his friend's appeal to human tradition.[33]

Job does not satirize his friends' view by sarcastically regurgitating what his friends have given to him. In comparison with Bildad's speech in 8:8-10, Job's appeal to nature is an earnest counterthesis clothed in biting parody. His friends rely on the lore of the fathers (8:8b, 10) in the same way the poet of the Song of Moses exhorts the reader to recall certain primal events through the testimonies of past generations: "Remember the days of old, consider the

28. The term for "animals" is *běhēmôt*, plural of *běhēmâ*, which suggests a proleptic identification with the imposing figure of Behemoth portrayed in 40:15-24 (see below).

29. The Hebrew can also be rendered as "consider the earth," since the term *śîaḥ* can function either as the verb "consider" or as a botanical term. The latter is preferable, since the parallelism is clearer with each line containing a reference to a form of life, animal or vegetable (so NRSV).

30. See, e.g., C. A. Newsom, "Job," in *The New Interpreter's Bible*, ed. L. Keck et al. (Nashville: Abingdon, 1996) 4:426-27.

31. The adversative particle *'ûlām* in this context (v. 7) neither overturns what Job has just said nor signals a senseless parody to follow, but introduces a startlingly new phase of his argument.

32. R. Gordis, "Quotations as a Literary Usage in Biblical, Oriental, and Rabbinic Literature," *HUCA* 22 (1949) 157-219; idem, *The Book of Job: Commentary, New Translation, and Special Studies* (New York: Jewish Theological Seminary, 1978) 523-24.

33. Contra D. J. A. Clines, *Job 1–20* (WBC 17; Waco: Word, 1989) 7-12; and N. C. Habel, *The Book of Job* (OTL; Philadelphia: Westminster, 1985) 266. Newsom presents a more nuanced perspective by admitting that although the dominant tone is one of parody, "these verses can be understood best as Job's forcing even a language of hypocrisy to bear witness to the truth" ("Job," 427).

years long past; ask your father, and he will inform you; your elders, and they will tell you" (Deut 32:7). In stark contrast, Job refrains from recalling the events and insights of the past borne by human tradents, but rather appeals to the immediacy of nature's wisdom, to the sagacity of animals and plants.[34] In short, wisdom's "bibliography" is different.

Job implies that the human pursuit of wisdom has fallen into the fallacy of arrogant "specieism." The sapiential enterprise has become needlessly circumscribed by human preoccupation with itself, the result of hubris, to the exclusion of nature's wisdom. Job's friends have illegitimately restricted the parameters of wisdom's *modus operandi,* thereby reaching patently false conclusions regarding his condition. In short, they have sold their souls to tradition.[35] In his bitter polemic against them, Job calls for a thoroughly inclusive view of wisdom's quest, an interdisciplinary approach, as it were. Job's appeal to nature is not so much an innovation as a recovery of a genuine domain of operation for wisdom. Proverbial wisdom, for example, relied frequently on the lessons of nature.[36] From leeches to lions, nature mirrors and informs the human social realm by example, both positively and negatively: "Go to the ant, you sluggard; consider its ways and be wise" (Prov 6:6); "Like a dog returning to its vomit is a fool who reverts to his folly" (Prov 26:11).

The scathing polemics of the dialogue between Job and his friends pit two legitimate sources of wisdom, nature and tradition, against each other, rending asunder what was seamlessly joined. The polarity gives rise to opposing epistemologies. The friends rely on past tradition for the acquisition of knowledge; the realm of nature comes to be foundational in Job's experience (Job 12:9 and 13:1-2). Once wedded in the sapiential household, experience and tradition, nature and culture, are suffering from irreconcilable differences.[37]

34. In addition, the contrast is all the more evident from the fact that Job casts his appeal in the present ("ask . . . and it will teach you"). Habel's suggestion that 12:7-8 is an appeal to ancient tradition concerning the primal era thus off the mark ("Appeal to Ancient Tradition as a Literary Form," *ZAW* 88 [1976] 266). There is nothing particularly primal about observing and gaining insight from nature. The force of Job's argument against his friends depends on the *overhaul* of past tradition, not appeal to it.

35. See also 15:17-19; Clines, *Job 1–20,* 355.

36. For example, Prov 6:6-11; 25:13-14, 26; 26:1-2, 11; 27:8, 15; 30:15-16, 18-19, 24-28, 29-31; cf. 1 Kgs 5:13.

37. The character of Elihu, who represents a later reading of Job (chs. 32–37), finds Job's appeal to nature as the true source of wisdom utterly specious: "[God] teaches us more than the animals of the earth and makes us wiser than the birds of the air" (35:11). Such a polemical statement fits well with Elihu's more general criticism of both traditional wisdom and Job's experience. See W. P. Brown, *Character in Crisis: A Fresh Approach to the Wisdom Literature of the Old Testament* (Grand Rapids: Eerdmans, 1996) 84-88.

In short, by recovering wisdom's inclusive parameters, Job adamantly insists that nature, too, is a repository of wisdom. Nature plays the role of instructor (vv. 7-8). Nature is not blind but in fact discerns what Job's friends cannot: the radical contingency of all life vis-à-vis Yahweh, the inscrutable (12:10).[38] The plants and animals perceive directly "that the hand of Yahweh has done this" (v. 9),[39] namely run roughshod over creation and Job. For Job radical dependence on God, to which nature bears witness, is demonstrated in the instability of the cosmic and social order: Job, a blameless man, has become an object of derision (12:4); robbers and idolaters remain secure (v. 6); and all creation is overturned (vv. 14, 22; cf. Prov 30:21-23). To be in God's hand is not a safe place to be, and there is no escape. The plants and animals clearly apprehend this indubitable fact, for they are firsthand witnesses to the oppressive nature of divine providence.

Like the sages who preceded him, Job draws existential examples from nature. Like a flower, human existence is fleeting (Job 14:2), and Job is a windblown leaf (13:25). Job recognizes that he is eminently biodegradable (13:28). Indeed, the trees have a distinct advantage over human beings: they can generate shoots after the ax fells them (14:7-12). They have hope, unlike humans, who dry up like wadis (v. 11). As the force of erosion destroys mountain and rock, so human hope is worn away to nothing (vv. 18-20). Propped up by pride, the hope of mortals is in fact an illusion, and nature knows this better than humans, and so does Job (13:1), whose experience of divine abuse has the potential to dismantle completely the pretentious traditions of the elders. Ask the earth, and it will tell of the ravaging effects of providence (v. 19). Ask Job, and he can testify to the travesty of divine justice. Both Job and the animals are ready to testify not on God's behalf, not to Yahweh's righteousness, but to divine depravity.

Job's derision of the Deity prompts an equally derisive response from his friends. Attempting to turn the tables, Eliphaz castigates Job for propping himself up as the font of wisdom. Recalling the words of Wisdom herself,

---

38. Job 12:9 is the only place in the poetic dialogues where the tetragrammaton is employed, suggesting that nature knows Yahweh more directly than humans do!

39. Much has been made regarding the attestation of v. 9b in Isa 41:20b. Without suggesting intertextual dependence, a close comparison is nonetheless telling. In Isaiah this cliché, somewhat akin to the English reference to an "act of God," marks the conclusion of an inquiry whose object is the arboretum richly detailed in the previous verse (see Chapter 3). In both Isaiah and Job, nature is the medium of the message. But the messages differ: the respective antecedents to the demonstrative object "this" (zō't) are diametrically opposed. In Isaiah the antecedent is Yahweh's deliverance and restoration of a people; in Job it is the demoralization of Job and the dissolution of the cosmos.

332

Eliphaz accuses Job of having a cosmic ego, of identifying himself with *sapientia revelata*: "Are you the firstborn of humanity (*'ādām*)? Were you brought forth before the hills? Have you listened in the council of God? And do you limit wisdom to yourself?" (15:7-8; cf. Prov 8:22-27). Like personified Wisdom, is Job privy to the secrets of the cosmos and thus to the mysteries of divine providence by virtue of some preexistent, supernal status he possesses? Such is the highest form of hubris, Eliphaz charges. Whereas tradition may be relative, wisdom is omniscient. By disparaging the accumulated wisdom of the sages, Job succumbs to the most egregious of sins, according to Eliphaz: abusing the vulnerable and questioning God's own knowledge (Job 22:5-14). To add insult to injury, Job has adopted the "old way" (*'ōraḥ 'ôlām*) of the wicked (v. 15). Turning Job's words against him, Eliphaz twists Job's lament in 3:3-28 into outright blasphemy with self-implicating results: Job has accused God of being wrapped in impenetrable clouds of ignorance and, in turn, has blinded himself to his own sinful behavior (22:12-14). Job has stripped the naked, starved the hungry, and oppressed widows and orphans (vv. 6-9), a classic case of wickedness roundly condemned by prophets and sages alike.[40] Job is no different from all the other abusers within his community.

Of Honor, Onagers, and Orphans

Job picks up the issue of just punishment in ch. 24. After lamenting over the hopeless prospect of gaining access to the throne room of God, his *Deus absconditus* (23:3, 8, 13-17), in order to present his case, Job reflects more generally on the conduct of the wicked and the resulting state of the oppressed. The wicked revel in abusing the orphan, widow, and poor (24:3-4). In two of the three cases, Job highlights their loss of movable property, of which the nondescript wicked[41] have dispossessed them (v. 3). But Job's focus is not so much on the perpetrators of such injustice as on their intended victims. With their domestic animals seized, including donkeys, the destitute are likened to "wild donkeys," or onagers (*pěrā'îm, equus hemionus*) that must scavenge the wastelands (*midbār, 'ărābâ*, v. 5). It is only appropriate that Job employs this particular creature of the wild (Ps 104:11), for the onager em-

40. For example, Isa 1:17; 10:2; Jer 22:3; Zech 7:10; Prov 15:25; 22:22-23; cf. Job 29:12-13.
41. The "wicked" are never referred to as such in vv. 2-4; they are simply described by their actions.

bodies social marginality in various ways. A deserted and desolate city is the "joy of wild asses" (Isa 32:14). Like the doe and the jackal, the onager depends on the rain and will die for lack of vegetation (Jer 14:5-6).[42] Embedded in the divine promise given in Hagar's "annunciation" in Gen 16:8-13 is the comparison of Ishmael to the onager, a paragon of antisocial defiance (v. 12; cf. 49:17, 27; Hos 8:9).

Job sees nothing noble in the onager, more a beast of burden than a wild beast. Its burden, however, does not come from human domestication and servitude,[43] but from frail dependence. This marginal animal must hastily glean from the cultivated fields. Bereft of clothing, the emblematic sign of civilization, it suffers the harsh vagaries of nature (Job 24:7-8). Job employs much of this same language to describe the dilemma of the defenseless in vv. 9-10: the poor and the orphan remain unclothed and hungry, the result of their enslavement by the wicked. The cruel treatment of the destitute is society's legacy, but nature is no different for the onager. In his description of the needy, Job freely moves from the domain of harsh and unforgiving nature to the brutal arena of human culture to describe the plight of the vulnerable. Abused by nature and society, the onager and the orphan share in common their status as victims. The poor have been forced, exiled, as it were, to the margins to become kin with the exploited class of asses.

The onager and the poor are objects of Job's pity. In his final words, however, they become objects of contempt (30:1-8), the conclusion of a natural movement in his case against God and humanity. In the summation of his lawsuit (chs. 29–31), Job brazenly defends his character despite all material evidence to the contrary. He begins with a profile of his former life "in the months of old" (29:1), in his prime when the "friendship of God was upon his tent" (29:4). Job's trek down memory lane is not nostalgic wallowing, however; it marks nothing less than an apotheosis of patriarchal character. Job once received the deference of old and young alike (vv. 7-8); his remarks were invariably met by respectful silence and sagacious commendation (vv. 9-11). As part and parcel of his character, Job was acknowledged by his community as the patriarch par excellence. Such is a character whose contours are shaped by the social codes of honor and esteem.

42. Part of a communal lament over a drought, Jer 14:2-6 contains a litany of sufferers that strategically moves from the urban elite (v. 3) to the rural farmers (v. 4), ending with the wild animals (vv. 5-6). The onager concludes the list.

43. Of note is that the onager was once domesticated by the Sumerians as a draft animal, but by 2000 BCE was replaced by the stronger and more docile horse. The onager is a liminal creature, one betwixt and between civilization and the wild, unthreatening yet stubbornly defiant.

The ostensible reason given for such self-praise is Job's treatment of the poor (vv. 12-17). The desperate needfulness of the poor, the orphan, and the widow is just as important for the moral constitution of Job's character as the honorable respect accorded him by the affluent. The rescue of the poor requires no less than the conduct of a conqueror (vv. 16-17). Extending comfort is tantamount to a campaign of royal proportions (v. 25). The exercise of virtue feeds on social need, and social deference is virtue's reward. For Job the salutary results of such moral achievement are long life and sustained vigor (vv. 18-20). Through this life of robust righteousness, Job's "bow" remains taught (v. 20). Job's former life, in short, fleshes out the cognate relation between virility and virtue; humility has no place in the equation (cf. 30:11). The maintenance of Job's character is founded on a mutual relationship of peer and poor; Job thrives on the esteem of his colleagues and glides on the gratitude of the indigent.

In the next stage of his defense, Job recounts how his bowstring has unraveled and his kingdom crumbled. In place of the blessings of deference, scorn is now heaped on Job by those whom he once helped. "Was not my soul grieved for the poor?" Job plaintively asks (30:25b); but when he sought their good, he received only evil (v. 26). Now he is their object of mockery and persecution (vv. 1, 9-15). Job begins his lament with a scathing characterization of the outcast (vv. 1-8). Bereft of "vigor,"[44] they lack socially defined virtues; castigated as thieves and fools, they are driven from the community (vv. 5, 8). As Job asks rhetorically at the outset of his lament, there is nothing to be gained "from the strength of their hands" (v. 2). More than manual labor is implied. The question is cast generally, literally reading "what's in it for me?" Given the link between vigor and virtue, Job indicts the poor for their lack of social utility, a veritable crime against humanity. Job, the erstwhile paragon of propriety, is a decimated city whose walls have been breached by barbarians (v. 14).

What good are these rejects to me? Job asks as he imagines their subsistence in the wastelands (vv. 3, 6-7). And what a vivid imagination he has! Like the animals of the wild, these social reprobates must scavenge the desolate land for sustenance and shelter (vv. 2-6). They "bray among the bushes" like wild asses, "whipped out of the land" (vv. 7-8; cf. 6:5). Recalling his characterization of the poor as pathetic onagers in 24:5-12, Job's pity has turned to contempt. Job now wants nothing to do with these despicable creatures, yet he concludes his diatribe with the bitter cry: "I am a brother of jackals and a companion of ostriches" (30:29). Like onagers, the jackals and ostriches in-

44. Heb. *kālaḥ*, v. 2b. See also 5:26; 20:11; 33:25-26.

habit lands no longer cultivated (Isa 34:13; 13:22; Jer 9:10; 10:22; 49:33). Like a ruined city that has become the haunt of jackals (Jer 49:33; 51:37), Job is utterly devastated, condemned to a life of subsistence in a godforsaken wilderness. Job is no longer among friends; indeed, his partners in the wilderness can be unremitting in their cruelty.[45] No help can be gained from them (Job 30:28b). Job finds himself in a no-man's-land. His misery eschews company of any kind: as in his initial lament, Job would prefer to be left alone to die. It is his cross to live among miscreants, virtual animals, as it has been his curse to suffer the verbal barbs of his friends. And the most bestial of them all is God (vv. 20-21).[46]

In Job's concluding address, certain wild animals come to embody his lamentable condition. They are apt symbols of a different breed of humanity, one that is for all intents and purposes subhuman. Jackals and ostriches populate the landscape of lament (cf. Mic 1:8; Ps 44:19 [MT 20]). The dog Job mentions at the beginning of his lament is associated with moral turpitude and filth (Job 30:1; cf. Ps 22:12, 16 [MT 13, 17]). The onager, which leads a life of pathetic subsistence devoid of contact with civilization, is vilified. Marginalized from civilization, such animals lack civility. Bereft of vigor, they lack moral fortitude. Consequently, these inhabitants of the wilderness become natural scapegoats for all social ills, even lawless cruelty.[47] Their subsistence in the wasteland is an imposed exile (30:5, 8). Job moves freely in his discourse from pity to contempt for these creatures, in the same way he moves from grief to bitter accusation toward the poor (30:24-25, 8-14). But he cannot escape these lawless animals. The poor he shall always have with him, much to his disgust.

The Oath of Virtue

Job's final challenge to God, cast in a series of compelling oaths (31:1-40a), marks the last stage in his discourse, paving the way for Yahweh's long-awaited response. Here he mentions no animals but focuses much attention on the needy. Proclaiming himself as their champion, Job once again cites the triad of the vulnerable — the poor, the widow, and the orphan (vv. 16-21) — in his oath of integrity

45. The ostrich embodies a certain cruelty, evidenced in neglecting its young (Lam 4:3; Job 39:13-18).

46. As Habel notes (*Job*, 421), the description of God as eminently "cruel" ('*akzār*, Job 30:21) is similar to the description of Leviathan's ferocity (41:10 [MT 2]).

47. The vilification of wild animals is also a staple of Western culture. See M. Midgley's classic study in *Beast and Man: The Roots of Human Nature* (2d ed.; London: Routledge, 1995), esp. 25-50.

(cf. 29:12-13). With typical hyperbole, Job claims to have guided the widow[48] from his mother's womb (31:18). Parental metaphors dominate this specific unit: Job is guide and father to the less fortunate (vv. 16-18). In return, he receives their blessing (v. 20).[49] As previously, Job profiles himself as the beneficent patriarch who is sustained by the deference of peer and poor alike.

Added to this taxonomy of destitution, however, is the figure of the slave, with whom he finds a certain biological solidarity: "Did not he who made me in the womb make them? And did not one fashion us in the womb?" (vv. 13-15). The tie between slave and master, between Job and servant, runs deeper even than the womb: Job and his slaves are bound up together from a juridical standpoint: they both have standing. As the administrator of perfect justice, Job claims that his slaves have the inalienable right of litigation (*rîb*, v. 13). Such is also the driving hope behind Job's lawsuit against God. Even as God's slave (1:8), Job thinks he has the right of redress. In principle the law court includes all social classes, whether slave or master, orphan or ruler, and lays the foundation for a vision of community that, like his vision of Sheol (cf. 3:18-19), reaches beyond reality. Indeed, such glimmers of a new social order will come back to haunt him like the jackals and ostriches whose companion — indeed, covenant partner — he has now become (30:29; 5:23).

Educating Job

As evident in both Job's and the friends' heated exchanges, references to animals and nature constitute an indispensable stock of ammunition in the rhetorical arsenal of metaphors the Joban poet employs. Even more can be found in the divine discourses of 38:29–39:30 and 40:15–41:34 (MT 26). Animal imagery dominates God's confrontation with Job from the whirlwind. References to animals proliferate in excess relative to the sum total of allusions to nature present elsewhere, whether cosmological (38:4-21, 31-33) or meteorological (38:22-30, 34-38). Given their literary arrangement, the cosmic, inanimate realm is in some sense prefatory to the animal realm.[50]

48. The objective verbal suffix is feminine.
49. This verse is best taken as a negative interrogative *('im-lō')*, contra NRSV.
50. See Y. Hoffman's analysis of Yahweh's discourse, noting the rise of literary attention given to each item of this catalogue: the first series of creation images (38:4-38) comprises 43 items presented in only 35 verses; the second section, which presents the animals (38:39–39:30), contains 33 verses and 15 items; and the final section concerning Behemoth and Leviathan (40:15–41:34 [MT 26]) consists of only 8 elements spread over 43 verses (A *Blemished Perfection: The Book of Job in Context* [JSOTSup 213; Sheffield: JSOT Press, 1996], 103).

337

Before analyzing these images drawn from nature, I must first address the issue of literary form and discursive style. The divine discourse that thunders from the whirlwind is harshly accusatory in tone and replete with biting rhetorical questions evidently designed to put Job back in his place as an ignorant creature. To be sure, God does not offer soothing words to assuage Job's suffering. To the contrary, the words come fast and furious, rife with challenge, divine fire meeting Job's inflammatory accusations. The language continues the "Lawsuit Drama" that is constitutive of the poetic discourse;[51] it is a *Streitgespräch*, a disputation intended to defend God before Job's accusation.[52] God angrily submits as a deposition against Job: "Will you even put me in the wrong? Will you condemn me that you may be justified?" (40:8-9). It is tempting to take the divine speeches as simply God's countersuit to Job's litigation.

Yet much more is operating underneath the surface. As James Crenshaw notes, form collides with content. "The first speech from the tempest presents Job ... with a fine example of the collision between literary form and its religious content. One can hardly say that in this instance the medium is the message."[53] Yet Crenshaw goes on to describe in only general terms how the reunifying function of the theophany clashes with the wholesale subversion of humanity's privileged status: "The portrayal of the deity in the speeches increases the distance between human beings and their maker. This distance takes place, paradoxically, despite a literary form that emphasizes incredible closeness."[54]

Crenshaw's reference to "literary form" is somewhat misleading. Theophany itself does not constitute a uniform genre; it is a divine act of self-disclosure that can be expressed in various ways, from an assurance of promise issued beside a tree (Gen 12:6-7) to a terrifying epiphany of vengeance (Nah 1:2-6).[55] Furthermore, it is not typical of biblical theophanies to induce

51. See B. Zuckerman's discussion of the legal metaphor with accompanying bibliography in *Job the Silent: A Study in Historical Counterpoint* (New York: Oxford University Press, 1991) 108-9n.298.

52. See the discussion on form in O. Keel, *Jahwes Entgegnung an Ijob: Eine Deutung von Ijob 38–41* (FRLANT 121; Göttingen: Vandenhoeck & Ruprecht, 1978) 24-35.

53. J. L. Crenshaw, "When Form and Content Clash: The Theology of Job 38:1–40:5" in *Creation in the Biblical Traditions* (ed. R. J. Clifford and J. J. Collins; CBQMS 24; Washington, D.C.: The Catholic Biblical Association of America, 1992) 70.

54. Crenshaw, "When Form and Content Clash," 84.

55. See the classic study of J. Jeremias, *Theophanie: Die Geschichte einer Alttestamentlichen Gattung* (Neukirchen-Vluyn: Neukirchener Verlag, 1965), which traces the development of this "form" primarily in hymns and prophetic proclamations and argues for an original Sitz im Leben in the victory song of the wars of Yahweh. Jeremias identifies Job 38:1 (= 40:6) as far removed from the standard literary form, since it conveys Yahweh's *answer*, not Yahweh's *approach* (pp. 69, 162).

"incredible closeness" between the earthly and heavenly realms.[56] More often than not, divine theophany strikes convulsive terror on the earthly plane rather than effect some sort of rapprochement.[57] To be sure, the theophanies of the Old Testament frequently occur in the context of desperate need on the part of Israel; theophanic manifestation can unveil a savior (e.g., Hab 3:13; Isa 29:1-6; Exod 15:1-18), as well as a lawgiver (Exod 19:3-23) and judge (Ps 94:1-3). But such results do not bring about intimate communion between the divine and human parties. Rather, they evoke dread, praise, or a combination thereof.

In addition, the theophany in Job is unlike any other. A fundamental characteristic of theophanies in Israel is their occurrence at locations considered particularly sacred, such as springs (Gen 16:7), rivers (32:23-33), trees (12:6-7), mountains (12:8; Exodus 19; Psalm 48), tabernacles (Num 12:5), and temples (Isaiah 6).[58] By contrast, the Joban theophany occurs without reference to any specific location. Indeed, theophany is mentioned only matter-of-factly: Yahweh's response is delivered "out of the whirlwind" (*min hassĕ'ārâ*, Job 38:1; cf. Hab 3:8; Ezekiel 1; Exod 19:16, 19; Ps 18:13 [MT 14]). A theophany of similar meteorological proportions is helpful for comparison:

> [Yahweh's] way is in the whirlwind (*šĕ'ārâ*) and in the storm; the clouds are the dust of his feet. He rebukes the sea and makes it dry, and he dries up all the rivers. Bashan and Carmel wither, and the bloom of Lebanon fades. The mountains quake before him, and the hills melt; the earth heaves before him, the world and all who live in it. Who can stand before his indignation? Who can endure the heat of his wrath? (Nah 1:3b-6a).

Personal longing for intimacy is clearly not the motivation behind Yahweh's self-disclosure in this whirlwind; rather, as the prophet makes clear, it is the implementation of justice (1:2-3a), a justice that indicts both the earth and its inhabitants. Consequently, is it any wonder that, in Crenshaw's words, the speeches of the Deity "increase the distance between human beings and their maker"? Crenshaw's "collision" is driven by the questionable assumption that the theophany in Job, irrespective of the discourse that follows, is intended to

56. Cf. the much-needed nuance Crenshaw provides in "When Form and Content Clash," 70n.2. Put more generally, theophany evokes the *mysterium tremendum* through a "strange harmony of contrasts" (R. Otto, *The Idea of the Holy* [tr. J. W. Harvey; 2d ed.; London: Oxford University Press, 1958] 1-40). In Job this is more evident in the formal dimensions and content of the divine discourse rather than from the factum of theophany per se.

57. See Hab 3:5-12; Judg 5:4-5; Nah 1:3-5.

58. See T. Hiebert, "Theophany in the OT," *ABD* (ed. D. N. Freedman; New York: Doubleday, 1992) 6.505-6.

reestablish the ties that bind Job and God. To the contrary, the formal rebuke and alleged demotion of humanity's privileged position in the created order are natural outcomes of the theophanic experience. Crenshaw's observations regarding the content of divine rebuke are in fact thoroughly entrenched within the dynamics of the *awe* before God. There is no clash here; "incredible closeness" is hardly a goal of divine self-disclosure in Job or elsewhere.

Yet there is a collision, and it is to be found within the formal dynamics of divine discourse. The tire marks can be observed by comparing the expected result of the literary form of the discourse, a blustery disputation in keeping with the tenor of theophany, with its underlying pedagogical intent. As noted above, divine discourse outweighs theophanic description.[59] This is significant and in keeping with the overall structure of the book of Job, in which speech figures so prominently. Although there is manifest power behind the words, Yahweh's theophany is not accompanied by brute force, as in the case of the whirlwind theophany described by Nahum, but by discourse. For the Joban poet, speech is the literary deposit of theophany as much as discourse is the tangible testimony of Job's and his friends' convictions. What does that discourse reveal? Nature in its ostensibly rawest form. Embedded within Yahweh's disputation "against" Job is an evocative series of images designed to limn the cosmos from Yahweh's standpoint and at the same time rehabilitate Job, whose righteous anger, according to Bildad, has ruptured himself and whose ego has forsaken the earth (Job 18:4).

Such is the clash between the harsh indictment of divine rebuke and the eventual fruition of Job's education. The series of cosmic and zoological images that parade by Job embody this tension, which can be most sharply felt when considering the role nature commonly assumes in contexts of legal trial and indictment. Within the so-called prophetic lawsuit, nature frequently assumes the roles of witness and jury in a suit called by God against Israel. Earth, mountains, and heaven have at one time or another been called to sit in judgment against Israel (e.g., Isa 1:2-3; Mic 6:1-2; Jer 2:12-13). In addition, the whole cosmos can bear witness on Yahweh's behalf. In Psalm 50 the "heavens declare [God's] righteousness" as God judges the people (vv. 4, 6). As stark testimony to a scathing indictment of Israel's breach of covenant, the land and its inhabitants languish (Hos 4:1-3).[60] In Yahweh's response to Job,

---

59. The ostensible lack of dramatic force traditionally associated with theophany in Job 38–41 is addressed in Elihu's discourse in 37:2-13, which explicitly associates God's speech with thunder, commanding the cosmic elements. In effect, Elihu backs up divine discourse with appropriate theophanic intensity.

60. For a more extended discussion, see K. Nielsen's discussion, which draws from Hermann Gunkel, in *Yahweh as Prosecutor and Judge: An Investigation of the Prophetic Lawsuit (Rîb-Pattern)* (tr. F. Cryer; JSOTSup 9; Sheffield: JSOT Press, 1978) 12-13.

all of nature is marshaled, and one would expect damning testimony from nature's witness, leading inexorably to a guilty verdict.[61]

Yet within the larger literary context, nature ultimately figures more in Job's vindication than in his condemnation. In the end, Job is exonerated by God before his friends (Job 42:7-8). Moreover, entirely lacking in Yahweh's discourse is any hint of punishment leveled against Job. In addition to its caustic language, Yahweh's litany of nature bears a positive function, indeed, a pedagogical purpose. The evocative series of images drawn from the realms of cosmology and zoology plays a critical role in broadening Job's moral horizon, as well as in demonstrating his innocence before his detractors. Yahweh's discourse is as much a didactic treatise and source of resolution for Job as it is a deposition against him. The blustery discharge that effectively silences Job's contentious discourse yet somehow confirms Job's innocence is a true coup de grâce, a final blow and a "stroke of grace."

The Cosmic Community

Preceding the extensive litany of wild creatures, the cosmic realm is limned with evocative descriptions of the basic elements of creation: earth, sea, and light (38:4-15), which then give way to the specific manifestations of these elements: the depths of sea and earth (vv. 16-18), the dwellings of light and darkness (vv. 19-21), various forms of precipitation (vv. 22-30, 34-38), and the movement of the constellations (vv. 31-33). Cosmology and meteorology are covered in the first half of this "lecture." Their respective functions and interrelationships serve to reestablish Yahweh's indomitable plan or design ($\`\bar{e}\d{s}\^{a}$, 38:2), which Job has challenged. As the climax of the dialogues, this cosmology is a model to supersede all other models, whether offered by Job or his friends.

Yahweh opens this catalogue of creation with a cosmic element that was noticeably missing in Job's initial lament: earth. The divine design is first demonstrated in the care and precision with which the earth is established (38:4-7). God is the architect and the earth is God's temple, not unlike the way in which the cosmos is patterned in Gen 1:2–2:3. Here, however, it is God's hands-on activities (e.g., measuring, setting, laying), rather than divine fiat, that imbue creation with cultic nuance. The celestial and heavenly beings supply the festive accolades (Job 38:4).[62] It is not fortuitous that Yahweh begins with a description

---

61. Moreover, in Job 40:2 Yahweh uses the language of lawsuit (*rîb*) to counter Job's litigation.

62. Cf. Ezra 3:10-11; Zech 4:7; 2 Chr 5:11-14.

of the earth in its cultically secure status. The earth, Yahweh assures Job, is a safe place to be, as much as the temple or cultic city is a refuge from hostile forces (e.g., Pss 23:6; 46:4-5 [MT 5-6]; 48:1-14 [MT 2-15]).

Abruptly, however, Yahweh's cosmic lecture leaps to the earth's antithesis, the sea, the traditional symbol of chaos. Earth and sea constitute a natural pair of opposites: solidity and fluidity, safety and danger. Frequently portrayed as a hostile force,[63] the mighty waters can overwhelm and destroy all manner of living space for earthbound creatures, as in the primordial flood of Genesis 6–9. Here, however, amorphous chaos is conveyed by the striking image of an enfant terrible, whose waves, like flailing limbs, must be restrained if some semblance of order is to prevail. Continuing the role of architect assumed in constructing the earth, God fastens doors and bars to restrict the sea's "proud waves" from overwhelming the temple-earth (Job 38:10-11). God's treatment of the sea implements a policy of containment in which absolute boundaries are prescribed (cf. Ps 104:5-9; Prov 8:29; Jer 5:22).

With the close juxtaposition of these two units, there is a disorienting dimension. Together, these two units effect a shift in Job's frame of reference. The change in topic, from earth to sea, dislocates Job's earthbound reference point. The sea is relegated to an appointed place and is viewed phenomenologically, that is, from the inside out. Moreover, Job is there. This displacement of Job's location is a defining characteristic of Yahweh's whirlwind tour of the cosmos. It is noteworthy that Yahweh's lecture on cosmology begins with the probing question: "Where were you ... ?" (Job 38:4) and throughout questions Job's location as well as his agency and ability (vv. 16, 19, 22, 24). Job was not there to witness the earth's foundation or the containment of the sea, but the evocative imagery of divine discourse is intended to take him and the reader there anyway.

This cosmic journey from land to sea is part of Job's journey of displacement, a foray into the frontiers of the cosmos inaccessible to common human experience. The journey presents the cosmos from Yahweh's vantage point, dynamic and ever shifting. On this cosmic expedition, Job's standpoint is uprooted and transported as he experiences the basic elements of creation from within rather than from any external, fixed perspective. Job's journey is an exercise in imaginative willpower; it is a journey of displacement not without, however, some attenuated sense of déjà vu. It is no coincidence that Job previously found himself, ironically, at home in the sea, hedged in by God (7:12; cf. 3:23). Now it is perhaps with some shock that Job sees the sea for what it really is: a

63. For example, Pss 18:4 (MT 5); 74:13-14; 77:16-20 (MT 17-21); 89:9-13 (MT 10-14); 144:7; Isa 17:12-14; 51:9-10. See H. G. May, "Some Cosmic Connotations of *Mayim Rabbîm,* 'Many Waters,'" *JBL* 74 (1955) 9-21.

child out of control, restrained yet nurtured, an object of containment and care. In the surging waters Job can see his distorted reflection (cf. 7:12).

Equally striking is Yahweh's role. With the sea depicted as an intemperate infant, God assumes the role of midwife and caretaker, not unlike the role God assumed in Job's own birth (10:18). Yahweh births the sea and wraps it in swaddling bands of dark clouds, an action of restriction as well as protection. The remarkable image of the sea bursting from the womb draws from the initial process of birth, the rupture of the amniotic sac, an event that Job himself cursed in his quest for the finality of rest (3:10-11; 10:18). But placid stillness is not in the sea's nature. Continually pushing the limits, the sea is associated with the "vigor of new life."[64] God is profiled as a confiner and protector, restrainer and nurturer, in short, a disciplining parent (cf. 38:28-29). Job, in turn, is a willful child in need of nurture and discipline, a work still in progress.

Yahweh's discourse, however, does not linger, however lovingly, on any one cosmic domain. Quickly off to the arena of the dawn (vv. 12-15), Yahweh questions Job if he has ever summoned the morning (cf. 3:9). An object of royal decree, sunlight rules the day by reinstituting justice in the land (cf. Gen 1:16). The daily establishment of order is itself a creative act that molds the earth like clay and colors it like a garment (Job 38:14). Again, the imagery is striking. The dawn shakes the "skirts of the earth" as if the earth were a cloak to be vigorously flapped to rid it of nocturnal vermin.[65] The wicked are expelled through the daily renewal of creation. For Job, the wicked — murderers, thieves, and adulterers — make their home in deep darkness, their "morning" (24:17). Consequently, dawn and dusk are inverted from the standpoint of the wicked, "those who rebel against the light" (24:13). Darkness is tantamount to moral anarchy. Yahweh's musings over the dawn, however, counter Job's dismal portrayal of darkness run amok. The dawn's power to differentiate and color the landscape, after darkness has reduced it to a formless mass, also imposes an order that distinguishes the good from the bad, so that the former can have their turn to take back the land. The dawn is the harbinger of justice, established daily by its rising.[66] The dawn and the darkness represent a cycle of order and disorder, similar to the daily cycle shared by animals and humans in Ps 104:20-23:

> You create darkness, and it is night,
> when all the animals of the forest come creeping out.
> The young lions roar for their prey,

64. Newsom, "Job," 602.
65. Ibid., 602.
66. The sun god in Mesopotamia, Šamaš or UTU, was considered the god of justice and righteousness.

> seeking their food from God.
> When the sun rises, they withdraw,
>   and lie down in their dens.
> Humans [in turn] go out to their work,
>   and to their labor until evening.

The poet's view of time is more foreboding than the psalmist's optimistic musings, but their comparison clarifies the wicked's place in the Joban cosmos. The wicked have, as it were, crossed the temporal boundaries by encroaching on the night, reserved for the nocturnal animals, to ply their trade. They are, for all intents and purposes, denizens of darkness. Yahweh's speech does not so much counter Job's gloomy portrayal as supplement it. Granted, the wicked, like darkness, may rule the night, but Job needs to be shown the light of day, where things are reversed. By wallowing in darkness (e.g., 3:4-6, 20; 10:20-22), Job has neglected the dawn and its restorative powers, both physical and moral. Yes, the wicked have a place in the scheme of things, but the same can also be said of the righteous. Similarly, Job's view of a disordered cosmos has its legitimacy, but it is woefully incomplete.

Yahweh follows up the transcendent dawn by highlighting the depths of sea and earth, the domain of death (38:16-17). Again, the imagery evokes the movement of a journey: Job's location is questioned and so also his knowledge: "Have you entered . . . walked . . . seen . . . comprehended . . . ?" Job has not surveyed the earth's boundless expanse to qualify for omniscient status.[67] Though Job has consistently yearned for death, he has never once been at its doorstep. Like the sea barricaded by doors and bolts, death too is demarcated by gates. Dangerous cosmic domains have their niche, their strongholds, as it were, yet Job has no clue where they are, even though he has invoked them throughout his complaints. Similarly, Job cannot lay claim to have forged a path to the dwellings of either light or darkness, let alone show them their way home (vv. 19-20)! Job may have the audacity to usher in chaos and overwhelm all of creation, but such brazenness only goes so far for anyone lacking deified status. Uncommon valor cannot lead the cosmic elements back to their respective — and respected — domains. Chutzpah cannot make up for wisdom, and chutzpah is precisely what Yahweh accuses Job of exercising:

67. Newsom suggestively compares this passage to Gilgamesh's heroic travels to escape the reality of death, travels that bring him to the gates of the sun, the underworld, and the waters of death (Newsom, "Job," 603; see *ANET*, 88-91). Although Job cannot claim to have made such a journey, the outcome for both him and Gilgamesh is the same: the acknowledgment of realistic limitations.

"Surely you know, for you were born then, and the number of your days is great!" (38:21)[68]

There are other domains still to be experienced, such as the sources of precipitation, snow and hail, rain and ice (vv. 22-30). Here precipitation is imbued with the language of violence: hail is reserved for battle; the rain comes down in thunderous torrents. Yet a life-giving dimension is also evident, of which Job remains unaware. Yahweh recounts the source and outcome of precipitation, from storehouses to distribution. The rain may fall in torrents, but it will only wreak destruction on the earth unless it is evenly distributed. The reference to water channels evokes distinctly cultural overtones (v. 25). Canals were essential for agriculture in ancient times. Mesopotamian kings frequently boasted of their prowess in cutting intricate water channels to sustain their people. The lower class Igigi-gods of the Babylonian pantheon, too, were assigned such a task, until humans were created to relieve them of the burdensome work, "the drudgery of god."[69] Yahweh's self-description as rain bringer resembles that of the Assyrian storm god Adad, found in the following inscription on a statue dedicated to Adad of Kurbail that commemorates Shalmaneser III's conquests:

> To the god Adad, canal-inspector of heaven (and) underworld,[70] the lofty, lord of all, almighty among the gods, the awesome (god) whose strength is unrivaled, who bears a holy whip which churns up the seas, who controls all the winds, who provides abundant water, who brings down rain, who makes lightning flash, who creates vegetation, at whose shout the mountains shake (and) the seas are churned up, the compassionate god whose sympathetic concern is life.[71]

In this invocation Adad assumes both destructive and creative roles. As a thunderstorm deity, he is equally at home on the battlefield as in the clouds. Frequently depicted as a "whirlwind,"[72] Adad was also invoked as the

68. Cf. the similar taunt in 15:7-8 and wisdom's self-described primordial nature in Prov 8:22-31.

69. *Atrahasis* (Old Babylonian version) I, including CT 44 20 (see B. R. Foster's translation in *Before the Muses: An Anthology of Akkadian Literature* [2 vols.; 2d ed.; Bethesda: CDL Press, 1996] 1.160-68).

70. H. Tadmor translates Adad's epithet as "Water Commissioner of heaven and earth" in a reconstructed part of the Iran Stele of Tiglath-pileser III (I.A.9; *The Inscriptions of Tiglath-Pileser III, King of Assyria* [Jerusalem: Israel Academy of Sciences and Humanities, 1994] 95).

71. *AR* 3.59 (A.O.102.12.1-8).

72. See the Prayer to Adad translated by Foster, *Before the Muses*, 2.540-41.

"irrigator of heaven and earth," whose abundant rains provoke joy from the fields and meadows, even reconciling the angry![73]

The Assyrian king also embodied this dual role. On the one hand, to highlight his military prowess, the king frequently conceived himself as the embodiment of "Adad, the devastator," who "rains down flames" upon the enemy,[74] a *Blitzkrieger* who storms defenses and overwhelms enemy territories like an undammable flood.[75] On the other hand, Mesopotamian kings regarded themselves as the consummate canal builders who built and maintained intricate water systems in order to preserve the life and productivity of their kingdom. Tukulti-Ninurta I's account of building his namesake city is telling: "I cut straight as a string through rocky terrain, I cleared a way through high difficult mountains with stone chisels, I cut a wide path for a stream which supports life in the land (and) which provides abundance, and I transformed the plains of my city into irrigated fields."[76] For the Assyrian king, the transformation of "uncultivated plains (and) meadows"[77] into livable space was foundational to urban planning. Similarly, Shalmaneser IV recounts with pride his achievement in establishing a city specifically "in the desert, in the wasteland."[78] For the monarchs of the Mesopotamian valley, canal construction was an agriculturally, and thus culturally, defining act.

Yahweh is similarly depicted in this dual role of both destroyer and restorer. "For the day of battle and war" are the cosmic reserves of hail and snow (Job 38:23). But precipitation is more than an instrument of royal domination or cultural imposition. Yahweh's "precipitous" role also has its salutary results for the land. Channels are cut in order to distribute the rain to "a land where no one lives, in the desert, devoid of human life, to satisfy the waste and desolate land" (vv. 26-27a). This is where, in the wasteland, the Mesopotamian king and Yahweh part company.

For Yahweh, water channels disburse the rain *beyond* the realm of civili-

73. Ibid., 2.542-43.

74. For example, Ashurnasirpal II (*AR* 2.210 [A.O.101.1.ii.106-7]; *AR* 2.250 [A.O.101.17.iv.73-74]; *AR* 2.275 [A.O.101.23.7]); Shalmaneser III (*AR* 3.29 [A.O.102.5.iii.3a.]; *AR* 3.16 [A.O.102.2.i.46]; *AR* 3.20 [A.O.102.2.ii.49b-50]; *AR* 3.23 [A.O.102.2.ii.97-98]). Without invoking the deity's name, Tiglath-pileser I frequently describes himself as a cloudburst annihilating his enemies (*AR* 2.13 [A.O.87.1.i.42-43]; *AR* 2.17 [A.O.87.1.iii.25]).

75. For example, Shalmaneser III (*AR* 3.60, 74, 110 [A.O.102.12.18, 16.5b, 32.6b]). Consonant with his royal name, Shamshi-Adad V, for example, carries the epithet "rider of the Deluge" (*AR* 3.182 [A.O.103.1.i.10]).

76. *AR* 1.273 (A.O.78.23.100-104).

77. *AR* 1.273 (A.O.78.22.94).

78. *AR* 3.242 (A.O.105.2.11).

zation to a land seemingly godforsaken. They are not the conduits of culture. For all the references about limits and borders in Yahweh's speeches heretofore, there is one boundary that is decisively overcome: the border between the desert and the sown, the desolate and the cultivated. The provision of rain cultivates what is, in principle, unsuitable soil by all human standards. Yet grass (*deše'*), the first and foremost sign of botanical life (cf. Gen 1:11), is produced in a wasteland. This is no miraculous event akin to the wondrous arboretum limned in Second Isaiah (Isa 41:17-20). Described, rather, is the seasonal occurrence of heavy rain, which causes the desert to bloom, however temporary. No mention is made of the kind of constant irrigation needed to sustain human culture; Yahweh specifically lifts up the marginal land that is devoid of human life (Job 38:26). For Job, it is a land of contempt where the outcast dwell like scavengers (30:3-8).[79]

Once again, Yahweh has displaced Job's frame of reference, and thereby broadened his moral horizons. By giving attention to no-man's-land, to the exclusion of "man-made" land, Yahweh has forced the periphery of Job's worldview into the center of his purview. Job now finds himself in a land that is not of his making, a land untouched by human hands, unfettered by the shackles of culturally imposed values, yet one that is eminently sustained by Yahweh. In Second Isaiah, watering the desert is a culture-creating act intended to restore the community of faith on barren soil (Isa 41:18-20; 43:19-21). In Job, however, the wilderness's domain remains a desert. Yahweh does not transform the desert into a lush oasis. God does not intervene in any fashion to reshape the topography of such rugged terrain, leveling out mountains and raising up valleys (cf. Isa 40:4). Yahweh simply provides (Job 38:26-27), and the "desolate" land is shown to be teeming with life.[80] The wilderness is presented *as is* from Yahweh's perspective, in all of its terrible beauty, populated with exotic creatures appropriate to their respective domains. In Job, Yahweh irrigates the wasteland to cultivate a community beyond culture.[81]

Behind the flash and thunder of torrential precipitation is a divine gratuitousness that sustains, by all human standards, an unsustainable land, a land associated with danger and chaos. Indeed, the desert can denote chaos as

---

79. The cognate expression "waste and desolate" (*šō'â ûmĕšō'â*) in 38:27 is replicated in 30:3.

80. The shock of witnessing such variegated life in the desert, as Job experiences, resonates with first-time visitors to the North American Southwest desert who commonly associate such a region with the Sahara.

81. Job's wilderness is to culture as the Yahwist's primordial garden is to society: both the wasteland and the garden lie beyond human culture per se, yet are generative of moral possibilities and values that can be embodied by culture.

much as can water (e.g., Jer 51:42-43).[82] Desert and sea are existentially bound up as common realms of fear and contempt situated at the very periphery of Job's ideological grid. From Yahweh's perspective, however, both warrant divine attention and care. Life-giving rain on the desert is indiscriminate from a morally retributive standpoint. Matitiahu Tsevat was the first to point to the crucial moral significance of this verse.[83] Tsevat interpreted this section as a tacit repudiation of retribution: rain is neither reward nor punishment (cf. Jer 3:3; Hos 6:3; Amos 4:7). His interpretation, however, has been criticized severely as missing the mark.[84] There is indeed moral significance demonstrated in Yahweh's care bestowed on the unsown desert, for such an act attests the desert's intrinsic worth. For Tsevat, the reference to rain quenching a parched land bears a distinctly *anti*-moral import, a conclusion that would be valid if the vast field of moral discourse could be narrowed to mechanistic retribution. But it cannot. Job is shown that this land, commonly associated with disdain and fear,[85] is also worthy of divine sustenance. Rain is harnessed by natural wadis to distribute water and quench the thirst of a desolate land and its inhabitants. The fall of rain on the parched soil is a morally indiscriminate act founded on divine gratuitousness rather than on human merit.[86] Divine attention is warranted not by entitlement but by need, a worth beyond merit. Sustaining a desert devoid of moral desert powerfully transforms the geo-ideological terrain of Job's moral landscape.

To evoke awe over Yahweh's activity, water's fluid nature erodes other forms of presumption as well. In vv. 28-30 Yahweh expounds on the various forms water can mysteriously assume: liquid, frost, and ice, like stone. In comparison with the discourse on the sea, it is now ice that comes forth from the primordial womb, and rain is begotten (vv. 28-29).[87] Not only is God's sustaining care unfettered, encroaching even on the godforsaken, it can take

82. Keel, *Jahwehs Entgegnung,* 58.

83. Tsevat, "Meaning," 99-100.

84. See Newsom, "Job," 604; idem, "The Moral Sense of Nature: Ethics in the Light of God's Speech to Job," *PSB* 15 (1994) 17-18.

85. The priestly legists, for example, regarded the wilderness as the domain of the "demon" Azazel, to whom the community's impurities were transferred on the Day of Atonement (Lev 16:8-10).

86. On the theme of divine gratuitousness and freedom, see G. Gutiérrez, *On Job* (tr. M. J. O'Connell; Maryknoll, N.Y.: Orbis, 1987) 72-75.

87. G. Vall's claim that the series of questions in 38:28-20 are to be answered in the negative, thereby eschewing the language of procreation, overlooks similar procreative language in 38:8-9, in which Yahweh is portrayed as midwife or even mother ("'From Whose Womb Did the Ice Come Forth?' Procreation Images in Job 38:28-29," *CBQ* 57 [1995] 504-13).

various, even hidden, forms. Water signifies a *gratia abscondita,* analogous to ice, which is, poetically speaking, water in "hiding" (38:30a).[88] The figure of water connotes God's mysterious ways as the bearer and sustainer of life.

As in the case of light's "territory" in v. 20, the issue of Job's ability is again broached in Yahweh's discourse on the constellations (vv. 31-33). Though some would find this unit better placed perhaps after v. 15 or v. 21, the key to this passage is the movement of the stars according to the seasons (v. 32a). Meteorology and agriculture remain the subjects.[89] The positions of the constellations determine the seasons of rain and drought, and Job can no more control the movements of the stars than turn water into stone. As the last unit on meteorology makes clear, only Yahweh can control the weather; Job cannot even predict it (vv. 34-37). Such prescience is to be found, rather, in two remarkable birds, the ibis and the cock (v. 36).[90] In Egyptian lore, the former is the symbol of Thoth, the Egyptian god of wisdom; it announced the Nile's rising, a critical event in the agricultural season. In a similar vein, the cock could announce the coming of the rain as well as the dawn. These two animals, rather than Job, are endowed with wisdom from on high. Job, however, cannot even predict, let alone control, the forces of nature, the genesis and distribution of water being a case in point. "Who can tilt the waterskins of the heavens?" so Yahweh concludes the remedial course on meteorology.

What is it about water that warrants such attention by God in Job's education? Signifying a host of contrasting results, water can be destructive as well as productive, depending on its distribution. Its mysterious qualities tug at the edges of Job's preconceived notions about nature and its operations. Water flows around earnest attempts at control, spilling over into the most unexpected, desiccated areas with torrential force, giving life to what was considered irredeemable. As a tangible sign of Yahweh's gratuitous care, water is present where it has no business being. Fundamental to culture, the sustaining power of harnessed water is considered coextensive with civilization. Water may occasionally flow into the desert, but only with fleeting effect, as Job has no doubt observed from within his community. Not so, Yahweh contends. Water in the desert is a sign of overflowing grace. Even in the most desolate of areas, water has its binding effect, causing the dust to "run into a mass and the clods [to] cling together" (v. 38), Yahweh concludes. Even in the land of the

88. Lit. "Water hides itself *(yithabā'û)* like a rock."

89. See the recent attempts to make sense of this passage in its present context: Newsom, "Job," 605; A. de Wilde, *Das Buch Hiob* (OTS 22; Leiden: Brill, 1981) 142-47, 366-67.

90. See J. A. Jaussen, "Le coq et la plui dans la tradition palestinienne," *RB* 33 (1924) 574-82; Gordis, *Job,* 452-53.

damned, water is formative of community.[91] Such a conclusion can only wreak havoc on Job's moral landscape, for it is from this land of the lost that an alien community springs forth for Job.

"Ask the Animals and They Will Teach You"

And the Spirit immediately drove him out into the wilderness. He was in the wilderness forty days, tempted by Satan; and he was with the wild beasts; and the angels waited on him.

Mark 1:12-13, NRSV

With effortless eloquence, Yahweh moves quickly from meteorology and agriculture to zoology (38:39–39:30). The issue of Job's limited ability and discernment vis-à-vis Yahweh's power and knowledge continues. Like earth and sea in 38:4-11 and light and darkness in vv. 12-21, the animals come two by two: lion and raven (38:39-41), mountain goat and deer (39:1-4), onager and auroch (39:5-12), ostrich and warhorse (39:13-25), and hawk and vulture (39:26-30). Why such a concentration on animals, particularly wild ones, can only be answered by gaining some familiarity with their significance in the larger ancient Near Eastern context.

Othmar Keel has significantly advanced this area of study in his examination of Mesopotamian and Egyptian iconography. His survey includes numerous depictions of royal figures hunting various wild animals, many of which are present in Job 39.[92] In addition, Keel identified a particular motif, which he called the "lord of the animals" *(Herr der Tiere):* a divine figure flanked by wild animals usually held in each hand.[93] From Keel's investigation, it becomes clear that the animals highlighted in Yahweh's answer to Job were by and large viewed as inimical forces to be eliminated or controlled, an expression of cultural hegemony over nature within the symbolic worldview of the ancient Orient.

Although it is always difficult to interpret iconography without accom-

91. The suggestive verb *dābaq* ("cleave"), which concludes Yahweh's description of the water's effect on the land, imbues water with community-binding force. It is frequently associated with human relationships, even intimacy (e.g., Gen 2:24 and 1 Kgs 11:2 [man and woman]; Ruth 1:14 [mother and daughter-in-law]; Num 36:7, 9 [tribe and land]; 2 Sam 20:2 [king and people]).

92. Keel, *Jahwes Entgegnung,* 71-81.

93. Ibid., 87-125.

panying texts, the following sample survey of royal inscriptions supplements and nuances Keel's observations. Animal imagery functions decisively, for example, in the maintenance of royal ideology in at least three categories of literary presentation: the enemy, the king, and the royal hunt.

Representations of the King's Enemies

In the Assyrian royal accounts of battle, the enemy was frequently likened to an animal to be vanquished. Of all the Assyrian kings, Tiglath-pileser I was perhaps the most prolific in this regard. The warriors of the land of Išdiš are, for example, "laid low like sheep."[94] More graphic, the combined troops of Murattas, Saradaus, and the city Hunusu are likened to lambs or sheep, decapitated and butchered before Assyrian might.[95] Prisoners are compared to oxen led by ropes run through their noses.[96] In all three cases, images of domestic animals are employed to underscore the enemies' weakness as well as their miserable fate: sheep for slaughter and oxen for servility.

On the less domestic side, the enemies of the king are frequently cast fleeing from the king's awesome might. Like jerboa they scurry off to remote regions for escape,[97] or like birds they fly off to inaccessible mountain ledges.[98] Like an ensnared bird, the enemy is trapped.[99] Shamshi-Adad V, in his pronouncement of victory over the royal city of Dur-Papsukkal, curiously likens his prisoners to locusts rounded up and transported to his land.[100] Tiglath-pileser III repeatedly refers to the wily queen of the Arabs, Samsi, fleeing to "an arid place, like an onager."[101] In a typical fit of disgust, the same king refers to the belligerent Ahlamaeans as "deer and wild goats who roamed about in the mountains."[102] Perhaps out of frustration, Shalamaneser III refers to his slip-

94. *AR* 2.16 (A.O.87.1.ii.80).
95. *AR* 2.19, 24 (A.O.87.1.iii.98-99, vi.6).
96. *AR* 2.34 (A.O.87.2.26).
97. *AR* 2.41 (A.O.87.4.12).
98. *AR* 2.18 (A.O.87.1.iii.68-69).
99. For example, Tiglath-pileser III's account of the defeat of the Chaldeans in the Calah Summary Inscription 7.15 (Tadmor, *Inscriptions of Tiglath-pileser III*, 161); Sennacherib's siege of Jerusalem, in which Hezekiah is made a prisoner in his own capital "like a bird in a cage" (*ANET*, 288); Esarhaddon's account of King Sanduarri's defeat: "Like a bird I snared him out of (his) mountain and cut off his head" (*ARAB* 2 §513).
100. *AR* 3.188 (A.O.103.1.iv.35).
101. Calah Summary Inscriptions 4.23'; 8.26'; 9.19 (Tadmor, *Inscriptions of Tiglath-pileser III*, 143, 179, 189).
102. Milga Mergi Rock Relief, 1.20 (Tadmor, *Inscriptions of Tiglath-pileser III*, 113).

pery enemy Marduk-bel-usati escaping "like a fox through a hole."[103] Similarly, Esarhaddon describes the seditious rebel Nab-zer-kitti-lisher fleeing to Elam like a fox, no doubt with his tail between his legs.[104] In a different kind of pursuit, Esarhaddon describes himself engaging in piscatorial activity to capture Sidon's king: "I pulled [Abdi-milkutti] out of the sea, like a fish. I cut off his head."[105]

Animal imagery is also applied to the enemies of Pharaoh in Egyptian epigraphy. In the Athribis Stela, which recounts Merneptah's Libyan campaign in his fifth year, the "families of Libya" are likened to mice scattering before the invincible raptor, the king of Egypt.[106] Indeed, his southern enemies are bereft of refuge, the court scribe goes on to state, and the survivors must scavenge for food like "[wild] cattle."[107] Similarly, Thutmose III describes in his most ambitious Asiatic campaign an encounter between the king of Mitanni and his forces: "They fled, forsooth, like a [herd] of mountain goats."[108] With disgust, Pharaoh Tanutamon describes his Delta foes as "beasts" who "crawl into their holes," refusing to fight.[109] Perhaps most graphic is Ramses III's inscription in the second court of the Medinet Habu temple, which commemorates his victory over the Libyans: "They flutter like wild fowl in the midst of the net, with legs struggling in the basket, made into a roast, laid low, prostrate on the ground."[110]

Although the choice of the particular animal depends on the military situation (e.g., mountain, sea battles), animal imagery serves to stress the flight, fear, and subordinated status of the king's enemies. Noble wild beasts are as a rule eschewed; the king's enemies are not worthy of such esteem.

Royal Self-Representations

Quite in contrast to the metaphorical depictions of enemies as pathetic or domesticated animals at the king's disposal, royal figures typically revel in self-depictions that employ wild, fearsome animals. The lion is frequently the animal of choice in both Mesopotamian and Egyptian annals. For example, mili-

103. *AR* 3.30 (A.O.102.5.v.1).
104. *ARAB* 2 §509.
105. *ARAB* 2 §527.
106. *ARE* 3 §598.
107. *ARE* 3 §598.
108. *ARE* 2 §479.
109. *ARE* 4 §930.
110. *ARE* 4 §41.

tary prowess is frequently associated with the figure of the lion. Shamshi-ilu, Adad-narari III's field marshal, describes his successful campaign against Urartu on two colossal stone lions with the following description for the first lion: "The lion . . . angry demon, unrivaled attack, who overwhelms the insubmissive, who brings success." The second lion is also described in appropriately military terms: "who charges through battle, flattens the enemy land, who expels criminals and brings in good people."[111] Ashurnasirpal II endearingly includes in his list of inflated epithets: "I am a lion and I am virile."[112] Nebuchadrezzar I "rages like a lion," who "frigh[tens] his distinguished nobles."[113] Ninurta-kudurri-usur, the governor of Suhu, roars "like a mighty lion" against his enemies, causing their arrows to quiver "like locusts over [my] forces."[114] Other wild animal imagery dressed with the emperor's clothes includes the "ferocious dragon" (Ashurnasirpal II),[115] the belligerent wild bull (Adad-narari II),[116] the slithering viper (Tiglath-pileser I),[117] the raging wolf (Esarhaddon),[118] the eagle (Esarhaddon[119] and Shamshi-Adad V[120]), the "swooping bird of prey" (Esarhaddon),[121] the mythic *anzu* bird (the army of Shalmaneser III),[122] wild oxen (Tiglath-pileser III),[123] and a swarm of locusts (Sargon II).[124]

The pharaohs also reveled in predatory imagery. Perhaps the greatest military pharaoh, the so-called Napoleon of ancient Egypt,[125] Thutmose III likened himself to a series of predators in his hymn of victory over various ene-

111. *AR* 3.233 (A.O.104.2010.21-24).

112. *AR* 2.196 (A.O.101.1.i.33). See similar references to Adad-narari II (*AR* 2.145 [A.O.99.2.15]) and Esarhaddon (*ARAB* 2 §561).

113. *ROB* 18 (B.2.4.5.1-3).

114. *ROB* 308 (S.0.1002.5.i.13'-16').

115. *AR* 2.195 (A.O.101.1.i.19).

116. For example, *AR* 2.157 (A.O.99.4.5b').

117. *AR* 2.16 (A.O.87.1.ii.75-76).

118. *ARAB* 2 §576.

119. *ARAB* 2 §561.

120. *AR* 3.184 (A.O.103.1.ii.52).

121. *ARAB* 2 §504.

122. *AR* 3.29 (A.O.102.5.iii.4).

123. Miscellaneous I.1.23-26 (Tadmor, *Inscriptions of Tiglath-pileser III*, 207). Here the king does not explicitly identify himself with the wild ox but rather describes two ox colossi with the language of royal valor and ability on the battlefield: "Fierce-Storm-[Which-Captures-Enemies-(and)]-Smashes-the-King's-Foes" and "One-That-Attains-Victories-for-the-King-[. . .]-and-Brings-Luck."

124. Letter to Assur (*ARAB* 2 §163).

125. P. A. Clayton, *Chronicle of the Pharaohs* (London: Thames and Hudson, 1994) 109.

mies: "crocodile, master of terror in the water, unapproached"; "youthful bull, firm-hearted, sharp of horns, invincible"; "fearsome lion, as you made corpses of them in their valleys"; "falcon-winged, who grasps what he espies as he desires"; "southern jackal, the racer, runner, roving the Two Lands."[126] Emulating his predecessor's penchant for such self-praise, Seti I describes himself with a similar litany of animals: "youthful bull," "crocodile," and "fearsome lion."[127] Elsewhere, Seti applies the following divine attributes to his royal eminence: "Mighty Bull," "Divine Hawk," "Prowling Wolf," and "Fierce-eyed Lion."[128] Ramses II evidently favored the lion image to convey his prowess on the battlefield.[129] The same can be said of his successor's namesake, Ramses III, who is depicted with his pet lion on a relief of his Medinet Habu temple:[130] "the heart of his majesty is violent with might, [like a] mighty [lion] falling upon the sheep."[131] Paired with the lion is the "valiant bull" whose "sharp horns are to tear open the mountains."[132] In his celebration over the Libyans in his fifth year, the same pharaoh gives this fulsome self-appraisal: "He is like the lion with a deep roar upon the mountain-tops, whose terror is feared from afar. A griffin swift in every stride, whose wings are iters of millions of years,[133] like the [. . .] of the gait of the panther, knowing his prey. . . . He sees the thick of the multitude like grasshoppers, smitten, ground down."[134]

These, along with countless other examples, establish a striking link between king and beast. The image of the wild animal is employed as a model of combat for the king to emulate. Intimidating in strength and courage, both king and wild animal have much in common on the battlefield. The king is by nature a predator, and all his enemies are, in turn, mere prey. The Libyans are quoted lamenting in the face of Ramses III's might: "The god has taken us for himself, as [prey], like wild goats creeping into the trap."[135] The royal campaign against foreign kingdoms that dare to defy the emperor's authority is a virtual small-game hunt.

126. M. Lichtheim, *Ancient Egyptian Literature* (3 vols.; Berkeley: University of California Press, 1973-80) 2.37.

127. See *ARE* 3 §117.

128. *ARE* 3 §§144, 147.

129. *ARE* 3 §§479, 498.

130. *ARE* 4 §49.

131. *ARE* 4 §41; see also §§49, 51, 62, 75, 104.

132. *ARE* 4 §41. Ramses III also likens himself to a panther, bull, and hawk (*ARE* 4 §§46, 62). Tanutamon and Amasis employ the image of the rapacious lion (§§921, 1005).

133. As Breasted explains, the expression means that the distances achieved with his wings would demand millions of years to cover under normal means (*ARE* 4 §46n.b).

134. *ARE* 4 §46.

135. *ARE* 4 §91.

Hunting Expeditions

Even more numerous than specific self-references to wild animals in the royal annals are accounts of the king's hunting expeditions. In light of the extant annals, Tiglath-pileser I appears to be the first Assyrian king to make mention of royal forays in the wild, thereby setting an example for future kings to follow in addition to empire building. His account is sandwiched between his battle and building reports:

> The gods Ninurta and Nergal gave me their fierce weapons and their exalted bow for my lordly arms. By the command of the god Ninurta, who loves me, with my strong bow, iron arrowheads, and sharp arrows, I slew four extraordinarily strong wild virile bulls in the desert, in the land Mittani. . . . I brought their hides and horns to my city Assur. I killed ten strong bull elephants in the land Harran and the region of the River Habur (and) four live elephants I captured. I brought the hides and tusks (of the dead elephants) with the live elephants to my city Assur. By the command of the god Ninurta, who loves me, I killed on foot 120 lions with my wildly outstanding assault. In addition, 800 lions I felled from my light chariot. I have brought down every kind of wild beast and winged bird of the heavens whenever I have shot an arrow.[136]

Of note is that this extended section appears immediately prior to Tiglath-pileser's statement of gaining "complete dominion over the enemies of the god Assur."[137] The wild animals slain by the king are at some level lumped together with Assur's rebellious enemies. One animal that is particularly associated with the sea is the so-called sea horse, the *nāḫiru*,[138] whose basalt replica, along with that of the mountain *burḫiš* (yak?),[139] was stationed at the palace entrance as a testimony to the king's unrivaled status as lord of land and sea. The royal hunt was thus no recreational exercise; it was akin to protecting his kingdom against hostile enemies, animal and human. The land of the wild was the king's proving ground for extending his rule to the far reaches of the world. As the "expert in the hunt,"[140] by vanquishing animal and human foe alike, the ruler could call himself "king of the universe."[141]

136. *AR* 2.25-26 (A.O.87.1.vi.58-84).
137. *AR* 2.25 (A.O.87.1.vi.85).
138. *AR* 2.37 (A.O.87.3.24).
139. *AR* 2.44 (A.O.87.4.67-71).
140. *AR* 2.25 (A.O.87.1.vi.57).
141. For example, *AR* 2.13, 66, 67 (A.O.87.1.i.29; A.O.87.24.2; A.O.87.25.2).

Following the account of his victories, Tiglath-pileser I offers his construction reports of various temples and fortifications. In connection with his monumental building programs, the king refers to forming herds of deer, gazelles, and ibex, "which the gods Assur and Ninurta, the gods who love me, had given me in the course of the hunt in high mountain ranges. I numbered them like flocks of sheep" for sacrifice.[142] In short, wild animals, including those that could be semi-domesticated, figured in the king's military and restorative activities. Hunting and herding were the tasks of empire building.[143]

Tiglath-pileser I, the consummate hunter, set an example for his successors. Cementing the genre of the hunt, Assur-bel-kala, who began his reign three years after Tiglath-pileser's tenure, boasts of his hunting spoils immediately following his account of plundering the troublesome Arameans: three hundred lions and six (?) wild bulls.[144] The opening statement: "The gods Ninurta and Nergal, who love my priesthood, gave to me the wild beasts and commanded me to hunt," henceforth serves as the formulaic preface to most hunting reports. A court scribe extended the list of wild game the king had bagged and left the numbers blank for future insertion or confirmation. Those that can be identified include wild bulls, elephants, panthers, bears, wild boars, ostriches, onagers, and wolves.[145] The "nāḫiru in the Great Sea" assumes pride of place as the first entry,[146] and the exotic "beasts of the Great Sea,"[147] including the crocodile and "river-man," all tribute from Egypt, round out the list, forming a literary envelope. As separate entries, similar to Tiglath-pileser's list, the herds, from gazelles to deer, are listed.[148]

Beginning with Adad-narari II, the demarcation between herded and hunted animal becomes blurred. Included in his herds are several of the more hostile animals, all maintained within Assur, the "Inner City": lions, wild bulls, elephants, along with onagers, deer, and ostriches.[149] The latter is a special target of Tukulti-Ninurta II's[150] and Ashurnasirpal II's predatory in-

142. AR 2.26 (A.O.87.1.vii.5-11).
143. Herding animals corresponds to the stock royal epithet of "shepherd" (e.g., AR 2.13 [A.O.87.1.i.34]; 2.194 [A.O.101.1.i.13]; Tiglath-pileser III's self-reference as the "shepherd of mankind" (Iran Stele I A.27; Tadmor, Inscriptions of Tiglath-pileser III, 97). Tukulti-Ninurta I's self-reference is particularly apt: "I set my foot upon the neck of the lands (and) shepherded the extensive black-headed people like animals" (AR 1.234 [A.O.78.1.i.29-31]).
144. AR 2.93 (A.O.89.2.iii.29'-35').
145. AR 2.103 (A.O.89.7.iv.22-25).
146. Line 3.
147. Line 29.
148. Lines 19-20.
149. AR 2.154 (A.O.99.2.126-27).
150. AR 2.175 (A.O.100.5.81).

stincts.[151] Along with the 450 strong lions and 390 wild bulls, Ashurnasirpal slays two hundred ostriches "like caged birds,"[152] as well as forms herds of wild bulls, lions, ostriches, and monkeys.[153] Ashurnasirpal's hunting expedition concludes with the following remark: "I added by force additional territory to Assyria (and) people to its population."[154] Given their literary juxtaposition, hunting and herding wild animals are associated with annexing and repopulating foreign territories.[155]

Beginning at least with Tiglath-pileser I, the hunting report continued as a staple of many royal annals: Shalamaneser III repeatedly employs the genre,[156] as well as lists in more matter-of-fact fashion his encounters with wild animals on his return trips from the Amanus range.[157] Ashurbanipal commissions a series of reliefs celebrating his might over wild lions, and for good reason.[158] Owing to Adad's abundant rains, his reign was faced with an unusual proliferation of lions, against which he had to conduct campaigns to ensure the safety of his kingdom.[159] Campaigns and hunting expeditions were often reported in close juxtaposition: for example, Shamshi-Adad V mentions killing "three startled lions" immediately prior to surrounding an enemy city.[160]

The hunting excursions of the pharaohs are also prominently featured in Egyptian records, although, from a literary standpoint, they are not as stereotypically conveyed as those described in Assyrian annals. Nevertheless, hunting was an important exercise of the royal office. Physical bravery demonstrated in the royal hunt became an important attribute of king and prince by the time of the New Kingdom. Amenmose, the younger son of Thutmose I and Queen Mutnofret, who assumed the title of "Great Army Commander," is described in a broken stela as hunting wild animals in the Giza desert near the Great Sphinx, a favorite playground of the royal

151. The importance attached to Ashurnasirpal's hunting expeditions is quite evident in the series of bronze bands that bear engraved epigraphs referring exclusively to his hunting successes over wild oxen and lions (AR 2.350 [A.O.101.92, 93, 94, 95]).

152. AR 2.291 (A.O.101.30.89).

153. Lines 97-99.

154. Lines 100-101.

155. For an overview of Assyria's policy in controlling satellites, vassals, and provinces, see J. M. Miller and J. H. Hayes, A History of Ancient Israel and Judah (Philadelphia: Westminster, 1986) 320-22.

156. AR 3.41 (A.O.102.6.iv.40-44); AR 3.84 (A.O.102.16.341'-47').

157. AR 3.54-55 (A.O.102.10.iii.42-43, iv.20-22).

158. ARAB 2 §§1021-25.

159. ARAB 2 §935.

160. AR 3.187 (A.O.103.1.iv.3-4).

princes.[161] Big game hunting became a major prestige sport during the New Kingdom, made all the more exciting by the development of the composite bow and horse-drawn chariot.[162]

Examples abound. One prominently displayed relief on the Medinet Habu temple is that of a dramatic lion hunt that "interrupts" the series of reliefs depicting Ramses III campaigning against the Northerners.[163] The tablet featured between the paws of the Great Sphinx describes the young pharaoh in training, Thutmose IV, hunting lions and wild goats on his chariot.[164] Amenemhab's biography of Thutmose III recounts a successful hunt in Naharin in which 120 elephants are bagged.[165] A scarab records the early hunting achievements of Amenhotep III in the Delta: mounted on a horse (or chariot) and with his whole army behind him, the king has a herd of wild cattle surrounded by an enclosure and slain in a fashion similar to the siege of a city.[166] In his tenth year Amenhotep issued numerous scarabs commemorating his success in lion hunting.[167] Even the female pharaoh Hatshepsut depicts herself on a lower portico that fronts her magnificent mortuary temple, *Djeser-Djeseru* (Deir el-Bahri), in the traditional role of the "18th Dynasty huntin', shootin', and fishin' pharaoh."[168]

In summary: fraught with ideological significance, the wild animal hunt had everything to do with the public maintenance of royal character. Indeed, it came to be an integral part of the exercise of royal office. It primarily confirmed the valor and strength of the king in combat. Frequently juxtaposed with accounts of military engagements, the royal hunt was a military campaign in miniature; it could even involve the royal army. Nevertheless, the royal hunt and the military campaign were different. Of the various accounts of military campaigns surveyed, rarely is the enemy likened to the dangerous animals that made up the big game hunt. Assyrian or Egyptian might was considered too overwhelming to be challenged by other foreign kingdoms in

161. J. A. Tyldesley, *Hatchepsut: The Female Pharaoh* (London: Viking, 1996) 75-76.

162. As Tyldesley points out, such freedom of movement stood in stark contrast to the Middle Kingdom style of hunting, which had the hunter standing before a penned group of "wild" animals (*Hatchepsut*, 76).

163. *ARE* 4 §74n.b.

164. *ARE* 2 §813.

165. *ARE* 2 §588.

166. As Breasted points out, the language is similar to Thutmose III's description of the siege of Megiddo (*ARE* 2 §864n.d).

167. *ARE* 2 §865.

168. Tyldesley, *Hatchepsut,* 174.

the role of noble predator. As a rule, the rebels of the king were disparagingly portrayed as pathetic animals, whether domestic or wild.

In combat the king had the sole prerogative of assuming the role of archetypal predator before his enemies. Yet in the hunt proper, the king was never a wild beast but always the fully armed king. At the top of both the food chain and the chain of command, the king was an armed warrior among predators and a fierce predator among human enemies. There is no honor in hunting sheep or mice, unlike stalking crocodiles and lions. Likewise, no king can afford to scurry from combat like a wild ass; no scavenger is he, whether in victory or in retreat. Job too recalls the imagery of the hunt when he proudly defends his royal worthiness: "I broke the fangs of the unrighteous, and made them drop their prey from their teeth" (29:17). Here Job likens the wicked to rapacious lions, not mice or grasshoppers, which he has disarmed. The wicked are deemed predatory, and the lions, similar to Eliphaz's disdain for them in 4:10-11, are guilty by association.

In addition to consuming wild animals and enemies along the path of empire building, kings give attention to capturing and herding predators for public consumption. For example, Ashurnasirpal II gives a comprehensive list of the various wild animal herds he captured and bred for the sake of displaying "to all the people of my land."[169] A vivid testimony to the king's prowess in ruling his kingdom was his ability to cause "the beasts of the plain" to lie down "as if at home."[170] As the crown of civilized culture, the king could domesticate the wild, even subdue and tame chaos itself. As savage predator, the king ruthlessly eviscerated his enemies like defenseless fish or fowl, vanquishing the chaos of rebellion. Whether slaying or domesticating the animals of the wild, annihilating or imprisoning his enemies, the ancient Near Eastern king was the consummate warrior/shepherd[171] who could proclaim himself lord over both nature and civilization, "king of the universe." In light of the plethora of predatory labels affixed to the king in the royal annals, this doublesidedness of royal character suggests a special bond between noble beast and king that was evidently not shared by the king and his pathetic human enemies. As in the case of Ramses's pet lion or of the *nahiru* replicas — in addition to the numerous bull and lion colossi,[172] the "beasts of mountain and seas" that graced the palace thresh-

169. *AR* 2.226 (A.O.101.2.31b-38a).

170. *ARAB* 2 §811.

171. See Tukulti-Ninurta I's self-proclamation as "prince," "shepherd," and "herdsman" (*AR* 1.273 [A.0.78.23.85-87]).

172. See Sennacherib's building report of his "palace without rival" in Nineveh, which featured eight bronze lion colossi and four mountain sheep of silver and copper set up at the entrances (*ARAB* 2 §367).

olds[173] — the predators of chaos were turned into instruments of human hegemony, conscripted into the arsenal of royal propaganda. Some were incorporated into the formation of the king's very identity.

Job in No-Man's-Land

Similar animals populate the landscape of Yahweh's response to Job. As noted earlier, Job concludes his magisterial defense (chs. 29–31) with two pertinent observations about himself: (1) recalling the prime years of his life, Job likens himself to a "king among his troops" (29:25); and (2) Job later despairs over his kinship with the jackal and ostrich (30:29). Together they represent the summit and nadir of Job's character. Moreover, both remarks are linked to the theme of mourning: as king, Job comforted mourners (29:25); in league with the animals of lamentation, Job's "pipe [is turned] to the voice of those who weep" (30:31). Confronted now by a gratuitous Creator and a populated cosmos, Job is about to discover a community in which the ravages of lament are displaced by the vitality of dignity and grace.

The series of animals of 38:39–39:30 populate a land utterly marginal to Job. As a consummate sage, Job was raised in a land of sages, as Eliphaz sternly reminds him: "I will show you . . . what sages have told, and their ancestors have not hidden, to whom alone the land was given, and no stranger passed among them" (15:17-19). Eliphaz's comment recalls a time when, conceivably, there was no alien *(zār)* in the land. But a pure land, swept clean of Canaanites and sojourners, was never realized, at least in Israel's turbulent history, although the ideal evidently existed as a fervent goal in the historical consciousness of certain ancient traditions (e.g., Josh 3:10; 6:21). The irony, however, runs much deeper when one recalls that Eliphaz is a Temanite instructing Job, an Uzite, both cultural outsiders from Israel's national purview. Yet what binds these national representatives is the common ideological landscape that gives rise to Eliphaz's statement. His instructive rebuke reflects the provincial landscape of national culture; the land is given to the ancestors of the wise *(ḥăkāmîm);* they alone possess it (15:18). By contrast, foreigners have no claim to the land; they are profiled as the wicked who writhe in pain and aimlessly roam the land for sustenance (vv. 20-23), anticipating Job's disparagement of the outcasts in his final defense (30:1-8). Both Eliphaz and Job, despite their differing nationalities, have had a hand in cultivating this land.

When Job is shown that the land sustains far more than the human

173. *AR* 2.276 (A.O.101.23.19-20 [Ashurnasirpal II]).

covenantal partners of the Lord of history, Job's ideological landscape suffers a tectonic shift. The land is now stocked with strange and foreboding creatures, and notably missing is any fellow sage.[174] Moreover, these exotic beasts are profiled in ways that are flagrantly at odds with their stereotypical portrayals attested elsewhere in ancient Near Eastern tradition. Each animal in its own way overturns certain values long cherished by Job and his community.[175]

The archetype of wild nobility and aggression, the lion opens Yahweh's litany of animals (38:39-40). Yet the lion's lordly status never sees the light of day in this vignette. The focus, rather, is on the lion's sustenance and dependency, not its ferocity: "Can you hunt the prey *for* the lion?" The lion is neither subject nor object of the hunt; rather it is its beneficiary. The lion, along with the raven, is simply another creature that must rely on divine sustenance, for human agents will have nothing to do with their care and feeding. For Job and his friends, the lion is worthy of only fear and contempt. Indeed, the contrast could not be sharper between Eliphaz's lurid description of the lion's demise (4:11-12) and Yahweh's implicit commitment to sustain the lion. In the former, lions, like those who "plow iniquity," must perish before an angry and just God (4:11). For Job, the extinction of the lion, a symbol of wickedness, is a good riddance (29:17). In Job's world the lion can symbolize the predacious greed that threatens the community to its core. In the divine economy, however, the lion's appetite is satisfied, but through no efforts of its own, suggesting a vulnerability also shared by the raven: "Who provides for the raven its prey, when its young ones cry to God and wander about for lack of food?" (38:41).

Divine discourse about the lion's sustenance treads where human discourse refuses to go: Job and his friends will have nothing to do with providing for the lion; they have rejected the lion, marked it for death in their calls for retributive justice, whether wrought by divine or human agency. Yahweh, however, sustains the lion and his pride, which are all too susceptible to hunger, if not to the slings and arrows of human prejudice. In short, this king of beasts is unveiled as a vulnerable creature in Yahweh's natural kingdom, "worthy," as it were, of divine gratuitousness. The lion's juxtaposition with the raven is striking. Linked by a wordplay — "ambush" (*'āreb*) and "raven" (*'ōrēb*)[176] — the pairing of these wildly different animals is made possible by their shared need for nourishment. Yahweh has transformed an object of fear and disdain to one of compassion. All of this flies in the face of Job's worldview, which is sharply

174. See, e.g., the figure of the ostrich, which is said to lack all wisdom (39:13-18).

175. For a general survey of wild animals in Palestine during biblical times see O. Borowski, *Every Living Thing: Daily Use of Animals in Ancient Israel* (Walnut Creek, Calif.: Alta Mira, 1998) 185-206.

176. J. E. Hartley, *The Book of Job* (NICOT; Grand Rapids: Eerdmans, 1988) 505n.4.

divided between the wild and the cultured. Job has no more need of lions on his land than he has need of the wicked in his community. Who provides for the lion and the raven? The rhetorical question is one that broaches not just ability but desire and will. Job once cast himself as a "father to the needy" (29:16), as one who wholeheartedly provided for the poor (31:16-19), but his beneficence cannot and will not extend beyond the borders of civility.

Mountain goats, deer, and onagers are of a different order. Birth, vitality, and freedom mark their livelihood. As browsing animals, they do not inspire dread, although they too are objects of the royal hunt, noted for their agility and flight.[177] Moreover, they are employed to typify the cowardly enemies of the king. Nevertheless, the wild goats are given their due as creatures of strength and dignity. Yahweh prompts Job to think about the calving of kids and fawns. The birthing event is a time when life hangs in a delicate balance. But vulnerability is not what is stressed in the birthing of goats and deer, as it was in the care and feeding of the lordly lion. Birth for these agile browsers marks a veritable explosion of new life that needs no guardianship.[178] From birth erupts offspring that quickly develop in strength and freedom, growing up "in the open" (babbār, 39:4a) without need of a shepherd or any other protective agent. Indeed, these animals mature never to return to their place of origin and nurture. Not contained in a herd, they exercise their individual freedom in excess. Such animals lead a life of absolute autonomy, irrespective of human agency. The questions concerning knowledge of their gestation periods and reproductive habits draw from the science of husbandry (cf. Gen 30:31-45). But Job must respond to such questions in abject ignorance; he is no herdsman, royal or otherwise. Neither is God in any traditional sense. Protective supervision in no way figures in this form of divine care. On the one hand, shepherding inevitably entails a return of the herd to some location for services rendered; on the other hand, providential care eschews any "return."

The onager (Equus hemionus hemippus or Equus hemionus onager) pushes the limits of autonomy by giving such freedom a defiant, polemical edge. The wasteland is where true independence lies, away from the commotion of city life. Home is where the wild ass roams. The demarcation between civilization and the wild could not be more sharply drawn, completely overturning Job's worldview. It is in the settled domain, the city (qiryâ), where chaos has its home: tumult (hămôn) and bondage define its identity. By contrast, the steppe and salt lands provide the necessary space for freedom and self-provision. As in

177. Newsom, "Job," 609; Keel, Jahwehs Entgegnung, 87-94.
178. Newsom appropriately stresses the protective nuance conveyed in the verb šmr in 39:1b ("Job," 609-10).

the case of the sea's birth, Job's ideological landscape is turned topsy-turvy by the onager's perspective. The "outside" is no longer the locus of lament; it is within the crown of human culture that cruelty and chaos are lodged, from the onager's perspective. Such a moral inversion also wreaks havoc on Job's caricature of the wild ass. As an object of both pity and disdain (24:5; 30:7), the image of the onager for Job evokes the category of the underclass, of banishment from communal existence, for the onager must forage on the bare heights for its sustenance. Yahweh implodes such prejudice by investing the onager with dignity, so much so that the emblem of culture is thereby construed as the arena of dehumanization. The city is a virtual prison from which the onager has been liberated. "Who has loosed the bonds of the swift ass?" Like Israel's exodus to freedom, the onager has been released from the urban house of bondage. But while the Israelites in their exodus replaced slavery with servanthood in their settlement in the promised land, the onager remains scot-free from any form of service in the wilderness. Such is the virtue of the wild.

Defiance of domestication is further stressed in the image of the wild ox or now extinct auroch (*Bos primigenius*, 39:9-11).[179] Versed in the art of eluding its captors, the onager poses no threat to human beings. The auroch is another matter. A favorite target of royal hunters, the wild ox used its horns as weapons for goring. Its strength, emphasized here, was something to be feared.[180] So Yahweh taunts Job to tame the auroch, to bind it for service, to rely on its strength to work the fields. But like the mountain goats, the wild ox remains ever free from any compulsion to "return" (v. 12).

The ostrich and the warhorse find common ground in their intrepid natures, yet they could not be more apart in their indigenous environments. The former's home is found in the uninhabited wasteland; the latter's livelihood is found in the heat of human combat. Their pairing is particularly telling, for although they share the same scene of conflict, they find themselves on opposite sides of the bow: the horse mounted by the hunter aiming the weapon at the ostrich. Yet their opposing roles are beside the point. Both share in the exercise of courage with only a difference in degree. Whereas the warhorse's bravery is harnessed and focused in battle, the ostrich exhibits an absurd courage when challenged, throwing all caution to the wind to the point of jeopardizing its young. The unique title for the ostrich in this passage is itself suggestive, "(joy) screecher" (*rěnānîm*, v. 13a; cf. v. 18b).[181] Earlier Job drew from the ostrich's tra-

179. See Borowski, *Every Living Thing*, 190-91.
180. See also Num 23:22; 34:8; Deut 33:17; Pss 22:21 (MT 22); 92:10 (MT 11).
181. See the use of the cognate *rěnānâ* in Job 3:7; 20:5; Ps 100:2. For further discussion over translation, see Newsom, "Job," 610-11; Keel, *Jahwes Entgegnung*, 67-68n.232.

ditional association with lamentation to highlight his own miserable state (vv. 29-31; cf. Lam. 4:3; Mic 1:8). This ostrich, however, connotes joy unbounded; its wild flapping and penetrating laughter exhibit the throes of ecstasy,[182] confounding Job's preconceived notions about the somber ostrich.

Lamentably, such abandonment confounds the ostrich as well, for it cannot distinguish between real danger and harmless threat. The ostrich stands its ground, wings outstretched and fully exposed, laughing at horse and rider to its own peril. Yet, remarkably, no shame is associated with such conduct. It is not the ostrich's fault, this creature of careless exuberance. Yahweh has made it this way, devoid of wisdom but resplendent in its heedless valiancy. An unnecessary but utterly glorious martyrdom awaits it, a fate preferable to the crushing burden of domestication. Associated with the barren desert are not only divinely fashioned creatures of dignity and cunning, but also that creature of rapture and nonsense, all exercising their freedom in unique ways, appropriate to the species. The ostrich strikes a poise that is as dignified as it is absurd in the face of clear and present danger.

Such danger comes from the warhorse, the ostrich's assailant,[183] yet it shares a courage equally heedless of the consequences. Laughing at fear itself, the warhorse lusts for battle as if in a sexual frenzy: snorting, pawing violently, ecstatic, and unrestrainable.[184] Its seemingly domesticated vocation as a harnessed weapon of war is rife with references to unbridled passion. In this respect, the warhorse is more a creature of the wild than of civilization, a veritable warrior god.[185] Its "taming" is only apparent, as ostensible as that of any ancient Near Eastern king on the prowl for combat: "For three days the hero explored the mountain, his bold heart yearning for battle,"[186] so Shalmaneser III describes his impatience with delayed gratification.

Lastly, flying raptors inspire wonder at their ability to traverse heights and distances humanly impossible (39:26-28). Their nests are as unattainably high as the horizontal distances they cover are vast. But awe is not the only response this final section on the animal kingdom is intended to provoke. This last scene concludes on a dissonant note that can only prompt revulsion: fledgling vultures[187]

---

182. Not only the name but also the verb denoting wing movement (ʿālas) suggests a display of irrepressible joy (v. 13).

183. Of note is that the warhorse is directed by its rider to hunt the ostrich, suggesting a *human* cause behind this scene of conflict, rather than a natural state of affairs.

184. For more lurid detail, see Newsom's treatment of this passage in "Job," 611-12.

185. Habel observes similar terminology applied to warrior deities (*Job*, 547).

186. *AR* 3.22 (A.O.102.2.ii.71).

187. The term *nešer* in v. 27 can be translated either as "eagle" (so, e.g., NRSV, NIV) or "vulture," but the subsequent context suggests the latter (see Mic 1:16; BDB, 676-77).

feasting on the blood of the slain in battle (v. 30). The scene is grotesquely disorienting. War provides fodder for carrion eaters; their prey are the mortally wounded. Yet such a horrifying scene is fitting, at least from a literary standpoint, within the larger catalogue of vignettes: the vulture's prey corresponds to that of the raven (38:41). In short, God provides, but in ways that invariably disturb human sense and sensibility. Job's education reaches a pause with the image of human battle, as seen through the eyes of horse and raptor, lingering in Job's mind.

At the conclusion of the first litany of animals, Job has witnessed firsthand the perceptions and sensibilities of particular wild animals. It is significant that the animals are not brought to Job, like those brought to the 'ādām of Gen 2:19 for their naming. Job is not a new Adam who classifies and defines the animals in relation to himself. Rather, he is catapulted into their domains. Instead of being presented with a parade of exotic animals, Job has come to see what they see, to prance with their hooves, to roam their expansive ranges, and to fly with wings to scout out prey. The poetry permits no escape; the captivating language is designed to take hold of Job and drive him to a heightened awareness of Yahweh's world and, ultimately, his own. Yahweh's response to Job is the supreme exercise in moral imagination, for in the realm of imaginative discourse empathy is born. What is it like to suffer hunger like the raven's brood, to spread one's arms and, like the falcon, soar the heights of heaven, to defy mortal danger like the ostrich? These are not pointless questions designed merely to titillate.[188] They are inherently imaginative questions, intrinsically moral inquiries.

Yahweh's intent is not to pique Job's curiosity but, in part, to disorient him. The moral horizons of Job's cultural landscape are infinitely broadened to take seriously the outward margins of existence. Shaken from his sheltered and dualistic worldview that thrived on the distinction between the righteous and the wicked, between culture and nature, between honor and contempt, Job must now think globally in empathetic ways. Empathy becomes the heuristic tool for new discoveries, transforming objects, whether of pity, disdain, or fear, into subjects of intrinsic worth. Job has come to discern some surprising things about these denizens of the margins. They are not what they seem from the outside looking in. From the inside out, they provoke outright reversals of commonly held assumptions: the vulnerable lion providentially sustained, the fiercely independent onager unencumbered by the trappings of

188. Midgley makes a similar point with the following series of questions: "What is it like to be an incubating gull? still more an emperor penguin? What are chimpanzee carnivals? Why do elephants interest themselves deeply in a dead elephant . . . ? Goodness knows. These are real questions" (*Beast and Man*, 351).

culture, the fearless ostrich laughing all the way to its death. An object of fear and contempt is transformed into one of providential care and intrinsic dignity. The image of the outcast doomed to a life of subsistence is now an icon of liberation and self-sufficiency. The plaintive cry of lamentation gives way to the laughter of defiance.

With the exception of the first pairing, a thread that runs throughout the sequence of presented animals is the theme of impossible domestication. These animals boldly indulge in their God-given freedom, controverting all attempts at taming them. To be sure, the mountain goat, wild ox, onager, and warhorse all have their more domestic counterparts. But any confusion between them and their sibling beasts of burden is laid to rest in their vivid descriptions. The mountain goat and wild ox are destined never to return for services rendered, the warhorse flexes its muscles to charge headlong into battle without reservation, the ostrich flaps its wings in defiant joy, and the onager roams and revels in unimpeded freedom. Liberated by Yahweh's leading hand, they are free of the human master's heavy hand.

By construing these wild creatures as icons of freedom and dignity, Yahweh indelibly associates civility with servility. Human culture is the chaos of oppression for the onager and the harness of slavery for the auroch. Where there is violence, a human hand is present: the driver directs the warhorse in the hunt and battle (39:18), and the slain in battle provide food for the fledgling vultures (v. 30). Although the ostrich ignorantly treats its young cruelly, outright malice has its home in human culture. There is a significant difference in the way human malice and the ostrich's cruelty are profiled. The latter is due to the ostrich's senseless abandonment of its brood under the threat of attack (vv. 14-16). By contrast, human beings are natural instigators of violence and masters of oppression. In the eyes of the wild, humans seem to thrive on oppression and slaughter. It is their way. But even more damning is the identity of those who stand to gain from the ravages of human conflict: not the human victors but the scavenging raptors, who "suck up" the blood of the slain, these nurslings of death (v. 30).

All this is called to Job's undivided attention, setting in motion the reformation of his moral identity. Where is Job qua human being in this cavalcade of exotic beasts? At first glance, one might claim nowhere. Often noted is that humanity has no place in this pageantry of the periphery, that creation presented by Yahweh is thoroughly unanthropocentric.[189] This is true as far

---

189. For example, R. A. Simkins, *Creator and Creation: Nature in the Worldview of Ancient Israel* (Peabody, Mass.: Hendrickson, 1994) 163; R. Gordis, "Job and Ecology," *HAR* 9 (1985) 189-202; Newsom, "Moral Sense of Nature," 23-27; G. M. Tucker, "Rain on a Land Where No One Lives: The Hebrew Bible on the Environment," *JBL* 116 (1997) 12-15.

as it goes, but it is important not to forget that Job is the one addressed throughout Yahweh's discourse; it is on *his* behalf that these animals proudly go before him for his scrutiny, their eyes and innermost passions becoming, in some sense, his own. They are presented by God for Job's moral education, forcefully leading him out *(educo)* to uncharted territory. As beasts of burden and of the wild were formative in maintaining the king's distinctly royal character, so these denizens of the margins help to reshape Job's identity. Job had earlier declared he would bind his written indictment on his crown and approach God "like a prince" (32:37). Job, the would-be king of his community who broke the fangs of the unrighteous, comforted mourners, and sustained the community (29:17, 25), is now pushed off his mountain. His familial kingdom has been ripped away and, like Daniel's Nebuchadnezzar (Dan 4:28-37 [MT 25-34]),[190] he has been cast out into a no-man's-land to experience the ways of the wild firsthand.

Job's response to Yahweh says it all: "I am small" (*hēn qallōtî*, Job 40:4a). The antithesis of "heaviness" or "honor" *(kbd)*, the state of smallness *(qll)* connotes self-humiliation. As Carol Newsom points out, Job's reference to covering his mouth (40:4b) recalls the gesture of respect that he once elicited from the leaders of his community (29:9).[191] Now Job refrains from responding to Yahweh's summons to make his case, an act of self-deprecating deference. This man of royal poise is now demoted to the rank of a commoner in unwelcomed league with the outcast animals. Yet Job's transformation has only begun. His newfound kinship with the beasts is not cause for disgrace and lamentation, as Job had thought (30:29). To his surprise, Job is not thrust out into utter isolation or into the company of miscreants, animal or human. Rather he has found himself in *good* company. Job had heretofore viewed life in the wild as impoverished and fragile, a drab wasteland of danger and deprivation. But Yahweh has landscaped a supposedly godforsaken terrain with the vivid contours of strength and dignity, of vitality and freedom, bringing rain on an empty land devoid of human life (38:26) and exposing Job's worldview as the product of misguided speciesism. Job is no superior, royal or otherwise, within the expanse of creation. In company with the worthy citizens of the marginalized, Job can, if he so chooses, find common cause with these members of the wild whose liberator and sustainer is the King of heaven. Like the wild man

190. After boasting of his power and glory, Nebuchadnezzar, as foretold by the prophet, is driven from human society to dwell with "the animals of the field" and "eat grass like oxen," where he comes to resemble a bird (Dan 4:28-33 [MT 25-30]). His experience of banishment prompts him to extol the "King of heaven" (vv. 34-37 [MT 31-34]).

191. Newsom, "Job," 613.

Enkidu prior to his incorporation into society,[192] Job can stand up, shake the dust off his feet, slough off his misconceptions, and run with the wild asses.

The issue of Job's identity and place in this new landscape of creation is more clearly delineated in Yahweh's final speech (40:6–42:6 [MT 41:26]), which lifts up the legendary beasts Behemoth and Leviathan for Job's consideration. Before these mythic animals present themselves, however, Yahweh issues one more challenge to Job (40:6-8). Job is summoned to govern the cosmos: "Deck yourself with majesty and dignity; clothe yourself with glory and splendor. Pour out the overflowings of your anger, and look on all who are proud, and abase them" (vv. 10-11). On the one hand, many scholars assume that Yahweh is challenging Job to be in some sense *like Yahweh* in theophanic majesty, governing the world with divine might.[193] On the other hand, Athalya Brenner contends that "God is conceding that he cannot dispose of the wicked and of evil, at least no more than Job can."[194] Yet it is curious that Yahweh eschews all self-references in this description of divine might and justice (vv. 9-13): not "my arm" but an "arm like El" is what Yahweh challenges Job to adopt (v. 9).

Furthermore, Yahweh makes explicit reference to Job's anger *('ap)*, not divine wrath, as the emotive basis of governance (v. 11). As Newsom points out, the language is thoroughly stereotypical, "almost clichéd."[195] And like the overturning of Job's cultural preconceptions about the arid wasteland, Yahweh is in the business of reforming Job's conception of God. Rather than challenging Job to emulate Yahweh per se, Yahweh invites Job to wreak his *own* brand of justice on the earth as if he were a god, to enforce the kind of justice that requires the subjugation of the proud (v. 12). In effect, Yahweh dares Job to project his brand of justice into the cosmic stratosphere, to rig it with the trappings of divinity, and to execute it. Granted, the challenge is an unfair one, but that is beside the point in a challenge fraught with unrelieved irony. Yahweh's challenge is meant to question Job in his self-righteous anger and suggest, without much subtlety, that human fury is no basis for cosmic governance.

192. Tablet I of the Epic of Gilgamesh. Enkidu, who "knew neither people nor country" and whose strength was like a "sky-bolt of Anu," had the reputation of helping the wild beasts escape the grasp of hunters. See S. Dalley's translation in *Myths from Mesopotamia: Creation, The Flood, Gilgamesh, and Others* (Oxford: Oxford University Press, 1989) 53.

193. For example, Habel, *Job*, 533; cf. A. Brenner, "God's Answer to Job," *VT* 31 (1981) 129-37.

194. Brenner, "God's Answer to Job," 133.

195. Newsom, "Job," 616.

It is on this issue of subjugating the proud that the larger-than-life creatures Behemoth and Leviathan are introduced. The former is modeled most likely after the water buffalo,[196] although precise identification is unnecessary. Like the auroch, Behemoth is known for its unsurpassed and untamable strength (40:24; cf. 39:10a). Yet like the domestic ox, it grazes peacefully (40:15). Like the warhorse, Behemoth is a liminal creature on the boundary between culture and chaos, sharing traits from both realms. Yet its strength is of a more settled nature. It does not lust after the heat of conflict, though lust there is for this ponderous beast.[197] Rather it can be found lounging lazily underneath the lotus or peacefully grazing while the wild animals play nearby (vv. 20-21). Moreover, its very title, a so-called majestic plural of the ordinary word for domestic animal, suggests the rendering "The Animal."[198] This consummate animal embodies elements from both realms, while still frustrating all attempts at domesticating it. Job had made an oblique reference to just such a being in 12:7 as a repository of wisdom. He must now learn from this animal in all of its singular glory.

What Job learns is that he and Behemoth share some solidarity of origin: "Look at Behemoth, which I made along with you" (ʿimmĕkā, 40:15). The significance of this reference is never explicitly spelled out;[199] one can only assume, however, some correspondence between Job and this mighty beast, his twin, as it were. The reference to its apparent primordial nature ("the first [rēʾšît] of the great acts of God") in v. 19 resonates with Eliphaz's sarcastic accusation that Job considers himself the "firstborn of the human race (hărî[ʾ]šôn ʾādām) . . . brought before the hills" (15:7). A temporal nuance is clearly meant, as in Prov 8:22, which describes the primordial origin of wisdom.[200] Nevertheless, the sense in Job 40:19 may be not so much temporal as essential. The Hebrew term for "first" can also connote primacy.[201] Corresponding to its name, Behemoth is quintessential animal. The following colon (v. 19b) is grammatically anomalous and most probably corrupt.[202] If it indeed refers to the Creator's approach to Behemoth with sword in hand, no mention is made of this beast's control, much less its demise. Indeed, most

196. See the range of possibilities in Newsom, "Job," 618; M. H. Pope, Job (3d ed.; AB 15; Garden City, N.Y.: Doubleday, repr. 1979) 320-22.

197. Verse 17 euphemistically describes an erection.

198. See Pope, Job, 320-21.

199. Newsom glosses over it as an incongruous referent ("Job," 618).

200. Indeed, the temporal expression in Prov 8:22 is identical to that found in Job 40:19a, suggesting a connection between wisdom and Behemoth.

201. So NIV and Newsom, "Job," 618. See Ezek 27:22; Exod 30:23; Ps 137:6.

202. See discussions by Newsom, "Job," 619; Pope, Job, 324-25.

translations render the verb modally ("can") rather than in the indicative. God could, if need be, tame the beast, but such a realization is nowhere developed or even mentioned elsewhere. Behemoth roves freely around mountains and rivers to suit itself; the need for control is moot. It appears that no domain is forbidden for this massive creature. Yet it does not roam the land attacking other creatures, animal or human. As a herbivore, it peacefully coexists with the frolicking animals of the wild.

In contrast to the warhorse, Behemoth's intrepid nature is exemplified in its stolid confidence, its mouth set against the onrushing waters of the Jordan (v. 23). Such a description alludes to previously discussed matters. Job had likened his friends to a "treacherous torrent bed" that flees and dissipates when the heat is on (6:15-18, 21), their confidence lost (v. 20). Zophar promises Job confidence and hope if he repents (11:18). Such confidence is modeled by Behemoth before the rushing waters. Perhaps unbeknownst to him, Job too has embodied such confidence by standing his ground before the verbal onslaught of his friends, controverting their arguments, and rendering them silent. Like Behemoth, Job's mouth remains pointed upstream, against the flow.[203] By his relentless defense, Job remains untamable and fearsome to his friends (40:24; cf. 6:21; 7:12). Likewise, Behemoth's fearless courage is a matter of defense, not assault. Behemoth is the archetypal animal, potent yet composed, that confirms as well as guides Job on his way toward archetypal humanity.

Finally, Leviathan, the crowning apex of Yahweh's creation, commands the scene. Like Behemoth, Leviathan is fearless (41:33 [MT 25]). Harpoons, arrows, clubs, and swords are of no avail against its coat of mail. Like that of Behemoth, Leviathan's mouth is a focus of much fascination: its tongue is irrepressible (41:1b [MT 40:25b]); its discourse is far from soothing or servile (41:3 [MT 40:28]), issuing forth fire and incinerating everything in its path (41:18-21 [MT 10-13]). This truly mythic creature associated with the watery depths is no harmless pet (41:5 [MT 40:29]; cf. Ps 104:26).[204] Its potential for

203. The reference to Behemoth's mouth is striking, suggesting some linkage with Job's character. For other possible associations between Behemoth and Job, see Brown, *Character in Crisis*, 104-6; J. G. Gammie, "Behemoth and Leviathan: On the Didactic and Theological Significance of Job 40:15–41:26," in *Israelite Wisdom: Theological and Literary Essays in Honor of Samuel Terrien* (ed. J. G. Gammie et al.; Missoula, Mont.: Scholars Press, 1978) 217-24.

204. Hostility between God and Leviathan or a comparable sea monster is unambiguously clear in other texts: Ps 74:13-14; Isa 27:1; cf. Pss 74:13; 89:10 (MT 11); Isa 27:1; 51:9; Ezek 29:3; 32:2; Job 9:13; 26:12. Indeed, Leviathan has deep roots in Ugaritic mythology as "Lotan, the Fleeing Serpent." For more comparison of the mythological allusions and roots, see Newsom, "Job," 621-23.

battle (Job 41:8 [MT 40:32]) seems to distinguish it from Behemoth, but again the graphic rhetoric focuses not on its prowess for battle but on its ability to defend itself. Leviathan too is no attack animal.

"Fantasy reigns in this description of a fire-eating dragon," so Crenshaw tersely comments in his notation for 41:18-21 (MT 10-13) in the NRSV.[205] Such poetic flights of fancy are not without purpose, however. By reveling in graphic detail about Leviathan's impregnable strength, the poet has exercised her moral imagination to the fullest.[206] As with Behemoth, the poet frequently takes leave of the caustic rhetoric of questioning Job and resorts to simple description of this formidable creature, as in the last twenty verses. Like Job among his friends, Yahweh refuses to muzzle Leviathan's mouth: "I will not silence his boasting, his mighty word, and his persuasive case" (41:12 [MT 4]).[207] Unsilenced discourse is what links Job and Leviathan. Like Leviathan's fiery discharge, Job's discourse with his friends was irrepressible, sharp, and scathing, turning their ineffectual proverbs into ashes (13:12).[208] That Yahweh refuses to silence Leviathan's boasting may indeed come as a shock to Job,[209] but it also carries literary precedent. Discourse and watery chaos also find their rhetorical intersection early on in Job's character. In the first cycle, Job decides to unloose his tongue before God and man and issue the following impassioned complaint: "Am I the Sea, or the Dragon that you place a muzzle on me?" (7:11-12).[210] Yet at no point is Job silenced before his friends; his mouth remains unrestrained, a discursive crescendo to the very end (chs. 29–31). Human agency is unable to bring Job's relentless discourse under control, and divine agency chooses not to stifle his voice.[211] Similarly, the flame of Leviathan's breath remains unquenchable.

Yet Leviathan, an earthly creature without equal, does exceed Job in

205. J. L. Crenshaw, Annotations on "Job" in *The HarperCollins Study Bible* (ed. W. A. Meeks; San Francisco: HarperCollins, 1993) 794-95.

206. Without any hard evidence, I simply suggest that given the emotive depth and poignancy of the poetry, as well as the nuanced critique of patriarchy, the ancient author/poet of Job could very well have been a woman.

207. Newsom's translation ("Job," 623). Contra Habel (*Job*, 551, 571) and Pope (*Job*, 335), the verse is not a question, although Habel's translation is preferable. Leviathan's "persuasive case" thus finds its antecedent in the previous verse, a quote from Leviathan itself: "Whoever confronts me I requite, for everything under the heavens is mine" (Habel, *Job*, 551).

208. For more ironic cross-references between Leviathan and Job, see Gammie, "Behemoth and Leviathan," 224-30; Brown, *Character in Crisis*, 106-7.

209. So Newsom, "Job," 623.

210. See M. J. Dahood, "*Mišmār* 'Muzzle' in Job 7:12," *JBL* 80 (1961) 270-71; Habel, *Job*, 153.

211. Nowhere does Yahweh command or exhort Job to shut up; indeed, God demands precisely more discourse from Job in the final scene.

sheer intensity and power. If Job even dares to domesticate this formidable beast, he does so at his own peril (41:8-9 [MT 40:32–41:1]). Job's "royal" status is once again overturned. Every kind of weapon at the king's disposal is woefully ineffective against the beast's impenetrable mail. As the final clincher, this monster of chaos bears an unrivaled royal poise: "It surveys everything that is lofty (gabōah), it is king over all that are proud (běnê-šāḥaṣ)" (41:34 [MT 26]). Leviathan is the king of kings within Yahweh's created realm, and its subjects are the intractably proud, present company included.

Yahweh's discourse comes to an abrupt end without any explanation of the significance of this lost horizon and its inhabitants. To the contrary, divine discourse concludes with the riveting image of an indomitable creature of chaos, whose rule is not of anarchy but of moral correction. Not simply the product of fantastical musings designed to inspire terror, every detail of the Leviathan's might is aesthetically limned and serves to heighten its royal stature. In the flow of presentation, this monster of the deep progresses from being an object of abject terror to a specimen of beauty (41:30-32 [MT 22-24]),[212] coming to rest within the arena of moral discourse. As king, Leviathan ensures some moral governance by towering above and surveying (lit. "seeing," r'h) the high and mighty. Yet nothing is said of any aggressive action undertaken to ensure a perfect world, as compared to Yahweh's challenge to Job in 40:11. Leviathan's penetrating gaze is somehow deemed sufficient: "its eyes are like the eyelids of the dawn" (41:18 [MT 10]), a simile that bears terrifying implications in its immediate context but conveys, nonetheless, a hint of aesthetic elegance.[213] For all its fantastic dimensions, Leviathan assumes a distinctly moral role. Its "dawnful" gaze resonates with the redemptive role the sun assumes in 38:12-15. More telling is the identical figure of speech attested in Job's initial lament in 3:9. Job pleads that the night of doom "not see the eyelids of the dawn" ('ap'appê-šāḥar). Such a dawn is the light that would impart life to Job, overturning his death wish. In its awful majesty, Leviathan wields the power of new life.

212. Newsom notes that 41:26-32 (MT 17-24) moves from images that are "progressively less violent and increasingly beautiful" ("Job," 624-25). Such beauty, however, is not simply an exercise in aesthetic appreciation but verges on the sublime. Kant's definition of sublimity is apropos: "Everything that provokes this feeling in us, including the might of nature which challenges our strength, is then . . . called sublime" (I. Kant, *Critique of Aesthetic Judgment* [tr. J. C. Meredith; Oxford: Clarendon, 1911] 114). For Kant, the sublime evokes a sense of limitlessness, which is present only in the mind of the judging subject. See T. J. J. Altizer, "The Apocalyptic Identity of the Modern Imagination," in *The Archaeology of the Imagination* (ed. C. E. Windquist; JAARS 48/2 [Chico, Calif.: Scholars Press, 1981] 20-22). This self-referential quality of the sublime, which somehow both highlights and internalizes the alien, is evident in Job's experience of the cosmos.

213. Cf. the Homeric formula, "rosy-fingered dawn."

With this horrifying image firmly planted in Job's sight, the final reversal of Job's moral worldview is set in motion. The consummate creature of chaos, the archenemy of all kings, is revealed to be the supreme king. Yet the human king, as noted above, reveled in predatory self-portrayals, whether as a ferocious dragon, slithering viper, or fierce-eyed lion on the prowl for human prey. Any ancient Near Eastern despot worth his or her salt would have eagerly welcomed Leviathan's description as a *self*-portrayal. But not Job. Leviathan is presented as the untouchable other, utterly alien but not utterly grotesque. Job cannot appropriate this creature as a king can incorporate the noble wild animals into his stock royal character. Job can only flee.

Nevertheless, a paradox runs persistently throughout this carnival of animals. All these dwellers of the outer limits are presented as wholly alien yet in some sense congruous with the developing constitution of Job's character evinced in the dialogues. Job's confident defiance before his friends is blown out of mythic proportion by Behemoth. His impenetrable defenses, which shielded him from his friends' verbal abuse, are taken into the cosmic realm by Leviathan. Unassailable dignity is modeled by the onager for the one who persisted in his integrity (2:9; 27:5). Job's combative spirit is emulated by the warhorse. Even the ostrich's absurd defiance before the hunter reflects Job's fearless approach to Yahweh, knowing full well that death is the outcome. No wonder the lordly lion is paired with the destitute raven at the outset of Yahweh's litany: both are shown to be eminently vulnerable creatures, as deprived of food and sustenance as Job was dispossessed of property and family. The former lordly patriarch, Job is found destitute by his friends. But in the heat of dialogue he finds strength and is reborn, like the mountain goats, to summon God to court and never turn back. Yahweh's litany opens where Job's conflicted saga began and it concludes where Job ended his own words (31:40), towering above his proud friends, who turn out to be mere sheep in sheep's clothing.[214]

The persistent theme of not "returning" is one that requires special attention, for both the animals and Job share this proclivity. The mountain kids go forth from their homes, never to return (*lōʾ-šābû*, 39:4); the onager enjoys its exodus of freedom from the city of slavery, roaming the mountain range (vv. 5, 8); no faith can be placed on the auroch's return *(Ketib: yāšûb)* to serve any master (v. 12); the ostrich is willing to leave (*ʿzb*) its eggs at the drop of a hat (v. 14); and the warhorse refuses to turn back *(lōʾ-yāšûb)* from conflict (v. 22). To "return" is to succumb to domestication, which is absolutely for-

---

214. Throughout his exchanges, Job frequently notes the friends' humiliating arrogance (e.g., 6:25-27; 12:2-4; 19:5).

eign to these animals' natures. Job also comes to share in this nature. Concluding his diatribe against God, Job proclaims his intent to "go, never to return *('ēlēk wĕlō' 'āšûb),* to the land of gloom and deep darkness" (10:21). Job wants God to release him from the misery of life so that he can make this journey to death unhindered (v. 20). Death is the place from which there is no return (16:22). Such is Job's hoped-for exodus.

On another front, Eliphaz exhorts Job to "return to the Almighty" *(tāšûb 'ad-šadday)* to be saved and restored (22:23; cf. 36:10).[215] This return is, of course, the turn toward repentance, the overt agenda of the friends' "consolations." But Job will have none of that. If he could ever find God, he would "approach him like a prince" (31:37), "lay [his] case before him," and "reason with him" (23:4, 7). Far from returning to God, Job intends to subpoena God and prosecute this promulgator of injustice! Thus he must resolutely "go forward" *(hlk,* 23:8a), searching in vain for the *Deus absconditus* (23:8-10) with righteousness firmly in his grasp (27:6). In short, Job and the animals share in this bold exercise of freedom to go where the culturally conditioned cannot. Through the use of similar terms denoting forward movement and return, the poet forges a common bond between beast and protagonist. They share in the proclivity to venture forth without a backward glance. The poet correlates repentance and domesticity. Job is as unrepentant as the wild animals are untamable. There is not an obsequious bone in Job's body, and the wild animals of Yahweh's harsh "indictment" confirm him in this.

Subtlety, paradox, and irony are commonly noted as the hallmarks of Joban rhetoric, even in the divine discourse.[216] But seldom noted is the final paradox, which is lodged within Job's own character vis-à-vis creation. The wild was a domain of dread as well as attraction, the landscape of *mysterium tremendum.* For the ancient Near Eastern kings, it was an arena to resist and combat, as well as annex and appropriate. Wild animals could be vanquished or tamed, as in the royal hunt, but the king, much to his credit, could also go wild, as in combat. The paradox runs deeper in Job's case. Job not only prided himself in vanquishing the wicked like wild animals, but also treated the outcast as objects of pity and disdain, as scavengers subsisting in the wild. Such classifications reflect a patriarchal prejudice that regards some members of the human race as subhuman. These values are subverted when Job finds

215. Cf. Elihu's portrayal of the repentant person, who is able to return to "his youthful vigor" (33:25).
216. See G. Fuchs's analysis of the irony behind the divine discourse in *Mythos und Hiobdichtung, Aufnahme und Umdeutung altorientalischer Vorstellungen* (Stuttgart: Kohlhammer, 1993) 288-90.

himself evicted from community and living on the mountain paths, like living on the streets with the destitute and mentally ill. Job must commiserate with the beasts of the field, and in so doing, with the outcasts of society. As the height of irony, Eliphaz's prophecy has come to fulfillment (5:22-23): Job has entered in league with the wild and found peace.

Yahweh's presentation of zoological exotica is intended to earn Job's respect, prompting him to discern incredible dignity in a land of shame, irrepressible vitality in a land of subsistence, and uncommon valor in the realm of fear. He sees himself "small" before these untamable creatures, yet at the same time finds confirmation in his own struggle and role within the arena of culture and community. Job comes to internalize these creatures of the wild, specifically the values they represent. Yet such values were already evident in attenuated form in Job's conduct with his friends. By insisting on his integrity throughout the heated exchanges, Job was to his friends a monstrous anomaly who threatened to collapse their provincial brand of moral theology. Yet for all their might, Job could not be tamed. Domesticating Job was an unmitigated failure; Job's true friends are his cohorts in the wild. Although they do not speak, by and large, their imposing yet alluring presence somehow suffices. The worth of humanless creation is an inherent worth, but the landscape also bears a functional worth in educating Job. Job is a changed man.

Job's Commencement: Dignity without Dominion

"Because we have all been brought up on a picture of the cosmos as a vast, ineluctably-grinding machine, any attempt to stress our continuity with the rest of nature tends to produce fatalism because it tends to make us feel like cogs," so moral philosopher Mary Midgley observes in the second edition of her provocative work.[217] The ancient story of Job and his brush with the wild proves otherwise. The world according to Job is anything but a dispassionate machine and Yahweh is, needless to say, no deus ex machina. Quite the opposite of fatalism, the result of Job's contact with the margins of creation grants him a new level of dignity, one that arises from within nature, not against it. Nature is a worthy partner and instructor for humankind.

No longer are conquering and controlling nature part of the equation for discerning human dignity.[218] Job discovers a self-forgetful awe in the "sheer alien pointless independent existence of animals," to quote Iris

217. Midgley, *Beast and Man,* xxix.
218. See the similar discussion in ibid., 196.

Murdoch,[219] and in so doing, discovers true integrity. Job's integrity is not what is threatened in his encounter with these creatures — he comes to see that he is a child of God as much as all these creatures are shown to be nurtured and set free by Yahweh. It is Job's patriarchal pride that is at stake, nurtured and sustained at the expense of nature and community. Job's groveling in "smallness" (40:4) does not satisfy Yahweh. Although a preliminary step, simply discerning one's contingent and insignificant status before the cosmos does not suffice.[220] Behemoth and Leviathan make their appearance only after Job's self-deprecating confession. Through their alien forms, Job discerns a link to himself: Behemoth's intrepid confidence was fashioned "along with" him; Leviathan's fire-breathing mouth was forged on the anvil of Job's own inflammatory discourse. These awesome beasts are neither projections of Job nor utterly alien or Other. They are creatures, like Job himself, but different. Consequently, they have earned Job's awe-filled respect and empathy, respect for their otherness and empathy in their God-given freedom. With all these creatures, human dominion has no place, but human dignity does.

The story of Job does not end with divine discourse; Job's response concludes the poetic discourse. He responds in a fashion in keeping with Yahweh's response to Job, in an open-ended paradox. Traditional translations that suggest repentance on the part of Job capture only one nuance of the evocative expression *wěniḥamtî ʿal* of 42:6b.[221] That the verb *nḥm* consistently denotes "comfort"[222] elsewhere in Job forces the possibility of such a meaning in Job's final words, a meaning that resonates with the book's prominent theme of consolation.[223] Job searched for the comfort of death while his friends tried to impose their brand of comfort on him by forcing his repentance. It would be a mistake, however, to limit this enigmatic expression to one meaning.[224] The ambiguity of this terse expression reflects the global ambiguity of the book. In the end, Job both retracts and finds resolution to his case against God. He repents yet finds vindication. He loses his life and comes

---

219. I. Murdoch, *The Sovereignty of Good* (New York: Schocken, 1971) 85.

220. Cf. Ps 8:2-4 (MT 3-5).

221. For the range of possibilities and the concomitant grammatical issues, see W. Morrow, "Consolation, Rejection, and Repentance in Job 42:6," *JBL* 105 (1986) 211-25.

222. Job 2:11; 7:13; 16:2; 21:34; 29:25; 42:11.

223. An alternative translation for the traditional "I repent in dust and ashes" of v. 6 is "I am comforted concerning dust and ashes," i.e., comforted by the recognition of human finitude. See Brown, *Character in Crisis*, 110; Perdue, *Wisdom in Revolt*, 237n.2; Newsom, "Moral Sense of Nature," 26.

224. So Morrow, "Consolation, Rejection, and Repentance," 211-25; Newsom, "Job," 628-29.

to find it. The outer limits of creation serve double duty for Job by deconstructing and restoring his character.

From Chaos to Community

In addition to reforming Job's own character, creation reveals the contours of
authentic community, whose diverse members exercise inalienable freedoms,
most particularly the freedom from control. Each has its appropriate domain
within the larger landscape, and yet they traverse freely, as in Behemoth's case
(40:20-23). Furthermore, a measure of interdependence is operative: the lion
and raven must feed off prey to survive, so also the vultures who clean up the
battlefield. Predation is present, but does not ultimately define the contours
of this wild community; rather freedom, vitality, fearlessness, and most of all
wondrous difference define it (see *niplā'ôt*, 42:3b). In the complexity of nature's distinctions, Job discovers something of himself.

Yahweh's praise of exotica suggests that an essential feature to human
life is being confronted with living beings that live and function in ways so
differently that they stagger us.[225] The ancient community of faith might have
found it shocking, for example, that the creatures so endearingly described by
Yahweh at no point bless or praise their Maker. To the contrary, divine pride
of workmanship is what pervades the litany. Missing is any mention of the
wild animals rendering due honor to God as a consequence of divinely rendered care, in contrast to the exilic prophet's vision of the transformed desert
(Isa 43:20). Nature does not praise God, in contrast to its role in the psalms of
praise.[226] The animals simply carry on their business, roaming, giving birth,
eating, and playing, each knowing its place. Yahweh does not present this carnival to wrench effusive words of praise from Job's lips. If so, then the experi-
ment has failed. Rather than praising God, Job comes to a clearer perception
of God and, consequently, of himself (Job 42:2-5).

The story of Job's transformation does not end in the desert either. He is
restored and returned back to the community whence he came. Job's place is
ultimately not in the wilderness among his wild compatriots, but back in the
community that once cast him out. Job's appropriate place is not in the wild;
he must turn homeward. His return does not connote repentance but restoration (42:10). Job does not arrive from the margins an erstwhile prodigal to

225. See Midgley, *Beast and Man*, 327.
226. For example, Pss 96:11-13a; 148:3-5, 7-10, 14b. See T. E. Fretheim, "Nature's
Praise of God in the Psalms," *Ex Auditu* 3 (1987) 16-30.

curry forgiveness, but as victor rejoined to family and community, comforted and restored. Job's transformation has come full circle, but has he learned anything? Indeed, Job's status as patriarch seems only heightened with his property doubled, including his draft animals (42:12; cf. 1:3). His beasts of burden are the counterparts to the animals of the wild; but their appropriate domain is Job's domicile, not the rugged mountains or bare heights. Their place remains with Job, servile and at home within Job's reestablished familial kingdom.

Many interpreters of Job have expressed their disappointment one way or another with the epilogue, and for apparent good reason. Mirroring the prose of the prologue, the conclusion of the book seems profoundly anticlimactic, comparable to a formulaic, Hollywood ending. Job has come home, and he and his new family live "happily ever after." It is as if the status quo of Job's old character has reasserted itself, but now with a vengeance, contravening all that was profoundly new in Yahweh's perspective of the world. The very fact that Job is restored to his former position as consummate patriarch is reason enough to despair, so it seems. Nevertheless, it is to the final editor's credit to have reworked the Joban folktale, filling it with combustible poetry, yet still allowing the composed prose of the epilogue to have the final say in the book.[227] For all the subversive speech, passionate dialogues, and iconoclastic revelations that constitute the bulk of the book, the Joban poet in the end reveals herself to be a master of understatement. Job has been flung out to the very margins of creation, cohabiting with alien beasts, beholding even the mighty Leviathan, only to be jerked back home. The periphery of culture and creation was for a while the hub of Job's existence, but Job has now returned to his comfortable center to live for another 140 years, no less!

Had Job remained (for whatever reason) in the wilderness, cohabiting with the beasts of the field, then an unavoidably banal message would have

---

227. The process leading to the final form of the book has been the focus of much discussion. Newsom suggests that as an alternative to the standard view in scholarship, a variant of which I endorse, a single author composed the entire book in order to generate dissonant interpretations ("Job," 323-24, 634; idem, "Cultural Politics and the Reading of Job," *BI* 1 [1993] 119-34). See also Y. Hoffman, "The Relation between the Prologue and the Speech-Cycles in Job," *VT* 31 (1981) 160-70; idem, *Blemished Perfection*, 267-70. I find it unlikely, however, that the final author of Job began from scratch, given the wholly different styles evinced in the poetry and prose. That is not to say that the poet/editor did not rework a so-called folk tale of Job, which I think she clearly did. The ironic consequence of the single-author thesis is that it entails for Newsom a thoroughly dissonant reading of Job that eschews much if not all thematic interconnection between the poetry and prose, particularly the epilogue. My view, based on a double-author/editor theory, strives to look at the subtle points of contact that the poetic editor wanted to convey in the prose.

forced itself into consideration: "Respect wild animals." But that is not the message of Job. These denizens of the margins are ultimately for Job symbols laden with the power to reorient his praxis *within* the community to which he must return. As Job had found something subtly familiar in an altogether alien terrain, something is now slightly awry in Job's all-too-familiar world. Something has changed in Job's patriarchal household, and although it does not call attention to itself with the blaring of trumpets, its silence is deafening. In light of the prologue, it is curious that no mention is made of Job rising early in the morning to offer burnt offerings on his children's behalf (1:5). No doubt the feast days continued with his new family, but Job is no longer the obsessive patriarch he once was. His sacrificial routine was motivated by fear and control. The festive gatherings of his late children signified some measure of independence from parental supervision and hinted of wanton revelry. Their activities, however, did not escape Job's attention; Job's sacrificial offerings served as the antidote to his children's potentially careless activities by warding off any possibility of incurring divine wrath. But in the absence of such fear-motivated conduct, freedom can finally take root in Job's familial kingdom.

In addition, Job takes a new course of action, and it is directed toward his three daughters, each of whom is named in endearing detail (42:14). Job grants them an "inheritance along with their brothers" (v. 15b). That the book of Job should conclude with this act suggests that this is no superfluous detail. Its very mention suggests a deviation from the normal practice in which the sons received their lot of inheritance and the daughters were left to fend for themselves through marriage (cf. Num 27:3-4).[228] As a recipient of gratuitousness himself (Job 42:11), Job responds in kind to his three daughters. Extending an inheritance gives them the material means of independence, comparable to that of Job's sons. As Yahweh's own discourse takes pains to demonstrate, such gratuitousness sustains the cosmos, providing a new basis for moral order. The ethic of merit and retribution has no home in the wild, so Yahweh's litany demonstrates. Now, it has lost its pride of place in Job's own home, so his new conduct indicates. Servility too is banished from the hearth: distinctly lacking in the epilogue is any mention of the numerous slaves in Job's household (cf. 1:3).

The epilogue, however, leaves unsaid anything about Job's involvement

---

228. For the textual relationship between Job 42:13-15 and Num 27:11, see P. Machinist, "Job's Daughters and Their Inheritance in the Testament of Job and Its Biblical Congeners," in *The Echoes of Many Texts: Reflections on Jewish and Christian Traditions*, ed. W. G. Dever and J. E. Wright (BJS; Atlanta: Scholars Press, 1997) 67-75.

in the larger community, but in light of Yahweh's address to Job, even here a hint is dropped. Job perceived the beasts of the field as objects of contempt, pity, and fear; consequently, Job was free to liken the outcast to wild asses scavenging the barren heights and the wicked to lions with voracious appetites. But Yahweh reveals to Job that the allegedly pathetic onager possesses a veritable lion's share of dignity and the ostensibly lordly lion receives its portion of vulnerability, owing to its constant need of sustenance and care. The result of such a reversal of animal roles is a transformed perception of people seemingly worthy only of contempt, whether as defenseless outcasts or oppressive tyrants. The clue to such a transformation at work is another series of remarkable reversals, which Job himself suffers, culminating in his restoration. The once lordly Job became the outcast of his community, loathsome to his family and abhorred by his friends (19:13-19), the archetypal stranger (zār/nokrî, v. 15). From patriarch to pariah, Job reenters his community now as a vulnerable partner.

For Job to reenter his community, he must become an object of sincere compassion. His extended family and acquaintances all succeed where his "friends" miserably failed (42:11; cf. 2:11). His own treat him as an equal; his "friends" considered him a foil and slave to their moral convictions. The narrative lingers over table fellowship and concludes with a remarkable scene in which offerings are given to Job. The heartfelt contributions empower Job, evincing Yahweh's blessing. No longer is Job the object of contempt or even pity; he is reestablished through the genuinely loving efforts of his community. The poignant scene demonstrates the restorative effects of true communion, not so much between Yahweh and Job as between Job and his community. Yahweh remains wholly Other both in theophany and in restoration, utterly sovereign and inscrutably free. In the end it is Job's community, not God, that relates in intimacy to Job. They recognize in Job one of their own. But then they have the advantage of memory. How much harder, the poet suggests, to recognize one's common identity in the derelict living on the margins. For help, the poet exhorts the reader to look again toward distant mountains and churning seas to recognize the stranger as one's own.

CHAPTER 7

Conclusion:
Cosmos and Ethos

High religion is distinguished from the religion of both the primitive and ultra-moderns by its effort to bring the whole of reality and existence into some system of coherence. The primitives, on the other hand, are satisfied by some limited cosmos, and the moderns by a superficial one.

Reinhold Niebuhr[1]

Place brings with it the very elements sheared off in the planiformity of site: identity, character, nuance, history.

Edward S. Casey[2]

Lord, you have been our dwelling place in all generations. Before the mountains were brought forth, or ever you had formed the earth and the world, from everlasting to everlasting you are God.

Psalm 90:1-2, NRSV

1. R. Niebuhr, *An Interpretation of Christian Ethics* (New York: Harper, 1935) 3.
2. E. S. Casey, *The Fate of Place: A Philosophical History* (Berkeley: University of California Press, 1997) xiii.

Creation in the Bible deals not so much with infinite *space* as with sustaining *place*. Biblical cosmology is essentially a "cosmo*topology*,"[3] a creational perspective that conveys a sense of place conducive for moral agency, in other words, an ethos. In this study, I have examined five creation-oriented placements or moral contexts in the Old Testament. These distinct yet interrelated cosmic ethoses (plural of ethos) are not reducible to any specific moral principle, evaluative framework, or systematic order from which particular codes of conduct are directly deducible. These ethoses of creation are more suggestive and symbolic than systematic, more inductive than deductive. Serving literally as "habitations" for moral agency, they provide the necessary contexts in which moral identity and character, relationship and conduct, are formed. An ethos of creation is constructed from the concrete images and contours by which an environment that sustains the moral life is depicted. Simplistically put, an ethos is the result of a dynamic engagement between the moral imagination and faith, on the one hand, and the empirical environment, on the other. In short, ethos is a matter of active discernment, of discovering the moral agent's placement in the world.

No hard-and-fast distinctions between a perceiving subject and an "objective" environment are to be had, however, in the work of moral epistemology. Ethos cements a seamless connection between the moral subject and the environment, for it addresses primarily the *location* of the self, an issue as basic as that of conduct in the matter of moral inquiry. Again, when God notes that something is awry inside and outside the garden, the first question posed is "*Where* are you?" or "*Where* is your brother Abel?" Only after the question of location is handled is the issue of moral conduct broached (Gen 3:9-13; 4:9-10). Indeed, the Yahwist's historiography narrates the quest for Israel's appropriate place in the moral landscape of creation, from garden to garden. Similarly, the ethos of parental instruction to the son in Proverbs is primarily concerned with the son's location vis-à-vis Wisdom's or the strange woman's domicile. An ethos places the moral subject, be it individual or community, into a discernible context that serves as the fundamental point of departure for ascertaining moral judgment. As the subject's moral space or dwelling place, ethos cuts to the heart of creation.

Any ethos of the cosmos provides a richness of context and background that sustains a constellation of basic beliefs and root values about the world that informs the self's identity and conduct. A vividly imaginative and arresting moral context, an ethos is the soil from which a coherent set of particular moral directives and principles, values and virtues, are cultivated. If the field

3. See Casey's use of the term in connection with Genesis 1 (ibid., 12).

of ethics is the study of the "logic of moral discourse and action"[4] or the "critical reflection upon the prescribed and proscribed,"[5] then ethos refers to the rhetorically identifiable context in which such reflection has its place. More than simply custom or habit, ethos refers to the full *habitation* of moral agency, the sustaining setting in which the logic of morality is operative, delineating what is both in and out of bounds, establishing limits as well as cultivating possibilities for moral reflection and conduct. Moreover, an ethos establishes a sustaining context in which the very identity of the moral agent is formed. Hence ethos bears a *creative* function; it is character forming.

It is commonly asserted that the ethics of the Bible is distinctly event oriented,[6] established by God's mighty acts in history, from the exodus to the resurrection and the consummation. Yet as both the *protos* and *telos* of divine activity, biblical creation itself is eminently historical, fashioned, redeemed, and sustained. For every redemptive event there is a creational context, an ethos that informs its wide-reaching moral significance. Although the relationship between ethos and ethic is complex, it would be fair to say that the connection is more organic than deductive. Ethos provides the creative juice and living space for the moral agent in which to live and act. More than simply worldview, ethos is the fertile landscape in which an ethic finds its place to flourish. Ethos designates the mode and product of the moral agent's discernment, not simply construction, of the environment; it is the "seeing-good" that makes for good.[7] Ethos provides the ontology for which and within which to live and embody integrity.

The various depictions of creation in the biblical tradition provide, inter alia, the moral space, the ethos, in which moral life and agency can flourish. Each abundantly suggestive in its own right, the various creation accounts provide a wealth of resources for informing and sustaining right conduct. Their diversity bespeaks a wellspring of moral imagination and discourse. Such suggestive richness I hope, at the very least, to have demonstrated by examining each creation tradition within its own literary integrity and context. Each portrayal

4. W. A. Meeks, *The Origins of Christian Morality: The First Two Centuries* (New Haven: Yale University Press, 1993) 4. Meeks makes the important distinction between morality, "a set of value-laden dispositions, inclinations, attitudes and habits," and ethics, a second-order discourse.

5. L. E. Keck, "Rethinking 'New Testament Ethics,'" *JBL* 115 (1996) 7.

6. Ibid., 10.

7. For a philosophical perspective of moral space and perception, see C. Taylor, *Sources of the Self: The Making of Modern Identity* (Cambridge: Harvard University Press, 1990) 517; W. Schweiker, *Responsibility and Christian Ethics* (Cambridge: Cambridge University Press, 1995) 170-76.

of creation is embedded in narrative, prophetic, exhortative, or dialogical discourse, and to divorce it from the narrated drama that follows or to disengage it from the poetic context that surrounds it is to truncate and distort creation's own message. Such has been the unfortunate result of treating creation as predominantly mythos at the expense of its ethos.

A clear example of the integral relationship between creation's ethos and human ethic, in addition to the ones examined in this study, is found in Psalm 19, whose first half (vv. 1-6 [MT 2-7]) establishes an evocatively cosmic context for the psalmist's subsequent meditation on the "law of Yahweh" (vv. 7-10 [MT 8-11]). The psalm is often viewed as an artificial composite, the result of joining two originally unrelated units. Regardless of its redactional history, however, the psalm establishes a natural connection between ethos and ethic. Law finds its home, its ground and integrity, in a thoroughly cosmic environment. Law has its dwelling in a cosmos in which divine *doxa* (glory) and *gnōsis* (knowledge) are transmitted by creation's nonverbal "discourse" (vv. 1-4b [MT 2-5b]). The soundless testimony of creation is matched and mirrored by the voice of *tôrâ*. Visual witness and verbal decree find a profound correspondence in this ode to the joy of law.

Moreover, the cosmic ethos of the psalm gravitates toward a particularly riveting image: the sun, "which proceeds like a bridegroom from his wedding canopy," full of joy and vigor as it makes its journey across the cosmos (v. 6 [MT 7]). As the mythological symbol of justice, the sun exudes virility in its penetrating heat. Like this celestial orb, the law enlivens and enlightens the one who appropriates it, imparting wisdom and integrity (vv. 7-8 [MT 8-9]). The heat of the sun, revealing as well as sustaining, vividly conveys the efficacy of *tôrâ*. Under the wedding canopy, a covenant is established and righteousness is consummated.

As with the concrete image of the wedding canopy in the psalm, the differences among the various creation traditions examined in this study are highlighted by their respective, culturally specific, settings. Each account or tradition is dominated by a central and arresting life context around which human interaction, moral and otherwise, is oriented. Each creation ethos identifies a cultural — or in Job's case a metacultural — counterpart by which creation is depicted. The Priestly cosmologist discerns the structural integrity of the sanctuary behind the differentiated cosmos, while the Yahwist lifts up and cultivates a lush garden in the land of myth, which Second Isaiah boldly transplants on Zion's summit. Wisdom plays in her cosmic domicile, while Job beholds the playfield of the wild, untransformed by human culture yet profoundly linked to it. Each creation account limns a unique setting that is consistent with a moral vision and conducive for the flourishing of moral

384

life and faith. In its literary context, each account imaginatively defines the parameters and context of human relations and moral reflection. In common with them all is that these various worlds are *populated* worlds. There is no place for the solitary individual, for an insulated island of human existence. From strange animals to intimate siblings, from God to human subject, creation is populated with the wondrous variety of life. The relationship between the self and the other is consequently of utmost significance among these creation ethoses: the native and the alien, man and woman, kin and stranger, human and animal, God and world are all collectively addressed.

By way of conclusion, it is necessary to return briefly to these suggestive traditions and encapsulate more pointedly their respective moral contexts. For each creation account, I want to identify and recapitulate a distinctive ethos and explore further the constructive moral possibilities each can bear, apart as well as together in their canonical context.

The Cosmic Sanctuary

The queen of the cosmogonies, the Priestly account of creation finds its home in the structural integrity of the sanctuary and its environs. The tabernacle is both the image projected onto the cosmos and the microcosmos lodged in the heart of Israel's own existence. An integrated pluralism[8] characterizes the Priestly cosmogony, as well as the tabernacle construction, in which the various elements and agents are ordained in the creative enterprise. Creation is characterized by "form-filledness": life fills the discrete domains of earth and sea, as the stars and planets populate the firmament's expanse. As space is differentiated, so time is segmented into days, setting in motion a rhythm of holiness and goodness. Culminating creation is the sabbath, the temporal side of holiness and vocational fulfillment, a tabernacle in time.

Like the tabernacle in the desert, the cosmic sanctuary is constructed by command and responsive stewardship, by ordination and service within a context of collaboration. Each element and agent exhibits its own dignity, assuming its place and yielding its appropriate product. But a *metaphysical*

8. I take "pluralism" to mean not a formless diversity or polyindividualism, but "a condition in which the testing of one's own judgments and goals against the judgments and goals of others becomes the rule" (M. Welker, "Pluralism and God's Creativity" [lecture given at the Carl Howie Center for Science, Art, and Theology at Union Theological Seminary in Virginia, Oct. 17, 1997]). Welker draws his definition from Immanuel Kant and appropriately shows how pluralism reflects "a highly developed form of living together socially, culturally, and religiously."

chaos ("Chaos") has no place in the cosmic congregation; without form and substance, Chaos is a veritable nonentity. The diversity of domain and life reflects creation's goodness and integrity. Each has its place in an order of differentiated interdependence, of boundness and boundedness. Boundaries are good, and so are the bridges.

The imperative of blessing arises naturally from creation's ethos. Blessing sets in motion the "filling" within the formfulness of creation's integrity, a perfect fit. Blessing is both gift and directive attuned to life's natural state and its inclination toward self-preservation from one generation to the next. But amid creation's stewardship, humanity's imperative to "subdue" the earth appears jarring. This unique blessing is intended to match in some form humankind's distinctive nature, fashioned not from the soil of the earth but from the collaboration of the heavenly council, spearheaded by the Overlord. In its aggressive and violent forms, subjugation has no place. In God's image, humankind "subdues" the earth by preserving and directing its natural powers for the flourishing of life. Like Noah, the nautical life preserver, Abraham, the equitable negotiator, and Oholiab, the creative artisan endowed with God's creative Spirit, humankind must respect the elements and agents while also employing them for their own good, a good that both includes and reaches beyond mere utility. Noah did not preserve the zoological diversity of life simply for his own sake. Moreover, what use humankind derives from nature requires some form of redress. From eating meat to negotiating land, the moral self must pay in full.

Holiness, too, has a perfect fit within the Priestly ethos of creation. Built into the very order of creation, holiness is the quintessential distinction that establishes the context and source of Israel's own ethic. Holiness elevates the movement toward differentiation, which characterizes all creation, to its optimal, transcendent level. As Israel is distinguished from the nations, so Israel's ethic is distinct from and distinctive of creation's common goodness. To the extent that holiness assumes its unique place in the order of creation in the sabbath, Israel assumes a unique place among the nations in its land. As the Noachic and Abrahamic covenants ensured the continuation of blessing for humanity in general and Israel in particular, preserving the vitality of progeny and culture, the sabbath covenant preserves the special nature of holiness, and thus Israel's distinctive ethic. In relation to cosmogony, sabbath marks the cessation of creative activity by implementing the divine *Gelassenheit* or "letting go" of creation. In relation to Israel's domain, sabbath ensures the distinction of its land, preserved and regularly restored, from all the lands that are cultivated by human labor. In relation to Israel's conduct, sabbath ensures proper worship of God in a relationship free from all forms of human manipulation. In the sabbath sanctuary, God and self meet, and the self rests and listens in the hushed silence, free of human discourse and filled with God's presence. Holiness is the consummation and counterbalance of all activity, human and divine. Sabbath is the temporal context of Israel's *imitatio Dei*. As the approbation of "goodness" denotes creation's ecological integrity, in which all life is preserved and promoted before God, holiness points to an ecology of restoration, in which the integrity of community is formed and reformed before God.

The relationship between ethos and ethic in the Priestly cosmogony is a natural and teleological one. As the distinction in excelsis, holiness finds its home at the climax and end of a differentiated creation. An ethic of holiness consequently builds on and fine-tunes the material discriminations by which creation was established. From dietary practice to sexual conduct, the practice of holiness ensures the integrity of distinctions at the highest level. As an ethic of restraint and self-denial, holiness prevents a contagion of human power from breaking down the boundaries and thus subverting creation's integrity, which once collapsed when violence "filled the earth." But never again: God instituted a covenantal prescription to check both the human propensity toward the kind of violence that overcomes ordained boundaries and the divine inclination to return creation back to the drawing board. As holiness fills both defined space and time, sanctuary and sabbath, so Israel must fill the domain of holiness by its moral conduct, the quintessential source of its distinction among the nations. Yet in that distinction lies Israel's role as cultic mediator, as "a priestly kingdom and a holy nation," on behalf of the nations that populate God's good earth. As a domain of creation to be filled, holiness constitutes Israel's ethos; as a calling to be fulfilled, it constitutes Israel's ethic in and on behalf of creation.

The indispensability of ethos to ethic can be underscored by considering the well-nigh incomprehensible question of where holiness would be without the bounded integrity of creation. Holiness would have no place except with God, alone and bereft of communion. Or, to view it another way, holiness would have no substance, infinitely diffused and uncontained, the antithesis of God's glory condensed in the sanctuary, God's dwelling place. Without creation, holiness has nothing to fill. Such imaginings are inconceivable, for they pose the impossible possibility of a Priestly ethic without creation's ethos, so intertwined they are. In short, holiness is sustained by a creation whose very integrity is founded on differentiated space. Similarly, the Priestly tradents establish an analogous situation in differentiated human activity, in the temporal rhythm of work and rest. Work without rest constitutes meaningless labor or enslavement, as evinced in the trauma of the Egyptian exile. The Priestly ethos is the differentiated landscape of integrity, a creational pluralism that supports an ethic of holiness. In Egypt's land Israel had no opportunity to maintain its holy distinction through its sabbath. The sabbath rest was meant for a holy land and a holy people. Conversely, rest without work is meaningless within the Priestly purview. Unbounded cessation connotes the loss of self and is akin to the reversal of creation from Day 7 to Day 0.

Finally, the Priestly ethos sets a context in which the self and the other are related. Most prominent are the figures of the native and the resident alien, much alike yet decidedly distinct. They share both common ground, namely, the land of Canaan, and common identity, that is, the experience of sojourn and oppression. Moreover, they participate together in certain cultic activities in the bond of common citizenship. Ethically, the neighbor and the alien receive, in principle, an equity of treatment. Yet the alien and the Israelite are never merged or assimilated. The alien can sojourn elsewhere, but the native must stay put. Thus the boundary between them is more a fence than a mote, and as the adage goes, "Good fences make good neighbors."

The Garden Community

The Yahwist's cosmogony is predominantly an anthropogony that unfolds in and around a garden. From beginning to end, this creation story is driven by a series of needs, identified and fulfilled. Lacks are filled, abundance flows, and a community of mutuality is born. Needs are met by a creative movement of differentiation from common sources: ground and flesh. The soil requires a tiller in order to be productive, and so a man is formed from the "dust of the earth." The man needs a counterpart for companionship, and so a woman is fashioned from the man's flesh. Such common essences, dirt and flesh, are the sources of mutual self-fulfillment. In the garden, primal man and woman have their home in work and companionship. As farmer, the man finds his vocational fulfillment in relation to the ground (and vice versa), and as companion, he finds relational fulfillment and delight with the woman (and vice versa). The lush garden is the natural context in which companionship and vocation, community and cultivation, are realized to their fullest potential in an ethos of mutuality in differentiation and symbiosis through common essence.

Yet there is more to this garden of delight. With the tree of knowledge standing in the middle of the grove and the divine interdiction barring human use of it, wisdom and *tôrâ* are also present in the garden. This tree, along with its counterpart, the tree of life, are out of bounds, and the human cou-

388

ple's placement within the garden is maintained by their adherence to the prohibition, by keeping within the bounds of *tôrâ*. But it does not last. Tempted by the false need for divine self-empowerment, the couple partakes. The ontology of the garden is preserved by the right exercise of the will. By introducing a primal *tôrâ* into the primordial garden, the Yahwist has driven a deep wedge into the heart of wisdom's ethos, splitting knowledge from life with the ax of the law. Unlike holiness, which has its natural home within the cosmic sanctuary, the law must cut its way into the garden's harmonious setting to find its place in verdant milieu. Amid the garden's abundant blessings, the law is the final arbiter of moral integrity, on which the goodness of the garden depends for the primal couple. Humankind's place in the garden has its limits, for the garden remains under divine ownership rather than human determination. Yet temptation comes, the couple disobeys, and the symbiotic relationship between community and garden is dramatically disrupted. Shame and blame, paralyzing fear and avoidance of responsibility take root. The common sources of origin, from which the fruits of delight and mutual fulfillment were cultivated, become the ground of alienation, burden, and bondage. Self-determining knowledge only dehumanizes the agents of disobedience, and so the man and woman hide in shame and fear within the garden, only to be expelled from it. And yet the garden itself does not wither away in the landscape of the Yahwist, as one might expect. Rather, the garden remains, firmly in view, as the ethos and *telos* of Israel's conduct.

The environment of sustenance and self-fulfillment, the garden's shalom, rests on the mastery of the inward, coiled impulse toward domination and self-apotheosis, reflected in the grab for power, whether from a tree or against a brother. The garden's primal blessing reflects an ontology of the human will in obedience to law. Its antithesis, the curse, reflects the corruption of the will and its tendency to abuse power. For example, the curse of Cain leads ineluctably to the garden's antithesis, the city, which becomes the scene for a collective coalescence of human pride, power, and violence. Back in the garden, the primal command, the alluring tree, and the wily serpent prompt the moral self's struggle toward relational equity and obedience, on the one hand, and against abusive power and self-denigration, on the other.

The moral dynamics of the Yahwist's narrative oscillates between a moral ontology, in which a mutuality of relationship between equals and the environment has its home, and an ethics of deontology, in which the moral will's status vis-à-vis the law powerfully comes into play. From the interplay between a divinely established ethos and ambivalent human conduct, moral conundrums emerge in the larger narrative that aim at both determining the mettle of the moral agent and providing the moral resources for resolution:

389

the primordial *tôrâ* of the garden, the rejection of Cain's offering of the fruit from the cursed ground, the planting of Noah's vineyard, the plague that drives Abraham and Sarah into Egypt, Jacob's flight from the land of promise, the manna and the sabbath in the wilderness, the law that anticipates the regaining of land, and Balaam's garden blessing. It all begins and ends in the garden. The garden's ethos imbues each episode within the Yahwist's historiographic sweep with moral pathos. The garden's ethos reflects a symbiosis between the will and its environment in which the struggle of the self sharpens the moral contours of the garden and the landscape beyond it, raising the stakes of human conduct to the moral level of blessing and curse. Through the curse, the will to power expels the agent from the natural and sustaining environment that was once its home; and wisdom, allegedly representing the unity of life and knowledge, is guilty by association with such an illegitimate act of self-assertion. Through the curse, the landscape of moral agency becomes a rugged terrain in which the exercise of power is at once a necessity and a danger. The wily serpent, the wisdom-hungry couple, the shrewdly oppressive pharaoh, and even the crafty patriarch, all embody overt or subtle abuses of power.

Power either sustains or undermines the integrity of relationships. Within the garden, life is one of discovering the mutuality of kinship and shared vocation with the sustainer of human life, the soil, all in a balance of power and fulfillment. Such is the life of primal blessing or shalom. In the striving for more power, however, the ethos of such equilibrium is shaken to the core and an ontology of strife and oppression erupts. Kinship consequently becomes a source of contention and mortal conflict. Cain, Abraham and Sarah, Esau and Jacob, Joseph and his brothers, all wander the earth as members of a dysfunctional family without a firm hold on either the land of promise or the integrity of community. Yet there is hope, for in addition to the ontology of curse is the reality of blessing that accompanies the errant family through thick and thin, opening up new vistas of moral possibilities and resources, including the prospect of familial reconciliation. As the curse marks the denigration of power, demonstrated in the bewildering array of abusive forms conveyed by the Yahwist, blessing exemplifies the edifying use and transfer of power in the formation of true community.

Through the inauguration of blessing in Gen 12:1-3, Abraham and Sarah begin their trek home, a journey that does not even come close to reaching its destination until generations later when an old seer hired to curse Israel out of existence is compelled to deliver a blessing aimed at bringing the desert-wandering Israel back to the garden, no longer as a helpless couple hiding among the trees in shame but as a victorious kingdom ready to dispense blessing to the nations. Yet such a kingdom cannot forget its rural roots, from which the contours of authentic community emerge. In the meantime, brothers are reconciled, covenants are forged, and oppressors are defeated, all for the sake of Israel's divinely ordained blessing and gift of land, the ground of the garden.

As formal ratification of divine blessing, Israel's covenant is the vehicle for reappropriating the gift of land and community, primally limned in the garden. Indeed, the covenant at Sinai sets the moral stage for the reception of such blessing. Obedience to the law preserves the blessing prefigured in the garden. The integrity of the will, sustained through obedience, preserves Israel's *telos*, which reflects humanity's *protos*. In the exercise of the moral will, in reconciliation with neighbors, familial and international, and in due acknowledgment of Yahweh with the fruits of the blessed ground in worship, Israel has the opportunity to cleave to the garden's ethos.

Within that ethos, a community of kinship is born, first in gender and ultimately in nationhood. As the garden of blessing contextualized and sustained mutual kinship between genders, so the land of Canaan ensures Israel's position as kin to the nations, as an instrument of blessing to the world. Beginning with Edom and Israel, fraternally represented by Esau and Jacob, the Yahwist envisions a time in which the kinship bonds of the nations are recovered as the result of Israel's position as a dispenser of blessing. From the intimacy of kinship between genders to the equity of international relations among kingdoms, the Yahwist's vision of the blessed Israel, even in its national apotheosis, remains garden grown.

The Temple Garden

In the hands of an exilic prophet, the primordial orchard is transplanted on Zion, the center of cult and *tôrâ* teaching. Second Isaiah has transformed the garden into a "temple grove," whose trees inspire true veneration of Yahweh rather than provide the raw material for the manufacture of idols. The remarkable biodiversity of the sacred grove symbolizes the social diversity of the community, gathered from the ends of the earth and transplanted on holy soil. On Zion foreigners and natives alike will be joined together in common worship, so claims the prophet's successor, and, according to his predecessor, to Zion the nations will come to receive *tôrâ*, the law of God. Grafting together images of sanctuary and garden, symbols of cult and cultivation, this exilic prophet has crafted the arresting symbol of the temple grove to transform a community laid waste by judgment into one fructified and restored, well-watered by the flowing streams of God's compassion. A garden grown in the desert symbolizes nothing less than the rescue and restoration of the cosmos from the ravages of chaos, the dry emptiness of death.

Second Isaiah's garden symbolically denotes Israel's vindication and Yahweh's victory over those forces that have enslaved and desiccated Zion. The garden is thus the sign of salvation, a vivid testimony to the liberating and restorative use of divine power. Furthermore, the garden denotes the birth of a new and just community. The symbol of the garden, in short, signifies the two defining factors of Israel's identity: Yahweh's deliverance and Israel's constitution, both inseparably conjoined in an ethos of righteousness. As a victory garden, the grove set on a hill is an enduring memorial of Israel's divinely wrought deliverance from captivity. Yahweh appoints a foreigner, a "messiah," to champion Israel's cause and prepare the soil of its regeneration, leveling the land and clearing out all obstacles, for the garden's sake. Cyrus serves as the instrument of Israel's vindication, imparting, in turn, judgment against those nations that had disabused Israel of its dignity, exceeding the bounds of divine judgment. But such deployment of divine power is essentially instrumental, for Yahweh also appoints a victim of violence to tend the garden, enabling it to flourish. A frail sapling himself, this servant embodies the once desiccated community Israel. As a victim of injustice and a light to the nations, Israel is to cultivate an ethic of justice rather than develop a craving for vengeance against the nations. Such is the calling of Israel's charter.

The garden ethos of Second Isaiah conveys both Israel's diversity and sanctity, an ecology of community. By listing the various species of the garden, the prophet delineates a taxonomy of community in all of its richness and plurality. His inordinate interest in the variety of trees within the forest reflects his view of covenant and conduct. As the forest widens its boundaries, incorporating divergent species, so the royal covenant of Judah's past is democratized: every member of the community, great and small, is now a Davidide, Yahweh's beloved. As the grove is sacred and off-limits to human manipulation, so the cult in the prophet's vision is undergirded by creation's adulation, from the trees of the forest and jackals in the desert to natives and foreigners, such as the foreign "shepherd" and the native "servant," all in a chorus of praise to Israel's Creator and Deliverer. In short, the ethos of the prophet's garden provides the formative context for the prophet's ethic of both praise to the Creator of new things and righteousness within the formation of new relationships.

Wisdom's Cosmic Domicile

Although Wisdom is likened to the tree of life, an association that the Yahwist undercuts in his own primordial garden, the sapiential ethos of Proverbs has its primary home neither in a garden in the desert nor in a tabernacle in the wilderness but in a household in the city. Wisdom at play in the house of the Lord, in creation itself, finds its earthly counterpart in the family, the defining ethos or moral setting of parental and marital relations. In every secure and steadfast household, Wisdom is one of the family, kin and friend, embodied by the faithful spouse and the edifying sage. In Wisdom's cosmic domicile, watery chaos is contained. From this sapiential household, the wicked and the scoffer, whose mouths spread strife and violence, are barred. But for the receptive, the door is flung wide open. To them the hostess offers a banquet of insight, of edifying discourse that sustains and promotes life of the highest order, shalom.

The ethic of Wisdom's ethos is eminently teleological. Righteous conduct beats a path straight to Wisdom's hearth, the context and culmination of the self's moral formation. By contrast, the crooked path is aimless and leads to the threshold of death. As Wisdom's play fills the cosmic household, claiming its security and celebrating its integrity, so the agent's righteous conduct promotes the community's integrity, creating a moral efficacy that fills and transforms the society at large. It all begins with the family: the journey of the moral agent in the metanarrative of Proverbs 1–9, indeed of the book as a whole, begins with the parental household and ends in Wisdom's domicile. As Wisdom builds her house, so the moral self constructs an abode of righteousness. As a counterpart to the Priestly ethic of holy *rest*oration is Wisdom's playful re*creation*. Her play is wholly integrative, engaging both God and the world in her all-encompassing mirth. From sexual chastity to cultic practice, Wisdom's play is as wide-ranging as it is familial. She is the bridge between family and community, between creation and Creator, discipline and joy. By her revelry creation itself is "familialized," the cosmos transformed into the household of God. By the moral agent's conduct, both family and community are sustained. To be sure, some are not Wisdom's kin; they are irredeemably alien. Either hopelessly intransigent or baneful, like chaos itself, they have no place within her domain of delight. Wisdom admittedly chooses her playmates with care. Nevertheless, her household, ever secure, is such that its threshold remains open to young and old alike, welcoming the poor and edifying the immature. In Wisdom's domicile, flowing water, like intoxicating love, is mutually shared and contained. In the stranger's household, the turbid waters of unbounded chaos wreak only havoc and death.

Wisdom's ethic is wholly theocentric. Adding levity to holy awe, Wisdom embodies the revelry of reverence. Her godly fear is the relaxed and

393

trustful posture of the faithful in her household, a knowing fear that apprehends the security of her dwelling amid the chaos that rages outside. Yet that chaos is contained by Yahweh's cosmic decree, and the conduct of the righteous effectively keeps the latch in place. The fear of Yahweh is the beginning of Wisdom, and her frolic before Yahweh is her end. Her exuberant delight marks the height of the self's fulfillment, realized in a relationship of reverence to God and of respect toward neighbor, the kin of the covenantal community. Strangeness, which forsakes both covenant and community, has no place in Wisdom's ethos, for contact with chaos is out of bounds and leads ultimately to the submergence of the self and its dissolution.

Job's Wild and Wondrous Wasteland

Although the cosmology in Job is all-encompassing, beginning with the earth's foundation and the sea's fluidity, the lion's share of attention is devoted to the vast, uncultivated wilderness. There, mostly wild animals, from lions to Leviathan, freely traverse the wasteland's expanse, sustained by Yahweh's gratuitous care and praise. The wilderness is where the wild things are, playing and feasting, giving birth and roaming, liberated from civilization and ever defiant of culture, even in death. Undomesticated and unbounded, these denizens of the margins revel in their heedless vitality and wanton abandonment, unashamed and unrepentant of their unbounded freedom, which rests on a providence of grace. In sharp contrast to Second Isaiah, the book of Job limns a wilderness that remains untransformed yet dignified, praised by Yahweh. What is transformed is Job's perception, his moral worldview and capacity for discernment. Moreover, strangeness has its rightful home in Job. The wasteland is the domain of strangeness, and Job, cast into the whirlpool of torment, is driven into the wilderness. As a stranger to his family and community, Job finds himself cohabiting with chaos.

As the ethos of the book of Job is lodged in the setting of the wilderness, so the ethic sustained in Job is defined wholly by its ethos. The relationship between ethic and ethos is nowhere more clearly evinced than in the dramatic transformation of the protagonist from Job the patriarch to Job the pariah, from Job the paragon of honor to Job the partner with ostriches. The book of Job moves from the ethos of patriarchy, squarely lodged in Job's familial kingdom, to the ethos of alien kinship, set in the wasteland. As patriarch, Job was crowned with honor and glory over his familial kingdom. In his suffering within the prosaic world of patriarchy, Job's silence fits well, indeed persists, in a deontologized view of righteousness, in an intractable sense of obligation even in the face of cosmic upheaval. *Fiat justitia ruat caelum,* so the Job of the prologue insists, and fall the heavens do. As pariah, Job sits on an ash heap afflicted with boils, a loathsome stranger to his family and the butt of despisement among his peers. Yet his wife begins to crack Job's iron will by scornfully suggesting that now is the time to forsake rightness and become defiantly self-authentic before a demonic deity. Job's quest henceforth is to find resolution between an inflexible obsession with the duties of will and its complete abandonment for the sake of self. What Job comes to discover is a new moral ontology where he never suspected: in the barren, uncultivated wasteland, in the land of "shame."

As the paragon of honor, Job looked with pity and contempt on the impoverished outcasts of his community, the scavengers of the margins. But as an outcast himself, Job becomes the object of disdain even among the disdained. All that he has left are the animals of the wild and their boastful, gratuitous Creator. Yet like Behemoth, they are made just as he is. "A brother of jackals and a companion of ostriches," Job has become kin to the wild and to a world seemingly without scruples. These aliens of the wasteland bear an inalienable dignity, an inherent, nonnegotiable worth that collapses Job's patriarchal kingdom based on desert and retribution. The "moral market" of patriarchy, the system of extending and withdrawing attention, honor, and respect, has crashed.[9] In this liminal landscape, dignity is not born from cultivated honor but of natural worth. Where there are no just deserts in the barren desert, shame and repentance also have no place. In the land beyond culture, Job has landed where Enkidu, the future partner of Gilgamesh, once roamed and ultimately forsook.

While Job does not forsake the wilderness, neither does he take up permanent residence there. Moreover, Leviathan, the monster of chaos, does not swallow the Joban self into oblivion, as the strange woman does to the unsuspecting youth in Proverbs. In the wilderness, Job has found his match in every sense with the creatures of the wild, made just as he is. Having become kin to these animals, Job retracts his patriarchy, both his honorable right to receive redress from the Lord of the whirlwind and his royal right to cultivate the nonarable landscape, and returns to his home and community, gratuitous of heart and humbled in spirit. Although restored with a new family, Job is no longer willing to see the despised and the disparaged as objects of contempt. Like the animals, they are his siblings in the wild; they have become partners in a kinship of altruism. Like his firstborn son, Job's daughters receive an equal inheritance. Such is Job's deconstructive "play" within the patriarchal household. He has found placement in the wilderness and brought a measure

9. See M. Welker, *God the Spirit* (tr. J. F. Hoffmeyer; Minneapolis: Fortress, 1994) 120.

of it back home. Job's family, consequently, is an altogether different beast, one that opens the way toward familializing chaos itself.

Creation and Community in Christ

It is beyond the scope of this study to explore the rich relationship between creation and ethics in the New Testament. Nevertheless, some attention is required in order to place, provisionally at least, the moral contours of the Old Testament creation traditions in the larger context of the Christian canon. Exploring how they come to bear on New Testament views of christology and ecclesiology is a critically necessary task for addressing the contemporary issues of community and ecology for the church. But, again, any exhaustive treatment deserves a full and separate study, which cannot be given here. The following modest observations, some more obvious than others, are meant to be only suggestive for further reflection.

As creation serves to delineate in various ways the multidimensional ethos of community in the Old Testament, beginning with the Priestly cosmogony of Genesis, so the new community profiled in the New Testament, the church, reflects in some measure the contours of the new creation embodied by Christ. As Richard Hays ably summarizes in his magisterial work, "the New Testament calls the covenant *community* of God's people into participation in the *cross* of Christ in such a way that the death and resurrection of Jesus becomes a paradigm for their common life as harbingers of God's *new creation*."[10] The emphasis on creation, along with cross and covenant, is entirely appropriate, for not only is the Christian community covenantal in nature, as was the Israel envisioned by the legists and prophets of old, but it is also creation oriented. Living "between the times," between the "already" and the "not yet," the ecclesial body of Christ prefigures in its life and hope the very redemption of creation. As the eschatological beachhead and harbinger of this new creation, the church lives the cosmic promise of Christ both in joyful anticipation of the consummation and in a solidarity of suffering with the present world, which is "groaning in labor pains," waiting "with eager longing" for its "freedom of the glory of the children of God" (Rom 8:18-22 NRSV).

For Paul, such apocalyptic rootage of the ecclesial community is crucial.

10. R. B. Hays, *The Moral Vision of the New Testament: A Contemporary Introduction to New Testament Ethics* (New York: HarperCollins, 1996) 292. Hays appropriately finds the theme of creation to be one of three indispensable "focal images" by which to synthesize the various New Testament witnesses in terms of their ethical import (e.g., 198).

Indeed, his cosmic vision of the end times provides the very framework for many of his ethical judgments.[11] Creation's anticipated freedom from "its bondage to decay" (v. 21) is prefigured by the church, the body of Christ, through whom the redemptive power of God to establish new creation and community has already broken into the present.[12] If the Old Testament has anything to add, it is that the establishment of God's kingdom is in some sense a reestablishment. The new creation, as reflected by the community of faith, is one that enjoys unsurpassed freedom, freedom from bondage and for service, bound up in an ethos of cosmic stewardship, not unlike that found in Priestly cosmology. So defines the ecclesial community Paul envisions, for example, in Corinth: a differentiated, interdependent whole — "many members yet one body" — in Christ (1 Cor 12:20). For Paul the church's *koinōnia,* its communal ethos, characterized by mutual fellowship and sharing, is the sign and seal of the new cosmos ushered in by Christ. As with the Priestly tradents of creation and sanctuary, *koinōnia* reflects *ktisis* or "creation." And reconciliation is the defining mark of new creation (2 Cor 5:17-19).[13] The ethos of the *Urwelt* lives on in the new. New creation is creation regained.

The Priestly view of creation, along with certain wisdom traditions, also finds much resonance in Johannine christology.[14] Watered by the conduit of Hellenistic philosophy, the prologue to John's Gospel (John 1:1-18) has its roots firmly planted in the soil of Priestly cosmology. As Word and Light, *logos* and *phōs,* Christ was "in the beginning" and "lived among us" (vv. 1, 14). According to Priestly lore, God's dwelling among a people was realized by the construction and consecration of a sanctuary in the desert. Christ, as the Word of God made flesh, enters creation anew to be identified with a new community in the flesh. Divine dwelling is no longer contained by temple or sanctuary but embodied by a human being, a *šĕkînâ* in the *sarx.* Although the Johannine literature lacks specific moral teaching, it does convey a strong sense of ethos, of ethical *placement* of community. As David Rensberger and Richard Hays point out, the Gospel's intracommunal focus requires a radical social relocation from the prevailing culture for the members of the Johannine community, resulting in a near isolationist

11. See ibid., 27.

12. Ibid., 21.

13. Cf. Eph 2:14-16, which Hays appropriately refers to as the ethic of a "cosmic ecclesiology" (ibid., 62-63). See also his discussion of the corporate nature of the new creation in relation to 2 Cor 5:14b-18 (p. 20).

14. See, e.g., P. S. Minear, *Christians and the New Creation: Genesis Motifs in the New Testament* (Louisville: Westminster John Knox, 1994) 82-84, 95, 101; H. Gese, "The Prologue to John's Gospel," in *Essays on Biblical Theology* (tr. K. Crim; Minneapolis: Augsburg, 1981) 167-222.

stance.[15] As the world had rejected Christ (1:11), so rejection is the community's fate. Yet all creation hangs in the balance, since through Christ "all things came into being" (v. 3). Similarly, the Priestly ethos of distinction between Israel and the nations reflects a predominantly intracommunal ethic of holiness, while maintaining a positive relationship to the created order, holding, that is, an integral place in the world. As God made the world good, so behind and beyond the polarity of a pagan world and a faithful community, Christ is the Word made flesh, which "affirms the goodness and significance of creation."[16] Through the incarnation of the one through whom creation was fashioned, the dualism of the cosmos is deconstructed.[17]

Another Old Testament foundation for Christology is found in the Priestly view of atonement as the means of restoring community, creation, and relationship with the Creator. Through the slaughtered Lamb (Rev 5:6), divine victory is wrought and new creation, as God's kingdom, supplants the old. That both creation and temple are in travail at the moment of Jesus' death (the cessation of light, the earth's quaking, and the tearing of the temple curtain) attests to the cosmic and cultic significance of the crucifixion (Matt 27:45, 51; Mark 15:33, 38; Luke 23:44-45). As the cultic mechanism of sacrifice worked to preserve and even further the domains of holiness and purity, so Christ's atoning work both intensifies and widens the parameters of holiness, making obsolete the confines of the temple precincts, and ushering in a new world without a sea (Rev 21:1) and a new Jerusalem without a temple (v. 22). The result is a new creation that is holy to the core, a world in which the brilliance of God's glorious effulgence serves as its all-encompassing light, a sun that never sets and a sabbath that never ceases. God's holy sanctuary has become cosmopolis, a temple city.[18] This "household of God" is a community of reconciliation and unity, founded on Christ's atoning work, as expressed in Ephesians 2 regarding the status of the Gentiles:

> But now in Christ Jesus you who once were far off have been brought near by the blood of Christ. For he is our peace; in his flesh he has made both groups into one and has broken down the dividing wall, that is, the hostility between us. He has abolished the law with its commandments and ordinances, that he might create in himself one new humanity in place of the two, making peace, and might reconcile both groups to God in one body,

15. D. K. Rensberger, *Johannine Faith and Liberating Community* (Philadelphia: Westminster, 1988) 26-27, 113-17; Hays, *Moral Vision*, 138-40, 147-48.

16. Hays, *Moral Vision*, 156.

17. Ibid., 157.

18. See also 1 Cor 3:16-17; 6:19; 2 Cor 6:16.

CONCLUSION: COSMOS AND ETHOS

through the cross, thus putting to death that hostility through it. . . . So then you are no longer strangers and aliens, but you are citizens with the saints and also members of the household of God, built upon the foundation of the apostles and prophets, with Christ himself as the cornerstone. In him the whole structure is joined together and grows into a holy temple in the Lord; in whom you also are built together spiritually into a dwelling place for God (vv. 13-16, 19-22, NRSV).

The temple sanctum has become the *ekklēsia*, the new "dwelling place for God," comprising Jews and Greeks alike in the common bond of unity. The peaceable community mirrors the Priestly, cosmic sanctuary, indeed creation itself, diverse yet joined together. Like the tabernacle, whose many parts are joined together "so that the tabernacle may be one" (Exod 25:6, 11), the community's "structure" *(oikodomē)* is "joined together and grows into a holy temple in the Lord" (Eph 2:21). While Ephesians' "cosmic ecclesiology" is conveyed in predominately architectural terms in this passage, the author mixes the metaphors by referring also to the temple's "growth" (*auxō*, v. 21),[19] suggesting an organic dimension of the community not unlike that found in Second Isaiah's image of the temple grove. Indeed, both the prophet and the "apostle" cultivate the image of the organic temple to underscore the inclusive nature of the elect community.

Organic imagery is also developed by Paul in his treatment of Gentile-Jewish relations in the new community. Employing the botanical image of the "wild olive shoot" grafted onto the branches of a "cultivated olive tree,"[20] Paul boldly makes the case for full inclusion of Gentile Christians into the family tree of God's planting (Rom 11:11-24). Paul employs an agricultural procedure as a metaphor for warning the Gentiles not to boast of their position within the household of faith by reminding them of their common roots with Israel (vv. 18-20): "If the root is holy, then the branches are also holy" (v. 16). This arbor of faith has its roots in Zion's arboretum, cultivated in Second Isaiah.

Yet on another tree Jesus is hung (Acts 5:30; 13:29) so that, according to Paul, "the blessing of Abraham might come to the Gentiles" (Gal 3:14). Reimagining Abraham's global blessing, Paul conflates the Yahwist's curse and blessing in claiming that the curse of the executioner's tree is the very means for

19. The verb is found, for instance, in reference to the mustard seed's growth (Matt 13:32; cf. Luke 12:27).

20. The specific choice of the olive tree by Paul may in part be governed by the evocative arboreal imagery found in Zech 4:1-3, 12-14, which is associated with the temple and community leadership.

extending blessing and promise to the nations (Gen 12:1-3; cf. Deut 21:23). In addition, the cross of Christ is symbolic of creation's pathos, of the "not yet" of creation's consummation and praise. As such, the community that lives between the times suffers in solidarity on creation's behalf.[21] Although the symbol of the cross is no doubt a "distinctively new contribution of the New Testament" relative to the Old,[22] the paradigmatic role of suffering is by no means an alien feature to the Old Testament's ethical vision.

The figure of the suffering servant, "crushed for our iniquities" and "a lamb that was led to the slaughter," plays an integral role in the formation of the community envisioned by the prophet of the exile (Isa 53:5, 7). Through his suffering, the servant is qualified, indeed empowered, to be the cultivator of a new community in which peace and justice reign. As sufferer and victim, Job also comes to appropriate a new vision of community and creation in the wilderness.[23] Job's suffering both provoked and was provoked by the dissolution of his world, from community to cosmos. As one rejected, Job's newfound perspectives, his anti-wisdom protests, were condemned as outright blasphemy. Yet in his subversive claims, as well as in his coming to know the inviolable integrity of the dispossessed, the denizens of the margins, Job is in the end vindicated. As Job's restoration serves to justify his words and posture, so the resurrection vindicates Christ's teachings and example.[24] As the marginalized become positively incorporated into Job's moral purview, so Jesus associates with sinners and tax collectors, prostitutes and lepers, incorporating them into God's holy kingdom. Job's ejection from his community into the wilderness to become a partner with the ostriches and the onagers is both his incarnation and his cross. Through the experience of painful wrenchings and surprising visions, this journey of passion, whether through Jerusalem's *via dolorosa* or on the desert's barren plains, a new community of empathy and solidarity is born.

---

21. For a trenchant analysis of the interconnected themes of creation, suffering, redemption, and community in Romans 1-8, see S. Kraftchick, "Creation Themes: A Test of Romans 1-8," *Ex Auditu* 3 (1987) 72-87. The precedent for such interconnections can be found in Second Isaiah.

22. Hays identifies the cross as an altogether new "paradigm for *ethics*" in the Bible, which requires some nuance (*Moral Vision*, 308). Cf., e.g., J. A. Sanders, *The Old Testament in the Cross* (New York: Harper & Bros., 1961); W. Brueggemann, "A Shattered Transcendence? Exile and Restoration," in *Biblical Theology: Problems and Perspectives* (ed. S. J. Kraftchick et al.; Nashville: Abingdon, 1995) 169-82.

23. Although Hays lists Old Testament contexts for Jesus' death, from the *Aqedah* to the royal lament psalms, nowhere does he mention the suffering figure of Job, who figures integrally in Jesus' suffering (Hays, *Moral Vision*, 308; cf. S. R. Garrett, *The Temptations of Jesus in Mark's Gospel* [Grand Rapids: Eerdmans, 1998] 32-33, 41-42, 100-101).

24. For Christ's resurrection as vindication, see Hays, *Moral Vision*, 166.

As the incarnation of divine wisdom in the cosmic domicile, Christ embodies a new household ethic. As scholars commonly note, the "prudential ethics of the wisdom traditions has its New Testament counterpart in the *Haustafeln* and the Epistle of James."[25] Wisdom's moral play in God's cosmic household does indeed find its christological counterpart in the taxonomy of household duties given in Eph 5:21–6:9; Col 3:18–4:1; Titus 2:1-10; and 1 Pet 2:18–3:7. The first citation is particularly noted for conveying a reciprocity of relations between husband and wife, a life of mutual submission (Eph 5:21).[26] Yet the husband is clearly identified as the "head of the wife just as Christ is the head of the church" (v. 22), a hierarchy that is, to be sure, thoroughly nuanced by the charge that the husband love his wife as himself (v. 28). Nevertheless, the larger legacy of the household ethos relativizes the mutuality of marital relations, since the wife's subordinate status is more thoroughly underscored in other texts (e.g., Col 3:18 [cf. v. 19]; 1 Pet 3:1 [cf. v. 7]; Titus 2:5). In the intertextual background lies an unfortunate misinterpretation of the Yahwistic account of man and woman in the garden, as cited by Paul, that serves to demonstrate the husband's superior status (e.g., 1 Cor 11:8-9; cf. Gen 2:18).[27] Here the proverbial view of wisdom's embodiment can serve as a necessary complement, if not a friendly corrective, to the "mutual" yet hierarchical ethos that the various *Haustafeln* promulgate. Wisdom's incarnation in the household in Prov 31:10-31 is analogously related to the wife, on whom the husband depends. The valiant wife, not the husband, is the "the image and reflection"[28] of Wisdom, to borrow from Paul's ascription of the man in 1 Cor 11:7. Together, Proverb's profile of the valiant woman and Paul's profile of the loving husband establish a household ethos that fosters a relationship of genuine mutuality. Indeed, to Paul's call for mutual submission wisdom adds the leavening element of faithful eros.[29] As sexual union is a matter of marital obligation for Paul, it is also a matter of equitable "play" for wisdom. Moreover, the marital relationship recaptures, however vesti-

---

25. Keck, "Rethinking," 15. For a brief survey of wisdom's influence in James, see W. P. Brown, *Character in Crisis: A Fresh Approach to the Wisdom Literature of the Old Testament* (Grand Rapids: Eerdmans, 1996) 160-64.

26. Hays, *Moral Vision*, 64-65.

27. On the other hand, Paul stresses elsewhere in the same epistle the *mutual* submission of both husband and wife by which the wife is accorded a measure of authority (7:3-4).

28. Gk. *doxa* (NRSV translation).

29. Hays perceptively notes the striking absence of love in connection with Paul's references to sexual union, although the apostle's argument targets those in the Corinthian congregation who find sexual intercourse alien to the Christian life (*Moral Vision*, 51).

gially, the primordial bliss of mutual equality created and cultivated within the garden (e.g., Gen 2:23-24).

Wisdom's irrepressible play, as a continual exercise of joy before God, is not without cultic nuance.[30] When Paul or the author of 1 Timothy, oscillating between domestic and ecclesial codes of conduct, enjoin that women keep silent and learn by submission (1 Cor 14:34-35; 1 Tim 2:11-12), the play and praise of Wisdom's worship before God is suppressed. If the woman's silence is grounded in the chronological observation that "Adam was formed first, then Eve" (1 Tim 2:13),[31] then it is the scourge of the curse, rather than the power of blessing, that is unwittingly proclaimed. Paul and, more so, the later epistolary authors hermeneutically deconstruct Wisdom's domicile by subordinating Wisdom's role as household manager and cultic player, as well as merge the garden and the ground, confusing the blessing with the curse. From the moral purviews of Wisdom's cosmic play and the Yahwist's garden of delight, the subjection of women in either home or worship counters the very ethos of creation. One can only hope that Paul's robust vision of a new creation and community, inaugurated by baptism into Christ and built on the integrity of primordial creation before its subjection (e.g., Gal 3:25-29; Rom 8:19-22), can provide the necessary critique of his more questionable legacy on this point. By faith, the Christian, male or female, is "no longer subject to a disciplinarian," the law (Gal 3:25).

For the Yahwist, the efficacy of the moral life is squarely lodged in the power of divine blessing. Through God's blessing, the garden can be embodied even by a community traversing a barren desert in search of land. In a similar vein, Paul claims the *theo-genetic* nature of moral character by affirming that the Holy Spirit is a "source of power enabling Christ's people to 'walk' in a way that fulfills the real meaning of the Law."[32] The Spirit of freedom empowers moral choice (Rom 8:1-11). The formative power of blessing and Spirit nuances the role of the law for both Paul and the Yahwist. For Paul, the law in and of itself is incapable of producing righteousness, although it bears a holy integrity, serving as the benchmark of righteousness (Rom 7:21-24).[33] For the Yahwist, the law of Sinai anticipates a community firmly settled in the land of blessing made possible only through the gift and appropriation

30. See also Sir 24:10.

31. The following verse, claiming that Adam was not deceived, and thus not a transgressor, is patently false. For a pointedly theological critique of woman's subordination in New Testament literature, see W. E. Phipps, "Eve and Pandora Contrasted," *TToday* 45 (1988) 34-48.

32. Hays, *Moral Vision*, 45.

33. Ibid., 44.

of blessing. That blessing was first given to Abraham (Gen 12:1-3), the patriarch before the law, as Paul rightly observes in Rom 4:1-25. Indeed, the blessing has its roots in the soil of Eden, the garden of shalom.

More broadly, God's Spirit or wind *(rûaḥ)*, which sets the primordial stage for creation (Gen 1:2) as well as invests an individual with the artistic know-how and skill to build a sanctuary (Exod 28:3; 31:1; 35:1), is instrumental in creating the new community, as demonstrated on Pentecost (Acts 2:1-13). On Pentecost the cultural world in all of its diversity is representatively gathered "in one place," the result of being "filled with the Holy Spirit" (vv. 1, 4). Like God's glory filling the tabernacle of old, a "wind . . . filled the entire house" (v. 2), bringing about a concentration of cultural diversity in the common bond of faith. As Michael Welker observes, what is imparted is not glossolalia but *xenolalia,* a public speaking in foreign tongues.[34] The community formed by the onrushing Spirit is thoroughly pluralistic, filled with different nationalities, "divided tongues," but is far from a mass of confusion, as in the case of Babel's fate (Gen 11:1-10). To the contrary, all come to understand "God's deeds of power" (Acts 2:11). Not fortuitously, Peter appeals to the prophecy of Joel 2:28-32 (MT 3:1-5), which describes the outpouring of God's Spirit:

> In the last days it will be, God declares
>   that I will pour out my Spirit upon all flesh,
> and your sons and your daughters shall prophesy,
>   and your young men shall see visions,
>   and your old men shall dream dreams.
> Even upon my slaves, both men and women,
>   in those days I will pour out my Spirit;
>   and they shall prophesy (Acts 2:17-18, NRSV).

The outpouring of the Spirit underscores, rather than washes out, the plurality of persons and groups, be they national, ethnic, gendered, or age differentiated. All receive equal status, seized and empowered by the Spirit, in an explosive diversity of prophecy and discourse. In short, the Spirit, present at creation and filling both individual and place, creates comm*unity* out of, but not at the expense, of diversity. The Spirit creates and preserves the pluralistic striving for God's righteousness.[35] The work of the Spirit constitutes the gathering of the ecclesial community in all of its differentiated wholeness. Moreover, God's Spirit is the "spirit of knowledge and the fear of the Lord," of

34. Welker, *God the Spirit,* 232n.7.
35. Ibid., 25.

righteousness and discerning judgment (Isa 11:2-4), a spirit to "bring forth justice to the nations" (42:1), "to bring good news to the oppressed, to bind up the brokenhearted, to proclaim liberty to the captives, and release to the prisoners" (61:1). The result is a "fruitful field" in which "justice" and "righteousness" can abide (32:15-16). Justice and mercy, liberty and righteousness, service and knowledge of God are the marks of the Spirit at work in cultivating the moral community, poured out like "water on the thirsty land" (44:3). Indeed, they are also the fundamental marks of the law, whose fulfillment is made possible by the Spirit.[36]

In addition to Pentecost, the Spirit's power is most dramatically felt in the fulfillment of the end times. By providential (and intertextual) design, the Yahwist's tree of life is given standing in the apocalyptic cosmopolis envisioned by the author of Revelation, whose leaves are "for the healing of the nations" and from which all curse is banished (Rev 22:2-3). The tree of the primordial garden is sustained by the "river of the water of life" that flows from the "throne of God and of the Lamb" (v. 1). The Lion-turned-Lamb (5:5, 6) marks a merging of the respective roles of the victorious Cyrus, Yahweh's "anointed" (Isa 45:1), and the suffering servant in Second Isaiah, both of whom are instrumental in the cultivation of Zion's garden. On the one hand, Christ is the conquering hero, the Word of God from whose mouth "comes a sharp sword with which to strike down the nations, and he will shepherd *(poimanei)* them with a rod of iron" (Rev 19:13, 15).[37] Such language recalls the victor "roused from the east," Yahweh's "shepherd" (Isa 41:2; 44:28). Both Cyrus and Christ bring about Babylon's fall (Rev 18:1–19:10) in order to release God's people (18:4). On the other hand, the image of the slaughtered Lamb also applies to Christ (e.g., 5:6, 9; cf. Isa 53:7), whose shed blood, paradoxically, is a conquering force (Rev 12:11; cf. 17:14). The robe of the conquering rider is dipped in his own blood, not that of his victims (19:13).[38] Jesus is the one who, like the servant in Isaiah, conquers through his suffering, even unto death, embodying a character of *kenosis*, as expressed in the early Christ Hymn of Phil 2:6-11, which lays claim to the invincible power of powerlessness.

The cosmic battle is won and a new creation ensues, a dramatic progression not unlike that found in the cosmogonic myths of the ancient Near East. But the final result that rides on the heels of victory is a kingdom differ-

---

36. See the extended discussion in ibid., 111-15.
37. See also 1:16; cf. Isa 41:2-3, 25; 45:1-4.
38. See Hays, *Moral Vision*, 175.

ent from that of Marduk. A new cosmopolis is envisioned by John of Patmos; a victory garden is cultivated by the prophet of the exile. Whether as architect or cultivator, God brings about a new community accompanied by new creation. Perhaps it is not fortuitous that John of the Gospel deliberately places Jesus' burial and resurrection in a "garden" (John 19:41)[39] and has Mary identifying the resurrected Christ, the new Adam,[40] as its gardener (20:15).

Toward an Ecology of Community

The church is a community that not only lives in between the times, "waiting for the consummation of its hope,"[41] but also at the juncture between places, between two gardens, two sanctuaries, two cities, the *Diesseits* and *Jenseits* of creation's consummation. Such was, in attenuated form, also the hope of certain prophets, priests, and sages of ancient Israel. The ethos of creation gave for them moral vision and coherence in a world that was on the brink of something new for a community that was on the verge of reconstituting itself. Creation was consequently ever redefining itself.

Placed side by side, the various cosmic ethoses of the Old Testament reveal the richly multidimensional character of creation, comprising a wealth of vital interconnections and variations. Creation pervades an ever changing ethos; no static or rigid moral order permeates the cosmos. Creation's multifaceted nature reflects dynamic cultural forces and pressing moral concerns at work within Israel's history in the face of new and challenging situations: for example, monarchy, exile, and restoration. Throughout these formative periods of history, creation was molded and remolded by the various authors and tradents of Scripture as much as the community was established, uprooted, and reestablished. Certain elements of creation gained special or transformed significance, while others were left by the wayside. More broadly, the moral settings changed, from the garden in the face of urban encroachment and the consolidation of royal power to the household embedded in urban life. In between lay a vast stretch of wilderness, one in which also stood a desert sanctuary. For the biblical tradents, creation was a matter of cultural craftwork. Cultural context helped to define creational setting, and moral imagination mediated both.

---

39. The Synoptic Gospels make no reference to a garden in connection with Jesus' burial or resurrection.

40. Cf. Rom 5:12-20; 1 Cor 15:21-22, 45-49.

41. Hays, *Moral Vision*, 20.

It would be a mistake, however, to view the various creation traditions and their divergent cultural settings in simply linear fashion. The diversity of traditions speaks also to a social complexity within Israel's historical existence, of which each sector offers its own constellation of values, from the priestly to the familial, from the rural to the urban, all coexisting within a communal pluralism. Rather than preferring one ethos over and against another, the task of the modern interpreter is to find a constructive synthesis that is morally suggestive without being wholly determinative for each and every new moral challenge. Each ethos exhibits its own integrity; each deserves a place at the table of moral discourse in so far as each has been included into the larger canonical chorus that constitutes the Testaments. Household and sanctuary, garden and wilderness, each has its place in the variegated landscape of creation and conduct.

Finding their convergence in the character of God, there are, to be sure, fundamentally common denominators among the various traditions: God is creator and sustainer of all life, covenant maker and provider, cultivator of community. As the psalmist proclaims, "the earth is the Lord's and its fullness" (24:1). Yet that fullness is evident not in homogeneity but in the integrity of differentiation. Inalienable distinctions are upheld by a common Creator, common sources, and mutual relations. On the one hand, amid the innumerable distinctions, from biological to cultural, creation is the shared, common arena of life, and any ethic of distinction must find its place in positive relationship to the whole. On the other hand, the distinctive ethoses of creation are not leveled out by the universalizing scope of the cosmos. For example, the domain of the family is not projected or diffused outward at its own expense. To the contrary, its integrity remains sharpened even when all of creation is perceived through it. At the same time, creation serves to contextualize the domain of distinction, be it family or sanctuary, garden or wilderness, and to safeguard it from scourge of provincialism or isolationism. The family is no more an enclave than the wilderness is a mere park reserve. Ethically, creation serves to liberate the communal self from the curse of cultural solipsism while preserving the distinctive integrity of every particular domain of moral existence. Creation both broadens and sharpens the moral contours of community.

In Scripture the relationship between creation and ethos is essentially built on analogy. The cosmos is *like* a household; hence the family is as morally valuable as the kinship of all humankind. The religious community of a distinctive people, symbolized by the sanctuary, is of equal import to the cosmic *templum* that shapes the very contours of creation. The particular and the universal are analogically related in the ethoses of creation, and they find their most profound connection in the identity and conduct of the moral self. As William Schweiker notes pointedly, "The struggle of the moral life is to integrate rightly the complexity of life against disintegration, fragmentation, and also false and tyrannous forms of personal and social unity."[42] The complexity of life is revealed in the multidimensional ways in which creation is morally perceived and in the various ways creation sustains and informs moral identity and praxis, maintaining a salutary balance between unity and distinction, an integrity of differentiation.

All the creation traditions examined above agree that the cosmos is meant to be a place of abundant and equitable provision. Again, the ancient authors and bearers of these traditions were by no means modern ecologists. Inconceivable to them was the earth's limited resources. Yet Israel was keenly aware that creation was something to be shared with all of life, not hoarded and exploited for the domination of one species, nation, family, or individual. Moreover, creation suffered from the community's lack of moral fortitude, bringing about a disintegration in both the social and natural realms, as evinced in curse and judgment. The ethic of rest and restoration explodes with ecological force today as it did with holy force to returning exiles from Babylon. Creation provides a panoply of goods meant to be used in life-sustaining ways that invariably configure the community in morally constructive ways. In the story of the multiplication of the loaves and fishes, for example, the five thousand in the wilderness are likened to "sheep without a shepherd," and preparatory to the miracle of the feeding, they are organized in groups, sitting on the verdant grass (Mark 6:30-44).[43] Ecology is of both nature and community. The dynamic structures of creation's goodness inform and sustain the salutary structures of human relations. Discerning and employing the goods of creation are addressed by an ethos, whether one that distinguishes between pure and impure goods to underscore Israel's holy distinction among the nations, or one that discerns invaluable worth in the most impure in order to forge new bonds of relationship. The creation ethoses of the Bible cover the vast spectrum of creation's value and goodness, from utilitarian to inherent. But in all cases, the moral self — individual or community — is placed in a morally formative context, be it household, city, sanctuary, or wilderness.

Establishing the moral self's appropriate "dwelling place" or ethos is most crucially a matter of discerning the right relationship between the self

42. Schweiker, *Responsibility and Christian Ethics*, 32.
43. I am indebted to János Bolyki for directing my attention to this dimension of the story.

and the other, distinct yet sharing some measure of common ground. Kinship and chaos are the opposite extremes, yet even they find an uncommon rapprochement in Job. In the more provincial traditions, creation trembles when "unnatural" associations are made, as when a slave becomes a king (Prov 30:21-23). Nevertheless, creation's integrity is heightened when the lowly are lifted up and the rich are sent away empty, as in the annunciation of Christ's birth (Luke 1:47-55; cf. Job 5:8-16). Indeed, cosmic integrity is raised to a new level when the earth trembles, the temple curtain is rent, and the dead burst out of their dark tombs, as if creation itself were in labor (Matt 27:51-53). In the crucifixion and the empty tomb, creation itself is reconfigured and a new community is born. The reality ushered in by Christ is a new creation, and yet that same Christ is the eternal and creative *logos,* through whom "all things came into being" (John 1:3). The holy and the common, the familiar and the strange, find their home within an ethos, established by Christ, that both builds on and reconfigures the dynamic goodness of God's creation that began as an inchoate mass and is moving in eager longing toward its redemption (Rom 8:19-25).

Biblical creation beckons the moral self to enter an ever dynamic yet secure space for moral dwelling. As Eric Auerbach observes, the world of the biblical narrative, in contrast to that of Homer, does not seek "merely to make us forget our own reality for a few hours, it seeks to overcome our reality: we are to fit our own life into its world, feel ourselves to be elements in its structure of universal history."[44] The same could be said of the elements and structures of creation itself. Comprising various cosmic dwelling

---

44. E. Auerbach, *Mimesis: The Representation of Reality in Western Literature* (tr. W. Trask; Garden City, N.Y.: Doubleday, 1957) 12. The words that follow the quotation also bear citing: "This becomes increasingly difficult the further our historical environment is removed from that of the Biblical books. . . . As late as the European Middle Ages it was possible to represent Biblical events as ordinary phenomena of contemporary life, the methods of interpretation themselves forming the basis for such a treatment. But when, through too great a change in environment and through the awakening of critical consciousness, this becomes impossible, the Biblical claim to absolute authority is jeopardized; the method of interpretation is scorned and rejected, the Biblical stories become ancient legends, and the doctrine they had contained, now dissevered from them, becomes a disembodied image" (pp. 12-13). Auerbach's observations serve as the impetus for H. W. Frei's classic work, *The Eclipse of Biblical Narrative: A Study in Eighteenth and Nineteenth Century Hermeneutics* (New Haven: Yale University Press, 1974) and has influenced the work of S. Hauerwas (e.g., "The Moral Authority of Scripture: The Politics and Ethics of Remembering," in *The Use of Scripture in Moral Theology,* ed. C. E. Curran and R. A. McCormick [Readings in Moral Theology no. 4; New York: Paulist, 1984] 245) and Schweiker, *Responsibility and Christian Ethics,* 92.

places, the Bible as a whole presents an all-encompassing environment for the formation of a faithful people. Populating these various habitations, the Bible is also like an intergenerational community, in which faithful readers are called to live.[45] The Bible offers more than a lame worldview or a flat, linear narrative. A worldview sees the cosmos as a three-tiered universe or a random multiverse; an ethos, however, reveals how Wisdom rejoices, Adam cultivates, Behemoth celebrates, God consecrates, and Christ conciliates, all in a vibrant cosmopolis in which the tree of life and the throne of God stand tall. In sum, cosmos and community find a powerful convergence in the biblical witness.

So, then, which is it? Are the biblical views of creation liberating or oppressive, as has been cast in recent discussions? The ones examined above, at least, are neither. Either/or polarities simply do not apply. Creation, rather, is all about transformation *and* preservation, stability and fluidity, pathos and praise, inviolable connections and irreducible differences, the universal and the particular, all in a dynamic coherence. God's creation establishes a community of complexity, of coherence and diversity that affirms the inherent richness of the self *and* the other/Other. In its canonical totality, biblical creation, on the one hand, eschews all superficial and naive attempts to *reduce* goodness to what already is, neglecting, as a result, the reality of sin and suffering and the need for redemption.[46] On the other hand, most biblical views of creation avoid *detaching* consummated value from what already is or was. The dynamic and teleological character of creation may very well force recognition of certain new forms of relationships that give evidence of integrity,[47] such as those conveyed by the bold pronouncements of an exilic prophet, the tortured imagination of a sage, and an encompassing vision of the Savior, all working to convey a thoroughly cosmic profile of God's reign of righteous-

45. See L. E. Keck, "The Premodern Bible in the Postmodern World," *Int* 50 (1996) 137-40.

46. So also Hays in his discussion of the problem of homosexuality in *Moral Vision*, 402.

47. According to F. M. Cross, "fidelity to the biblical text," in light of pressing modern cultural and ecological concerns, enjoins one to "develop new forms of family life, . . . new tolerance for different modes of human association, including the homosexual, new modesty as to our place in the history of nature" ("The Redemption of Nature," *PSB* 10 [1989] 103). The moral status of homoerotic associations remains highly controversial in modern theological and ethical discourse, as evidenced by the diametrically opposing views represented by Hays and Cross, both careful biblical scholars in their own right. Whether there is a mediating resolution to this most contentious issue, which I believe there must be, remains to be seen as the church continues to interpret the Bible *and* contemporary culture.

ness and peace. The redemption of creation builds on what already is, for without Christ "not one thing came into being" (John 1:3). In continuing creation, the vibrant pluralism of a richly differentiated community is formed and sustained, whether it is Israel and the nations in blessing, Job and the animals in dignity, man and woman in intimacy, or Jews and Gentiles in the Christ who "holds all things together" (Col 1:17).

When members and visitors of a thriving African-American congregation deep in a poor section of inner-city Chicago are exuberantly greeted each Sunday morning in the language of blessing, an empowering and faithful community is being formed. In their "playful" worship, embracing both lament and praise, freedom and moral direction, God's kingdom in Christ is cultivated on earth.[48] God's reign of righteousness and mercy, as the ancient cosmologists would remind us, can emerge from the ground up like a sprout pushing through the parched soil. Indeed, its roots are already firmly planted.

48. The congregation I have in mind is the Apostolic Church of God as studied by D. Browning in *A Fundamental Practical Theology: Descriptive and Strategic Proposals* (Minneapolis: Fortress, 1991) 243-77. Browning describes the worship service as "grandly playful and gravely serious" (p. 243; see also pp. 244-45, 257, 262-63).

Bibliography

Ackerman, S. *Under Every Green Tree: Popular Religion in Sixth-Century Judah.* HSM 46. Atlanta: Scholars Press, 1992.

Albertz, R. *Weltschöpfung und Menschenschöpfung untersucht bei Deuterojesaja, Hiob und in den Psalmen.* CThM 3. Stuttgart: Calwer, 1974.

Allegro, J. M. "The Meaning of *byn* in Isaiah xliv 4," *ZAW* 63 (1951) 154-56.

Alonso-Schökel, L. "God's Answer to Job," in *Job and the Silence of God,* ed. C. Duquoe and C. Floristan. Edinburgh: T. & T. Clark, 1983, 45-51.

———. "Motivos sapienciales y de alianza en Gn 2–3," *Bib* 43 (1962) 295-316.

Alter, R. *Genesis: Translation and Commentary.* New York: Norton, 1996.

Altizer, T. J. J. "The Apocalyptic Identity of the Modern Imagination," in *The Archaeology of the Imagination,* ed. C. E. Windquist. JAARS 48/2 Chico, Calif.: Scholars Press, 1981, 19-30.

Anderson, B. W. *From Creation to New Creation: Old Testament Perspectives.* OBT. Minneapolis: Fortress, 1994.

———. *Creation Versus Chaos.* 1967. Repr. Philadelphia: Fortress, 1987.

———. "Theology and Science: Cosmic Dimensions of the Creation Account in Genesis," in idem, *From Creation to New Creation,* 97-110 (repr. from *Drew Gateway* 56 [1986] 1-13).

———. "Human Dominion over Nature," in idem, *From Creation to New Creation,* 111-31 (repr. from *Biblical Studies in Contemporary Thought,* ed. M. Ward. Somerville, Mass.: Greeno, Hadden, 1975, 27-45).

Anderson, E. "The Code of the Streets," *Atlantic Monthly* (May 1994) 81-94.

Anderson, G. A. *A Time to Mourn, a Time to Dance: The Expression of Grief and Joy in Israelite Religion.* University Park: Pennsylvania State University Press, 1991.

411

Antonaccio, M. "Imagining the Good: Iris Murdoch's Godless Theology," in *The Annual of the Society of Christian Ethics, 1996*. Washington, D.C.: Georgetown University Press, 1996, 223-42.

Arden, E. "How Moses Failed God," *JBL* 76 (1957) 50-52.

Auerbach, E. *Mimesis: The Representation of Reality in Western Literature*, tr. W. Trask. Garden City, N.Y.: Doubleday, 1957.

Bailey, L. R. *Genesis, Creation, and Creationism*. New York: Paulist, 1993.

―――. "Gehenna: The Topography of Hell," *BA* 49 (1986) 187-91.

Bakhtin, M. M. *The Dialogic Imagination*, tr. C. Emerson and M. Holquist. Ed. M. Holquist. Austin: University of Texas Press, 1981.

Barbour, I. "Science, God, and Nature." Lecture given at the Carl Howie Center for Science, Art, and Theology at Union Theological Seminary in Virginia, Nov. 30, 1995.

―――. "Creation and Cosmology," in *Cosmos as Creation*, ed. T. Peters. Nashville: Abingdon, 1989, 115-51.

Barr, J. *Biblical Faith and Nat

―――. "The Image of God inural Theology. Oxford: Clarendon, 1993.

―――. *The Garden of Eden and the Hope of Immortality*. Minneapolis: Fortress, 1993.

the Book of Genesis — A Study in Terminology," *BJRL* 51 (1968) 11-26.

Barré, M. "The Portrait of Balaam in Numbers 22–24," *Int* 51 (1997) 254-67.

Batto, B. F. *Slaying the Dragon: Mythmaking in the Biblical Tradition*. Louisville: Westminster John Knox, 1992.

―――. "Creation Theology in Genesis," in *Creation in the Biblical Traditions*, ed. R. J. Clifford and J. J. Collins. CBQMS 24. Washington, D.C.: Catholic Biblical Association of America, 1992, 16-38.

―――. "The Covenant of Peace: A Neglected Ancient Near Eastern Motif," *CBQ* 49 (1987) 187-211.

Beaulieu, P.-A. "An Episode in the Fall of Babylon to the Persians," *JNES* 52 (1993) 241-61.

Bechtel, M. "Shame as a Sanction of Social Control in Biblical Israel: Judicial, Political, and Social Shaming," *JSOT* 49 (1991) 46-76.

Becker, J. *Gottesfurcht im Alten Testament*. AnBib 25. Rome: Pontifical Biblical Institute, 1965.

Bendor, S. *The Social Structure of Ancient Israel*. JBS 7. Jerusalem: Ben Zvi Press, 1996.

Bergant, D. *Israel's Wisdom Literature: A Liberation-Critical Reading*. Minneapolis: Fortress, 1997.

―――. "My Beloved Is Mine and I Am His' (Song 2:16): The Song of Songs and Honor and Shame," *Semeia* 68 (1996) 23-40.

Berger, P. *Invitation to Sociology: A Humanistic Perspective*. Garden City, N.Y.: Doubleday, 1963.

412

Bettis, J. "Theology and Politics: Karl Barth and Reinhold Niebuhr on Social Ethics after Liberalism," *Religion and Life* 48 (1979) 53-62.

Biddle, M. E. "The 'Endangered Ancestress' and the Blessing for the Nations," *JBL* 109 (1990) 599-611.

Birch, B. *Let Justice Roll Down: The Old Testament, Ethics, and the Christian Life.* Louisville: Westminster John Knox, 1991.

————, and L. Rasmussen. *Bible and Ethics in the Christian Life.* Rev. ed.. Minneapolis: Augsburg, 1989.

Bird, P. A. "'Male and Female He Created Them': Gen 1:27b in the Context of the Priestly Account of Creation," *HTR* 74 (1981) 129-59 (repr. in *"I Studied Inscriptions from before the Flood": Ancient Near Eastern, Literary, and Linguistic Approaches to Genesis 1–11,* ed. R. S. Hess and D. T. Tsumura. SBTS 4. Winona Lake, Ind.: Eisenbrauns, 1994, 362-82).

Blank, S. *Prophetic Faith in Isaiah.* New York: Harper & Bros., 1958.

Blenkinsopp, J. "An Assessment of the Alleged Pre-Exilic Date of the Priestly Material in the Pentateuch," *ZAW* 108 (1996) 495-518.

————. *Wisdom and Law in the Old Testament: The Ordering of Life in Israel and Early Judaism.* New York: Oxford University Press, 1995.

————. "The Social Context of the 'Outsider Woman' in Proverbs 1–9," *Bib* 72 (1991) 457-73.

————. "The Structure of P," *CBQ* 38 (1976) 275-92.

Boomershine, T. "The Structure of Narrative Rhetoric in Genesis 2–3," *Semeia* 18 (1980) 113-29.

Booth, W. C. *Critical Understanding: The Powers and Limits of Pluralism.* Chicago: University of Chicago Press, 1979.

Borowski, O. *Agriculture in Iron Age Israel.* Winona Lake, Ind.: Eisenbrauns, 1987.

————. *Every Living Thing: Daily Use of Animals in Ancient Israel.* Walnut Creek, Calif.: Alta Mira, 1998.

Boström, G. *Proverbiastudien: Die Weisheit und das fremde Weib in Spr. 1–9.* LUÅ 1/30/3. Lund. Gleerup, 1935.

Breasted, J. H., ed. *Ancient Records of Egypt.* 4 vols. Chicago: University of Chicago Press, 1906-7.

Brenner, A. "God's Answer to Job," *VT* 31 (1981) 129-37.

————. "Proverbs 1–9: An F Voice," in idem and F. van Dijk-Hemmes, *On Gendering Texts.* Biblical Interpretation Series 1. Leiden: Brill, 1993.

Brett, M. "Nationalism and the Hebrew Bible," in *The Bible in Ethics: The Second Sheffield Colloquium,* ed. J. W. Rogerson et al. JSOTSup 207. Sheffield: JSOT Press, 1995, 136-63.

Brettler, M. Z. *God Is King: Understanding an Israelite Metaphor.* JSOTSup 76. Sheffield: JSOT Press, 1989.

Brichto, H. C. "On Slaughter and Sacrifice, Blood and Atonement," *HUCA* 47 (1976) 19-37.

Brown, F., S. R. Driver, and C. A. Briggs. *A Hebrew and English Lexicon of the Old Testament*. Oxford: Clarendon, 1906.

Brown, W. P. "*Creatio corporis* and the Rhetoric of Defense in Psalm 139 and Job 10," in *God Who Creates*. Grand Rapids: Eerdmans, forthcoming.

———. *Character in Crisis: A Fresh Approach to the Wisdom Literature of the Old Testament*. Grand Rapids: Eerdmans, 1996.

———. "Divine Act and the Art of Persuasion in Genesis 1," in *History and Interpretation: Essays in Honour of John H. Hayes*, ed. M. P. Graham et al. JSOTSup 173. Sheffield: JSOT Press, 1993, 19-32.

———. *Structure, Role, and Ideology in the Hebrew and Greek Texts of Genesis 1:1–2:3*. SBLDS 132. Atlanta: Scholars Press, 1993.

Browning, D. S. *A Fundamental Practical Theology: Descriptive and Strategic Proposals*. Minneapolis: Fortress, 1991.

Brueggemann, W. "The Loss and Recovery of Creation in Old Testament Theology," *TToday* 53 (1996) 177-90.

———. "A Shattered Transcendence? Exile and Restoration," in *Biblical Theology: Problems and Perspectives*, ed. S. J. Kraftchick et al. Nashville: Abingdon, 1995, 169-82.

———. "Response to J. Richard Middleton," *HTR* 87 (1994) 279-89.

———. "The Social Significance of Solomon as a Patron of Wisdom," in *The Sage in Israel and the Ancient Near East*, ed. J. G. Gammie and L. G. Perdue. Winona Lake, Ind.: Eisenbrauns, 1990, 117-32.

———. *Israel's Praise: Doxology against Idolatry and Ideology*. Philadelphia: Fortress, 1988.

———. "Imagination as a Mode of Fidelity," in *Understanding the Word: Essays in Honour of Bernhard W. Anderson*, ed. J. T. Butler et al. JSOTSup 37. Sheffield: JSOT Press, 1985, 13-36.

———. *The Message of the Psalms: A Theological Commentary*. Minneapolis: Augsburg Fortress, 1984.

———. *Genesis*. Interpretation. Atlanta: John Knox, 1982.

———. "The Kerygma of the Priestly Writers," in idem and H. W. Wolff, *The Vitality of Old Testament Traditions*. 2d ed. Atlanta: John Knox, 1982, 101-14 (repr. from *ZAW* 84 [1972] 397-413).

———. *The Prophetic Imagination*. Philadelphia: Fortress, 1978.

———. "Isaiah 55 and Deuteronomic Theology," *ZAW* 80 (1968) 191-203.

Budd, P. J. "Holiness and Cult," in *The World of Ancient Israel: Sociological, Anthropological and Political Perspectives*, ed. R. E. Clements. Cambridge: Cambridge University Press, 1989, 275-98.

Burnham, F. B. "Maker of Heaven and Earth: A Perspective of Contemporary Science," *HBT* 12/2 (1990) 1-17.

Burrell, D., and S. Hauerwas. "Self-Deception and Autobiography: Theological and Ethical Reflections on Speer's *Inside the Third Reich,*" *JRE* 2 (1974) 99-117.

Camp, C. "What's So Strange about the Strange Woman?" in *The Bible and the Politics of Exegesis: Essays in Honor of Norman K. Gottwald,* ed. D. Jobling, P. L. Day, and G. T. Sheppard. Cleveland: Pilgrim, 1991, 17-32.

————. "Woman Wisdom as Root Metaphor: A Theological Consideration," in *The Listening Heart: Essays in Wisdom and the Psalms in Honor of Roland E. Murphy,* ed. K. G. Hoglund et al. JSOTSup 58. Sheffield: JSOT Press, 1987, 45-76.

————. *Wisdom and the Feminine in the Book of Proverbs.* BLS 11. Sheffield: Almond, 1985.

Campbell, A. F. *The Study Companion to Old Testament Literature.* OTStudies 2. Wilmington, Del.: Glazier, 1989.

————, and M. A. O'Brien. *Sources of the Pentateuch.* Minneapolis: Fortress, 1993.

Carmichael, C. M. "The Paradise Myth: Interpreting without Jewish and Christian Spectacles," in *A Walk in the Garden: Biblical, Iconographical and Literary Images of Eden,* ed. P. Morris and D. Sawyer. JSOTSup 136. Sheffield: JSOT Press, 1992, 47-63.

Carr, D. "The Politics of Textual Subversion: A Diachronic Perspective on the Garden of Eden Story," *JBL* 112 (1993) 577-95.

Carroll, M. P. "One More Time: Leviticus Revisited," in *Anthropological Approaches to the Old Testament,* ed. B. Lang. IRT 8. Philadelphia: Fortress, 1985, 117-26 (repr. from *AES* 99 [1978] 339-46).

Casey, E. S. *The Fate of Place: A Philosophical History.* Berkeley: University of California Press, 1997.

Cassuto, U. *A Commentary on the Book of Genesis, Part II: From Noah to Abraham,* tr. I. Abrahams. Jerusalem: Magnes, 1964, repr. 1992.

————. *A Commentary on the Book of Genesis, Part I: From Adam to Noah,* tr. I. Abrahams. Jerusalem: Magnes, 1961, repr. 1989.

Cazelles, H. "La mission d'Esdras," *VT* 4 (1954) 113-40.

Charry, E. "Academic Theology in Pastoral Perspective," *TToday* 50 (1993) 90-104.

Childs, B. S. *Old Testament Theology in a Canonical Context.* Philadelphia: Fortress, 1985.

————. *The Book of Exodus.* OTL. Philadelphia: Westminster, 1974.

————. *Memory and Tradition in Israel.* SBT 1/37. Naperville, Ill.: Allenson, 1962.

Clark, W. M. "A Legal Background to the Yahwist's Use of 'Good and Evil' in Genesis 2–3," *JBL* 88 (1969) 266-78.

Clausen, C. *The Moral Imagination: Essays on Literature and Ethics.* Iowa City: University of Iowa Press, 1986.

Clayton, P. A. *Chronicle of the Pharaohs.* London: Thames and Hudson, 1994.

Clements, R. E. *Loving One's Neighbour: Old Testament Ethics in Context*. Ethel M. Wood Lecture. London: University of London Press, 1992.

————. *Wisdom in Theology*. Didsbury Lectures, 1989. Grand Rapids: Eerdmans, 1992.

Clifford, R. J. *Creation Accounts in the Ancient Near East and in the Bible*. CBQMS 26. Washington, D.C.: Catholic Biblical Association of America, 1994.

————. "The Hebrew Scriptures and the Theology of Creation," *TS* 46 (1985) 507-23.

————. *Fair Spoken and Persuading*. New York: Paulist, 1984.

————. "The Function of Idol Passages in Second Isaiah," *CBQ* 42 (1980) 450-64.

Clines, D. J. A. "Deconstructing the Book of Job," *BR* 11 (1995) 30-35, 43-44.

————. *Job 1–20*. WBC 17. Waco: Word, 1989.

Coats, G. W. "Another Form-Critical Problem of the Hexateuch," in *Narrative Research on the Hebrew Bible*, ed. M. Amihai et al. *Semeia* 46 (1989) 65-73.

————. *Rebellion in the Wilderness: The Murmuring Motif in the Wilderness Traditions of the Old Testament*. Nashville: Abingdon, 1968.

Cohen, N. J. "Sibling Rivalry in Genesis," *Judaism* 32 (1983) 331-42.

Cohn, R. L. *The Shape of Sacred Space: Four Biblical Studies*. AARSR 23. Missoula, Mont.: Scholars Press, 1981.

Colson, F. H. *Philo*, vol. VI. LCL. Cambridge: Harvard University Press, 1935.

Coogan, M. D. "Canaanite Origins and Lineage: Reflections on the Religion of Ancient Israel," in *Ancient Israelite Religion: Essays in Honor of Frank Moore Cross*, ed. P. D. Miller Jr., P. D. Hanson, and S. D. McBride. Philadelphia: Fortress, 1987, 115-24.

Cook, S. L. *Prophecy and Apocalypticism: The Postexilic Social Setting*. Minneapolis: Fortress, 1995.

Coote, R. B., and D. R. Ord. *In the Beginning: Creation and the Priestly History*. Minneapolis: Fortress, 1991.

————. *The Bible's First History*. Philadelphia: Fortress, 1988.

Crenshaw, J. L. "When Form and Content Clash: The Theology of Job 38:1–40:5," in *Creation in the Biblical Traditions*, ed. R. J. Clifford and J. J. Collins. CBQMS 24. Washington, D.C.: The Catholic Biblical Association of America, 1992, 70-84.

————. Annotations on "Job," in *The HarperCollins Study Bible*, ed. W. A. Meeks. San Francisco: HarperCollins, 1993, 751-96.

Cross, F. M. "The Redemption of Nature," *PSB* 10 (1989) 94-104.

————. *Canaanite Myth and Hebrew Epic*. Cambridge: Harvard University Press, 1973.

————. "The Priestly Tabernacle," in *The Biblical Archaeologist Reader* (vol. 1), ed. G. E. Wright and D. N. Freedman. New York: Anchor Books, 1961, 201-28.

Crüsemann, F. "Jahwes Gerechtigkeit im AT," *EvT* 36 (1976) 427-50.

Dahood, M. "*Mišmār* 'Muzzle' in Job 7:12," *JBL* 80 (1961) 270-71.

Dalley, S. *Myths from Mesopotamia: Creation, The Flood, Gilgamesh, and Others.* Oxford: Oxford University Press, 1989.

Damrosch, D. *The Narrative Covenant: Transformations of Genre in the Growth of Biblical Literature.* San Francisco: Harper & Row, 1987.

Daube, D. "The Culture of Deuteronomy," *Orita* 3 (1969) 27-52.

Davies, E. W. *Numbers.* NCBC. Grand Rapids: Eerdmans, 1995.

Davies, P. C. W. "The Intelligibility of Nature," in *Quantum Cosmology and the Laws of Nature,* ed. R. J. Russell et al. Vatican City State: Vatican Observatory. Berkeley: Center for Theology and Natural Sciences, 1993, 145-61.

Davis, E. "Job and Jacob: The Integrity of Faith," in *Reading between Texts: Intertextuality and the Hebrew Bible,* ed. D. N. Fewell. Louisville: Westminster John Knox, 1992, 203-24.

Day, J. "Asherah in the Hebrew Bible and Northwest Semitic Literature," *JBL* 105 (1980) 385-408.

Dearman, A. J. *Religion and Culture in Ancient Israel.* Peabody, Mass.: Hendrickson, 1992.

Di Vito, R. A. "The Demarcation of Divine and Human Realms in Genesis 2–11," in *Creation in the Biblical Traditions,* ed. R. J. Clifford and J. J. Collins. CBQMS 24. Washington, D.C.: Catholic Biblical Association of America, 1992, 39-56.

Donaldson, M. E. "Kinship Theory in the Patriarchal Narratives: The Case of the Barren Wife," *JAAR* 49 (1981) 77-87.

Donner, H., and W. Röllig, eds. *Kanaanäische und aramäische Inschriften.* 3 vols. Wiesbaden: Harrassowitz, 1962.

Douglas, M. *Purity and Danger: An Analysis of the Concepts of Pollution and Taboo.* London: Routledge & Kegan Paul, 1966, repr. 1970.

Dozeman, T. B. *God on the Mountain: A Study of Redaction, Theology, and Canon in Exodus 19–24.* SBLMS 37. Atlanta: Scholars Press, 1989.

Duff, N. "Introduction," in P. L. Lehmann, *The Decalogue and a Human Future.* Grand Rapids: Eerdmans, 1995, 1-12.

Elliger, K. "Sinn und Ursprung der priesterliche Geschichteserzählung," *ZTK* 49 (1952) 121-43.

Elnes, E. "Creation and Tabernacle: The Priestly Writer's 'Environmentalism,'" *HBT* 16 (1994) 144-55.

Enslin, M. S. "Cain and Prometheus," *JBL* 86 (1967) 88-90.

Farmer, K. A. *Who Knows What Is Good? A Commentary on the Books of Proverbs and Ecclesiastes.* ITC. Grand Rapids: Eerdmans, 1991.

Fewell, D. N., and D. M. Gunn. "Shifting the Blame: God in the Garden," in *Reading Bibles, Writing Bodies: Identity and the Book,* ed. T. K. Beal and D. M. Gunn. London: Routledge, 1997, 16-33.

Fishbane, M. *Biblical Interpretation in Ancient Israel.* Oxford: Clarendon, 1985.

————. *Text and Texture: Close Readings of Selected Biblical Texts.* New York: Schocken, 1979.

————. "Jeremiah iv 23-26 and Job iii 13: A Recovered Use of the Creation Pattern," *VT* 21 (1971) 151-67.

Fontaine, C. R. *Traditional Sayings in the Old Testament.* BLS 5. Sheffield: Almond, 1982.

Foster, B. R. *Before the Muses: An Anthology of Akkadian Literature.* 2 vols. 2d ed. Bethesda: CDL Press, 1996.

Fox, M. V. "*'Āmôn* Again," *JBL* 115 (1996) 699-702.

————. "World Order and Ma'at: A Crooked Parallel," *JANES* 23 (1995) 31-48.

————. "Words for Wisdom," *ZAH* 6 (1993) 159-70.

————. *The Song of Songs and the Ancient Egyptian Love Songs.* Madison: University of Wisconsin Press, 1985.

————. "Sign of the Covenant: Circumcision in the Light of the Priestly *'ôt* Etiologies," *RB* 81 (1974) 557-96.

Frame, G. *Rulers of Babylon: From the Second Dynasty of Isin to the End of Assyrian Domination (1157-612 BC).* RIMB 2. Toronto: University of Toronto Press, 1995.

Frei, Hans W. *The Eclipse of Biblical Narrative: A Study in Eighteenth and Nineteenth Century Hermeneutics.* New Haven: Yale University Press, 1974.

Fretheim, T. "The Plagues as Ecological Signs of Historical Disaster," *JBL* 110 (1991) 385-96.

————. *Exodus.* Interpretation. Louisville: John Knox, 1991.

————. "The Reclamation of Creation: Redemption and Law in Exodus," *Int* 45 (1991) 354-65.

————. "Nature's Praise of God in the Psalms," *Ex Auditu* 3 (1987) 16-30.

————. "The Priestly Document: Anti-Temple?" *VT* 18 (1968) 318-29.

Fritz, V. *Israel in der Wüste.* Marburger theologische Studien 7. Marburg: Elwert, 1970.

Frymer-Kensky, T. "Patriarchal Family Relationships and Near Eastern Law," *BA* 44 (1981) 209-14.

————. "The Atrahasis Epic and Its Significance for Our Understanding of Genesis 1–9," *BA* (1977) 147-55.

Fuchs, G. *Mythos und Hiobdichtung, Aufnahme und Umdeutung altorientalischer Vorstellungen.* Stuttgart: Kohlhammer, 1993.

Galambush, J. "*'ādām* from *'ădāmâ,* *'iššâ* from *'îš:* Derivation and Subordination in Genesis 2.4b–3.24," in *History and Interpretation: Essays in Honour of John H. Hayes,* ed. M. P. Graham et al. JSOTSup 173. Sheffield: JSOT Press, 1993, 33-46.

Gammie, J. G. *Holiness in Israel.* OBT. Minneapolis: Fortress, 1989.

————. "Behemoth and Leviathan: On the Didactic and Theological Significance of Job 40:15–41:26," in *Israelite Wisdom: Theological and Literary Es-*

says in Honor of Samuel Terrien, ed. J. G. Gammie et al. Missoula, Mont.: Scholars Press, 1978, 217-31.

Ganoczy, A. *Schöpfungslehre*. Leitfaden Theologie 10. Düsseldorf: Patmos, 1987.

Garbini, G. *History and Ideology in Ancient Israel*, tr. J. Bowden. New York: Crossroad, 1988.

Garrett, S. *The Temptations of Jesus in Mark's Gospel*. Grand Rapids: Eerdmans, 1998.

Geertz, C. *The Interpretation of Cultures: Selected Essays*. New York: Basic Books, 1973.

Gerhardsson, B. *The Ethos of the Bible*, tr. S. Westerholm. Philadelphia: Fortress, 1979.

Gerstenberger, E. S. *Leviticus*. OTL. Louisville: Westminster John Knox, 1996.

Gese, H. "The Prologue to John's Gospel," in *Essays on Biblical Theology*, tr. K. Crim. Minneapolis: Augsburg, 1981.

———. "The Question of a World View," in *Essays on Biblical Theology*, tr. K. Crim. Minneapolis: Augsburg, 1981, 223-46.

Glacken, Clarence J., *Traces on the Rhodian Shore: Nature and Culture in Western Thought from Ancient Times to the End of the Eighteenth Century*. Berkeley: University of California Press, 1967.

Good, E. *In Turns of Tempest: A Reading of Job*. Stanford: Stanford University Press, 1990.

Gordis, R. "Job and Ecology," *HAR* 9 (1985) 189-202.

———. *The Book of Job: Commentary, New Translation, and Special Studies*. New York: Jewish Theological Seminary, 1978.

———. "Quotations as a Literary Usage in Biblical, Oriental, and Rabbinic Literature," *HUCA* 22 (1949) 157-219.

Gorman, F. H., Jr. *The Ideology of Ritual: Space, Time, and Status in the Priestly Theology*. JSOTSup 91. Sheffield: JSOT Press, 1990.

Gowan, D. E. *Theology in Exodus: Biblical Theology in the Form of a Commentary*. Louisville: Westminster John Knox, 1994.

Grayson, A. K., ed. *Assyrian Rulers of the Early First Millennium* BC *II (858-745* BC*)*. RIMA 3. Toronto: University of Toronto Press, 1996.

———. *Assyrian Rulers of the Early First Millennium* BC *I (1114- 859* BC*)*. RIMA 2. Toronto: University of Toronto Press, 1991.

———. *Assyrian Rulers of the Third and Second Millennia* BC *(to 1115* BC*)*. RIMA 1. Toronto: Toronto University Press, 1987.

———. *Assyrian and Babylonian Chronicles*. Locust Valley, N.Y.: Augustin, 1975.

Green, A. "Sabbath as Temple: Some Thoughts on Space and Time in Judaism," in *Go and Study: Essays and Studies in Honor of Alfred Jospe*, ed. R. Jospe and S. Z. Fishman. Washington, D.C.: B'nai B'rith Hillel Foundations, 1980, 287-305.

Greenfield, J. C. "The Seven Pillars of Wisdom (Prov. 9:1) — A Mistranslation," *JQR* 76 (1985) 13-20.

Gregersen, N. H. "Theology in a Neo-Darwinian World," *ST* 48 (1994) 125-49.

Guevin, B. M. "The Moral Imagination and the Shaping Power of the Parables," *JRE* 17 (1989) 63-79.

Gunkel, H. *Genesis.* HAT 1. 8th ed. Göttingen: Vandenhoeck & Ruprecht, 1969.

Gutiérrez, G. *On Job,* tr. M. J. O'Connell. Maryknoll, N.Y.: Orbis, 1987.

Habel, N. C. *The Land Is Mine: Six Biblical Land Ideologies.* OBT. Minneapolis: Fortress, 1995.

———. *The Book of Job.* OTL. Philadelphia: Westminster, 1985.

———. "Appeal to Ancient Tradition as a Literary Form," *ZAW* 88 (1976) 253-72.

———. "The Symbolism of Wisdom in Proverbs 1–9," *Int* (1972) 131-57.

Hackett, J. A. *The Balaam Text from Deir ʿAllā.* HSM 31. Chico, Calif.: Scholars Press, 1980.

Hadsell, H. "Creation and Theology and the Doing of Ethics," *HBT* 14 (1992) 93-111.

Hall, R. G. "Circumcision," *ABD,* ed. D. N. Freedman. New York: Doubleday, 1992, 1:1026-27.

Hanson, P. *Old Testament Apocalyptic.* IBT. Nashville: Abingdon, 1987.

———. *The Dawn of Apocalyptic.* Philadelphia: Fortress, 1978.

Harrelson, W. *From Fertility Cult to Worship.* Garden City, N.Y.: Doubleday, 1969.

Hart, S. "The Cultural Dimension of Social Movements: A Theoretical Reassessment and Literature Review," *Sociology of Religion* 57 (1996) 87-100.

Hartley, J. E. *The Book of Job.* NICOT. Grand Rapids: Eerdmans, 1988.

Hauerwas, S. *A Community of Character: Toward a Constructive Christian Social Ethic.* Notre Dame: University of Notre Dame Press, 1981.

———. "The Moral Authority of Scripture: The Politics and Ethics of Remembering," in *The Use of Scripture in Moral Theology,* ed. C. E. Curran and R. A. McCormick, S.J. Readings in Moral Theology no. 4. New York: Paulist, 1984, 242-75.

———. *Character and the Christian Life: A Study in Theological Ethics.* TUMSR 3. San Antonio: Trinity University Press, 1975.

———, and D. Burrell. "From System to Story: An Alternative Pattern for Rationality in Ethics," in *Why Narrative?* ed. S. Hauerwas and L. G. Jones. Grand Rapids: Eerdmans, 1989, 158-90.

Hauser, A. J. "Genesis 2–3: The Theme of Intimacy and Alienation," in *Art and Meaning: Rhetoric in Biblical Literature,* ed. D. J. A. Clines et al. JSOTSup 19. Sheffield: JSOT Press, 1982, 20-36 (repr. in *"I Studied Inscriptions from before the Flood": Ancient Near Eastern, Literary, and Linguistic Approaches to Genesis 1–11,* ed. R. S. Hess and D. T. Tsumura. SBTS 4. Winona Lake, Ind.: Eisenbrauns, 1994, 383-98).

———. "Linguistic and Thematic Links between Genesis 4:1-16 and Genesis 2–3," *JETS* 23 (1980) 297-306.

Hayes, J. H. "Atonement in the Book of Leviticus," *Int* 52 (1998) 5-15.

————, and S. A. Irvine. *Isaiah the Eighth-Century Prophet: His Times and His Preaching.* Nashville: Abingdon, 1987.

Hays, R. B. *The Moral Vision of the New Testament: A Contemporary Introduction to New Testament Ethics.* New York: HarperCollins, 1996.

Hefner, P. *The Human Factor: Evolution, Culture, and Religion.* Minneapolis: Fortress, 1993.

Heidegger, M. "Letter on Humanism," in *Basic Writings from* Being and Time *(1927) to* The Task of Thinking *(1964),* ed. D. F. Krell. New York: Harper & Row, 1977, 20-36.

Hendel, R. S. *The Epic of the Patriarch: The Jacob Cycle and the Narrative Traditions of Canaan and Israel.* HSM 42. Atlanta: Scholars Press, 1987.

Hepper, F. N. *Illustrated Encyclopedia of Bible Plants.* Grand Rapids: Baker, 1992.

Herion, G. A. "Why God Rejected Cain's Offering: The Obvious Answer," in *Fortunate the Eyes That See: Essays in Honor of David Noel Freedman in Celebration of His Seventieth Birthday,* ed. A. B. Beck et al. Grand Rapids: Eerdmans, 1995, 52-65.

Hermisson, H.-J. "Observations on the Creation Theology in Wisdom," in *Israelite Wisdom: Theological and Literary Essays in Honor of Samuel Terrien,* ed. J. G. Gammie et al. Missoula, Mont.: Scholars Press, 1978, 43-57.

Heschel, A. *The Prophets.* 1962. Repr. in 2 vols. New York: Harper & Row, 1975.

Hiebert, T. *The Yahwist's Landscape: Nature and Religion in Early Israel.* New York: Oxford University Press, 1996.

————. "Re-Imagining Nature: Shifts in Biblical Interpretation," *Int* 59 (1996) 36-46.

————. "Theophany in the OT," *ABD,* ed. D. N. Freedman. New York: Doubleday, 1992, 6:505-11.

Hoffman, Y. *A Blemished Perfection: The Book of Job in Context.* JSOTSup 213. Sheffield: JSOT Press, 1996.

————. "The Relation between the Prologue and the Speech-Cycles in Job," *VT* 31 (1981) 160-70.

Hurowitz, V. A. "The Priestly Account of Building the Tabernacle," *JAOS* 105 (1985) 21-30.

Hurvitz, A. "The Date of the Prose Tale of Job Linguistically Reconsidered," *HTR* 67 (1974) 17-34.

Hutter, M. "Adam als Gärtner und König," *BZ* 30 (1986) 258-62.

Hyers, C. *The Meaning of Creation: Genesis and Modern Science.* Atlanta: John Knox, 1984.

Isaac, E. "Circumcision as Covenant Rite," *Anthropos* 59 (1965) 444-56.

Jacob, I., and W. Jacob. "Flora," *ABD,* ed. D. N. Freedman. New York: Doubleday, 1992, 2:803-17.

Janowski, B. "Temple und Schöpfung. Schöpfungstheologische Aspekte der priesterschriftlichen Heiligtumskonzeption," in *Schöpfung und Neuschöpfung,* ed. I. Baldermann et al. JBT 5. Neukirchen-Vluyn: Neukirchener, 1990, 37-70.

———. *Rettungsgewissheit und Epiphanie des Heils*. WMANT 59. Neukirchen-Vluyn: Neukirchener, 1989.

Janssens, L. "Norms and Priorities in a Love Ethics," *Louvain Studies* 6 (1977) 207-26.

Janzen, W. *Old Testament Ethics: A Paradigmatic Approach*. Louisville: Westminster John Knox, 1994.

Jaussen, J. A. "Le coq et la plui dans la tradition palestinienne," *RB* 33 (1924) 574-82.

Jensen, P. P. *Graded Holiness: A Key to the Priestly Conception of the World*. JSOTSup 106: Sheffield: JSOT Press, 1992.

Jeremias, J. *Theophanie, Die Geschichte einer Alttestamentlichen Gattung*. Neukirchen-Vluyn: Neukirchener Verlag, 1965.

Johnson, L. T. "Imagining the World Scripture Imagines," *Modern Theology* 14/2 (1998) 165-80.

Joines, K. R. "The Serpent in Gen 3," *ZAW* 87 (1975) 1-11.

———. *Serpent Symbolism in the Old Testament*. Haddonfield, N.J.: Haddonfield House, 1974.

Jones, M., Jr. "Just Too Good to be True: Another Reason to Beware of False Eco-Prophets," *Newsweek* (May 4, 1992) 68.

Junger, S. *The Perfect Storm: A True Story of Men against the Sea*. New York: Norton, 1997.

Kaiser, W. C., Jr. *Toward Old Testament Ethics*. Grand Rapids: Zondervan, 1983.

Kant, Immanuel. *Critique of Aesthetic Judgment*, tr. J. C. Meredith. Oxford: Clarendon, 1911.

Kaupel, H. *Die Dämonen im Alten Testament*. Augsburg: Filser, 1930.

Kaufmann, Y. *The Religion of Israel*, tr. and abridged by M. Greenberg. New York: Schocken, 1960.

Kautsch, E., ed. *Gesenius' Hebrew Grammar*, tr. A. E. Cowley. 2d ed. Oxford: Clarendon, 1910.

Kayatz, C. *Studien zu Proverbien 1–9*. WMANT 22. Neukirchen-Vluyn: Neukirchener, 1966.

Keane, P. S. *Christian Ethics and Imagination: A Theological Inquiry*. New York: Paulist, 1984.

Kearney, P. J. "Creation and Liturgy: The P Redaction of Ex 25–40," *ZAW* 89 (1977) 375-87.

Keck, L. E. "The Premodern Bible in the Postmodern World," *Int* 50 (1996) 137-40.

———. "Rethinking 'New Testament Ethics,'" *JBL* 115 (1996) 3-16.

Keel, O. *The Song of Songs*, tr. F. J. Gaiser. Continental Commentary. Minneapolis: Fortress, 1994.

————. *Jahwes Entgegnung an Ijob: Eine Deutung von Ijob 38–41*. FRLANT 121. Göttingen: Vandenhoeck & Ruprecht, 1978.

————. *Die Weisheit Spielt vor Gott*. Freiburg: Universitätsverlag; Göttingen: Vandenhoeck & Ruprecht, 1974.

————, and C. Uehlinger. *Göttinen, Götter und Gottesymbole*. QD 134. Freiburg: Herder, 1992.

Kingsolver, B. *High Tide in Tucson*. New York: HarperCollins, 1995.

Klein, R. "Back to the Future," *Int* 50 (1996) 264-76.

Klopfenstein, M. A. *Scham und Schande nach dem Alten Testament*. ATANT 62. Zurich: Theologischer Verlag, 1972.

Knierim, R. "Cosmos and History in Israel's Theology," *HBT* 3 (1981) 59-124 (repr. in idem, *The Task of Old Testament Theology: Method and Cases*. Grand Rapids: Eerdmans, 1995, 171-224).

Knohl, I. "Between Voice and Silence: The Relationship between Prayer and Temple Cult," *JBL* 115 (1996) 17-30.

————. *The Sanctuary of Silence: The Priestly Torah and the Holiness School*. Minneapolis: Fortress, 1995.

Korsack, M. P. *At the Start: Genesis Made New*. New York: Doubleday, 1993.

Kosinski, J. *Being There*. New York: Bantam, 1985.

Kovacs, B. W. "Is There a Class-Ethic in Proverbs?" in *Essays in Old Testament Ethics (J. Philip Hyatt, In Memoriam)*, ed. J. L. Crenshaw and J. T. Willis. New York: Ktav, 1974, 171-89.

Kovacs, M. G. *The Epic of Gilgamesh*. Stanford: Stanford University Press, 1989.

Kraftchick, S. "Creation Themes: A Test of Romans 1–8." *Ex Auditu* 3 (1987) 72-87.

Kutsch, E. "Die Paradieserzählung Genesis 2–3 und ihr Verfasser," in *Studien zum Pentateuch. Walter Kornfeld zum 60. Geburtstag*, ed. G. Braulik et al. Vienna: Herder, 1977, 9-24.

L'Heureux, C. *In and Out of Paradise*. New York: Paulist, 1983.

Laato, A. *The Servant of YHWH and Cyrus: A Reinterpretation of the Exilic Messianic Programme in Isaiah 40–55*. ConBOT 35. Stockholm: Almqvist & Wiksell International, 1992.

Landes, G. M. "Creation Tradition in Proverbs 8:22-31 and Genesis 1," in *A Light unto My Path: Old Testament Studies in Honor of Jacob M. Myers*, ed. H. N. Bream et al. Philadelphia: Temple University Press, 1974, 279-294.

Landy, F. "The Song of Songs and the Garden of Eden," *JBL* 98 (1979) 513-28.

Lang, B. *Wisdom and the Book of Proverbs: An Israelite Goddess Redefined*. New York: Pilgrim, 1986.

————. "Die sieben Säulen der Weisheit (Sprüche IX 1) im Licht israelitischer Architektur," *VT* 33 (1983) 488-91.

Lehmann, P. *Ethics in a Christian Context*. New York: Harper & Row, 1963.

Levenson, J. *The Death and Resurrection of the Beloved Son: The Transformation of*

Child Sacrifice in Judaism and Christianity. New Haven: Yale University Press, 1993.

————. *Creation and the Persistence of Evil: The Jewish Drama of Divine Omnipotence*. San Francisco: Harper & Row, 1988 (2d ed. Princeton: Princeton University Press, 1994).

————. "The Theologies of Commandment in Biblical Israel," *HTR* 73 (1980) 17-33.

Lichterman, P. *The Search for Political Community: American Activists Reinventing Commitment*. Cambridge: Cambridge University Press, 1996.

Lichtheim, M. *Ma'at in Egyptian Autobiographies and Related Studies*. OBO 120. Freiburg: Universitätsverlag; Göttingen: Vandenhoeck & Ruprecht, 1992.

————. *Ancient Egyptian Literature, vol. 2: The New Kingdom*. Berkeley: University of California Press, 1976.

————. *Ancient Egyptian Literature, vol. 1: The Old and Middle Kingdoms*. Berkeley: University of California Press, 1975.

Lind, M. C. "Monotheism, Power, and Justice: A Study in Isaiah 40–55," *CBQ* 46 (1984) 432-46.

Loewenstamm, S. E. *Comparative Studies in Biblical and Ancient Oriental Literature*. AOAT 204. Kevelaer: Butzon & Bercker; Neukirchen-Vluyn: Neukirchener, 1980.

Lohfink, N. *Theology of the Pentateuch: Themes of the Priestly Narrative and Deuteronomy*, tr. L. N. Maloney. Minneapolis: Fortress, 1994.

————. "God the Creator and the Stability of Heaven and Earth," in idem, *Theology of the Pentateuch*, 116-35.

————. "Original Sins in the Priestly Historical Narrative," in idem, *Theology of the Pentateuch*, 96-115.

————. "The Priestly Narrative and History," in idem, *Theology of the Pentateuch*, 136-72.

————. "The Strata of the Pentateuch and the Question of War," in idem *Theology of the Pentateuch*, 173-226.

————. "'Subdue the Earth?' (Genesis 1:28)," in idem, *Theology of the Pentateuch*, 1-17.

Lotman, Y., and B. Uspensky. "On the Semiotic Mechanism of Culture," *New Literary History* 9 (1978) 211-32.

Luckenbill, D. D., ed. *Ancient Records of Assyria and Babylonia*. 2 vols. Chicago: University of Chicago Press, 1926-27.

Machinist, P. "Job's Daughters and Their Inheritance in the Testament of Job and Its Biblical Congeners," in *The Echoes of Many Texts: Reflections on Jewish and Christian Traditions*, ed. W. G. Dever and J. E. Wright. BJS, Atlanta: Scholars Press, 1997, 67-80.

Maier, C. *Die "fremde Frau" in Proverbien 1–9: Eine exegetische und sozialgeschichtliche Studie*. OBO 144. Freiburg: Universitätsverlag; Göttingen: Vandenhoeck & Ruprecht, 1995.

Malina, B. J. *The New Testament World: Insights from Cultural Anthropology*. Rev. ed. Louisville: Westminster John Knox, 1993.

Marböck, J. "Im Horizont der Gottesfurcht: Stellungnahmen zu Welt und Leben in der alttestamentlichen Weisheit," *BN* 26 (1985) 47-70.

Mathews, C. R. *Defending Zion*. BZAW 236. Berlin: de Gruyter, 1995.

Mathys, H.-P. *Liebe deinen Nächsten wie dich selbst: Untersuchungen zum alttestamentlichen Gebot der Nächstenliebe (Lev 19,18)*. OBO 71. Freiburg: Universitätsverlag; Göttingen: Vandenhoeck & Ruprecht, 1986.

Matthews, V. H., and D. C. Benjamin, eds. *Honor and Shame in the World of the Bible. Semeia* 68 (1994).

Matties, G. H. *Ezekiel 18 and the Rhetoric of Moral Discourse*. SBLDS 126. Atlanta: Scholars Press, 1990.

May, G. *Creatio ex Nihilo: The Doctrine of "Creation out of Nothing" in Early Christian Thought*, tr. A. S. Worrall. Edinburgh: T. & T. Clark, 1994.

May, H. G. "Some Cosmic Connotations of *Mayim Rabbîm*, 'Many Waters,'" *JBL* 74 (1955) 9-21.

Mays, J. G. "Justice: Perspectives from the Prophetic Tradition," in *Prophecy in Israel: Search for an Identity*, ed. D. L. Petersen. IRT 10. Philadelphia: Fortress, 1987, 144-58 (repr. from *Int* 37 [1983] 5-17).

McBride, S. Dean, Jr. "The Yoke of Torah," *Ex Auditu* 11 (1995) 1-16.

———. "Divine Protocol: Genesis 1:1–2:3 as Prologue to the Pentateuch," in *God Who Creates*. Grand Rapids: Eerdmans, forthcoming.

———. "Polity of the Covenant People," *Int* 41 (1987) 229-47.

———. "The Deuteronomic Name Theology." Ph.D. dissertation. Harvard University, 1969.

McCarter, P. K., Jr. "The Balaam Texts from Deir 'Alla: The First Combination," *BASOR* 239 (1980) 49-60.

McCreesh, T. P. "Wisdom as Wife: Proverbs 31:10-31," *RB* 91 (1985) 25-46.

McEvenue, S. "The Style of a Building Instruction," *Semitics* 4 (1974) 1-9.

———. *The Narrative Style of the Priestly Writer*. AnBib 50. Rome: Pontifical Biblical Institute, 1971.

———. "Word and Fulfillment: A Stylistic Feature of the Priestly Writer," *Semitics* 1 (1970) 104-10.

McKane, W. *Proverbs*. OTL. Philadelphia: Westminster, 1970.

———. *Prophets and Wise Men*. SBT 1/44. Naperville, Ill.: Allenson, 1965.

Meeks, W. A. *The Origins of Christian Morality: The First Two Centuries*. New Haven: Yale University Press, 1993.

———. *The Moral World of the First Christians*. LEC 6. Philadelphia: Westminster, 1986.

Melcher, S. J. "The Holiness Code and Human Sexuality," in *Biblical Ethics and Homosexuality*, ed. R. L. Brawley. Louisville: Westminster John Knox, 1996, 87-102.

Mettinger, T. N. D. *The Dethronement of Sabaoth: Studies in the Shem and Kabod Theologies.* ConBOT 18; Lund: Gleerup, 1982.

Meyers, C. L. "'To Her Mother's House': Considering a Counterpart to the Israel-ite *bêt 'āb*," in *The Bible and the Politics of Exegesis: Essays in Honor of Nor-man K. Gottwald on His Sixty-Fifth Birthday,* ed. D. Jobling, P. L. Day, and G. T. Sheppard. Cleveland: Pilgrim, 1991, 39-52.

—————. *Discovering Eve: Ancient Israelite Women in Context.* New York: Oxford University Press, 1988.

—————. "Gender Roles and Genesis 3:16 Revisited," in *The Word of the Lord Shall Go Forth: Essays in Honor of David Noel Freedman in Celebration of His Six-tieth Birthday,* ed. C. L. Meyers and M. O. Connor. Winona Lake, Ind.: Eisenbrauns, 1983, 337-54 (repr. in *A Feminist Guide to Genesis,* ed. A. Brenner. FCB 2. Sheffield: Sheffield Academic Press, 1993, 118-41).

—————, and E. M. Meyers. *Haggai, Zechariah 1–8.* AB 25B. Garden City, N.Y.: Doubleday, 1987.

Middleton, J. R. "Creation Founded in Love: A Rhetorical Reading of Genesis 1:1–2:3." Paper presented at the annual SBL meeting, Nov. 19, 1995.

—————. "Is Creation Theology Inherently Conservative? A Dialogue with Walter Brueggemann," *HTR* 87 (1994) 257-77.

Midgley, M. *Beast and Man: The Roots of Human Nature.* 2d ed. London: Routledge, 1995.

—————. *Science as Salvation: A Modern Myth and Its Meaning.* London: Routledge, 1992.

Milgrom, J. "Encroaching on the Sacred: Purity and Polity in Numbers 1–10," *Int* 51 (1997) 241-53.

—————. "The Changing Concept of Holiness in the Pentateuchal Codes with Em-phasis on Leviticus 19," in *Reading Leviticus: A Conversation with Mary Douglas,* ed. J. F. A. Sawyer. JSOTSup 227. Sheffield: JSOT Press, 1996, 65-83.

—————. *Leviticus 1–16.* AB 3. New York: Doubleday, 1991.

—————. *Numbers.* JPS Torah Commentary. Philadelphia: Jewish Publication So-ciety, 1990.

—————. "Magic, Monotheism, and the Sin of Moses," in *The Quest for the King-dom of God: Studies in Honor of George E. Mendenhall,* ed. H. B. Huffmon et al. Winona Lake, Ind.: Eisenbrauns, 1983, 251-65.

—————. "The Biblical Diet Laws as an Ethical System: Food and Faith," *Int* 17 (1963) 288-301 (repr. in idem, *Studies in Cultic Theology and Terminology.* SJLA 36. Leiden: Brill, 1983, 104-18).

—————. "Leviticus," *Interpreter's Dictionary of the Bible: Supplementary Volume,* ed. K. Crim. Nashville: Abingdon, 1976, 541-45.

Miller, J. M., and J. H. Hayes. *A History of Ancient Israel and Judah.* Philadelphia: Westminster, 1986.

Miller, P. D., Jr. "Creation and Covenant," in *Biblical Theology: Problems and Perspectives,* ed. S. J. Kraftchick et al. Nashville: Abingdon, 1995, 155-68.

———. "Syntax and Theology in Genesis XII 3a," *VT* 34 (1984) 472-76.

———. "*Yeled* in the Song of Lamech," *JBL* 85 (1966) 477-78.

Minear, P. S. *Christians and the New Creation: Genesis Motifs in the New Testament.* Louisville: Westminster John Knox, 1994.

Mitchell, C. W. *The Meaning of BRK "to Bless" in the Old Testament.* SBLDS 95. Atlanta: Scholars Press, 1987.

Mitchell, H. G. *The Ethics of the Old Testament.* Chicago: University of Chicago Press, 1912.

Mitchell, S. *Genesis.* New York: HarperCollins, 1996.

Moore, R. D. "The Integrity of Job," *CBQ* 45 (1983) 17-31.

Morrow, W. "Consolation, Rejection, and Repentance in Job 42:6," *JBL* 105 (1986) 211-25.

Mott, S. C. *Biblical Ethics and Social Change.* New York: Oxford University Press, 1982.

Mowinckel, S. *Tetrateuch — Pentateuch-Hexateuch: Die Berichte über die Landnahme in den Drei altisraelitischen Geschichtswerken.* BZAW 90. Berlin: de Gruyter, 1964.

Mudge, L. S. "Paul Ricoeur on Biblical Interpretation," in Paul Ricoeur, *Essays on Biblical Interpretation,* ed. L. S. Mudge. Philadelphia: Fortress, 1980, 1-40.

Müller, H.-P. "Segen im Alten Testament. Theologische Implikationen eines halb vergessenen Themas," in idem, *Mythos — Kerygma — Wahrheit: Gesamelte Aufsätze zum Alten Testament in seiner Umwelt und zur Biblischen Theologie.* BZAW 200. Berlin: de Gruyter, 1991, 220-51 (repr. from *ZTK* 87 [1990] 1-32).

Murdoch, I. *Metaphysics as a Guide to Morals.* New York: Viking Penguin, 1992.

———. *The Sovereignty of Good.* SEPR. New York: Schocken, 1971.

Murphy, N., and G. F. R. Ellis. *On the Moral Nature of the Universe: Theology, Cosmology, and Ethics.* Minneapolis: Fortress, 1996.

Murphy, R. E. "Wisdom and Eros in Proverbs 1–9," *CBQ* 50 (1988) 600-603.

———. "Wisdom and Creation," *JBL* 104 (1985) 3-11.

Nel, P. J. *The Structure and Ethos of the Wisdom Admonitions in Proverbs.* BZAW 158. Berlin: de Gruyter, 1982.

Nelson, R. D. *Raising Up a Faithful Priest: Community and Priesthood in Biblical Theology.* Louisville: Westminster John Knox, 1993.

Newsom, C. "The Book of Job," *The New Interpreter's Bible,* ed. L. Keck et al. Nashville: Abingdon, 1996, 4:319-637.

———. "The Moral Sense of Nature: Ethics in the Light of God's Speech to Job," *PSB* 15 (1994) 9-27.

———. "Cultural Politics and the Reading of Job," *BI* 1 (1993) 119-38.

———. "Women and the Discourse of Patriarchal Wisdom: A Study of Proverbs

1–9," in *Gender and Difference in Ancient Israel*, ed. P. L. Day. Minneapolis: Fortress, 1989, 142-60.

Niditch, S. *Underdogs and Tricksters: A Prelude to Biblical Folklore*. San Francisco: Harper & Row, 1987.

———. *Chaos to Cosmos: Studies in Biblical Patterns of Creation*. SPSH; Chico, California: Scholars Press, 1985.

Niebuhr, R. *Moral Man and Immoral Society: A Study in Ethics and Politics*. New York: Charles Scribner's Sons, 1953.

———. *An Interpretation of Christian Ethics*. New York: Harper, 1935.

Nielsen, K. *Yahweh as Prosecutor and Judge: An Investigation of the Prophetic Lawsuit (Rîb-Pattern)*, tr. F. Cryer. JSOTSup 9. Sheffield: JSOT Press, 1978.

Noth, M. *A History of Pentateuchal Traditions*, tr. B. W. Anderson. 1972. Repr. Chico, Calif.: Scholars Press, 1981.

———. *Numbers*, tr. J. D. Martin. OTL. Philadelphia: Westminster, 1968.

———. *Exodus*, tr. J. S. Bowden. OTL. Philadelphia: Westminster, 1962.

Ollenburger, B. C. "Isaiah's Creation Theology," *Ex Auditu* 3 (1987) 54-71.

Olson, D. *The Death of the Old and the Birth of the New: The Framework of the Book of Numbers and the Pentateuch*. BJS 71. Chico, Calif.: Scholars Press, 1985.

Olyan, S. M. "Honor, Shame, and Covenant Relations in Ancient Israel and its Environment," *JBL* 115 (1996) 201-18.

Oppenheim, A. L. "On Royal Gardens in Mesopotamia," *JNES* 24 (1965) 328-33.

Otto, E. *Theologische Ethik des Alten Testaments*. TW 3/2. Stuttgart: Kohlhammer, 1994.

Otto, R. *The Idea of the Holy*, tr. J. W. Harvey. 2d ed. London: Oxford University Press, 1958.

Overbye, D. "The Cosmos according to Darwin," *The New York Times Magazine* (July 13, 1997) 26.

Perdue, L. G., ed. *Families in Ancient Israel*. FRC. Louisville: Westminster John Knox, 1997.

———. "The Israelite and Early Jewish Family: Summary and Conclusion," in *Families in Ancient Israel*, 163-222.

———. *Wisdom and Creation: The Theology of Wisdom Literature*. Nashville: Abingdon, 1994.

———. *The Collapse of History*. OBT. Minneapolis: Fortress, 1994.

———. *Wisdom in Revolt: Metaphorical Theology in the Book of Job*. BLS 29: JSOTSup 112. Sheffield: Almond, 1991.

———. *Wisdom and Cult*. SBLDS 30. Missoula, Mont.: Scholars Press, 1977.

Peristiany, J. G., ed. *Honour and Shame: The Values of Mediterranean Societies*. London: Weidenfeld & Nicholson, 1966.

———, and J. Pitt-Rivers, ed. *Honor and Grace in Anthropology*. Cambridge: Cambridge University Press, 1992.

Phillips, A. "Uncovering the Father's Skirt," *VT* 30 (1980) 38-43.

Phipps, W. E. "Eve and Pandora Contrasted," *TToday* 45 (1988) 34-48.

Plantinga, C. *Not the Way It's Supposed to Be: A Breviary of Sin.* Grand Rapids: Eerdmans, 1995.

Plath, S. *Furcht Gottes: Das Begriffe jr' im Alten Testament.* AzT 2/2. Stuttgart: Calwer, 1962.

Pleins, J. D. "Poverty in the Social World of the Wise," *JSOT* 37 (1987) 61-78.

Pola, T. *Die ursprüngliche Priesterschrift: Beobachtungen zur Literarkritik und Traditionsgeschichte von P*ᵍ. WMANT 70. Neukirchen-Vluyn: Neukirchener, 1995.

Polkinghorne, J. "The Laws of Nature and the Laws of Physics," in *Quantum Cosmology and the Laws of Nature,* ed. R. J. Russell et al. Vatican City State: Vatican Observatory; Berkeley: Center for Theology and Natural Sciences, 1993, 437-48.

Pope, M. *Job.* 3d ed. AB 15. Garden City, N.Y.: Doubleday, repr. 1979.

Pritchard, J. B. *Ancient Near Eastern Texts Relating to the Old Testament.* 3d ed. with supplement. Princeton: Princeton University Press, 1969.

Propp, W. H. "The Rod of Aaron and the Sin of Moses," *JBL* 107 (1988) 19-26.

————. *Water in the Wilderness: A Biblical Motif and Its Mythological Background.* HSM 40. Atlanta: Scholars Press, 1987.

von Rad, G. *Genesis,* tr. J. H. Marks. Rev. ed. OTL. Philadelphia: Westminster, 1972.

————. *Wisdom in Israel,* tr. J. D. Martin. Nashville: Abingdon, 1972.

————. "Some Aspects of the Old Testament World-View," in *The Problem of the Hexateuch and Other Essays,* tr. E. W. Trueman Dicken. London: SCM, 1966, 144-65.

————. "The Theological Problem of the Old Testament Doctrine of Creation," in *The Problem of the Hexateuch and Other Essays,* tr. E. W. Trueman Dicken. London: SCM, 1966, 131-43.

————. *Das Gottesvolk im Deuteronomium.* BWANT 47. Stuttgart: Kohlhammer, 1929.

Rensberger, D. K. *Johannine Faith and Liberating Community.* Philadelphia: Westminster, 1988.

Ricoeur, P. *The Rule of Metaphor,* tr. R. Czerny et al. Toronto: University of Toronto Press, repr. 1981.

————. *The Symbolism of Evil,* tr. E. Buchanan. Boston: Beacon, 1960.

Riemann, P. A. "Am I My Brother's Keeper?" *Int* 24 (1970) 482-91.

Ringgren, H. *Word and Wisdom: Studies in the Hypostatization of Divine Qualities and Functions in the Ancient Near East.* Lund: Ohlssons, 1947.

Rogers, C. "The Meaning and Significance of the Hebrew Word *'mwn* in Proverbs 8,30," *ZAW* 109 (1997) 208-21.

Rolston, H., III. "The Bible and Ecology," *Int* 50 (1996) 16-26.

————. "Does Nature Need to be Redeemed?" *HBT* 14 (1992) 143-72.

Rouillard, H. *La péricope de Balaam (Nombres 22–24): La prose et les "oracles."* Ebib 4. Paris: Gabalda, 1985.

Rosenberg, J. *King and Kin: Political Allegory in the Hebrew Bible.* Bloomington: Indiana University Press, 1986.

Rossi, P. J. *Together toward Hope: A Journey to Moral Theology.* Notre Dame: University of Notre Dame Press, 1983.

———. "Moral Interest and Moral Imagination in Kant," *The Modern Schoolman* 57 (1980) 149-58.

———. "Moral Imagination and the Narrative Modes of Moral Discourse," *Renascence* 31 (1979) 131-41.

Sakenfeld, K. D. "Theological and Redactional Problems in Numbers 20.2-13," in *Understanding the Word: Essays in Honour of Bernhard W. Anderson,* ed. J. T. Butler et al. JSOTSup 37. Sheffield: JSOT Press, 1985, 133-54.

Sampson, R. J., S. W. Raudenbusch, and F. Earls. "Neighborhoods and Violent Crime: A Multilevel Study of Collective Efficacy," *Science* 277 (Aug. 15, 1997) 918-24.

Sanders, J. A. *From Sacred Story to Sacred Text.* Philadelphia: Fortress, 1987.

———. *The Old Testament in the Cross.* New York: Harper & Bros., 1961.

Sasson, J. M. "The Worship of the Golden Calf," in *Orient and Occident: Essays Presented to Cyrus H. Gordon on the Occasion of His Sixty-Fifth Birthday,* ed. H. A. Hoffner. AOAT 22. Kevelaer: Butzon & Bercker; Neukirchen-Vluyn: Neukirchener, 1973, 151-60.

Schäfer, P. "Temple und Schöpfung: Zur Interpretation einiger Heiligtumstraditionen in der rabbinischen Literatur," *Kairos* 16 (1974) 122-33.

Schama, S. *Landscape and Memory.* New York: Knopf, 1995.

Schmid, H. H. "Creation, Righteousness, and Salvation: 'Creation Theology' as the Broad Horizon of Biblical Theology," tr. B. W. Anderson and D. G. Johnson, in *Creation in the Old Testament,* ed. B. W. Anderson. IRT 6. Philadelphia: Fortress, 1984, 102-17.

———. *Gerechtigkeit als Weltordnung: Hintergrund und Geschichte des alttestamentlichen Gerechtigkeitsbegriffes.* BHT 40. Tübingen: Mohr (Siebeck), 1968.

Schmidt, L. *Studien zur Priesterschrift.* BZAW 214. Berlin: de Gruyter, 1993.

Schmidt, W. H. *Die Schöpfungsgeschichte der Priesterschrift.* WMANT 17. Neukirchen-Vluyn: Neukirchener, 1964.

Schweiker, W. *Responsibility and Christian Ethics.* Cambridge: Cambridge University Press, 1995.

Scott, R. B. Y. "Wisdom in Creation: The *'Āmôn* of Proverbs VIII 30," *VT* 10 (1960) 213-22.

Seitz, C. *Isaiah 1–39.* Interpretation. Louisville: John Knox, 1993.

———. *Zion's Final Destiny.* Minneapolis: Fortress, 1991.

————. "The Divine Council: Temporal Transition and New Prophecy in the Book of Isaiah," *JBL* 109 (1990) 193-206.

Seow, C. L. *Myth, Drama, and the Politics of David's Dance.* HSM 46. Atlanta: Scholars Press, 1989.

Sheldon, B. *Prophetic Faith in Isaiah.* New York: Harper & Bros., 1958.

Simkins, R. *Creator and Creation: Nature in the Worldview of Ancient Israel.* Peabody, Mass.: Hendrickson, 1994.

————. *Yahweh's Activity in History and Nature in the Book of Joel.* ANETS 10. Lewiston, N.Y.: Edwin Mellen, 1991.

Skehan, P. W. "The Seven Columns of Wisdom's House," in *Studies in Israelite Poetry and Wisdom.* CBQMS 1. Washington, D.C.: Catholic Biblical Association of America, 1971, 9-14 (revised from *CBQ* 9 [1947] 190-98).

————. "Wisdom's House," in *Studies in Israelite Poetry and Wisdom,* 27-45 (revised from *CBQ* 29 [1967] 468-86).

Slayton, Joel C. "Manna," *ABD,* ed. D. N. Freedman. New York: Doubleday, 1992, 4:511.

Smith, D. L. *Religion of the Landless.* Bloomington, Ind.: Meyer Stone, 1989.

Smith, M. S. "The Near Eastern Background of Solar Language for Yahweh," *JBL* 109 (1990) 29-39.

Smolin, L. *The Life of the Cosmos.* New York: Oxford University Press, 1997.

von Soden, W. *Akkadisches Handwörterbuch.* 3 vols. Wiesbaden: Harrassowitz, 1965-81.

Speiser, E. A. *Genesis.* AB 1. Garden City, N.Y.: Doubleday, 1964.

Spina, F. A. "The 'Ground' for Cain's Rejection (Gen 4) *'ᵃdāmāh* in the Context of Gen 1–11," *ZAW* 104 (1992) 319-32.

————. "Israelites as *gērîm,* 'Sojourners,' in Social and Historical Context," in *The Word of the Lord Shall Go Forth: Essays in Honor of David Noel Freedman in Celebration of His Sixtieth Birthday,* ed. C. Meyers and M. O'Connor. Winona Lake, Ind.: Eisenbrauns, 1983, 321-35.

Springsted, E. O. "'Thou Hast Given Me Room': Simone Weil's Retheologization of the Political," *Cahiers Simone Weil* 20/2 (1997) 87-98.

Stecher, R. "Die persönliche Weisheit in den Proverbien Kap. 8," *ZKT* 75 (1953) 411-51.

Steck, O. H. *Bereitete Heimkehr: Jesaja 35 als redaktionelle Brücke zwischen dem Ersten und dem Zweiten Jesaja.* SBS 121. Stuttgart: Katholisches Bibelwerk, 1985.

————. "Die Paradieserzählung: Eine Auslegung von Genesis 2,4b–3,24," in idem, *Wahrnehmungen Gottes im Alten Testament. Gesammelte Studien.* TBü 70. Munich: Kaiser, 1982, 9-116 (reprint from Biblische Studien 60; Neukirchen-Vluyn: Neukirchener Verlag, 1970).

————. *World and Environment.* BES. Nashville: Abingdon, 1980.

Steinmetz, D. "Vineyard, Farm, and Garden: The Drunkenness of Noah in the Context of Primeval History," *JBL* 113 (1994) 193-207.

Stratton, B. J. *Out of Eden. Reading, Rhetoric, and Ideology in Genesis 2–3.* JSOTSup 208. Sheffield: Sheffield Academic Press, 1995.

Stuhlmueller, C. *Creative Redemption in Deutero-Isaiah.* AnBib 43. Rome: Pontifical Biblical Institute, 1970.

Sykes, S. "Time and Space in Haggai–Zechariah 1–8: A Bakhtinian Analysis of a Prophetic Chronicle." Ph.D. dissertation. Richmond: Union Theological Seminary in Virginia, 1997.

Tadmor, H. *The Inscriptions of Tiglath-Pileser III, King of Assyria.* Jerusalem: Israel Academy of Sciences and Humanities, 1994.

Taylor, C. *Sources of the Self: The Making of Modern Identity.* Cambridge: Harvard University Press, 1990.

Terrien, S. "The Play of Wisdom: Turning Point in Biblical Theology," *HBT* 3 (1981) 125-54.

Toulmin, S. *Cosmopolis: The Hidden Agenda of Modernity.* New York: Free Press, 1990.

———. *The Return of Cosmology: Postmodern Science and the Theology of Nature.* Berkeley: University of California Press, 1982.

Towner, W. S. "Interpretations and Reinterpretations of the Fall," in *Modern Biblical Scholarship: Its Impact on Theology and Proclamation,* ed. F. A. Eigo. Villanova, Pa.: The Villanova University Press, 1984, 53-85.

Trible, P. *God and the Rhetoric of Sexuality.* OBT. Philadelphia: Fortress, 1978.

Tsevat, M. "The Meaning of the Book of Job," *HUCA* 37 (1966) 73-106 (repr. in idem, *The Meaning of the Book of Job and Other Biblical Studies.* New York: Ktav, 1980, 1-38).

Tucker, G. M. "Rain on a Land Where No One Lives: The Hebrew Bible on the Environment," *JBL* 116 (1997) 3-17.

Tuell, S. S. *The Law of the Temple in Ezekiel 40–48.* HSM 49; Atlanta: Scholars Press, 1992.

Tyldesley, J. A. *Hatchepsut: The Female Pharaoh.* London: Viking, 1996.

Vall, G. "'From Whose Womb Did the Ice Come Forth?': Procreation Images in Job 38:28-29," *CBQ* 57 (1995) 504-13.

Van Houten, C. *The Alien in Israelite Law.* JSOTSup 107. Sheffield: JSOT Press, 1991.

Van Seters, J. *Prologue to History: The Yahwist as Historian in Genesis.* Louisville: Westminster John Knox, 1992.

———. "The Creation of Man and the Creation of the King," *ZAW* 101 (1989) 333-42.

———. *In Search of History: Historiography in the Ancient World and the Origins of Biblical History.* New Haven: Yale University Press, 1983.

Vawter, B. "Prov. 8:22, Wisdom and Creation," *JBL* 99 (1980) 205-16.

Volf, M. *Exclusion and Embrace: A Theological Exploration of Identity, Otherness, and Reconciliation*. Nashville: Abingdon, 1996.

Wagner, V. "Zur Existence des sogennanten 'Heiligkeitsgesetzes,'" *ZAW* 86 (1974) 307-16.

Wallace, H. N. "The Toledot of Adam," in *Studies in the Pentateuch*, ed. J. A. Emerton. VTSup 41. Leiden: Brill, 1990, 17-33.

———. *The Eden Narrative*. HSM 32. Atlanta: Scholars Press, 1985.

Wallis, G. "Die Stadt in den Überlieferungen der Genesis," *ZAW* 78 (1966) 133-48.

Walsh, J. T. "Genesis 2:4b–3:24: A Synchronic Approach," *JBL* 96 (1977) 161-77 (repr. in *"I Studied Inscriptions from before the Flood": Ancient Near Eastern, Literary, and Linguistic Approaches to Genesis 1–11*, ed. R. S. Hess and D. T. Tsumura. SBTS 4. Winona Lake, Ind.: Eisenbrauns, 1994, 362-82).

Walters, S. D. "Jacob Narrative," *ABD*, ed. D. N. Freedman. New York: Doubleday, 1992, 3:599-608.

Waltke, B. K. "Lady Wisdom as Mediatrix: An Exposition of Proverbs 1:20-33," *Presbyterion: Covenant Seminary Review* 14 (Spring 1988) 1-15.

Wander, N. "Structure, Contradiction, and 'Resolution' in Mythology: Father's Brother's Daughter Marriage and the Treatment of Women in Genesis 11–50," *JANES* 13 (1981) 75-99.

Ward, W. A. "Goshen," *ABD*, ed. D. N. Freedman. New York: Doubleday, 1992, 2:1076-77.

Washington, H. C. "The Strange Woman (נכריה/זרה אשה) of Proverbs 1–9 and Post-Exilic Judaean Society," in *Second Temple Studies*, vol. 2: *Temple and Community in the Persian Period*, ed. T. C. Eskenazi and K. H. Richards. JSOTSup 175. Sheffield: JSOT Press, 1994, 217-43.

———. *Wealth and Poverty in the Instruction of Amenemope and the Hebrew Proverbs*. SBLDS 142. Atlanta: Scholars Press, 1994.

Watts, J. D. W. *Isaiah 34–66*. WBC 25. Waco: Word, 1987.

Weimar, P. "Sinai und Schöpfung: Komposition und Theologie der priesterschriftliche Sinaigeschichte," *RB* 95 (1988) 337-85.

Weinfeld, M. *Social Justice in Ancient Israel and in the Ancient Near East*. Minneapolis: Fortress, 1995.

———. "Sabbath, Temple and the Enthronement of the Lord — The Problem of the Sitz im Leben of Genesis 1:1–2:3," in *Mélanges bibliques et orientaux en l'honneur de M. Henri Cazelles*, ed. A. Caquot and M. Delcor. AOAT 212. Kevelaer: Butzon & Bercker; Neukirchen-Vluyn: Neukirchener, 1981, 501-12.

———. "Cult Centralization in Israel in the List of a Neo-Babylonian Analogy," *JNES* 23 (1964) 202-12.

———. "God the Creator in Gen. 1 and the Prophecy of Second Isaiah," *Tarbiz* 37 (1968) 105-32 [Heb.].

Welker, M. "Pluralism and God's Creativity." Lecture given at the Carl Howie Center for Science, Art, and Theology at Union Theological Seminary in Virginia, Oct. 17, 1997.

——. *Schöpfung und Wirklichkeit*. Neukirchen-Vluyn: Neukirchener, 1995.

——. "Creation: Big Bang or the Work of Seven Days?" *TToday* 52 (1995) 173-87.

——. *God the Spirit*, tr. J. F. Hoffmeyer. Minneapolis: Fortress, 1994.

——. "What Is Creation? Rereading Genesis 1 and 2," *TToday* 48 (1991) 56-71.

——, and W. Schweiker. *Integrity — Dignity — Truth: Beyond the Crisis of Christianity in the West* (forthcoming).

Wellhausen, J. *Prolegomena to the History of Ancient Israel*, tr. A. Menzies and J. Black. 1885. Repr. Gloucester, Mass.: Peter Smith, 1983.

——. "Die Composition des Hexateuchs," *Jahrbücher für Deutsche Theologie* 21 (1876) 392-450, 531-602 (repr. in *Die Composition des Hexateuchs und der historischen Bücher des Alten Testaments*. 4th ed. Berlin: de Gruyter, 1963, 1-134).

Westermann, C. *The Roots of Wisdom: The Oldest Proverbs of Israel and Other Peoples*, tr. J. D. Charles. Louisville: Westminster John Knox, 1995.

——. *Genesis 12–26*, tr. J. J. Scullion. Continental Commentary. Minneapolis: Augsburg, 1985.

——. *Genesis 1–11*, tr. J. J. Scullion. Continental Commentary. Minneapolis: Augsburg, 1984.

——. *Blessing in the Bible and the Life of the Church*, tr. K. Crim. Philadelphia: Fortress, 1978.

——. *Creation*, tr. J. J. Scullion. Philadelphia: Fortress, 1974.

——. "Creation and History in the Old Testament," tr. D. Dutton, in *The Gospel and Human Destiny*, ed. V. Vajta. Minneapolis: Augsburg, 1971, 11-38.

——. *Isaiah 40–66*, tr. D. M. G. Stalker. OTL. Philadelphia: Westminster, 1969.

Wevers, J. W. *Notes on the Greek Text of Genesis*. SBLSCS 35. Atlanta: Scholars Press, 1993.

White, E. B. "Introduction," in K. S. White, *Onward and Upward in the Garden*, ed. E. B. White. Toronto: McGraw-Hill Ryerson, 1979, i-xix.

White, L., Jr. "The Historical Roots of Our Ecological Crisis," *Science* 144 (March 10, 1967) 1203-7.

White, R. E. O. *Biblical Ethics*. Atlanta: John Knox, 1979.

Whybray, R. N. "City Life in Proverbs 1–9," in *Jedes Ding hat seine Zeit . . .": Studien zur israelitischen und altorientalischen Weisheit*, ed. A. A. Diesel et al. BZAW 241. Berlin: de Gruyter, 1996, 243-50.

——. *Wealth and Poverty in the Book of Proverbs*. JSOTSup 99. Sheffield: JSOT Press, 1990.

Wilcoxen, J. A. "Some Anthropocentric Aspects of Israel's Sacred History," *JR* 48 (1968) 333-50.

Wildberger, H. "Das Abbild Gottes," *TZ* 21 (1965) 245-59, 481-501.

de Wilde, A. *Das Buch Hiob.* OTS 22. Leiden: Brill, 1981.

Willey, P. T. K. *Remember the Former Things: The Recollection of Previous Texts in Isaiah 40–55.* SBLDS 161. Atlanta: Scholars Press, 1997.

Williams, J. G. "Job and the God of Victims," in *The Voice from the Whirlwind: Interpreting the Book of Job,* ed. L. G. Perdue and W. C. Gilpin. Nashville: Abingdon, 1992, 208-31.

Williamson, H. G. M. "The Concept of Israel in Transition," in *The World of Ancient Israel: Sociological, Anthropological and Political Perspectives,* ed. R. E. Clements. Cambridge: Cambridge University Press, 1989, 141-61.

Willis, J. T. "An Important Passage for Determining the Historical Setting of a Prophetic Oracle — Isaiah 1.7-8," *ST* 39 (1985) 151-69.

Wilson, A. *The Nations in Deutero-Isaiah: A Study on Composition and Structure.* ANETS 1. Lewiston, N.Y.: Edwin Mellen, 1986.

Wilson, F. M. "Sacred and Profane? The Yahwistic Redaction of Proverbs Reconsidered," in *The Listening Heart: Essays in Wisdom and the Psalms in Honor of Roland E. Murphy,* ed. K. G. Hoglund et al. JSOTSup 58. Sheffield: JSOT Press, 1987, 313-34.

Wink, W. "Biblical Theology and Social Ethics," in *Biblical Theology: Problems and Perspectives,* ed. S. J. Kraftchick et al. Nashville: Abingdon, 1995, 260-75.

Wiseman, D. J. "Mesopotamian Gardens," *AnSt* 33 (1983) 137-44.

Wolff, H. W. "The Kerygma of the Yahwist," tr. W. A. Benware, in W. Brueggemann and H. W. Wolff, *The Vitality of Old Testament Traditions.* 2d ed. Atlanta: John Knox, 1982, 41-66 (repr. from *Int* 20 [1966] 131-58).

Wolters, A. M. "The Meaning of *Kîšôr* (Prov 31:19)," *HUCA* 65 (1994) 91-104.

———. "Proverbs XXXI 10-31 as Heroic Hymn: A Form-Critical Analysis," *VT* 38 (1988) 446-57.

———. *Creation Regained: Biblical Basics for a Reformational Worldview.* Grand Rapids: Eerdmans, 1985.

———. "*Ṣôpiyyâ* (Prov 31:27) as Hymnic Participle and Play on *Sophia*," *JBL* 104 (1985) 577-87.

Wright, C. J. H. "Jubilee, Year of," *ABD,* ed. D. N. Freedman. New York: Doubleday, 1992, 3:1025-30.

———. *Walking in the Ways of the Lord: The Ethical Authority of the Old Testament.* Downers Grove, Ill.: InterVarsity Press, 1995.

Yee, G. A. "The Theology of Creation in Proverbs 8:22-31," in *Creation in the Biblical Traditions,* ed. R. J. Clifford and J. J. Collins. CBQMS 24. Washington, D.C.: Catholic Biblical Association of America, 1992, 85-96.

———. "'I Have Perfumed My Bed with Myrrh': The Foreign Woman (*'iššâ zārâ*) in Proverbs 1–9," *JSOT* 43 (1989) 53-68.

Ziegler, J. "Die Hilfe Gottes am Morgen," in *Alttestamentliche Studien:*

Fr. Nötscher zum sechsigsten Geburtstag, ed. H. Junker and J. Botterweck. BBB 1. Bonn: Hanstein, 1950, 281-88.

Zimmerli, W. "The Place and Limit of the Wisdom in the Framework of the Old Testament Theology," *SJT* 17 (1964) 146-58 (repr. in *Studies in Ancient Israelite Wisdom*, ed. J. L. Crenshaw. New York: Ktav, 1976, 314-26).

Zohary, M. *Plants of the Bible*. Cambridge: Cambridge University Press, 1982.

Zuckerman, B. *Job the Silent: A Study in Historical Counterpoint*. New York: Oxford University Press, 1991.

Zvi, E. Ben. "Isaiah 1:4-9, Isaiah, and the Events of 701 BCE in Judah: A Question of Premise and Evidence," *SJOT* 5/1 (1991) 95-111.

Index of Authors and Subjects

437

Index of Scripture References

449